RAPE, SEXUAL VIOLENCE AND ME

CONNOR WHITELEY

DEDICATION

Thank you to all my readers without you I couldn't do what I love.

BREAKING THE SILENCE

CONNOR WHITELEY

Any questions about the book, rights licensing, or to contact the author, please email connorwhiteley@connorwhiteley.net

DEDICATION

Thank you to all my readers without you I couldn't do what I love.

INTRODUCTION

We need to break the silence, even within clinical psychology.

My life changed forever on the 13th April 2024. I was raped. I was traumatized. I almost lost everything that night.

Over the course of the next 7 months, my mental health died. I developed Post-Traumatic Stress Disorder, depression and anxiety, as well as I would jump at the smallest thing. Also, I would have constant nightmares, wake up screaming and so much more that it has been a hellish 7 months.

In addition, during this time and even now, I encountered so many myths, misconceptions and invalidation over my rape. Most of the time it was from people who have never experienced sexual violence (lucky them), my friends and my family and sometimes it was even from mental health professionals.

There is such a lack of awareness about even the basics of sexual trauma that this creates a perfect breeding ground for sexual violence itself, its devastating impact on survivors and it means these myths thrive.

I want to change that.

I am a researcher, psychology graduate, podcaster, writer and so many more things besides being a rape survivor. I wanted to use this to my advantage. Over the past 7 months, I have done more research into rape and other forms of sexual violence than I ever thought possible. I've explored the mental health, forensic psychology, biological psychology and so many more aspects that I understand a lot of truths about sexual violence.

The majority of people, let alone the professionals within psychology, do not even know a fraction of these truths.

This is why the silence must be broken.

<u>Who Is This Book For?</u>

I've written this engaging, easy-to-understand book for psychology students and psychology professionals that want to deepen their understanding of sexual violence and its impact. As well as this is a great book for anyone wanting to learn more about the truth behind sexual trauma.

You'll learn:

- Male and female sexual violence.

- How sexual violence impacts a survivor at a biological, social and psychological level.
- Why men *and* women commit sexual violence.
- How to support and help rape survivors, including a look at trauma therapies.
- And more.

By the end of this great, engaging book, you'll have a deep foundational knowledge on sexual violence, its effects and most importantly how you can start supporting clients with sexual trauma in the future.

Who Am I?

In my other psychology books, I include this section because I like to know who the author is so I know the information is coming from a reliable and good source, but I'm including this section for a different reason.

I'm Connor Whiteley, the internationally bestselling author of over 40 psychology books, I am the host of *The Psychology World Podcast,* a weekly show exploring a new psychology topic each week and delivering the latest psychology news. Available on all major podcast apps and YouTube. As well as I am a psychology graduate who studied a Clinical Psychology undergraduate and Masters at the University of Kent, England.

Also, I am a survivor, not a victim.

I love psychology, spending time with my friends, going out and living. Also, I like fiction books of all types especially books by Dean Wesley Smith, and I like watching films with my friends.

I am a normal person with a normal, fun, exciting life but when I was raped, he took everything from me.

I thought I was a weak victim but I am not. I am slowly rebuilding my life, I am slowly living again and I am recovering from what he did to me.

I am a survivor, not a victim, but it wasn't always that way.

This is my exploration of sexual violence so I could understand what the hell was happening to me and my trauma responses.

This allowed me to survive and heal so I could be a survivor and no longer a victim.

Psychology has the power to make other people feel better about themselves and heal after trauma. Please turn over the page and let's start breaking the silence around sexual trauma.

PART ONE:
SEXUAL VIOLENCE

WHAT ARE THE FACTS AND FIGURES FOR SEXUAL VIOLENCE ON UNIVERSITY AND COLLEGE CAMPUSES?

I've mentioned before one of the ways how I deal with trauma and understanding why different things happen in the world is through research. Therefore, in the months following my sexual assault, I've read a lot about rape, sexual assault and all the different facets of sexual violence. Sometimes this has only made me even more distressed and sometimes it has helped.

Therefore, one of the areas I came across during my rape research was related to the how common it is amongst the university or college population, and this seems to be a finding that applies to both the United Kingdom and the United States. Also, to be honest, I seriously doubt it is different anywhere else in the world.

As a result, in this chapter, I'm going to be explaining the facts and figures about how common sexual violence is amongst college students. You can see the full list of references at the back of the book in the reference section.

Introduction To Sexual Violence Amongst University Campuses

A moment ago, I mentioned that sexual violence is very common on university campuses because 13% of all university students (regardless if they're undergraduate or postgraduate) experience sexual assault or rape through physical force, physical violence or incapacitation during their time as a student. As well as, if we focus only on graduate and professional students then 2.5% of males and 9.7% of females will experience sexual assault or rape through physical violence, force or incapacitation.

Unfortunately, this increases when we focus on undergraduate students (probably because there are more of them) since 6.8% of males and 26.4% of females will also experience sexual assault or rape through physical violence, force or incapacitation during their time as a student.

Also, 5.8% of students regardless of sex or gender have experienced stalking since they started university.

This is even worse for transgender individuals because 23.1% of transgender, gender-nonconforming and genderqueer college students have been sexually assaulted.

Finally for this section, it's worth noting that regardless of whether a person is a student or not, being aged 18 to 24 means they are at a high risk of experiencing sexual violence. I was 22 years old when I was raped so I guess I'm proof of these statistics. Since there's a very interesting finding when it comes to risk factors because female college-aged students are actually 20% less likely than non-students of the same age to experience rape or sexual assault. Whereas male students are 78% more likely to experience rape or sexual assault compared to non-students of the same age.

Personally, I flat out hate all the statistics in this chapter because they are disgusting, wrong and so messed up. No one should ever be raped or experience sexual violence, and it is even more disgusting that university campuses seem to be a breeding ground for this sort of evil behaviour.

I know I can only speak for UK universities, but I know the research I'm basing this chapter on was done in the USA. And from everything I know about the USA's student population and their college hierarchy, I can unfortunately understand how these numbers are so common. There's a much larger focus in the USA on fraternities and sororities, drinking and having massive frat parties. Of course, the UK has a similar culture about drinking and having sex at university, but the USA version seems to be on an industrial scale by comparison.

My point is, I don't like these statistics. These are heartbreaking, troubling and outrageous. That's one of the reasons why I'm writing a psychology research-based book on sexual violence and a memoirish book on the aftermath of my own rape.

I want to educate people and help fellow survivors so maybe, just maybe these statistics can decrease in the future.

Sexual Violence Is More Common Than Other Crimes At University

Another tragic research finding is that sexual violence is more common than other crimes at university because in the general population, there are 5 robberies for every 4 sexual assaults meaning that robberies are more common to experience. Yet when it comes to college-aged women, there are 2 sexual assaults for every one robbery.

In other words, they are more likely to experience a sexual assault than being robbed at university.

That is flat out disgusting and that is rather soul-destroying for me. I've researched the consequences of criminal behaviours and the effects that crimes have on victims, and whilst being robbed can be very difficult for victims. Experiencing a robbery doesn't even remotely compare to being sexually assaulted.

Unfortunately, it's even worse that only 1 in 5 female survivors receive assistance from a victim services agency.

Now that really makes me uncomfortable because in the upcoming book, you'll see and hear how I've struggled immensely with my mental health since my rape, and I've been in contact with an agency. In fact, at the time of writing, I should be getting my rape counselling appointment in the next two weeks (at the very earliest). Therefore, I cannot begin to imagine how hard, how devastating and how bad their mental health has been if they didn't seek the support of some kind of agency.

I hope those female survivors are doing okay, but I unfortunately doubt it.

Moreover, there are certain times of the year when sexual violence is more common on university campuses. For instance, more than 50% of college sexual assaults happen in August, September, October or November. As well as students are at an increased risk of sexual violence in the first few months of their first and second terms at university.

Why Don't College-Aged Students Report Their Sexual Assault To Law Enforcement?

Now this is a fascinating topic because it is very uncommon for a sexual assault survivor to report it to the police. I didn't report my assault and I have an upcoming chapter explaining why this was the case. According to the research, I'm basing this chapter on, only 32% of nonstudent female survivors at college age report their assault to the police, whereas only 20% of female students report it to law enforcement.

This means 4 out of 5 students don't report their sexual assault to the police and 66% of nonstudents don't report their assault either.

Now if I had read this research before my own rape, I would have been confused, I wouldn't have understood why they didn't report it and I would have been judgmental because it was only after my rape I started to learn the truth about rape myths and misconceptions.

In addition, below are the different reasons why female students didn't report their sexual assault, and because participants were allowed to pick more than one reason, the percentages below don't add up to 100%.

- 4% reported it but not to the police
- 9% believed the police wouldn't or couldn't do anything to help them
- 10% didn't want to get their attacker in trouble
- 12% believed it wasn't important enough to report it
- 20% had a fear they would suffer some kind of reprisal for reporting it.
- 26% believed it was a personal matter and didn't concern the police
- 31% had other reasons not for reporting it.

Below is the list of reasons with percentages for nonstudents:

- 5% reported it but not to the police
- 10% believed the police couldn't or wouldn't do anything to help
- 14% didn't want to get their attacker in trouble
- 19% didn't believe it was important enough to report
- 20% had a fear of reprisal.
- 23% believed it was a personal matter
- 35% had other reasons for not reporting it to the police.

Interestingly, I actually agree with all those reasons based on my personal experience, and I've struggled with every single one of those factors, and I talk about why in a future chapter.

Yet I think it's always interesting to see why different survivors don't report it. If you did report it then more power to you and you have a hell of a lot of courage and I am proud of you for doing it. And even if you didn't report it like me, I am proud of you because you're alive, you survived and you are reading this book in an effort to recover.

It might not always seem like you survived or that you're healing, but you are. It might be extremely slow but you're being proactive by reading this book.

I'm proud of you for that.

WHY AN ERECTION ISN'T CONSENT?

This is the psychology article that started everything, because without this podcast episode, this book would not be possible. Also, this article allowed to subtly talk about what had happened to me, it made me want to speak up about rape and male rape more generally so I could educate people against the many myths and misconceptions about rape.

Even though any podcast episode on sexual violence is going to do badly because 99% of people just want to avoid the topic of sexual violence and pretend it doesn't exist, I am proud that I did this podcast episode.

It gave me a chance to find my voice, get comfortable talking about my experience and it gave me a drive to fight. It gave me hope that I could fight against the veil of silence that society created for itself around this topic and it gave me hope that I might be able to help at least one single person in case they're experienced something similar.

Please enjoy the psychology article that started everything.

***

Research suggest that men get raped and sexually assaulted as often as women by both men and women. Yet male rape is a lot less reported because of societal factors, gender roles and a whole bunch of horrible myths that stop men from reporting rape and sexual assault. Also, it's important to note that talking about male rape isn't about stopping or taking the focus away from female rape, instead it's actually about highlighting something that isn't spoken about in society. All rape and sexual assault whether it's against a man or woman is flat out wrong and it should never happen. Therefore, in this forensic psychology podcast episode, we'll explore male rape and why an erection isn't consent. If you like learning about forensic psychology, sexual crimes and why people do this crime then you'll enjoy today's episode.

<u>Why Am I Talking About Male Sexual Assault and Rape?</u>

Just as a little introduction to this episode and why I'm personally doing this, I wanted to be upfront and honest with you about my own personal position. So I'm a victim of sexual assault, it happened about three weeks ago and I cannot emphasise how distressing, awful and foul it was. I don't wish it on anyone and whilst you won't hear any major details about my assault in this episode, this did happen to me. As well as I will add in my personal thoughts like always in this episode to help it come alive.

Since one of the awful things that happened after my assault was that I worked an Open Day at my university and I was talking to a lecturer that I always talk to. I really like her, she's great and she studies forensic psychology. Even though I completely forgot her topic was sexual violence so she started talking about it and I just couldn't listen not one week after what had happened.

And the entire reason for this podcast episode was researching sexual assault and rape really did help me during that first intense, horrific week. It helped me to understand what had happened, this was common and it really wasn't my fault.

Therefore, even if I can help one person or inform a few people about male sexual assault then I would have done my job with today's episode.

Some Data On Male Sexual Assault

Before we start talking about the content in any more depth, let's look at some data, the Rape, Abuse and Incest National Network found that 1 in 33 men have experienced a completed or attempted rape in their lifetime and 1 out of every 10 rape victims are male. And remember, these figures are out of the reported figures, so the real numbers could be a lot, lot higher.

Furthermore, the US's Centre for Disease Control and Prevention have shown in research that men and women are equally likely to be sexually assaulted and victims of sexual violence. Yet sexual assault against men has been severely, severely underrecognized, undertreated and underreported.

Finally, the National Crime Victimisation Survey shows that a lot of men report being sexually assaulted by women through forced penetration and coerced erections.

Overall, I hope this goes to show that male sexual assault isn't rare and it is a lot more common than any of us realise.

Male Sexual Assault And Rape

Whilst it is very rare that male sexual assault is reported in a given year, it is true that men are victims of sexual harassment, rape and molestation on a daily basis. Also, whilst it's tempting to think that male sexual assault is *only* committed by other men, in reality, it is actually an even spilt with female and male rapists.

As a result of male rape by women is a lot more common than we will ever see in the Criminal Justice System and the news as well as social media. Part of this underreport is shame and the stigma of a man "not being manly enough" because of the stupid idea that "only weak men get raped". Yet another reason is that when women rape men, they generally get the man to have an erection and even ejaculation so this confuses and paralyses the man.

Mainly because society teaches us that if a man gets an erection then they enjoy it and that isn't rape.

I actually remember one of my schoolfriends saying this back in my secondary school years and back then I sort of knew that wasn't 100% right, but I had no idea how flat out wrong it was until three weeks ago.

Also, on the underreporting, why I didn't report it was because I was embarrassed, I felt dirty, I felt so violated that I didn't want many people to know. And I was scared to be honest. I was scared of getting hurt yet again, I was scared of the stigma and I was scared about what my friends and family would think. Of course, they loved me, supported me and they have been great since they found out. Then there is the legal issue too because I had cleaned my teeth when I got home and I had showered the next morning because I was in extreme denial. And it took me two days to admit I had been sexually assaulted and by that point there was no one DNA left on me.

There were other reasons why a prosecution would have been difficult but that isn't the focus of this episode.

And I didn't want to go through the whole legal process, but if someone listening does want to do this that is very important, critical and you should. If you want to press charges then you absolutely should.

In addition, having an erection isn't consent or a sign that the person is willing or ready to have sex because an erection and ejaculation are physiological responses that we cannot control. Also, these physiological responses can occur due to pain, anxiety, fear and sexual desire or excitement.

Lastly, a final note on the underreporting, a lot of men don't label themselves as sexual assault victims and they don't call it what it is. Since typically when men learn that other men have been sexually assaulted they meet the disclosure with insensitivity and mockery.

Personally, it took me two full days, my two good friends and a specialist at the university to help me realise and call my assault what it was. I was in such extreme denial that I refused to label myself as a victim of sexual assault because I knew how those people were viewed in society. Yet I am a victim and once I "accepted" or realised that, it got a little bit easier because I could talk to people, contact my therapist and start recovering.

This podcast episode is part of that recovery because I want to help someone possibly.

What About Male On Male Sexual Assault? A Brief Look

So far in the episode, we've looked at what happens when women assault men, but let's focus on male-on-male sexual assault. When a man is sexually assaulted by another man this carries another strand of stigma as the victim fears that other people might question their sexual preferences and their sexual orientation and there is a concern about they might be seen as "less manly" because of the assault.

This is why I don't understand gender roles and the whole idea that men have to behave a certain way. Male mental health would be so much better if these gender-based rules of behaviour weren't around.

Anyway, a lot of men don't report male-on-male sexual assault because of the shame and humiliation or the perception of being weak for not fighting their attacker.

That's actually an interesting myth about sexual assault and rape that I learnt from the specialist at the university. Everyone thinks that when someone is raped or sexually assaulted, the victims screams, fights and tries to break free. But that is very, very rare. In reality, and this happened to me, you basically get so numb and cold and an emotion that I lately realised was fear, that you don't want it to happen, you say stop but when the attacker keeps grabbing you and carrying on. You get it over with so you can escape and run like hell after towards. Since my fear was my attacker was a lot larger than me unfortunately, so I was scared if I tried to fight back he would grab me, hurt me and the situation would be even worse.

That is why people rarely fight back.

It doesn't make them weak or stupid and it doesn't make what happened to them any less traumatic.

It just makes them a survivor.

Myths That Contribute To The Challenge Of Recognizing Male Sexual Assault

Below are some myths in society that contribute to people not talking, recognising and treating male sexual assault as seriously as female sexual assault (And yes, I realise there is still a long, long way to go before female sexual assault treatment is perfect).

- Men are only raped by other men.
- Erections only happen when the man is excited.
- Erections are a sign of consent.
- Men always want sex no matter what.
- Men can never have enough sex.
- Men secretly like being sexually assaulted.
- There is something wrong with a man if he doesn't want sex.
- Ejaculation is a sign of sexual enjoyment.
- "Real men" don't get sexually assaulted.
- Men like to be in charge in the bedroom.

All these myths are extremely harmful when it comes to recognising male sexual assault, but they don't help the aftermath of the assault too. Since our culture views sexual violence against men as disenfranchised abuse and this means men don't get the same emotional, legal or medical support as women do.

Therefore, these myths about men only being sexual predators that have an extreme need for sex that is engrained in the mental health, public health, medical as well as Criminal Justice Systems, they only hurt men. Since having an erection and ejaculation makes people debate if it was actually assault or not, because people believe they had to be aroused and enjoying it for that to happen.

I can personally protest that this isn't the case. Sure, I was rock hard during my assault but I was never ever going to ejaculate and I was not enjoying it. I did not enjoy being grabbed and having a lot of different things done to me.

Interestingly, as I'm an aspiring clinical psychologist, in psychotherapy, a therapist might question the validity of the rape claim by the male victim and they might not be very convinced of the traumatic effects of the incident. So the therapist's behaviour and attitudes tend to leave male victims feeling undermined and delegitimatized.

Another factor I want to add here is that after a sexual assault, it takes even more courage to reach out to a therapist than normal. Since I have a great relationship with my therapist and she is brilliant because I work well with her and she helped me with my child abuse trauma. Something that was slightly connected to my assault. Yet I didn't want to contact her because I didn't want to admit that my assault had happened. I only contacted her and had a brilliant session with her because a good friend basically ordered me to see her.

Thankfully, it worked out well.

Conclusion

Before I wrap up the podcast episode with a little more information, I want to mention that I have really enjoyed this episode. It has been tough and at the moment, I've only written the episode out. I am a little nervous about saying this stuff because I think having to say the R-word and the A-word so many times will be hard. But I'm still proud of myself for doing this really hard episode, because I'm revealing to the general public what happened to me and some people won't like what I'm saying because of the myths. Other people will thankfully support me and it's those people that I will listen to and treasure.

But ultimately, I'm doing this episode to help people. There might be another listener who has experienced an assault, rape or they might know someone who has been. I hope this episode shows these people that it's okay, things do get better and it wasn't their fault. This is a common experience and it flat out doesn't make you a failure.

Society and the myth spreaders, they are the failures.

And for people who have never been a victim, I seriously hope that never changes, but I hope you now know the truth and you'll actively challenge these myths when they pop up. Then if you work with clients and if this happens to a friend or loved one then you know more facts to help them.

Just love them, support them and listen to them. Those are my biggest takes from my experience.

Anyway, on the whole, we need to realise that when our systems don't make victims feel like they're taken seriously and they minimise the assault and don't tend to take action. Then this continues the harm and suffering that male victims experience from the trauma of sexual violence.

As a result, as a society, we need to stop this minimisation and break this stigma of male sexual assault because it isn't helpful and it certainly isn't right. A lot of this can be done by deconstructing traditional gender stereotypes because the main problem is that currently men aren't allowed to demonstrate their feelings besides anger, and this isn't good. Especially when people see pain and trauma responses as a degradation of manhood and this isn't helpful to us achieving true feminism.

In other words, true gender equality where men and women are true equals.

Additionally, we need to continue to work on deconstructing traditional ideas about what it means to be a victim. Since it's important to note that "force" isn't always about physical strength and being overpowered. Rapists and predators typically groom, coerce and emotionally manipulate or threaten their targets into nonconsensual sex.

Most importantly, this podcast episode and the entire point of advocating for male sexual assault victims isn't about delegitimising or undermining violence against women. Instead I am highlighting that men can be victims too and the gender stereotype that women are helpless victims is another unhelpful and undeserved gender stereotype. In turn, this only reinforces silly ideas what about it means to be a man or woman and even more outrageous ideas that male victims are "failed" men.

No victim of sexual violence is a failure. They are a victim that needs to be supported, helped and listened to.

Overall, when it comes to male sexual violence (or women for that matter) using gender-sensitive approaches in our work is critical. We need to understand that societal norms and expectations will always impact men and women disproportionately, and this should never come at the cost of undermining boys and men that have been sexually abused. Instead we need to use inclusive approaches to our work that allow us to advocate and support victims regardless of their gender, so we can enable a culture shift to happen.

Ultimately allowing us to have more conversations about healing, prevention and providing good care for victims whatever their gender is.

5 HARMFUL MYTHS ABOUT CHILD SEXUAL ABUSE

As much as no one wants to look at the disgusting act of child sexual abuse, it is a massive area of concern around the world. As well as since this is a criminal act it firmly falls under the remit of forensic psychology and the podcast, and it's important to try to combat dangerous myths that only hurt children and enable the abuse to continue. So if you're interested in sexual abuse and forensic psychology, you need to keep reading!

5 Harmful Myths About Child Sexual Abuse

I have spoken briefly about some myths in my Forensic Psychology book, but in this chapter we're going to explore some more myths, and most importantly, why are they harmful to children?

Myth: Sex Offender Registries Prevent Sexual Abuse

This is actually a myth that I fell for because I just presumed that this was a measure that worked to prevent sex crimes. But it turns out that sex offender registries show no effect on re-offending positive or negative.

As a result of a meta-analysis by Zgoba and Mitchell (2021) found that over the past 25 years, which was when sex offender registries were first introduced. There has been no effect on reoffending. Meaning there was no decrease in reoffending for these people on the registry.

In addition, Sanler, Freeman and Socia (2008) found that only 5% of sex crimes were committed by people on the sex offender registry.

In other words 95% of all sex crimes are committed by people not on these registries. Therefore, it really does beg the question, why do people think they work?

Personally, I think it comes down to people just not looking into it and believing what politicians and the police tell them about how effective they are. But that's why I love these sorts of myth busting chapters because we get to learn different truths about the world.

Myth: Child Sexual Abuse Is A Spontaneous Crime

I can't specifically say I've ever believed this one but it makes perfect sense why people believe this myth. Since if you watch any crime drama on TV or film they always show you a sex offender grabbing a random kid off the street without any planning or thought behind the act.

However, the truth is many sex offences made against children involve sexual grooming behaviour where the act is planned for days or weeks or even years before the disgusting act happens. And in this time frame the offender is grooming the child, their community and their family (this ties into another myth we'll talk about in a moment).

In addition, sexual grooming refers to when an offender exercises a process of deceit where they select a victim, gain access to them and isolates the child. They do this by developing a bond of trust with them and the other adults in their life and the would-be offender desensitises the minor to sexual content and physical contact.

Subsequently, after the sexual act (abuse) has happened then the offender could engage in maintenance strategies to facilitate future abuse and/or to prevent the minor telling others about the abuse.

In terms of the sexual grooming literature, there's evidence (see the references below) from two 2016 studies that show whilst the main literature believed only sexual abuse against children used grooming tactics. These two studies show that sexual abuse against adults and teenagers may use grooming tactics as well.

Additionally, it was commonly believed that only around half of all sexual abuse offences involved grooming tactics but Winters and Jeglic (2021) found 99% of all self-reported sexual offences against children used grooming tactics.

Overall, child sexual abuse is hardly a spontaneous crime.

<u>Myth: Only Strangers Commit Sex Offenses</u>

Whilst I mentioned this in my forensic psychology book, it is very much worth mentioning this myth again. Due to not only is it extremely dangerous as it could cause children not to be believed if they report sexual abuse against them by a family member. But it ties into the myth above.

As a result, only 7% of child sexual abuse and 19.5% of adult sexual abuse is committed by a stranger.

Furthermore, another reason why this is so dangerous is because this is the myth that drives most sexual abuse prevention strategies. So even our prevention strategies are highly flawed and don't work because of this single myth.

The truth is 34% of children are sexually abused by family members and 59% of them are abused by acquaintances. Then for adults, 39% are sexually abused by an acquaintance and 33% are abused by a former or current partner.

<u>Myth: Only Adult Men Commit Sex Offenses</u>

I should probably combine this myth slightly with the silly idea that only gay people commit sexual offences against children. Both are flat out wrong.

Because it turns out that up to 12% of sex offenders are women and 25% to 35% are under 18s.

Now the reason why this is a dangerous myth is because when it comes to teaching sexual violence prevention, we tend to without a shadow of a doubt identify the perpetrators of sexual offenses are men. And whilst it is completely true that the vast majority of sex offenses are carried out by men a meta-analysis by Cortoni, Babchishin and Rat (2016) found in 12% of sexual abuse cases the offender was female.

As well as in 40% of sexual abuse against men the offender was a woman compared to only 4% in those committed against a woman.

Finally, 33% of people who abuse children and 25% of people who abuse adults are minors and under 18s themselves.

Therefore, none of these are small percentages and by failing to teach people about the risk of female and minors committing sexual abuse. It can only harm innocent people in the long term as it may negatively affect prevention reporting and detection.

Myth: There Is Only A Specific Type Or Profile Of A Person Who Commits Sexual Abuse

At the time of writing this post in early-Mid June 2022, I've started researching terrorism and the criminal psychology behind it. And personally I do not understand people's obsession with finding a specific set of traits, personalities or something to give them a specific profile of a criminal. You just have to read or listen to my Criminal Profiling book to know how stupid that idea is and how much it doesn't work.

Anyway off my little soapbox, the truth is there is absolutely not one profile of a typical sex offender. If you watch any TV then there is a set profile of a sexual offender that makes it easy to identify based on their behaviours and characteristics, but in the real world it doesn't work like that.

The people who commit sexual offenses come from all walks of life with different looks, sizes and backgrounds. Some sex offenses come from respectable members of the community like Priests, Teachers and doctors. Other offenders come from less respectable sections of the community (which I think is just harsh to put it like that).

Conclusion:

However, what we do know is that teaching our children and young people about healthy sexuality, relationship skills and affirmative consent can go a very, very long way to preventing future sexual violence.

And understanding the myths and the realities of sexual offending is just flat out critical for preventing it, so we know who to target.

But the thing I want to leave you with today is the true damage of myths and misconceptions in all areas of life. Due to with our laws and prevention strategies being based on these myths and misconceptions, we are not only failing to protect ourselves but we could be putting ourselves at an increased risk too.

THE EFFECTS OF SEXUAL ASSAULT

Trigger warning: this following reflection contains references to sex, sexual assault and the aftermath of the assault and mental health. If the following will trigger you then please skip this reflection for the sake of your own mental health.

Sometimes things happen in my personal life that make me want to write these clinical psychology reflections a lot earlier than I normally would. For example, I know I won't write the rest of these reflections for another few months but I need to write these two now.

I was sexually assaulted two nights ago and I had an appointment today to discuss it at my university, the very nice woman helped to me to understand that it was sexual assault. I wasn't making it up or overreacting and she was really helpful.

I easily cried 2 or 3 times during that 30-minute appointment.

There is a clinical psychology point in the next chapter that I might be able to generalise to our profession. Yet I want to explain the effects of sexual assault on a victim in this chapter because I was surprised to learn what was normal behaviour in these cases when I spoke to the specialist at the university today.

Disclaimer

I've been watching the news, looking at social media and I've heard a lot of conversations with different people over my lifetime. I know I will get slated for writing these next two reflections, I know people will say I was asking for it and I know people will say I am disgusting and all that shit.

But honestly, unless you have experienced sexual assault then you don't have a leg to stand on.

I promise I am not having a go at 99% of readers because I know my audience are genuinely lovely and I love you all, you allow me to write and do what I love.

I am instead talking to the 1% of people that will read this and want to bully me because of it. To you I say kindly fuck off.

What Happened?

Before I explain what the effects of this event on me were specifically, I want to explain what happened in a way similar to how I described it to the woman at the university. I will brushstroke some stuff because what actually happened was too detailed for a book.

Therefore, if you're familiar with me and if you've been listening to The Psychology World Podcast then you might be aware that I was abused and traumatised as a kid for being gay. My social environment was extremely homophobic, I was in fear for my life for a decade that led to a lot of bad mental health outcomes. So I was never ever allowed to be gay at all. Much less hookup, have sex or kiss someone.

Thankfully, in that department my life is a million times better than it was and I'm generally happy with my life. It was so much better than before.

So I was free at the weekend, my friends have a lot of relationships and my best friend is currently abroad visiting the woman that They really want to start a relationship with. So I thought yeah it would be great if I could experience something.

I went on Grindr (for people who don't know that is a gay dating app but it is a more sex-focused one) so I had some nice conversations with two people that wanted to have sex with me. They couldn't do that particular night so I started talking with a third guy.

He seemed nice enough, he knew I was a virgin and had never ever done anything before with anyone. His photo seemed nice enough (something that was a minor con in the end) so we arranged to meet and I went to his house.

For starters, I realised he had lied on his profile because the photo he sent me he had hidden his body in such a way that he was very overweight.

For clarification I am not fatshaming, I am simply raising a point that he made sure to hide that fact and he used his weight to his advantage later on.

I went inside the house and he grabbed me and started kissing and grinding himself against me. I said "No, I haven't done this before". Expecting him to stop and we could talk about this hookup, what I wanted and we could go slow.

That didn't happen.

He stopped for a moment and then he grabbed me again and started *really* grinding himself against me, kissing me and forcing his tongue down my throat. And let me tell you, considering I have never kissed anyone in my entire life before, that wasn't nice and it is awful having someone force their tongue down your throat.

I hated it.

Now typical stereotypes would make you question why I didn't punch, kick, scream in this situation if I hated it so much. I have been a survivor my entire life and I was always focused on doing what I needed to do to survive, so I simply let it happen because once it happened this would be over and I could get the hell out of there without anything violent happening to me.

When I was talking to the woman at the university, this is a very normal response. The vast majority of sexual assault and rape victims do this strategy because this is what happens.

So the guy kept touching me, taking off my clothes, he kept kissing me and getting really really excited.

Only an idiot couldn't tell I wasn't enjoying it because I wasn't touching him back, I wasn't smiling and I wasn't doing anything to him in return. Mainly because he was massive. I might have touched him on the head to be nice and polite but that was it.

Then he took my boxers off and this is where I skip over some details. Let's just say he really, really liked my manhood so let's skip over that section.

Afterwards he ordered me to lie down and I am very thankful for the next bit. Because he was so fat, his dick didn't work in the sense that it didn't get long so this couldn't graduate from sexual assault to rape (the legal difference being rape requires penetration).

He grabbed me and covered me in his hulk in a tight hug as he tried to penetrate me and once he realised he wasn't able to. (He wasn't even using a condom or lube which is extremely bad sexual practice but I was too numb and feeling bad to mention it) He stopped and called it over.

I got out of there.

<u>The Effects</u>

During this entire process, I felt very numb, uncomfortable and I expect this is the autism here. I didn't feel in danger or too distressed at the time.

Interestingly when I spoke to the woman at the university, she said that this is also very normal because victims go into survival mode. Similar to fight or flight response, there is "fawn" or "freeze" response and I think I did both of these in the moment. Since fawn is about being a people pleaser in the end where you just allow shit to happen because it would make the other person happy and that reduces any unseen things happening to you. Like him getting angry and lashing out.

Equally, "freeze" is definitely what I did once he grabbed me for the second time.

In addition, something I notice with myself and I expect this is an autistic trait, so autistic people don't always know what they're feeling in the moment and there can be a delay between what happened and an emotion. Turns out, according to the woman at the university, this is common for victims too.

Since when I got home the night it happened, I felt numb and uncomfortable but I didn't feel distressed. Yet my problem was I couldn't sleep, I couldn't stay still in my bed and it wasn't awful. I woke up with a massive headache the next morning.

Also, the next morning I was really distressed, scared and I started to spiral. In other words, my brain and emotions caught up with the reality of the situation.

I cleaned my teeth a lot yesterday because I wanted to make sure my mouth was clean after he tongued me. Also, I had my normal trauma reaction of whenever I ate or drank it felt like swallowing glass. I've experienced that before whenever I'm distressed.

And the most major one and you might want to skip the next few paragraphs if you're sensitive. Because the guy liked my dick so much, I really hated having a dick. Yesterday morning I wanted to cut it off and just get rid of it forever.

Thankfully, that only lasted yesterday morning and then it shifted into a case of "I don't like seeing my dick but I don't want it gone anymore". Even now, I'm *better* with my dick but I still haven't looked at it and I haven't really touched it.

So going to the toilet is a bit annoying.

Moreover, something that is distressing as hell is yesterday when I was trying to keep myself busy and focus on everything but what happened (it didn't work). I could be doing something, like lying on my bed playing Duolingo or reading something, and I could *feel* him touching me.

Then I would get scared and almost cry because my body literally felt like he was touching me exactly how he did the night before. I know there's a name for this in psychology but I don't want to look it up.

It was weird and scary and awful.

Finally, the last major effect of the assault was I had a very weird panic attack last night in my own bed. Now this guy didn't try to have sex with me in a bed, it was in his living room.

Therefore, I was very surprised that when I went into my bed last night in my normal way of only wearing boxers. I had a panic attack because I wasn't wearing many clothes and I had to use grounding techniques about what I could feel, hear, smell and taste (I couldn't use see because I had my bedroom lights off) to make me focus back on the present moment.

And where I actually was.

So I'll admit I am very nervous about going to bed tonight but if I have another panic attack then I'll do what the woman from the university said and wear more clothes going to bed. That's a good idea to be honest and it's easy.

The Response From Others

Yesterday I was spiralling, trying to focus on what had happened and I was just scared because of a bunch of other trauma and what had happened before in my life (it wasn't sexual assault related but my brain didn't care), so I contacted one friend. The problem was they're in another country and they were away so they didn't have access to Wi-Fi (we communicate via WhatsApp a lot), so they didn't get back to me.

Also, my other close friend is very innocent and they wouldn't have any clue about this. As well as my other close friend is a sexual abuse victim from childhood so I couldn't talk to him about it.

Therefore, this morning actually did contact my friend that had been sexually abused as a child with the massive caveat that he needs to say no if he isn't comfortable with this. He messaged me back hours later saying we could take this conversation slowly and thankfully he didn't get triggered but he confirmed this was rape.

Before that though, I contacted my university because they have a Specialist Support Service as part of their mental health team. I had a 30-minute appointment with her and she's great and I told her what happened, she told me about my options and some support I could get.

The only real support I am concerned I might need is academic because I have two stats exams coming up and I'm concerned that I can't seem to focus. I know I'm getting ahead of myself because it was only two days ago but I am scared that I won't be able to focus on revision for the exams next month.

Thankfully, she said mitigation is an option and she can help with that.

Then she mentioned the name of a service with an extremely problematic name and we spoke about groups and some interesting stuff including some denial about terms on my part. Like I didn't want to admit I was a sexual assault victim until three people confirmed what happened was sexual assault.

I really didn't want to admit it but that is what happened.

Finally, I had a lovely, deep conversation with my best friend who finally read my messages and I'm looking forward to seeing them in a few weeks when they're back.

Ending Note

I'll admit that it took a lot for me to write this reflection because I didn't want any of this to happen, I am better than I was in the morning but that's only because I spoke to people about it. I feel better that I'm supported and the people important to me socially are aware of this.

Like, I'm seeing a friend on Thursday (it's Monday today), I'm spending a few days with my best friend anyway, I'm hoping to see my innocent friend next week so I thankfully have the social support.

Will I be 100% okay?

Of course not. No one ever is but I am better than I was and I'm happy about that.

Now, because this reflection is a little longer than I intended I will leave the rest for another reflection. Which will be a lot more general towards clinical psychology and mental health as a whole.

Let's check it out.

GROUP IDENTITIES AND PROBLEMATIC NAMES OF SEXUAL ASSAULT AND RAPE SERVICES

Trigger warning: *the following clinical psychology reflection contains details and references of rape, sexual assault and the stories of victims. Please do not read this reflection if you would find it distressing.*

The Group Identities and Labels

As a clinical psychology student, author and podcaster, I've thought a lot about the stigma and social perceptions surrounding labels and names. It's one of the reasons why I hate the diagnostic system with a passion and it's why I've spoken a lot about the damaging impact of labels in these reflections before.

However, I was a little surprised by my own denial and resistance to terming myself as a victim or a sexual assault victim. I think mainly because I thought maybe only someone who's been kicked, punched, beaten with an inch of their life could say they're a victim of rape or sexual assault.

Again, just me going off the societal myths about this sort of crime.

Maybe I thought only certain people get raped and assaulted. Maybe I didn't want to admit what had happened and how serious and bad that was.

Then as the woman at the university said along with my good close friends, this was rape and this was bad and this never ever should have happened.

I slowly had to acknowledge that this was sexual assault and I was a victim.

Therefore, as a clinical psychology person, I find it interesting that people don't want to attach certain labels to themselves. In all honesty, I know this from my previous lectures and comments on labels because they are stigmatised. I bet you're thinking I am a very specific type of person because I've been sexually assaulted.

Some of you are probably thinking I'm weak, not manly (I'm non-binary anyway) and I'm a failure because real people fight back.

You would only be going off cultural stereotypes so I hardly blame you. I might even do the same if I was in your shoes.

And I think the reason why I was so resistant to terming myself as a sexual assault victim was because I didn't want to see myself as a victim anymore. I've been a victim my entire life from child abuse and trauma, living constantly in fear for my life and so on.

I just wanted to live a little and then this happened.

And I know from my family and my social environment that being a victim of sexual assault isn't always something you get supported in. Like I know I will tell my family but I won't at the moment because that will make me a victim in their eyes and they will look at me every day like I'm a victim.

Also, there is a lot of stigma and social pressure on victims. People will say I was asking for it, I should have fought back, I should have done X, Y and Z. or even well, I'm gay so this was bound to happen (an utter bullshit comment if there ever was one but I have heard a variation of it in real life).

So I was very resistant to it.

Overall, when it comes to clinical psychology work in the future and you have a client that refuses to be termed or included in a group of people. I would unofficially recommend respecting them and maybe even gently question why.

Since when the woman at the university said in a paraphrased way "Something-Something Rape Services for victims of sexual violence, I don't know if you would include yourself in those groups,"

I said: "I don't want to but I know the definition is anything that isn't consensual sex is rape. But I *know* I'm a rape victim but I don't want to admit it,"

That is perfectly okay and she respected me and I later admitted it in my own time. That is something you can and should do with clients too.

Naming Services

Continuing with the same vein of thinking and reasoning, I wanted to comment on the name of a charity or mental health service that offers counselling and other support for sexual assault and rape victims. I can't say its actual name for privacy reasons but it was "Something-Something Rape Crisis Centre"

I didn't like the name and the name immediately put me off the service.

As well as the woman at the university admitted the name was problematic because for starters, it implies only rape victims can go there, not sexual assault victims.

Also, the name is very loaded because it suggests that if you go to this place then you are a victim of rape and sexual assault and it carries all that social stigma with it. I did not want to contact or deal with this charity whatsoever because I didn't want to admit to myself that I was a victim and I did not want to go there and be seen to everyone at this charity as a weak victim.

Again, this isn't me being difficult. This is me just using what limited knowledge I have about victims from what I've seen on TV, the news and social conversations over the years. I only researched it more this afternoon after others confirmed and helped me to realise what had happened.

On the whole, I think if this service and charity didn't have such a loaded name then I would have considered it. I might have contacted them, and the woman at the university wouldn't have had to explain that other people have had similar reactions to me. And then she gently made sure I explained what support network I have in place at the moment as she knew I wasn't going to contact the service.

In future, I think, as future or current clinical psychologists, if we ever rise to a position of power where we are in a position to name mental health and support services. Then we need to be mindful about the words we use in the name so they aren't loaded, they aren't going to turn people away and they aren't going to stop the people we aim to help.

Just an interesting thought-provoking idea that I would have liked never to learn or have to think about.

UPDATE ON USE OF INCULSIVE LANGUAGE IN MENTAL HEALTH SERVICES

Whilst this next chapter might not immediately seem linked to working with rape survivors, this is a critical chapter to understanding how simple (to you) language can create additional barriers to psychological treatment.

Back in *Clinical Psychology Reflections Volume 5*, I did an entire reflection on the great topic of why inclusive language is needed within clinical psychology, mental health services and the assessment tools we use. That is still one of my favourite reflections because it's very adept, useful and it is critical to understand.

Even more so when we understand that minority groups, including sexual and gender minorities, tend to have a lot of mental health difficulties due to minority stress and other societal-level factors as well as interpersonal factors.

Back in the last reflection on this topic, I gave a personal therapy example because the day I wrote that reflection I went for my first appointment at my university's counselling service. Please read that volume to find out more.

However, two days ago when I went for the appointment with the university sexual assault specialist, she was a brilliant example of why it is beyond critical to use people's preferred names and pronouns. Since I have dropped the name "Connor" in recent months but I still keep it as an author and business name.

Therefore, in this reflection, I want to briefly explain what happened in regards to this preferred name and inclusive language topic, before explaining how and why it benefited the appointment as much as it did.

What Happened?

Even though I've recently changed my preferred name at the university and I am officially my preferred name on the vast majority of systems. I know that occasionally I still pop-up as my legal name, which is a bit annoying but I can live with it.

Also, because I wasn't convinced at the time and I seriously didn't want to admit that I was sexually assaulted, I wanted to talk to my old counsellor at the university. The problem was he only knew me as Connor because that was the name I went by back then.

Therefore, I emailed the student support service the following (It's easier than explaining what I wrote):

"Hello, I hope you're well.

I'm not really sure how to start this email but I would like to request some support please, so maybe counselling or maybe just a one-off appointment. I know I had my 5 allotted sessions back in the Autumn term but *counsellor's surname* said things calm down in April and Summer so... maybe that request could be okay.

It's just I think what happened to me Saturday night might have been approaching the sexual harassment/assault threshold. I'm autistic so I don't know but I said no and it kept happening. And I've been jumpy, had a panic attack and a few other things other the event.

So I would like to talk to someone at the uni about this please as soon as possible. Maybe *Counsellor's name* because he was my counsellor before when I went by my deadname Connor.

Thank you for reading.

Have a good week,

Preferred name."

As you can probably tell from that email, I really wasn't sure and I really didn't want to admit what had happened to me.

Anyway, the university student support service didn't bat an eyelid towards my name and gender, they just accepted it and got on with the job itself. Their job was to see me and make sure that I was okay.

Hence, I got a phone call a few hours later with the wonderful woman I always see at reception when I used to go there, she explained to me my old counsellor wasn't about but the specialist was free at 2pm on Teams and I should see her. She kept using my preferred name and I was more than happy with that.

I agreed to see the specialist.

At 2 pm, I went on Teams and met with the woman as I've explained before and it was great that she called me by my preferred name. Since it removed any additional barriers to the appointment anyway then she explained stuff about confidentiality, how this would work and more.

Granted, I highly expected she thought I was a transwoman because of my name, but thankfully I mentioned about gender dysphoria and being non-binary. So we clarified pronouns and just cracked on with the appointment and we focused on what had happened, any support I might need and so on.

Why Is This Language Important?

The main reason why this was important to me in the appointment was because it removed any additional barriers that didn't need to be there. For example, the woman could have just called me "he" throughout the entire appointment, she could have kept referring to me as a man and she could have asked what my "real" name was (I hate it when people say that because that is beyond disrespectful).

And at the time of writing, I've just finished a blog post on Culturally Sensitive Therapy and there's a concept that I really like. There's a concept about distance between the therapist and the client, and the more distant a client feels from the therapist, the less successful a therapy is likely to be.

I think the same concept can be applied here because if the woman from the university put up those additional barriers by not using my preferred name or pronouns then I would have felt uncomfortable, distant and I wouldn't have trusted her as much as I did. And I certainly wouldn't have told her as much as I did about what happened.

Therefore, it's important to respect a client's preferred name and their pronouns because it helps to strengthen the therapeutic alliance, it tears down any additional barriers and concerns that the client has, and it helps to improve the experience of the client.

This is even more important when we think about how scary, intimidating and nerve-racking going to a sexual assault or rape service is.

And if you're concerned about asking about pronouns would be a "waste of time", I've had private therapy, I've had a few university counselling sessions and I've had a specialist appointment now. Every single time I have heard the exact same talk about confidentiality and its limitations.

It's boring and as a client after I've heard it once or twice, I consider briefing me time and time again about confidentiality as a waste of time.

However, I know in reality confidentiality is beyond critical in psychotherapy and other settings. Yet my point is, there are already some longish and critical pieces of information to get across to a client before any session or therapy works start in order to set the session off in the right direction.

So why don't we add in a tiny little section about pronouns that will take no more than 20 seconds to make sure that clients feel safe, comfortable and respected in our therapy room.

If it helps a client to see us as equals who respect them and want to hear from them, then this is something we absolutely need to do. It just might be the difference between getting a client to open up about an event and them choosing to delay it when it could have been dealt with earlier in therapy.

WHAT IS INTENT TO SURVIVE?

"You need to have the Intent To Survive this,"

Those were the words of my therapist towards the end of our session shortly after my sexual assault. They were powerful words to hear both as a clinical psychology student and a sexual assault survivor. I think a lot of their power came from me not understanding what it meant and me still reeling from what happened, but I also think they're powerful words because they are so true.

To be able to survive any traumatic event, you need to make sure you want to survive it.

As a result, I want to take the opportunity of this reflection to explain what Intent To Survive means to me personally as a survivor, but first I want to talk about this as an aspiring clinical psychologist.

What Is Intent To Survive In Clinical Psychology Terms?

As we know from our clinical psychology experiences, lectures and various conversations with professionals, we all know that we can give a client a lot of psychological help and support yet until a client is willing to change and use the tools and techniques we give them. Then our help only has a limited value.

For example, we can teach our clients ways to change their biased cognitive processes in depression and other mood disorders. Yet unless a client puts what they learn in therapy into practice in the real-world then the client cannot improve their lives.

To some extent, I think "Intent To Survive" is the trauma term of capacity to change, because a trauma causes a lot of psychological and physiological changes within a client. For instance, my sexual assault caused me to have a lot of panic attacks, rapid heartbeats, shaking and more.

Those were the physiological changes.

When it comes to psychological changes, I have a fair amount of social anxiety, my mood changes from normal and positive to depressed so I can't move some days, and as bad as this sounds I do have a minor fear of overweight people. Since my attacker was severely overweight so I might overweight people triggering.

Therefore, the term *intent to survive* means that a client has to do double duty when recovering from trauma. Since not only have they got to want to change and improve their life so they don't "suffer" from the physical and psychological manifestations of their trauma, but they have to want to survive it and move past it.

I know that won't make sense for people, because surely it is perfectly obvious that our clients will want to survive their trauma.

No.

Trauma really doesn't work like that in my personal experience and conversations I've had with some survivors.

Due to in trauma, death really can seem so much easier, and surviving trauma seems so pointless. It really does.

One example I had in May 2024 about 3.5 weeks after my assault was I had had a few panic attacks at a social group I go to normally and my friends and some of the other people at the social group went to a local pub in Canterbury. They asked if I wanted to go but I just broke down a little and ran out of there.

I texted my best friend and another friend about five minutes later saying how I just wanted to kill myself, I didn't want to do this anymore and death just seemed so much easier. I wasn't really suicidal that night but the thoughts were starting to come up.

This is rather normal in trauma survivors because surviving something traumatic just seems impossible and such a far away future that it doesn't seem real at all.

Therefore, as aspiring or qualified clinical psychologists or other mental health professionals, you might benefit from thinking about trauma in terms of *intent to survive*. Since helping a client focus specifically on surviving instead of healing straight away might be really, really useful.

Of course, the process will and should always be on the healing as well as recovery process. Yet healing takes a long, long time and it is that time in-between that is stupidly difficult.

Also, even though me and my therapist aren't really focus on the concept of *intent to survive* too much in my session. I still found those three words useful over the past few weeks because whenever I was struggling or in a "dark place", I could say to myself "I need to have *intent to survive* this,".

It was useful.

Overall, the concept of *intent to survive* within clinical work might have two places. Firstly, it is an effective way to reframe initial trauma sessions even more so when a client has just recently suffered the trauma. This is where (to my knowledge) survival is the main priority as healing seems so far away and impossible and trauma survivors aren't really in a position to heal at this point in time.

Secondly, *intent to survive* might be a useful phase to say to clients so they can remember they need to have an *intent to survive* their trauma whenever they're struggling or in a really dark place.

What Does *Intent To Survive* Mean To Me?

This is something I have seriously struggled with over the past few weeks because as an aspiring clinical psychologist, I know what this means. I think it is a great term and way to frame our own thinking about trauma like I mentioned above.

However, as a two-time trauma survivor, I have struggled to work out what this means to me as a human being. When my therapist first mentioned this, I didn't really register it because of course I wanted to survive this, I wanted to move past this and I thought I was going to be fine.

Because come on, it was only sexual assault.

Then May happened with my panic attacks, meltdowns and everything else that went negatively with my mental health. So it was nasty and I didn't know if I had the *intent to survive* because I wasn't sure what it meant.

Nonetheless, it's been 7 weeks exactly since The Event and I have a *better* idea about what it means to me. I've had my counselling assessment, I'm on the waiting list and I've learnt how great my friends are, so I have built a social support network around myself.

I think in the beginning *intent to survive* literally meant I wanted to see my best friend again because they were in Switzerland. I know this sounds odd because I wanted to see my best friend and I wanted to spend my birthday with them. I wanted my family to meet them, I wanted to go up to London to do the virtual reality escape room and I wanted to catch up with them.

They are my best friend for a reason.

Also, to me *intent to survive* initially meant just processing and dealing with it, because I was having a lot of physical reactions and problems. For example, the shaking, the fear of going to sleep and the problems of having a toilet.

After this happened the definition of *intent to survive* changed as I started to experience more and more psychological symptoms and trauma reactions. Like the depression, the meltdowns in public because of triggers, the intense social anxiety and so on.

When this happened *intent to survive* meant rather sadly just putting one foot in front of the other, taking each day as it came and trying to live as normal as a life as I possibly could.

This was really hard because there was another minor change in the definition as I couldn't see a future. The future and the idea of healing seemed so extreme and so impossible that I did not believe I could have a future.

This wasn't helped by my exams, my best friend experiencing awful harassment and accusations by their psychotic exboyfriend, and then a whole bunch of other things were going on in my own life.

Therefore, *intent to survive* took on a very meaningless or opaque definition. Since I sort of wanted to live and survive my assault but I also couldn't see a future. I couldn't see how I could ever have a relationship, I couldn't see how I could ever have sex, love someone or how I could ever not feel like a weak, pathetic, violated victim.

Thankfully, I did meet with the specialist at the university again and it was nice to have that referral.

This is where the definition of *intent to survive* changed again to what it currently means, and it's actually rather lovely to think about it for a change.

I know me and my best friend we are still operating on the assumption that I am a moderate suicide risk until we move into together at the end of June 2024 (exactly four weeks away). Personally, I think if I can make it after Pride weekend (that triggers a lot of past child abuse and trauma for me) then I should be okay.

Also, there will be a lot of people at Pride and a lot of couples and my concern is my mind will twist seeing couples and lots of happy people enjoying their day as "you can never have this because of your child abuse and your sexual assault so what's the point of living,"

Thankfully, me and my best friend have a plan in place anyway for Pride weekend and we're going with a lot of other friends too.

Anyway, going back to *intent to survive,* because I've had my counselling assessment and I'm on the waiting list with East Kent Rape Crisis Centre, I have a sense of hope. I am not 100%, I am still not completely sure that I can date, I can have sex and I can have relationships in the future.

But I will get the support I need, even if it takes two or three months.

There is hope.

So for me that is what *intent to survive* means at the moment. It means I have the hope to live and survive my sexual assault long enough to see what happens to me in the future.

Additionally, it means I have the curiosity as well as capacity to change because I want to survive this, so I can explore relationships, dating and what consensual sex actually looks like. That would be lovely. Also, I am curious about the therapy process as an aspiring clinical psychologist because I know sexual violence work is very specialised so I want to see how this differs from "normal" clinical work.

And it is perfectly okay if that is a reason that increases my *intent to survive*. As long as I can intend to survive my trauma then that is okay.

Lastly, *intent to survive* means to me that I want a future. I have no idea what this future will look like, I don't know if it's filled with relationships, love and respect. I don't know if it's filled with trauma, pain and suffering. I don't even know if it's filled with job possibilities and me having a successful career in clinical psychology.

Yet I want to try and I want to explore my future what it might be.

That is what *intent to survive* means to me because if I don't survive this trauma then I will never ever know what my future will be and hell, right now this is a half-joke to myself but I hope in a few months this will be something I truly believe in.

If I don't survive this then I might deny a hot, sexy guy or masculine person a chance to meet me, and come on now, that really would be cruel.

WHAT IS POST-TRAUMATIC STRESS DISORDER?

There is no denying that experiencing sexual violence is a massively traumatic event that changes your life forever. Therefore, it makes sense that the majority of survivors go on to develop PTSD after their trauma. However, not all aspiring or qualified clinical psychologists are aware of what PTSD actually is, what are the symptoms and some of the other important pieces of information that you need to know about PTSD. As a result, our next chapter focuses on PTSD so you can increase your awareness about this distressing, traumatic mental health condition that is unfortunately all too common amongst sexual assault survivors.

In addition, the vast majority of people have heard of Post-Traumatic Stress Disorder (PTSD) before when it comes to veterans and soldiers. Also, we know this mental health condition involves flashbacks, intrusive memories and panic attacks, but beyond that a lot of laypeople don't know that much about Post-Traumatic Stress Disorder. I'm only starting to learn more about PTSD because I have it because of my sexual assault, so whilst I don't talk about it in this chapter, my own experiences make this important to look at. Therefore, in this clinical psychology podcast chapter, we'll be looking at what is Post-Traumatic Stress Disorder, what causes Post-Traumatic Stress Disorder and what are the symptoms of PTSD. I won't cover treatments for Post-Traumatic Stress Disorder in this chapter because that's a massive area and I've already spoken about that in different chapters on The Psychology World Podcast before. So if you enjoy learning about mental health, trauma and clinical psychology then this is a great chapter for you.

What Is Post-Traumatic Stress Disorder?

As you can imagine Post-Traumatic Stress Disorder is a mental health condition classed as a trauma and stress-related disorder that can develop in response to being exposed to an event or ordeal where severe physical harm or death was threatened or happened. People can develop PTSD after rape, violence, bombings, shootings, military service and rescue workers can develop PTSD too.

In terms of prevalence rate, I talk more about Post-Traumatic Stress Disorder in sexual violence populations briefly in a moment, but about 6.8% of Americans develop the condition in their lifetime. This information is from the National Institute of Mental Health.

Furthermore, Post-Traumatic Stress Disorder can develop at any age, including childhood, and women are more likely to develop it than men. Also, there is some evidence that PTSD runs in families, as well as Post-Traumatic Stress Disorder is often comorbid with conditions like depression, anxiety and substance use disorders. Then when these other conditions can be diagnosed and treated, the likelihood of the overall treatment being successful increases.

In addition, something we need to know about Post-Traumatic Stress Disorder is you can only get diagnosed with the condition if you have PTSD symptoms for over a month. If you have the symptoms for less than a month then you don't have PTSD (at least in diagnosis terms), instead you have Acute Distress Disorder.

Also, with the right care and support, a lot of PTSD symptoms can abate within trauma survivors within that first month so a lot of people never go on to develop Post-Traumatic Stress Disorder.

Interestingly, Post-Traumatic Stress Disorder can be delayed in its manifestations because this occurs if PTSD symptoms show themselves six months or more after the onset of the trauma.

Post-Traumatic Stress Disorder And The Military

I couldn't really do a Post-Traumatic Stress Disorder-focused podcast chapter without talking about the military as this is where a lot of our common knowledge about PTSD comes from.

The prevalence rate of Post-Traumatic Stress Disorder in the military is moderately high because about 30% of the Vietnam War veterans developed PTSD, and 10% of soldiers who took part in Operation Desert Storm (the Gulf War) developed PTSD. As well as between 12% and 20% of soldiers serving in the Iraq war developed PTSD too.

As you can imagine, it is the combat element that increases the risk of developing Post-Traumatic Stress Disorder for veterans amongst other mental health conditions, because severe harm and death happens around them. There are other risk factors too, including the politics surrounding the war, the type of enemy the soldier faces and where the war is fought.

All these risk factors can interact to cause Post-Traumatic Stress Disorder to develop and be maintained in a soldier.

Moreover, there is a type of trauma that is never spoken about in the military and this is Military Sexual Trauma and sexual assault or sexual harassment connects to this topic too. This certainly can cause Post-Traumatic Stress Disorder.

Since Military Sexual Trauma can happen to both men and women regardless of whether it's wartime, peacetime or during training with figures suggesting 23% of women have been sexually assaulted in the US military and 55% of women and 38% of men have been sexually harassed in the military too.

Personally, I suspect the real numbers are a lot, lot higher because no one likes to report this stuff and get it on public record. And I say this as a survivor myself, the people that made this research possible are amazing and a lot more courageous than me.

Overall, there are a lot of different traumatic experiences that can lead to a person developing Post-Traumatic Stress Disorder. Including terrorist attacks, natural disasters, sexual assaults and physical attacks.

Post-Traumatic Stress Disorder And Sexual Violence: Why Am I Talking About PTSD Now?

A few weeks ago leading up to Canterbury Pride in early June, I wanted to go by myself to a Warhammer event at my university with a Pride twist. I would be going alone and I wanted to go because it would be nice to meet new people, get back into Warhammer and it would be a good event. Yet I had a lot of social anxiety, I felt physically sick about going and I had seen photos of the Warhammer group at my university and some of the people there were rather triggering for me.

A lot popped up that week because of me wanting to go to this event.

I was really distressed so I texted my best friend and they mentioned I have PTSD, so I pooed-pooed. I wasn't listening to them, not that they knew it at the time. Yet I thought about it, researched it a little more and then found out it is very common amongst survivors of sexual violence.

This was hammered home last week too when I went to Wales because in the evening, my parents were asleep on the sofa and I was still watching the crime drama that had on and it turned out the killer was getting revenge on her rapists. And the programme showed the implicated rape scenes, so I got really distressed, I couldn't change the TV over so I shouted and it was a little messy.

There are other reasons why I'm certain I have PTSD and I'll probably sprinkle them in throughout the chapter to help show examples of this in real life.

Anyway, the reason why I'm talking about Post-Traumatic Stress Disorder now is I want to understand it is more and it is scarily common. For example, Campbell (2009) who looked at studies dating back to the 1980s found that between 17% and 65% of women who experience sexual assault develop PTSD. As well as a peer-reviewed article from the University Of Washington School Of Medicine/Uw Medicine found 81% of survivors had PTSD one week after their attack and 75% of sexual assault survivors had PTSD a month after their attack. Lastly, an article from Verywell Mind in 2023 explained nearly 48% of survivors had PTSD after a year of being assaulted.

I want to note that the specific type of Post-Traumatic Stress Disorder that sexual violence survivors develop is known as Rape Trauma Syndrome.

So now we understand how common it is in another area besides military veterans, let's explore the symptoms of Post-Traumatic Stress Disorder in more depth.

What Are The Symptoms Of Post-Traumatic Stress Disorder?

A lot of people with Post-Traumatic Stress Disorder tend to relive and re-experience the traumatic event or different aspects of it. There is a wide range of triggers, something I am finding out more and more, but there are some common themes. For example, anniversaries of traumatic events and similar people, situations or places can trigger the distressing memories.

A similar person example for me was my attacker was very fat and very overweight so I can be extremely triggered when I see a fat man. This isn't me being fatphobic, it is just fat people trigger my rape memories.

In addition, Post-Traumatic Stress Disorder causes a person to experience flashbacks, intrusive thoughts, distributed sleep, anxiety, sadness, intense guilt, emotional numbness, outbursts of anger and dissociative experiences.

And whilst people with PTSD try to avoid situations that remind them of the traumatic event, they can still be surprised by what triggers them and when the symptoms last for longer than a month, a diagnosis of PTSD might be relevant.

Now I want us to look at the different types of PTSD symptoms.

What Are The Avoidance Symptoms Of PTSD?

Because no one with Post-Traumatic Stress Disorder wants to be reminded of the traumatic event, we all avoid certain triggers so avoidance symptoms include:

- Avoiding activities, places and people associated with the event
- Avoiding conversations, feelings or thoughts about the event

As I mentioned earlier, I avoid fat men like the plague because they remind me too much of my rapist, and I avoid any crime drama with a sexual violence theme. Thankfully, I never watched *Law and Order: Special Victims Unit.*

What Are The Reexperiencing Symptoms Of Post-Traumatic Stress Disorder?

When it comes to the reliving the traumatic experience over and over again, symptoms include:

- Experiencing intense emotions when you're reminded of the event
- Feeling or behaving as if the event was actually happening all over again (flashbacks)
- Having distressing memories and bad dreams of the event
- Having dissociative reactions and/ or loss of awareness of your present surroundings
- Having intense physical sensations when reminded of the event. Such as, feeling faint, feeling a loss of control, sweating, pounding heart and so on.

One of the ways I've experienced these symptoms include very distressing physical sensations all over my body about how he was touching and doing things to me, and that's all I'll say about that one. As well as I used to have this one a lot more but it has thankfully mellowed out a little nowadays, I would have a complete loss of awareness that worked with these physical sensations so I would need to use grounding techniques to get me to focus back on the present.

What Are The Reactivity and Arousal Symptoms Of PTSD?

When it comes to the reactivity and arousal symptoms of Post-Traumatic Stress Disorder, they can include:

- Feeling easily startled.
- Excess awareness (also known as hypervigilance)
- Sleeping difficulties including having trouble falling or staying asleep
- Difficulty concentrating
- Outbursts of anger or being irritable

An unfortunately good example of this area for me was during my Statistic Theory online exam in May. Since it was bad enough that I couldn't concentrate enough to do any revision whatsoever until a week before the exam, as well as because the exam was online and made up of 40 multiple choices, my mind wondered after question 20. Which led to a full-on meltdown and panic attack during my exam.

That wasn't nice but thankfully I passed, only by 3 points by still.

What About The Mood and Cognitive Symptoms Of Post-Traumatic Stress Disorder?

When someone has PTSD, they'll experience negative changes in their mood and thoughts, these symptoms can include:

- An inability to experience positive moods
- A lack of interest in social activities
- Feeling detached and numb from things
- Having difficulty remembering an important part of the traumatic event
- Pessimism about the future

In terms of clinical psychology, one thing I do want to mentiom is you can see why depression and anxiety are common conditions to find alongside PTSD. For example, a lack of interest in social activities and pessimism about the future, they're both common with depression too.

Going back to personal experience, I've already mentioned the social anxiety I have about going to something new and I have basically stopped that now, and even social events I've been going to since before my assault. It still takes me a while to actually go to them before I do. For example, I am not that ashamed to admit, I spent twenty minutes in the university toilets with my social anxiety before I went to a social last week.

Are There Other Symptoms Of Post-Traumatic Stress Disorder?

Some other symptoms of PTSD that don't really fit into the other categories include:

- Depersonalisation- feeling like you're outside of your body
- Derealisation- experiencing unreality of surroundings

These symptoms are rarer for people but some clients can experience them.

What Causes Post-Traumatic Stress Disorder?

Whilst we don't know the definitive cause of Post-Traumatic Stress Disorder, we know that there are biological, psychological and social factors that interact together to develop the condition. Since Post-Traumatic Stress Disorder causes changes in how the body responds to stress so it impacts our stress hormones as well as neurotransmitters that carry information between our nerves.

As a result, people who experience childhood abuse or other traumatic experiences are likely to develop PTSD months or even years after the trauma. Also, temperamental variables, like externalising behaviours or other anxiety difficulties, can increase the risk of developing the condition too.

Additionally, environmental factors can cause PTSD. For instance, childhood adversity, family dysfunction, family mental health history, cultural variables, and more importantly, the more traumatic the event, the greater the risk of developing Post-Traumatic Stress Disorder. This is why witnessing atrocities and severe personal injury are major, major risk factors.

Moreover, having maladaptive coping mechanisms, a lack of social support, financial stress and family instability can all worsen the mental health outcomes for people with Post-Traumatic Stress Disorder.

Personally, because my best friend is the only social support I actually have since my sexual assault because other people just don't know how to help me and the most important people in my life just want to pretend it never happened and I am perfectly fine. I am seriously not. That can decrease my mental health a lot because I feel guilt towards my best friend because they are all I've got until my specialise counselling starts and my best friend isn't always around, so I have had to do some maladaptive coping mechanisms just to survive.

Having more social support is critical when it comes to PTSD.

On the other hand, there are resilience factors that can decrease the risk of a client developing Post-Traumatic Stress Disorder. Some of these resilience factors are present before the trauma and other resilience factors can become more importantly learnt during and after the traumatic event. For example, seeking out support including mental health professionals, finding a support group, feeling good about your own actions in the face of danger, being able to act and respond effectively despite fear and having a coping strategy are all resilience factors that can help reduce the development of Post-Traumatic Stress Disorder.

Conclusion

We've covered a lot of ground when it comes to Post-Traumatic Stress Disorder because we've looked at what is PTSD, how common is PTSD in the military and sexual violence survivors, what are the symptoms and what are the causes. After this chapter, we've all deepened our knowledge about this mental health condition a lot and I'm pleased that we've all learnt about PTSD more.

Since PTSD is a horrible, horrible condition to have but there is hope. There are treatments and you can still live a long, happy life with the condition.

Even though I've been having panic attacks, distressing memories, distressing physical experiences and so on, there are still happy, joyful moments. Like I love spending time with my best friend, I enjoy Outreach work at my university and I still love writing. There are moments of positivity so I focus on them.

And another reason why I liked today's chapter is that I could start to see what I'm experiencing is normal and it's a natural response to an extremely unnatural situation.

I am not a problem and no one with PTSD is a problem.

Therefore, I want to conclude this chapter by saying that if you ever meet, become friends with or get to know someone with PTSD. Offering them some social support (that accurately reflects the level of friendship of course), listening to them and signposting them to some mental health services could have a massive positive impact on that person.

And it really could change their life for the better.

WHAT IS COERCIVE CONTROL?

Continuing with our focus on domestic violence for one more chapter, I wanted to talk about coercive control because this is an outrageous behaviour that can be seen in rapists and other sexual abusers that try to control their victims. As well as after I came across a woman's domestic violence survival story and her wish to raise awareness about domestic violence and Coercive Control. I really wanted to help honour her survival in a way so I wanted us to look on the podcast at this critical topic. So we can understand the psychology behind this outrageous behaviour, and in future episodes hopefully focus on helping ourselves avoid Coercive control.

Why Psychology Needs To Look At Coercive Control And Abusive Relationships?

I always think it's important to highlight why these are important topics to discuss on the podcast because that way I know I tend to focus on them, and you might enjoy them more because of their importance. I don't know why I like to lay down a psychological foundation too before we dive into the meat of the topic.

In terms of Coercive Control and abusive relationships, many people simply ask questions: *why don't victims simply leave the relationship?*

And of course that is a reasonable question, I think when I was younger I wondered that too. Yet from social psychology and the Need To Belong Theory, humans are resistant to breaking any relationship even ones that are bad for us.

In addition, as we are all hopefully outside the abusive relationship the answer seems so simple to the abuse. Just report it and leave the relationship. But this is where the reality is different from the ideal and it was a lot, lot more complicated than this.

As well as whilst there are many different reasons why victims don't leave the relationship. One of the most common reasons is fear, and whilst the exact definition of fear is hard to pin down. A good definition is something along the lines of a very unpleasant strong emotion caused by a person's anticipation and/ or awareness of danger.

Due to like most emotions, fear can range from minor to severe, and the fear could be real or perceived to be real. And what's critical to understand here is that the victim's perception and whether the danger is real or not doesn't matter. What does matter is that fear can be psychological or physical and it can be rather incapacitating and debilitating. Making leaving the relationship quite impossible.

And I want to mention that the reason why I'm not mentioning gender here is because whilst women are the victims in the vast majority of cases. They are not in every single case and men can be and are still abused in some cases, so I don't want to put a gender here instead of the word *victim* and help to reinforce a damaging stereotype.

Additionally, to help show the importance of this topic some more, here are some numbers from the United States' National Coalition Against Domestic Violence. For example, 1 in 9 men and 1 in 4 women experience severe intimate partner physical violence, intimate partner contact, sexual violence, intimate partner stalking with impacts. These impacts include fearfulness, post-traumatic stress disorder, use of victim services, injury and more.

Furthermore, 1 in 3 women and 1 in 4 men have experienced some kind of physical violence in the past by an intimate partner. This includes a range of behaviour, like slapping, pushing and shoving, and in some cases might not be considered "domestic violence" when it actually is.

1 in 4 women and 1 in 7 men have been victims of severe physical violence. For example, beating, strangling and burning by an intimate partner in their lifetime. As well as 1 in 7 women and 1 in 25 men have been injured by an intimate partner.

Therefore, as you can clearly see (or hear) regardless of the situation (except maybe the last one) regardless of gender a sadly high number of both have experienced domestic violence. And this only highlights why it's critical to increase awareness of the topic.

What Is Coercive Control?

Moving onto the next section of the episode, one of the leading authorities on this area is a person called Dr Evan Stark and he defines Coercive Control as the following:

"a strategic course of oppressive behavior designed to secure and expand gender-based privilege by depriving women of their rights and liberties and establishing a regime of domination in personal life."

As well as one of the problems with the literature on Coercive Control is that there is no, or no easy to find studies that have men as the victims. Now it would be great to imagine that meant no men fall under this area, but given how the myth of men being domestically abused is false. I personally doubt this and think this is a massive gap in the literature. You cannot seriously imagine that out of every single man on the planet, not a single one of them is being Coercively Controlled.

Moreover, Stark adds in his work that 60% to 80% of all abused women experience Coercive Control beyond the use of physical abuse. Meaning the physical abuse might have stopped but the Coercive Control continues.

And Coercive Control can have deadly consequences as Stark argues Coercive Control is strongly correlated with murder. For example, for the sake of illustration only, between the years 2000 and 2006 3200 American soldiers were killed in combat, but during the same time three times as many women were murdered by their husbands or boyfriends. As well as 1 woman is murdered every 16 hours in the United State either by a current or former male partner.

With the victims most at risk of being murdered are the people in which domestic violence, stalking and Coercive Control happen at the same time. And domestic violence and stalking is common.

The Role of Narcissistic Personality Disorder:

Interesting, there is some evidence that Narcissistic Personality Disorder is involved in Coercive Control alongside antisocial personality disorder, as all three of them are common among perpetrators of domestic violence. With people having Narcissistic Personality Disorder being described as manipulative, demanding, arrogant and self-centred. And they exhibit at least 5 of the following traits:

- Exploitation of others
- A lack of empathy
- Envy of others
- Have a need for excessive admiration
- A grandiose sense of self-importance
- Busy with fantasies of unlimited power, beauty, ideal love, success and brilliance.
- A belief about themselves being special and can only be understood by or associated with special people and institutions.
- Arrogant, condescending attitudes or behaviours
- Sense of entitlement

How Is Coercive Control Criminalised?

Moving onto the last section of the episode, we need to address the very harsh topic of Coercive Control and the legal system. Due to very few elements of Coercive Control are technically a crime and criminal and psychological abuse is always harder to get evidence for and prosecute compared to physical abuse. And yes, I know physical abuse getting prosecuted is hard enough.

This sadly results in the identification, criminally charging and prosecution of the Coercive Control cases is very much beyond challenging.

To make matters worse, successfully prosecuting Coercive Control cases are incredibly rare.

Yet there is a bit of hope because if a case does move forward to trial then the case will most likely be plea-bargained.

In addition, if you live in Ireland, England, Wales, Scotland and France. Then you're in luck because those countries have criminalised Coercive Control but the United States does not. New York State has become the first state in the entire country to start introducing criminalising legalisation for Coercive Control as a class E felony. Which for myself and our non-US audience, it means that Coercive Control is punishable by a maximum fine of $250,000 dollars and/ or a maximum of 5 years imprisonment but more than 1 year.

And I just checked the New York State Senate Website for the bill and it says it is currently in committee. So it has another 4 stages to pass until it is signed or vetoed by the New York governor.

Conclusion:

At the end of this episode, I want to say that Coercive Control isn't just another facet of abuse to look at it. It is very serious that we need to address and I truly hope that none of you listening or reading this will ever experience it. And whilst we didn't look at how to avoid it and recognise the signs in this episode, I do want to do that in the future just to help protect all of us a little more.

But until then, Coercive Control and abuse might be a dark topic to look at. But it is fascinating and very much worth investigating, because you never know when it might be useful.

WHAT IS DISEMPOWERMENT IN MENTAL HEALTH? AND SOME LIVED EXPERIENCE

Disempowerment is a concept I've sort of heard a lot about in clinical psychology lectures, textbooks and in my own reading for The Psychology World Podcast, but no one has actually highlighted just how important it is to understand.

Since disempowerment refers to the lack of control and, well, power that a person feels like they have over their own life, decisions and what they do.

Furthermore, disempowerment targets a person's self-worth, self-perception and it can lead to feelings of shame and guilt. Granted I'm remembering what I read about disempowerment from sexual assault, but the same applies to other events and conditions too.

In turn, these feelings of guilt and shame that disempowerment can create and/ or reinforce can lead to a multitude of maladaptive coping mechanisms. Like alcohol and substance abuse, self-harm, suicidal ideation and more.

As a result, this idea of disempowerment is flat out critical to understand in mental health, because a wide range of mental health conditions are very disempowering. To some extent, this is probably why we don't really focus on disempowerment in mental health and clinical psychology, because we just know our clients are disempowered in their own lives so us, as aspiring or qualified mental health professionals, we don't really need to know or focus on it.

I agree to some extent.

However, I do believe we should think about mental health in terms of disempowerment from time to time, because once you start thinking about mental health conditions or difficulties as something that disempowers our clients. Then this opens up new ideas about how to conceptualise, understand and even empathise with our clients.

In addition, I should note that clinical psychology sometimes focuses on disempowerment in terms of minority groups and mental health services. I think I've actually spoken or reflected on this topic in a previous volume. Therefore, whilst it is flat out critical that therapists and services never disempower our clients, this isn't what we're focusing on in this reflection.

Instead, to give you some examples of mental health conditions as disempowerment, let's talk about social anxiety. This is the easiest example to understand but if a client has social anxiety then they likely feel like they can't go outside, they can't go out with friends and they can't do something that they want to because they're scared of feeling anxious, having a panic attack or being judged negatively.

Normally, we think about this in terms of normal social anxiety because these are symptoms, biased cognitive processes and some of the safety behaviours seen in social anxiety.

Nonetheless, if we think about this in terms of disempowerment, we can see that social anxiety as a condition and the biased cognitive processes has actually decreased the control and ability of the client to live their own life. The client wants to go out, be social and do things that bring them pleasure but it is the social anxiety that makes them feel like they don't have the power to do that.

Another example is depression, because a client feeling unable to get out of bed, they catastrophizing about everything and the client has a low mood. Through a disempowerment lens, you could argue that that isn't the client feeling that part, it is the depression taking away the client's power and ability to control what they do in their own life.

A final example which serves as a minor segway into our next section is Post-Traumatic Stress Disorder. Since the intense thoughts, flashbacks and panic attacks seen in PTSD robs a client of the control they have over their lives to the point where they get extremely distressed when triggered and they avoid potentially triggering stimuli all together.

Overall, my point is that a wide range of mental health conditions robs clients the control they have over their lives. Due to our clients want to improve their lives, they want to be able to do whatever they want and they want to regain their independence so their mental health difficulty or condition is no longer ruling their lives.

Of course, in an attempt to be balanced here, you could argue that there is no point thinking about mental health in this way because disempowerment is obvious. Of course, if you're anxious, depressed, whatever you're going to lack control over your life.

Therefore, you might argue that disempowerment is a waste of time and it's better to think of mental health in terms of the symptoms, interventions and what you're going to do to improve the client's life.

All of those points are valid.

Although, I would counter-argue by saying that thinking about disempowerment is important too for a very simple and important reason. Thinking about mental health as disempowerment is extremely humanising.

Instead of thinking about a client in terms of their symptoms, what can be done to help them so we can move onto our next client to reduce waiting lists (which is a very real, valid and understandable pressure we all face in mental health). If we think about a client in terms of what *they* have lost and how *they* are disempowered. Then we're taking a moment to think about the client and that's it.

And actually, I'm not going to explore it here but you might be able to get some useful information from disempowerment-thinking for your clinical formulation.

On the whole, I would argue disempowerment-thinking helps us to take a moment to think about the client, what they've lost and what they want to gain from the therapeutic work. This might help you understand the client so you can phase things in a certain way, help them and benefit the therapeutic alliance somehow.

Ultimately, disempowerment work is the main point of therapy.

Therapy is about subtly empowering our clients so using the tools and techniques we give them, the client can go back out into the world and conquer it. By empowering our clients we can obviously improve their lives, but we can decrease their psychological distress and give them control over their lives again.

And it is that sense of control that I'm focusing on in this reflection.

Since I'm actually going to come back in the next one and talk about why I'm discussing this and give you some examples about my own disempowerment in terms of my assault (which was a short extremely intense event) and my child abuse and trauma (a long-term, low intensity trauma that happened every single day for a decade).

Definitely turn over the page to see this disempowerment thinking in action.

WHAT MIGHT DISEMPOWERMENT LOOK LIKE IN RESPONSE TO TRAUMA?

The reason why I'm writing this chapter looking at disempowerment is because in the past two days, I've realised, truly realised how disempowering sexual assault can be. I've felt this way for a while but it took me some time and a good few internet searches to find the terminology.

Of course, once you know the terminology you feel like an idiot because you knew it all along.

Anyway, I'll get to the disempowerment I feel because of my assault later in the chapter, and please relax, I don't even talk about the assault itself so it isn't graphic at all.

Therefore, in this chapter, I'm going to be sharing my own experience of disempowerment in hope that this helps your own understanding, it might help you with your clinical work in the future and it might reinforce what we spoke about in the last chapter.

Disempowerment From Long-Term Trauma

I have to admit here that my long-term abuse and trauma that started in my childhood and went on for a decade thankfully stopped nine months ago, so my memory might be blocking some of the nuances of disempowerment but I remember the it for the most part.

And in fact a lot of my current difficulty actually stem from that disempowerment.

As a result of because my social world (a slightly vague term for who abused me) taught me, drummed it into my skull from 12 years old onwards and made threats and perform actions that made me believe those threats, I was terrified for my life for that decade if these people found out I was gay.

Therefore, because I couldn't afford to be gay because I didn't want to die, I didn't want to be beaten and I didn't want to be homeless. This was actually extremely disempowering and it's really interesting to look at my childhood in terms of disempowerment.

Since I basically had no control over large aspects of my life.

I couldn't really afford to have any gay friends because I wanted to protect gay people, and I didn't want these people to think I was gay. That would have been a direct threat to my life and safety.

Also, I couldn't date, have a first kiss or have anything that heterosexual teenagers enjoy as a matter of course. Again, experiencing any type of normal adolescent behaviour would have been a risk to myself, the person I was kissing or whatever and I didn't want to die.

It was as simple as that.

Also, these people in my social world were very critical of my friendships as it was so friendships were difficult enough as a young, gay autistic kid who struggled anyway.

Moreover, my entire family were deeply homophobic so combined a lack of familial support with a tiny and basically non-existent friendship network. My emotional dependency (you can hear more about that on the Psychology World Podcast) is seriously no surprise.

Since if we think about emotional dependency and how I was (to some extent) "addicted" to a close friend I made who accepted me for me. You might argue that my emotional dependency was me trying in an extremely unhealthy way to take control of my life again. In terms of me having a gay friend that liked me for me and wasn't berating or abusing me.

Overall, my current relationship and friendship difficulties certainly come from that disempowerment and lack of control I had over my own life. Since with disempowerment impacting someone's self-perception and self-worth judgment. I am awful for saying that I don't deserve love, no one will ever love me and I don't deserve happiness.

If not believing you deserve the same happiness everyone else has the right to feel isn't disempowerment, then I seriously don't know what is.

<u>What Might Disempowerment Look Like After A Sexual Assault?</u>

Ever since my assault, even though I didn't realise it until yesterday, I've been feeling really disempowered because there are times my life feels like it's in freefall. I don't feel like I have control over my life and I am fearful what might happen in certain situations.

As I mentioned a few chapters ago, this mainly manifested itself after my assault as a crippling, intense fear of seeing my best friend again because I'm into them romantically. I was fearful of being alone with them, I was scared of sleeping in the same room as them and I was scared they would do something to me.

Of course that would never ever happen because they are the nicest person you would ever meet. Yet as much as it annoys me, sometimes when I think about my best friend it triggers thoughts of my assaulter. According to one of my other friends, that's a normal assault/ rape response because both are to do with physiological arousal.

As a result, when everything happened over my birthday weekend like my panic attack on the Tube, like my inability to sleep comfortably in the same room as my best friend and me having panic attacks at the social group I go to. That is such a disempowering feeling.

I don't know what I can do, where I can go and who I can be with so I don't have a panic attack or something else.

Below is a Whatsapp message I quickly sent my best friend and then I'll explain the context in terms of disempowerment:

"I acknowledge this isn't a logical concern but X isn't the type of person to touch and hug people she's only just met right?

I know she's lovely from our conversations. She's Y's girlfriend, right? I want to meet her.

I'm generally okay. Past few days have been nice.

Last night was tough. I'm just a little nervous about Friday. I'm coming no matter what but that's a lot of people in a (maybe locked) room. And I don't want to spoil it for people if I have a panic attack or something. If needed, I'll ask Z not to lock the door but I hate drawing attention to my discomfort. It just makes what happened even more real and reminds me I'm disempowered and it will take time to heal and get empowered again."

Firstly, I want to focus on getting back to a sense of empowerment does take time because it takes time to heal and for therapy to happen and for you to process stuff.

Also, the context for Friday is I'm going to a one-shot game of Dungeons and Dragons because a friend is doing it, he invited me and some others and I am refusing to let my social anxiety and assault control my life too much.

I don't want to accidentally lock myself away in my room because I'm too scared of being assaulted and hurt again.

Yet I am nervous about Friday for illogical reasons but to me they are very real. I mentioned some of the reasons in that text to my best friend, but there's another reason I will probably keep exclusively for these pages. I am scared about someone who's going to be playing this one-shot with us will be triggering to me.

There's a player and he's kind, very nice and we've spoke a few times. Yet he has long hair and he's slightly on the larger side of life and he has an oval-type of face. All those 3 things are similar to my attacker.

I think he might trigger me so there are very real but illogical reasons why I might have problems on Friday. Then I'm scared that a lot of negative thoughts will pop up about me not being able to enjoy my life anymore and stuff like that.

Personally, I know if something happens, no one will actually care in the sense that they won't judge me for it. Everyone but two of the seven people at the game knows to differing extents what happened to me. And that's something else I'm not thrilled about, I think I'm scared people are going to see me as a weak victim.

Of course, I know as an aspiring clinical psychologist that victims are flat out far from weak. But as a person, I feel a little weak, violated and I'm still reeling from what happened. I don't wish it on anyone and I don't want this to ever happen again.

That is why I feel disempowered because I feel like I don't have control over my reactions, my decisions to do things and I have this constant fear to be honest. Fear that something bad's going to happen, fear that people will judge me for having a panic attack and a fear that people will stop inviting me to stuff because they don't know how I'll react.

I know none of that is logical because my friends are amazing and even though I don't really care much about Dungeons and Dragons (sorry friends and readers), I want to be social and make sure I don't retreat into my room for the rest of my life.

Disempowerment isn't always pretty but if you give a client (or myself) time to process, heal and go to therapy then they can be empowered once more so they can retake control of their lives, decisions and more once again.

And that is an amazing feeling to have after being disempowered for so long.

YOU ONLY KNOW SO MUCH WITHOUT LIVED EXPERIENCE

Originally taken from one of my *Clinical Psychology Reflection* books, I wanted to add in this chapter because it shows why this book and my memoir book is flat out critical to read and understand. This book and my memoir gives you the information and first-hand account of the consequences and what being raped is like. And as this chapter shows you, you cannot hope to understand what life is like for a client without any sort of lived experience.

This chapter is great at hammering that point home, so this is an important chapter to read for any aspiring or qualified clinical psychologist.

***

As aspiring or qualified clinical psychologists, we want to be the best in clinical psychology. We want to know as much as we possibly can about the clinical populations that we work with or want to work with in the future, and we want to listen to their lived experiences to better understand them.

I've spoken a lot in the past about the importance of listening to service users, their experiences and their thoughts about mental health. Since these are the people we are trying to help and support so they are the experts in the mental health conditions.

Whereas us psychologists are experts in the theory, treatment and applied nature of psychotherapy. Yet our expertise in theory and applied topics only goes so far without the knowledge that people with lived experience give us.

I know generally clinical psychologists and students alike acknowledge that they can read all the textbooks, watch all the videos and listen to all the podcasts they want and even then, they will still not be experts in lived experience and a mental health condition.

By the end of our clinical psychology journey (at least the point where we get qualified) we will have a brilliant understanding of mental health, various conditions and psychotherapy. We will be able to help a lot of people and improve lives and give people hope when they might not have any.

But then there are other students and even psychologists that I've met.

Thankfully, these students are the minority but some people are just arrogant. I've met students that think they can understand the nuances and exactly what a client goes through because of their condition or mental health difficulties even though they have never ever experienced it themselves.

If you know a student like this or if you are one of these students yourself then I can respectfully say that this arrogance is futile.

It is beyond critical within clinical psychology that we listen to service users and we put them, their interests and their experiences at the core of everything we do. It is critical that aspiring and qualified clinical psychologists learn as much as they can about their clinical population and more.

This helps us to improve our understanding, our empathy and it helps improve the therapeutic relationship so we can improve lives.

Yet you need to know that you will never be an expert in a condition or exactly what a client experiences every day. Since we are not our client and we are not living inside their minds and we are not living their lives.

That is an extremely hard concept for a lot of students to understand, because we think our lectures, textbooks and essays are training us perfectly for the future. But there is always a disconnect between theory and practice.

Sometimes those differences are thankfully small, other times they are massive.

What Made Me Think Of This Topic?

There are two main areas of clinical psychology that made me think about this topic, because it's starkly clear. I thought about it because depression is the main mental health condition we learn about in the UK. Depression is common, it is something the NHS focuses on and if you can treat depression then your employability is high.

And I understood depression in terms of how overwhelming it is, how it can bias your thinking processes and everything. I understood how it can hurt people, disrupt your routine and make you feel like you can't even move.

I understood all of that at a textbook level, but to actually experience it is something else.

Here's an extract from something I wrote about experiencing an intense depressive episode back in November 2023:

"When I left my private therapist back in August, I had no intention of seeing her again because she had helped me to save my own life, she had helped me get my life back and she had changed my life for the better. Also, I was still going to have the university's Student Support Service available to me so I thought I was going to be fine.

Yet of course mental health recovery is difficult and I do appreciate that now. Therefore, what happened was about a week or two after my last university therapy appointment, I was texting this girl that I was thought I was friends with and she had said a lot of times before that she was going to be alone for Christmas. Now in my family that is a no-no, no one should be alone at Christmas so I invited her to ours for Christmas.

Little did I realise as an autistic that kind of offer is very big, it requires a good level of friendship and it was a rather intense offer according to this girl because she really appreciate it, but it was a lot to offer her considering she believed we didn't really know each other.

I didn't want to argue with her considering I know tons about her, but anyway.

So we had a lot of conversations back and forth and we agreed that we don't have a problem with each other, we would like to be friends at some point but we need to hang out more before that happens.

Which is fair enough.

However, my problem was that she used the words "intense" and a few other words very innocently, but they were very triggering for me. Since the last time I was called "intense" was when a dear friend of mine put us on pause during my breakdown and I lost one of the best friendships I had ever had, so I didn't exactly want to still be making these same mistakes.

I wanted to learn how to have good, healthy friendships.

As a result, I got seriously depressed that Wednesday afternoon, it was so bad actually that I couldn't go to my statistics workshop that was only a 2 or 3 minute walk from where I was sitting being depressed. I literally couldn't move.

It was interesting to experience from a psychological point of view but it was awful to experience firsthand."

Overall, it was awful to experience and now I have a much better understanding of how crippling, draining and horrific depression can be at times. This is something you cannot learn from a textbook and whilst I hope no one ever experiences this, much less for a long period of time. This helps me appreciate and want to support our clients even more.

In addition, the second example was my sexual assault. We all know that being sexually assaulted is bad, awful and traumatic. We sometimes cover trauma stuff in lectures, we sometimes talk about sexual assault.

Yet again, we only really know that sexual assault and rape is bad and traumatic. I used to feel confident, like I understood how bad sexual assault was. I understood that it was triggering, distressing and everything else.

But no one understands sexual assault until it happens to them.

And I'm actually writing this reflection coming up to the 4-week mark since it happened. It's been a bloody tough week filled with panic attacks, anxiety and I don't really think I've slept properly in days, because whenever I get in bed. All the memories just come back along with the sensation of being touched like he's actually in the room with me.

So yes, I used to pretend that I had at least a surface-level understanding of sexual assault and rape and how bad it actually was. No one can know that until it happens and no one can know the consequences until they pop up.

For example, one of the really distressing things at the moment is that I actually don't know what's going to trigger me and the memories and the sensations. I go to a social group every two weeks and I've been there since The Event and didn't have a problem. But last night I was there and had two panic attacks.

One because there were a lot of people in the kitchen area and I felt trapped. The second one I don't really understand what happened, it was something about my best friend who I was taking home wanted to change plans and they asked me if I wanted to go to a bar in Canterbury with everyone else.

I think it was the idea of the bar with so many other people that made me have the panic attack.

Conclusion

Overall, at the end of this reflection, I am saying as an aspiring or qualified clinical psychologist. You have to keep learning about the clinical populations you work with, you need to keep listening to the lived experience of our clients and you need to keep wanting to deepen your knowledge about them.

Yet just understand you will never know everything or all the little details and every single client can teach you something new about *their* experience of the event, condition or mental health difficulty.

This not-knowing-everything flat out doesn't make you a bad clinical psychologist, not in the slightest. It just means you're lucky but you still have the power to change lives, improve them and decrease a client's psychological distress.

You can still do amazing things, but only if you keep learning.

WHY SHOULDN'T YOU INVALIDATE YOUR TRAUMATIC EXPERIENCES?

After someone experiences a traumatic event, a common trauma response is minimising and invalidating what happened to them by saying that other people have had it worse than them so they shouldn't be affected. This is something I tried to do for the first two days after my sexual assault, because I tried to tell myself that I was fine because other people who were raped were beaten, bloodied and had bones broken. That was me trying an extreme version of minimising and invalidating my sexual trauma because I flat out didn't want to deal with what had happened to me. Nonetheless, this kind of minimisation and denying your traumatic experience blocks your path to healing, recovery and improved mental health.

Therefore, in this chapter, you'll learn about why you shouldn't minimise your traumatic experiences, how you can overcome this minimisation and most importantly, why your traumatic experiences are just as valid as other people who have had "worse" experiences than you. If you enjoy learning about clinical psychology, mental health and trauma responses then you will love this chapter.

Why Do Sexual Assault Survivors Minimise Their Experiences?

There are a lot of different ways why sexual assault survivors minimise their traumatic experiences and we'll look at some of these in this chapter. Yet when it comes to minimisation, this tends to come in the form of survivors saying that their experiences weren't "that bad" or "other people had it a lot worse than me". People tend to do this because it helps them to believe that their feelings and their reactions are easier to manage.

I know frequently over the past 17 weeks, I've had to catch myself thinking my sexual assault wasn't "that bad" because I was beaten, bruised and it wasn't rape by the legal definition because there was no penetration. Even though in reality, that definition is stupid and it came so close to becoming rape in the eyes of the law. Anyway, I told myself these lies because I wanted to feel better and make it seem like my trauma responses were just overreactions.

Of course they weren't and I was seriously hurting and dealing with negative mental health outcomes because of my assault.

In addition, we tend to minimise our traumatic experiences because sexual assault can feel too overwhelming for survivors to deal with, so minimising it makes it easier until we're ready to deal with our emotions and what the hell happened to us.

Also, whilst this minimisation can be an effective coping mechanism for us, it isn't healthy in the long term. Since there will come a point when we absolutely have to deal with our trauma and our emotions because our mind will make us as our trauma responses will make us deal with it. For example, survivors can start feeling more fearful, anxious, stressed, shutting down emotionally or engaging in unhelpful maladaptive coping mechanisms like drinking or eating disorders.

How To Deal With Other People Having It Worse?

I've literally just told you that minimising your own or your loved one's experience is a very unhealthy, negative and maladaptive coping mechanism. Yet what happens when other people actually do have it worse than you, because it will happen.

If we take what happened to me for example, I *know* other sexual assault survivors had it worse than me. I wasn't beaten, I wasn't physically injured and I didn't experience any penetration. I almost did but because the idiot was so fat he couldn't. Yet other people have experienced everything I didn't so technically, other people have had it a lot worse than me.

Although, what we need to realise is that this doesn't make our experiences any less valid, painful or traumatic.

Since pain and loss do exist on a spectrum and different experiences will impact people in different ways so for me, my sexual assault has been extremely painful and it has led to devastating and crippling mental health difficulties most days. Yet for someone, they might have coped slightly better with and felt less pain than me and that's okay.

It does not make my experience any less valid.

Moreover, a lot of therapists refer to something known as "Big T" and "little T" traumas. This is an idea I've heard of a few times but it wasn't until I was researching this chapter I realised I had to focus on it a lot more. Therefore, "Big T" traumas include events that are typically associated with the development of Post-Traumatic Stress Disorder and these can be caused by single, significant traumatic events. Like rape and other forms of sexual violence as well as being in combat, witnessing a violent crime, being in a severe car accident or experiencing your life being threatened.

It's normal for people who have experienced Big T traumas to try and minimise their experience by focusing on how someone else *might* have had it worse than them. And this is a valid thing to do as long as you realise that your traumatic experience is valid and it's okay that these experiences are painful, traumatic and have a long, profound impact on you.

That's why getting professional support is so important.

On the other hand, "little t" traumas might not seem as bad as Big T traumas but they can still have a major impact on your life. Since "little t" traumas don't involve experiences that are life-threatening but they can still include series of events or single events that cause you emotional dysregulation and difficulties coping with what happened. For instance, financial hardships, an abrupt relocation, a difficult relationship with a parent, interpersonal conflict, chronic illness amongst others.

Also, these "little t" traumas can compound because when you experience "little t" traumas over time then these can exacerbate their impact on your mental health and emotional functioning. Leading to increases in anxiety, fatigue, grief and irritability as well as decreases in self-esteem.

Therefore, whilst "little t" traumas mean you don't tend to meet the diagnostic criteria for Post-Traumatic Stress Disorder like Big T traumas, it can still have major negative impacts on your wellbeing.

Finally, whilst the majority of people in society agree that Big T traumas are major events that are likely to have a significant negative impact on a person's life and wellbeing, a lot of people fail to realise the extent of the impact "little t" traumas can have on a person too. Typically, people who experience "little t" traumas are told unhelpful things like they simply need to give it time or move on from the past. These aren't helpful messages because this can lead to the person internalising the messages that their experiences are not bad or severe enough to have the impacts and negative mental health outcomes that they're experiencing.

This is not okay because your experience is valid no matter what other people say.

Conclusion

Whilst I'm writing this chapter in a book dedicated to sexual violence, this chapter applies to all trauma. Since it doesn't matter if you've experienced a Big T trauma or a "little t" trauma or multiple traumatic events in your life, your experiences are valid whatever they are.

At the end of the day, trauma is trauma no matter how you experienced it.

No one ever chooses to experience trauma, like I certainly did not choose to be raped, so if you're struggling then please know that your experience was bad enough. It was severe enough to make you experience whatever you're going through now.

It doesn't matter if someone went through something similar or worse and they're dealing with it differently to you. Your experience is still valid and your trauma responses are normal reactions to an extremely abnormal situation.

Lastly, I talk a lot about mental health and clinical psychology on my podcast so even though I have no intention of dipping into therapy and trauma treatments today. If you are experiencing trauma responses and negative mental health outcomes because of something that happened to you, please seek professional help.

Healing and recovery from trauma is possible but everyone needs a helping hand.

You are never alone in your trauma so please get the help you need and start your journey towards trauma recovery.

HOW ARE SEXUAL ASSAULT, SELF-HARM AND SUICIDE CONNECTED?

In a past chapter, I've spoken about the wide range of negative mental health outcomes that sexual assault can cause a survivor to experience. I've spoken about Post-Traumatic Stress Disorder, anxiety and depression. Yet in comparison to self-harm and suicide resulting from being sexually assaulted, these are somewhat "lighter" negative mental health outcomes. In this chapter, you'll learn about the connection between sexual assault, suicide and self-harm and most importantly, what do we do to prevent this connection.

Brief Introduction To The Effects of Sexual Trauma

In case it's been a while since you last picked up this book, I wanted a briefly recap the devastating impact that sexual trauma can have on a person. Since sexual trauma causes a survivor immense physical, emotional and mental distress and scars that they'll experience and have to deal with for years or decades to come. As well as survivors of sexual assault are at increased risk of developing a range of mental health conditions, like post-traumatic stress, depression, anxiety, substance use disorders and eating disorders compared to people who didn't experience sexual trauma.

Moreover, when any kind of trauma occurs, including sexual trauma, the brain doesn't process the event properly so this leaves the trauma to be bubbling away in the back of someone's mind so it can be triggered again in the future. This is one of the reasons why substance abuse disorders can develop because it helps a person to avoid the feelings and thoughts associated with the traumatic event. As well as the disordered thoughts and behaviours associated with the addiction are done to help the survivor suppress any unwanted emotions. This is an unhealthy coping mechanism the survivor develops to help them cope with the trauma and sometimes, it can sadly be done to the point where the addiction takes over their life.

And sometimes kills them.

How Does Self-Harm Relate To Sexual Trauma?

A lot of sexual assault survivors engage in self-harming behaviours, as well as substance use behaviours, as a form of self-punishment. To this end, it isn't uncommon for survivors to use thoughts and behaviours like *I deserve to be punished and I will punish myself, I am a bad person so I need to hurt myself,* and *I have no control over my trauma but I can control my self-harm behaviour so I'm doing it.*

I would add here that another reason why survivors self-harm going off my own experience is the control angle, but also because physical sensation can stop the rape memories and the physical sensations that pop up during an intense flashback. This is a maladaptive coping mechanism but in the first month after my assault, I didn't feel like I had another choice.

This is why getting professional help is so important.

No one should ever feel like self-harm is their only choice.

Furthermore, this is why during therapy and other examples of mental health support, it's important to help survivors rebuild their internal and external dialogue so we can tear down these distorted thinking processes and behaviours and replace them with more adaptive coping mechanisms. As well as whilst self-harm and addiction are common amongst sexual assault survivors, it's important to treat each mental health condition separately whilst understanding that sexual trauma is the underlying trigger.

Another maladaptive coping mechanism is survivors often cut themselves off from their bodies to numb the pain of the assault. This means they might not look at their bodies in the mirror and they might neglect their body as a form of coping with everything that happened to them. Leading to addiction, eating disorders and self-harming behaviour to numb their mind from the emotional distress, discomfort and emotional void that being assaulted creates for them.

Overall, to explicitly say this, the link between sexual trauma and self-harm is that self-harm is a maladaptive coping mechanism that survivors use to help them deal with their sexual trauma. As well as it helps them deal with the emotional distress and negative feelings that being assaulted leaves them with.

Other Consequences Of Being Sexually Assaulted and The Link Between Sexual Trauma and Suicide

Unfortunately, it isn't just an increased risk of developing a substance abuse disorder, an eating disorder or engaging in self-harm that act as consequences for sexual assault survivors. Some other negative impacts include 31% of all rape survivors will develop Post-Traumatic Stress Disorder in their lifetime (and I've seen research suggesting it's higher than this), and sexual assault survivors are 13.4 times more likely to develop two or more major alcohol difficulties and 26 times more likely to develop two or more serious drug abuse issues in their lifetime.

Also, rape survivors are three times more likely when compared to people who have never experienced sexual trauma to have a major depressive episode.

Finally for this section, rape victims are 13 times more likely to attempt suicide when compared to people who haven't experienced sexual trauma.

13 times more likely to attempt suicide.

I've been there at least twice in the past 17 weeks and that is why supporting sexual assault survivors is so important and that's why we need to work towards a world where sexual violence does not happen. Period.

Thankfully, there's a chapter at the end of the book about how we do just that.

Yet 13 times more likely to attempt suicide. That is a heartbreaking fact.

How Do We Break The Connection Between Self-Harm, Suicide and Sexual Trauma?

Professional psychological support is the answer.

Since by a survivor going to get therapy, counselling or any other form of mental health support, they're going to get the support and help they need to process what the hell happened to them and talk about any trauma responses and maladaptive coping mechanisms that they've developed. I firmly believe that every survivor should seek mental health support even if they feel okay because there will come a time when they shatter.

This is why getting mental health support early on is so important.

In addition, a survivor should look for a mental health professional who specialises in trauma-informed care. For example, some professionals swear by Eye Movement Desensitization and Reprocessing for sexual assault survivors which is an 8-phase psychological treatment that involves talking about and processing your trauma whilst you do eye movement tracking and you recall the emotions and feelings associated with the traumatic event in a safe and controlled space. I've done a podcast episode before on the therapy if you want to learn more and it is a highly effective therapy.

Another option is trauma support groups so you can get support from other people who have experienced similar trauma to you. As well as counselling is a great choice too.

Overall, there are a lot of different options for you to get mental health support for your sexual trauma, and this is important as it helps you deal with the psychological distress and other trauma responses. So you don't feel like you have to lean on substance abuse, self-harm and even suicide to give you a break from the trauma.

Recovery, healing and hope for a better life are all possible following a sexual assault. Reading or listening to me say this might seem impossible or even disingenuous at times because of how hard the aftermath of sexual assault can be.

Yet if you or your loved one or your client gets mental health support from someone who specialises in trauma. Then it is possible for you to work *with* them so you can disconnect the idea between sexual trauma means you need to use self-harm and substance use to survive, and in the most extreme and tragic cases, we can prevent suicide seeming like the only way out.

Suicide is never the answer because there is always hope for a better life. I am living proof of that so please hang on, get mental health support and believe life gets better.

Because it seriously does.

HOW DOES TRAUMA AFFECT THE HEART?

I wanted to include this next chapter because it takes us slightly outside the realm of clinical psychology and merges our trauma interest with biological psychology. As well as whilst you might initially think that heart health has absolutely nothing to do with us, as aspiring or qualified psychologists, in reality, it might not hurt us to discuss cardiovascular health from time to time.

And this chapter explains why.

As a result, as someone who's experienced a range of trauma over their life, I'm always interested in learning about the different ways how trauma affects someone. Normally, I focus on the mental health implications, like panic attacks, social anxiety and Post-Traumatic Stress Disorder. I'm experiencing all of these symptoms at the time of writing but trauma doesn't only affect us psychologically. Trauma can have profound physical consequences too. Therefore, this chapter merges clinical psychology and biological psychology so you can learn how trauma affects the heart, why trauma has physical impacts on our body and what can we do about these impacts. If you enjoy learning about trauma psychology, biopsychology and mental health, then this is a great episode for you.

Brief Introduction To Trauma

Whilst I talk about trauma on the podcast a fair bit, I wanted to briefly recap the importance of trauma within clinical psychology in case there are any new readers or listeners tuning in to this episode. Therefore, trauma is the term given to an extremely difficult experience in a person's life that has a profound impact on them. This can include being involved in or witnessing life-threatening diseases, severe injuries or accidents, assaults, sexual violence and deaths of loved ones and so on. As well as trauma is common within society with at least 50% of adults in the United States experiencing one or more traumas in their lifetime (Wisco et al., 2022). Also, I've mentioned before in a chapter, this is why trauma-informed approaches are so important, because they're about recognising trauma is common and we need to support people.

Furthermore, I'm guilty of this too but when it comes to trauma, we particularly only think about trauma as a psychological concept with psychological impacts. Which come to think of it doesn't make a lot of sense, because traumatic events are physical, tangible events that happen to a person so it makes no sense why its impacts would only be psychological in nature.

In this chapter, you're going to be learning about the physical impacts of psychological trauma and why we need to acknowledge their existence. Since if we ignore the physiological impacts of trauma and Post-Traumatic Stress Disorder then this could prove deadly for our clients.

Why Is Trauma A Mind-Body Condition?

To some extent, I have no issue with the current official and extremely oversimplified dialogue about psychological trauma is very focused on the psychological and mental experience of trauma. You only need to look at the DSM-5 to see how trauma focuses on the intense emotional and behavioural responses that the traumatic event causes. For instance, the PTSD and acute stress disorder symptoms as listed in the DSM-5 focus on the anxiety, avoidance of trauma-related stimuli and situations and hypervigilance. Personally, I have no issue with that whatsoever because these are the things I severely struggle with after my sexual assault and these intense emotions and severe behavioural responses are horrific at times and rather debilitating. It was only three nights ago at the time of writing that I was watching a romance because I didn't read the trigger warnings and I saw a sex scene. I screamed, panicked and I felt paralysed for 20 minutes just dealing with the perfectly innocent scene I had just witnessed.

Needlessly to say, I will be reading trigger warnings a lot more carefully in future.

However, the issue is that trauma probably needs to be reconceptualised a little more because there is a growing body of neuroscience research showing how trauma has a major impact on our biology and our physical body (O'Donnell et al., 2016).

Now there are some researchers saying trauma has a greater physical impact than the psychological impact, and I have some thoughts on this argument. I have no doubt there is research demonstrating how significant and damaging trauma is on our physical body, but as someone who has experienced two major types of trauma in their life, I have to admit I don't buy this argument. It is the anxiety, Post-Traumatic Stress Disorder, depression, suicidal ideation and on and on and on that causes me to struggle because of my trauma. It is the intense emotions and psychological aspects of dealing with being sexually assaulted that causes me to be paralysed as times as I deal with the intrusive thoughts and physical sensations of what happened to me.

It is the psychological aspects that hurt me the most.

The only physical aspects of the trauma I have to deal is the sweating and increased heart rate and rapid breathing whenever I have a panic attack. As well as the physical sensations of my body effectively remembering what he did to me amongst a few other bits. I don't doubt all these physical trauma responses are having a physical impact on my body, but to say physical impacts are the *most* damaging and the *most* painful for a trauma survivor just doesn't sit right with me.

You might disagree but this is my lived experience.

One of the areas most impacted by trauma is the heart.

How Does Psychological Trauma Impact The Cardiovascular System?

As you can imagine, whenever we experience a traumatic event, the brain activates our flight-fight-freeze response which is a biological process. During this process, the pituitary gland, hypothalamus and adrenal glands (typically referred to as the HPA axis) work together to produce a powerful and rapid stress response that floods the body with neurotransmitters and hormones in an effort to protect and save us.

It is these hormones and neurotransmitters that are believed to alter the normal functioning of our major organs including the heart.

Interestingly, whilst our fight-or-flight response is meant to save us during traumatic situations, it can be deadly too. Due to there are times when people have had heart attacks as well as strokes during natural disasters so it is possible to die from stress-induced cardiovascular events. There are even times when these cardiovascular events kill more people than the natural disaster in question (Babaie et al, 2021).

In addition, whilst our flight-or-fight response is a biological mechanism that evolved as an emergency response to help our ancestors thrive. Our ancestors were almost always able to rest and recover after the activation of this mechanism, whereas in this modern era we cannot do that because of chronic stress. This is a modern problem because modern trauma and modern stressful events mean the fight-or-flight response gets activated more often so this response can be activated for months or even years after the traumatic event.

I know this might sound strange or impossible but I agree with it. Since I sort of believe my fight-or-flight response is starting to only calm down after 17 weeks after being assaulted but whenever I go outside, whenever I go into certain situations and whenever I am inside, even more so when I'm in a locked room, all the physical stress responses return and I am on high alert. I know if I need to escape in case someone hurts me again, my body is only a second away from activating my flight-or-fight response. As well as there have been plenty of major incidents over the past 17 weeks where I have been okay in one moment, something small has happened and then I have freaked out and my flight-or-fight has been activated.

I doubt my flight-or-fight has rested in the past 17 weeks.

Therefore, with humans not resting and able to recover after each activation of our flight-or-fight response, our physical body is getting battered by our endless stress responses. This means our cardiovascular system and heart slowly become dysfunctional and damaged so this raises the risk of heart attack and stroke over time.

Why Is The Trauma-Heart Relationship Bidirectional?

Lastly, what's interesting about trauma and its physical impacts is that trauma is both a cause and an outcome of heart problems. Due to there is research, like Edmondson and von Kanel (2017), showing a strong link between trauma and chronic and acute cardiovascular risk. As well as there is separate evidence showing how strokes and heart attacks cause trauma reactions amongst the survivors (O'Donnell et al., 2021).

This shows the trauma-heart relationship is bidirectional and they can both cause and be a consequence of each other.

However, the issue with trauma and cardiovascular health problems is that because trauma is psychological in nature as are the emotional and behavioural responses, these aren't assessed in emergency rooms or cardiovascular wards. This means the trauma symptoms that are causing clients a massive amount of psychological distress and are causing further damage to their heart, these are not being treated. Meaning the cardiovascular damage and the trauma symptoms simply continue.

Which is why I flat out love holistic work and the biopsychosocial model, despite the jokes about it being the bio bio bio model. I'm an idealist at heart so I still believe in the aim of the biopsychosocial model.

Conclusion

On the whole, if you take anything away from today's episode, it needs to be that trauma survivors and other people experiencing chronic or acute stress need to be educated on how to reduce potential cardiovascular risk, and they need to be treated. As well as whenever someone goes into a medical setting to have treatment for a cardiovascular-related health problem, they should be screened and assessed for psychological trauma so they can be helped, supported and their trauma treated if needed so their cardiovascular symptoms don't get worse.

Of course, I am very cynical when it comes to medical settings embracing psychological concepts because most medical settings in my experience are ruled over by white older men who firmly believe in the biomedical model and they have little time or patience for psychology. There is absolutely nothing wrong with white older men but I wish they were more accepting towards psychology.

Anyway, a great argument to make to them and other medical directors about this issue might be to mention, if you spend the time and money assessing clients for trauma and treating it earlier on. It means their symptoms will not get worse, they won't need as long or as intense medical treatment and they can be discharged sooner from the hospital. That means the hospital can save money, which is something hospitals and medical settings love. I don't blame them because their budgets are beyond awful at this point.

Penultimately, I want to mention that I know a lot of this chapter doesn't directly apply to us aspiring or qualified psychologists. We are trained to become experts in psychological matters so our knowledge about physical health is limited and I don't always think that is a bad thing. Since the worst thing that could happen with this neuroscience research is that people use it to shift trauma treatment into the biomedical model where the main focus is on the physical symptoms, the hormones and neurotransmitters and everything that is physically happening to a client.

That just will not work for trauma treatment.

Of course, there always needs to be psychoeducation about how trauma impacts a client physically, especially when it comes to PTSD, panic attacks and anxiety. Yet I think it's okay that psychologists mainly focus on the psychological aspects instead of letting the medical doctors rush in and focus on the biological aspects, like they do with depression with their anti-depressants that don't actually work. I still love Read and Moncrieff (2022) for their brilliant work against the biomedical model for depression.

Anyway, the real point of this episode is two-fold. Firstly, we all need to become aware, appreciative and acknowledge that psychological trauma has a physical impact. Secondly, we need to pressure medical settings to realise psychological trauma impacts physical health and if we want to save lives, improve the physical health of clients and decrease cardiovascular-related health problems that cost medical settings a lot of money each year. Then psychologists and medical doctors need to work together as equal partners to help tackle the physical aspects of trauma.

Awareness is always a good first step towards change.

Ultimately, I've mentioned on the podcast a lot of times how trauma is common in society, and I am a total fan-person of the trauma-informed approaches that we are starting to shift towards in clinical psychology. Therefore, if we fail to appreciate the physiological impact that psychological trauma has on a person then not only are we negatively impacting the physical health of our clients but we could be risking major public health consequences with an increase in cardiovascular-related deaths.

Something we have to avoid at all costs.

HOW TO STOP TEENAGE DATING VIOLENCE?

Typically, we think that teenage love is innocent, joyful and it is without a doubt the purest form of love. The media and books are filled with the idea that teenage love is perfect, and it is an amazing feeling to be in love for the first time as we feel positive, light and we feel high on life. For the majority of people, this is thankfully the case but violence within teenage relationships is very common and a major problem in society is the physical, psychological and sexual abuse within teenage relationships.

Therefore, in this chapter, you'll learn how we can stop teenage dating violence to protect everyone including all present and future teenagers and honour the past teenagers who experienced this horrific abuse. If you enjoy learning about the social psychology of relationships and the forensic psychology of violence, abuse and sexual trauma then this will be a fascinating experience for you.

How To Stop Teenage Dating Violence?

Unfortunately, teenage dating violence is common and it is very harmful because of its range of effects on teenage survivors. Sometimes teenage dating violence can be physical, psychological or sexual, or even technological abuse. Therefore, we need to teach young people how to have healthy relationships and we need to do the three things below to help stop teenage dating violence.

Recognise The Different Forms Of Adolescent Dating Abuse

Whenever we think of dating violence, we only tend to think of sexual violence or physical violence, and whilst this is true to a large extent, there are other types too. Since part of the problem with dating violence and our conception that dating violence is *only* sexual and physical abuse, is that we fail to recognise other forms of abuse. This means that abusers can keep on harming their so-called teenage love because no one recognises the signs of their abuses and this makes it harder to stop.

Thankfully, once we realise that there are some forms of abuse, we can become more open, aware and vigilant against teenage dating violence. Allowing us to call it out, stop abusers and hopefully protect teenage survivors in the long term.

In terms of the data, Wincentak et al. (2017) showed that 1 in 5 teenage girls and 1 in 5 teenage boys report physical victimisation in their relationships. So it is right for us to imagine dating violence has a physical element that really harms their target, but this isn't always the majority of dating violence.

Instead, teenage dating abuse can take many forms. It can include sexual, emotional and technological abuse amongst others. For instance, Wincentak et al. (2017) found that roughly 14% of teenage girls and 8% of teenage boys were sexually abused in their relationships. As well as emotional abuse is even more common (Francis & Pearson, 2019) and emotional abuse is devastating because it chips away at a person's self-esteem and self-worth over time. Furthermore, emotional abuse can include name calling, threats, actions, shaming, and controlling behaviour like isolating them from their friends and family members.

Unfortunately, the rates of emotional, physical and sexual abuse might be higher for some groups of young people. For example, LGBT+ youth (Reuter & Whitton, 2018).

When it comes to technological abuse, this is where it gets even more heartbreaking because this isn't an area I typically focus on or even remember exists at times. I know cyberbullying is a major issue but I had never connected it to relationship abuse before now. Therefore, as Ouytsel et al. (2016) pointed out both teenage boys and girls experience their partners trying to control them through their phones, social media and other forms of technology. As well as teenage girls are more likely than boys to be sexually coerced and victimised through technological means.

And I don't really have an issue with showing my own blindness to the topic, because I want you to know I am not perfect, I am human and I have flaws. I've always heard my female friends talk about issues they were having with their partners online, through their phones and their texts and calls. I knew it was wrong of their partners to harass them over text, ask about their social media and track them through their phones. I knew that it was flat out wrong and outrageous.

But I did not know that classes as technological abuse, which might be a sad commentary on society. Did I not know this was abuse because it's so common, I just thought this was an outrageous part of bad behaviour in relationships that needed to be stomped out.

Maybe. Maybe I did just assume that. Maybe technological abuse is so normalised in our culture as part of the dating scene that we don't consider it abuse.

If that's true then that is a very sad reflection of society and that needs to change urgently.

We Must Always Take Relationship Abuse Seriously

As my example above shows, relationship abuse is so normalised that a lot of us don't even recognise it anymore. This is even worse when we're been through trauma itself or we are so used to abuse that we believe it is simply a part of life or it is a normal thing to say or do. For example, I remember working an Outreach event once and a student said something abusive about their family member who went to the same school that I didn't even recognise it as a safeguarding issue, until I mentioned it to someone just in case and it turned out it was.

Therefore, it is an unfortunate truth that in society, we can intentionally or accidentally minimise or dismiss relationship abuse.

In addition, there are reasons why relationship abuse is difficult to detect because abusive behaviours can occur besides desirable and very healthy behaviours (Goldman et al., 2016). Even though there are at times, warning signs that emerge across a range of behavioural patterns which the organisation Love Is Respect has several resources to help you detect them.

Furthermore, depending on how you and researchers define teenage dating violence, relationship abuse seems to be very common. For instance, a normal healthy relationship would use emotion regulation and conflict resolution skills to resolve conflict, but relationship abuse is used instead in dating violence. This relationship abuse can include less severe forms of aggression like pushing. In other words, the abusers that make teenage dating violence matter might resort to aggression to solve any conflicts in their relationships.

On the whole, you've learnt why relationship abuse is common because whenever something is common, we tend to take it less seriously. Sometimes this is because we think it is simply the way things are but there are other reasons too. Yet when it comes to teenage dating violence, thinking for even a second that relationship abuse isn't serious can lead to devastating consequences. Such as relationship abuse that includes physical violence can lead to injuries, this is especially true for girls and older youth (Munoz-Rivas et al., 2007). Another awful consequence of relationship abuse is it increases psychological distress in survivors, so much so that the negative impact ranges from depression to disordered eating and substance abuse to suicide risk (Lee and Wong, 2020; Smith et al., 2020).

Teenage dating violence devastates lives.

In addition, if we turn our attention to the sexual violence angle, when young girls are raped in their teenage years, they're more likely to be raped again in their first year of college (Carey et al., 2015). And this compounds the existing sexual trauma and further damages their physical and mental health.

Ultimately, a final reason why we need to take teenage relationship abuse seriously is because this can turn very deadly. Relationship abuse can lead to partners killing the other. Most murder victims are teenage girls that are killed by their current or former partners being motivated by the break-up, arguments or partner jealousy.

I want to mention here that even though there are "only" three sections to this chapter, I am having to stop and take breaks after every section because this is hitting hard. I am so annoyed at these awful, twisted abusers that think it is okay to abuse anyone at all, let alone their partner. Let alone their teenage partner.

Abuse is wrong on so many levels. It destroys the partner's life, it devastates their mental health and it causes such severe trauma that it will take them months and years to heal from the stupid actions of a pathetic abuser.

I would have loved to be safe enough and felt free enough to enjoy a relationship during my adolescence but I wasn't. I wish everyone experienced what I couldn't, but some people are just so weak and pathetic that they feel the need to abuse others and abuse the person they are meant to love to feel powerful.

It disgusts me and that is why teenage dating violence must end immediately.

We Must Help Young People Build Skills For Healthy Relationships

For our final section of this chapter, let's look at the specific factors that can help prevent teenage dating violence. Thankfully, there has been a good amount of research into this topic over the years and we know from the literature that there are key actions that can be done to prevent relationship abuse. For example, Spencer et al. (2019) found that teaching young people conflict resolution skills helps to decrease dating violence as there is no reason for the young person to resort to violence to achieve their aims and to deal with conflict within the relationship. On the other hand, a meta-analysis by Pusch (2022) found that dating violence is more likely to occur when young people have friends who used violence or if they believed there were benefits to using violence in helping them get what they want.

If we bear this in mind, it shows the need for society to help teach young people how to have healthy relationships (Wolfe et al., 2009) and how to decrease relationship aggression (National Institute Of Justice). Personally, I know from my experience with the English education system, this is something we greatly fail at because the closest I ever came to formally learning about healthy relationships was this video about consent using the Tea metaphor. For example, just because your friend wanted tea (sex) yesterday doesn't mean they want it now so you give them tea (sex) now just because they wanted it yesterday.

Given I was raped I don't believe this silly video works at all.

Anyway, it's good to know that some countries aren't completely useless at teaching their young people how to have healthy relationships. Since across the Western world, there are a range of programmes to help teach young people these relationship skills in schools, and they all have similar things in common (Lee and Wong, 2020). For instance, these programmes teach young people the difference between healthy and abusive relationships as well as develop the skills and attitudes needed to engage in positive relationship behaviours. Like how communication and conflict resolution works in healthy relationships compared to abusive ones. Also, these programmes help to explore and challenge the expectations young people have about gender equality and gender roles within a relationship.

Thankfully, these programmes have been found to effectively change young people's attitudes, knowledge and reports of dating violence perpetration (Lee and Wong, 2020).

Personally, I am really grateful and pleased that there are programmes out there that help us to teach young people the relationship skills they need to be able to have healthy relationships. Since relationships are meant to be loving, heartwarming and non-abusive. There is no place for abuse in our society, let alone in our loving relationships, so as much as I want this to be rolled out globally (of course with it being adapted for different cultures to prevent cultural imperialism), it makes me feel good that there is a starting point for this change.

Lastly, for this section, it doesn't matter if you live in a community, country or region that regularly offers dating violence prevention programmes. It is the responsibility of all of us to help prevent relationship abuse and there is something all of us can do to help transform lives for the better and prevent future young people becoming survivors. Some things you can do to prevent relationship violence includes parents and carers talking to their young people about how to have healthy relationships with consent, boundaries and conflict resolution at the core of it.

Moreover, we can help our young people access resources that explain answers to common questions they might have about relationships. You can go to VAWNet and Love is Respect for more information. As well as us adults can learn about therapy and other support services within our local area so we can be prepared to connect young people with local services if the worst happens.

In my experience, once the worst happens to you or the Ultimate Betrayal as I've started calling it, it is best to access mental health support as soon as possible.

Conclusion

In the future, I want to live in a world where there is no teenage dating violence, and I want to live in a world where there is no sexual violence or abuse at all. This is why this chapter is important, useful and it shows us what we can proactively do to help bring this violence to an end.

We all want to protect our children, our communities and we want to help make the world a better place. Doing these three simple things is how we do that and achieve it.

I don't have children, I don't know if I ever will but I have nieces and nephews and I will have friends in the future that have children. I do not want any of them to suffer because of relationship violence, I certainly do not want them to be raped or experience sexual violence.

Therefore, at the end of this chapter, I am asking you, wonderful listener or reader, to please try and incorporate these simple steps into your own life. If you know a young person then please talk to them about healthy relationships, talk to them about the importance of consent, healthy boundaries and what positive behaviours look like in relationships. As well as never stop learning about relationship abuse and violence because the more you understand, the more you'll be able to help and change young people's lives for the better.

I want to stop teenage dating violence and we all have a role to play in that. So now you have this information, let's change the world together.

HOW TO MANAGE THE AFTERMATH OF SEXUAL ASSAULT?

I know from personal experience that being sexually assaulted is devastating, it changes your life forever and it leads to a wide range of very negative and distressing mental health outcomes. I suffer from panic attacks, intense social anxiety and Post-Traumatic Stress Disorder to only name a few and some of the "lighter" mental health outcomes I've experienced since my sexual assault.

Therefore, in our next chapter, you'll learn 5 tips on how to manage the aftermath of sexual assault so you can support yourself, your friends and your family if the worst ever happens to them. If you enjoy learning about forensic psychology, mental health and sexual violence then this will be a fascinating chapter for you.

Why Do We Need To Talk About The Aftermath of Sexual Assault?

I've mentioned before in this book just how common sexual violence is in the world unfortunately and just as a reminder in the paragraph below I want to remind us how disgustingly common sexual violence is in the world, let alone university campuses:

"I mentioned that sexual violence is very common on university campuses because 13% of all university students (regardless if they're undergraduate or postgraduate) experience sexual assault or rape through physical force, physical violence or incapacitation during their time as a student. As well as, if we focus only on graduate and professional students then 2.5% of males and 9.7% of females will experience sexual assault or rape through physical violence, force or incapacitation.

Unfortunately, this increases when we focus on undergraduate students (probably because there are more of them) since 6.8% of males and 26.4% of females will also experience sexual assault or rape through physical violence, force or incapacitation during their time as a student.

Also, 5.8% of students regardless of sex or gender have experienced stalking since they started university.

This is even worse for transgender individuals because 23.1% of transgender, gender-nonconforming and genderqueer college students have been sexually assaulted."

As a result, you can see that sexual violence is very common and this leads to a wide range of very distressing mental health outcomes for survivors. For example, according to Resick (1993), a survivor can experience post-traumatic incursions, severe fear, anxiety, adjustment as well as mood difficulties and difficulties with sexual functioning and intimacy. That's only to name a few of the devastating effects that sexual assault can have on a person.

Yet there is hope for survivors to manage the aftermath of sexual assault. It won't be easy and it will be very distressing at times but these 5 tips will help you or your loved one to manage sexual assault a little better.

Managing The Physical Impacts and Collect Evidence

Personally, I find the whole conversation around "evidence" to be very triggering and upsetting for me because I was denied this chance because of how my rapist operated. Yet I still want to mention it here in case other people find it useful.

As a result, we tend to forget that sexual violence can at times have some significant physical impacts so if this happened to you or your loved one then getting medical assistance is flat out critical. I want you to be okay and medical assistance is a great way for your physical injuries to be tended to. As well as it's helpful to know that your body right now is already hurt and I didn't realise it for a few days until after my assault but my body was basically shattered after what he did to me, and I didn't have any physical injuries. I was terrified of getting them in the moment but that's a conversation for a different time.

Therefore, if you have physical injuries, it is critical that you have been medically treated so you can start healing. And if they're professionally treated then they should heal sooner and the physical reminders of what your attacker did should go a little quicker.

I understand for a lot of survivors, it is very, very difficult for them to have someone touch them in their private area. This means it is difficult for both the survivor and the medical staff to treat any injuries in these sensitive, private areas but please know, most doctors and nurses who work at sexual violence centres have been specially trained to support you or your loved one through this process. As well as you should be allowed to ask for a support person or a nurse to sit in with you whilst the doctor treats you.

Personally, that paragraph was very tough for me to write and I almost teared up. Even though I never went to a rape centre for treatment, I was in denial at the time. I still struggle so much with the idea of being touched in that area that it utterly terrifies me and I tend to have really bad panic attacks.

So I understand how difficult this is but please trust the people at the rape centre or wherever you go for professional medical help.

Moreover, if the sexual assault involved physical contact then it might be important for a rape kit to be conducted so the professionals can collect any evidence that you might exist on you. And it's critical to know that you don't need to make any decisions about pressing charges or contacting the police right now, you seriously don't have to make those decisions for a while. Yet if the evidence is collected, it is there to use against your attacker if you decide that is what you want to do.

And I know I've mentioned this a few times on the podcast before, but it is perfectly okay if you decide not to report. It doesn't make the rape or sexual assault any less real, it doesn't mean your trauma responses are any less valid and it doesn't mean anything.

If you want to report, then more power to you and I hope you nail the attacker whoever they are.

<u>You Should Seek Support</u>

As an aspiring clinical psychologist, I will always advocate and slightly demand that sexual assault survivors should go and get professional psychological support. Since what happened to us was outrageous, disgusting and it has such a why range of psychological impacts that we simply cannot do this alone. Therefore, you might benefit from researching any rape charities, specialists or organisations in your local area so you can get the support you need. Since you might feel okay after a sexual assault because you're so intensely in denial, and I know because I've been there.

But at some point you or your loved one will realise they are seriously not okay and when the penny drops and when the tidal wave of what the hell happened to you slams into you. You will need help and that is okay.

Of course, I will note as someone born male, that a lot of sexual assault services are aimed at female survivors. It is hard enough for female survivors to come forward because of the stigma surrounding sexual assault, but this can make it difficult for male survivors to come forward too and report their assault and get support. This is an extra consideration when you're seeking support.

Please do get support though.

Personally, even though I've been on a waiting list for rape counselling for close to three months now, I still think I'm doing a lot better than I would have been if I wasn't on the waiting list. Since I am on the list, there is hope that I will get counselling and there is hope that my life will get better. That is enough for me for now and it has helped me deal with the aftermath a little better.

I still have crippling days and there isn't a week that goes by that I don't struggle with something, but I have hope.

And that is enough.

<u>You Should Know It Wasn't Your Fault</u>

If you take anything away from this chapter, please let it be that it was NOT your fault.

I'm not really talking about all the rubbish, outrageous and foul myths that say people who get sexually assaulted were asking for it. I actually had a dear family member tell me "lesson learnt" after I revealed my sexual assault. I am not talking about these myths, like if you wear a skirt that's too short then it's your fault. Those myths are harmful, outrageous and they are flat out wrong.

Instead, I'm talking about the trauma response that is when someone has been sexually assaulted, they try to rationalise it and explain why it happened. A large part of this is the survivor believing that they caused the assault and at first this is a protective belief because it gives them a sense of control over their rape. Yet over time, it causes you a lot of difficulties with anxiety, avoidance and other safety behaviours in the long-term.

Therefore, you need to understand that absolutely nothing you or your loved one did was the cause behind the sexual assault. And if you did what I did during my rape where I froze, please know this is an extremely normal response to overwhelming and extreme danger.

The attacker, rapist, perpetrator, whatever you want to call them. They are the only person you should be blaming.

It is not your fault.

<u>You Need To Give Yourself Time To Process The Sexual Assault and Accept and Expect Some Impacts</u>

As much as I have issues with the advice about "give it time" because it is extremely wrong. Time doesn't heal all wounds, especially when it comes to sexual violence, and it is only through processing the trauma and receiving professional support that you can heal and recover. You do need to give yourself the time needed to process what the hell happened to you.

In this book, I remember writing a line that I still love because it is so true.

If you don't deal with your sexual assault, it will deal with you.

I love that line because it's true. There have been times when I have refused to deal with certain aspects of my sexual assault and it's seriously come back to haunt me later on, often with a lot more intense and negative mental health outcomes compared to if I had only dealt with it in the moment.

Whatever happens you need to give yourself the time and space to process the assault instead of simply assuming that you're going to be okay and you're ready to jump back into your normal, everyday life.

It's true that resembling a sense of normality in your life is important and it can be very helpful, but it's okay if you need time away from the things you normally do or if you don't feel the same for a while after your assault. There's no way to predict how you're going to react in certain situations or whilst doing certain things after a sexual assault so give yourself the time to process it.

Personally, me continuing to do my student ambassador work at the university has been a massive, massive help in dealing with the aftermath of sexual assault. Since it is very difficult to focus on sexual assault when you're working with younger students, and I've always enjoyed the people, the work and it makes me happy.

Even though I cannot start new things since my assault. I have way too much anxiety, too many panic attacks and my PTSD is too severe to risk starting new things. It annoys me more than I want to admit but I've accepted that this is just a normal part of trauma recovery.

As well as accept and expect that things will be different now for a while. You'll have to deal with triggers, responses and mental health challenges and that's okay.

Accepting that this was a normal part of trauma recovery was helpful to me. It was annoying as hell but it was helpful and I have noticed small increases in my mental health because of it.

<u>You Need To Allow Yourself To Feel Your Emotions</u>

Building upon the last point, after a sexual assault, a lot of people have different emotional responses. I responded with intense denial and me pretending that I was okay even though all the signs were there that I seriously wasn't. Other people respond with fear, anxiety, sadness, anger, disgust and numbness. I experienced all those emotions later on and I'm still experiencing them 17 weeks later.

All these emotions are normal trauma responses and considering how horrific sexual assault is, it is more than okay for you to experience all these different emotions.

However, please reject one emotion. Please reject shame being directed towards you. *You* have nothing to be ashamed of because whilst there is no right or wrong way to feel, you truly have nothing to be ashamed of.

It wasn't your fault after all.

Overall, to help you or your loved one deal with the aftermath of sexual assault, please allow yourself to feel whatever you're feeling. Never push away or try to repress your emotions because it isn't healthy and it will only hurt you in the long-term. As well as please express your emotions in any way that you want. Be it writing, crying, talking, shouting, painting, drawing.

Just do whatever helps you to get the emotions out.

<u>Conclusion</u>

Sexual assault is one of the worst things someone can ever experience and I wouldn't wish it on my worst enemy because it leads to so many negative mental health outcomes. It's been 17 weeks since my sexual assault at the time of writing and it is still extremely difficult for me. There are a lot of reasons for that but the main one is I cannot sleep well more than two nights in a row without intense sexual assault popping up. And it didn't even happen in a bed.

However, my mental health is improving, slowly, and I am dealing with the aftermath better as time goes on. Even though I do wish I had known these tips and tricks earlier on because dealing with the aftermath of sexual assault would have been slightly easier for me.

Therefore, please make sure you manage your physical injuries and collect evidence, you understand this was NOT your fault, you need to seek support, give yourself time to process your assault and accept and expect trauma responses, and allow yourself to feel your emotions.

Those five tips should help you manage the aftermath of your sexual assault.

Your road to recovery and healing will not be easy but it is possible. I am living proof of that so it will take time, a lot of crying and bad mental health. Yet the road to recovery is always dark but there can still be plenty of joyous moments along the way.

WHAT IS THE NEUROLOGICAL IMPACT OF SEXUAL ASSAULT?

If experiencing sexual violence has taught me anything, it is that the body reacts, remembers and gets scared by trauma. My body experiences rapid breathing, shaking, panic attacks, burning sensations and more whenever my brain activates intrusive thoughts. This is all because of the effect trauma has on the nervous system, and whilst this is not an exhaustive chapter on all the ways sexual trauma impacts the nervous system and the brain.

In this chapter, you'll learn about the impact sexual trauma has on a neurological level and how it impacts our memory, nervous system and more. If you enjoy learning about trauma, neuropsychology and biopsychology then this is a brilliant chapter for you.

Why Does Sexual Assault Impact The Nervous System?

Personally, it took until 4 months after being raped that I realised just how much this was impacting my nervous system, because I don't really focus on the nervous system too much in general. Yet as I learnt more and more about sexual trauma and I healed just enough to allow myself to listen to my body and all the ways it was screaming at me, I finally realised that my nervous system was on fire because of my rape.

It's actually been something you focus a lot on in rape counselling, if you follow the trauma model, and you go through the Stabilization stage. You get to learn about how the nervous system reacts to responds and how a lot of the trauma responses are all linked to the nervous system. Then thankfully, this focus on the nervous system and me allowing myself to focus on my body allowed for a wonderfully healing moment the other week.

All leading us to question, how does sexual assault impact the nervous system?

As I've implied sexual trauma in any form can have a major, major impact on the nervous system and someone's neurological state that lasts far longer than the traumatic event itself. As well as in order to heal from the sexual trauma, survivors need to get back to a physical and emotional state where they feel safe. This was my massive healing moment last week, because I actually learnt how to *feel* safe in my own skin.

However, this is difficult for sexual assault survivors because we struggle to activate our parasympathetic nervous system that allows us to feel calm and safe. This struggle to activate the parasympathetic nervous system can have lasting negative impacts on our memory, mental function and brain structure.

Unfortunately, this is made even worse when survivors are revictimized by the criminal justice system and what happens when they come forward. Due to lawyers, the media and other people can attack, deny the survivor's claims and use their line of questions to blame the survivor when it wasn't their fault. When this happens, the survivor needs to develop strong resilience and coping skills to help them endure life after the awful trauma.

Thankfully, this can happen because survivors can be taught how to regulate their physiological reactions to be more resilient and tolerant over time to repeated stress, so they can effectively return their brains to a calming state by activating the parasympathetic nervous system.

How Does Sexual Assault Impact Memory?

Despite popular belief, sexual assault survivors don't remember every single detail of their assault like a perfect picture, because it is simply too painful and too horrific for them. As a result, survivors often have a very tough time remembering specific details or putting their attack into words. The reason for this difficulty is because the brain has to cope with the trauma as best it can, so typically the brain buries these memories so the survivors can continue to function in their everyday lives.

Personally, this is something I find very horrific at times, because whenever I "unlock" or remember a new trigger or an aspect of my rape, it is rather crippling. It causes me to experience massive PTSD reactions and recently I've been literally running out of rooms as soon as possible because it's been so overwhelming. I'm slowly healing in a lot of areas so this just makes the new triggers even harder. It was only a few days ago that I realised hearing the sound of people making out was a massive trigger for me because my first kisses were from my rapist, so that was horrific. Also, three weeks after my rape, me and my best friend were sleeping in the same room and they took their belt off and taking a belt off has a very distinctive sound.

I freaked and it was an awful night.

Those are some examples of how the brain can make us forget details in order to help us survive.

In addition, the brain tries to protect itself as much as possible so you're hardwired to survive, and this is where the fight-or-flight response comes into play. Since whenever something bad happens, your brain tells your body to run like hell, but when this does happen, it's important you try to remember that is a hardwired response and that you are safe. As well as it's important to learn over time not to be annoyed at yourself because this is important that you don't blame yourself or get annoyed at yourself because these are the body's trauma responses related to extremely abnormal situations.

Ultimately, if a sexual assault survivor cannot balance their fight-or-flight response with self-regulation skills (something I maintain is very hard but extremely possible to learn over the course of months), then the survivor might see the world as a negative and scary place. That's why repeated trauma worsens this negative bias and this makes it even harder for survivors to appreciate, remember and act on the positive aspects of their life.

Personally, because I've experienced at least two types of trauma in my life, this is why I've been so suicidal after my rape. And why I have to do positive psychology techniques these days to help me recognise the good parts of my life when I am really struggling.

Thankfully, social support and most importantly, therapy are extremely useful tools in helping survivors.

How Does Sexual Assault Impact Brain Structure?

Interestingly, any form of trauma, especially sexual trauma, causes our brains to change in a few different ways. Some of these changes are structural changes in the brain and others are functional changes in the brain in response to sexual trauma. The difficulty for sexual assault survivors is that we need to get our brains back to a point of homeostasis where we can feel safe and function properly once again. I've written a lot on the podcast over the past few months about how my brain and nervous system have been impacted by my rape so I won't recap it all here.

One of the brain changes that sexual violence can cause in survivors is hypervigilance because repeated trauma (or any kind of sexual trauma) can enlarge the amygdala, and this is the brain region in charge of our fight-or-flight response. And when we get triggered because of trauma, in an effort to protect us, the brain inhibits communication between the amygdala and our prefrontal cortex (the brain area in charge of executive functioning). In other words, this means our brain stops us from thinking rationally about the trigger and the brain ensures we only feel the emotion so we can run away or freeze just to survive.

Moreover, the brain changes because sexual trauma impacts our breathing and other bodily reactions too. Since to live a healthy lifestyle, humans need to be calm for long periods of time and humans breathe 6 cycles per minute, we access the right brainwave of our sensory-motor rhythm that's between 12-15 hertz and we regulate our skin temperature to be above roughly 90 degrees F. However, when we experience trauma, what matters is that we live our lives in a constant state of tension with erratic breathing and constant sympathetic nervous system activation.

In other words, our sexual trauma impacts our brain's ability to regulate our body so we lose control of our mental and physical abilities. Therefore, in therapy, this is why it is critical that survivors are taught how to regulate the symptoms of trauma so eventually they can live life and function once more at their fullest capacity.

This is another reason why I seriously recommend H*ealing Sexual Trauma Workbook by Erika Sherman.* It's a brilliant workbook that has helped me massively in regulating my nervous system and it is a brilliant companion for specialist counselling.

How Does Sexual Assault Impact Post-Traumatic Stress Disorder?

Building upon these brain changes even more, I've already spoken in the book about the prevalence of Post-Traumatic Stress Disorder amongst sexual assault survivors, so now I want to focus on the neurological aspect of the condition. Therefore, a lot of neuroimaging studies on the brain of people with PTSD have shown that there are several brain regions that are functionally and structurally different to people without PTSD. For example, the amygdala, ventromedial prefrontal cortex as well as the hippocampus are all critical in triggering the symptoms of PTSD. Also, the volume of the hippocampus reduces in survivors so this causes sexual assault survivors to possibly lose the ability to discriminate against past and present experiences or even appropriately interpret environmental contexts.

In practical terms, for survivors, this means that survivors might tie specific things about their attack into their life, like the time of day or year or a particular place where they were assaulted. In turn, this leads to survivors having mental triggers that lead to sensations of re-experiencing the attack months or unfortunately even years after the sexual assault happened.

This is what I've been eluding to over the past few months because there are key aspects and triggers that I have integrated into my life by accident and now I'm starting to break those patterns very, very slowly. For example, my mental health always used to dip like clockwork in the evening because I was raped roughly between 23:20 and 23:40 on the 13th of April 2024. As well as I was distressed Sunday night at the time of writing so I went for a walk but the issue I had found out very quickly was that where I've moved to, at night, the house look scarily similar to the house of my rapist and I "remembered" that I was raped on a cold night.

I did not enjoy re-remembering that little sensory detail.

Conclusion

At the end of this clinical psychology chapter, you know that a lot of sexual assault survivors struggle to activate their parasympathetic nervous system. Then it is our job as mental health professionals, including clinical psychologists, to teach our clients that have experienced sexual trauma how to become more tolerant to stressors and how to activate their parasympathetic nervous system so they can feel calm after the ultimate betrayal. Thankfully, we can teach clients how to regulate the variability of their heart rate, breathing and skin temperature then these basic biofeedback skills are what clients can use on a daily basis or whenever to deal with stressors and trauma triggers.

Ultimately, if the past six months have taught me anything it is that, survivors need to learn self-regulation skills so they can work through their distress, panic and anxiety that will pop up whenever they re-experience the sexual assault. These skills have taken me roughly 6-months to truly start embracing, understanding and incorporating them into my own life (you can do them a lot sooner but still) and it is a very weird feeling. I actually feel safe, secure and loved for the first time since my rape, maybe even my life.

It is weird but oddly wonderful to go from a state of constant and utter fear into a state where you still get triggered on occasion but you can handle the world so much better.

In addition, whilst sexual trauma will impact us survivors forever, it doesn't have to control us forever because by getting professional help where mental health professionals can listen to us without judgement and they can help teach us self-regulation skills to help us cope with the past, present and future stressors. We can all heal and that is a powerful and brilliant realisation to come too.

Since survivors need professionals to teach them and guide them towards allowing survivors to activate their brain's social engagement system where clients feel safe enough to form attachments and ask and think about their own safety needs. These two features and so many more typically get shut off after sexual trauma so the client can survive in a world that becomes terrifying. So these biofeedback skills become even more important as professionals work with survivors to activate the parasympathetic nervous system so clients can feel calm and safe in their recovery.

The brain is an amazing organ that protects us at all costs, but after experiencing trauma the brain scrambles and moves heaven and earth to protect us. It manages that very well but the results can be devastating to our lives so we must learn over time to overcome the neurological impact of sexual trauma so we can live, heal and enjoy life once more.

I know it may sound impossible, but I promise you, over time as you learn more, heal more and get professional help. It is very possible and an extremely positive feeling to experience.

It actually might be one of the best feelings you'll ever experience.

WHAT MAKES A PSYCHOLOGIST TRAUMA-INFORMED?

Our next chapter focuses on one of my favourite areas of clinical psychology because as you'll see in this chapter, trauma-informed approaches are critical in modern clinical psychology. Yet they are even more important when working with rape survivors.

As a result, in recognition of how common trauma is in society and in an effort to help address its devastating consequences on people's mental health, clinical psychology has shifted towards becoming more trauma-informed. In the UK at least, it is an area of interest that candidates are being asked about more often during their doctorate interviews. Therefore, if you want to work in clinical psychology and if you're an aspiring clinical psychologist then trauma-informed approaches are a critical area to understand.

In this psychology chapter, you'll learn what makes a psychologist trauma-informed, what are the 6 core principles of trauma-informed approaches and more. If you enjoy learning about trauma, mental health and clinical work then this is a great chapter for you.

<u>What Is A Trauma-Informed Approach?</u>

As I mentioned in the introduction to today's chapter, there is a big move within clinical psychology to become more trauma-informed. Due to psychologists need to be trauma-informed in recognition of how common trauma is in the world and as psychologists we need to respond to this harsh reality that trauma causes. For example, if I go off my own experience here, I've been through two types of trauma, one a single event and another form of trauma that stretched on for over a decade. As well as trauma is a wide-ranging umbrella term for different traumatic situations that might not affect some people but they might affect others. These can include child abuse, sexual violence, witnessing a murder, being a soldier and so on.

Therefore, being trauma-informed means psychologists need to be aware of how trauma can impact an individual personally and societally too as well as psychologists need to anticipate how trauma survivors might respond to our actions and words so we don't compound the damage and suffering that the trauma causes.

In addition, this concept connects to the idea of secondary traumatisation. This is normally seen in forensic psychology where victims of crimes are traumatised again by going through the criminal justice system. Yet I see no reason why this cannot be extended to clinical psychology because if you have a clinical psychologist who isn't trained in dealing with trauma and they make a mistake with a client by saying the wrong thing. Then I can easily see how this would retraumatised the client.

For example, let's take a personal example and talk about my child abuse during my adolescence and let's use this situation in when I went to therapy last August. If my therapist wasn't aware of trauma or LGBT+ issues and she said something that was blaming me for my abuse, my mental health and my situation then that would have been extremely damaging and it would only add to my trauma. Since in my mind, if a therapist cannot accept me and support me being gay and all the trauma I'm experiencing around it then no one can accept me. So my mental health would continue to decline.

This is why psychological training is so important as well as having trauma-specific training is critical.

Ultimately, being trauma-informed means psychologists are helping to create a world that can foster a client's resilience, growth as well as healing.

What Are The 6 Core Principles of Trauma-Informed Approaches?

As you can probably imagine, all of us aspiring and qualified psychologists can say we want to be trauma-informed as much as we want but this intention isn't enough alone. Also, when we consider just how many different examples of traumatic experiences there are and all the different types of trauma survivors, it's very difficult to land on a narrow set of clinical guidelines that are going to be useful in every situation. This is why clinical psychologists have managed to come together to create a set of 6 guiding core principles that we can apply flexibly to each client as well as situation.

The source behind these guidelines are the Substance Abuse and Mental Health Service Association (SAMHSA) in 2014, and now we'll look at these 6 core principles.

What Is Trustworthiness And Transparency In Clinical Trauma Work?

The first principle we'll look at isn't directly linked to client work but trustworthiness and transparency is a principle focusing on helping clients to feel more willing to engage with the mental health service that we work in. When it comes to being trustworthy, this means we need to keep our promises, be reliable and we need to clearly show this towards our clients. Such as, we might say to our clients one thing and then follow up with the client with evidence to show that we've done this for them. One example is that if you say you're going to email a medical doctor for some reason then you could show them the email you sent, of course whilst sticking to data protection and any other rules your service has in place.

Furthermore, transparency helps clients to understand what your intentions and priorities are so the clients know where they stand with you as well as the mental health service. One way of putting this concept is it is the equivalent of "showing your work" when you try to solve a problem, so you might tell your client your thought process and what factors you considered when trying to make the clinical decision.

Personally, I only just realised how brilliant transparency is because when I went for my counselling assessment for my sexual violence therapy, the psychologist doing the assessment told me a lot of "extra" information. For example, she explained why I wouldn't be suitable to see a placement or trainee counsellor and she would talk to me and tell me what she was thinking as she was making notes. Therefore, she might have "only" been a psychologist assessing me but because she was completely transparent with me and she kept me informed of everything she was thinking, I felt really comfortable. And I am really looking forward to working with the service whenever I come off the waiting list.

How Does The Safety Principle Make A Psychologist Trauma Informed?

Whenever it comes to trauma, it is very common and a natural response for people not to feel safe. For example, me and my best friend were talking the other night because they asked me a question from the kitchen, they found it weird that whenever they asked me something I stop everything immediately and "ran" to them. I said that it was because if I didn't come quickly in the past to someone asking me a question or if I didn't do something quick enough then I would be shouted at or occasionally worse, and my best friend wanted me to learn that I am safe with them in our new house. And the same goes for the intense social anxiety I often have because of my sexual assault.

It can be extremely difficult for trauma survivors to feel safe but without a feeling of safety clinical work is often doomed to fail.

As a result, safety encourages clients to focus on the psychological intervention and support that is being offered so clients can feel emotionally and physically protected from danger. Also, it's important that psychologists understand what makes clients feel unsafe so this can be very different across different trauma experiences and across different cultures. Such as when it comes to what makes me feel unsafe due to my sexual assault, big crowds, a dimly lit room and large men make me feel very unsafe. Then again before I dealt with my abuse, homophobia and older straight men would make me feel very unsafe, so it is different depending on the situation.

In addition, it's worth noting that safety doesn't mean that things will always be easy for the client or even comfortable and it's important to make this distinction at times. Since the idea of safety is built on the idea that a lot of trauma survivors lack a basic sense of safety (this is why I have so many panic attacks when I'm in public and meeting new people), and a lot of non-trauma survivors take their basic sense of safety for granted.

As a result, when it comes to applying the safety principle in clinical work, it's about levelling the playing field so all your clients can enjoy a basic sense of safety whenever they're with you. So an individual might report feeling safe when they're able to just stop scanning their environment for any threats or dangers for the hour they are with for you, and they're no longer having to focus on defending or protecting themselves.

And it is this basic sense of safety which causes me a lot of issues in my life at the moment because whenever I'm out and in a busy place, I am hypervigilant and hyperfocused on scanning my environment, watching out for anyone who would hurt me and so on. I understand that these are all illogical thoughts but it is still scary.

How Does Empowerment, Voice And Choice Make A Psychologist Trauma-Informed?

Our next principle focuses on making sure psychologists help clients to use their voice and power. Since trauma is a very disempowering experience so clients can be fearful and reluctant to step forward so it is up to psychologists to gently help and support clients to develop skills in this area that will help them become more empowered. For instance, helping to develop a client's assertiveness and advocacy. As well as the interesting thing about all 6 of these core principles is that the more you embody all of them, the more likely clients are to be empowered too.

As a brief personal example, one major issue I've had following my sexual assault is my disempowered and my inability to make decisions. For example, there are times when I simply cannot make decisions at all, including really tiny ones like in what cupboards to put my kitchen stuff in when I moved into my student accommodation. I simply couldn't make a decision because I didn't trust myself, I didn't have self-worth and so on. And there are lots of different examples of disempowerment in the past few months and it is absolutely horrible. I don't wish being paralysed with fear so you cannot function and make basic decisions on anyone.

How Does Mutuality And Collaboration Make A Psychologist Trauma-Informed?

In addition, our next principle takes this even further because it encourages clients to focus on who has power and who might be vulnerable to its misuse. Due to this principle is about a psychologist embodying collaboration and mutuality, a psychologist can help a client to reduce this power differential and its risks by engaging in more active collaboration across different levels of the service between clients and staff. For instance, a mental health service might get clients to give their input on the service (Collaboration and Mutuality) when considering a new policy or procedure then share how that information was used when the service was making its final decision (transparency).

Ultimately, I think this connects to all clinical work and the importance of the therapeutic alliance. I know all therapy work is effectively a collaboration depending on the therapy module being used, but in trauma work, this is even more important because trauma survivors are already so disempowered. Then if a psychologist walked in, did a lot of things to the client without working *with* them and then kept doing this then the trauma survivor wouldn't see any benefit because nothing would change. This so-called clinical work would only be a continuation of their disempowerment and trauma without anything changing.

How Does Understanding Cultural, Historical And Gender Issues Make A Psychologist Trauma Informed?

There are a lot of historical, cultural and gender issues that exist in the world and the vast majority of these impact trauma survivors, so it is flat out critical to understand how these issues impact trauma-informed work. This is why psychologists need to pay attention to the culture and world we live in so we can see the strengths, core values, social connections and resources that people might ignore. As well as psychologists need to understand how a historical context or how a client experiences discrimination might impact them but also how these experiences might frame how a client perceives our actions or policies. Due to by understanding these historical issues, we can have a better understanding of how to implement the other core principles in this chapter.

And when it comes to my personal trauma, these historical, cultural and gender issues are a major problem for me. Since my childhood trauma was caused by the cultural and historical issues around homophobia and how older people see and treat gay people. As well as when it comes to my sexual assault, the gender issue of being male and how the vast majority of people believe males don't experience sexual violence is very challenging and it has compounded my trauma in more ways than I want to admit.

So please, try to understand the different cultural, historical and gender issues that will impact your clients. It is a fascinating topic and it is flat out critical for trauma-informed work.

How Does Peer Support Make A Psychologist Trauma-Informed?

Our final trauma-informed principle focuses on how peer support can help clients find opportunities to learn and grow with other people who have lived experiences of trauma. Before on the podcast I've spoken about the benefits of group therapy and peer support groups is one of the three types. Peer support can be useful because it gives trauma survivors a chance to develop a stronger sense of belonging and it can support empowerment too because it is normally easier to speak up as a group than as a single individual.

Conclusion

When it comes to trauma-informed work, this is flat out critical for aspiring and qualified psychologists because a trauma-informed approach isn't just about the students or clients that we work with, to be honest. It is about our fellow psychologists, staff and our leaders at our mental health services, as well as ourselves, who could be trauma survivors. Our clients are not the only trauma survivors in the world.

Therefore, these 6 core principles can be used in everyday context and setting, even if you're not working with trauma survivors explicitly, because all these principles can be useful in clinical work. As well as even when you're working with your peers, it is always good to make them feel safe, be transparent and collaborate with them and more. Sometimes I feel like just knowing how to be more trauma-informed helps you to become a better person and after this chapter, I believe that even more.

To wrap up this trauma chapter, it needs to be said that these principles need to be applied flexibly because chances are they will look very different depending on the type of trauma you are working with now or in the future. Yet they are still important because these principles have the power to transform and heal our relationships, our mental health services and maybe even ourselves if we're trauma survivors.

Working with trauma might sound scary to a lot of people, but as a trauma survivor myself, yes what I experienced and went through was utterly terrifying. But I am not a victim that needs to be treated carefully, like a child or like I am anything other than a regular human being who has been through hell and back. I am simply a survivor trying to live my life as much as I can but I need psychological help for that and that is where all of us come in now or in the future.

Clinical trauma work might sound scary but it can probably be some of the most rewarding work we might ever do as psychologists. And we might transform lives for the better even more than usual.

TRIGGERS CAN COME FROM ANYWHERE

Within clinical psychology, we are all well-aware that clients with different mental health conditions can be triggered in a few different ways. For example, if we take the most obvious example of anxiety, then we know that clients can be triggered in limited ways.

For instance, clients with social anxiety will likely be triggered in social situations whereas clients with a spider phobia will likely only be triggered in a situation involving a spider. Also, clients with generalised anxiety disorder can get anxious about everything and anything.

This content we all learn through our clinical psychology lectures, textbooks and we can hear about it from service users. Yet this comes back to the previous point I made in another reflection, I did not truly understand this idea of triggers and how extremely distressing and random they can be until my assault.

I'll briefly and lightly tell you some things that happened to me this week and then I'll reflect on them in terms of clinical psychology. Although, this is more of a lived experience post compared to a "hardcore" clinical psychology reflection.

<u>What Happened?</u>

It was my birthday over the bank holiday weekend and my best friend stayed with me at my parents' house, and because of my Great-Aunt was staying, They couldn't sleep in the room they normally did whenever they stay over.

They had to sleep on a camp bed in my room, and I had been concerned about that for a different reason for weeks after my assault. I was concerned how I would react to have someone I really like sleeping in the same room as me.

I just never expected it to trigger me as much as it did.

Since my friend was wearing jeans with a belt and when we turned the lights off my friend started to get undressed for bed. Like any normal person would and I was trying to get to sleep because I had undressed and got into bed when they were cleaning their teeth.

Yet the sound of them undoing their belt and taking their clothes off was beyond awful. I wrapped myself up so tightly in my bedsheets just so nothing could happen.

And in hindsight I should have gone downstairs and slept on the sofa. Yet I stayed in my room with my friend and it was a rough night. My friend slept fine but whenever they moved in the night, whenever they made a sound and whenever they did anything. I would get so anxious, so scared and so hypervigilant that I couldn't sleep.

On the second night, I slept downstairs but I still couldn't really sleep because our sofa is a lot less comfortable than it was 2 years ago at Christmas. And the camp bed was on a dodgy floorboard so again whenever my friend moved in the night I would hear it.

Thankfully, the third night, I got a better night's sleep because I was sleeping again in my room but closer to my friend. And I trained my brain to tell me that if there's a noise in the night, my friend would never ever let anything bad happen to me. They would protect me.

That worked for the most part and the only bad part was the floor next to the camp bed was, well, a floor so I wasn't perfectly comfortable.

Anyway, so you can see how just something as normal as two friends sleeping in the same room can be triggering. As well as simple sounds or movements can be triggering to assault survivors.

Personally, I found this a logical thing to be triggered by because in my sexual assault, there were no clothes on, the assaulter was wearing jeans and he had to take them off and the rest. So I can understand why this was triggering.

Yet I was surprised how this trigger had spread to other domains in my life. Since my assault did not happen with a friend, it did not happen in a bedroom and it did not happen with someone that I trust with my life. Much less someone I'm romantically into.

However, I think this trigger is a good example of how traumatic events and what reminds victims of them can spread into other areas of their lives to the point where they are extremely distressed.

It was horrible not sleeping for those three nights then it took me another two nights to start sleeping normally again.

The Tube Incident

On my actual birthday when my friend stayed with me, we both went up to London to do this Virtual Reality escape room that was brilliant fun and I seriously recommend it. The day was lovely, I really enjoyed the VR thing and I had a great time with my friend.

Yet I was already tired from not sleeping for two nights and then we were on the Tube in London to get some dinner. And there was a sign, a very noble and innocent sign on the Tube opposite me.

Pressing Up Against Someone On Purpose is Sexual Harassment. Then it was something like *Don't Do It* or *Stop!*

And my body and mind just got scared and triggered to my utter annoyance. I tried to make myself as small as possible, I could only look at the floor and my friend had to call my name to make me look at them. They told me things were okay, we didn't have long left and they were asking if I wanted to get off the Tube for a breather.

They are a brilliant friend.

But I really didn't want to be on that Tube, because in my mind, pressing up against someone is the same as grinding against something. Which is something my assaulter did to me constantly so I was tired, stressed and seeing that sign really didn't help.

I hated it and when me and my friend were back in my room, I asked them point blank *what was it like seeing me like that*? They could only say it was concerning and they worry about me enough anyway so to have their worries confirmed probably really wasn't nice for them.

Overall, I'm really annoyed that I was triggered by such a stupid sign. I hated how I was triggered that easily and I think there is an embarrassment aspect because I was crying my eyes out on the Tube and all this happened in front of other people who didn't know me, didn't know what had happened and they were judging me. Especially this elderly man with grey hair and big bushy eyebrows. He was seriously judging me.

So I hated that I could be triggered that easily since there is a disempowering element too.

Part of me no longer knows if I can go up to London by myself, because what if I get triggered and there's no one around to help me? What if all the assault memories flood me and I'm trapped? What if someone hurts me again on the Tube?

Of course the last one isn't a logical or realistic thought, but it happens. As well as I know giving myself time to heal needs to be my main focus but it is still annoying.

<u>Reading Survivor Stories</u>

Finally, on the Wednesday, I was still tired and I was at university away for a revision lecture and I had a social group thing that evening. I was still a bit distressed because after I dropped my friend off back home, they experienced something really bad because of their housemates. And I know it's bad because they refuse to tell me over text and we can have massive text conversations lasting hours at times.

Anyway, the distress from my birthday weekend was still lingering so I thought in my eternal wisdom to look up male sexual assault survivor stories. So I wouldn't feel so alone, so I would know other people were coping and surviving and they were thriving.

Note to self, do not read stuff like that less than a month after the assault.

I found a story exactly like mine down to every detail accept the ages were slightly different. And that was distressing as hell to realise that had happened to someone else and it was even worse that 5 years later they couldn't really date, they couldn't have sex and they couldn't live a normal life.

My mind didn't want to accept that, because when I was really distressed I was in the mind of "I want everything to go back to how it was before the assault". Of course that can never happen.

Reading that story was so triggering and distressing that I was crying and I had to do something very stupid to stop the pain.

Then I tried to read another story (clearly not learning my lesson) about a guy who had a completely different assault to me. The last line of the opening paragraph was "now I've lost everything I love" and that really sent me over the edge because I don't want to lose everything.

I know I won't but reading that survivor story wasn't helpful to me personally at this moment in time. Because this has always been my fatal fault, I try to do healing things before I am ready for them because I want to be further along than I am.

I never give myself time to heal and that's a massive mistake on my part.

Overall, when it comes to this triggering experience, I think we can all understand why this was triggering. It was reliving in words what had happened at a point where I was already distressed, tired and I hadn't slept in days.

Although, the interesting thing about this is that it shows that feeling that you aren't alone and that there are others like you, that come with time. Since some survivors and clients aren't ready for that straight away (I don't think anyone is straight away) and I think sometimes in clinical psychology when the conversation does turn to a sense of community, the nuance about whether this is right for a client or if they're ready for this, is missing at times.

I know I miss it in my personal life and my clinical psychology interests, but every client is different. That is what I've learnt from this week even more than normal, so some clients will enjoy and benefit from hearing stories and feeling apart of a larger community of victims. But some clients aren't ready at the moment and maybe they never will be.

That's okay because there are still so many ways to help them improve their lives, take back control and decrease their distress.

A WERID SITUATION, BEING NOT DEFENSIVE AND NOT JUDGEMENTAL

Originally, this next chapter came from *Clinical Psychology Reflections Volume 6* and whilst this chapter doesn't explicitly add anything to working with people who have experienced sexual violence, it is important. Since this chapter teaches us aspiring and qualified psychologists the importance of being non-judgemental, not being defensive and not letting clients attacking us impact us too much (easier said than done I know).

This is an invaluable chapter for sure.

***

There are times in our lives when we meet certain people, go through certain experiences and in the moment you don't know whether you're coming or going, what's actually happening and you feel that life is extremely chaotic. Yet afterwards, when the dust has settled you realised you did a really good job and you actually might be more cut-out for a job in clinical psychology and mental health than you previously thought.

Our next reflection is a chance for me to reflect on lessons learnt after the past few days when I was badly attacked via WhatsApp Messenger and in a few Group chats and this had very real-world implications too.

Now I talk about this because I only realised last night that the person doing this (who I do know) she has a few mental health conditions that I know about and from what I've read and heard from her, I am fairly sure she has psychotic features too.

Therefore, I'll tell you what happened, how I dealt with it and why I think this is a useful experience for the future.

And for the purpose of this reflection, I will be calling this woman, Jane, as in Jane Doe.

What Happened?

For context, me and Jane have clashed before because our personalities and sense of humour don't mix well. And because of this and the fact she is extremely sensitive, I don't talk to her, I avoid perfectly normal topics like me and my best friend living together next month and a whole range of other things because I know she gets extremely jealous of me.

Anyway, on Monday night, me and my friends were finishing off a one-shot (short campaign) of Dungeons and Dragons, because even though this isn't really my thing, I like the social side and it's not as bad as I make out in my head. It is actually rather fun at times.

Anyway, Jane was getting really annoyed at some rules and how the other players weren't using them properly. And I couldn't have cared less about these rules so I told her to calm down.

Later on that night when I got home after driving through the back and beyond because of a motorway closure, she texted me asking me if I had said what I had said. I knew whatever I replied with there would be an argument because this has happened before.

I was half-tempted to lie to her but I didn't want to gaslight her and I just wanted to see how she would argue with me. So I told her the truth and that I had asked her to calm down.

About ten minutes later, she sent me this very impressive and long message attacking me. Saying I was a meanie, a bully and I was a horrible person that had it out for her and I was always targeting her with my jokes and my "jabs".

It was a rather interesting message to read because it made basically no sense and everything was so over the top.

I will admit that I am not a perfect human being and I am autistic so social interactions can be a little difficult at times. And I have made one or two general jokes that hit her trauma because I didn't know it.

I haven't repeated those jokes but my personal approach is you shouldn't be angry with someone for accidentally and innocently hitting your trauma if they don't know it.

For example, in the first session of this one-shot, a new player who I knew about from a friend but I had never met made a comment about I should have had time to learn a new class of character because she learnt it in a few hours. She is actually lovely in reality, but that comment annoyed me because the reason why I hadn't had time to learn a new class is because I had been really struggling with rape stuff that week so I didn't have the mental energy.

Then I realised she wasn't attacking me because she didn't know what was going on, so I wasn't going to judge her or hate her for hitting something she didn't know was there.

Anyway, so Jane sent me this message and she threatened to pull out of my best friend's DnD campaign if I didn't stop being such a foul person.

Now me and my best friend we have been through this before with Jane, so I said to my friend (who was in bed at the time) that I need to leave your campaign and I wrote a long message to my best friend about why I should leave and Jane should stay. In essence, Jane enjoys it more and after everything she's been through I do want her to be happy and being in this DnD campaign will definitely help that.

The next day my best friend replied back saying "I'll think about how to navigate this". Which I mean is typical them because they want me and Jane in this campaign and I love my best friend but they are an extreme peacekeeper. They want to make sure everyone is happy no matter what the future conflict.

I am more practical because even though I played this entire situation as a peacekeeper and I did not engage with these attacks at all. I know I cannot do any right in Jane's eyes so these attacks would only continue in the future unless I did something.

However, because I felt bad for my best friend because I knew this wasn't what I wanted at all and I have an awful habit of blaming myself for a lot of stuff (something I thankfully didn't do too much), I decided to leave the DnD campaign.

So I posted a nice little message saying I was leaving, it's been great playing with you all and I highlighted a favourite player of mine and I wished everyone luck with the future. Since a few of the other players are leaving the university and Kent this year.

Jane flew at me in the group chat.

Now it's useful to note here that another odd habit of mine is I like writing out "important" messages in my personal email drafts, I sit on them for a bit and then I edit them. My original leaving message pointed out how me and Jane didn't get on and it named a few of our issues. It wasn't blaming but it would have highlighted Jane was a problem.

And judging from the response I got from leaving without blaming anyone, I think a lot of people would have sided with me anyway.

Yet I didn't want to turn this into a fight where people needed to pick sides and stuff, so I did a very vague, lovely message.

Jane still flew at me.

I've been accused of a lot of stuff by lying people before, especially in my childhood who would lie because they didn't understand I was autistic. But I have never been accused of such horrible things in front of my friends where they could see so many lies and I've never been accused of looking for sympathy before.

I was half-tempted to message back on the group chat saying "as if I would want sympathy from these people". Which would have made me look bad, because it makes it sound like I'm not friends with them, when in reality, I knew everyone (But Jane) in that group chat really liked me.

Anyway, I texted my best friend saying *are we good* and I just saw Jane's message. My best friend replied saying *yeah we're good and I'm talking to* Jane now.

I later found out that my best friend spoke to Jane and she left the group chat for my best friend's DnD campaign, got really angry with said best friend and actually kicked the best friend out of the DnD campaign she was running.

My best friend isn't that bothered but I feel for them, and they deleted Jane's hateful messages from the group chat too.

That's basically the whole story.

Lessons Learnt And Why Am I Talking About This?

I think what happened has a few different lessons that we can learn, because Jane does have a few mental health conditions and from conversations with Jane, our friends in common and what I've read about her conditions, they do make a person act a certain way.

This is why I don't have a problem with Jane at all because my perspective is, she isn't attacking me, it's her other personalities and psychotic symptoms.

These lessons can be applied to working in clinical psychology too.

Firstly, I think it's important to not get defensive when you're attacked by a client or someone with a mental health condition. Because the past few days have been really bad with these attacks and the specific ways Jane's attacked me.

Equally, it would have been a lot worse if I had replied, defended myself and argued the toss with her. It would have made her get more and more angry, she would have attacked me even more and this could have spilt out into other areas of our life.

For example, I managed to keep this argument focused on DnD but it could have spilled out into the friends we have in common, the shared social activities we have and it could have gotten awkward in other ways.

But I didn't interact with her or get defensive or try to defend myself.

I defended myself to my best friend because they are the Dungeon Master (the person in charge of the DnD campaign) so I had to tell them this issue and I wanted to explain why these were lies. Something they already know thankfully.

Yet I didn't engage with Jane and I blocked her after the attacks in the group chat.

Therefore, I think in future clinical work, I will need to make sure I take the same approach about being attacked. Since let's face it, we will not be perfect with every single client and there will be clients that don't like us, don't like our service and they will berate us.

It doesn't happen constantly but this happens in real life.

Overall, in terms of you, it's important to realise you shouldn't get defensive or judgemental when a client is attacking you and don't react negatively. You will only make it worse and by reacting badly you will not be helping anyone.

Approach A Situation Without Hate, Dislike or Judgement

Something I was rather proud of myself about during this entire situation was I didn't hate Jane, I didn't dislike her and even though it's over now because I know me and my best friend are fine, I've left the conflict-filled situation and Jane has been dealt with.

I still don't dislike or hate Jane because it isn't her fault her psychotic features and persecutory delusions make her believe all this stuff.

Personally, I would like her to go and get professional help and be in weekly therapy, but that isn't my place. It isn't my concern and as I have said a thousand times, you cannot send someone to therapy unless they admit they need it and they have a capacity for change.

Therefore, I think if you are being attacked badly based on lies, it might be helpful to take a similar position to me in this case. And instead view the person attacking you as the "attacking" behaviour being a result of their mental health difficulties.

This is not a perfect solution though.

Due to you need to make sure you aren't automatically dismissing what the client is saying, because there might be something wrong, you should always seek to improve and the client might have good feedback for you.

This is why one of the texts I sent to my best friend last night was something the lines of "if you can see anyway I could have handled this better, let me know and I'll improve if a similar situation happens again,"

My best friend completely skipped out that part but I do acknowledge that reflective practice is important in clinical work, and I think there can be a place for that in the real world when something happens.

Don't Let It Get To You

I did fail at this final lesson.

Since every single week in May, I have had to deal with something major, I did let this get to me a lot more than it should have. Part of that was because I didn't want to leave DnD because I like it, I like seeing my friends and my best friend was going to invite someone I find seriously attractive in the future so I wanted to see this person. Then my best friend was planning other fun social things too around the main DnD campaign.

Anyway, I basically lost two full days to this issue, the Tuesday and the Wednesday, with me only having the energy to do the things I had scheduled in my calendar. Like a few meetings and some Student ambassador leadership training because I got a job promotion.

I shouldn't have been bothered by these attacks as much as they did and I should have done more self-care. Part of the problem is I only have a few very, very close friends and my best friend wasn't really talking to me in any great depth until the Wednesday with the group chat attacks. Mainly because they're busy revising for an exam tomorrow and they wanted to think up a solution to keep everyone happy.

On the whole, when you are being attacked, it isn't nice and it can be quite distressing, so it is okay if it bothers you. I would unofficially recommend that you make sure you do self-care, you talk to people and look after yourself.

Do not suffer because someone attacked you. If they attacked you and it was badly framed criticism for improvement, then learn from it because we can all be better.

If it's an attack that isn't based in reality, then try to shrug it off and look after yourself.

Just don't engage at all and if you absolutely have to, do not engage negatively you won't be helping anyone.

WHY HAVING EVENING APPOINTMENTS IS AMAZING?

One of the two major things that I learnt during my counselling assessment was how brilliant it is when mental health services have evening appointments. This is a topic I've heard spoken about in my clinical psychology lectures before and I have fully agreed and supported the idea as an aspiring clinical psychologist. Yet it was only during my counselling assessment that I realised just how incredible it is as a client for evening appointments to be available.

Therefore, in this reflection, I'll explain why mental health services need evening appointments from a clinical psychologist perspective, then I'll talk about my own experience as a client.

Why Does Clinical Psychology Need To Have Evening Appointments?

As the vast majority of us know as aspiring or qualified clinical psychologists, mental health services tend to run 9 am until 5 pm in the evening. This happens because this is the normal working day, the entire working world is oriented towards these hours and it is just a part of our society and culture. People always go to work between these times and once the clock goes outside this 8-hour timeframe then people do not have to work anymore.

Of course, I understand this is a generalisation. My dad did continental shift patterns for over twenty years and even now he works 6 til 2, so I understand how general my argument is here.

However, this 9 am until 5 pm window that mental health services operate under is very good. It gives us eight hours to see clients, transform lives and decrease psychological distress. That's amazing and it is these eight hours a day that allow clinical psychology to be as amazing as it is.

There is a downside.

Unless you can get time off work, you cannot have therapy.

Mainly because *everyone* works 9 am until 5 pm in the evening. That means if you do not finish your work until this window finishes then mental health services cannot see you because they are closed.

In addition, if we think about the types of people that generally have poor mental health. For example, people from lower socioeconomic backgrounds and deprived areas then this means these people generally cannot afford to take time off work.

Equally, if they do have a day-off by some miracle then they tend to have caring responsibilities because they can't afford childcare or the like.

On the whole, this means clinical psychology as a profession and how mental health services are currently setup are failing these people. This is not good and I really don't like it.

Granted, there is the additional problem about staffing because if we pretend for one moment that the National Health Service and other mental health services have perfect staffing levels (which they do not have), then clinical psychologists are unlikely to want to work (let's say) a 12 hour shift so they can see clients in the evening.

This would mean that mental health services would need to hire even more clinical staff and mental health professionals to offer these evening appointments. This costs extra money and budgets are tight enough for the public sector.

In other words, I understand why this isn't available but it isn't morally right.

The entire point of clinical psychology is to help everyone who experiences a mental health difficulty, condition or psychological distress to clinically significant levels. And if our mental health services are not arranged in a way that means they can come and see us and get the support they need, then we are failing these people.

That is not good enough.

Why Are Evening Appointments Brilliant? A Client's Perspective

I mentioned before that I was extremely concerned about my counselling assessment for my sexual violence counselling. Due to the charity was going to ask me what my availability was in the next few weeks and that scared me because I couldn't give them much.

In fact, the charity specifically said, try to give the counselling department as much availability as possible so they can pair you up quickly and your waiting list will be shorter.

I translated that in my mind to mean, you need a good availability so you can get the help you really need.

My main issue is me and my best friend are working the Summer Core period of my university's Outreach department as student ambassadors. This means we need to be available to work every working day between 17th June 2024 to the 12th July 2024 from 9 am to 3 pm.

That would be relatively okay by itself but we don't get our timetables until the Friday before for the following week, as well as we could be working at the Medway or Canterbury campus or anywhere else in the county of Kent. So one bit of traffic and we are screwed trying to get back to Canterbury for my counselling.

As a result, I wanted to give them something so I feared I would only be able to give the charity 4 pm until 5 pm Monday to Friday. That is only 5 available slots a week that is not very good. Also, I think they are very popular times so I would hardly be the only person asking for those times.

As a client, this made me very scared, very nervous and it didn't really help me when I was suicidal the other week. It only made the idea of me healing, moving on and having a future seem more distant and like it was impossible.

Since as a client (and I always say this about people who come to mental health services), it took me a lot of courage to agree to come to a sexual violence centre. Partly because I was in denial, I didn't want to admit it was real and I didn't want even more people to know I was a victim.

It is hard for me to know others see me as a sexual violence victim.

Nonetheless, I knew how bad my mental health, my psychological and physiological symptoms were so I didn't have another choice. I need the specialist counselling immediately.

That's why the idea of having such an extremely limited availability scared me so much and it upset me.

So I went for the counselling assessment and I was ready to admit how awful my availability was. Then the amazing woman said they have appointments up until 8 pm at night.

As a client, I was amazed.

As an aspiring clinical psychologist, I was like a kid in a candy store because it was mind-blowing and I fully understand why mental health services need to be like this charity.

Moreover, when I heard that there were evening appointments that meant my availability increased to anytime between 4 pm and 8 pm Monday to Friday that's 16 possible sessions a week I could be scheduled in for. That is good availability and that might mean the waiting list might still be 3-months for me but the chance of it being shorter is still greater than if I only had 5 chances a week.

I am extremely happy for that.

Furthermore, I would describe the feeling of knowing I had greater availability as a mixture of pure and utter relief, pure joy and hope.

Hope was the biggest one.

I felt hope because now I fully believe there is a genuine sense of hope for me to heal, recover and be a position in the future where I can date, have sex and have a romantic life. Something I have never ever been able to have before, even before my sexual assault.

Conclusion

Overall, when it comes to setting up mental health services and thinking about the opening times. We shouldn't just do the normal 9 til 5 because it is the norm, we should try to arrange for evening or later appointments because it helps our clients and it helps the profession.

Even if a mental health service runs until 8 pm or 9 pm at night for a single day of the week, it is so much better than the alternative of restricting our clients, the people that need mental health support the most, to an impossible schedule that they simply cannot attend or abide by.

If we don't change our mental health services to have later appointments and if we keep denying clients that cannot take time off work to see us, mental health support then we are failing.

And we are straying from the ideals of clinical psychology.

Evening appointments allow clinical psychologists to access more clients so we can decrease psychological distress, improve lives and give our amazing clients access to the tools and techniques they need to thrive.

That is why evening appointments are critical and why we must start incorporating them into our standard opening times.

WHAT HAPPENS DURING A COUNSELLING ASSESSMENT?

In the last reflection, I told you (rather passionately) why I love evening appointments in mental health services, and in this reflection, I want to talk about what actually happens in a counselling assessment.

I want to do this because I've had two now and they are very similar, and these are very standard within mental health services. Therefore, in case you ever have to do one or to give you a little bit of extra knowledge, I want to explain how counselling assessments work.

Of course, every mental health service will have slight differences, but this is for information purposes only based on my own experience as a client (and a clinical psychology Masters student at the time of writing).

<u>What Happens During A Counselling Assessment?</u>

My counselling assessment for the sexual assault counselling was done over Zoom at 7:30 in the evening (again it was very suitable and a great time for me) and I always have a problem getting onto Zoom, but I managed it.

As I mentioned in few reflections ago, being a well-rounded person is critical within clinical psychology, because the lovely lady who was doing my assessment told me something. She told me about her dogs and that she was working at home and a takeaway person was going to ring the doorbell at some point during our call for other people in the house.

This wasn't her being unprofessional but it was her making it clear that her dogs would probably bark and she didn't want to alarm me. And honestly, I found this short conversation very reassuring because it showed to me that she was a kind, normal person and she was a person who I could get along with. As well as it showed me that even though I had literally only said "hello" that she already had my best interests at heart.

I appreciated that fact a lot considering how nervous I had been about this counselling assessment.

Next she explained how the counselling assessment was going to work and how long it would last, and she asked me some questions about myself. For example, what Doctors am I registered at, am I living in Canterbury and just some more information about me.

Afterwards, we spoke about the counselling itself. This included information on what I was hoping to gain out of this counselling, my physiological and psychological symptoms and what my availability was.

Now as a client, this shows the power of being a well-rounded and likeable clinical psychologist. Since in my last counselling assessment for the university, when the woman doing it asked me questions I would give her the answer but I wouldn't add context or additional information.

I didn't want to do this because I didn't like her. She was way too smiley, she interrupted and I didn't have a natural rapport with her.

However, the lovely lady at the charity, I was very open with so I told her about the physiological symptoms, me being suicidal the other week and I gave her more context than I normally would. She appreciated this and as an aspiring clinical psychologist, I think this goes to show how important it is to just be friendly, respectful and open with the client.

And try to build that therapeutic alliance or those interpersonal skills as soon as possible.

Especially, because the lady was able to add information to my assessment forms that would help the counsellor in the future. I think one of the "extra" notes was something in the next section about "have I ever thought that being dead would be easier". Now she asked on a Likert scale that I'll talk about in a moment and because it was "only" for one day, on the scale, it wouldn't be a lot but because I was honest and open with her she was able to add a note that would be useful for my future counsellor.

Furthermore, in this section, the lady asked me about past mental health, am I on any medication and those sort of general mental health questions. I am not on any medication but I do have past mental health and past trauma.

Leading to an interesting discussion about why if I ever requested my notes, I would see "Not For A Placement Counsellor" written on them. Since the charity has a handful of placement counsellors who want experience with sexual violence survivors, but the charity doesn't allow these placement counsellors to help survivors with additional trauma.

This might sound harsh but I seriously understand it.

Due to, I am only speaking for myself here, but my child abuse and trauma directly impacted my sexual assault. And to be honest, if I wasn't abused as kid then I never would have been sexually assaulted so they're connected in that way. Yet they are connected through the mental health impact after the sexual assault too.

For example, the same sort of abusive and negative thoughts that popped up in my childhood popped up after my sexual assault. My mind tried to use my sexual assault as proof that everything my abusers "taught" me in my childhood was true and so on.

There is a massive connection and overlap, and as a client, I would prefer a fully-qualified counsellor with a LOT of experience to help me.

Even as an aspiring clinical psychologist, I seriously wouldn't want someone like me as my first few cases.

Moving onto the final section of the counselling assessment, this is the section reserved for the mental health questionnaire. Now as psychology is a science, I am no stranger to questionnaires and I have made some questionnaires myself.

However, even I have to admit mental health questionnaires are almost funny at times because they are so cold and calculating that they miss so much nuance.

Although, my counselling assessment was a little messed up in this section because this week had been extremely weird in terms of my mental health. I wasn't dealing with rape or sexual assault stuff this week because I was spending so much time dealing with being publicly and privately attacked by someone I know who has Dissociative Identity Disorder with psychotic features.

Even though I will admit that as soon as all that was dealt with the sexual violence stuff returned with a vengeance. Unfortunately, this was after my assessment was done.

Anyway, there were 34 questions in total and some of them she didn't ask because I had already answered them in the other sections in response to other questions. As well as these were done as a Likert Scale ranging from "None Of The Time" to "Most of The Time" with "Often" and "Some of The Time" and "Occasionally" being in the middle.

In addition, the actual questionnaire has a timeframe of the past 7 days, but because of the weirdness of my week, the lady proposed the past 7 to 10 days which I wasn't going to reject.

I need the counselling way too much to not help myself.

For the rest of the counselling assessment, we went through the questions that asked how happiness, social functioning, suicidality, anxiety and a bunch of other domains of functioning too.

It was a good set of questions I admit and the lady did something I did appreciate.

She kept it fun.

She didn't make it seem like a deep, depressing task that would ultimately decide my future, and if I didn't answer something right it would be the end of the world.

No, instead she kept it light and fun and she worked with me as well. Due to let's face it, in my mind, there is very little difference between "Often" and "Some of The Time" so sometimes me and her did need to think about certain answers because the "real" answer was between those two points but I needed to put something as my official answer.

And that ability and patience to work with me was important. I am really grateful that she wanted to do that with me because she could have easily made me feel uncomfortable and awkward so I could say random answers to get it over and done with.

Yet she didn't.

She made me feel listened too, respected and she actually did some empowerment stuff without me or her even realising even now. She waited for me to give a response so I could make a real choice for the first time since my sexual assault.

And that feels amazing.

Now I'm realising that I actually made a choice for myself, that feels incredible and wonderful and I know for a precious few minutes, I don't feel like a weak, pathetic victim (yes I realise that self-perception is something I need to work on in counselling).

Then we wrapped up with whether I had any questions for her now, next steps and she spoke about how if I needed support or had a major meltdown I could reach out to the helpline or the woman at the charity who referred me to the counselling department because she is my dedicated sexual violence worker.

Personally, I still think I should have been given some kind of resource or a Brief Psychological Intervention, especially as the waiting list could be three months long. But the charity is brilliant and I am happy with my experience.

On the whole, when it comes to counselling assessment, as an aspiring clinical psychologist, I've learnt that you need to be kind, respectful and patient with the client. Since they will be nervous, they will be scared and they will probably be feeling so disempowered about the world around them.

Therefore, if you can give them a positive experience using your good interpersonal skills that make them feel respected, listened to and cared about. Then even though this is not a counselling session, you are going to have an insanely positive impact on them.

I've had a good and a bad counselling assessment and after comparing the two in my head, I know the main difference is the person performing the assessment. You are the main factor that will impact the client's experience.

Of course, the client has to want therapy, they want to have to change and improve their lives, and they have to want to work *with* the therapist. I know that.

However, if you don't treat the client with respect, patience and you don't empower them, like the first woman at my university. Then you might make them have a negative experience and that isn't what we want.

It will happen at some point in your career, that's normal and you can learn from the experience, but if you can nail it and make a client feel great and hopeful about the future. Then you already might have helped a client more than you could ever realise and it isn't even the first counselling session yet.

I know it can happen from my own experience, so I have no doubt it can happen again and again and again.

THOUGHTS ON THE GAP BETWEEN BOOKING THE APPOINTMENT AND THE COUNSELLING ASSESSMENT

One thing I did want to reflect on is, is there a need for charities and mental health services to automatically provide some kind of "help" or other resource to people who have made some kind of appointment but have to wait a while until they get a counselling assessment or they are actually seen?

For context, I'm asking this because last Monday, me and the sexual violence specialist at my university met, we spoke and she referred me to East Kent Rape Crisis Centre for specialised counselling. They took the referral, I had a meeting and they referred me to the counselling department.

Then on Friday (two days after I met with a woman from the charity to refer me to counselling) I had a phone call from the counselling department asking if I wanted a counselling assessment next Friday. I said yes and I have my counselling assessment tomorrow.

I will probably do a reflection on it because I find the idea of needing an assessment interesting. Although I know it is really standard practice. I already had one when I went for university counselling last year.

Anyway, there is a gap between me booking the assessment and me actually getting the assessment, and then there will be another long gap until I actually start counselling.

The reason I want to reflect on if it should be standard for resources to be given out is because last Friday I was extremely suicidal. I wanted to die because of my sexual assault and other things that were going on in my life.

I said to my friend later that night because they really wanted me to go out with them to play some Tennis, that I'm disappointed that it's a week away. To me especially in that depressed and suicidal mindset, a week was so, so far away and I said to my friend "that is a long time to live for".

As a result, I do wonder if the charity should have sent me some kind of resource anyway just to give me something to focus on whilst I wait for this assessment, let alone counselling. Since the waiting list for counselling could be two months.

I'm not entirely sure what this "resource" would look like. It could be a booklet talking about recovering from sexual violence, stressing that it is possible and it could give me some facts to think about.

In addition, it could be a type of Brief Psychological Intervention (Clinical Psychology: Second Edition) or even a form of bibliotherapy (Introduction To Types Of Psychotherapies). Due to this would allow me to get some form of psychological help that would allow me to start feeling like I'm in control, I can have a future and my sexual assault doesn't have to define me.

I think the development of a Brief Psychological Intervention could be extremely useful.

Moreover, I think the development of resources or a Brief Psychological Intervention would be beneficial for the charity or any mental health service too.

It would allow the client to start healing sooner so I think you might find the client requires fewer sessions of in-person (or online) therapy. In turn, this would mean they could be discharged sooner and the waiting lists would be shorter as the therapist could see more people in less time.

However, I am developing a Brief Psychological Intervention for people with Parkinson's at the moment, and it is time-consuming, you need to conduct research on it to see if it works or not and it has to be evidence-based.

All these factors cost time and money and these charities and all mental health services are already stretched to breaking point, so I get why this hasn't been done sooner. For example, when I spoke to East Kent Rape Crisis Centre, the woman mentioned they have 40 counsellors in the department and all of them are really busy.

That shows the scale of the problem of sexual violence.

As a result, whilst I think there is a clear need for some kind of resource for victims or anyone seeking mental health support so they can feel hope and empowered in that weird gap between making an appointment and an assessment or counselling starting, there are issues. Mainly, there are time and cost issues in the development of these resources because if they're going to be good resources then you need to put in the time and research.

Furthermore, I do acknowledge that a lot of charities do not have research expertise readily at their disposal. These are volunteers and the therapists are already giving up their time for free counselling. You can't really ask them to do more. And it's expensive to pay researchers for their time.

Personally, after writing this reflection, I think I would like to make some kind of Brief Psychological Intervention because I know there is a need for it. Yet I know it involves a lot of work, I would have to find a supervisor for the project and I would need to have charities and services that would be willing to give me access to their clients.

Which given the sensitive nature of sexual violence will be extremely difficult because if I was in charge of a service, unless I knew, liked and trusted the researcher, I wouldn't let them anywhere near my clients.

However, if this is something you're interested then please research it, research it and make a Brief Psychological Intervention.

And if you want to hear from someone with lived experience, please contact me and I would like to work with you.

Questions

What do you think?

Do you think there needs to be some kind of support in this gap between making and having a counselling assessment or appointment?

If so, what should this support look like?

WHAT'S IT LIKE TO EXPERIENCE A MAJOR DEPRESSIVE EPISODE?

I've mentioned before how sexual violence survivors are more likely to experience depression amongst other negative mental health outcomes. However, as aspiring and qualified psychologists and people interested in psychology, we read, listen and learn a lot of content about different mental health conditions. And as great as academic content is for helping us understanding a mental health condition, depression and anxiety, it is only lived experience that can possibly help us to truly understand what a condition is like for a client or service user.

In other words, you can read as many academic papers on depression as you want but until you talk or listen to people who have or are currently experiencing depression then you will never be able to fully understand how depression impacts a person. Especially in their everyday life. Therefore, in our next chapter, I'll be talking about my experience of a major depressive episode, which is still on-going as I finish off this chapter. You'll learn about how it's impacting me, what triggered my depression, the challenges depression gives me and more.

This major depressive episode all comes back to my sexual violence and my extremely bad mental health at the moment.

Why Am I Talking About Experiencing Depression?

Note: this is a cleaned-up audio transcription from the recording I made when I was experiencing a wave of depression. I did not realise I was as depressed as I was when I was making the record, so there will be grammatical errors. Since this is spoken word and not written word.

I've hinted at my depression and declining mental health in the past two episodes. Therefore, the reason why I'm talking about this is because since Saturday, so seven days now, I've been having quite a major depressive episode, and I've never actually had this before. Sure, I've had one or two days of being depressed, and I mean going through quite crippling depression, but I've never had it for seven days.

And yes, it's sort of gotten a little better, but I'm still quite depressed now, though. For example, the only reason why I can actually record this and sound relatively normal in terms of this is what I normally sound like, at least I hope so, is because I've just been texting my best friend because they wanted to know about what plant pot they had in their bedroom. And I was like, "Oh God, I'm gonna have to go and look."

So, I did that, and we were talking, and we were texting to and fro for a bit, and I was making fun of them for their mason jars here. Thankfully, this helped me to have quite a bit of energy. But I know that will seriously dip, though. I thought, right now I feel good, I've got to do this.

Overall, the reason why I'm talking about this is, one, because of the practical issue that I just spoke about. Two, as a future clinical psychologist, or maybe even qualified psychologists and people interested in lived mental health experiences, it is really important that we do understand not only what academia says about a mental health condition, but we also hear about it from those people with a life experience. Of course, I do not have a depression diagnosis. To be honest, I do have a scary feeling that I'm not actually gonna get any better by saying "over the next week." And because I have been feeling depressed for two weeks, this is just off the top of my head, so don't quote me on this, that's actually all you need for a depression diagnosis, of course, as long as you meet the other criteria too, though.

So, at the moment, I don't have a depression diagnosis, and I'm hoping that I won't ever have to get one. So, I'm talking about this just so we can all understand lived-like experiences here.

An Overview Of My Week

I already mentioned earlier that this all started on Saturday, but there's something larger that's going on here. So, as you guys know, I experienced sexual violence back in April, and that has really messed with my mental health. That has been quite debilitating, and I've been doing tons of different bits to try and get better in that sense. But I'm still on a waiting list for specialist rape counselling, which is taking a toll on my mental health because I need this support, but I can't get it because it turns out there's a lot of people that get raped. So, it takes a while for a place to open up for you, which is tragic. And I'm basically coping as best I can with my mental health getting worse as the months go by, especially my PTSD. And I mean, like, I think I've had two days of depression since my, so to like 19 weeks ago tomorrow at the time of recording.

I've not had it for seven days before.
In addition, what happened was that on Saturday, I started to feel quite depressed. I started to feel really down, and it was a struggle to get out of bed. Thankfully, I had a friend coming round at 2:00 just because we had already planned it, and I wanted to spend time with him because we get on really well. But the problem was, was that I couldn't get out of bed. It took me a long time to have a shower, not as much as the next day though. And it took me a while to do everything. So, thankfully, I was ready for when he came around at 2:00, but I wanted to do stuff before then. I wanted to do some writing, I wanted to do some podcast work and other stuff, but that really didn't happen.

Me and my friend had a really nice four and a half hours. It was really nice talking. We spoke about Halo Lore. We basically talked about a bunch of nerd stuff, then we talked about relationships and other bits and pieces, basically stuff you normally talk with your friends about. Then he left, and then I was just like, oh, right, I'm actually quite sad now. I'm actually feeling ridiculously lonely and everything. And then it was a full-on night of just PTSD. I mean, if there was a sound, I would have a massive reaction. There were tons of intrusive thoughts about sexual violence.

That was not fun.

On the Sunday, it was even worse. And because it was so dark and so bad, I can't actually go into all of the details, but it was absolutely horrific.

All I'll say is it took me 3 hours and 20 minutes just to have a shower because the interesting thing about depression is that because it's a low mood, it really impacts your energy levels. So then what happened was that around 2:00 pm, I finally decided, right, I am gonna have a shower. I'm gonna move heaven and earth to have a shower.

Well, the issue with that is that you need to get up from the sofa, then you need to go upstairs, then you need to get your clothes, get your towel, go into the bathroom, have a shower, get changed, etc. So, when you think about it, there are actually quite a few steps to anything that we do. And normally, I can normally do that all in, like, 20 minutes.

On Sunday, it took me 3 hours, 20 minutes to have a shower. I mean, that was just like... It took me 15 minutes just to get up the stairs. But then I actually had to come back down, so I was depressed about that, and it was ridiculous. It wasn't until I actually got in the shower at 5:00 pm, and I was just like, there's no point in me actually having a shower because it's 5:00, and to me, that's pointless. But I was like, I've been trying to do this for three hours. I've got to try.

And then, as the night went on, my mental health deteriorated. I broke my favorite mug. I smashed my favorite mug ever. Oh, God. I mean, I was actually quite devastated because it's this half-liter mug, which is just amazing. I've had it since 2019, since I first came to university, so I broke it, and then I just called my best friend, and we spoke for, like, an hour and a quarter, and then they were just like, "Right. You need to go home. You need to be around people," and, etc. So, I went...

I got back to my parents at half past midnight that night because me and my friend had a really heartfelt conversation. We'd had a really detailed one. Over the next two days, it was just constant depression. I was in and out of it because my parents work during the days, I was alone. Again, quite depressed. I couldn't really do anything. I had no energy. And then when they were back, it was fine because I was around people, so we could talk and stuff. Some stuff happened, but, I mean, that's just family.

And then I came back Wednesday because I saw my great aunt, who lives, like, nearby. Then I came back. Now, bear in mind, when my mug had shattered that night, I actually hadn't cleaned it up because I was just like... My mental health was so bad, I didn't have the capacity to actually clean it up. So, then I walked in at Wednesday, and I was just like, "Oh, my God, I'm back here. I've got to clean the mug. I've got to do tons of stuff." It took me an hour and 40 minutes just to clean that mug up. And that did not make me feel great. So that all happened.

Following on from this, yesterday, thankfully, I was able to do a few bits, but it was the energy levels that were really concerning me, because it was more of a thing about being in and out of depression and it basically not stopping and me not being able to reliably do stuff. I managed to do, I don't know, let's say four hours of stuff. It really wasn't that, it was more, like, two and a half because I tried to do some stuff. It was so unproductive. And considering I'm normally used to doing seven hours with ease of different bits and pieces, that was quite shocking, and that was actually quite bad. Quite bad.

Unfortunately, today it's just been more of the same. There has been a lot of other very traumatic things going on in the background. But again, just to keep this podcast easy to listen to, or at least nice to listen to, I'm not gonna go into it.

I just had to pause the podcast because I thought I heard a noise outside. I thought I was going to have a bad reaction. And then I felt a massive hit of depression almost hit, though. So, I've got to keep going with this, otherwise, it's not gonna get done.

<u>What Triggered This Depressive Episode?</u>

As with all mental health conditions and difficulties, there are always goning be triggers and different aspects of this which make your mental health worse. Thankfully the only highlight of being depressed for seven days is that there are moments when you can actually think clearly. Oh, believe me, it happens extremely rarely, but they still happen.

As a result, the thing that really triggered my depression and the thing that keeps making me feel worse is one, of course, the sexual violence. Two, just being really lonely because I really don't have many friends. And my best friend, they went back to the midlands to see their family and spend time with their friends. As well as basically, everyone I know is out there doing really cool stuff. They're going away, they're having fun, they're seeing their other friends. And because of my PTSD, because of everything else, my issue is that I actually can't do the same.

Then there's also been some relationship stuff that were present. My best friends have been doing some relationship stuff. The LGBT+ society at my university, some of those conversations have been about past and current romantic relationships. And as someone who's been through sexual violence and also child abuse that was very homophobic, it's sort of like... I don't know if I can have that.
I know logically, I can, but I mean, like, there's gonna be so much work to actually do that for. So that really didn't help me. And also, PTSD is bad enough, but when it comes to going outside, that doesn't help. But also, something I've been finding a lot lately when I've been going outside, like, going shopping is a nightmare. For instance, I tend to forget a lot. I find it really hard to focus. So as you can expect, it's really tough going out. As well as in my mind, if you're going go out properly, like, you're going to go somewhere, you do tend to need a friend just to make it more, enjoyable. And you can do it as a shared experience.

But because my only real friend is actually not here at the moment, that's really tough.

<u>What Are The Challenges Of Experiencing Depression?</u>

Moreover, there are four main challenges which I'm really struggling with at the moment. The first one is an inability to watch stuff because it's bad enough when I'm in and out of being depressed, which is another major problem because I can just be going along, then a wave of depression can just hit me. It can also be linked to triggers. For example, I can be doing stuff, then an intrusive thought comes out that's really bad, quite traumatic. Then it knocks me for six, and then

I get depressed, and I just lay on the stairs, on the sofa, or wherever I am for half an hour to an hour.

That's bad enough.

But when I'm depressed, I also have a massive problem. I can't watch stuff because I can't watch things on the TV or any streaming service because of sexual references and sex scenes, which never used to bother me whatsoever. But because that's how bad my mental health is at the moment, I can't watch any of that because it's too distressing, it's too triggering, which is annoying.

As a result, that was another reason why me and my best friend, we were on the phone for two and a quarter hours last night, as they were going through and compiling me a list of different series and films which I might be able to watch. But as I said to them, the main problem with that is, and just know I am extremely grateful that they did that. And I'm definitely gonna start watching some of it at some point. But some of it is that, yeah, you can have this list, you can have stuff to do, but you don't have the energy to actually do it, or you don't have the executive function to do it, which is an issue.

My third major challenging of experiencing depression is loss of pleasure. I've always known this is a depression symptom, but I've never had to experience it before. So, you can be doing stuff which you normally flat-out love. Like earlier today, I was flat-out loving doing some business stuff, but I wasn't enjoying it. It was just like, "Wow, this is actually quite boring." And sure, I sort of picked the more mundane aspects, but I still enjoy it. I still don't mind doing it. It's so important to me. I did not enjoy it.

Normally, I can do some reading, I can do a hobby, or I can do anything that I find really fun. No, not this week. I've just lost pleasure in most things, which is why I'm a bit concerned about this list that my friends put was they really love all of these programs. I don't wanna be the type of person who turns around and says, "Oh, thank you for doing this, but I really don't like this. I couldn't really care less about this." I'm pretty sure that's just the depression, but still, I don't want to do that even though I think that might be the case. But I will honestly try and enjoy this stuff.

But the main issue that I've been having is energy.

I know this is linked to a low mood, but the energy is that I really only have so much energy to be able to do stuff in the day. And I like to think of this in terms of spoons theory.

I've done an autism podcast episode maybe two years ago on spoons. So, the idea of this, and this is done by Christina someone, is that there's the idea that you only have so many spoons in terms of energy throughout the day, and every time you do something, you take away a spoon.

Let's say you have 10 spoons. Then what happens is that if you get up, then you could lose a spoon. If you go to work, if you have a shower, then you lose another spoon. Then if you get the kids ready, take them to school and get to work, that's another spoon. Then you have a really hard day at work, you have lots of meetings, you're working a very high-pressure job.

Let's say that actually takes five spoons away from you. That means you've only got two spoons left by the time you get home from work. But then let's say you've got to pick up the kids, and then you've got to do dinner. Both of those activities takes away your two spoons. Therefore, after you've cooked dinner, you might not have even served it up yet. You're completely exhausted, and you have no energy whatsoever. That's how you can think about energy levels in terms of spoons. That's something I found quite annoying yesterday, was that I was trying to do stuff, I wanted to do stuff, I had no energy after a while to do it whatsoever.

What am I trying to do to feel better?

I'm between a rock and a hard place.

The reason why I'm sort of in a rock and a hard place is quite simply because what I need is my rape counseling to start.

Nonetheless, that can't happen because I'm still on the waiting list. And my contact at this charity that I'm gonna be seen by, she's on annual leave until the 27th of August. That's five days away, at the very least. And in the meantime, I sort of keep suffering. Of course, it's not the charity's fault. This is just how life works. But she can't chase it, and she can't say, "Right, this person needs help ASAP. Can we please try and fit them in?"

So that's what I really, really need, and that's the sort of the solution. As soon as I start processing my rape and everything, then everything will get better. But until then, I am trying to do one or two things. I'm calling my best friend every night. We're having quite long conversations about each other's day, how I'm doing. And it's nice because it's social connection when I normally wouldn't get any social connection, which is quite a depressing fact, but that's just my life at the moment.

And then the only other thing which I'm really doing because this week's been quite difficult because, I mean, I can't go back to my parents again because they're away, and the whole point is that I'm lonely. So I can't just go somewhere else to be lonely. That defeats the whole point.

The only other thing I'm doing is I'm seeing my private therapist this week and next week. Both of us have agreed she's not a rape specialist. So, it's a case of me just talking to her. To be honest, like, I'm educating her about sexual violence because I've done so much research in the past 19 weeks. And I mean, it's nice just having someone to talk to, but I know it's sort of just sticking plaster on a very crumbling wall at the moment.

Oh, no. Actually, the only other last thing that I'm doing, though, is that next week, I'm going up to see my best friend in the midlands. So, we can see each other, we can go to this city that I've always wanted to go to, more for a laugh than anything else. But this got quite a reputation. And originally, I wanted to go by myself, but my best friend was like, "You can't. You just can't. Like, I don't think you'll be able to cope."

Of course, they said in much more polite terms than this, but I was just like, "You're right," and I'm really annoyed that I just can't go out without having a meltdown, without having an inability to make decisions and just getting overwhelmed, anxiety, PTSD, etc.

So, all fun, not.

As a result, I'm going up to see them, and their parents are going be there. And, I mean, I get on great with their parents. Their parents are lovely. And I might be able to meet their brother, which would be nice because I've been wanting to meet him for ages.

Ultimately, there's a lot's going on. I'm just trying to hang in there. And I don't know if this was a useful podcast episode, but I hope you got something out of it.

WHAT TO DO WHEN DEPRESSION MAKES IT IMPOSSIBLE TO GET OUT OF BED?

I wanted to include this next chapter because as a mental health professional supporting a survivor of sexual trauma, it is very, very likely they have depression. Survivors might differ in terms of whether they have Major Depressive Disorder or their depression is part of their Post-Traumatic Stress Disorder or another mental health condition altogether, this is why I'm critical of the DSM-5 and I support the social-constructivist viewpoint. If there were concrete types of mental health conditions then there shouldn't be this much overlap.

Anyway, when it comes to clinical work with rape and sexual assault survivors, you might come across the symptom called "leaden paralysis" in the form of it taking hours for clients to get out of bed in the morning. Or clients might not get out of bed at all because it takes too much energy and it feels impossible.

As a result, I wanted to include this next chapter to help you understand this consequence of sexual trauma and how you might want to support a client in therapy.

Of course, whilst nothing in this book is any form of official advice, this will hopefully still be very interest, useful and insightful.

Enjoy.

***

With depression being one of the most common mental health conditions in the world, a lot of a clinical psychologist's workload will be supporting people with depression. A common depression symptom is what's known as "Leaden Paralysis" and one of the effects of the symptoms is that everyday tasks take a million times more energy to complete. This can make the "simple" task of getting out of bed feel impossible for people with depression. Therefore, in this chapter, you'll learn what is leaden paralysis, why leaden paralysis impacts people's mental health and what to do when depression makes it impossible to get out of bed.

What is The Weight of Depression?

If you've ever experienced depression then you might be aware that there are some days where your depression will weigh you down so much that it feels like your body is made of lead and concrete. This makes the very notion of doing anything, much less leave your bed feel flat out impossible. As well as the sheer weight of depression might make you cancel plans, spend more time at home and/ or you might miss or be late for work.

This weight of depression and a struggle to get out of bed can take a massive toll on your work, relationships and your quality of life.

Personally, during August until October 2024 when I had quite severe depression, it always took me about two hours to get out of bed in the morning. Getting out of bed just felt hard because I had fun things to do, I could see my friends and everything but it wasn't good enough motivation to actually want to get out of bed. I just wanted the day to be over so I could sleep and I didn't have to deal with all the trauma responses that I was having every single hour of every single day.

What Is Leaden Paralysis?

As a result, there is a symptom of depression called "leaden paralysis" that causes people with depression to experience a severe drop in energy and as Qi et al. (2020) highlights this makes everyday tasks a million times harder for the individual. This is important to bear in mind because a lot of people who have never experienced depression or severe depression before might argue that people should just get up. Yet it isn't that easy. And this is one of the reasons why depression is a leading cause of disability round the world (Friedrich, 2017).

One of the clearest examples for me of leaden paralysis was on the very first day of my severe depression when it took me 5 hours just to have a shower. After struggling to get up for two or three hours, I managed to eventually make breakfast and at midday I decided to try to have a shower. Yet everything felt so heavy, I was so drained, I had no energy and my body might as well have had 20kg kettlebells tied to it.

It took so long to go through the living room, up the stairs, grab my towel and clothes, go across the landing, go into the bathroom, undressed, etc, etc.

Every one of those steps felt so impossible and each one took so long.

That is what leaden paralysis is like and that's why supporting people with depression is so important. You can probably imagine but having leaden paralysis doesn't make you feel great and it can make you feel even worse about yourself as your quality of life starts to crumble, so this is why mental health support is critical.

What To Do When Depression Makes It Impossible To Get Out Of Bed?

Here are three strategies to help people with depression overcome leaden paralysis and get out of bed in the mornings.

Firstly, you can break the day down into "hoops". This strategy involves breaking down your day into sections then you visualise these tasks as hoops. For example, getting up or brushing your teeth can be seen as two hoops that need to be conquered. After completing each task, you could imagine yourself jumping through each hoop and this can be an encouraging visual so you get a sense of achievement, and it helps to make the day less overwhelming. As well as on the really difficult days, seeing tasks as hoops can help you determine what tasks or hoops can be done on other days.

Secondly, you need to try to be kind to yourself because one of the ways how depression impacts us is makes us criticise ourselves more often. Therefore, to define your depression and how it criticizes you every chance it gets, you might want to practise self-kindness by using compassionate words when you realise your self-dialogue is getting more negative and harsher.

For example, today is actually a good example for me because my mental health definitely dipped today, and I was tired, overwhelmed and I was anxious about seeing my partner tomorrow because of trauma responses. My partner has done nothing wrong by the way. This meant I didn't get up for over an hour this morning and when I had a nap in the late afternoon in an effort to make myself feel better, I napped for 40 minutes but I didn't get out of bed for another two hours.

At first I was judging myself harshly because that was such a waste of time, I had so much to do and on and on and on. But I realised that it's okay I couldn't get out of bed earlier because this is what happens when my mental health dips. I need to listen to myself, figure out what's causing my mental health to dip and just keep going. Things will get better later on or tomorrow and as long as I focus on just going forward then that's okay. As well as I am hardly alone because this happens to everyone at different times in their life, even more so when you have depression and other mental health difficulties.

This is what works for me, you might need other self-compassionate and self-kindness thoughts.

The key is to not feed into your depression by criticising and hating yourself because you can't get out of bed. This will only make it feel even harder to do everyday tasks.

Finally, reach out for mental health support, because if you're experiencing depression that is so severe you find it really difficult to get out of bed. It is important that you seek mental health support as soon as possible because if you don't get support then your symptoms might get worse and your risk of suicide and self-harm increase. I really don't want that for you. As well as your depression might make you want to be alone and isolate yourself, but when you're struggling, it is a really good idea to be surrounded by other people. These people can include friends and family, but make sure you reach out to mental health professionals like a therapist or a mental health helpline too. Since if you isolate yourself then you might quickly find yourself in an echo chamber surrounded by your negative thoughts and inactivity and this will only maintain your depression.

And make you feel worse and worse until you don't see another way out.

Whenever I go through depression and mental health difficulties, reaching out to mental health support is always the best thing I could have done. It is always nerve-racking, I try to put it off as long as possible and I try to deal with things on my own at first. Yet ultimately seeing a counsellor, therapist or another form of mental health support is always best and I grow and develop so much and I flat out love the process too.

Conclusion

Whether you're an aspiring or qualified psychologist or person with depression, we've learnt a lot in this chapter. For psychologists, a lot of our future work will be with people with depression and we will encounter leaden paralysis the majority of the time because it is a common symptom. I know as someone who has experienced the inability to get out of bed frequently in the past, this is very distressing, it makes you feel awful about yourself and it can play into suicidal thoughts. Especially, when every single other everyday task seems to require so much effort that your quality of life just crumbles and is reduced to nothing.

This is why learning about strategies to support clients with leaden paralysis is so important.

For people with depression, I hope you now have some strategies to help you get out of bed in the morning and I hope you realise that you aren't alone. What you're experiencing is normal for depression and it is a normal response for whatever is causing your difficulties and that's why talking to a mental health professional is critical.

Here are some questions at the end of this chapter:

- Have you ever encountered leaden paralysis before? Either through personal or clinical experience.
- How have you dealt with these experiences of leaden paralysis?
- Do you know how to practise self-kindness?
- How could you learn more about self-kindness?
- What would you say to a loved one and/ or client who struggles to get out of bed in the morning because of their depression?

HOW TO BE A TRAUMA-INFORMED PARTNER?

I can never be 100% sure of the different reasons why people pick up my books, especially when it comes to psychology. You might be an aspiring or qualified psychologist, you might be someone you experienced a particular traumatic experience or mental health condition and you want to learn more or you might have a friend or loved one who experienced something and you want learn more in an effort to help them. Or you might be a combination of all three.

As a result, our chapter is more aimed at non-sexual assault survivors because this brilliant chapter focuses on how to date a survivor and the types of things you're going to need to know so you can support them and be informed. Interestingly enough, this chapter has its root in a podcast episode I did two months before I was raped, but it still stands up and I think this is going to be a critical resource for me and my future relationships.

I hope you enjoy it.

***

In recent years, there has been an increase in awareness within clinical psychology about the importance of a trauma-informed approach to mental health care. As well as considering trauma is relatively common, there is a chance we will meet and maybe form romantic relationships with people who have experienced trauma. Therefore, in this chapter, I wanted to combine clinical and relationship psychology to expand upon a list of tips and ways to be a trauma-informed partner. Since this will allow us all to become more trauma-informed and this might be an extremely useful guide if you learn your partner has trauma. This could be the difference between a relationship working or not. If you enjoy learning about relationships, mental health and trauma then you'll love this chapter.

Note: as always absolutely nothing in this book is any sort of official medical, relationship, career or any form of official advice.

Why Do We Need To Learn About Trauma-Informed Approaches?

Personally, I think there are three main reasons why it is critical to understand trauma-informed approaches. Firstly, this is a psychology podcast that aims at providing psychology students, professionals and other people with psychological knowledge and we mainly focus on clinical psychology. Since this is my main interest. Therefore, trauma-informed approaches are becoming more and more recognised and valued within clinical psychology so you need to learn about them. In fact, if you're in the UK, then you will probably be asked about trauma-informed approaches when you go for your interview to get onto the DClinPsych. You don't want to risk not knowing about an important area that might pop up.

Secondly, humans, like you and me, are social creatures, we all like social relationships, and these include romantic ones. Therefore, there is a good chance that at one point in our lives, we will date and maybe even fall in love with a person has experienced trauma. These relationships will have unique challenges at no fault of either party, but how these challenges are dealt with might become problems in their own right. Therefore, in this chapter, I want to give you the knowledge so you know how you might want to navigate these challenges and make your partner feel safe.

Finally, I just think this is a great topic and personally, I am fascinated by the concept of trauma-informed approaches because of my own abuse and trauma. I seriously want to understand this better and maybe I'll find some extra healing or relaxation in this knowledge. I don't know but that's why I'm here learning and having fun along the way.

Also, I should note the main points for this chapter came from the University of Kent's Student Support Service's Instagram page from a post they did on the 16th of February 2024.

Understand What Your Partner Needs

At first, this might seem like a very simple and almost silly point to make. Due to I can imagine a lot of people just dismissing this idea because surely we all know what our partner needs. They only need a bit of love, support and some fun and then they'll be happy. Surely, it's as simple as that?

Maybe in other relationships that don't involve trauma but even then I highly doubt it.

Since when it comes to trauma and life in general, we need to remember that everyone has had different experiences with intimacy, sex and sexual relationships. Some people would have had brilliant relationships and they have no relationship issues or baggage. Yet other people might have been abused, assaulted or hit in past relationships so this can bring complications into relationships.

As a result, it is critical that you try to understand your partner's experiences to find out what they were, how positive or negative they were and if they were negative then you need to approach this relationship with a trauma-informed manner or mindset.

Personally, drawing on my own experience here, whilst I have never been in a relationship, more than enough mental health and trauma stuff pops up in close friendships for me to understand (even roughly) how I would react in romantic relationships. And it's good that everything I do and all my reactions, I can trace back to a particular event so now it's just about overcoming them. Yet in a relationship I would need a partner who was willing to be patient, support and listen to my experiences.

Communication Is Key In Relationships

Of course, this is a brilliant rule for life because honest conversations are extremely powerful, but not everyone is ready to share in relationships.

One example I can think of, is how it took me two months to tell my closest friend about my past, how traumatised I was and everything that can happen to me at times because I was so scared of losing them because of it. That had happened before and then it took another two months for me to kill that fear outright, and now I am a lot more open with them. That's just an example of how people aren't always willing to open up about trauma, how it affects them and how all types of relationships can be difficult.

Therefore, when it comes to relationships, it's important that you try to create and encourage a safe emotional and physical space where your partner and yourself are both comfortable enough to share things openly.

Understand Trauma

Given how I sometimes feel that laypeople use trauma as a buzzword with absolutely no understanding of what trauma actually is, I can understand why some people in relationships might not understand the role of trauma and how it affects people. Yet if you truly care or even love your partner then you need to understand what trauma is.

Since trauma affects a person physically, emotionally and psychologically. No part of a person's life escapes trauma completely. When it comes to their physical body, your partner's nervous system will be affected by the trauma. For example, my heart rate can make me have extreme reactions in certain situations because of my trauma and what people have done to me before. Like two Sundays ago at the time of writing, my friend started texting me in a strange way because it turned out they wanted to ask me something massive. But considering I had made an innocent mistake a few days before (that turned out to be nothing) my heart rate was pounding because my trauma made me believe my really, really close friend was going to end the friendship with me.

It still took me another five minutes to get my heart rate back to normal, because it had "only" been caused by my friend texting me.

As a result, I wanted to highlight how trauma can make partners react in ways that aren't always in their control and most of it is just automatic. These responses aren't done on purpose and the partner isn't trying to hurt you, this is just how the trauma has affected them.

Then over time hopefully, as you both work on helping each other and your partner tries to improve their life and deal with the past, these responses will decrease or maybe stop entirely.

Be Observant In Relationships

There are a lot of different ways this point can be applied to relationships, but let's take the most innocent and probably most common one. You and your partner have just had a great night out, you had a lot of fun and you laughed a lot. Then you start acting flirty and you press them a little to come back to your place for a "nightcap". Even if you seriously mean it as a nightcap and no adult fun.

Watch your partner's body language.

It might change to show they're uncomfortable but they're too nervous or unsure how you'll react if they try to say anything.

If their body language changes then just step back, relax and act if their feelings escalate. Since not everyone communicates verbally all the time.

For example, when a friend of mine stayed over a few months ago, I could tell they were uncomfortable and slightly bored whilst we were talking with my parents. And then later on they told me, they were anxious and nervous and they only did that for my benefit.

I know this was a friendship example but the same could apply in a relationship. If this was a relationship then I should have asked my friend what was wrong and if they were okay. They would have been better than noticing it and not recognising it for whatever it might have been. In this case it was anxiety. Which for this particular friend does go back to trauma.

Just Be Open

As we slowly take some steps towards dealing with adult activities in relationships, it's important to know you need to have open conversations. Since people who have experienced trauma can have very difficult relationships with sex and similar things.

That's why it's important to talk to your partner about both of your likes, dislikes and just talk about sex beforehand. You need to make them feel comfortable and what they need from you if they get overwhelmed.

Personally, I am flat out terrified of sex. I will happily admit that and I have no doubt it will cause massive issues in the future. Part of my fear comes from the touch difficulties in autism, but 90% of it is trauma-related because without saying too much, I am scared to let people close enough to me to touch me where they could hurt me. Logically, it is a silly fear but from a trauma perspective it is very practical.

Which is why there are only really four people that I've met in my 22 years of living that I wouldn't mind twice about having sex with. Simply because I know these four people would never hurt me, none of those things happened though.

Anyway, it just comes to show you how trauma can seriously affect sexual relationships and why it's important to be honest and open in conversations. Due to I know when I eventually find someone, I won't be comfortable with the idea of sex until a deep conversation about it. As that is another test to see if they care about me very much. If they don't want the talk then they clearly aren't that bothered by me.

Check In With Your Partner During Sex

I'll fully admit that I have never spoken about or said the word "sex" so many times in my life than this chapter, and you realise how uncomfortable you are with the idea when you struggle saying and writing it a lot. I suppose that's why I write sweet romance instead of steamy romances.

Anyway, building upon the last section, when you and your partner finally decide to have sex and it is perfectly okay if this doesn't happen for a while. Be it weeks, months or even years. It's important to check in with them during sex to see if they're still okay.

You can do this by occasionally asking your partner if what you're doing is okay and if they're still enjoying it. Also, you can remind that them you can stop at any time and they can withdraw their consent whatever they want. As well as you can agree on safe words or another way to communicate that means this needs to stop immediately.

This is just flat out critical I think to making anyone who's been through trauma feel safe, secure and cared for.

Learn Grounding Techniques

Finally, if your partner starts reacting or panicking or having some sort of negative reaction during sex then help them. One of the forms of help could be encouraging them to use grounding techniques so they become grounded in the present moment and not their traumatic past.

These grounding techniques can include reassuring them that they're safe, referencing the present location, date, time and other immediate sensations. Like anything you hear or whatever you see. This is all about helping to ground them in the present moment and making it harder for them to focus on the past and traumatic event they're re-experiencing.

Conclusion

At the end of the day, when it comes to being a trauma-informed partner, it's about realising none of us can remove all the harm that the trauma has caused our partner. It simply cannot be done. Yet what can be done is you can understand and support your partner by being patient and supportive and then you can do your best to minimise the harm caused by their trauma.

This isn't going to be easy and I have had friends that have found dealing with my trauma difficult to say the least. So I have no idea how a future boyfriend or partner would find it. Yet I know if they care about me or even love me, then they will be patient, understanding and supportive.

That's what you need to do to if you want to be a trauma-informed partner.

Therefore, just as a reminder here are the ways you can be an informed partner:

- Know what your partner needs
- Communicate with them
- Understand trauma
- Be observant
- Talk openly about adult activities
- Check in with your partner during sex
- Use grounding techniques

Just because a partner has trauma in their past, it doesn't mean they can never be loved. A relationship with a traumatised person can still be as magical, wonderful and loving as a relationship with anyone else. But only if you both put the work in and you become a trauma-informed partner that loves, supports and understands your partner.

HOW TO HELP A TEENAGE SEXUAL ASSAULT SURVIVOR?

Whether you're an aspiring psychologist, psychology student or loved one of a teenager, this chapter will be immensely useful to you.

Since my audience is mainly psychology students and aspiring and qualified psychologists, I want to mention that depending on the mental health service you work in, there is a chance you'll encounter a survivor of sexual violence. As well as I've already mentioned in the book before unfortunately how common sexual assault is for men and women. Yet unfortunately teenagers can be subjected to sexual assault too, and this presents us with an issue because some of the advice about how to help adult survivors doesn't work for teenagers. As well as because teenagers are still children and as parents or friends or loved ones, we want to protect them at all costs, we aren't always sure how to help them. Therefore, in this chapter, you'll learn a range of tips on how to help a teenage sexual assault survivor.

Introduction To The Heartbreaking Event of Teenage Sexual Assault

It's heartbreaking enough to know that sexual assault exists in the world and I flat out hate that sexual assault happens in the first place. Yet it is even more heartbreaking to know that 44% of sexual assault survivors are under the age of 18, so when we discover that our teenage child, loved one or friend has been sexually assaulted then this is heartbreaking. Your teenager will be in pain, they will be suffering and they will be going through hell and back as they try to process what the hell happened to them and why.

Moreover, because 44% of sexual assault survivors are so young, we need to rethink the traditional advice we give people, so we can make sure it's applicable to the young men and women that experience this awful traumatic event. As well as whilst the research and voices this episode is based on are mainly women-focused, this should apply to all teenage survivors regardless of their gender identity. That's why I'll be using gender-neutral language in this episode.

When it comes to yourself, you will be angry that some idiot did this to your teenager, you will be scared about the future and you will be scared or terrified for your teenager. As well as you will probably be powerless to help them and it is that sense of powerlessness that I want to talk about in this episode.

You might experience grief too.

When you feel powerless, please know you are never alone and neither is your teenager. There are rape crisis centres, there are support groups and there are other parents and allies that have been or are where you are right now so you can walk hand-in-hand with them through the healing and recovery process. Also, you can learn from them too because you are all there to support each other.

In addition, there are plenty of ways how you can support your teenager compassionately and that's the focus for the rest of this episode.

Also, all the references for today's episode are at the bottom of the blog post like always.

Encourage Your Teenager To Express Themselves

Sexual assault survivors are three times more likely to develop depression compared to non-survivors, and psychologist Dana C. Jack refers to depression as a condition that silences a person. This basically means that depression stops the survivor from experiencing, expressing and feeling all the emotions they have as they process the distressing life event. Therefore, one option to help a teenage sexual assault survivor is to find a mental health professional who uses expressive art therapy in their work. Since expressive arts can be very useful for teenagers because it helps them connect with as well as process the truth about the traumatic experience.

Personally, even though I'm not a teenager, I think that's why I've thrown myself into my fiction and nonfiction writing. It's why I'm writing a personal book and then a psychology-focused book based on sexual violence so I can process, reflect and express what I feel about this horrific situation. Yet you might be able to try painting, modelling, clay stuff and a wide range of other creative art forms in a therapeutic setting.

Visit the *Rape, Abuse, Incest National Network* (RAINN) Website

Even though this is a website for the United States, this is still a brilliant website wherever you are in the world. For the past 17 weeks, I've been reading a fair amount of different articles, websites and a single academic paper to help me process what on earth happened and the RAINN website is one I have kept coming back to. They have some good statistics and facts that I like, and it's very useful for finding the location of any local rape crisis centres near you and learning more about sexual assault. As well as your teenager might find their Online Hotline useful, which is an instant messaging section where your teenager will be able to connect with a trained advocate who can answer any questions that they have.

In addition, after your teenager has connected with their local crisis centre, you can research recovery groups and ask for referrals. Ultimately, this is about knowing that your teenager is never alone and when they hear the stories of other sexual assault survivors, they can heal and reduce their shame and self-blame.

As an adult, I know contacting a support service has been immediately healing, beneficial and it has given me hope for the future. I'm still on the waiting list for rape counselling but making the referral was still one of the best decisions I've ever made because in all the dark moments, all the dark times when I am suffering so much and I want it all to end, I know I just need to wait a little longer and I'll be able to get help as I come off the waiting list.

There is hope for a good life after sexual assault.

Help Your Teenager Explore Contemplative Practices

In case you're like me and it took you a little longer than it should to remember what a contemplative practice was, it is a practice that quiets the mind so you can cultivate a personal capacity for insight and deep concentration. This can include tai chi, prayer, yoga as well as meditation. Also, these practices can be very helpful in healing any dissociation experienced by your teenager or your client because disassociation is where a trauma survivor disconnects from their experience and sometimes their own body in an effort to survive.

In addition, I really shouldn't need to say this but just in case, I do want to mention it. If your teenager has been sexually abused by a religious figure. Do not push religion as a source of healing or power or light in this dark time. If your teenager is religious then please, give them the space to find their own spiritual or religious path as they process what happened to them. And if they reject religion forever after their sexual assault then that's okay.

Talk About Healthy Relationships with Your Teenager

A terribly unfortunate research finding is surviving a teenage sexual assault is one of the greatest predictors of them experiencing some type of relationship violence in the future. Therefore, it's important to talk with your teenager about the difference between a healthy, respectful relationship and an abusive one, and this is something you should model in your own life. This allows your teenager to actually see it and understand it in the real world.

Whilst as an adult, me and my best friend haven't had too many discussions about this topic, I remember one extremely helpful conversation that we had about consent. Since my best friend took the virginity of their ex-boyfriend and they were using it as an example of how informative consent works. In essence, actual consent isn't a simple "yes" or "no" at the beginning of sex, it is asking frequently throughout sex if is it okay if they do X then y then z and so on to you and not doing it until you enthusiastically consent to it. And it is that need for enthusiasm that is important because you can say "yes" out of fear, out of concern for your safety and out of terror that the person doing things to you will hurt you badly. Thus, if you give consent with enthusiasm then that means you actually want it and that is the whole point of consent.

That's a relatively cruel explanation of this conversation but it proves the importance of having these honest, open conversations.

Honour Your Teenager's Boundaries

Something I cannot stress enough because I understand I am not a teenager but my family did this to me and it really distressed me in secret. But please, ask permission before hugging and touching the teenage survivor, because if you don't and if you just touch or hug them without permission. It can bring up a lot of distressing memories, a lot of pain and a lot of terror because this is likely exactly what the person did who attacked the teenager in your life.

Of course, logically this is very different, but the brain doesn't work like that and your teenager's brain will not distinguish between these two types of sudden hugs and touches that happened without permission.

Ultimately, the teenager in your life needs to be in control of their body at all times so you can discuss safety planning and ask permission before hugging and touching. Yet make sure you don't take away their freedoms out of your own fear. For example, I know you can track phones and I know certain communities have safety apps that you can download, so you can talk about these with your teenager. Just make sure they don't feel restricted or controlled in the process.

The reason why I'm mentioning this is because my social environment (the term I use to subtly refer to something) have a Ring doorbell camera and whenever I would go out, leave the house or do something, they would ask me about it later on. They thought it was funny that they could see who was coming or going from the house but it seriously negatively impacted my mental health but I felt so controlled, I lacked all freedom that it was actually something that played a minor role in my sexual assault.

Furthermore, after my sexual assault, my social environment was struggling with me telling them what had happened and one day someone was seriously angry with me that I didn't want to hug them. So I forced myself to and I hated it, I felt so disrespected and that's one of the main reasons why I don't consider my social environment a good place for support. Them not caring about my requests not to be touched for a little while whilst I recovered and started healing a little (my sexual assault had only happened three days before), set up the emotional tone in the relationship that they didn't want to hear me out, respect me or move heaven and earth to help me.

Please listen and respect your teenager's boundaries no matter how hard they are.

Never Blame The Teenager In Your Life

I've already mentioned why you should never ever blame a sexual assault survivor in other chapters. However, you should remind the teenager in your life that their sexual assault was never their fault and all the trauma responses and whatever happened during the sexual assault was what they had to do to survive. Therefore, what you can do as a parent, a friend or loved one is simply to give the teenager in your life the patience and be the empathetic listener they deserve. There are a lot of online resources and books to help you become an empathetic listener in case you need some extra support. For instance, *Non-Violent Communication* by Marshall Rosenberg.

On the whole, as someone who did have their social environment blame them for the sexual assault before claiming a few weeks later this wasn't true (gaslighting), this is extremely damaging. I cannot stress enough how you should avoid doing this at all costs, because this will place a massive wedge between you and the teenage survivor, and you might not notice, you might think that everything in your relationship is going okay. Yet in my experience, the survivor will remember what you said, what you implied and how you made them feel.

I don't want that for you, because if you're hunting down information and reading or listening to this chapter. Then you are actually amazing as far as I'm concerned because no one did that for me. No one wanted to support me so badly that they hunted down information in an effort to support you.

Just make sure your teenager feels loved, supported and listened to and the road to recovery should be a little easier even if it doesn't seem like it some days.

Conclusion

I know this chapter was mainly aimed at parents, loved ones and friends of teenage sexual assault survivors whereas my normal audience is aspiring and qualified psychologists and people interested in psychology. Yet here's the tragic truth about sexual violence, it doesn't matter who you are, what your job is or what your future or current job is. You yourself or someone you know or someone you love can be a sexual assault survivor.

This is critical information to know whoever you are so that's why I have no issue having this in the book at all.

Overall, during this difficult time of recovery, please be kind to yourself and your teenager because self-care is flat out critical for both of you. Definitely reach out to a mental health professional and/ or a rape crisis centre for support as you process what on earth happened to the teenager in your life.

There will be dark times, dark moments and you will be terrified for your teenager at times because you love them, you want to support them and you will struggle with how to handle this aftermath.

However, whilst sexual assault does devastate lives, there is hope for a better life if you want to heal. There are other survivors, specialist mental health professionals and a lot of other great people that want to help you and your teenager heal and recover.

It is possible regardless of how difficult processing sexual assault is on both of you.

WHAT ISSUES CREATE BARRIERS FOR ABUSED MEN?

As we continue our look at sexual violence, we've learnt a few times about how common it is for males to be the victim of sexual violence instead of exclusively being the abusers. In past chapters, we've learnt about the devastating impact that sexual violence can have on men and women and we learnt Why An Erection Isn't Consent.

Therefore, in this chapter, you'll learn some of the Issues that abused men experience, how these issues stop male survivors coming forward and I'll comment on how things could be improved as well. If you enjoy learning about sexual violence, forensic psychology and the criminal justice system then this is a great chapter for you.

What Issues Create Barriers For Abused Men?

Whilst I talk more in depth about this issue in the chapter, *Why An Erection Isn't Consent,* I want to stress here that these Issues and misconceptions about male survivors are devastating. They can stop men coming forward to the police so their abusers and attackers can face justice, it stops them getting the psychological and medical support they might need after sexual violence and it can ruin their lives. Just like how sexual violence impacts women.

In addition, I should note all the Issues and misconceptions about male survivors mentioned in this chapter comes from Bates (2020) who researched the lives of 161 men between the ages of 20 and 82. He found that abused men experienced consistent issues.

Abused Men DO Face Mental Health Challenges After Sexual Violence

As society doesn't typically believe that men can be survivors of sexual violence and coupled with the myth that men shouldn't show emotion or any so-called sign of weakness (that really is utter rubbish), people don't believe that men can experience mental health challenges after sexual violence.

However, Bates (2020) demonstrates that men can experience a lot of mental as well as physical health difficulties and conditions after being abused. For example, abused men can experience social isolation, depression, scars, self-esteem difficulties and sometimes chronic physical health difficulties.

Overall, whenever an abused man comes forward saying they were abused and that is what is causing them a lot of mental and physical health difficulties then we need to believe them and support them. We need to allow them to access sexual violence-specific mental health and physical health services so they can heal from the abuse and hopefully thrive in the future.

Abused Men Fear Losing Their Children By Coming Forward

When men experience intimate partner violence at the hand of their girlfriend, wife or partner, most men know there is a likely risk that if they leave the abusive relationship. They will not be able to see their kids anymore since perhaps the abused men believe their female abuser will lie to family court making them out to be the abuser instead, or the abuser will use the children as leverage to control the abused man. This fear could be based in a wide range of concerns.

Unfortunately, Bates (2020) found that after leaving an abusive relationship, a lot of men did lose access to their children but this wasn't always the case.

This is a hard one to talk about because no one, man, woman or anyone else, should ever lose access to their children because they want to leave an abusive relationship. The best thing we can try and do is investigate better and approach these family situations with an open mind that both men and women can be abusers.

Abused Men Struggle Trusting Future Partners

Even though I'm non-binary, I totally get this issue because this is something I'm really scared of in my own future relationships, even though my rape was different.

A lot of men reported to Bates (2020) that they were scared that they would never be able to trust any partner in any future relationship because of the intimate partner violence that they experienced. As well as these abused men fear that they will be alone for the rest of their lives if and when they leave their current (abused) relationships.

This is the dramatic thing about human behaviour, because we are such social creatures that need social groups for our own survival, we would rather be in an abusive relationship than alone. Most of the time us wanting to be in groups is a wonderfully useful, helpful and joyous behaviour that doesn't harm us, but it does when it comes to abusive relationships.

I know from my personal experience, this is something I constantly get scared, distressed and panicked about. I am scared that because I was raped, I will never find someone who is interested in me, I'll never be able to have a relationship and I'll never be good enough for someone else because I have such severe trauma in this department.

In reality, I know that if I keep working on trauma healing with my counselling and my workbook then things will get better, because they have already. I am slowly eating and things are getting better, even if they are taking an extremely long time in my biased opinion. Therefore, I know that I will get better over time, I'll focus on working on my own self-compassion and I'll get there.

And I'll keep healing and trying to find someone slowly so when I do, it will be a good relationship where there is a good chance that I will feel safe, secured and I will be able to give the relationship a good shot.

Because that is what *I* deserve.

Abused Men Experience A Lot Of Barriers To Services

Unfortunately, as I mentioned in the chapter *Why An Erection Isn't Consent*, when men want to come forward, they experience a lot of barriers when it comes to accessing sexual violence support services. This is largely because a lot of people believe that men could never possibly experience sexual violence and they can only ever be the abusers and attackers themselves, so this prevents males from getting the help they need. Also, this isn't limited to the mental health or physical health services, this extends to the biases within the police and criminal justice system too. Therefore, when a lot of men come forward to the police about their abuse, law enforcement doesn't always believe them and a lot of police officers, and the criminal justice system as a whole, see these men as the abusers so these male survivors don't get the help they need or deserve.

Thankfully, Bates (2020) shows that this wasn't always the case and there are times when law enforcement believes male survivors and helps them.

I've mentioned it before on the podcast and in my books, but this is why I didn't report what happened to me because I was already experiencing enough invalidation about my rape. I hardly needed the police and criminal justice system to deny what happened to me.

Friends and Family Don't Always Believe Male Survivors

As a result of me experiencing invalidation, it breaks my heart to know that a lot of male survivors in the study had negative experiences when confiding in their friends and family. This annoys me so much because it is a very brave and courageous action to tell someone about what sexual trauma happened to them, so the fact that someone would invalidate or not believe the male survivor, just annoys me so much.

People do not lie about sexual violence.

Unfortunately, the men in the study were often told by friends and family members to act "more like a man" and the survivors were often shamed and humiliated by their so-called friends and family members. This finding just makes me sick because these people are not real friends, they are not true loving family members and they don't deserve to know you if they can minimise trauma so easily. It's awful that even happens and it is beyond stupid that friends and family members think throwing outdated and harmful gender stereotypes is going to be helpful when you need love, support and someone to listen to you more than ever.

This is beyond outrageous and I'll say this a final time, if someone discredits, invalidates or shames you because of your sexual trauma. Then they are not your friend and they are not a caring, loving family member.

On the whole, this is why it's so important to be respectful when a male confides in you about their experience. They are showing you so much trust, so much faith and so much bravery by opening up. If you disrespect them because of what an idiot did to them then that is outrageous and wrong on so many levels.

Conclusion

At the time of writing and as my mental health improves, I'm finally getting round to finishing up all these chapters on sexual trauma because I've almost achieved what I wanted to when I first set out these chapters. I wanted to understand what the hell had happened to me, why I was having these extreme reactions and I wanted to understand sexual violence in as many little ways as possible, even if it didn't affect me directly. There is such a vow of silence in society that stops people from talking, learning and stopping sexual violence that I wanted to help break this silence so we can become more aware of sexual trauma.

Part of them is turning the world on its head a little when it comes to our collective understanding of sexual violence. We need to understand that men can be sexual assault survivors and women can be predators and sexual offenders too at times. We need to unlearn the false ideas that sex offenders are exclusively men and the survivors are exclusively women. The vast majority of sexual assault survivors will be females and the majority of sex offenders will be males but if we ever want to reach a point where there is true gender equality then we need to realise that everyone can experience sexual violence and everyone has the potential to unfortunately commit the ultimate act of betrayal and violation.

We will never be able to stamp out sexual violence until we, as a society, accept this heartbreaking truth.

Will you accept it?

WHY IS IT DIFFICULT TO RECOGNISE DOMESTIC VIOLENCE AGAINST MEN?

Domestic violence can fall under the umbrella of sexual violence if there is a sexual element to the domestic violence. Hence, the need to focus on this outrageous behaviour in our next chapter.

Whenever domestic violence is mentioned, you never hear about the countless men that are abused as well. It is outrageous that any man or woman is abused by their partners, and this needs to stop for everyone. But whilst there is plenty of research focusing on men assaulting women, there is barely any research on women attacking men. This is extremely harmful to everyone and this needs to change. But why is it so hard to recognise abuse against men?

Why Is It Difficult To Recognise Domestic Violence Against Men?

Even in 2022, there are so few research studies that focus on men as the victims of domestic abuse, and the studies that do exist tend to focus on homosexual couples. Creating and reinforcing the extremely damaging stereotype of an adult straight man cannot be abused by a woman.

Of course it is flat out wrong. But the stereotype exists and it is what people believe.

In addition, the national coalition against domestic violence reports that 1 in 9 men experience domestic violence in the USA. But when you consider the damaging impact of the stereotypes, the tendency for men to underreport it and the so-called accompanying embarrassment, this number is likely to be very low compared to the real number.

And I call the embarrassment so-called because there shouldn't be any negativity towards the male victims. They should be able to get support and stop the awful things they are experiencing.

Additionally, whereas male abusers tend to use physical methods to inflict pain onto their victims. Women don't necessarily have that option, not only because of their small size and possible inability to overpower a man. But also it comes back to how women are socialised in our society.

Therefore, women abusers tend to use psychological warfare instead. By using revenge-seeking behaviour (like posting horrible things on social media and spreading rumours), emotional abuse and stalking.

And most experts and people who work with domestic violence survivors actually say this form is more harmful than physical aggression. Due to it is harder to spot and prove, as well as even more our legal systems are not designed to effectively deal with the non-physical side of abuse.

Meaning that this psychological abuse is far more likely to continue, go unnoticed and unstopped for much longer than any physical abuse would.

Personally, I think this is tragic because in society, we should want to protect everyone, regardless of gender, so it is a shame that we cannot detect and even legally deal with psychological abuse. And this goes for any gender.

All abuse is flat out wrong!

Male domestic violence and stereotypes:

Nonetheless, when it comes to men being victims of domestic abuse, men don't only feel weak, embarrassed and shame because of the abusive woman. But because of the damaging stereotypes too. As the men aren't only learning how to deal with the trauma of the partner abuse, they are learning how to survive the societal pressure and stereotypes too.

Because clearly if a man gets abused, he isn't a real man.

What utter rubbish!

In addition, these stereotypes only increase the self-doubt the victim is already experiencing and can actually lead them to put up with it, because they ask themselves questions like, *is the abuse really that bad?* And *how much damage can a woman do?*

Again it isn't helpful and it is even worse when people around the victim ask them this. It doesn't help them to fight, deal or survive the trauma. It only makes it worse.

Societal expectations and the law:

Of course in this chapter, I am not saying men are the majority of domestic abuse victims. That unfortunate and outrageous statistic goes to women. But I am highlighting that men are victims too.

Also the very idea of straight men being abused by women was laughable up until recently in research. As well as even in the legal system, men aren't given the same amounts of legal protection against abusers.

This is not good because surely as a society, we should try to make things equal for everyone. And yes, I know this is very idealist but ideally we should have a society where everyone gets the same amount of legal protection.

Of course, it will never ever happen. But we should still try to come as close as we can!

Additionally, because of the intimate and tight-lipped nature around domestic violence all victims feel alone and isolated in their experiences. Like they're trapped forever. And being a man in our culture only adds to this difficulty, because of the utter rubbish expectations we have about men.

Like the rubbish about real men don't talk about their feelings, they don't cry and they leave the emotional wrecks to women. It is rubbish and we need to stop these harmful beliefs.

Also it is worth noting that most people (I was no exception a few years ago) believe that a man would be able to stop the abuse and therefore don't think about it nor do they take it too seriously. This only creates an environment that isn't conducive to supporting men who have been domestically abused.

Signs to watch out for:

As always in my books, I like to mention some useful unofficial tips toward the end. Therefore, if you think you are experiencing, or suspect a man that you care about might be going through what we've spoken about today, here are some signs to watch out for:

- He is concerned about his partner's reaction to social media, calls or texts from other women.
- Their partner is extremely jealous and/or possessive. For example, they aren't able to go out with friends alone or allowed other forms of privacy.
- The partner tells people very personal details about him or the relationships out of spite or malice. Basically making fun of him.
- Having the partner's friends do their dirty work for them. For example, driving past his house and checking up on him.
- The partner threatens to kill herself if he doesn't behave in a certain way or do certain things she asks of him.

- She brags about trying to get him fired from his job or another form of punishment for leaving the relationship.

Conclusion:

Domestic abuse should not happen to anyone. Regardless of their gender, sexuality and all the other outrageous causes of abuse. It shouldn't happen full stop. But hopefully after today you can see that domestic abuse can happen to everyone and we still have a lot of work to do to help both women and men from being abused.

HOW TO BUILD RESILIENCE AFTER TRAUMA?

Everyone needs psychological resilience because it is being resilient that allows us to effectively pick ourselves up after something goes wrong. As well as resilience refers to our ability to quickly recover from a difficulty so this can refer to something going wrong at work, us not getting a certain grade at school or university or resilience can refer to trauma. Since after witnessing or experiencing a traumatic or difficult event, be it sexual violence, physical violence or more, resilience can help us with our recovery from the trauma.

Therefore, in this chapter, you'll learn about how to build resilience so you can use it in your everyday life and if you ever experience trauma, your resilience can help you with your recovery.

Why Do We Need To Talk About Resilience?

Back in the early days of my podcast, I did the podcast episodes called *3 Tips To Build Psychological Resilience* and *3 New Tips To Build Psychological Resilience*. As you can see, I was very creative with my episode names back in 2020 and 2021, yet as I preluded to in the introduction, experiencing trauma and surviving traumatic events can be very physically, emotionally and psychologically difficult for people and the amount of resilience a person had was an important factor in their ability to deal with the trauma.

Now before we continue I want to jump in here and add two very important pieces of information. Firstly, I can only speak for sexual trauma in the context of this chapter but you can still be an extremely resilient person like me and seriously struggle with the aftermath of your sexual assault. If you're struggling, it doesn't mean that you're not resilient and all those disgusting myths that exist around being a "victim". Experiencing sexual trauma can shatter your resilience.

Also, resilience can be learnt so if you aren't a very resilient person or you're a trauma survivor who feels like they have no resilience (even though you probably have more resilience than you realise. That's a lesson I have to keep teaching myself) then that's okay because you can learn to be more resilient over time.

In addition, the content for this chapter largely comes from Roeckner et al. (2021) who concluded that individual differences in threat cue processing are related to the person's resilience whilst their higher-order executive functioning is less consistent and their relationship with resilience changes over time. In other words, both resilience and higher-order executive functioning are both stable factors in predicting how your brain responds to threats that will impact the likelihood of your resilience and how it changes over time.

Also, the researchers found that whilst trauma is very common, even people who experience trauma most often can recover over time. Their resilience is a major protective factor during the aftermath of their trauma so it's important to help grow people's resilience.

That's why we're going to look at five different ways to help people grow their resilience so we can help people recover following trauma.

How To Build Resilience?

Let Yourself Carefully Think About The Traumatic Experience

Now I say carefully because I have tried, and I'm sure a lot of other people have to, to think about the traumatic experience in great depth without much care. This was a massive mistake for me personally and I always end up getting a lot more distressed after the fact, because it wasn't carefully.

Therefore, carefully thinking about a traumatic event can be useful because it allows you to think about the trauma in the context of the event. As well as you don't need to come to any conclusions about why this happened to you, and instead by thinking carefully about the trauma, you're preventing your brain from overgeneralising. In other words, you're stopping your brain from taking the trauma and applying it to other parts of your life. This is a massive problem that I'm having at the moment and for the past 17 weeks, because whenever I see a very overweight man, I get extremely distressed because it reminds me of my attacker.

This is an unfortunate example of how my brain has overgeneralised my sexual assault to other areas of my life so much so that even going out in public can be a minefield of distress for me. I still go out and live my life but there is a lot of distress and anxiety that accompanies me.

Overall, carefully thinking about the traumatic experience can be helpful for processing the emotions associated with the experience and over time the intensity of the experiences and all the negative, distressing emotions it evokes should decrease.

Let Yourself Engage In Positive Self-Care

Whenever you experience a traumatic event, you still need to look after yourself and I'm smiling as I write this because I seriously did not do this at certain times in the last 17 weeks. I remember back in very early July because me moving in with my best friend was so distressing, so triggering and so bad for me. My eating disorder had activated so badly and my best friend was really worried for me, and I basically did everything against self-care. Thankfully I am fine now in that department and me and my best friend really enjoy living together, but after trauma and when you face triggers, it can be very easy not to look after yourself.

Please try to remember to look after yourself.

You are the most important person and you need to look after yourself.

Therefore, you need to eat healthy foods, stay active, get good sleep (I would flat out love that at the moment) because all these are important supporters of your resilience. Due to doing all these self-care things helps our brains to work better and our anxiety and mood improves when we're rested and well-fed.

Please take care of your mind and body.

Allow Yourself To Reach Out To Trusted People For Support

Let's face it, this is a clinical psychology book in all but name and I am an aspiring clinical psychologist so I will always bring up this point. You cannot deal with trauma alone, you seriously can't so please reach out to other people for support.

When it comes to support after a traumatic experience, this can take different forms depending on the other person and the level of your relationship with them. For example, you might just want to hang out with a friend that you have a positive connection with because you enjoy spending time with them. Actually, a relatively new friend just Whatsapped whilst I was writing this blog post saying he wants to come round tomorrow. This new friend isn't a person I could ever have rape conversations with but I really like spending time with him and I find that really relaxing and it gives me a few hours away from all the distress and rape stuff coming on in my head.

That is one option for you.

Equally, on the side of the spectrum of friendships, you can talk to friends and family members that you have a close relationship with for specific support. For instance, whilst my best friend is currently 181 miles away (we joked about the distance, it isn't weird I know the exact distance from where I live to the town their parents live in), they were still very firm with me about contacting them if I need anything or need any contact. And over the past week, we've had some in-depth supportive conversations but mostly, it's been a case of them letting me talk or send them long, distressed messages because that's what I need.

I sent them one yesterday where I literally had to write down what I was going to do next because something that happens in rape survivors is they sometimes cannot make any decisions. That popped up for me yesterday, so my hack around that is after making sure I actually can't make decisions (it's always the case) I text my best friend and I talk myself through it.

In other words, get support however you need it and have open and honest conversations with your friends and loved ones about what they need from you.

Ultimately, getting this support will help to improve your mood and this increases your resilience. As well as if you share your experience with them then this can be even more helpful. It is very healing to say things out loud to another person who wants to be there for you and support you.

Let Yourself Consider Your Core Values and How To Connect With These During Distressing Times

This is advice I have seen time and time again and it is still something I really struggle with.

There are a lot of different ways you can do this, but the entire point of this tip is to help you do what matters to you, brings you joy and improves your mental health. For example, it's important that you take a few minutes to decide what matters most to you. Such as, it could be your community, connecting with your friends or family, your religious or spiritual practices or a hobby.

For me, what matters most is my writing, being a good friend, my business, psychology, my podcast helping people and so on.

As a result, I've been trying to focus on my fiction and nonfiction writing as much as possible during the past 17 weeks. It has been flat out impossible but I am happier in this great month of August 2024 because I am able to dedicate so much time to my fiction and nonfiction projects. I am still having to balance my writing with business stuff and me working on my academic paper, but I still really enjoy those aspects of my life too.

And it helps me manage all the distress, negative mental health and sheer crippling Post-Traumatic Stress symptoms that paralyse me on a weekly or daily basis. Doing what I enjoy just helps me realise how good my life is when I'm not experiencing these hellish mental health outcomes.

Okay, maybe I have been doing this tip more than I thought.

In terms of yourself, you might want to do something really basic to help you engage in your core values. You might read a book, watch films with a friend or loved one or go out to specific places that you enjoy. Like a museum, a park or a woodland.

On the whole, this helps to increase your resilience because you are doing what matters most to you and when we all live a life that is consistent with our values, then our mood increases, our mental health improves and we're happy.

<u>You Need To Avoid Unhelpful Patterns Of Substance And/ or Alcohol Abuse</u>

When I was putting this chapter together, I was very, very careful to make sure the subheadings didn't sound like I was ordering you to do anything. I made an exception for this one because I've seen and I've read a lot of very heartbreaking literature on the consequences of substance and alcohol abuse on survivors and I don't want that for you.

Since for a lot of people who have survived trauma or distress, they really want to push away these feelings by numbing their emotions with substances or alcohol. This works for a time but the problem tends to get worse and grow over time and this leads to a wide range of mental and physical health complications later on. A very bad liver is one that springs to mind.

As a result, it's important that you're mindful about alcohol and substance use if you've been through a difficult and traumatic situation because this helps to reduce the chance of unhelpful responses developing as a coping mechanism.

And I'm not going to sit here and say that this is easy. Back when I was having my mental breakdown in August 2023 because of my insanely homophobic and dysfunctional social environment and all the decade-long trauma and abuse that led to, I was so tempted to try and find some drugs. I was seriously considering trying substance abuse because I just wanted the pain to stop, but I didn't. Since I knew substance abuse wasn't helpful, it wasn't healthy and it would only damage me even more in the long term.

I did therapy instead and it helped me more than I could ever express.

<u>Conclusion</u>

Ultimately, resilience is a critical skill for life because it enables us to pick ourselves up after we've experienced a negative life event. Yet resilience isn't a given for everyone and if you've been through trauma then your resilience can be shattered. The latter is what I've found after my sexual assault.

Thankfully, resilience can be improved, practised and you can become more resilient over time as you put in the time and effort to improve this trait. The key to building resilience is knowing it will take some time, this won't be something that happens overnight and if you rush it, you will be frustrated and you might risk quitting. So please, be kind to yourself, reach out for support when you need it and remember, there is life after trauma.

Your trauma doesn't have to define, control or ruin your life. You can heal and recover, and resilience is just one part of that great journey.

WHAT IS RAPE GRIEF?

Previously in the book, I've spoken a lot about how after my rape I researched sexual violence and Post-Traumatic Stress Disorder, because I wanted to understand what was happening to me, why I was having such extreme trauma responses and how I could heal. A lot of people who experience various types of trauma and mental health conditions do this and we all find various psychology facts, techniques and revelations that stick with us. For me, understanding rape grief was profoundly helpful, stabilizing and for the first time, it gave me words to describe a unique aspect of my rape and its consequences that no one had spoken about.

Therefore, in this chapter, you'll learn what is rape grief, why is this a powerful concept for rape survivors and more. If you enjoy learning about trauma recovery, healing from sexual violence and mental health, then this will be a great chapter for you.

What Is Rape Grief?

I think I found the concept of "rape grief" extremely powerful and important to me because it captured so much of what I was experiencing in the early days after my rape.

Therefore, grief is an intense emotional response to significant personal loss, and this painful emotional experience can include us wanting what we had lost back, concerns and fears about the future, as well as remorse for what we did and didn't do in a given moment.

Now everyone experiences grief at some point in their life and it isn't always around death despite popular opinion. For instance, yes, when someone dies we want our loved one back, we get fearful and concerned about how we will deal with them no longer being there in the future and we question whether they knew we loved them or not.

Equally, when it comes to jobs, we can yearn for that job promotion we never got, we can question if we said the right thing or not in an interview and we might question how we will work at the company now someone else is your boss or got the promotion.

We can experience grief around anything as long as there is that personal loss.

In addition, grief isn't a bad thing. Whilst it is a painful emotional experience, grief is a natural part of our lives and everyone will go through grief at some point in their life. It only becomes a clinical difficulty or "condition" if the grief causes clinically significant levels of psychological distress and impaired functioning in multiple domains of life. Like home life, work and school. As well as if it generates thoughts of self-harm, self-neglect and sometimes grief can be powerful enough to harm our own immune system.

As a result, when it comes to rape and other examples of sexual trauma, this "rape grief" follows the initial shock of the attack. This shock eventually leads to feelings of loss and fear amongst the sexual assault survivors because the survivors can lose a lot because of the attacker. For instance, survivors can feel a loss of their sense of safety and the following too:

- Loss of their lifestyle
- Loss of their physical and mental health.
- Loss of trust in other people
- Loss of their ability to work
- Loss of their hopes and dreams about the future
- Loss of virginity if their rape was their first sexual encounter
- Loss of important relationships. This is mainly if the attacker belongs to their family or group of friends.
- Loss of interest in physical intimacy
- Loss of ability to resume their normal roles like going to school.
- Loss of self-esteem

Personally, I don't believe there is a single one of those bullet points that I haven't experienced myself. Although, I will add in my book *I Am Survivor, Not A Victim* I do comment in there I firmly reject the idea that rape counts as losing your virginity. That was a very healing moment for me.

However, during the first 7 months of my rape, I felt a massive sense of loss because I had lost my sense of safety, my sense of hope about the future and the idea that I could ever work again or live a normal life. As well as I completely lost my ability to live my lifestyle and do my normal roles.

Moreover, when we consider how significant and how many of these sense of losses combine, it is no surprise that sexual assault survivors experience rape grief to extreme levels. The process of healing from rape grief isn't linear or easy or straightforward in the slightest. When I consider my own mental health journey, there have been major breakthrough moments where I thought my life was changed and healed forever, then new triggers, new fears and new experiences cause that all to change so this requires more healing. Trauma recovery ebbs and flows and it depends on the triggers that the client experiences as these act as reminders of what the client has lost.

In addition, one of the most annoying things but equally, it was this fact that I found healing. It is the fact that survivors experiencing rape grief will have conflicting emotions. For example, I remember this clearly because I had just found out about rape grief, I was sitting on the ugly red sofas in our shared house and me and my best friend had moved in together whilst the other two didn't until two months later. After a month, we were sitting on the sofa in the afternoon, I was depressed and I wanted to be alone. Yet I wanted to be with my best friend. I wanted to share everything with my best friend including the nightmares about them raping me (my best friend would never ever do that to me) but I didn't want to tell them because it would hurt them. And so many more conflicting emotions and thoughts.

I felt insane half the time.

And it is that simple realisation that it is okay for rape survivors to feel so many conflicting emotions.

It is normal. As difficult, insane and awful as you feel when you're experiencing all these different emotions, you are reacting normally to an extremely abnormal situation.

Why You Should NOT Tell A Rape Survivor "Time Heals All Wounds"?

There are a lot of different phrases and other rubbish that has been said to me as a rape survivor that have been the opposite of helpful. I cover a whole bunch of them in my book *I Am A Survivor, Not A Victim* but I flat out hate the phrase "Time Heals All Wounds" and "Give It Time".

Interestingly when it comes to this "well-intentioned" advice, this isn't helpful but it isn't done with malice. These pieces of advice simply reflect myths and misconceptions that people have about trauma and rape. Since this bad advice can create self-doubts within survivors as survivors can get concerned and fearful and their mental health can be further harmed if they believe they should be healing more because it's been months or more since their attack.

This was one of my major struggles after my rape.

In addition, "time heals all wounds" is a bad phrase because whilst it takes time to heal from grief and trauma, what actually impacts healing the most is the degree of support and acceptance that the survivor receives in the long term. I completely agree with this because it seriously wasn't the time since I was raped that healed me. It was living in a supportive and loving environment as well as my rape counselling. It was the support I got that made the difference, not the time.

Furthermore, if you tell a rape survivor to "just give it time" then this can seriously trivialise the gravity of the situation for the survivor and everything they are going through. As well as "just giving it time" doesn't help the emotional turmoil and hell that the survivor is going through and it makes the survivor feel powerless. Due to it explains to survivors that it doesn't matter what they do or how they try to cope, time (a factor that they do not control) will determine how long it takes for them to heal.

This suggests to the survivor that waiting is the only way to cope instead of any deliberate action.

Why You Should NOT Say "Don't Think About It" To A Rape Survivor?

When my mental health really got bad during August 2024 and I had to go back to my parents to stay with them for a few days, I remember one of them saying "Just don't think about it" and it annoyed me so much. I flat out hate this silly saying or piece of advice. Since the issue with "don't think about it" is that you are telling someone to ignore or bury these powerful feelings and it doesn't allow a survivor to create an emotional space where they can process what happened to them and heal. Instead "just don't think about it" encourages the survivor to not feel a certain way so this denies the survivor the right to truly feel how they feel and it can even imply that the survivor isn't good enough because they can't control their emotions.

This is similar to why "keep busy" isn't a good piece of advice either. Due to why I strongly encourage survivors to do self-care things that make them happy, give them structure and purpose. It is important not to "keep busy" because keeping a survivor busy doesn't make them "snap out" of the trauma, it simply allows them to escape processing and healing from what happened to them. I always like to mention that you can only go without processing trauma for so long. If you don't deal with your trauma, your trauma will deal with you. This can be depression, a mental breakdown, severe Post-Traumatic Stress Disorder (as if any form of PTSD isn't severe) amongst others.

Of course, like I mentioned in the last paragraph, there are mental health benefits to having structure and engaging in normal activities and routines. Like I found it extremely helpful during the worst of my PTSD to have my Outreach work at the university, my writing and my business. Then again, this is only useful if the survivor has a good support system around themselves, because keeping busy does not and will never eliminate the intrusive thoughts, feelings and other trauma responses.

"Keeping busy" is only ever a temporary distraction and trauma will be dealt with. It can be by the survivor with a social support network and therapy, but the trauma can make you deal with it.

<u>What Are The Outcomes of This Misguided Advice?</u>

When dealing with rape grief, this so-called advice that people give rape survivors just isn't helpful and it can be very harmful to their healing and recovery. For example, it can lead to the survivor becoming guarded in expressing how they feel to others out of concern for being judged or being hurt further. This is what happened to me because I only really open up to my best friend because I know they would never ever hurt me. It's only recently I've started to become less guarded around my family and a new friend that I'm making.

In addition, this unhelpful advice can make a survivor feel guilty about feeling or acting or not in a certain way. As well as this silly advice suggests that rape survivors should ignore or bury their powerfully distressing and negative emotions. This leads to the survivor becoming confused about what they're feeling or how they're expected to feel.

Ultimately, the reason why this is so harmful to survivors is because trauma healing is all about living in an environment that is supportive and allows the survivor to be honest with themselves and get in touch with their true emotions. If a survivor lives in an environment that isn't supportive and encourages denial, guilt as well as an inability to share their feelings with other people then they will not heal and their mental health will die.

Their sense of rape grief will only be prolonged and as a survivor myself, that is something we cannot allow.

That is why supportive friends, family and therapists are the most important thing in trauma healing. Especially after sexual violence which for me is the ultimate act of betrayal and violation. A violation so severe it creates an immense sense of loss and grief that must be overcome in order to heal.

It might feel impossible to heal from sexual violence but it is possible. It might be cheesy but this always makes me smile. I don't know who said it but I like the saying "Nothing is impossible because impossible actually reads I'm Possible,"

And that is even truer when it comes to sexual trauma recovery.

PART TWO:
ANXIETY DISORDERS

WHAT IS PANIC DISORDER AND ANXIETY DISORDERS?

I talk a lot about social anxiety and panic attacks in this book and a lot of us survivors know how it feels to be constantly anxious, especially if we develop PTSD. Therefore, I want to put in this anxiety content so we can learn what social anxiety is, why a survivor might develop it and what triggers social anxiety and how can social anxiety be treated through Cognitive Behaviour Therapy or Exposure Therapy.

As a result, in this next section of the book, I want to know on some psychology facts, theories and research findings on social anxiety so you can understand what and why your current or future clients might be feeling this way as well as I'll make you aware of some psychological therapies that your clients might benefit it, or some therapeutic models you might want to draw on in your own practice.

All the chapters in this section are taken from CBT For Anxiety, available anywhere you got this book from, so if you want to learn more definitely check it out.

Our first chapter focuses on understanding what are panic and social anxiety disorders.

Note: whilst the next few chapters is taken from a book aimed at psychology students, it should be still be accessible to you and help you understand what anxiety is, how and why it effects you and how psychological therapies are an effective treatment option for the condition and allow you to live a happier and less anxious life.

***

What Is Panic Disorder And Agoraphobia?

Personally, I always think that panic disorders are one of the worst anxiety disorders because this is a type of anxiety disorder that can be characterised by a person having repeated or debilitating panic attacks. With these attacks being a sudden episode of horrific bodily symptoms. Like: choking, chest pains and distress.

As well as whilst all anxiety disorders do involve panic attacks to various extents and normally a panic attack in any other disorder is limited to only the anxious stimuli like a social situation or spiders, but a panic disorder involves panic attacks that come out the blue.

For instance, whilst I once knew a girl that suffered from Social Anxiety Disorder so she had panic attacks in social situations, it was only those situations. Where a person with Panic Disorder would suffer from a panic attack in any situation. As well as panic disorders are found in 5% of women and 2% of men. (Barlow, 2002).

As a result, when it comes to understanding panic disorders, we need to look at the following three types:

- Panic disorder without agoraphobia
- Panic disorder with agoraphobia
- Agoraphobia without a history of panic disorder

Also, agoraphobia without panic disorders are the same as the above but this condition is focused on panic-like symptoms and not full-blown panic attacks.

What Is Agoraphobia?

Personally, I feel that agoraphobia isn't a very well-used word and it really isn't known about so agoraphobia is a form of anxiety coming from a person being in situations where escape is embarrassing or difficult or help isn't perceived to be available in the event of a panic or panic-like symptoms. For example, agoraphobia can be found in situations when a person is far from home because the person might not know who to turn to for help, and the same goes for travel and crowds.

Consequently, the person with agoraphobia will avoid these situations or if they go into these situations this will produce a lot of anxiety or they will need a companion to enter these situations. This helps with the issues surrounding the situation being difficult to escape and helping not being available. As well as if a person does want a diagnosis of agoraphobia then this condition needs to be able to explain the person's symptoms better than another disorder.

What Would A Panic Attack and Panic Disorder Diagnosis Require?

When it comes to getting a diagnosis, we all know that a set list of criteria has to be met in the Diagnostic and Statistical Manual Version 5 (DSM-5) for a diagnosis to be made, so all this information is from the DSM-5 (APA, 2013).

Therefore, for a person to meet Criterion A for Panic Disorders (and as this is the Criterion that gives you the best idea about the feelings a Panic Disorder gives a person, this is the only one we'll look at), a person must experience an abrupt surge from a calm or anxious state to one of intense discomfort or fear that peaks within minutes and during this time four or more of the following symptoms must happen:

- Sweat
- Tremble
- Shake
- Have a feeling of choking
- Experience palpitation, accelerated heart rate or pounding heart
- Experience chest pains or discomfort
- Feel dizzy, unsteady, faint or light-headed
- Have a fear of dying

- Experience a sense of smothering or shortness of breath
- Have a sense of numbness or tingling
- Nausea or abdominal distress
- Chills or heat sensations
- Fear losing control or "going crazy"
- Experience a feeling of unreality (Derealisation) or being detached from themselves (depersonalisation)

This is why I rather like looking at the diagnostic criteria for different mental health conditions, because they help to give a real sense about what it is like to experience these conditions, and then using this knowledge we can start to think about possible ways to treat these symptoms.

Social Anxiety Disorder (APA, 2013)

This definitely has to be the most famous anxiety condition so whilst I probably don't have to introduce it too much, I still really want to. As a result of social anxiety disorder is defined as high levels of fear or anxiety about one or more social situations where the person is exposed to scrutiny by others.

This fear and anxiety are caused by the person's fear that they will act in a way or show their anxiety symptoms that will lead to the other people negatively evaluating them. In other words, negatively judging them so the person will be humiliated, embarrassed and rejected by the other people.

Also when I was first learning this topic, I found it rather surprising that social anxiety disorder isn't one thing. Since a person could be fine at parties but have social anxiety disorder when talking in public, talking in a classroom or not at all. The entire point of social anxiety disorder is that a person's anxiety and fear could be provoked by a single type of social situation, most or all social situations. It really does depend on the person.

Furthermore, men and women are affected equally by this disorder as well as it typically manifests itself in childhood or adolescence (Robins and Regier, 1991).

A Social Anxiety Disorder Diagnosis

When it comes to a person wanting a diagnosis, there is a set list of symptoms and behaviours they have to meet. For instance, for a person to have social anxiety disorder they need to experience a high level of fear or anxiety about one or more social situations where the person is exposed to possible scrutiny by other people.

For example, the DSM-5 includes examples like social interactions, like meeting unfamiliar people and having a conversation, performing in front of others, like doing public speaking, and being observed, like eating or drinking.

In addition, the anxiety or fear they experience has to be out of proportion to the real threat posed by the social situation and the sociocultural context. This is an idea we'll return to in the Specific Phobia chapter.

Moreover, the social situation must almost always provoke a fear or anxiety reaction in a person, as well as the person must show that they avoid these situations or when they are exposed to these situations, the person has to endure them with intense anxiety or fear.

And then because the DSM-5 loves a good old time factor (a very common theme throughout the book), the person has to have a persistent fear, anxiety or avoidance of these situations for at least 6 months or more. As well as (by the end of this first section you'll be saying this with me) the fear, anxiety, or avoidance of social situations must cause clinically significant distress or impairment for the person in social, occupational, or other important areas of functioning.

INTRODUCTION TO COGNITIVE BEHAVIOURAL THERAPY

Now we understand what social anxiety and panic disorder involve, I want to point out some possible treatment options you might want to investigate more if you experience severe social anxiety. Therefore, in the next three chapters, you'll learn about Cognitive Behavioural Therapy, including this introductory chapter so you understand what Cognitive Behavioural Therapy (CBT) is, as well as Exposure Therapy. Both of these types of psychotherapy are highly effective for treating social anxiety.

And my favourite thing about CBT is that it is fascinating and a very fun read if you're interested in mental health, so please enjoy.

***

Now that we're getting onto the part of the book we've all been waiting for, let's start learning about the amazing topic of Cognitive Behavioural Therapy.

As a result, we first need to know both the cognitive and behavioural theories that Cognitive Behavioural Therapy is built on before we can ever hope to understand how CBT works for anxiety disorders.

Therefore, as you can probably imagine Cognitive Behavioural Therapy is based (at least in part) on the cognitive approach to behaviour. As well as Westbrook, Kennerley & Kirk (2007) noted that there is evidence that a lot of mental health conditions are associated with a wide range of cognitive factors. For example, many conditions cause people to have information processing biases, faulty belief schemas as well as dysfunctional ways of thinking.

Then if we apply this logic to anxiety disorders then we've already discussed in the book how anxiety causes a person to have faulty belief systems about how dangerous the stimuli is, the dysfunctional ways they develop to "cope" with the anxiety and their bias information processing because how they perceive the stimuli.

Also, the cognitive approaches to treatment were first pioneered by Albert Ellis (1962) and Aaron Beck (1967) with their aim being to incorporate cognitive processes into psychology, all whilst still maintaining an empirical approach to this because they wanted to avoid ungrounded speculation.

In other words, they wanted to make sure their findings withstood empirical scrutiny and it is a brilliant thing that they set out with this in mind.

In addition, when it comes to cognitive approaches, this view focuses on the idea that a mental health condition is caused by a person developing irrational beliefs, dysfunctional ways of thinking and biased information processing like we saw earlier. And this leads to the person's mental processes being impacted heavily.

For instance, the way a person behaves and emotionally reacts to a stimuli is strongly influenced by their cognition. Like their beliefs, thoughts and interpretation. As well as this impacts how a person reacts to an event too.

For example, because I personally don't find spiders anxiety-provoking, if I see a spider then I don't interpret this as dangerous, life-threatening and I'm not overwhelmed by the emotion of fear. Yet if an anxious person saw a spider then their cognitive processes would tell them this is a life-threatening situation and they will react completely differently to me because the anxious person has biased cognitive processes.

Furthermore, the cognitive approach believes mental health conditions develop and the mental health difficulties onset because of cognitive factors (obviously) but both functional and dysfunctional beliefs develop earlier on, and these beliefs may not cause difficulties for a long period of time.

And this is something that I personally find very interesting about mental health. A person could have depression, ADHD, autism or another condition and function absolutely perfectly. They can hold down a job, have tons of friends (if they want) and live a perfectly happy life, but it is only when they start to struggle and need help is when clinical psychology is really needed.

And something that I personally love to remind people is that a mental health condition isn't a death sentence like some people sadly believe it is. Sure a person with a mental health condition might need a little more support, guidance and treatment but given all of those things there is a good chance they could live a very happy and relatively clinically "normal" life.

Nonetheless, if the person does experience a critical incident event, also known as encounters the anxiety-provoking stimuli, then this would be a disturbing event to them, this could activate their negative beliefs and then lead to a distressing emotional response.

What's The Cognitive-Behavioural Approach?

Building on both the cognitive approaches, to form Cognitive Behavioural Therapy, this approach has to be combined with behavioural approaches. Therefore, whilst the cognitive approach focuses on a person's cognitions and beliefs and how these might lead to particular behaviours. It is these behaviours that are actually a core factor in maintaining or changing beliefs and emotions. Meaning this can become a very vicious cycle.

In other words, a person's negative cognition and beliefs cause negative behaviours. Then these behaviours reinforce the cognitions and beliefs and so on. Since it's the behaviour in a person's response to a negative experience or cognition that could have a significant effect on whether the emotion persists.

For example, if a person reacts badly to a spider then of course the person will want to avoid spiders to avoid this feeling again. Hence, they develop avoidance behaviours. Like, avoiding the situation and event completely, escaping it or engaging in safety behaviours.

Now personally, I love safety behaviours and I think they are truly fascinating because to be honest they have to be some of the biggest cons in psychology. Due to safety behaviours are fully intended to protect us from threat or prevent harm coming to us. As a result, these safety behaviours might reduce our anxiety in the short term, but they always have the unintended consequence of maintaining anxiety in the longer term.

That's why I think safety behaviours are very interesting cons that we pull on ourselves because we convince ourselves that we're helping ourselves to be less anxious, and if we don't do these behaviours we're going to basically die. But in reality, they're making us "worse", not "better.

Core Treatment Components

When it comes to what CBT actually involves, there are a few flat out critical elements that make up this amazingly effective and fascinating therapy.

Firstly, there is a lot of cognitive restructuring involved. This component involves challenging and modifying a person's negative thoughts as well as their dysfunctional beliefs. This is typically done by examining the evidence for a person's beliefs.

For example, we'll talk a lot more about cognitive intervention in two chapters' time but an anxious person will believe their safety behaviours save them and without their safety behaviours they will basically die. That is how powerful these behaviours are, so as you'll see in two chapters a therapist can challenge these beliefs by using experiments and testing whether or not there is evidence to support these beliefs.

Another core feature of CBT is it involves a therapist helping to modify a person's tendency to indulge in unhelpful thinking processes, this relates to the cognitive biases we spoke about earlier, so the therapist works with the client to modify and reduce these unhelpful mental processes. Like, how a person pays excessive attention to the threat, how they ruminate on the anxiety provoking stimuli and they engage in mental checking.

As well as when it comes to helping a person reduce their unhelpful behaviours, this includes things like reducing their avoidance, safety and checking behaviours. Also CBT involves behavioural experiments (definitely more on that later) and exposure and response prevention (again more on that in a later chapter).

Levels Of Cognition

Of course, we could never ever hope to learn about cognitive approaches and CBT without looking at levels of cognition, and this is absolutely critical when it comes to Cognitive Behavioural Therapy. Since a person's levels of cognition are as follows:

- Their automatic thoughts
- Their intermediate beliefs, attitudes and rules which are assumptions about the world and the self.
- Their core beliefs. Their basic beliefs about their self, others and the world.

And this idea about levels of cognition is flat out critical in CBT because a therapist has to be very careful when they do cognitive restructuring because you cannot hope to change someone's core beliefs automatically. That just isn't how things work but you can start off with challenging and modifying a person's automatic thoughts then their intermediate beliefs and then their core beliefs.

You need to work "slowly" and gradually for the therapy to work.

An anxiety example of how a therapist might go about finding out what a person's core belief is, is as follows:

- I'm terrified of spiders (automatic thought)
- I know if a spider gets near me it could attack me (potential intermediate belief)
- If a spider touches me then I know for a fact I'm going to get bitten and I'll be rushed to hospital (potential core belief)

Now I have to admit that it is far, far easier to come up with potential levels of cognitions with depression for teaching purposes but you get the general idea. A CBT therapist would have to effectively peel back the layers of a person's cognition to truly understand why they have these biased mental processes.

Thinking Errors/Biases

If you've studied depression then you might be familiar with this section of the chapter because there are a lot of commonalities between all types of CBT (at least "first-wave" therapies) and the types of cognitive biases and errors a CBT therapist would encounter. Therefore, here are the following cognitive errors a therapist is likely to encounter and I have broken them up so you can clearly see the error and an example of what it is like:

- All or nothing- if I can't love all dogs then I'm scared of all of them.
- Exaggerated standards/expectations- if I can't pet a dog then I'm a failure (a potential example at least)
- Catastrophising- my life is over because if I go outside I might see a dog and it might kill me.

- Selective attention to the negative/threat- a person is basically always drawn to anxiety provoking stimuli.
- Over-generalising- "I'm scared of my brother's pet dog so I'm scared of all dogs"
- Dismissing the positive- I might be able to stroke my sister's dog but I feel worthless and scary around all other dogs. I'm so lame.

- Magnifying/minimising- minimising the positive and magnifying the bad
- Jumping to conclusions
- Emotional reasoning- being irrational and basing your reason on emotion, not fact.
- Personalising
- Internalising/externalising

Again, some of those examples might sound similar to depression and that is to be expected considering there is a comorbidity between depression and anxiety in some people.

Role Of Avoidance And Safety Behaviours

Returning to my topic and building upon what we learnt earlier, a very good definition of a safety behaviour can be found in Salkovskis (1988, 1991):

"A behaviour which is performed in order to prevent or minimise a feared catastrophe"

As well as we know that safety behaviours have several effects on a person's beliefs. Like they prevent a person from getting disconfirming evidence about their beliefs (this is flat out critical for the information in two chapters' time), this can increase the sensation a person experiences like their anxiety and fear, and safety behaviours increase their rumination and preoccupation with the anxiety provoking stimuli.

Overall, all these effects on behaviour that safety behaviours cause are linked together to make the person focus on the stimuli they find threatening and this of course isn't helpful.

CBT FOR ANXIETY DISORDERS

Something that I really like about this book is that as the other chapters have shown us, there is an awful lot that goes into CBT, and CBT is nowhere near as straight forward as you might have previously believed since it is only now that we are getting onto CBT. As well as there is plenty more information after this chapter to deepen your knowledge even further.

Therefore, we know that anxiety disorders develop due to people believing that situations are a lot more dangerous than they really are. As well as this means psychologists need to help clients to consider alternative, less threatening explanations of their mental difficulty.

And yet, this isn't straight forward as each anxiety disorder has its own unique facets and this means a client has to learn and test these alternative ways of interpreting their experience.

Ultimately, this helps the person to make changes to their own unique, personal situation so CBT is critical in helping them to adopt and try out these new ways of understanding themselves, their experience and most importantly their future assumptions.

How Does CBT For Anxiety Work?

The entire point of all CBT models of anxiety disorders is to help the client consider their own threatening interpretation of the experience as well as how this is maintained by their emotion and behaviour as discussed in previous chapters.

In addition, all CBT models use behavioural activation and cognitive restructuring to help the client learn alternative ways of interpreting their experience and helps them to make changes to their situation by trying out their new ways of understanding themselves, others and the world.

But that is basically where the similarities end. Every CBT model is different for each anxiety disorder.

CBT For Panic Disorder

When it comes to panic disorder, the cognitive theory proposes that people have a relatively enduring tendency to interpret a range of bodily sensations catastrophically. In other words, people with panic disorder think their bodily sensations is the end of the world and they're going to die. That's an example of how exaggerated their biased cognitive processes are.

As a result, these bodily sensations are the ones that are mainly involved in normal anxiety responses, like heart palpitations, dizziness and breathlessness, but they aren't always triggered by anxiety. Hence, the person's catastrophic interpretation involves them perceiving these sensations as indications of an immediately impending physical or mental disaster.

And come on, anyone could find this absolutely terrifying and they would rightly have a major panic attack.

Afterwards, a person might start catastrophising these sensations but that doesn't mean they should automatically be maintained and a person should have these catastrophic interpretations forever, so what maintains panic disorders?

A lot of research finds that once a person has developed a tendency to interpret body sensations in a catastrophic way, then several other processes engage and it is these processes that contribute to the maintenance of panic disorder. For example, a person's safety behaviours, imagery, emotional reasoning and their selective attention to bodily cues.

Overall, when it comes to treating panic disorder with CBT, the therapy needs to focus on cognitively restructuring these catastrophic misinterpretations, reducing their unhelpful attentional processes and helping them to reduce their safety and avoidance behaviours. This is typically done through Behavioural Experiments (my absolute favourite topic in the entire book coming up in the next chapter).

CBT For Generalised Anxiety Disorder (GAD)

Additionally, if we look at Generalised Anxiety Disorder (this will be examined more in the free bonus essay at the back of the book), the cognitive model of GAD was proposed by Wells (1995; 1997; 2000; 2009) and he proposed that the excessive worry and anxiety common in GAD was maintained by a range of factors.

For instance, Wells found that GAD was maintained by a person's hypervigilance to threats, so they're always looking out for threats and I think we can all imagine how if a person is always looking for threats they will always find them in the end.

A GAD sufferer has information processing biases like attention and interpretation biases as well that have a maintaining role too. As does the person's dysfunctional beliefs about their worry and its function. Leading people to believe that it's perfectly necessary to run through this process of avoidance because they believe it is critical to avoid future catastrophes. Despite the worry this process causes them being uncontrollable and harmful. Then like always safety seeking behaviours and avoidance also play a role in maintaining GAD.

Therefore, when a CBT therapist comes to treating GAD, they focus on the self-monitoring aspect of the person with them constantly watching out for anxiety and worry.

This is done through cognitive restructuring by challenging the beliefs they have about the likelihood and cost of the negative events, they challenge the client's dysfunctional beliefs about their worrying as well as they carry out behavioural experiments to test out their beliefs about worry.

Moreover, the therapist would help the client to reduce and disengage from their worrying and reduce their safety behaviours, like reassurance seeking.

Overall, as you can see so far and we'll come back to this point at the end of the chapter, but

CBT is like a core when it comes to anxiety disorders (and pretty much all mental health conditions) and it needs to be adapted and changed to meet the needs of the client with a specific mental health condition.

No two CBTs are the same because no two conditions are the same.

What CBT Works For Social Anxiety Disorder?

To wrap up this chapter, we'll look at one final anxiety disorder because Social Anxiety Disorder is always interesting to look at. Consequently, CBT for the condition aims to help clients reduce their negative mental processes and beliefs about social situations, their overly negative view of their performance in social situations, their excessive fear of negative evaluations by others as well as their excessive importance attached to social performance.

Additionally, to put this into a perspective for those of us without social anxiety disorder can understand, whenever we go to a social situation, we always want to do well, not look like an idiot and we want people to like us at these social situations but our entire identities aren't obsessed with that and our world will not end if we make a fool of ourselves.

But that is how social situations and negative evaluations feel to people with social anxiety disorder.

As a result, CBT for this condition seeks to reduce a person's self-focused attention, getting them to stop their safety and avoidance behaviours and get them to reduce their attentional bias to the social threat.

Ultimately, now that we've looked at CBT for three different anxiety disorders, hopefully you can see how CBT is adapted to each condition, and how there are similarities and there are some fairly stark differences as well.

And it is those differences that make this topic so fascinating to learn about.

EXPOSURE THERAPY

We seriously couldn't do a section on treatments for anxiety disorders without investigating exposure therapy, and this is a therapy that is so often used in books, TV and films that I just know a lot of people would have been disappointed if I didn't write about it. And personally, I would have been disappointed too because exposure therapy is flat out brilliant.

What Is Exposure Therapy?

Exposure therapy is a psychological treatment that was developed to help people confront their fears. Since whenever people are fearful or scared of something, they tend to avoid the feared object, situation or activity. For example, if a person is fearful of social situations or spiders then the person will avoid said social situation and spider.

Furthermore, as we know from earlier chapters, this avoidance behaviour might help the person to reduce their feelings of fear in the short term, in the long term it can make the fear even worse. Basically, this has the complete opposite effect than intended.

As a result, in exposure therapy, psychologists create a safe environment so the client can get "exposed" to the anxiety provoking, fearful objects, situations and activities that they avoid and find fearful. If the therapy is done correctly (more on that later) then this leads to a reduction in their fearful response and avoidance behaviour.

Moreover, exposure therapy isn't some guru rubbish that doesn't have supportive literature, it has been scientifically shown to be an effective treatment or treatment component for a wide range of mental health conditions. Such as:

- Social Anxiety Disorder
- Generalized Anxiety Disorder
- Phobias
- Obsessive-Compulsive Disorder
- Panic Disorder
- Posttraumatic Stress Disorder

<u>How Is Exposure Therapy Done?</u>

Now this is why I really enjoy learning about exposure therapy because the therapy really has come such a long way since its beginning. Especially since when I think about Exposure Therapy I only imagine a client looking at a spider in a glass box and it then crawling up on the client's arm.

Even though I don't have a spider phobia, I seriously couldn't imagine me willingly having a massive spider crawling up my arm. That's just goes to show how amazingly brave our clients are.

However, this is only one of the ways exposure therapy is done.

The first way exposure therapy is done is by what's known as "In vivo exposure" and this is basically what I mentioned above. Since this is when you directly face the feared situation, object or activity in real life.

For example, to use a different example, if a person is terrified of horses then they might be instructed to handle a horse, or a person with social anxiety might be asked to give a speech in front of an audience.

Another method is "Imaginal Exposure". This involves a person vividly imagining the feared situation, object or activity. And a great example here is from PTSD sufferers, because they might be asked to recall and describe their traumatic experience in great detail to reduce the feelings of fear.

Penultimately, Virtual Reality (VR) can be used as a form of exposure because in some cases, VR technology can be used in cases where In Vivo exposure just isn't practical. For example, we can all see that if a person has a fear of flying then the psychologist isn't going to rent a plane and take the client flying for the hour of their therapy appointment. It would be cool if they did but that really isn't practical in the slightest.

So VR comes in very handy in cases like this, especially as the VR equipment in the psychologist office's can be used to provide the sights, smells and sounds of an aeroplane.

Finally, "Interoceptive Exposure" can be used. This is a very interesting one because it involves bringing on physical sensations that are harmless to the client but fearful. Such as, if you're working with a client with panic disorder, they might be instructed to run on the spot to make their heart speed up so the person learns that the sensation isn't dangerous.

That's brilliant because the whole "problem" with a panic disorder is that the person is fearful of the physical sensation.

<u>What Is Graded Exposure?</u>

Originally in my weird little notes the three next sections were later in the chapter but as you'll see that just flat out wouldn't work.

Anyway, graded exposure is an absolutely critical feature of Exposure Therapy because it involves a fear hierarchy. This is a list of a person's triggers that makes them feel afraid or anxious, and these triggers are ranked from the trigger that is least anxiety provoking to the most provoking.

For example, if you have a client that is terrified of spiders then the least anxiety provoking situation might be seeing a photo of a spider, followed by watching a video of a spider, being in the same room as a spider and then allowing a spider to crawl up your arm.

This is a good example for a hierarchy for spider phobias, but of course a real one depends on the client.

Additionally, it's important in Exposure Therapy to try and have these items by distress number (another way of saying the amount of distress it causes goes up linear) so there are no big jumps. Then the idea is to make sure the client and the therapist work their way through the list from the lowest number to the highest number also known as the most anxiety-provoking.

Also, it's a good idea to make sure the theme of the list is relevant to the goals of the therapy. Therefore, a therapist could experiment with each item several times until the client no longer feels distress in that situation.

For instance, going back to our spider example, a therapist wouldn't move from getting the client to look at images of a spider before moving onto watching a video. As well as the therapist might have the client look at images of small, medium and massive spiders to make sure the client no longer feels anxious after looking at images before moving onto the next one.

Equally, sometimes therapists might "only" keep experimenting until the distress in a given situation is about half of what it was. This makes sense because it isn't until a client reaches the top of their hierarchy that their anxiety responses are a lot better than before treatment.

That's the easiest way to explain it.

How Does Exposure Therapy Work?

This is what we all want to know because as psychology is a science, we want to know why and how something works. Therefore, there are four main mechanisms that help change to occur during a course of Exposure Therapy.

Firstly, the client goes through a process of habituation where over time, people find that their reactions to the feared objects, situations or activities decrease because of their exposure to them. This links with the challenging of their biased beliefs because if a client is being exposed to the feared object without the world ending then this helps them to learn that maybe their beliefs were wrong.

Secondly, the cognitive process of extinction occurs where exposure helps to weaken the previously learnt associations between feared objects, activities or situations and bad outcomes.

And yes, this has a lot to do with the psychology of learning, which you can read more about in *Cognitive Psychology: A Guide To Neuropsychology, Neuroscience and Cognitive Psychology*.

Thirdly, and this is something I think is so, so important in therapy work. A client learns about their own self-efficacy. Meaning the exposure helps to show the client that they're perfectly capable of confronting their own fears as well as they can manage the feelings of their anxiety.

This links to the brilliant concept of CBT Pie Charts, a very powerful and fascinating therapy tool, that I discuss more in *Clinical Psychology Reflections Volume 4*.

Finally, exposure therapy is great for emotional processing since during the exposure, the client can learn to attach new, more realistic beliefs about feared objects, activities or situations, and they can become more comfortable with the experience of fear.

What Are The Four Rules of Exposure Therapy?

I have to admit that psychologists love rules, methods and having to do things a certain way and this is definitely true for CBT, but when it comes to Exposure Therapy, these four rules are particularly important because if a therapist doesn't stick to the rules then chances are the therapy will fail and the client will only be worst off.

Therefore, the first rule of Exposure Therapy is the exposure absolutely has to be graded. If we look back at our spider example, you seriously cannot go from getting a client to look at photos of spiders to having a spider crawling up their arm. That will end so badly and the client will never improve and yeah, it will not be pretty.

Just don't do that.

In addition, and see this as a sub-rule of the first one, when it comes to creating the Hierarchy of Anxious Situations, it's best to start with the most anxiety-provoking and then work down. Remember, this is the creation phase because if a therapist asks a client about the object that causes them the least anxiety. Chances are they will not know.

They only know the *most* anxiety-provoking one so it's best to start there and then it breaks the ice, allowing you to ask more questions, investigate more and slowly work your way down towards the least anxiety-provoking ones.

Remember, therapy is a process and so is the creation of this hierarchy.

Secondly, these exposures have to be prolonged since the therapists need to wait until the anxiety comes down to about half of what it was before they started before they get the client to stop. Since if the therapist stops it too soon then they risk reinforcing the very behaviour they are trying to get the client to stop.

Thirdly, these exposures have to be repeated so the client should continue doing the exposure of the same activity until their pre-activity anxiety comes down to about half what it was when the therapist planned the activity.

Again, if a therapist shows a client a photo of a spider and the client starts rapidly breathing, they would wait until the rapid breathing decreases before moving on to the next task.

Finally, these exposures have to be done without distraction. The client has to be focused on these exposures and learn that their biased beliefs are not based in reality and the danger is nowhere near what they believe it is. And distractions only make this learning or unlearning even harder.

Exposure And Response Prevention

This next aspect is very similar to standard graded exposure and this is when a therapist and a client work together, much like how they do in CBT, to develop a hierarchy like we saw in the last few sections and the four principles still apply.

However, the difference is that the client needs to resist the urge to respond to a compulsive desire and it is important for the client to sit with the distress until it comes down to about half.

The clearest fictional example of this is with OCD. For example, a client might have the urge to start cleaning whenever they see dirt so their compulsion might be hand cleaning so at least they are clean. In this situation, the client would have to sit with that compulsion and *not* clean their hands.

Of course, this would cause a lot of distress and anxiety but it will also show the client that nothing bad will happen to them if they don't wash their hands the second the compulsion manifests itself.

What Are The Common Difficulties With Exposure?

Of course, nothing in psychology like life is straight forward and therapy is no different. Therefore, there will be problems a therapist encounters with their clients when it comes to exposure therapy. Some of these problems include:

- The client doesn't want to get started and the therapist can't encourage them.

You cannot do a therapy if the client isn't willing to put in the work and at least try it, but exposure therapy is terrifying for people.

- Missing activities or missing steps in the hierarchy. That will almost always end badly.
- The client or therapist or both tries to do too much too soon.
- Jumping ahead in the hierarchy.
- The client doesn't drop their safety behaviours so they still believe it is their safety behaviours that are protecting them.
- Both the client and therapist have difficulties categorising activities in the hierarchy.

This is problematic because if a therapist can't categorise activities properly then it is so much harder to understand how to properly go up the hierarchy without the risk of jumping steps and trying to do too much at once.

- Stopping an activity before the anxiety drops.

How To Address Safety behaviours In Exposure Therapy?

Some of you might have realised that normally in CBT (which is completely separate from Exposure Therapy), you carry out cognitive interventions including behavioural experiments to challenge and address a person's beliefs and safety behaviours. And I'm sure there is a good argument that Exposure Therapy is a good form of cognitive intervention, but Exposure Therapy does not have a good way of addressing safety behaviours. At least from what we've seen so far.

The first step of getting rid of any safety behaviour is obviously identifying them, you can't get rid of something if you don't know what it is.

As well as we need to remember that safety behaviours try to distract us from the experience of our anxiety, and this is important because it reduces the opportunities for habituation. As well as this is why it's sometimes a very good idea to make a list of safety behaviours that might get in the way of habituation with the client.

As a result, a person might say to a therapist "I can look at spider photos if I do…"

We don't want them to say that. And whilst it is sometimes "okay" to allow a safety behaviour in order to make a jump in the hierarchy, this isn't ideal in the slightest, but when this is done, the next step should be completed without the safety behaviour before moving on to the next.

A practical example would be the one we've been using all chapter, if a client couldn't even look at a photo of a spider but we saw there was a decrease of about a quarter to a third in anxiety. Then maybe a therapist could allow them to do a safety behaviour before moving on to the next one.

Again, this really, really does come down to clinical judgement and the therapist's experience.

Overall, at the end of this great chapter, I have to admit that Exposure Therapy is definitely a serious but potentially fun therapy because we get to help our clients, and get very creative at the same time, and it is that creativity that I just love.

PART THREE:
FEMALE SEXUAL OFFENDING

INTRODUCTION TO FEMALE SEXUAL ABUSE OF CHILDREN

Out of everything I've written so far and everything I will write later on in this book, this is probably the first chapter I've written that has honestly made me feel sick to write, because no one likes to think about women sexually abusing children. No I don't like thinking about any form of sexual violence. However, when it comes to female sexual abuse against children, there are a lot of gender stereotypes at play and this explains why female sexual offenders are a very understudied and underreported issue. Therefore, in this chapter, you'll learn why females sexually abuse children, how denying the existence of female sexual abusers only prolongs the suffering of survivors and how do we fix this mess.

Introduction To Female Sexual Abuse of Children

I've spoken a lot on the podcast before about the pervasive impact of gender stereotypes on society and its extremely harmful and damaging impact on sexual assault survivors. In the context of this chapter, the gender stereotypes that females can only ever be perfect, innocent, protective mother figures who could never ever hurt a child is a harmful belief that results in the idea of female sexual abuse of children becoming unthinkable. This makes it very difficult for survivors to come forward and it only prolongs their suffering.

Another myth that negatively impacts child sexual abuse survivors is the idea that women could only possibly hurt a child if a man ordered or coerced them into doing the behaviour. This is a damaging myth because it places the blame on a man instead of people realising that female sexual perpetrators are real so this blinds people to the reality of child sexual abuse.

This is something we are very slowly starting to realise as more women are prosecuted for child sexual abuse without the involvement of male coercion. Yet academics believe the real number of women sexually abusing children is likely to be higher.

As a result of the official statistics in the United States suggest that between 12% and 17% of the sex offender population are women and research shows that the perception of what sex is more dangerous is biased against men. Also as you'll see in a following chapter, you'll know that women's sexual offences are often minimised or discounted, especially when women sexually assault men. As well as this could explain why the conviction rates against female sex offenders could be underestimated as a lot of children abused by women aren't disclosing what happened to them out of fear of not being taken seriously.

Some evidence supporting the number of female sex offenders being greater than the official statistics show is if we look at call centres for children, these call centres show a much greater number of children reporting female sexual abuse compared to the official court records. For instance, in the United Kingdom, Childline found 40% of children calling them reported being sexually abused by a female.

This is a lot higher than the official statistics, so now we have to ask a painful question.

Why Are Children Who Are Being Abused by Females Not Reporting It?

Of course, there is no single answer to this painful question and I've already mentioned a wide range of possible answers in other chapters. Yet another reason why children might not be reporting their female sexual abuse is because if the victim is a boy then it is more difficult for them to report abuse. Since boys are taught by society that they're always meant to want sex and that men are only ever the perpetrators of sexual assault and society tells them that it is impossible for them to be victims of sexual abuse and sexual violence.

As a result, this leads to the male victims feeling ashamed and they don't believe that they actually were sexually assaulted. This stops them from coming forward and it stops them from getting the psychological support they need.

Furthermore, whilst I won't go into the details and the ins and outs, the film May-December is a great depiction of what an abusive relationship looks like when there's a female sexual predator. It's based on a true story about 36-year-old Mary Kay Letourneau who was a teacher who had a sexual relationship with a 12-year-old student. Since it features a woman in her 30s sexually abusing a 13-year-old boy through manipulation, coercion and constant invalidation of his experiences and opinions on their relationship so he ends up being completely submissive to her. He doesn't know any other type of life so this traps him inside the abusive relationship because he doesn't see it as abusive. He doesn't know another way to live.

This connects to this section of the chapter because this is another reason why sexually abused children might not come forward. Not only do they not realise they're being abused, like the boy in May-December who protested for years that their relationship was consensual and nothing was wrong. Yet abusers use manipulation tactics to invalidate and control their victims to stop them escaping their control.

As well as for victims to confront the distortions, lies and normalisations of the abuse, that is profoundly painful for them. This is another limiting factor behind them wanting to come forward.

On the whole, May-December reminds us how just like men, women can find wielding power over vulnerable people very gratifying and if we allow ourselves to disregard female sexual abuse then this only increases these damaging, harmful myths that ignore the capacity that women have for hurting and abusing children. As well as this disregard of female sexual abuse only intensifies the shame that stops children from coming forward and getting justice against their abusers.

This is wrong and we must make sure sexual abuse survivors are capable and empowered to stand up against their abusers and get justice.

A Note On Cognitive Distortions Of Female Sexual Abusers

As we head towards the end of this chapter, I wanted to mention how anyone, whether they're a sexual abuser or not, likes to maintain a positive self-image so they feel good about themselves and have high self-esteem. Therefore, in an effort to achieve this positive self-image, sex offenders need to justify their foul actions and this leads to several cognitive distortions of their actions.

In terms of female sexual abuse, sex offenders believe that they aren't exploiting the child whatsoever and instead they firmly believe they're in a loving and consensual relationship where both of them are so-called equals. Of course, the reality of their so-called relationship is the complete and utter opposite so sex offenders engage in rigid and stalwart rationalisations and defences to stop them and their victims from realising the truth.

And it is the stigma of the crimes that makes acknowledgement even more unlikely.

Overall, films and criminal cases like the one that May December is based on are good at highlighting issues surrounding female sexual abuse, even showing us how women are vilified and they don't reflect the reality of real-world female sexual predators. In the film, the female sexual abuser is painted as a monstrous, clearly evil woman that is sensationalised, whereas in reality, female sexual abusers can seem perfectly normal and they mainly manipulate and coerce their child victim into their so-called loving and equal relationship.

Moreover, May December and other such media falls into the classic trap of not showing how young boys can be victimised, just like young girls. Since films like May December use the "teacher lover" trope to demonstrate how the young boy is so-called lucky to be seduced by a hot teacher. This is a problem because it is this damaging trope that hides how actual child sexual abuse happens because males can and are raped by female predators and women can misuse their authority, power and their role as an adult teacher to abuse young boys. Very similar to how men can do the exact same.

Conclusion

Ultimately when it comes to female sexual abuse, as a society, we need to stop just condemning these crimes where females are the abusers as weird and morally outrageous. We need to go a lot further because as aspiring or qualified psychologists we need to explore and address the historical as well as psychological factors that underlie these outrageous acts against children. We need to reduce the stigma around female sexual abuse so the victims feel like they can come forward, and this helps to reduce further abuse and victimisation too.

And it is about time we acknowledge, the disgusting, hard truth that women are capable and actively do abuse children to sexually meet their own needs. It is not only males that are capable of this disgusting act.

Finally, urgent psychological treatment needs to be developed as soon as possible so these women (and the same goes for men) can be treated, supported and rehabilitated so they no longer feel the need to sexually abuse children. Due to it is only through the development of psychological treatments that we will finally be able to put this awful cycle of trauma, abuse and harm to an end once and for all.

WHY DO GIRLS COMMIT SEXUAL OFFENCES?

Typically, in society, it's commonly believed that only men and boys can possibly commit sexual offences. Since a lot of people believe it is simply impossible for women and young girls to do the same, but it is a lot more common than previously thought for women to be abusers and perpetrators. Also, whilst the majority of perpetrators of sexual violence are men, women can be abusers too. Including young girls.

Therefore, in this chapter focusing on females as perpetrators of sexual violence, you'll specifically learn about young girls that commit sexual offences. For example, why they do it, factors that make young girls commit sexual offences and more. If you enjoy learning about criminal psychology, sexual offending and more then this is a great chapter for you.

Why Do Girls Commit Sexual Offences?

In the book, we've already spoken a lot about sexual violence, the devastating impact it has on survivors and how healing from sexual trauma is very difficult, but very possible. Therefore, I'm not going to recap any of that information, but I will mention that Finkelhor et al. (2014) demonstrated that one in 20 boys and one in four girls are sexually victimised during their childhood in the United States, let alone in other countries.

In addition, as impossible as it might be to hear, not all these sexual offences are committed by grown men. In previous chapters, you've learnt how women can be perpetrators of sexual abuse, but in this chapter, we're going to be focusing on a fellow child committing a sexual offence against another. More specifically, you'll learn how young females commit sexual offences.

At first, this might seem like an impossible idea because of gender stereotypes and other factors, but the FBI Crime Data Explorer reveals that juvenile sexual offending (sex offenders aged between 10 and 19 years old) make up 16% of rape offences in the USA between 2011 and 2021. As well as other research studies demonstrate how juvenile sexual offending is a massive, complicated and dire issue faced by countries all over the world.

Furthermore, research shows that the early life experiences, like their environment and psychological factors, of juvenile sexual offenders have a large impact on their sexual offences. Since Oliver and Holmes (2015) found that domestic violence within the home environment and a chaotic family system were a common feature in the home environments of female juvenile sexual offenders. As well as this shouldn't come as a surprise but it was unfortunately common for female juvenile sexual offenders to be sexual violence survivors themselves, experiencing at least one sexual assault at an early age. Also, Matthews et al. (1997) highlighted how female offenders were more likely to have sustained sexual and physical abuse compared to male offenders.

Other family factors common amongst female juvenile sexual offenders were substance and alcohol abuse in the family and poor parental control.

On the other hand, female juveniles that specifically targeted younger children were less likely to run away from home, experience conduct or school performance issues and less likely to have parental alcohol abuse problems.

Why Do Female Juvenile Offenders Have Unhealthy Sexual Boundaries?

I think one of the aspects that people struggle most with when it comes to understanding why children, and in particular young girls, commit sexual offences is that we don't instantly understand how these young girls develop such unhealthy sexual boundaries. That's why in this next section, you'll learn how these unhealthy sexual boundaries develop.

As part of Oliver and Holmes's research, they found that young juvenile sex offenders have two additional risk factors for sexual offending, these are inadequate relationship and social skills. Since most of the teenagers in van der Put (2013)'s sample showed that the female juvenile offenders had insufficient healthy relationships and they were associated with other antisocial young people. As well as between 16% and 27% of the subjects reported being socially isolated during their childhood and adolescence, and less than 7% of the sample maintained gang membership across all subtypes. Additionally, these two researchers showed that female sexual offenders had high rates of Post-Traumatic Stress Disorder, conduct disorder and Attention-Deficit Hyperactivity Disorder.

Furthermore, as I mentioned earlier, school performance was a common issue amongst female sexual offenders, so this can lead to intellectual and conduct difficulties in an academic setting. Additionally, this isn't a hard and fast rule though because van der Put (2013) found that school performance and conduct issues were only actually common in about 25% to 50%, so there are other factors at play here as well instead of it simply being down to a lack of education and school dropout. As well as van der Put et al. (2014) found that in a sample of 40 female sexual offenders, 20% of them did drug and alcohol abuse but their previous research in 2013 showed that drug abuse can be as high as 47% and alcohol abuse can be as high as 33% in the teenage girl sexual offending population.

When we turn our attention to the psychological factors, almost 50% of female offenders have come into contact with mental health services at some point in their lifetime, a similar number to male offenders, according to Matthews et al. (1997). As well as juvenile sex offenders experience high rates of suicidal ideation and attempts for both sexes, and over 40% of these suicide-related mental health difficulties occur during adolescence and childhood.

Also, something I find interesting is that when we look at Bumby and Bumby (1997), another study that confirms that male and female sex offenders have a lot of similarities between their suicidal behaviour (Oliver & Holmes, 2015). It just goes to show that male and female sexual offenders aren't as different as everyone imagines and I suppose there is some hope in that. Since if there are criminological factors we can target to prevent males from becoming sexual offenders then hopefully they will work to prevent female sexual offenders going the same way, as well as if there are treatment programmes designed for males then maybe they can work for females with a little adaptation.

It's a hope at the very least.

Nonetheless, Matthews et al. did point out that compared to male juvenile sex offenders, female offenders are less likely to have a learning disability (45% versus 23%). This was supported by Van de Put (2013) who found that 24% and 39% of female sexual offenders in their sample experienced mental health difficulties.

In addition, if we look at a biological factor and some more on mental health, Manestsch et al. (2021) demonstrated that over half of female sexual offenders in their research sample reported somatic complaints, over 33% of participants reported having significant angry-irritation problems as well as nearly 40% of participants reported depression-anxious difficulties above the clinical cutoffs for the MAYSI-2 screening tool. Hence, in this regard, female sex offenders are actually a lot more similar to male sex offenders than non-sexual offending females because of their mental health profiles on the MAYSI-2 tool.

What About The Different Crime Characteristics Of Teenage Girl Sex Offenders?

When it came to the characteristics of the crimes that female juvenile sex offenders committed, Matthews et al. concluded that these juvenile sex offenders were more likely than male offenders to be their victims' older sibling, babysitter, stranger or acquaintances. As well as the researchers reported that female sex offenders were more likely to offend against children aged 0-5 years old and these female sex offenders were at a heightened risk of offending against male and female victims.

These results are supported by Wijkman et al. (2013) as well, because these researchers found that the female sex offenders were mostly known to their victim. As well as female juvenile sex offenders focused on victims with an average age of 13 years old but their victims' ages can range from 0 years old to 23 years old. Additionally, Kubik et al. (2002) found that just like males, female offenders were just as likely to use verbal threats, weapons, mental aggression, force and physical restraint in their sexual assaults.

Moreover, Wijkman et al. (2013) mentioned that roughly 60% of female juvenile sex offenders tended to sexually abuse their victims with the support and assistance of other perpetrators. 9% of these cases had help from their boyfriend as a co-offender. Also, what I think is heartbreaking but rather interesting is that as much as these researchers focused on and stressed the male influence in the majority of group sexual offending, when it comes to female juvenile sex offenders, they play an active role in the sexual abuse in 74% of cases.

That's shockingly high when we consider the traditional conception of females in sexual abuse cases are either the survivor, or they are passive in the abuse and mainly forced by their boyfriend to do so.

Do Female Juvenile Sex Offenders Reoffend?

For our final section, if we look at the recidivism rate amongst this population, Cortoni et al. (2010) performed a meta-analysis and found that only 3% of this criminal population reoffended through sexual offences. Although another 6% reoffended in violent ways. In total, according to this meta-analysis around 25% of female juvenile sex offenders reoffended in all crimes including the crimes coded as *violent, sexual* as well as other non-violent offences. Then when we compare these rates to reoffending amongst male juvenile sexual offenders, we find that compared to females, 14% of male offenders reoffend sexually, 25% of male offenders reoffend violently and 37% commit an offence overall.

Finally, it's worth noting that whilst young girls committing sex offences is very understudied, according to Finekelhor et al. (2009) and Roe-Sepowitz and Krysik (2008), they do make up between 5% and 10% of the sexually aggressive juvenile offenders.

Conclusion

Whilst when it comes to these more information-heavy chapters so I can't add too many of my own thoughts and feelings, I have to say that this is still heartbreaking. Sexual violence in any form, whether you are an adult, a child, a male, female and regardless of your background is wrong on every single level. Sexual violence should not exist and it needs to be stamped out more than ever.

As a result, as much as it makes me uncomfortable and feel physically sick that we need to learn about young girls committing sexual offences, this is important. This is critical to research and study so we know the factors that make this possible in the first place. This will allow us to target those criminogenic factors so we might be able to prevent more young girls developing into sex offenders, and this will help us figure out possible interventions, so no one, absolutely no one ever reoffends sexually.

You might call this vain hope or idealism. Maybe you're right but just like how we have treatments for a wide range of offenders with varying effectiveness. I think and I hope it is possible to prevent sexual violence because it is the worst thing a person could ever experience.

So that is why research is important and beyond critical.

Even if it means we have to learn and hear about the unfortunate reality that some young girls become juvenile sex offenders.

WHAT HAPPENS WHEN FEMALE PREDATORS SEXUALLY ASSAULT MALE VICTIMS?

Following on from the last chapter, we need to learn about female sexual predators in more depth. Since whenever we typically think about sexual violence, myself included, we always think of men as the predators and women are the victims or survivors of their sexual violence. Nonetheless, female sexual predators exist and female predators actively conduct sexual assault against children and adults of all genders.

Therefore, in this chapter, you'll learn about the impact of female predators on male victims and what happens when females sexually assault men. We'll cover what happens to male victims, the mental health implications and most importantly, how do we get justice for male survivors just like female survivors. Whilst the criminal justice system is far from perfect for any sexual assault survivor, becoming aware of how to help survivors is the first step towards ending sexual violence for good.

Introduction To Female Sexual Predators and Male Victims

A multitude of research studies show that female sexual predators are more common than we once thought. For example, a 2014 study referred to in Stemple and Meyer (2017) found that men are sexually victimised more often than previously believed and women were perpetrators of these sex crimes more commonly than previously believed as well. As well as surveys were analysed by the Bureau of Justice Statistics and the Centre For Disease Control and they found that over a one-year period, men and women were just as likely to experience non-consensual sex (also known as sexual violence) as each other and most of the male victims reported being victimised by female perpetrators.

In addition, Stemple and Meter found that 79% of men forced to penetrate someone, which most researchers include as rape, reported being victimised by female perpetrators. Similarly, most men who experienced unwanted sexual contact and sexual coercion were assaulted by women.

Moreover, the researchers found that gender-based stereotypes, like the idea that males are sex hungry beasts with a massive sexual appetite, can prevent people from effectively responding to male victims. Then this has another negative impact because male victims are aware of the common misconception that apparently men cannot be victims and females cannot be predators. This only adds to the feelings of shame and negative mental health outcomes experienced by male victims so they're less likely to report their victimisation and unfortunately the traumatic experience of male victims is often minimised because others believe they don't suffer any harm. All because they're men.

Research supports this heartbreaking truth time and time again.

This means whenever female predators sexually assault men, male victims unfortunately feel unable to come forward because of the cultural misconceptions about what a sexual assault victim and perpetrator look like.

What Is Sexual Coercion And The Perceived Responsibility of Male Victims?

It should come as no surprise to any of us that regardless of a person's gender, any form of sex that is not consensual is sexual assault. There are no exceptions to this fact whatsoever. Even though when it comes to dealing with sexual assault committed by females, this isn't how people perceive sexual assault cases where women are the attackers and the victim is a male.

As a result of gender stereotypes impacting how people perceive the idea of sexual coercion. This form of coercion is where someone pressures or persuades an unwilling sexual partner to engage in sexual activity. Therefore, when men are sexually coerced into performing sexual acts against their will by a female perpetrator then people tend to see the men as more responsible than when females are the sexual assault victims.

Personally, I find this flat out disgusting because I don't care who the sexual assault survivor is, they are not responsible for what happened to them. It is not their fault and it is outrageous that anyone would blame or believe the survivor is responsible, regardless of their gender. All survivors of sexual violence deserve to be treated equally.

In addition, Katz et al. (2007) studied people's perceptions of victims and their responsibility for their sexual assault when exposed to sexual coercion. The researchers found that after participants were exposed to fictional sexual coercion scenarios, the participants perceived verbal coercion as more controllable than rape in scenarios with a male dating partner, so they perceived the male victims as more responsible for their sexual assault. Then as you would expect when it was a male perpetrator and female victim, the participants believed the opposite.

In other words, the participants believed that female-to-male sexual coercion was more controllable than male-to-female coercion so the participants always showed that males, whether they're victims or perpetrators, had more control over their actions than the female perpetrator who verbally coerced them into sexual activities.

On the whole, with there being such a stark gender bias showing that male victims are seen to be more responsible for their sexual assault than the females actually coercing them. It is a very unfortunate finding that male victimisation is taken less seriously. Also, in the *Why An Erection Isn't Consent* chapter, I explained why this isn't about detracting from female victims and I explain how this gender bias negatively impacts female survivors too.

Why Are Male Sexual Assault Victims Taken Less Seriously?

Building upon the last section, Huitema et al. (2016) conducted a study to see how sexual coercion was perceived by people depending on whether the fictional scenario involved a man coercing a woman or vice versa. The results showed that when men are sexually coerced into sexual activity with a woman, this isn't taken seriously compared to women being sexually coerced by a man. This finding was strongest for the Dutch men in the research sample, so this could suggest that men just cannot understand or see how other men could possibly be sexual assault victims. Especially by a woman.

Therefore, this goes to show the extreme power and just how embedded these "victim" and gender myths are in our society. It shows how women are seen as weak, easy victims that could never hope to attack or beat a man in anything. That is a complete and utter myth because I know plenty of strong women that can hold their own. Yet it is only when we start looking at sexual violence that we start to realise just how damaging these myths truly are.

Conclusion

After investigating what happens when female perpetrators sexually assault male victims, we've learnt a lot about sexual coercion, the damaging impact of gender stereotypes on victims and how men feel unable to come forward and report their assault as a result. You can probably guess that this is an urgent problem we need to solve and there are ways to help this issue.

Research shows that as a society, we need to accept and acknowledge that men can be and are victims of sexual assault as well. And we need to acknowledge that female perpetrators of sexual violence are subject to the exact same laws and punishment as males. No one is above the law regardless of their gender.

In addition, as time goes on and more men start feeling comfortable enough to report their sexual assault then we'll be able to understand the scope of the issue and ensure that justice is done.

As I mentioned before, acknowledging how men can be victims of sexual assault is never about detracting from the awful experiences of female victims. It seriously isn't. Instead highlighting male sexual assault is about highlighting that men can be victims as well and the gender stereotype that women are helpless victims is another unhelpful and undeserved gender stereotype. In turn, this only reinforces silly ideas about what it means to be a man or woman and even more outrageous ideas that male victims are "failed" men.

No one deserves to be a victim of sexual violence.

And it is only after we ensure that both male and female victims can speak up, get the support they need and ensure everyone has an equal chance of justice can we even begin to believe we're making good progress towards ending sexual violence.

It is possible but there is a long way to go.

PART FOUR: THERAPIES

WHAT IS EMDR?

To kick off the next section of the book that focuses on introducing you to different types of psychotherapies that might be useful when supporting with sexual assault survivors, I wanted to focus on a fun one. Since EMDR stands for Eye Movement Desensitization Reprocessing and this is a type of psychotherapy that I've become more aware of in recent months. Since a close friend of mine mentioned they had EMDR and a good podcast I listened to mentioned that she went for EMDR too.

And before this chapter, I knew it was an effective psychotherapy but I had no idea what it actually involved and I knew there was a sort of stigma around it within the psychology community. Therefore, in this clinical psychology chapter, you'll learn what is EMDR, how does EMDR work and much more. If you enjoy learning about mental health, clinical psychology and psychotherapy then you will love today's chapter.

<u>What Is EMDR?</u>

EMDR isn't really a psychotherapy in and of itself, it is more of a psychotherapy technique that is designed to relieve the psychological distress associated with a client's disturbing memories. As well as it involves a client recalling a specific negative experience while following a side-to-side visual stimulus delivered by the therapist. A client needs to do this in EMDR because the lateral eye movements that following this stimulus causes that are thought to help reduce the emotional impact of this memory. This helps the negative experience to become easier to discuss with the therapist as the memory is effectively stripped of its power to trigger avoidance behaviours and anxiety within a client.

In addition, there have been a lot of empirical studies that show that EMDR works for some clients, but it is very, very controversial. There are a lot of reasons for this but one of the main reasons is that we just don't know how it works. There are a lot of theories that try to explain how EMDR works but there isn't a universally accepted theory. Another reason why EMDR is controversial is because there isn't much clear evidence that EMDR is better than other forms of exposure therapy. Since EMDR and other exposure therapies are basically the same in terms of you have a client recalling a traumatic memory in the safe environment provided by a therapist. As well as the client repeatedly talks about the event in this safe context and this leads to a decrease in avoidance and fear responses.

Personally, when I first learnt those two reasons I wasn't very surprised, because I completely understand that EMDR is basically the same as other exposure therapies. They all follow the same principles and whilst it is good that we know EMDR works for some clients. Clinical psychology is a science after all, and we need to understand how and why EMDR works. Not just as a whole but why does it work for some clients and not others, and once we understand what are the important elements or components of EMDR then we might be able to distil EMDR and combine it with other treatment models. There is a lot of work to do in EMDR research as you'll see later on.

How Does EMDR Work?

Whilst as I mentioned a moment ago, there are no widely accepted theories that explain EMDR, but I'm going to tell you about some of the theories. None of these are conclusive and these are all just theories, but I think having at least a basic understanding of how EMDR *might* work is more important here.

Therefore, EMDR is meant to be based on the so-called Adaptive Information Model and this is meant to target the way a distressing memory is stored in the brain. The idea behind this is that the experience is distressing because of how it's stored in the brain so if you can change how the memory is stored then you can change how distressing it is to a client. As well as when these memories are triggered in the present they contain all the same emotions, physical feelings and thoughts as the experience did in the past. All because the experience wasn't processed properly in the first place.

I'm just going to say upright that I find this theory very suspect already, but let's continue.

Interestingly, there have been studies that have called into question whether the eye movement part of EMDR is even needed. Due to these studies suggest that EMDR actually works because the desensitisation involves recalling, confronting as well as reprocessing the aversive memories under the careful supervision of a therapist.

And you know what that's called. It's called exposure therapy.

On the other hand, there have been some new theories suggested in recent years to explain how EMDR works. For example, Andrew Huberman of Standford University supports the eye movements as an important part of EMDR because he proposes that the movements seen in EMDR copy optic flow and this decreases a person's fear system as well as temporarily decreases the sense of threat that the traumatic memory holds.

Additionally, the eyes are a part of the central nervous system and research Huberman conducted shows when the eyes are relaxed, a client adjusts their inner state to match. This is supported by additional research, including a study done by Dutch researchers and published in the *Journal Of Neuroscience*.

Also, I want to add in this quote from Huberman that further supports his theory: "It makes sense from an evolutionary perspective. We've always been confronted with threats—animal threats, interpersonal threats. Forward movement is the way you suppress the fear response." Then when it comes to the visual system, he says, "is a steering wheel and brake of the nervous system. The brain will follow the visual system in many ways."

Overall, I think this theory makes a lot of sense because it helps to explain how EMDR works, the biological mechanisms behind it and how this has a knock-on effect for our mental processes. However, there are still other questions that have yet to be answered about EMDR's workings. For example, the interpatient factors that explain the variance in why it works for some and not others, and this almost sounds a little reductionist in a sense. Since this theory only focuses on the biological aspects of the eye movements. It fails to explain how the social factors, like being in a safe environment of the therapist's office, helps to explain how works.

<u>When Is EMDR Used?</u>

Whilst originally this therapy technique was developed to treat PTSD, it's now used for a wide range of conditions. For instance, anxiety disorders, depression, eating disorders, some personality disorders, obsessive-compulsive disorders and a few others.

However, it's important to note that for a client to be a good fit for EMDR, they need to be comfortable with some emotional discomfort. Also, they shouldn't be too easily overwhelmed by their feelings and not shut down emotionally when they face discomfort. As well as clients should be able to use their emotional and cognitive resources to help them reprocess their memories.

I will just add there that I don't think a single one of those points is actually unique to EMDR. I think they are basic assumptions of all clients going in psychotherapy because you can't do therapy successfully if you aren't willing to confront and process the past and you need to have a capacity for change too.

<u>What Should Someone Expect In EMDR?</u>

Whilst some clients might need fewer sessions, a typical course of EMDR lasts between 6 and 12 sessions that are delivered once or twice a week. With some studies showing that reprocessing a single distressing memory can be processed within three sessions.

Then after the client and therapist talk about the client's history and the therapist explains the procedure, the two work together to decide on which past experiences will be the subject of the treatment. Afterwards, the therapist activates the distressing memory by asking the patient to visualise and/ or experience their thoughts.

I find that term "activate" quite funny because it makes it sound like the therapist has a switch into a client's head.

Anyway, once the memory is activated, the therapist assesses the level of negative thoughts and feelings within the client about the event, and the positive beliefs the client wants to increase about themselves. Next, the therapist administers the bilateral visual stimulation.

In addition, the client can almost always expect to experience some physical and emotional discomfort here because they'll be recalling the distressing memories. Then as the procedure continues, new thoughts and feelings will emerge and these are discussed. Also, the therapist samples the nature and level of the client's emotional and cognitive distress as well as any physical distress.

Finally, the session ends when the client feels manageably calm and the therapist gives them instructions about how to handle any disturbing thoughts and feelings in-between their sessions. As well as in the following sessions, these begin with an assessment of the memories that might have emerged since the last treatment.

Conclusion

I have to admit that this has been a rather fun chapter for me because we've looked at how EMDR works, what EMDR is, what to expect in EMDR and more. And whilst I have made fun of EMDR in at least two sections of this chapter, I think this therapy does have a place in clinical psychology. Of course, more research has to be done so we can actually understand how it works because psychology is a science and we have to use empirical tools in therapy. Also, there needs to be more research into how EMDR is different to other forms of exposure therapy because I am personally not convinced it's as different as it claims to be.

However, at the end of the day, there will be clients that need EMDR to improve their lives, decrease their psychological distress and function clinically normally. My friend's proof of that and so is the podcast host that I listen to from time to time. I think as long as we admit the limitations, we try to fix the limitations and we don't overstate how effective or great EMDR is compared to other therapies. Then this is a good compromise because EMDR is good for some people, but it isn't for others. And even for the people who it works for, we just don't know why.

And that little bit of controversy is why psychotherapy can be important, fascinating and seriously fun to think about.

WHAT IS PERSON-CENTRED THERAPY?

As a rape survivor and as I've mentioned in previous chapters, I'm on a waiting list for specialist rape counselling that will probably draw on a lot of humanistic and personal approaches towards mental health.

Therefore, you'll definitely get a greater sense of this approach to mental health in the chapter itself, but this type of therapy is very personal to me, I know from personal experience that it can be extremely helpful and life changing. Also, I think when we consider combining approaches to mental health, the personal or humanistic approach works wonderfully with a lot of other approaches.

This is going to be a fascinating chapter for sure.

***

Interestingly enough in August 2023, I started four weeks of psychotherapy to help me deal with trauma and abuse from my past and I have only recently learnt that the counsellor (or as I call her 'therapist') uses a person-centred approach to therapy. I have only just heard about this approach to mental health to be honest, so I want to explore it further. Since I found it rather useful. Therefore, in this clinical psychology podcast episode, we'll explore what is person-centred therapy, how does it work, what to expect and so much more. If you're interested in psychological therapy, mental health and clinical psychology, then you'll be in for a treat.

<u>What Is Person-Centred Psychotherapy?</u>

Person-centred therapy is a client-based psychotherapy that uses a non-authoritative approach to mental health difficulties that allows clients to take the lead in therapy sessions so they can discover their own solutions to their difficulties.

This particular approach to mental health was started by Carl Rodgers because he believed that every person is unique (which we are) and everyone's view of their world should be trusted. In other words, he believed we should never ever doubt our clients and how they describe the world, because to them that actually is how the world works.

Personally, I do understand this because everyone interprets different situations and events differently depending on their past experiences. This is basically what the cognitive approach is saying just with different words. Due to the cognitive approach believes it isn't the events themselves that cause mental health difficulties it is our beliefs and interpretations of them that lead to difficulties.

Furthermore, Carl Rodgers firmly believed in self-actualisation. This is the idea that all of us have the solutions, knowledge and power to make the changes we need in our lives. As well as this therapy is non-directive so the therapist doesn't take the lead and instead follows the client and doesn't engage in any direct discussions.

However, something I am seriously starting to notice is that all these different approaches to mental health are basically just rehashing what another has already said. For example, every single psychotherapy I can think of is about self-actualisation and making sure the client realises *they* can make the changes needed in their lives using the tools and guidance the therapist gives them. Yet only they can make the changes for themselves.

This actually isn't unique to any approach.

Moreover, I will admit that the non-directive part of person-centred therapy does require a bit of getting used to. Since I love cognitive-behavioural therapy, which is very structured, I had to let go of the idea that she was going to lead, and I had to lead instead. Thankfully I have so much mental health difficulties tied up in different parts of abuse and trauma that I have more than enough things to talk about, but it still did require a bit of relearning.

Anyway, during person-centred therapy, a therapist isn't the lead as we know. Instead the therapist is known as a "compassionate facilitator" because they listen to the client without judgement, they acknowledge the client's experiences without changing or moving the conversation and they are there to support the client without interrupting them. Or impacting on their own process of self-discovery.

In my experience that acknowledgement and "validation" in a fashion is extremely important and it does feel great to have someone else call your abuse and trauma, well, abuse and trauma. And I will happily admit that the process of self-discovery it is scary how much you can actually discover about yourself when we free yourself up. Like I literally cannot share everything I've discovered about myself on the podcast because that's like another twenty episodes in itself, but it's a lot of fun. And honestly, as much as really don't want to discover anything more about myself, I know I will and that's okay.

Overall, the reason why the therapist doesn't interrupt this process of self-discovery and lead is because it is down to the client to uncover what hurts them and what they need to do to repair it. That is a very powerful realisation when it hits you.

How Does Person-Centred Therapy Work?

The entire point of person-centred therapy is to step away from the more traditional psychotherapeutic models where the therapist is the leader and expert and instead the client is the expert in themselves. Again that is something I have mentioned a thousand times before on the podcast and in books.

Therefore, person-centred therapy has three central tenets that allow the therapy to be successful. Firstly, the therapist has an unconditional positive regard so they are empathetic and non-judgemental. Due to the therapist accepts what the client is saying as true and they want to convey to the client that they are understood, confident, trusted and they are valued. As well as the client is free to make their own better choices and decisions in their life.

This tenet I think is very powerful and helpful because I have tried to talk about my past before and there are only ever three outcomes really. None of which I blame on people. Firstly, they call me a liar because they don't want to hear it because what I have to say is too painful. Secondly, they are sorry for what's happening but they can ultimately never ever understand it at a deep level. Thirdly, they understand it but the problem with that is it is common trauma and abuse so they aren't comfortable listening to it and because of emotional dependency and other difficulties, I burn them out too much.

That's why having a therapist that can just listen to me talk is extremely helpful.

Secondly, there is congruence or genuineness so the therapists have no air of authority to them. Instead they present themselves as an accessible and their true self that clients can see is honest and transparent. And this is definitely true, I might be autistic so reading and understanding people is always going to be hard but I know my therapist is very honest and transparent.

Finally, there is empathetic understanding where the therapist wholeheartedly accepts and understands the client's views as well as feelings in a way that can be helpful in reshaping the client's sense of their experiences.

Normally, I think this final part is done by "accident" in a fashion because just by talking and listening and offering up good psychological insights. My therapist has helped me to realise a lot about myself and how I view my Self and my past and my relationships.

On the whole, in this therapy, whenever the therapy is working well the clients feel they are better understood in these sessions and this leads them to feel better understood in other areas of their lives as well. This does have research support, especially whenever a client identifies the unconditional positive regard in their therapist there is an increased chance in positive outcomes. Since the therapeutic relationship between the therapist and the client is a type of therapy in itself.

When Is Person-Centred Therapy Used?

A person-centred therapeutic approach might be used with groups and individuals, be it adults or adolescents in a short- or long-term fashion. The people that tend to take this approach and benefit from it are people that want more self-confidence, a stronger sense of identity and authenticity, increased trust in their own relationships and more success in establishing (and maintaining I will add) their interpersonal relationships.

In addition, like other approaches to mental health, the person-centred approach doesn't have to be used only because it can be combined with other therapies to treat depression, grief and anxiety. Although, it can also be treated to treat trauma, family stressors, abuse and so much more.

And because this is a client-led psychotherapy, it is the more motivated and determined clients that tend to do better and be more successful at the therapy.

Personally, even though I didn't choose person-centred therapy, I am more than glad I ended up with it. Since I've only had two sessions so far and I have found it so useful in understanding my own relationships, my identity, self-confidence and it has basically taught me to let go of what other people want from me and their expectations. I talk about this a little more next week in the Emotional Dependency and Locus of Evaluation podcast episode but person-centred therapy has been immensely useful to me.

What To Expect In Person-Centred Therapy?

Even though I've mentioned my own experience through the podcast episode, the only other thing I want to say is that the therapist might repeat your words. This isn't them trying to be annoying or anything, it is simply them trying to understand what happened, what you mean and how you feel. It is them trying to draw out a little more information from you too.

Of course, they might have misunderstood you and I think that's happened once or twice with myself. One time was when, because I laugh as a coping mechanism when I have seriously screwed up, she didn't understand why I was laughing about something extremely serious (well at least it was to me). This allowed me to rephrase my response in a way both of us could understand.

Moreover, there might be moments of silence in the therapy and this can be good because it allows us to process our thoughts and realisations. Since person-centred therapy is all about self-acceptance and self-discovery. Or if you're like me and you have so many things to unpack, you basically don't stop talking for the entire session.

Then you end up at the end of the therapy feeling a little overwhelmed because of everything you've learnt, discussed and it can take a little while for you to realise what the takeaways are for you.

Conclusion

Overall, person-centred therapy is all about allowing a client to talk, explore their difficulties and find the solutions for themselves. This is extremely helpful in my experience but then again I've learnt recently I have very high emotional intelligence, which is funny because I used to be extremely bad at it.

A Person-centred Therapist should always have the ability to be calm in sessions and they need to let a client verbalise their frustrations and disappointments too. Since this can all help a client to gain insights into what's hurting them and most importantly how they can move forwards.

Personally, I am willing to say that person-centred therapy has already changed my life for the better and I still have two more sessions, so I am actually really excited to see what will happen, what will I learn and most importantly how else can *I* change my life for the better.

Therapy can be seriously fun, interesting and life changing if you want it to be.

WHAT IS ACCEPTANCE AND COMMITMENT THERAPY?

Whilst our next therapy isn't one that is normally given as a treatment option for trauma survivors, I wanted to talk about Acceptance Commitment therapy (ACT) because there are a lot of useful ideas in the therapy that you can use in everyday life in addition to therapeutic settings. Also, I hear a lot of talk about ACT and it's nice to actually learn what it is, how it works and just have a more solid understanding of ACT.

Since sometimes I believe we all talk about it but no one actually sits us down as aspiring clinical psychologists and explains exactly what it is.

I hope this next chapter fills that gap.

***

Within clinical psychology, there are a few types of psychological therapy that you hear about time and time again. These include cognitive behavioural therapy, interpersonal psychotherapy amongst others. As well as I often hear about Acceptance and Commitment Therapy but because this therapy isn't really available on the National Health Service in the UK, we don't really learn about it in any great depth. Therefore, in this psychology podcast episode, you'll learn what is Acceptance and Commitment Therapy, how it works, when it used and more. If you enjoy learning about psychotherapy, clinical psychology and mental health then you'll love today's episode.

Note: as always absolutely nothing on this podcast is ever any sort of professional, medical or official advice.

What Is Acceptance and Commitment Therapy?

Acceptance and Commitment Therapy is a therapy stemming from the more traditional behavioural and cognitive behavioural therapies. Since Acceptance and Commitment Therapy is an action-oriented approach to therapy because it gets the client to stop denying, struggling and avoiding their inner emotions. Instead, the therapy gets the client to accept their deeper feelings as appropriate responses in a given situation that they shouldn't prevent themselves from experiencing, because trying to stop these responses stops the client from moving forward in their lives.

As a result, Acceptance and Commitment Therapy gives the client an understanding that they need to begin accepting their mental health difficulties and commit to making the needed changes in their behaviour regardless of what's going on in their lives and how they feel about it.

Personally, I really like the sound of Acceptance and Commitment Therapy because I think all therapies need a touch of this to be successful. Since if we take Cognitive Behavioural Therapy for example, we need a client to accept that their depression, anxiety, whatever can't actually be cured. But if they commit to the therapy and have a capacity for change then they can develop adaptive coping mechanisms that will decrease their psychological distress and improve their lives.

So I could argue that the idea of acceptance and commitment is an undertone in all psychotherapies, but this therapy just focuses on it a lot more.

In addition, in the 1980s psychologist Steven C. Hayes from the University of Nevada developed Acceptance and Commitment Therapy based on his own experiences. Since the professor had a history of panic attacks and in the end, he promised himself he would no longer run from himself. Instead he would accept himself and his experiences.

How Does Acceptance and Commitment Therapy Work?

From a theoretical perspective, Acceptance and Commitment Therapy works because it is counterproductive for a client to try and control their painful emotions and their psychological experiences. As well as it is the suppression of these feelings that leads the client to experience even more distress.

As a result, Acceptance and Commitment Therapy proposes that a client needs to develop the belief system that there are valid alternatives trying to change the way they think. Including mindful behaviour, commitment to action and attention to personal values. This leads to taking steps to change their behaviour to decrease their psychological distress, but the client is still learning to accept their psychological experiences at the same level.

This eventually leads to a client changing their emotional states and attitudes.

What Should A Client Expect From Acceptance and Commitment Therapy?

Building upon this further, when a client works with a therapist for this type of psychotherapy, the client will learn to listen to their own self-talk and this includes how they talk about problematic relationships, traumatic events, physical limitations and other challenges. Then it is up to the client to decide if a problem requires any immediate action or a change, or if the problem can be accepted for what it is whilst the client learns to make the behavioural changes to modify the situation.

To do this a client might have to look at their past to see what has or hasn't worked for them, and the therapist can help the client stop repeating the same thought patterns and behaviours as the past so they don't cause more problems in the future.

Additionally, after a client has faced and accepted their current challenges, the client can make a commitment to stop fighting the past and their emotions. Instead, the client can start practicing more optimistic as well as confident behaviour based on their personal values and goals.

Ultimately, Acceptance and Commitment Therapy aims to develop a person's psychological flexibility. A concept that encompasses emotional openness and the ability to adapt their behaviours and thoughts to better align with the client's own values and goals.

Personally, I really like the idea of psychological flexibility and a lot of what Acceptance and Commitment Therapy aims to do. Since being flexible in the way we think and feel in a given situation is critical to our mental health. We can't be strict and inflexible so we only feel a certain way in a given situation because this will make us feel awful and experience a lot of distress. Yet if start to explore other ways that make us feel slightly better then that will definitely improve our mental health over time if we accept and commit to changing our thoughts and behaviour.

A little personal example here is actually rather funny in a way, because I have a friend that I really want to date and everything, I asked them out and they said no. Fair enough, and we're both really open about the fact that I like them. Yet whenever they talked about them dating or seeing someone, I used to feel like utter rubbish and I had some very bad thoughts towards myself but that wasn't healthy. So over time I taught myself to think in other ways, accept how bad I felt and I have committed to take steps to change certain aspects of my life. Like, trying to meet other people. I know this isn't like professional Acceptance and Commitment Therapy at all, but what I'm trying to say is that the concepts are useful even outside of therapy.

Moreover, there are six core processes used in Acceptance and Commitment Therapy to promote psychological flexibility:

- Acceptance

This core process involves the client acknowledging as well as embracing the full range of their emotions and thoughts rather than trying to deny, change or avoid them.

- Being Present

This core process comes from mindfulness in the sense that a client should try to be mindful in the present moment, so the client can observe their feelings and thoughts without judging them or trying to change them. instead, the client should experience events clearly and this can directly help them to promote behavioural change.

- Cognitive Defusion

Thirdly, cognitive defusion involves a client distancing themselves from their distressing thoughts and feelings as well as changing the way they react to them. This decreases their harmful effects. Also, some ways how this defusion is done include singing the thought, labelling the automatic response the client has to them and observing a thought without judgment.

- Values

Fourthly, values are important for developing psychological flexibility because this encompasses a client choosing personal values in different domains of their life, and trying as hard as they can to live according to these principles.

Now this is interesting because this is in direct contrast to when a client's actions are being driven by their desire to avoid distress or to adhere to other people's expectations.

- Self As Context

Penultimately, self as context is the idea that expands the notion of self and identity because it proposes that people are more than their feelings, experiences and thoughts.

Something I completely agree with, because it is true. All of us are way more than our past, our thoughts and how we feel in a given moment.

- Committed Action

Finally, committed action involves a client taking concrete steps to incorporate changes into their lives that will align with their values and lead to positive changes. For example, the client could do some goal setting, skill development or expose themselves to difficult thoughts and experiences.

When Is Acceptance and Commitment Therapy Used?

Lastly, Acceptance and Commitment Therapy is a useful therapy for a wide range of mental as well as physical conditions. For instance, depression, anxiety disorders, psychosis, eating disorders, workplace stress, chronic pain, substance use disorders and obsessive-compulsive disorder.

Conclusion

I have to admit that I have rather liked this podcast episode because I have heard a lot about Acceptance and Commitment Therapy over the years through my lectures, but it is only now that I have learnt about the therapy in any great depth. And I know I say this in a lot of these therapy-based podcast episodes, but I think a lot of these concepts can be transplanted into other therapies too.

For instance, the idea of getting your client to accept that their experiences aren't something to be avoided, cured or ashamed of. That is nothing new and I know that is a large part of Cognitive Behavioural Therapy, which is where this therapy stems from in the first place.

Equally, getting a client to commit to taking actionable and concrete steps to improve their lives. Again, I don't exactly think that is anything new because surely that is the same as a client having a capacity to change.

Therefore, if you like the idea of acceptance and commitment but you don't practice Acceptance and Commitment Therapy, then maybe think about incorporating those concepts into your own practice in the future. It's just an idea but I know it's something interesting to think about.

What do you think?

WHAT IS TRAUMA-FOCUSED COGNITIVE BEHAVIOURAL THERAPY?

Considering I flat out love trauma topics within clinical psychology and I really enjoy learning about Cognitive Behavioural Therapy, I'm so excited to give you a chapter that combines both my major areas of interest.

This is a brilliant chapter to have in a book about sexual violence because I know first hand that rape can heavily impact your cognitive processes and it can teach you a lot of "safety" behaviours that only harm you in the long run.

This means CBT is a very good therapy for dealing with the cognitive and behavioural aspects following an experience of sexual violence.

I enjoy writing this chapter a lot so I hope you enjoy reading it as much as I did writing the chapter.

***

One of my many interests within clinical psychology is certainly trauma. Partly this is because of my own various experiences and I know first-hand how damaging it can be to our mental health. Therefore, I suppose my interest is me reminding myself that there is hope and there is a wide range of therapies to help people who have been through trauma. That's why in this podcast episode we get to learn about the combination of two of my major interests. Trauma-Focused Cognitive Behavioural Therapy combines my interest in trauma and Cognitive Behaviour Therapy. Hence, in this psychology podcast episode, you'll get to learn about what Is Trauma-Focused Cognitive Behavioural Therapy, how does it work, when is it used and more. If you're interested in mental health, trauma and psychological interventions then this is a great episode for you.

What Is Trauma-Focused Cognitive Behavioural Therapy?

This form of psychotherapy tends to be shortened to FT-CBT, and it is a therapy to support children, teenagers and families suffering from the effects of early trauma. Therefore, Trauma-Focused Cognitive Behavioural Therapy is very attuned for helping the specific and rather unique difficulties that children with PTSD and mood disorders experience. These mental health difficulties and conditions can be a result of sexual or physical abuse or violence, or grief.

Also, because the client in Trauma-Focused Cognitive Behavioural Therapy is normally a child, this therapy is rather unique in the sense that non-offending parents and other caregivers can brought into the therapy and it incorporates a lot of principles from family therapy.

This makes the therapy rather interesting I think because one, it is relatively uncommon to bring caregivers into a therapy setting, so it's interesting to know how this works. Two, I find it interesting personally because this is actually the second time I've tried to write this post. I couldn't even start writing the first time round because this therapy hit me in a few unexpected ways.

Yet the three main ways were, I had tried to write it originally less than a week after being sexually assaulted so that was a mistake. I might have been grieving because I would have loved to have had an option like this as a child myself. Thirdly, I hate the idea of another child going through trauma because I don't wish it on anyone.

So I just wanted to share that with you so you know my personal position on this therapy.

Moreover, Trauma-Focused Cognitive Behavioural Therapy was developed in the 1990s by a psychiatrist called Judith Cohen alongside psychologists Anthony Mannarino and Esther Deblinger. Originally, the therapy was designed to better help sexually abused children as well as adolescents. Then over the years, the therapy has expanded to include services for young people who have experienced over forms of severe abuse and trauma.

How Does Trauma-Focused Cognitive Behavioural Therapy Work?

I talk more about how the family therapy and the cognitive behavioural therapy aspects help Trauma-Focused Cognitive Behavioural Therapy to be the effective therapy it is towards the end of the podcast episode. Yet TF-CBT combines cognitive-behavioural techniques with trauma-sensitive approaches to help the client process their traumatic experiences, build resilience and develop more adaptive coping mechanisms.

In addition, Trauma-Focused Cognitive Behavioural Therapy is made up of the following five components that help to make it an effective therapy for trauma.

Firstly, there is a heavy focus in the therapy on skills-building. This is where relaxation techniques, emotion regulation strategies and coping skills are taught to the client to help them manage their emotion and any challenging situations.

Secondly, there is cognitive restructuring where the client's maladaptive thoughts, beliefs and behaviours are targeted and replaced to more with realistic and adaptive thinking patterns.

Thirdly, psychoeducation is important in Trauma-Focused Cognitive Behavioural Therapy because clients learn about trauma and its effects on us. This helps the client to understand their reactions and behaviours and this normalises their experiences.

Fourthly, trauma-narrative is another component. In this area of the therapy, clients are guided through the process of sharing and processing their traumatic experience in a safe and supportive environment.

Personally, this is a critically important area of therapeutic work, because when I was talking about my assault with my therapist it was lovely to have a safe space to talk about it. Of course, it was still distressing and really uncomfortable but I couldn't have processed it in another environment where I didn't feel safe and supported. This is why trauma-informed therapists are flat out critical, because they can help clients to feel safe enough to process and share what happened when other people can't.

Finally, gradual exposure is another important area of the therapy. Since this is where clients are gently exposed to trauma reminders in a controlled way to reduce their fear and avoidance.

Whilst I never had Trauma-Focused Cognitive Behavioural Therapy, after my assault, a small part of me did just want to crawl up in bed and never leave the house again. I didn't really want to see my friends, I didn't really want to see my parents and I just wanted to stay in my room because it was safe in there and I controlled it. Yet I knew that wasn't healthy but I did need to start slowly introducing myself back in the world and it's been lovely. And you definitely know what people think of you and how good they are as friends when you tell them you've been assaulted.

Things still pop up when I go out and when I introduce myself to situations, but doing it in a controlled way is very helpful and it minimises the risks.

When Is Trauma-Focused Cognitive Behavioural Therapy Used?

As mentioned earlier, Trauma-Focused Cognitive Behavioural Therapy isn't only for young people who have experienced sexual abuse. Nowadays, it's used for children and adolescents who have experienced a single or repeated incidents of mental, physical or sexual abuse or who young people who have developed post-traumatic symptoms, anxiety or depression.

Nonetheless, Trauma-Focused Cognitive Behavioural Therapy might not be the best option for children and adolescents who do show serious suicidal ideation, substance abuse or behavioural issues. In this case, other forms of psychotherapy might be better for the client, like dialectical behavioural therapy, as an initial intervention and then a trauma-sensitive approach could be used as a follow-up.

What Can Clients Expect From Trauma-Focused Cognitive Behavioural Therapy?

Trauma-Focused Cognitive Behavioural Therapy is a short-term psychological intervention that typically lasts anywhere from 8 to 25 sessions that can take place in a wide range of settings. For example, the therapy can be done in a group home, a community centre, school, hospital, in-home setting or an outpatient mental health clinic. Also, the therapy takes place with a non-offending caregiver or parent and often the therapy starts with separate therapy sessions for the child and caregiver. Then they advance into joint therapy sessions.

Furthermore, as this is a form of Cognitive Behavioural Therapy, a lot of CBT techniques are used to help modify the unhelpful and distorted thinking and the negative behaviours and reactions the child has because of the trauma. Then the child focuses on learning how to challenge their invasive thoughts of fear and guilt so they can reorganise their thinking in a more adaptive and positive way.

Subsequently, there is a major aspect of family therapy to Trauma-Focused Cognitive Behavioural Therapy too. Since the family therapy aspects focus on the issues the family members might be dealing with, because of the trauma suffered by the child. This is why a range of communication, parenting and stress management skills are taught here.

On the whole, research investigating the effectiveness of Trauma-Focused Cognitive

Behavioural Therapy against other treatment models show that TF-CBT demonstrates significantly greater gains in the well-being for children and their parents.

Personally, this section reminds me about why I love clinical psychology and psychotherapies so much. Since family therapy and cognitive behavioural therapy alone would have only a positive on trauma work to a certain extent, because they focus on different things. But when you combine them and use cognitive-behavioural and family approaches together, now there is where the magic happens and that is where you can start to transform the lives of clients for the better.

I flat out love combining approaches to target a difficulty from different angles.

Conclusion

I have really enjoyed today's episode because I like looking at trauma and I like Cognitive Behavioural Therapy, so combining them into a single episode was great fun for me. And I know within clinical psychology, there is a shift towards becoming more trauma-informed so it is critical that we take every opportunity we can to learn and develop our understanding about trauma.

The last thing we ever want to do as aspiring or qualified clinical psychologists is to add to someone's trauma, because that is wrong, unfair and it isn't what the profession is meant for at all.

I think for me today's episode has reminded me that I like trauma work, therapy and it reminds me a lot about my own life. Sure, this is painful at times, but it is also reassuring. That there is hope for other people, trauma doesn't have to define a person and there is a good chance for recovery given the right tools and therapist.

For you, I hope that you're inspired to learn more about therapy, or at least you're inspired to think about combining and mixing different therapeutic approaches more. Due to the results, when done right and backed up by evidence, can be powerful, supportive and life-changing for our clients.

And as aspiring or qualified psychologists, that truly is all we want for them.

WHAT IS COGNITIVE PROCESSING THERAPY?

Even though I flat out love trauma content because I find it really interesting, engaging and it's nice to understand my experiences through an academic lens, I wanted to return to some trauma-based therapies for this book on sexual violence.

Since whenever you work with someone who's experienced sexual violence, they will need psychological support and because of the sheer traumatic nature of sexual violence, a "tradition" psychological intervention might not be very effective. This is why learning about trauma-based therapies might be a good idea because this might prove very valuable to be aware of.

Also, I like learning about trauma because it's personal, I know how awful it is and I always like hope.

Hope that there is a post-trauma life.

And Cognitive Processing Therapy really helps with sense of hope because it is designed for trauma survivors and you can see how helpful and useful it is with my personal thoughts and examples in the article below.

Please enjoy.

***

It turns out that I have a minor interest in treatments for Post Traumatic Stress Disorder, so when I came across Cognitive Processing Therapy, I realised I had to do a podcast episode on it. Not only because the therapy is a treatment option for PTSD but also because this is a specialised form of Cognitive Behavioural Therapy, an approach that I really enjoy. Therefore, in this clinical psychology podcast episode, you'll find out what is Cognitive Processing Therapy, how does it work and more. If you enjoy learning about PTSD, trauma and different psychological therapies then you'll definitely enjoy today's episode.

What Is Cognitive Processing Therapy?

This form of psychotherapy is a specialised form of Cognitive Behavioural Therapy that is used to treat clients who have experienced traumatic life events. Such as violence, natural disasters, abuse amongst others, as well as it has been found to be an effective treatment for PTSD.

Cognitive Processing Therapy was first developed in the late 1980s and thankfully, it's been found to be a highly effective treatment for PTSD. All the references are at the end of the blog post but a large meta-analysis found that Cognitive Processing Therapy was more effective than a placebo immediately after treatment and at follow-up sessions regardless of the client's age. Also, the same conclusion was drawn whether it was group or individual Cognitive Processing Therapy with the American Psychological Association strongly recommending the therapy too.

In addition, Cognitive Processing Therapy is typically delivered in 12 sessions where the therapist helps a client who has had a traumatic experience evaluate their thoughts surrounding the trauma. Even more so for any self-blaming or maladaptive thoughts that might be maintaining or increasing the severity of the mental health difficulties. Afterwards the client will learn how to challenge these thoughts and take a new perspective when they need to with homework being used like in most other forms of CBT.

Now we'll look at this information in a little more depth in the rest of the episode.

How Does Cognitive Processing Therapy Work?

When we experience significant trauma, we can develop PTSD and this makes a person think about ourselves and our environment differently. At least when compared to before the trauma. For example, before my sexual assault, I was perfectly happy being in my bed or being in certain situations, but after the assault, I seriously wasn't okay in my own bed for a while. Even in different public situations, I was very, very nervous about because my assault changed how I saw certain environments.

Additionally, there tends to be five areas of life that people who have experienced significant trauma notice changes. Firstly, they see changes in safety in terms of the client might doubt their ability to protect themselves, others and their loved ones.

Secondly, the client might see changes in their intimacy, so they might feel incapable of connecting with and being understood by others, let alone accepted. To be honest, even though my abuse was spread over a decade period, this was my main concern and I was so closed off for so long and I refused to have any sort of emotional intimacy simply because I saw that as too dangerous.

Thirdly, the client might lack a sense of control so they don't feel capable or able of controlling their own life or influence the lives of the people they care about.

Fourthly, a client could see changes in trust. This means they might question the judgement and/ or intention of other people and they might doubt their own judgement.

Finally, esteem could be a massive issue because the client could see themselves and other people differently after the trauma and see themselves as "broken" and other people as "evil".

Personally, I'll talk about this briefly but it's that idea that you're "broken" or "messed up" or a "victim" that can be really hard for people who have experienced trauma. And it took me ages and a lot of therapy to start realising that I am a great person that isn't broken and my experiences don't define me.

Also, just today as I write this, I've learnt about the concept of Post-traumatic Growth which is an idea I love. I need to read and research it more but if you enjoy trauma work definitely learn that idea.

Anyway, these thoughts tend to lead our clients towards experiencing negative emotions, like guilt, fear, anger and anxiety and this can stop a person's recovery dead in its tracks. It seriously can. Therefore, Cognitive Processing Therapy can help people by teaching them skills that will help the person challenge their negative thoughts.

Overall, Cognitive Processing Therapy is based on the social cognitive theory of Post-Traumatic Stress Disorder. This theory argues that a client makes the traumatic event a part of their worldview and this is counterproductive and leads to maladaptive beliefs. As a result, Cognitive Processing Therapy focuses on repairing the damage the event has done to someone's beliefs about themselves, others and the world.

Typically, this is done by teaching the client and using specific cognitive restructuring techniques so a client can challenge these thoughts and instead gain a healthier perspective about their trauma in turn.

And before we move onto when is Cognitive Processing Therapy used, one almost heartbreaking example of how trauma impacts beliefs about the world is from my assault. Since about 3 weeks after the assault, my friend was returning from a little trip to celebrate my birthday with me and we were going to go to London, do a virtual reality thing and have dinner out. I remember begging my friend over Whatsapp to bring their brother who studied in London along because I was so scared of for starters being in a one-on-one situation because that was what happened in my assault. As well as I was so scared of the idea of needing a toilet that I really wanted my friend to come with me because I was terrified of something happening in the toilet.

Thankfully, therapy helped me get rid of that fear but it's an example about how trauma can warp a person's beliefs about the world.

When Is Cognitive Processing Therapy Used?

I've already mentioned a few different times in this episode that Cognitive Processing Therapy is an effective treatment for adult clients with PTSD, but it can be useful for people with other mental health conditions too. For example, older adolescents with PTSD is another ideal clinical population for this treatment.

Now, there is some research suggesting Cognitive Processing Therapy might be good for people who experience secondary traumatisation and people who anticipate encountering additional traumatic events. Such as, paramedics, police officers and other emergency workers. There isn't tons of research on this area, but this is thought to be good for these groups because the therapy aims to change the way clients process and interpret their trauma on an ongoing basis.

However, Cognitive Processing Therapy shouldn't be used for people without a diagnosis of PTSD nor if they have literacy difficulties, because this therapy involves written homework. Also, Cognitive Processing Therapy isn't a good idea for people with substance abuse, comorbid bipolar disorder or suicidal ideation. Instead people with these mental health difficulties should go for a research-supported trauma treatment called Prolonged Exposure Therapy.

What Can A Client Expect In Cognitive Processing Therapy?

When a client goes for this type of therapy, they can expect to either have group or individual therapy sessions or even a combination of both for 12 weekly sessions. Each session is about an hour to an hour and a half long depending on the needs of the clients.

The first few sessions are focused on the psychoeducation aspects of trauma so the client learns about PTSD as well as what they can expect to get out of treatment.

Afterwards, in the next few sessions, the therapist and client work together to identify and explore the different ways that the trauma has impacted and changed how the client thinks, feels and behaves. Then the therapist helps to pick out thoughts that act as barriers to the client's recovery.

Next the patient learns a set of strategies to challenge and modify the thoughts that aren't accurate and/ or unhelpful. Then the client practices these strategies with the therapist and with the homework in the form of exercises and worksheets.

And briefly jumping in here, trauma can make you develop some random thoughts that flat out aren't helpful. For example, since my assault, I've struggled with the idea of going out and even though I've managed to force my way through some rather intense episodes of social anxiety. I was talking about some of these thoughts and excuses with my therapist and it was almost funny saying them out loud because of how illogical and unhelpful they were. Of course, I laugh as a coping mechanism and because I've managed to get a little emotional distance from my Event, so I can look at it a little more psychologically. But working with a therapist and exploring these thoughts is absolutely critical for moving forward.

Moreover, the client might be asked to write about the traumatic event including some sensory detail or they might be asked to write more broadly about how their experience made them feel and how they tend to think it happened. Then if the client is having individual therapy then their writing might be read aloud during the session but the same isn't required for group therapy.

I can't even begin to imagine how scary that would be in a group setting.

On the whole, a client can expect Cognitive Processing Therapy to be very emotionally and cognitively intense, even more so when they're talking or writing about the experience itself. Due to clients tend to feel discomfort, and a lot of clients report that this discomfort was brief and the benefits gained from the therapy definitely outweigh the discomfort after completing the full course of therapy.

Again, I know I've never had Cognitive Processing Therapy but I like adding in some paragraphs here and there because I think it helps to bring the material alive. I had a therapy session yesterday related to my assault and I've been for therapy for other trauma before. But because my assault was more recent and acute, I was surprised at how draining it was emotionally. I normally have to do other stuff for about 30 minutes when I get home because I cannot be productive straight away after therapy.

This time it took a good two hours before I even thought about being productive, but I did feel a lot better afterwards.

Conclusion

I think I'll always have a soft spot for people with PTSD and other people that go through trauma. Maybe I feel a certain kinship, maybe I feel like I understand them a little better and maybe I just want them to be okay whatever happens. Personally, I think it's a mixture of all three.

Therefore, I really like Cognitive Processing Therapy because I've read a lot of psychology textbooks in my time and sometimes there is a sense of hopelessness and a lack of effective treatment options for people with PTSD. So I'm happy and grateful that there is an option for people with PTSD and other traumatic experiences so they can get support to improve their lives, decrease their psychological distress and have their lives effectively given back to them.

And that's what I love about our profession and I want to be a clinical psychologist in the future. We can help people to take back control of their lives, we help them feel better and to help them realise they can get past their trauma no matter how bad it seems.

Having the ability to do that is special and that's why I'll always defend, advocate and encourage people to join or take an interest in clinical psychology. Because you never truly know what amazing things you can do until they happen.

PART FIVE: WRAP UP

HOW DO WE TAKE ACTION TO END SEXUAL VIOLENCE?

For our final chapter, I want to focus on how do we end sexual violence once and for all, because as much as I hope the information in this book is interesting, useful and insightful. I truly wished that this book wasn't needed in the first place and ultimately that is what we should be focusing on. We always need to heal and help sexual assault survivors, but we need to make sure there are no more people experiencing this awful event.

There, over the years, we've spoken a lot about sexual violence and its devastating impact on the lives and mental health of survivors. I've tried to use my podcast and this book as a tool for increased awareness so we can all be more informed about the truth behind sexual violence, but that isn't enough because taking action against sexual violence can seem daunting.

As a result, in this chapter, you'll learn how we can move from sexual violence awareness into taking action to end sexual violence once and for all. If you enjoy learning about criminal psychology, clinical psychology and sexual violence then you'll find this chapter interesting.

Why Is Sexual Violence Awareness Not Enough?

There are a lot of different campaigns and efforts to try and increase awareness of sexual violence and its devastating impacts. For example, February is Teen Dating Violence Awareness and Prevention Month and April is sexual assault awareness month. As well as these awareness campaigns are effective in decreasing the taboo and vow of silence that society has created for itself around sexual violence, because it enables survivors to talk openly about their experiences. This leads to a decrease in alienation and an increase in mental health and getting support.

However, the real point of these awareness campaigns is to bring about lasting change, and awareness of sexual violence and its devastating impacts is not enough to help survivors. Since sexual violence against people of all genders is still extremely common across society and there are still a lot of myths, misconceptions and stigma attached to sexual violence that stop people from getting the support they need.

Overall, awareness isn't enough because it isn't enough to bring about the action needed to end sexual violence. A massive problem that directly and/ or indirectly affects all of us through its impacts on education, healthcare and legal systems. And it is these direct and indirect effects that mean it is in all of our interests to end sexual violence forever. Just think about it this way, if healthcare systems didn't have to support sexual violence survivors because no one experienced it anymore then more money, staff and resources could be put into cancer patients for example and so on.

Everyone benefits if sexual violence is stomped out forever.

How Do We Take Action To End Sexual Violence?

Now we'll look at the three different ways how we can turn awareness into action.

You Need To Learn About Sexual Violence And Share It With Others

I know I'm preaching to the converted here but if we're going to end sexual violence then you need to learn about it, what it is and the truth behind sexual violence. In other words, you need to overcome all the myths and misconceptions that we've created for ourselves in society, because these myths are harmful and extremely common. Therefore, it's good to know that online resources, like my podcast, have made it easier than ever before to get accurate information about sexual violence as well as how common it is within our communities and how it devastates lives.

Knowledge is power against sexual violence, so please, make sure you read about it and learn about sexual violence.

The next step is sharing what you've learnt with other people.

Now I know from my own experience of being a sexual assault survivor that sharing what you've learnt about rape and other forms of sexual violence is very difficult and some people just don't want to hear about it. That is a massive shame, and honestly, those people that don't want to learn the truth and they want to enjoy believing in the myths and misconceptions, they are part of the problem against us survivors.

However, when you share what you've learnt with someone else, you're doing a lot of good. You're helping to combat the harmful and common myths so you're able to educate people about the truths of sexual violence. As well as you're practising talking about sexual assault and this helps it become easier over time to talk about it and gets rid of the taboos against speaking about this form of violence more broadly.

Personally, as a survivor, when I was first raped, it was extremely hard for me to talk about sexual violence at all with anyone. Including my closest friends, because this was impossible for me and I was so constricted by the stigma and fear of the myths. Yet 17 weeks later, I am a lot freer and able to talk about sexual violence because this is the reality of the world and it is something I don't wish on anyone.

So I will talk about sexual violence and I will educate people and hopefully I will help people along the way.

You Can Advocate For Youth Prevention Programs

As I've spoken about before in the book, the majority of perpetrators of sexual violence are teenagers and young adults. Therefore, if we're going to stop sexual violence then we need to give young people the knowledge and tools for healthy relationships. This includes tools to help them understand consent and to help them have a healthy sexuality.

Thankfully, over the years, there has been a lot of work done on the development of youth prevention programs to help give young people the tools to have healthy relationships without them believing they have to commit sexual violence. The webpage below belonging to the United States Centre For Disease Control has lots of good information on sexual violence prevention strategies if you want to learn more:

https://www.cdc.gov/sexual-violence/prevention/?CDC_AAref_Val=https://www.cdc.gov/violenceprevention/sexualviolence/prevention.html

In addition, after you've looked to see if your local community offers any of these programs maybe through a local community centre, school or charity. You could advocate to expand these programs or advocate to start a program within your community. You might do this by encouraging your elected official to support prevention programmes to end sexual violence in your community.

Something I'm hoping to do related to this point is in September 2024, I should be in charge of a team of students within the School Of Psychology at my university who will organise different events for the psychology students. Part of my job will be organising speakers and talks so I want to get East Kent Rape Crisis Centre in to do one of their talks about sexual violence on campus. Since whilst this is still more awareness, it will help make people aware of the charity and I'm hoping beyond hope here that this will have some kind of knock-on effect that will benefit their prevention programmes. And in all fairness, the specific talk I want to book them for is billed as a prevention-ish talk.

Hopefully, it will have some sort of positive impact at the university.

<u>You Can Identify Organisations And People Working With Sexual Assault Survivors In Your Community And Connect With Them</u>

To help take action against sexual violence within your community, you can see who's doing prevention and response work in the local area. For example, this can include a family justice centre, a rape crisis centre and local political groups in charge of legislating against sexual violence. This can be a powerful way to take action to end sexual assault because by reaching out to these organisations and people you can get involved in their networks and be an active member of them so you can use your interests, skills and abilities to support them. For instance, if you identify a gap in their resources, like there being no way for people to donate to the local cause, then you could help them fill that gap in the community's network.

Personally, this is why I'm intending at some point to connect more "formally" with East Kent Rape Crisis Centre after I've "recovered" (I have no idea what that word means exactly at this point in time) and I want to have them on the podcast. This will help the charity to raise awareness about them, their services and the way how people can support them and other rape charities. As well as in the future after my rape counselling, I want to donate some money to them as a thank you, and if there's any feedback I have for them, I want to give it to them so I can help them fill any gaps they have in their services.

Also, in an ideal world, but I doubt I'll be in a mental headspace to do this for years, I would like to volunteer as a mental health professional for them, so I can support them and the survivors that come through their doors. Since let's face it, there is always a critical shortage of mental health professionals in the world.

Finally, something I would flat out love to do in the future, but I am pretty sure I am never going to be able to do this research project. I would seriously love to create a Brief Psychological Intervention to support rape survivors in between the time they're unsupported from the counselling assessment appointment (or booking the assessment appointment) to the first counselling session. This is a time period I have seriously struggled with and I have been a little suicidal at times, even though I would flat out never commit suicide. Hence, this would be a major gap I could fill within rape services to help support my fellow rape survivors.

Overall, even if you aren't a mental health professional, you can still help and support prevention programmes in your local community by volunteering, identifying and helping to fill gaps in services and being proactive about taking action in support of local efforts to end sexual violence.

Conclusion

At the end of the day, we have a long way to go before we're able to end sexual violence forever, and everything I've included in this chapter is just a starting point. Since there is never a better time than the present to start exploring other ways to take action nationally and locally against sexual violence because it is possible to end sexual violence.

It might be years or decades, but it is possible. It is possible to help create a world where no one regardless of their gender is at risk of sexual assault.

I know ending sexual violence seems like a massive, daunting task that can never be done because it is such a massive task and problem that is so common within society. Yet I firmly believe if each of us simply commits to doing one small thing a day or one small thing a week then over time, sexual violence will dramatically decrease as these small things add up into a massive tidal wave of change.

A tidal wave that will lift up survivors and hopefully drown perpetrators.

Sexual violence can be stopped if we simply take action, one small step at a time.

CONCLUSION

The silence needs to be broken, never forget that.

During the course of this book, I don't doubt there would be facts, sections or maybe entire chapters that made you feel disgusted, uncomfortable and sick. I get that because there were lots of times in this research and writing this book when I just needed to stop and come back to a topic later.

Sexual violence is disgusting, but that is why reading, learning and understanding it is so important.

Understanding sexual violence isn't about feeling good, feeling relieved or anything like that. You need to understand sexual violence so we can help make the world a better place. If you're a psychology professional then understanding sexual trauma helps you understand your clients better, it makes you more empathetic and it helps you know the truth and myths about this ultimate betrayal.

Since if I have learnt anything since my rape, it is that sexual violence is far more common than you ever thought possible. I returned to university in the September after my rape in April for a new academic year and I met 3 people who had been raped in Freshers Week alone.

Sexual violence must end. The silence must be broken.

If you're a psychology student then the knowledge contained in this book might help your future clinical work, but it will help you be a better, kinder, more empathetic friend too. I mentioned near the beginning of the book that sexual violence is common on university campuses so there is a chance you will become friends with someone who's been through sexual violence. Now you know how to respond to that revelation, how much courage it took for them and all the mental health responses that your friend will be experiencing.

You know the myths and truths about what happened to them so you can be a better person to them.

Finally, if you're not a survivor, a psychology student or a psychology professional, then firstly I want to thank you for picking up this book. You might not be my intended audience but I am very, very grateful for you picking this book up.

In addition, it means you have the knowledge about sexual violence too. It means you, like all of us, now have the knowledge, power and ability to combat and openly challenge these myths too. You have the power to help change minds and shine a light on the truth of sexual violence so these harmful, damaging and destructive myths can be wiped out over time.

Survivors will only be able to heal, thrive and their lives will start to become easier when these myths are stamped out. I've had to deal with a lot of challenges over the past 7 months related to the myths and misconceptions that are ingrained in our society. If these myths weren't about then maybe I could have healed a lot quicker.

Whatever the case, we all have this knowledge, these facts and studies in our minds now. We need to use this knowledge in the real world, we need to challenge and openly condemn any invalidation, minimising or any other lie about sexual violence.

We need to encourage and have conversations with our friends and family about sexual violence so other people can learn what actually happens too. Instead of having them rely on the lies, misconceptions and myths that idiots have created to allow sexual violence to go unchecked in our society.

The silence must be broken and we are all capable of helping to break it over time. As a survivor, it will take me longer to feel comfortable and healed enough to be as challenging as I want to be, and that's okay. I wrote this book, I will continue to talk about it on my podcast and in time I will openly challenge others too.

I will break the silence in my social world, and everyone else do be their part too.

We are in this together because sexual violence can and does impact everyone. It doesn't matter your age, your gender, your sexuality, you can be raped and that is why we are all in this together no matter what.

Even if you do something you consider small like simply share a post about sexual violence support on your social media, or you have a light conversation about it when you next see a friend, you are doing so much more than you ever realise.

You are breaking the silence and that means you are amazing.

We will break the silence one step at a time.

REFERENCES

ABS (Australian Bureau of Statistics) 2011. Australian and New Zealand Standard Offence Classification (ANZSOC), 2011 (third edition). ABS cat. no. 1234.0. Canberra: ABS.

Adhia, A., Kernic, M. A., Hemenway, D., Vavilala, M. S., & Rivara, F. P. (2019). Intimate partner homicide of adolescents. JAMA pediatrics, 173(6), 571-577.

AIHW (Australian Institute of Health and Welfare) 2019a. Family, domestic and sexual violence in Australia: continuing the national story. Cat. no. FDV 3. Canberra: AIHW.

AIHW (Australian Institute of Health and Welfare) 2020. Sexual assault in Australia. Media Release. Canberra: AIHW.

Alshehri, T., Mook-Kanamori, D. O., de Mutsert, R., Penninx, B. W., Rosendaal, F. R., le Cessie, S., & Milaneschi, Y. (2023). The association between adiposity and atypical energy-related symptoms of depression: a role for metabolic dysregulations. *Brain, Behavior, and Immunity*, *108*, 197-203.

American Journal of Psychiatry

Annual Review of Psychology

Armatta, J. (2018). Ending sexual violence through transformative justice. *Interdisciplinary Journal of Partnership Studies*, *5*(1), 4-4.

Au, T. M., Dickstein, B. D., Comer, J. S., Salters-Pedneault, K., & Litz, B. T. (2013). Co-occurring posttraumatic stress and depression symptoms after sexual assault: A latent profile analysis. *Journal of affective disorders*, *149*(1-3), 209-216.

Augarde, S., & Rydon-Grange, M. (2022). Female perpetrators of child sexual abuse: A review of the clinical and empirical literature–A 20-year update. *Aggression and violent behavior*, *62*, 101687.

Augarde, S., & Rydon-Grange, M. (2022). Female perpetrators of child sexual abuse: A review of the clinical and empirical literature–A 20-year update. *Aggression and violent behavior*, *62*, 101687.

Augarde, S., & Rydon-Grange, M. (2022). Female perpetrators of child sexual abuse: A review of the clinical and empirical literature–A 20-year update. *Aggression and violent behavior*, *62*, 101687.

Babaie, J., Naghipour, B., & Faridaalaee, G. (2021). Cardiovascular diseases in natural disasters; a systematic review. *Archives of academic emergency medicine*, *9*(1).

Banyard, V. L., & Cross, C. (2008). Consequences of teen dating violence: Understanding intervening variables in ecological context. Violence against women, 14(9), 998-1013.

Bates, E. A.(2020) "No one would ever believe me": An exploration of the impact of intimate partner violence victimization on men. Psychology of Men & Masculinities.Vol.21(4) 497-507.

Bates, E. A., & Weare, S. (2020). Sexual violence as a form of abuse in men's experiences of female-perpetrated intimate partner violence. *Journal of Contemporary Criminal Justice*, *36*(4), 582-595.

Bichard, H., Byrne, C., Saville, C. W., & Coetzer, R. (2022). The neuropsychological outcomes of non-fatal strangulation in domestic and sexual violence: A systematic review. Neuropsychological rehabilitation, 32(6), 1164-1192.

Biological Psychiatry

Blanco, L., Nydegger, L. A., Camarillo, G., Trinidad, D. R., Schramm, E., & Ames, S. L. (2015). Neurological changes in brain structure and functions among individuals with a history of childhood sexual abuse: A review. Neuroscience & Biobehavioral Reviews, 57, 63-69.

Bordere, T. (2017). Disenfranchisement and ambiguity in the face of loss: The suffocated grief of sexual assault survivors. Family Relations, 66(1), 29-45.

Bourke, A., Doherty, S., McBride, O., Morgan, K., & McGee, H. (2014). Female perpetrators of child sexual abuse: Characteristics of the offender and victim. *Psychology, crime & law*, *20*(8), 769-780.

Bremner, J. D., Vythilingam, M., Vermetten, E., Southwick, S. M., McGlashan, T., Staib, L. H., ... & Charney, D. S. (2003). Neural correlates of declarative memory for emotionally valenced words in women with posttraumatic stress disorder related to early childhood sexual abuse. Biological psychiatry, 53(10), 879-889.

Brown, A. L., Testa, M., & Messman-Moore, T. L. (2009). Psychological consequences of sexual victimization resulting from force, incapacitation, or verbal coercion. *Violence against women*, *15*(8), 898-919.

Budd, K. M., & Johnston, S. (2021). Female youth convicted of sex offenses: Public opinion on public notification. *Criminal justice policy review*, *32*(7), 675-692.

Bullock, C. M., & Beckson, M. (2011). Male victims of sexual assault: Phenomenology, psychology, physiology. *Journal of the American Academy of Psychiatry and the Law Online*, *39*(2), 197-205.

Bumby, N. H., & Bumby, K. M. (1997). Adolescent female sexual offenders. In B. Schwartz, & H. Cellini (Eds.), The sex offender: New insights, treatment, innovations, and legal developments (Vol. 2, pp. 10.1–10.16). Kingston, NJ: Civic Research Institute.

Burgess, A. W., & Holmstrom, L. L. (1978). Recovery from rape and prior life stress. Research in nursing & health, 1(4), 165-174.

Campbell, R. (2009). Trauma, Violence, & Abuse, Vol. 10, No. 3.

Campbell, R., Greeson, M. R., Fehler-Cabral, G., & Kennedy, A. C. (2015). Pathways to help: Adolescent sexual assault victims' disclosure and help-seeking experiences. *Violence against women*, *21*(7), 824-847.

Campus Sexual Assault Study, 2007; Matthew Kimble, Andrada Neacsiu, et. Al, *Risk of Unwanted Sex for College Women: Evidence for a Red Zone*, Journal of American College Health (2008).

Canadian Journal of Psychiatry

Carey, K. B., Durney, S. E., Shepardson, R. L., & Carey, M. P. (2015). Incapacitated and forcible rape of college women: prevalence across the first year. The Journal of adolescent health : official publication of the Society for Adolescent Medicine, 56(6), 678–680. https://doi.org/10.1016/j.jadohealth.2015.02.018

Castillo, J. (2022). *What Happened to Make You Anxious?: How to Uncover the Little "t" Traumas that Drive Your Anxiety, Worry, and Fear.* New Harbinger Publications.

Centers for Disease Control and Prevention. Intimate Partner Violence, Sexual Violence, and Stalking Among Men.

Chae, W. R., Baumert, J., Nübel, J., Brasanac, J., Gold, S. M., Hapke, U., & Otte, C. (2023). Associations between individual depressive symptoms and immunometabolic characteristics in major depression. *European Neuropsychopharmacology*, *71*, 25-40.

Champine, R. B., Lang, J. M., Nelson, A. M., Hanson, R. F., & Tebes, J. K. (2019). Systems measures of a trauma-informed approach: A systematic review. American Journal of Community Psychology, 64(3-4), 418-437.

Chang, E. C., Lee, J., Wright, K. M., Najarian, A. S. M., Yu, T., Chang, O. D., & Hirsch, J. K. (2019). Examining sexual assault victimization and loneliness as risk factors associated with nonlethal self-harm behaviors in female college students: is it important to control for concomitant suicidal behaviors (and vice versa)?. *Journal of interpersonal violence*, *34*(21-22), 4443-4458.

Chang, J. J., Ji, Y., Li, Y. H., Yuan, M. Y., & Su, P. Y. (2021). Childhood trauma and depression in college students: Mediating and moderating effects of psychological resilience. *Asian Journal of Psychiatry*, *65*, 102824.

Chu, Y. C., Wang, H. H., Chou, F. H., Hsu, Y. F., & Liao, K. L. (2024). Outcomes of trauma-informed care on the psychological health of women experiencing intimate partner violence: a systematic review and meta-analysis. *Journal of Psychiatric and Mental Health Nursing*, *31*(2), 203-214.

Collins, K. A., Eng, G. K., Tural, Ü., Irvin, M. K., Iosifescu, D. V., & Stern, E. R. (2022). Affective and somatic symptom clusters in depression and their relationship to treatment outcomes in the STAR* D sample. *Journal of Affective Disorders*, *300*, 469-473.

Cortoni F., Babchishin K. M., Rat C. (2017). The proportion of sexual offenders who are female is higher than thought: A meta-analysis. Criminal Justice and Behavior, 44(2), 145–162.

Cortoni, F., Babchishin, K. M., & Rat, C. (2017). The proportion of sexual offenders who are female is higher than thought: A meta-analysis. *Criminal Justice and Behavior*, *44*(2), 145-162.

Cortoni, F., Hanson, R. K., & Coache, M. È. (2010). The recidivism rates of female sexual offenders are low: A meta-analysis. Sexual Abuse, 22(4), 387-401.

Cunningham, S., Hudson, C. C., & Harkness, K. (2021). Social media and depression symptoms: a meta-analysis. *Research on child and adolescent psychopathology*, *49*(2), 241-253.

Cutuli, J. J., Alderfer, M. A., & Marsac, M. L. (2019). Introduction to the special issue: Trauma-informed care for children and families. Psychological Services, 16(1), 1.

David Cantor, Bonnie Fisher, Susan Chibnall, Reanna Townsend, et. al. Association of

American Universities (AAU), *Report on the AAU Campus Climate Survey on Sexual Assault and Sexual Misconduct* (January 17, 2020). ("Victim services agency" is defined in this study as a "public or privately funded organization that provides victims with support and services to aid their recovery, offer protection, guide them through the criminal justice process, and assist with obtaining restitution." RAINN presents this data for educational purposes only, and strongly recommends using the citations to review any and all sources for more information and detail.)

Davies, M. (2002). Male sexual assault victims: A selective review of the literature and implications for support services. *Aggression and violent behavior*, *7*(3), 203-214.

Department of Justice, Office of Justice Programs, Bureau of Justice Statistics, Rape and Sexual Victimization Among College-Aged Females, 1995-2013 (2014).

Department of Justice, Office of Justice Programs, Bureau of Justice Statistics, Campus Law Enforcement, 2011-2012 (2015).

DeSalvo, L. (2000). *Writing as a way of healing: How telling our stories transforms our lives*. Beacon Press.

Diagnostic and Statistical Manual of Mental Disorders, Fifth Edition

DiMarco, D., Mizzoni, J., & Savitz, R. (2022). On the sexual assault of men. *Sexuality & Culture*, 1-9.

Dong, C., Xu, R., & Xu, L. (2021). Relationship of childhood trauma, psychological resilience, and family resilience among undergraduate nursing students: A cross‐sectional study. *Perspectives in Psychiatric Care*, *57*(2), 852-859.

Downing, B. (2018). The aftermath of rape: Innovative approaches to understanding sexual violence against Australian women and children. *Coolabah*, (24&25), 322-336.

Dworkin, E. R., DeCou, C. R., & Fitzpatrick, S. (2022). Associations between sexual assault and suicidal thoughts and behavior: A meta-analysis. *Psychological Trauma: Theory, Research, Practice, and Policy*, *14*(7), 1208.

Dworkin, E. R., Menon, S. V., Bystrynski, J., & Allen, N. E. (2017). Sexual assault victimization and psychopathology: A review and meta-analysis. *Clinical psychology review*, *56*, 65-81.

Edmondson, D., & von Känel, R. (2017). Post-traumatic stress disorder and cardiovascular disease. *The lancet. Psychiatry*, *4*(4), 320–329. https://doi.org/10.1016/S2215-0366(16)30377-7

Fenster, R. J., Lebois, L. A., Ressler, K. J., & Suh, J. (2018). Brain circuit dysfunction in post-traumatic stress disorder: from mouse to man. *Nature Reviews Neuroscience*, *19*(9), 535-551.

Feuereisen, P. (2018). *Invisible girls: The truth about sexual abuse*. Seal Press.

Finkelhor, D., Ormrod, R., & Chaffin, M. (2009). Juveniles Who Commit Sex Offenses Against Minors. Juvenile Justice Bulletin.

Finkelhor, D., Shattuck, A., Turner, H. A., & Hamby, S. L. (2014). The lifetime prevalence of child sexual abuse and sexual assault assessed in late adolescence. The Journal of Adolescent Health, 55(3), 329–333.

Ford, H. (2006) Women Who Sexually Abuse Children Wiley: London

Forkey, H., Szilagyi, M., Kelly, E. T., & Duffee, J. (2021). Trauma-informed care. Pediatrics, 148(2).

Francis, L., & Pearson, D. (2021). The recognition of emotional abuse: Adolescents' responses to warning signs in romantic relationships. Journal of interpersonal violence, 36(17-18), 8289-8313.

Friedrich, M. J. (2017). Depression is the leading cause of disability around the world. Jama, 317(15), 1517-1517.

Fuchs, S. F. (2004). Male sexual assault: Issues of arousal and consent. *Clev. St. L. Rev.*, *51*, 93.

Galli, F., Lai, C., Gregorini, T., Ciacchella, C., & Carugo, S. (2021, July). Psychological traumas and cardiovascular disease: a case-control study. In *Healthcare* (Vol. 9, No. 7, p. 875). MDPI.

Gilmore, A. K., Ward-Ciesielski, E. F., Smalling, A., Limowski, A. R., Hahn, C. K., & Jaffe, A. E. (2020). Managing post-sexual assault suicide risk. *Archives of women's mental health*, *23*, 673-679.

Goldman, A. W., Mulford, C. F., & Blachman-Demner, D. R. (2016). Advancing our approach to teen dating violence: A youth and professional defined framework of teen dating relationships. Psychology of Violence, 6(4), 497.

Guo, Z. P., Chen, L., Tang, L. R., Gao, Y., Qu, M., Wang, L., & Liu, C. H. (2025). The differential orbitofrontal activity and connectivity between atypical and typical major depressive disorder. *NeuroImage: Clinical*, *45*, 103717.

Haiyasoso, M. (2023). The aftermath of sexual violence: Consequent grief and loss. In Disenfranchised Grief (pp. 170-186). Routledge.

Hammond, L., Ioannou, M., & Fewster, M. (2017). Perceptions of male rape and sexual assault in a male sample from the United Kingdom: Barriers to reporting and the impacts of victimization. Journal of Investigative Psychology and Offender Profiling, 14(2), 133-149.

Han, H. R., Miller, H. N., Nkimbeng, M., Budhathoki, C., Mikhael, T., Rivers, E., ... & Wilson, P. (2021). Trauma informed interventions: A systematic review. PloS one, 16(6), e0252747.

Haskell, L., & Randall, M. (2019). Impact of trauma on adult sexual assault victims: What the criminal justice system needs to know. Available at SSRN 3417763.

Hippocampal Volume in Women Victimized by Childhood Sexual Abuse.

https://crimesolutions.ojp.gov/ratedprograms/safe-dates

https://rainn.org/

https://vawnet.org/sc/preventing-and-responding-teen-dating-violence

https://www.eurekalert.org/news-releases/630084

https://www.loveisrespect.org/

https://www.loveisrespect.org/wp-content/uploads/media/sites/3/2022/12/2211-TDVAM-Action-Guide_FINAL.pdf

https://www.psychologytoday.com/gb/blog/awareness-action/202203/3-ways-take-action-end-sexual-assault

https://www.psychologytoday.com/gb/blog/healthy-communication-in-hard-situations/202405/your-experience-is-still-valid-even-if-others

https://www.psychologytoday.com/gb/blog/the-crime-and-justice-doctor/202107/coercive-control-entrapped-fear

https://www.psychologytoday.com/gb/blog/the-new-teen-age/201207/7-ways-to-help-a-teen-survivor-of-sexual-assault

https://www.psychologytoday.com/us/blog/beyond-mental-health/202407/when-it-feels-impossible-to-get-out-of-bed

https://www.psychologytoday.com/us/conditions/post-traumatic-stress-disorder

https://www.scientificamerican.com/article/sexual-victimization-by-women-is-more-common-than-previously-known/

https://www.verywellmind.com/symptoms-of-ptsd-after-a-rape-2797203#toc-symptoms-of-ptsd-after-sexual-assault

Huitema, A., & Vanwesenbeeck, I. (2016). Attitudes of Dutch citizens towards male victims of sexual coercion by a female perpetrator. *Journal of sexual aggression*, *22*(3), 308-322.

i. National Crime Victimization Survey, 1995-2013 (2015); ii. Department of Justice, Office of Justice Programs, Bureau of Justice Statistics, Rape and Sexual Victimization Among College-Aged Females, 1995-2013 (2014).

Jeglic, E.L., & Calkins, C (2018). Protecting your Child from Sexual Abuse: What You Need to Know to Keep your Kids Safe. Skyhorse, New York

Johnson, T. C. (1989). Female child perpetrators: Children who molest other children. *Child Abuse & Neglect*, *13*(4), 571-585.

Journal of Psychopharmacology

Journal of Traumatic Stress

Katz, J., Moore, J. A., & Tkachuk, S. (2007). Verbal sexual coercion and perceived victim responsibility: Mediating effects of perceived control. *Sex Roles*, *57*, 235-247.

Kirby, P. (2015). Ending sexual violence in conflict: the Preventing Sexual Violence Initiative and its critics. *International Affairs*, *91*(3), 457-472.

Kirkner, A., Relyea, M., & Ullman, S. E. (2018). PTSD and problem drinking in relation to seeking mental health and substance use treatment among sexual assault survivors. *Traumatology*, *24*(1), 1.

Kruis, N. E., Ménard, K. S., Choi, J., Rowland, N. J., Frye, T., Kosaka, R., & Williams, A. (2023). Perceived Dangerousness Mediates Punitive Attitudes Toward Sex Offenders: Results From a Vignette Experiment. Crime & Delinquency, 0(0). https://doi.org/10.1177/00111287231170106

Kubik, E. K., Hecker, J. E., & Righthand, S. (2003). Adolescent females who have sexually offended: Comparisons with delinquent adolescent female offenders and adolescent males who sexually offend. Journal of Child Sexual Abuse, 11(3), 63-83.

Kumar, S. A., Jaffe, A. E., Brock, R. L., & DiLillo, D. (2022). Resilience to suicidal ideation among college sexual assault survivors: The protective role of optimism and gratitude in the context of posttraumatic stress. *Psychological trauma: theory, research, practice, and policy*, *14*(S1), S91.

Larsen, M. L., & Hilden, M. (2016). Male victims of sexual assault; 10 years' experience from a Danish Assault Center. Journal of Forensic and Legal Medicine, 43, 8-11.

Lee, C. (2019). Examining the effects of dating violence prevention programs: A systematic review and meta-analysis.

Lee, C., & Wong, J. S. (2020). Examining the effects of teen dating violence prevention programs: A systematic review and meta-analysis. Journal of Experimental Criminology, 1-40.

Lei, M. K., Beach, S. R., & Simons, R. L. (2018). Childhood trauma, pubertal timing, and cardiovascular risk in adulthood. *Health Psychology*, *37*(7), 613.

Little, N. (2019). Rape-related mourning on a social network site: Leah Parsons"'Facebooked" grief and the Angel Rehtaeh Parsons page. Feral Feminisms: Critical Interventions in Rape Culture, 8, 57-79.

Maghfira, R., & Lailiyah, M. (2021). Coping strategies of a rape victim as reflected in Chanel Miller's Know My Name memoir. *EnJourMe (English Journal of Merdeka): Culture, Language, and Teaching of English*, *6*(1), 63-69.

Malgaroli, M., Calderon, A., & Bonanno, G. A. (2021). Networks of major depressive disorder: A systematic review. *Clinical Psychology Review*, *85*, 102000.

Manetsch M, Nelson Aguiar RJ, Hermann D, van der Put C, Grisso T and Boonmann C (2021) Mental Health Problems in Girls Who Committed Sexual Offenses: Similarities and Differences Compared to Girls With Non-sex Offenses and Boys With Sex Offenses. Front. Psychol. 12:721927. doi: 10.3389/fpsyg.2021.721927.

Mathews, R., Hunter, J. A., & Vuz, J. (1997). Juvenile Female Sexual Offenders: Clinical Characteristics and Treatment Issues. Sexual Abuse, 9(3), 187–199. https://doi.org/10.1177/107906329700900304.

Maynard, B. R., Farina, A., Dell, N. A., & Kelly, M. S. (2019). Effects of trauma-informed approaches in schools: A systematic review. Campbell Systematic Reviews, 15(1-2).

Messing, J. T., Mohr, R., & Durfee, A. (2015). Intimate partner violence and women's experiences of grief. Child & Family Social Work, 20(1), 30-39.

Miles, L. W., Valentine, J. L., Mabey, L. J., Hopkins, E. S., Stodtmeister, P. J., Rockwood, R. B., & Moxley, A. N. (2024). A systematic review of evidence-based treatments for adolescent and adult sexual assault victims. *Journal of the American Psychiatric Nurses Association*, *30*(3), 480-502.

Mohammed, G. F., & Hashish, R. K. (2015). Sexual violence against females and its impact on their sexual function. *Egyptian Journal of Forensic Sciences*, *5*(3), 96-102.

Moore, C. L., & Van Vliet, K. J. (2022). Women's experiences of nature as a pathway to recovery from sexual assault. *Journal of Humanistic Psychology*, *62*(1), 123-150.

Muñoz-Rivas, M. J., Graña, J. L., O'Leary, K. D., & González, M. P. (2007). Aggression in adolescent dating relationships: Prevalence, justification, and health consequences. Journal of Adolescent Health, 40(4), 298-304.

Munroe, C., & Shumway, M. (2022). Female-perpetrated sexual violence: A survey of survivors of female-perpetrated childhood sexual abuse and adult sexual assault. *Journal of Interpersonal Violence*, *37*(9-10), NP6655-NP6675.

Munroe, C., & Shumway, M. (2022). Female-perpetrated sexual violence: A survey of survivors of female-perpetrated childhood sexual abuse and adult sexual assault. *Journal of Interpersonal*

Violence, *37*(9-10), NP6655-NP6675.

National Center for PTSD, U.S. Department of Veterans Affairs

National Coalition Against Domestic Violence. https://ncadv.org/statistics. Accessed 12/15/2021.

National Comorbidity Survey Replication

National Institute of Mental Health

National Institutes of Health - National Library of Medicine

Navalta, C. P., Polcari, A., Webster, D. M., Boghossian, A., & Teicher, M. H. (2006). Effects of childhood sexual abuse on neuropsychological and cognitive function in college women. The Journal of neuropsychiatry and clinical neurosciences, 18(1), 45-53.

Neofytou, E. (2022). Childhood trauma history of female sex offenders: A systematic review. *Sexologies*, *31*(2), 99-106.

Noble, N. C., Merker, J. B., Webber, T. K., Ressler, K. J., & Seligowski, A. V. (2023). PTSD and depression severity are associated with cardiovascular disease symptoms in trauma-exposed women. *European Journal of Psychotraumatology*, *14*(2), 2234810.

O'Callaghan, E., Shepp, V., Ullman, S. E., & Kirkner, A. (2019). Navigating sex and sexuality after sexual assault: A qualitative study of survivors and informal support providers. *The Journal of Sex Research*, *56*(8), 1045-1057.

O'Donnell, C. J., Longacre, L. S., Cohen, B. E., Fayad, Z. A., Gillespie, C. F., Liberzon, I., ... & Stein, M. B. (2021). Posttraumatic stress disorder and cardiovascular disease: state of the science, knowledge gaps, and research opportunities. *JAMA cardiology*, *6*(10), 1207-1216.

Oliver, B. E., & Holmes, L. (2015). Female juvenile sexual offenders: Understanding who they are and possible steps that may prevent some girls from offending. Journal of Child Sexual Abuse, 24(6), 698-715.

Panisch, L. S., & Tam, L. M. (2020). The role of trauma and mental health in the treatment of chronic pelvic pain: a systematic review of the intervention literature. *Trauma, Violence, & Abuse*, *21*(5), 1029-1043.

Perryman, K., Blisard, P., & Moss, R. (2019). Using creative arts in trauma therapy: The neuroscience of healing. *Journal of Mental Health Counseling*, *41*(1), 80-94.

Peter, T. (2009). Exploring taboos: Comparing male-and female-perpetrated child sexual abuse. *Journal of interpersonal violence*, *24*(7), 1111-1128.

Petersson, C. C., & Plantin, L. (2019). Breaking with norms of masculinity: Men making sense of their experience of sexual assault. Clinical Social Work Journal, 47(4), 372-383.

Petreca, V. G., & Burgess, A. W. (2024). Long-Term Psychological and Physiological Effects of Male Sexual Trauma. *The Journal of the American Academy of Psychiatry and the Law*, *52*(1), 23-32.

Psychiatric Clinics of North America

Pusch, N. (2024). A meta-analytic review of social learning theory and teen dating violence perpetration. Journal of Research in Crime and Delinquency, 61(2), 171-223.

Qi, B., MacDonald, K., Berlim, M. T., Fielding, A., Lis, E., Low, N., ... & Trakadis, Y. (2020).

Balance problems, paralysis, and angina as clinical markers for severity in major depression. Frontiers in psychiatry, 11, 567394.

Quidé, Y., Cléry, H., Andersson, F., Descriaud, C., Saint-Martin, P., Barantin, L., ... & El-Hage, W. (2018). Neurocognitive, emotional and neuroendocrine correlates of exposure to sexual assault in women. Journal of Psychiatry and Neuroscience, 43(5), 318-326.

Raghavan, S., & Sandanapitchai, P. (2020). The relationship between cultural variables and resilience to psychological trauma: A systematic review of the literature. *Traumatology.*

Rauch, S. A. M., & Rothbaum, B. O. (2023). *Making Meaning of Difficult Experiences: A Self-Guided Program.* Oxford University Press. https://doi.org/10.1093/med-psych/9780197642573.001.0001

Read, J., & Moncrieff, J. (2022). Depression: Why drugs and electricity are not the answer. *Psychological Medicine*, *52*(8), 1401-1410.

Reed, L. A., Tolman, R. M., & Ward, L. M. (2017). Gender matters: Experiences and consequences of digital dating abuse victimization in adolescent dating relationships. Journal of adolescence, 59, 79-89.

Resick, P. A. (1993). The psychological impact of rape. Journal of interpersonal violence, 8(2), 223-255.

Ressler, K. J., Berretta, S., Bolshakov, V. Y., Rosso, I. M., Meloni, E. G., Rauch, S. L., & Carlezon Jr, W. A. (2022). Post-traumatic stress disorder: clinical and translational neuroscience from cells to circuits. *Nature Reviews Neurology*, *18*(5), 273-288.

Rice, S. M., Easton, S. D., Seidler, Z. E., & Oliffe, J. L. (2022). Sexual abuse and mental ill health in boys and men: what we do and don't know. *BJPsych open*, *8*(4), e110.

Rodríguez-deArriba, M. L., Nocentini, A., Menesini, E., & Sánchez-Jiménez, V. (2021). Dimensions and measures of cyber dating violence in adolescents: A systematic review. Aggression and Violent behavior, 58, 101613.

Roeckner, A. R., Oliver, K. I., Lebois, L. A. M., van Rooij, S. J. H., & Stevens, J. S. (2021). Neural contributors to trauma resilience: a review of longitudinal neuroimaging studies. *Translational Psychiatry*, *11*(1), 508. https://doi.org/10.1038/s41398-021-01633-y

Roe-Sepowitz, D., & Krysik, J. (2008). Examining the sexual offenses of female juveniles: The relevance of childhood maltreatment. The American Journal of Orthopsychiatry, 78(4), 405–412. https://doi.org/10.1037/a0014310.

Rosenberg, M. B., & Chopra, D. (2015). *Nonviolent communication: A language of life: Life-changing tools for healthy relationships*. PuddleDancer Press.

Rothbaum, B. O., & Rauch, S. A. M. (2020). *PTSD: What everyone needs to know.* Oxford University Press.

Sandler, J. C., Freeman, N. J., & Socia, K. M. (2008). Does a watched pot boil? A time-series analysis of New York State's sex offender registration and notification law. *Psychology, Public Policy, and Law*, *14*(4), 284.

Sargent, A. (2010). Representing Prison Rape: Race, Masculinity, and Incarceration in Donald Goines's" White Man's Justice, Black Man's Grief". Melus, 35(3), 131-155.

Seelau EP, Seelau SM, Poorman PB. Gender and role-based perceptions of domestic abuse: does sexual orientation matter? Behav Sci Law. 2003;21(2):199-214. doi: 10.1002/bsl.524. PMID: 1264504

Shorey, S., Ng, E. D., & Wong, C. H. (2022). Global prevalence of depression and elevated depressive symptoms among adolescents: A systematic review and meta-analysis. *British Journal of Clinical Psychology*, *61*(2), 287-305.

Siegel, J., & Fix, R. L. (2020). Court outcomes among female juveniles with sexual offences. *Journal of sexual aggression*, *26*(2), 263-273.

Smith, A. U., Reidy, D., & Norris, A. E. (2020). Teen dating violence and suicide risk among bisexual adolescents. Journal of adolescent health, 67(5), 685-691.

Smith, M. M., Sherry, S. B., Ray, C., Hewitt, P. L., & Flett, G. L. (2021). Is perfectionism a vulnerability factor for depressive symptoms, a complication of depressive symptoms, or both? A meta-analytic test of 67 longitudinal studies. *Clinical Psychology Review*, *84*, 101982.

Song, S., Yang, X., Yang, H., Zhou, P., Ma, H., Teng, C., ... & Zhang, N. (2021). Psychological resilience as a protective factor for depression and anxiety among the public during the outbreak of COVID-19. *Frontiers in psychology*, *11*, 618509.

Stefanidou, T., Hughes, E., Kester, K., Edmondson, A., Majeed-Ariss, R., Smith, C., ... & Lloyd-Evans, B. (2020). The identification and treatment of mental health and substance misuse problems in sexual assault services: A systematic review. *PLoS One*, *15*(4), e0231260.

Substance Abuse and Mental Health Services Administration. SAMHSA's Concept of Trauma and Guidance for a Trauma-Informed Approach. HHS Publication No. (SMA) 14-4884. Rockville, MD: Substance Abuse and Mental Health Services Administration, 2014

Thomas, J. C., & Kopel, J. (2023). Male victims of sexual assault: a review of the literature. *Behavioral Sciences*, *13*(4), 304.

Thomas, S. (2021). *The Impact of Sexual Assault Disclosure on Mental Health and Recovery* (Doctoral dissertation, The Chicago School of Professional Psychology).

Troy, A. S., Willroth, E. C., Shallcross, A. J., Giuliani, N. R., Gross, J. J., & Mauss, I. B. (2023). Psychological resilience: an affect-regulation framework. *Annual review of psychology*, *74*(1), 547-576.

Türk-Kurtça, T., & Kocatürk, M. (2020). The Role of Childhood Traumas, Emotional Self-Efficacy and Internal-External Locus of Control in Predicting Psychological Resilience. *International Journal of Education and Literacy Studies*, *8*(3), 105-115.

Tutchell, E., & Edmonds, J. (2020). *Unsafe spaces: Ending sexual abuse in universities*. Emerald Publishing Limited.

Ullman, S. E., Lorenz, K., Kirkner, A., & O'Callaghan, E. (2018). Postassault substance use and coping: a qualitative study of sexual assault survivors and informal support providers. *Alcoholism treatment quarterly*, *36*(3), 330-353.

US Department of Health and Human Services

Valencia-Agudo, F., Kramer, T., Clarke, V., Goddard, A., & Khadr, S. (2020). Correlates and predictors of self-harm in a prospective sample of sexually assaulted adolescents. *Clinical child psychology and psychiatry*, *25*(4), 847-859.

van der Put, C. E. (2013). The prevalence of risk factors for general recidivism in female adolescent sexual offenders: A comparison of three subgroups. Child abuse & Neglect, 37(9), 691-697.

van der Put, C., van Vugt, E. S., Stams, G. J. J. M., & Hendriks, J. (2014). Psychosocial and Developmental Characteristics of Female Adolescents Who Have Committed Sexual Offenses. Sexual Abuse, 26(4), 330–342. https://doi.org/10.1177/1079063213492342.

Van Ouytsel, J., Van Gool, E., Walrave, M., Ponnet, K., & Peeters, E. (2016). Sexting: adolescents' perceptions of the applications used for, motives for, and consequences of sexting. Journal of Youth Studies, 20(4), 446–470. https://doi.org/10.1080/13676261.2016.1241865

Vreijling, S. R., Fatt, C. R. C., Williams, L. M., Schatzberg, A. F., Usherwood, T., Nemeroff, C. B., ... & Lamers, F. (2024). Features of immunometabolic depression as predictors of antidepressant treatment outcomes: pooled analysis of four clinical trials. *The British Journal of Psychiatry*, *224*(3), 89-97.

Waegemann, A. (2020). When no one believes you: redesigning rape kits and responses in the aftermath of a sexual assault. *Scitech Lawyer*, *16*(4), 8-13.

Walker, J., Archer, J., & Davies, M. (2005). Effects of rape on men: A descriptive analysis. Archives of sexual behavior, 34, 69-80.

Watters, K. N., & Yalch, M. M. (2022). Relative effects of sexual assault and other traumatic life events on self-harm. *European Journal of Trauma & Dissociation*, *6*(1), 100244.

Wessells, M. G., & Kostelny, K. (2021). Understanding and ending violence against children: A holistic approach. *Peace and Conflict: Journal of Peace Psychology*, *27*(1), 3.

Whiteley, C. (2024) CBT For Depression: A Clinical Psychology Introduction To Cognitive Behavioural Therapy For Depression. CGD Publishing. England.

Whiteley, C. (2024) Social Media Psychology: A Guide To Clinical Psychology, Cyberpsychology and Mental Health. CGD Publishing. England.

Whiteley, C. (2024) Working With Children and Young People: A Guide To Clinical Psychology, Mental Health and Psychotherapy. CGD Publishing. England.

Widanaralalage, B. K., Hine, B. A., Murphy, A. D., & Murji, K. (2022). "I didn't feel i was a victim": a phenomenological analysis of the experiences of male-on-male survivors of rape and sexual abuse. *Victims & Offenders*, *17*(8), 1147-1172.

Wijkman, M., Bijleveld, C., & Hendriks, J. (2014). Juvenile female sex offenders: Offender and offence characteristics. European Journal of Criminology, 11(1), 23-38.

Wincentak, K., Connolly, J., & Card, N. (2017). Teen dating violence: A meta-analytic review of prevalence rates. Psychology of Violence, 7(2), 224–241. https://doi.org/10.1037/a0040194

Winters, G. M., & Jeglic, E. L. (2021). The Sexual Grooming Scale–Victim Version: The Development and Pilot Testing of a Measure to Assess the Nature and Extent of Child Sexual Grooming. *Victims & Offenders*, 1-22.

Winters, G., & Jeglic, E.L (2016). Stages of sexual grooming: Recognizing potentially predatory behaviors of child molesters. Deviant Behavior, 1-10. http://dx.doi.org/10.1080/01639625.2016.1197656

Winters, G., & Jeglic, E.L. (2016). I knew it all along: The sexual grooming behaviors of child molesters and the hindsight bias. Journal of Child Sexual Abuse, 25(1). 20-36. doi: 10.1080/10538712.2015.1108945

Wisco, B. E., Nomamiukor, F. O., Marx, B. P., Krystal, J. H., Southwick, S. M., & Pietrzak, R. H. (2022). Posttraumatic stress disorder in US military veterans: Results from the 2019–2020 National Health and Resilience in Veterans Study. *The Journal of Clinical Psychiatry*, *83*(2), 39779.

Wright, H. (2015). Ending Sexual Violence and the War System–Or Militarizing Feminism?. *International Feminist Journal of Politics*, *17*(3), 503-507.

Ybarra, M. L., & Mitchell, K. J. (2013). Prevalence rates of male and female sexual violence perpetrators in a national sample of adolescents. *JAMA pediatrics*, *167*(12), 1125-1134.

Zack, E., Lang, J. T., & Dirks, D. (2018). "It must be great being a female pedophile!": The nature of public perceptions about female teacher sex offenders. Crime Media Culture, 14(1), 61-79. https://doi.org/10.1177/174165901667404

Zgoba, K. M., & Mitchell, M. M. (2021). The effectiveness of Sex Offender Registration and Notification: A meta-analysis of 25 years of findings. *Journal of Experimental Criminology*, 1-26.

Zilkens, R. R., Smith, D. A., Mukhtar, S. A., Semmens, J. B., Phillips, M. A., & Kelly, M. C. (2018). Male sexual assault: Physical injury and vulnerability in 103 presentations. Journal of forensic and legal medicine, 58, 145-151.

I AM NOT A VICTIM, I AM A SURVIVOR

CONNOR WHITELEY

DEDICATION

Thank you to all my readers without you I couldn't do what I love.

INTRODUCTION

On the 13th April 2024, my life changed forever because I was raped. This is what happened over the next 5 months before my specialist counselling started.

This is my truth.

Whenever a person experiences sexual violence (the ultimate violation), we need to start our healing journey and healing from sexual violence is a journey that takes time, as annoying as that is to realise. Since as this book shows there'll be a lot of twists and turns, highs and lows, heart-warming and heart-breaking moments as you start to heal.

During healing you can have a breakthrough, a time of happiness where most of the trauma responses go away, then you remember a new detail or realised you have a new trigger, and this can feel devastating. Almost like you will never heal fully, never get better and you are doomed to be ruled by your trauma forever.

Healing is very possible, even if it feels like it's taking forever.

Nonetheless, as this book shows as I talk you through my life and mental health week-by-week for the first 5 months after my rape. You can see that the healing journey isn't linear, and there is no such thing as a finish line. You will heal in time, as you learn, go to therapy and try to recover, but it is a journey.

In this book, you'll be able to see my highlights, my low points and how I helped myself survive with the help of my friends. As well as on your own healing journey, you will encounter something that you think is a setback, this will be another piece of trauma that your body and mind are revealing to you so you can heal. It is annoying when this happens but it is a good thing because it means you can heal it and recover over time.

It is these small healing pieces that allow you to be successful over time and allows you to face more and more challenges. Trauma is essentially the gift that keeps on giving and it is exactly like an onion or artichoke, you peel back layers then you find the centre. The centre of you that wants to live, wants to be healed and the centre that can never be defeated.

A lot of people might believe that me writing about my rape as soon as it happened is strange, but I am a writer, I am a researcher, I am a psychology Masters student. For me, writing and researching rape was how I dealt with it because I knew I couldn't heal from this alone.

At the time of writing this introduction, it's 7-months since my rape and now I am at the point where I can confidently say that I am healing because I still go through hell-and-back some days, but my triggers are decreasing and everything is getting better very slowly.

However, this book shows that wasn't always the case, so I want you to know that are never alone in your feelings, your experiences and whatever you're going through.

What Is The Purpose Of This Book?

Personally, I call this book a mixture of memoir and psychoeducation information. A lot of the book focuses on my experiences, my PTSD, my mental health after my rape. I wrote about these topics with you in mind and whenever I can, I focus a lot on tips and tricks that helped me survive these periods.

In addition, there are chapters in this book that are solely dedicated to providing you with psychology facts and information about the sexual violence and therapy options, so you can understand the topic for yourself if you're comfortable. Even though I talk more about sexual violence in my book *Breaking The Silence.*

This book is designed to help you in small ways so you don't feel alone, but professional help is always best.

Furthermore, if anything in the book starts to overwhelm you then please, give yourself permission to stop, use the self-soothing exercises I introduce in a moment and come back to the book later.

Never forget you, and only you are in charge. You have choice in what you read, what you do and how you relate to this book.

Lastly, whenever you're healing from sexual trauma, it is perfectly okay if you don't, but it might be useful to include a dear friend or family member or therapist in the process. You may feel vulnerable at times, but their support will help you heal.

Who Am I?

In my other psychology books, I include this section because I like to know who the author is so I know the information is coming from a reliable and good source, but I'm including this section for a different reason.

I'm Connor Whiteley, the internationally bestselling author of over 40 psychology books, I am the host of *The Psychology World Podcast,* a weekly show exploring a new psychology topic each week and delivering the latest psychology news. Available on all major podcast apps and YouTube. As well as I am a psychology graduate who studied a Clinical Psychology undergraduate and Masters at the University of Kent, England.

I am a survivor, not a victim.

I love psychology, spending time with my friends, going out and living. Also, I like fiction books of all types especially books by Dean Wesley Smith, and I like watching films with my friends.

I am a normal person with a normal, fun, exciting life but when I was raped, he took everything from me.

I thought I was a weak, victim but I am not. I am slowly rebuilding my life, I am slowly living again and I am recovering from what he did to me.

I am a survivor, not a victim, but it wasn't always that way.

This is my story and this is my truth.

WHAT ARE SOME SELF-SOOTHING STRATEGIES?

I'm almost embarrassed that I didn't think to include this chapter when my sexual assault counselling started (that's the focus of another book), but I wanted to include this first chapter so in case you get overwhelmed, triggered or distressed by anything in this book then you have some strategies to help your body relax.

The very last thing I want is for you to get triggered or distressed by anything in this book and for you not to have tools or strategies to help you.

As a result, the ability to self-soothe is beyond critical to mental health because it allows us to calm ourselves down, we can relax and return to our window of tolerance. Yet some people aren't able to self-soothe so to relax, calm down and maintain their mental health they need others to soothe them. This is a strategy that works for a time but it is far from perfect and it doesn't solve anything.

I struggle a lot with my inability to self-soothe because this was the focus of the topic this week in my specialist counselling session. Therefore, in this chapter, you'll learn what is self-soothing, how can you self-soothe and why it's so important to your mental health.

What Is Self-Soothing?

A person's ability to self-soothe is their efforts to calm themselves down when they're in an emotional state as proposed by Wright (2009). As well as this is beyond critical for our psychological well-being because it helps people to stay calm and emotionally regulated.

I know this is a massive issue for me because my ability to self-soothe has always been bad, but after my rape, over time it got worse and worse. Currently, at the time of writing, I essentially cannot self-soothe at all, which is a massive problem. This is why I'm focusing on this in therapy.

Moreover, a lot of people learn how to self-soothe when we're babies because when our caregivers soothe us, we internalise this soothing and learn how to do it ourselves (Wright, 2009). Yet there are a wide range of reasons why people (like me) are unable to learn these self-soothing skills and use them as adults.

Thankfully, it is perfectly possible to learn how to self-soothe as an adult and that's the focus of this chapter. Granted, self-soothing requires self-insight, we need to develop our skills and we need to be able to effectively use these skills in an effort to calm ourselves down.

This is an important bit I believe because we can read and learn everything we want to about self-soothing. Yet unless we practice and get better *over time* then we will never actually improve our self-soothing skills.

What Are Some Self-Soothing Strategies?

Take Some Deep Breaths

I wanted to start us off with an extremely simple one because I know from personal experience, it is this extremely simple and extremely useful technique that we tend to forget the most. As well as I want to take advantage of the primacy and recency effect. Therefore, whenever we want to self-soothe we need to deactivate our sympathetic nervous system. This means we need to activate our parasympathetic nervous system because this nervous system helps to stop the fight-or-flight response and helps us to calm down.

Thankfully, the parasympathetic nervous system can be very easily activated by taking a few long, deep breaths, including box breathing. Box breathing involves you breathing in for a count of 4 then you hold for a count of 4 and breathe out for a count of 4. Finally, you hold for a count of 4.

You do this a few times until you start to feel calmer.

Again, you need to practice this, so let's try it right now together.

- Breathe in for a count of 4.
- Hold your breath for a count of 4
- Breathe out
- Hold

You would do this a few times but I hope you already start to feel calmer. I know I do.

You Need To Listen To Relaxing Music

Something I've only just realised is that when my mental health is bad and I cannot focus on doing something on my laptop, I play relaxing music as a matter of habit. I never do it when my mental health is good, but I still do it to self-soothe. I never realised that until now. In fact, on YouTube, I'm currently listening to "*Cozy Autumn Vibes, Beautiful Relaxing Music, Peaceful Soothing Instrumental Music, By Tim Janis*".

It's very good by the way.

Anyway, listening to relaxing music is a good idea for self-soothing because this type of music helps to reduce the stress hormone called Cortisol (Khalfa et al., 2003). As a result, if you're feeling distressed and you're spiralling, try listening to relaxing music because this calming music might help you change your mood, help you to breathe deeper and decrease the negative emotions that you're experiencing.

If you have a Go-To music service that you love (my friends still don't understand why I prefer YouTube for my music over Spotify), then maybe create a playlist of relaxing music so you can listen to it when you're distressed.

Then remember to actually play it and listen to it.

You Should Do Pleasant Activities To Self-Soothe

Personally, I know how difficult, impossible and awful it can be when you're depressed, spiralling or in a mental health crisis, because we all know we need to do pleasant activities to maintain our mental health. Yet when we're spiralling and urgently need to self-soothe, it can be so impossible to do these things that we enjoy.

However, Dialectical Behavioural Therapy suggests that we can self-soothe by doing activities that bring us joy and make us happy (Linehan, 1993). Especially as us doing a pleasurable activity when we're distressed can make us feel better.

As a result, when you're distressed, try to do activities you enjoy. Be it reading, gardening, exercise, whatever. Just try to do something that makes you happy.

When I'm distressed, I try to watch something I'll enjoy, listen to podcasts, cook, read or hang out with friends. Since these are the activities that make me happy and they help to make me feel better. Of course that doesn't mean they're easy to do in the slightest when I'm distressed but over time as you practise to self-soothe more and more then these strategies become a lot easier.

Conclusion

In my opinion, none of these strategies are useful alone and in isolation. In reality, whilst all these are highly effective self-soothing strategies, they feed into each other. For example, when you're distressed you cannot simply start doing pleasurable activities because in my experience, you cannot focus and you cannot enjoy them. Therefore, you can start to self-soothe by doing box-breathing to activate our parasympathetic nervous system so you can calm down or listen to relaxing music. Then you can start to do pleasurable activities to help you self-soothe for longer.

So much of psychology and mental health advice can never be done effectively in isolation.

Therefore, to end this chapter, I want to finish by saying that having an inability to self-soothe can be very damaging to your mental health, and it is so annoying. Yet it is more than possible over time to practise and improve your self-soothing skills. I never thought I would be able to self-soothe but last night I got triggered by a stupid sex ad on YouTube and I got distressed yet I practised box-breathing and managed to self-soothe for the first time in my life.

And I am very proud of myself for managing that.

Now I just need to keep practising, keep trying and keep strengthening my ability to self-soothe. It is possible regardless of how impossible and scary it seems. Just keep trying and using the strategies included in this chapter and one day you will get there.

And it will be a wonderful feeling when you do.

PART ONE:
MY PERSONAL EXPERIENCE OF RAPE

THE EFFECTS OF SEXUAL ASSAULT

Trigger warning: this following reflection contains references to sex, sexual assault and the aftermath of the assault and mental health. If the following will trigger you then please skip this reflection for the sake of your own mental health.

Straight after my assault and before I knew I needed to write a book on my experience as a survivor and the first 6-months of my recovery, I wrote what I call "clinical psychology reflections". This is one of the psychology series I have and they're easy-to-understand experience- and fact-based reflections written to inform and educate aspiring or qualified clinical psychologists.

This is one of those chapters.

However, please rest assured that nothing in this book is going to be dull, academic and unreadable. This is a very personal and insightful chapter that you're going to learn a lot from, so please sit back, relax and read how I was sexually assaulted.

***

Sometimes things happen in my personal life that make me want to write these clinical psychology reflections a lot earlier than I normally would. For example, I know I won't write the rest of these reflections for another few months but I need to write these two now.

I was sexually assaulted two nights ago and I had an appointment today to discuss it at my university, the very nice woman helped to me to understand that it was sexual assault. I wasn't making it up or overreacting and she was really helpful.

I easily cried 2 or 3 times during that 30-minute appointment.

There is a clinical psychology point in the next chapter that I might be able to generalise to our profession. Yet I want to explain the effects of sexual assault on a victim in this chapter because I was surprised to learn what was normal behaviour in these cases when I spoke to the specialist at the university today.

<u>Disclaimer</u>

I've been watching the news, looking at social media and I've heard a lot of conversations with different people over my lifetime. I know I will get slated for writing these next two reflections, I know people will say I was asking for it and I know people will say I am disgusting and all that shit.

But honestly, unless you have experienced sexual assault then you don't have a leg to stand on.

I promise I am not having a go at 99% of readers because I know my audience are genuinely lovely and I love you all, you allow me to write and do what I love.

I am instead talking to the 1% of people that will read this and want to bully me because of it. To you I say kindly fuck off.

What Happened?

Before I explain what the effects of this event on me were specifically, I want to explain what happened in a way similar to how I described it to the woman at the university. I will brushstroke some stuff because what actually happened was too detailed for a book.

Therefore, if you're familiar with me and if you've been listening to The Psychology World Podcast then you might be aware that I was abused and traumatised as a kid for being gay. My social environment was extremely homophobic, I was in fear for my life for a decade that led to a lot of bad mental health outcomes. So I was never ever allowed to be gay at all. Much less hookup, have sex or kiss someone.

Thankfully, in that department my life is a million times better than it was and I'm generally happy with my life. It was so much better than before.

So I was free at the weekend, my friends have a lot of relationships and my best friend is currently abroad visiting the woman that They really want to start a relationship with. So I thought yeah it would be great if I could experience something.

I went on Grindr (for people who don't know that is a gay dating app but it is a more sex-focused one) so I had some nice conversations with two people that wanted to have sex with me. They couldn't do that particular night so I started talking with a third guy.

He seemed nice enough, he knew I was a virgin and had never ever done anything before with anyone. His photo seemed nice enough (something that was a minor con in the end) so we arranged to meet and I went to his house.

For starters, I realised he had lied on his profile because the photo he sent me he had hidden his body in such a way that he was very overweight.

For clarification I am not fatshaming, I am simply raising a point that he made sure to hide that fact and he used his weight to his advantage later on.

I went inside the house and he grabbed me and started kissing and grinding himself against me. I said "No, I haven't done this before". Expecting him to stop and we could talk about this hookup, what I wanted and we could go slow.

That didn't happen.

He stopped for a moment and then he grabbed me again and started *really* grinding himself against me, kissing me and forcing his tongue down my throat. And let me tell you, considering I have never kissed anyone in my entire life before, that wasn't nice and it is awful having someone force their tongue down your throat.

I hated it.

Now typical stereotypes would make you question why I didn't punch, kick, scream in this situation if I hated it so much. I have been a survivor my entire life and I was always focused on doing what I needed to do to survive, so I simply let it happen because once it happened this would be over and I could get the hell out of there without anything violent happening to me.

When I was talking to the woman at the university, this is a very normal response. The vast majority of sexual assault and rape victims do this strategy because this is what happens.

So the guy kept touching me, taking off my clothes, he kept kissing me and getting really really excited.

Only an idiot couldn't tell I wasn't enjoying it because I wasn't touching him back, I wasn't smiling and I wasn't doing anything to him in return. Mainly because he was massive. I might have touched him on the head to be nice and polite but that was it.

Then he took my boxers off and this is where I skip over some details. Let's just say he really, really liked my manhood so let's skip over that section.

Afterwards he ordered me to lie down and I am very thankful for the next bit. Because he was so fat, his dick didn't work in the sense that it didn't get long so this couldn't graduate from sexual assault to rape (the legal difference being rape requires penetration).

He grabbed me and covered me in his hulk in a tight hug as he tried to penetrate me and once he realised he wasn't able to. (He wasn't even using a condom or lube which is extremely bad sexual practice but I was too numb and feeling bad to mention it) He stopped and called it over.

I got out of there.

The Effects

During this entire process, I felt very numb, uncomfortable and I expect this is the autism here. I didn't feel in danger or too distressed at the time.

Interestingly when I spoke to the woman at the university, she said that this is also very normal because victims go into survival mode. Similar to fight or flight response, there is "fawn" or "freeze" response and I think I did both of these in the moment. Since fawn is about being a people pleaser in the end where you just allow shit to happen because it would make the other person happy and that reduces any unseen things happening to you. Like him getting angry and lashing out.

Equally, "freeze" is definitely what I did once he grabbed me for the second time.

In addition, something I notice with myself and I expect this is an autistic trait, so autistic people don't always know what they're feeling in the moment and there can be a delay between what happened and an emotion. Turns out, according to the woman at the university, this is common for victims too.

Since when I got home the night it happened, I felt numb and uncomfortable but I didn't feel distressed. Yet my problem was I couldn't sleep, I couldn't stay still in my bed and it wasn't awful. I woke up with a massive headache the next morning.

Also, the next morning I was really distressed, scared and I started to spiral. In other words, my brain and emotions caught up with the reality of the situation.

I cleaned my teeth a lot yesterday because I wanted to make sure my mouth was clean after he tongued me. Also, I had my normal trauma reaction of whenever I ate or drank it felt like swallowing glass. I've experienced that before whenever I'm distressed.

And the most major one and you might want to skip the next few paragraphs if you're sensitive. Because the guy liked my dick so much, I really hated having a dick. Yesterday morning I wanted to cut it off and just get rid of it forever.

Thankfully, that only lasted yesterday morning and then it shifted into a case of "I don't like seeing my dick but I don't want it gone anymore". Even now, I'm *better* with my dick but I still haven't looked at it and I haven't really touched it.

So going to the toilet is a bit annoying.

Moreover, something that is distressing as hell is yesterday when I was trying to keep myself busy and focus on everything but what happened (it didn't work). I could be doing something, like lying on my bed playing Duolingo or reading something, and I could *feel* him touching me.

Then I would get scared and almost cry because my body literally felt like he was touching me exactly how he did the night before. I know there's a name for this in psychology but I don't want to look it up.

It was weird and scary and awful.

Finally, the last major effect of the assault was I had a very weird panic attack last night in my own bed. Now this guy didn't try to have sex with me in a bed, it was in his living room.

Therefore, I was very surprised that when I went into my bed last night in my normal way of only wearing boxers. I had a panic attack because I wasn't wearing many clothes and I had to use grounding techniques about what I could feel, hear, smell and taste (I couldn't use see because I had my bedroom lights off) to make me focus back on the present moment.

And where I actually was.

So I'll admit I am very nervous about going to bed tonight but if I have another panic attack then I'll do what the woman from the university said and wear more clothes going to bed. That's a good idea to be honest and it's easy.

The Response From Others

Yesterday I was spiralling, trying to focus on what had happened and I was just scared because of a bunch of other trauma and what had happened before in my life (it wasn't sexual assault related but my brain didn't care), so I contacted one friend. The problem was they're in another country and they were away so they didn't have access to Wi-Fi (we communicate via WhatsApp a lot), so they didn't get back to me.

Also, my other close friend is very innocent and they wouldn't have any clue about this. As well as my other close friend is a sexual abuse victim from childhood so I couldn't talk to him about it.

Therefore, this morning actually did contact my friend that had been sexually abused as a child with the massive caveat that he needs to say no if he isn't comfortable with this. He messaged me back hours later saying we could take this conversation slowly and thankfully he didn't get triggered but he confirmed this was rape.

Before that though, I contacted my university because they have a Specialist Support Service as part of their mental health team. I had a 30-minute appointment with her and she's great and I told her what happened, she told me about my options and some support I could get.

The only real support I am concerned I might need is academic because I have two stats exams coming up and I'm concerned that I can't seem to focus. I know I'm getting ahead of myself because it was only two days ago but I am scared that I won't be able to focus on revision for the exams next month.

Thankfully, she said mitigation is an option and she can help with that.

Then she mentioned the name of a service with an extremely problematic name and we spoke about groups and some interesting stuff including some denial about terms on my part. Like I didn't want to admit I was a sexual assault victim until three people confirmed what happened was sexual assault.

I really didn't want to admit it but that is what happened.

Finally, I had a lovely, deep conversation with my best friend who finally read my messages and I'm looking forward to seeing them in a few weeks when they're back.

Ending Note

I'll admit that it took a lot for me to write this reflection because I didn't want any of this to happen, I am better than I was in the morning but that's only because I spoke to people about it. I feel better that I'm supported and the people important to me socially are aware of this.

Like, I'm seeing a friend on Thursday (it's Monday today), I'm spending a few days with my best friend anyway, I'm hoping to see my innocent friend next week so I thankfully have the social support.

Will I be 100% okay?

Of course not. No one ever is but I am better than I was and I'm happy about that.

Now, because this reflection is a little longer than I intended I will leave the rest for another reflection. Which will be a lot more general towards clinical psychology and mental health as a whole.

Let's check it out.

GROUP IDENTITIES AND PROBLEMATIC NAMES OF RAPE AND SEXUAL ASSAULT SERVICES

Trigger warning: *the following clinical psychology reflection contains details and references of rape, sexual assault and the stories of victims. Please do not read this reflection if you would find it distressing.*

Originally, I debated whether to include this chapter in or not but I want to. Since our next chapter touches on how us survivors can be in denial about what happened to us, as well as how the names of services can stop us from accessing them.

In other words, this chapter, like a few other chapters in this book, is about letting you know that you aren't alone and if you're experiencing things that you might call "weird" then chances are, you are far from the only one.

You are never alone.

<u>The Group Identities and Labels</u>

As a clinical psychology student, author and podcaster, I've thought a lot about the stigma and social perceptions surrounding labels and names. It's one of the reasons why I hate the diagnostic system with a passion and it's why I've spoken a lot about the damaging impact of labels in these reflections before.

However, I was a little surprised by my own denial and resistance to terming myself as a victim or a sexual assault victim. I think mainly because I thought maybe only someone who's been kicked, punched, beaten with an inch of their life could say they're a victim of rape or sexual assault.

Again, just me going off the societal myths about this sort of crime.

Maybe I thought only certain people get raped and assaulted. Maybe I didn't want to admit what had happened and how serious and bad that was.

Then as the woman at the university said along with my good close friends, this was rape and this was bad and this never ever should have happened.

I slowly had to acknowledge that this was sexual assault and I was a victim.

Therefore, as a clinical psychology person, I find it interesting that people don't want to attach certain labels to themselves. In all honesty, I know this from my previous lectures and comments on labels because they are stigmatised. I bet you're thinking I am a very specific type of person because

I've been sexually assaulted.

Some of you are probably thinking I'm weak, not manly (I'm non-binary anyway) and I'm a failure because real people fight back.

You would only be going off cultural stereotypes so I hardly blame you. I might even do the same if I was in your shoes.

And I think the reason why I was so resistant to terming myself as a sexual assault victim was because I didn't want to see myself as a victim anymore. I've been a victim my entire life from child abuse and trauma, living constantly in fear for my life and so on.

I just wanted to live a little and then this happened.

And I know from my family and my social environment that being a victim of sexual assault isn't always something you get supported in. Like I know I will tell my family but I won't at the moment because that will make me a victim in their eyes and they will look at me every day like I'm a victim.

Also, there is a lot of stigma and social pressure on victims. People will say I was asking for it, I should have fought back, I should have done X, Y and Z. or even well, I'm gay so this was bound to happen (an utter bullshit comment if there ever was one but I have heard a variation of it in real life).

So I was very resistant to it.

Overall, when it comes to clinical psychology work in the future and you have a client that refuses to be termed or included in a group of people. I would unofficially recommend respecting them and maybe even gently question why.

Since when the woman at the university said in a paraphrased way "Something-Something Rape Services for victims of sexual violence, I don't know if you would include yourself in those groups,"

I said: "I don't want to but I know the definition is anything that isn't consensual sex is rape. But I *know* I'm a rape victim but I don't want to admit it,"

That is perfectly okay and she respected me and I later admitted it in my own time. That is something you can and should do with clients too.

Naming Services

Continuing with the same vein of thinking and reasoning, I wanted to comment on the name of a charity or mental health service that offers counselling and other support for sexual assault and rape victims. I can't say its actual name for privacy reasons but it was "Something-Something Rape Crisis Centre"

I didn't like the name and the name immediately put me off the service.

As well as the woman at the university admitted the name was problematic because for starters, it implies only rape victims can go there, not sexual assault victims.

Also, the name is very loaded because it suggests that if you go to this place then you are a victim of rape and sexual assault and it carries all that social stigma with it. I did not want to contact or deal with this charity whatsoever because I didn't want to admit to myself that I was a victim and I did not want to go there and be seen to everyone at this charity as a weak victim.

Again, this isn't me being difficult. This is me just using what limited knowledge I have about victims from what I've seen on TV, the news and social conversations over the years. I only researched it more this afternoon after others confirmed and helped me to realise what had happened.

On the whole, I think if this service and charity didn't have such a loaded name then I would have considered it. I might have contacted them, and the woman at the university wouldn't have had to explain that other people have had similar reactions to me. And then she gently made sure I explained what support network I have in place at the moment as she knew I wasn't going to contact the service.

In future, I think, as future or current clinical psychologists, if we ever rise to a position of power where we are in a position to name mental health and support services. Then we need to be mindful about the words we use in the name so they aren't loaded, they aren't going to turn people away and they aren't going to stop the people we aim to help.

Just an interesting thought-provoking idea that I would have liked never to learn or have to think about.

WHY ISN'T AN ERECTION CONSENT?

This is the psychology article that started everything, because without this podcast episode, this book would not be possible. Also, this article allowed to subtly talk about what had happened to me, it made me want to speak up about rape and male rape more generally so I could educate people against the many myths and misconceptions about rape.

Even though any podcast episode on sexual violence is going to do badly because 99% of people just want to avoid the topic of sexual violence and pretend it doesn't exist, I am proud that I did this podcast episode.

It gave me a chance to find my voice, get comfortable talking about my experience and it gave me a drive to fight. It gave me hope that I could fight against the veil of silence that society created for itself around this topic and it gave me hope that I might be able to help at least one single person in case they're experienced something similar.

Please enjoy the psychology article that started everything.

***

Research suggest that men get raped and sexually assaulted as often as women by both men and women. Yet male rape is a lot less reported because of societal factors, gender roles and a whole bunch of horrible myths that stop men from reporting rape and sexual assault. Also, it's important to note that talking about male rape isn't about stopping or taking the focus away from female rape, instead it's actually about highlighting something that isn't spoken about in society. All rape and sexual assault whether it's against a man or woman is flat out wrong and it should never happen. Therefore, in this forensic psychology podcast episode, we'll explore male rape and why an erection isn't consent. If you like learning about forensic psychology, sexual crimes and why people do this crime then you'll enjoy today's episode.

Why Am I Talking About Male Sexual Assault and Rape?

Just as a little introduction to this episode and why I'm personally doing this, I wanted to be upfront and honest with you about my own personal position. So I'm a victim of sexual assault, it happened about three weeks ago and I cannot emphasise how distressing, awful and foul it was. I don't wish it on anyone and whilst you won't hear any major details about my assault in this episode, this did happen to me. As well as I will add in my personal thoughts like always in this episode to help it come alive.

Since one of the awful things that happened after my assault was that I worked an Open Day at my university and I was talking to a lecturer that I always talk to. I really like her, she's great and she studies forensic psychology. Even though I completely forgot her topic was sexual violence so she started talking about it and I just couldn't listen not one week after what had happened.

And the entire reason for this podcast episode was researching sexual assault and rape really did help me during that first intense, horrific week. It helped me to understand what had happened, this was common and it really wasn't my fault.

Therefore, even if I can help one person or inform a few people about male sexual assault then I would have done my job with today's episode.

<u>Some Data On Male Sexual Assault</u>

Before we start talking about the content in any more depth, let's look at some data, the Rape, Abuse and Incest National Network found that 1 in 33 men have experienced a completed or attempted rape in their lifetime and 1 out of every 10 rape victims are male. And remember, these figures are out of the reported figures, so the real numbers could be a lot, lot higher.

Furthermore, the US's Centre for Disease Control and Prevention have shown in research that men and women are equally likely to be sexually assaulted and victims of sexual violence. Yet sexual assault against men has been severely, severely underrecognized, undertreated and underreported.

Finally, the National Crime Victimisation Survey shows that a lot of men report being sexually assaulted by women through forced penetration and coerced erections.

Overall, I hope this goes to show that male sexual assault isn't rare and it is a lot more common than any of us realise.

<u>Male Sexual Assault And Rape</u>

Whilst it is very rare that male sexual assault is reported in a given year, it is true that men are victims of sexual harassment, rape and molestation on a daily basis. Also, whilst it's tempting to think that male sexual assault is *only* committed by other men, in reality, it is actually an even spilt with female and male rapists.

As a result of male rape by women is a lot more common than we will ever see in the Criminal Justice System and the news as well as social media. Part of this underreport is shame and the stigma of a man "not being manly enough" because of the stupid idea that "only weak men get raped". Yet another reason is that when women rape men, they generally get the man to have an erection and even ejaculation so this confuses and paralyses the man.

Mainly because society teaches us that if a man gets an erection then they enjoy it and that isn't rape.

I actually remember one of my schoolfriends saying this back in my secondary school years and back then I sort of knew that wasn't 100% right, but I had no idea how flat out wrong it was until three weeks ago.

Also, on the underreporting, why I didn't report it was because I was embarrassed, I felt dirty, I felt so violated that I didn't want many people to know. And I was scared to be honest. I was scared of getting hurt yet again, I was scared of the stigma and I was scared about what my friends and family would think. Of course, they loved me, supported me and they have been great since they found out. Then there is the legal issue too because I had cleaned my teeth when I got home and I had showered the next morning because I was in extreme denial. And it took me two days to admit I had been sexually assaulted and by that point there was no one DNA left on me.

There were other reasons why a prosecution would have been difficult but that isn't the focus of this episode.

And I didn't want to go through the whole legal process, but if someone listening does want to do this that is very important, critical and you should. If you want to press charges then you absolutely should.

In addition, having an erection isn't consent or a sign that the person is willing or ready to have sex because an erection and ejaculation are physiological responses that we cannot control. Also, these physiological responses can occur due to pain, anxiety, fear and sexual desire or excitement.

Lastly, a final note on the underreporting, a lot of men don't label themselves as sexual assault victims and they don't call it what it is. Since typically when men learn that other men have been sexually assaulted they meet the disclosure with insensitivity and mockery.

Personally, it took me two full days, my two good friends and a specialist at the university to help me realise and call my assault what it was. I was in such extreme denial that I refused to label myself as a victim of sexual assault because I knew how those people were viewed in society. Yet I am a victim and once I "accepted" or realised that, it got a little bit easier because I could talk to people, contact my therapist and start recovering.

This podcast episode is part of that recovery because I want to help someone possibly.

What About Male On Male Sexual Assault? A Brief Look

So far in the episode, we've looked at what happens when women assault men, but let's focus on male-on-male sexual assault. When a man is sexually assaulted by another man this carries another strand of stigma as the victim fears that other people might question their sexual preferences and their sexual orientation and there is a concern about they might be seen as "less manly" because of the assault.

This is why I don't understand gender roles and the whole idea that men have to behave a certain way. Male mental health would be so much better if these gender-based rules of behaviour weren't around.

Anyway, a lot of men don't report male-on-male sexual assault because of the shame and humiliation or the perception of being weak for not fighting their attacker.

That's actually an interesting myth about sexual assault and rape that I learnt from the specialist at the university. Everyone thinks that when someone is raped or sexually assaulted, the victims screams, fights and tries to break free. But that is very, very rare. In reality, and this happened to me, you basically get so numb and cold and an emotion that I lately realised was fear, that you don't want it to happen, you say stop but when the attacker keeps grabbing you and carrying on. You get it over with so you can escape and run like hell after towards. Since my fear was my attacker was a lot larger than me unfortunately, so I was scared if I tried to fight back he would grab me, hurt me and the situation would be even worse.

That is why people rarely fight back.

It doesn't make them weak or stupid and it doesn't make what happened to them any less traumatic.

It just makes them a survivor.

Myths That Contribute To The Challenge Of Recognizing Male Sexual Assault

Below are some myths in society that contribute to people not talking, recognising and treating male sexual assault as seriously as female sexual assault (And yes, I realise there is still a long, long way to go before female sexual assault treatment is perfect).

- Men are only raped by other men.
- Erections only happen when the man is excited.
- Erections are a sign of consent.
- Men always want sex no matter what.
- Men can never have enough sex.
- Men secretly like being sexually assaulted.
- There is something wrong with a man if he doesn't want sex.
- Ejaculation is a sign of sexual enjoyment.
- "Real men" don't get sexually assaulted.
- Men like to be in charge in the bedroom.

All these myths are extremely harmful when it comes to recognising male sexual assault, but they don't help the aftermath of the assault too. Since our culture views sexual violence against men as disenfranchised abuse and this means men don't get the same emotional, legal or medical support as women do.

Therefore, these myths about men only being sexual predators that have an extreme need for sex that is engrained in the mental health, public health, medical as well as Criminal Justice Systems, they only hurt men. Since having an erection and ejaculation makes people debate if it was actually assault or not, because people believe they had to be aroused and enjoying it for that to happen.

I can personally protest that this isn't the case. Sure, I was rock hard during my assault but I was never ever going to ejaculate and I was not enjoying it. I did not enjoy being grabbed and having a lot of different things done to me.

Interestingly, as I'm an aspiring clinical psychologist, in psychotherapy, a therapist might question the validity of the rape claim by the male victim and they might not be very convinced of the traumatic effects of the incident. So the therapist's behaviour and attitudes tend to leave male victims feeling undermined and delegitimatized.

Another factor I want to add here is that after a sexual assault, it takes even more courage to reach out to a therapist than normal. Since I have a great relationship with my therapist and she is brilliant because I work well with her and she helped me with my child abuse trauma. Something that was slightly connected to my assault. Yet I didn't want to contact her because I didn't want to admit that my assault had happened. I only contacted her and had a brilliant session with her because a good friend basically ordered me to see her.

Thankfully, it worked out well.

Conclusion

Before I wrap up the podcast episode with a little more information, I want to mention that I have really enjoyed this episode. It has been tough and at the moment, I've only written the episode out. I am a little nervous about saying this stuff because I think having to say the R-word and the A-word so many times will be hard. But I'm still proud of myself for doing this really hard episode, because I'm revealing to the general public what happened to me and some people won't like what I'm saying because of the myths. Other people will thankfully support me and it's those people that I will listen to and treasure.

But ultimately, I'm doing this episode to help people. There might be another listener who has experienced an assault, rape or they might know someone who has been. I hope this episode shows these people that it's okay, things do get better and it wasn't their fault. This is a common experience and it flat out doesn't make you a failure.

Society and the myth spreaders, they are the failures.

And for people who have never been a victim, I seriously hope that never changes, but I hope you now know the truth and you'll actively challenge these myths when they pop up. Then if you work with clients and if this happens to a friend or loved one then you know more facts to help them.

Just love them, support them and listen to them. Those are my biggest takes from my experience.

Anyway, on the whole, we need to realise that when our systems don't make victims feel like they're taken seriously and they minimise the assault and don't tend to take action. Then this continues the harm and suffering that male victims experience from the trauma of sexual violence.

As a result, as a society, we need to stop this minimisation and break this stigma of male sexual assault because it isn't helpful and it certainly isn't right. A lot of this can be done by deconstructing traditional gender stereotypes because the main problem is that currently men aren't allowed to demonstrate their feelings besides anger, and this isn't good. Especially when people see pain and trauma responses as a degradation of manhood and this isn't helpful to us achieving true feminism.

In other words, true gender equality where men and women are true equals.

Additionally, we need to continue to work on deconstructing traditional ideas about what it means to be a victim. Since it's important to note that "force" isn't always about physical strength and being overpowered. Rapists and predators typically groom, coerce and emotionally manipulate or threaten their targets into nonconsensual sex.

Most importantly, this podcast episode and the entire point of advocating for male sexual assault victims isn't about delegitimising or undermining violence against women. Instead I am highlighting that men can be victims too and the gender stereotype that women are helpless victims is another unhelpful and undeserved gender stereotype. In turn, this only reinforces silly ideas what about it means to be a man or woman and even more outrageous ideas that male victims are "failed" men.

No victim of sexual violence is a failure. They are a victim that needs to be supported, helped and listened to.

Overall, when it comes to male sexual violence (or women for that matter) using gender-sensitive approaches in our work is critical. We need to understand that societal norms and expectations will always impact men and women disproportionately, and this should never come at the cost of undermining boys and men that have been sexually abused. Instead we need to use inclusive approaches to our work that allow us to advocate and support victims regardless of their gender, so we can enable a culture shift to happen.

Ultimately allowing us to have more conversations about healing, prevention and providing good care for victims whatever their gender is.

TRIGGERS CAN COME FROM ANYWHERE

Within clinical psychology, we are all well-aware that clients with different mental health conditions can be triggered in a few different ways. For example, if we take the most obvious example of anxiety, then we know that clients can be triggered in limited ways.

For instance, clients with social anxiety will likely be triggered in social situations whereas clients with a spider phobia will likely only be triggered in a situation involving a spider. Also, clients with generalised anxiety disorder can get anxious about everything and anything.

This content we all learn through our clinical psychology lectures, textbooks and we can hear about it from service users. Yet this comes back to the previous point I made in another reflection, I did not truly understand this idea of triggers and how extremely distressing and random they can be until my assault.

I'll briefly and lightly tell you some things that happened to me this week and then I'll reflect on them in terms of clinical psychology. Although, this is more of a lived experience post compared to a "hardcore" clinical psychology reflection.

What Happened?

It was my birthday over the bank holiday weekend and my best friend stayed with me at my parents' house, and because of my Great-Aunt was staying, They couldn't sleep in the room they normally did whenever they stay over.

They had to sleep on a camp bed in my room, and I had been concerned about that for a different reason for weeks after my assault. I was concerned how I would react to have someone I really like sleeping in the same room as me.

I just never expected it to trigger me as much as it did.

Since my friend was wearing jeans with a belt and when we turned the lights off my friend started to get undressed for bed. Like any normal person would and I was trying to get to sleep because I had undressed and got into bed when they were cleaning their teeth.

Yet the sound of them undoing their belt and taking their clothes off was beyond awful. I wrapped myself up so tightly in my bedsheets just so nothing could happen.

And in hindsight I should have gone downstairs and slept on the sofa. Yet I stayed in my room with my friend and it was a rough night. My friend slept fine but whenever they moved in the night, whenever they made a sound and whenever they did anything. I would get so anxious, so scared and so hypervigilant that I couldn't sleep.

On the second night, I slept downstairs but I still couldn't really sleep because our sofa is a lot less comfortable than it was 2 years ago at Christmas. And the camp bed was on a dodgy floorboard so again whenever my friend moved in the night I would hear it.

Thankfully, the third night, I got a better night's sleep because I was sleeping again in my room but closer to my friend. And I trained my brain to tell me that if there's a noise in the night, my friend would never ever let anything bad happen to me. They would protect me.

That worked for the most part and the only bad part was the floor next to the camp bed was, well, a floor so I wasn't perfectly comfortable.

Anyway, so you can see how just something as normal as two friends sleeping in the same room can be triggering. As well as simple sounds or movements can be triggering to assault survivors.

Personally, I found this a logical thing to be triggered by because in my sexual assault, there were no clothes on, the assaulter was wearing jeans and he had to take them off and the rest. So I can understand why this was triggering.

Yet I was surprised how this trigger had spread to other domains in my life. Since my assault did not happen with a friend, it did not happen in a bedroom and it did not happen with someone that I trust with my life. Much less someone I'm romantically into.

However, I think this trigger is a good example of how traumatic events and what reminds victims of them can spread into other areas of their lives to the point where they are extremely distressed.

It was horrible not sleeping for those three nights then it took me another two nights to start sleeping normally again.

The Tube Incident

On my actual birthday when my friend stayed with me, we both went up to London to do this Virtual Reality escape room that was brilliant fun and I seriously recommend it. The day was lovely, I really enjoyed the VR thing and I had a great time with my friend.

Yet I was already tired from not sleeping for two nights and then we were on the Tube in London to get some dinner. And there was a sign, a very noble and innocent sign on the Tube opposite me.

Pressing Up Against Someone On Purpose is Sexual Harassment. Then it was something like *Don't Do It* or *Stop!*

And my body and mind just got scared and triggered to my utter annoyance. I tried to make myself as small as possible, I could only look at the floor and my friend had to call my name to make me look at them. They told me things were okay, we didn't have long left and they were asking if I wanted to get off the Tube for a breather.

They are a brilliant friend.

But I really didn't want to be on that Tube, because in my mind, pressing up against someone is the same as grinding against something. Which is something my assaulter did to me constantly so I was tired, stressed and seeing that sign really didn't help.

I hated it and when me and my friend were back in my room, I asked them point blank *what was it like seeing me like that*? They could only say it was concerning and they worry about me enough anyway so to have their worries confirmed probably really wasn't nice for them.

Overall, I'm really annoyed that I was triggered by such a stupid sign. I hated how I was triggered that easily and I think there is an embarrassment aspect because I was crying my eyes out on the Tube and all this happened in front of other people who didn't know me, didn't know what had happened and they were judging me. Especially this elderly man with grey hair and big bushy eyebrows. He was seriously judging me.

So I hated that I could be triggered that easily since there is a disempowering element too.

Part of me no longer knows if I can go up to London by myself, because what if I get triggered and there's no one around to help me? What if all the assault memories flood me and I'm trapped? What if someone hurts me again on the Tube?

Of course the last one isn't a logical or realistic thought, but it happens. As well as I know giving myself time to heal needs to be my main focus but it is still annoying.

Reading Survivor Stories

Finally, on the Wednesday, I was still tired and I was at university away for a revision lecture and I had a social group thing that evening. I was still a bit distressed because after I dropped my friend off back home, they experienced something really bad because of their housemates. And I know it's bad because they refuse to tell me over text and we can have massive text conversations lasting hours at times.

Anyway, the distress from my birthday weekend was still lingering so I thought in my eternal wisdom to look up male sexual assault survivor stories. So I wouldn't feel so alone, so I would know other people were coping and surviving and they were thriving.

Note to self, do not read stuff like that less than a month after the assault.

I found a story exactly like mine down to every detail accept the ages were slightly different. And that was distressing as hell to realise that had happened to someone else and it was even worse that 5 years later they couldn't really date, they couldn't have sex and they couldn't live a normal life.

My mind didn't want to accept that, because when I was really distressed I was in the mind of "I want everything to go back to how it was before the assault". Of course that can never happen.

Reading that story was so triggering and distressing that I was crying and I had to do something very stupid to stop the pain.

Then I tried to read another story (clearly not learning my lesson) about a guy who had a completely different assault to me. The last line of the opening paragraph was "now I've lost everything I love" and that really sent me over the edge because I don't want to lose everything.

I know I won't but reading that survivor story wasn't helpful to me personally at this moment in time. Because this has always been my fatal fault, I try to do healing things before I am ready for them because I want to be further along than I am.

I never give myself time to heal and that's a massive mistake on my part.

Overall, when it comes to this triggering experience, I think we can all understand why this was triggering. It was reliving in words what had happened at a point where I was already distressed, tired and I hadn't slept in days.

Although, the interesting thing about this is that it shows that feeling that you aren't alone and that there are others like you, that come with time. Since some survivors and clients aren't ready for that straight away (I don't think anyone is straight away) and I think sometimes in clinical psychology when the conversation does turn to a sense of community, the nuance about whether this is right for a client or if they're ready for this, is missing at times.

I know I miss it in my personal life and my clinical psychology interests, but every client is different. That is what I've learnt from this week even more than normal, so some clients will enjoy and benefit from hearing stories and feeling apart of a larger community of victims. But some clients aren't ready at the moment and maybe they never will be.

That's okay because there are still so many ways to help them improve their lives, take back control and decrease their distress.

WHAT IS INTENT TO SURVIVE?

"You need to have the Intent To Survive this,"

Those were the words of my therapist towards the end of our session shortly after my sexual assault. They were powerful words to hear both as a clinical psychology student and a sexual assault survivor. I think a lot of their power came from me not understanding what it meant and me still reeling from what happened, but I also think they're powerful words because they are so true.

To be able to survive any traumatic event, you need to make sure you want to survive it.

As a result, I want to take the opportunity of this reflection to explain what Intent To Survive means to me personally as a survivor, but first I want to talk about this as an aspiring clinical psychologist.

What Is Intent To Survive In Clinical Psychology Terms?

As we know from our clinical psychology experiences, lectures and various conversations with professionals, we all know that we can give a client a lot of psychological help and support yet until a client is willing to change and use the tools and techniques we give them. Then our help only has a limited value.

For example, we can teach our clients ways to change their biased cognitive processes in depression and other mood disorders. Yet unless a client puts what they learn in therapy into practice in the real-world then the client cannot improve their lives.

To some extent, I think "Intent To Survive" is the trauma term of capacity to change, because a trauma causes a lot of psychological and physiological changes within a client. For instance, my sexual assault caused me to have a lot of panic attacks, rapid heartbeats, shaking and more.

Those were the physiological changes.

When it comes to psychological changes, I have a fair amount of social anxiety, my mood changes from normal and positive to depressed so I can't move some days, and as bad as this sounds I do have a minor fear of overweight people. Since my attacker was severely overweight so I might overweight people triggering.

Therefore, the term *intent to survive* means that a client has to do double duty when recovering from trauma. Since not only have they got to want to change and improve their life so they don't "suffer" from the physical and psychological manifestations of their trauma, but they have to want to survive it and move past it.

I know that won't make sense for people, because surely it is perfectly obvious that our clients will want to survive their trauma.

No.

Trauma really doesn't work like that in my personal experience and conversations I've had with some survivors.

Due to in trauma, death really can seem so much easier, and surviving trauma seems so pointless. It really does.

One example I had in May 2024 about 3.5 weeks after my assault was I had had a few panic attacks at a social group I go to normally and my friends and some of the other people at the social group went to a local pub in Canterbury. They asked if I wanted to go but I just broke down a little and ran out of there.

I texted my best friend and another friend about five minutes later saying how I just wanted to kill myself, I didn't want to do this anymore and death just seemed so much easier. I wasn't really suicidal that night but the thoughts were starting to come up.

This is rather normal in trauma survivors because surviving something traumatic just seems impossible and such a far away future that it doesn't seem real at all.

Therefore, as aspiring or qualified clinical psychologists or other mental health professionals, you might benefit from thinking about trauma in terms of *intent to survive.* Since helping a client focus specifically on surviving instead of healing straight away might be really, really useful.

Of course, the process will and should always be on the healing as well as recovery process. Yet healing takes a long, long time and it is that time in-between that is stupidly difficult.

Also, even though me and my therapist aren't really focus on the concept of *intent to survive* too much in my session. I still found those three words useful over the past few weeks because whenever I was struggling or in a "dark place", I could say to myself "I need to have *intent to survive* this,".

It was useful.

Overall, the concept of *intent to survive* within clinical work might have two places. Firstly, it is an effective way to reframe initial trauma sessions even more so when a client has just recently suffered the trauma. This is where (to my knowledge) survival is the main priority as healing seems so far away and impossible and trauma survivors aren't really in a position to heal at this point in time.

Secondly, *intent to survive* might be a useful phase to say to clients so they can remember they need to have an *intent to survive* their trauma whenever they're struggling or in a really dark place.

What Does *Intent To Survive* Mean To Me?

This is something I have seriously struggled with over the past few weeks because as an aspiring clinical psychologist, I know what this means. I think it is a great term and way to frame our own thinking about trauma like I mentioned above.

However, as a two-time trauma survivor, I have struggled to work out what this means to me as a human being. When my therapist first mentioned this, I didn't really register it because of course I wanted to survive this, I wanted to move past this and I thought I was going to be fine.

Because come on, it was only sexual assault.

Then May happened with my panic attacks, meltdowns and everything else that went negatively with my mental health. So it was nasty and I didn't know if I had the *intent to survive* because I wasn't sure what it meant.

Nonetheless, it's been 7 weeks exactly since The Event and I have a *better* idea about what it means to me. I've had my counselling assessment, I'm on the waiting list and I've learnt how great my friends are, so I have built a social support network around myself.

I think in the beginning *intent to survive* literally meant I wanted to see my best friend again because they were in Switzerland. I know this sounds odd because I wanted to see my best friend and I wanted to spend my birthday with them. I wanted my family to meet them, I wanted to go up to London to do the virtual reality escape room and I wanted to catch up with them.

They are my best friend for a reason.

Also, to me *intent to survive* initially meant just processing and dealing with it, because I was having a lot of physical reactions and problems. For example, the shaking, the fear of going to sleep and the problems of having a toilet.

After this happened the definition of *intent to survive* changed as I started to experience more and more psychological symptoms and trauma reactions. Like the depression, the meltdowns in public because of triggers, the intense social anxiety and so on.

When this happened *intent to survive* meant rather sadly just putting one foot in front of the other, taking each day as it came and trying to live as normal as a life as I possibly could.

This was really hard because there was another minor change in the definition as I couldn't see a future. The future and the idea of healing seemed so extreme and so impossible that I did not believe I could have a future.

This wasn't helped by my exams, my best friend experiencing awful harassment and accusations by their psychotic exboyfriend, and then a whole bunch of other things were going on in my own life.

Therefore, *intent to survive* took on a very meaningless or opaque definition. Since I sort of wanted to live and survive my assault but I also couldn't see a future. I couldn't see how I could ever have a relationship, I couldn't see how I could ever have sex, love someone or how I could ever not feel like a weak, pathetic, violated victim.

Thankfully, I did meet with the specialist at the university again and it was nice to have that referral.

This is where the definition of *intent to survive* changed again to what it currently means, and it's actually rather lovely to think about it for a change.

I know me and my best friend we are still operating on the assumption that I am a moderate suicide risk until we move into together at the end of June 2024 (exactly four weeks away). Personally, I think if I can make it after Pride weekend (that triggers a lot of past child abuse and trauma for me) then I should be okay.

Also, there will be a lot of people at Pride and a lot of couples and my concern is my mind will twist seeing couples and lots of happy people enjoying their day as "you can never have this because of your child abuse and your sexual assault so what's the point of living,"

Thankfully, me and my best friend have a plan in place anyway for Pride weekend and we're going with a lot of other friends too.

Anyway, going back to *intent to survive,* because I've had my counselling assessment and I'm on the waiting list with East Kent Rape Crisis Centre, I have a sense of hope. I am not 100%, I am still not completely sure that I can date, I can have sex and I can have relationships in the future.

But I will get the support I need, even if it takes two or three months.

There is hope.

So for me that is what *intent to survive* means at the moment. It means I have the hope to live and survive my sexual assault long enough to see what happens to me in the future.

Additionally, it means I have the curiosity as well as capacity to change because I want to survive this, so I can explore relationships, dating and what consensual sex actually looks like. That would be lovely. Also, I am curious about the therapy process as an aspiring clinical psychologist because I know sexual violence work is very specialised so I want to see how this differs from "normal" clinical work.

And it is perfectly okay if that is a reason that increases my *intent to survive.* As long as I can intend to survive my trauma then that is okay.

Lastly, *intent to survive* means to me that I want a future. I have no idea what this future will look like, I don't know if it's filled with relationships, love and respect. I don't know if it's filled with trauma, pain and suffering. I don't even know if it's filled with job possibilities and me having a successful career in clinical psychology.

Yet I want to try and I want to explore my future what it might be.

That is what *intent to survive* means to me because if I don't survive this trauma then I will never ever know what my future will be and hell, right now this is a half-joke to myself but I hope in a few months this will be something I truly believe in.

If I don't survive this then I might deny a hot, sexy guy or masculine person a chance to meet me, and come on now, that really would be cruel.

HOW CAN SEXUAL VIOLENCE IMPACT YOUR SEXUALITY AND ATTRACTION AND A POSSIBLE WAY FORWARD

First of all, when I included sexuality in the title of this chapter, I flat out do not mean that going through sexual violence will make a straight person gay and vice versa. Everyone has a sexuality whether you're straight, gay, bisexual-plus, etc. You have a sexuality no matter what so in this context I am talking about how sexual violence impacts your relationship with your sexuality.

Secondly, if you ever wonder what chapter or idea made me want to do this book, it is this chapter. Since originally, I was never really going to talk about this with anyone until my specialist counselling started but then I brought it up with my best friend and we spoke about it.

Now I want to talk about it in an effort to normalise what happens to sexual assault survivors, because I've read a lot about this topic and every sexual assault survivor goes through this in one form or another.

Therefore, in this chapter, I'm going to talk about the information more generally then I'll talk about my relationship with my sexuality and my attraction since my sexual assault. Then I'll finish off discussing something my best friend said about as a potential way forward, because right now, that is helping me.

It might help you, and just for the sake of context, I am writing this chapter as a sexual assault survivor at the 9-and-a-half-week mark since The Event happened.

General Information

I would include a lot of different references and links to different websites and articles, but if you type in something along the lines of "dating after rape" you'll find out a lot of this information. Since I made the massive mistake of reading up all about this one night when I was on holiday in Wales and my parents were asleep.

My mind wandered and I looked up assault stuff instead of happy stuff. I have to admit this is probably the topic I've handled best but it's taken me this long to be relatively okay with it.

Anyway, generally speaking, after experiencing sexual violence, a survivor's sexual behaviour and attraction can either go to the extremes. For example, all they want is sex, porn and masturbation. They're basically obsessed with it. Or a survivor can go to the extreme of swearing off all sexual contact, all members of their attacker's gender and they don't want to be attracted to anyone ever again.

Those are the two extremes and whilst some survivors do fall on the extreme ends of the spectrum, most people fall in between these extremes.

That's a good thing.

Another issue about sexuality, attraction and sexual violence (and this is something that upset my best friend because they weren't impressed by it) is even when you are ready to start dating, you face the massive challenge of finding someone who can support you when you need it and you have to tell them about your sexual assault at some point in the relationship.

There is no right or wrong way to do this.

Also, you are NOT damaged goods whatsoever, because you are a wonderfully bright, caring person who deserves love, romance and everything you could ever want in a relationship.

And if someone can't see how brilliant you are, then they don't deserve you.

Furthermore, from what I've read, there are different ways of telling people about sexual assault, but it's important to remember you don't have to tell them everything. You could simply tell them you are a sexual assault survivor and leave it at that, and tell them more over time as your level of emotional intimacy increases.

Equally, you could tell them before the first date, during the first date or you could not tell them at all until you're ready or before something physical happens.

The whole idea about telling someone is that you want them to be understanding if you freeze during a physical act, you get nervous or you have a meltdown.

Also, you want your partner to be understanding that you might (more like) will have certain needs that they HAVE to meet, because you are a brilliant person and you need to be respected.

Personally, thinking about it now, some of my needs at this week-9 point, would be I would want sex in a bright room that isn't the living room and I couldn't do kissing, I couldn't have my frontal private area dealt with and I don't want my partner kissing my body like it's the most amazing thing on earth.

Even now it's making me upset and anxious and awful just thinking about it.

It is okay to feel like that and your partner needs to respect these boundaries and your needs.

In addition, I am really scared and nervous about telling a future partner about my sexual assault, because they will have to know on my timetable. They might be really into me and try kissing me and I might freak out and feel sick. So that would be a good time to tell my partner why I reacted like that.

But how the hell do you tell someone that that happened to you?

That is hard and it is why you have to be kind to yourself and you need to respect yourself and your boundaries no matter what the partner wants.

Also, the thing that upset my best friend was when I told them, there are three typical reactions that a partner has when you reveal your history of sexual assault to them:

- They're shocked and speechless and they ask if you're okay.

- They're stupid and fall into the myths and they ask moron questions that subtly blame you.
- They're pathetic and leave you.

My best friend used the c-word to describe people who fall into the latter two reactions and I agree. Therefore, it is hard to deal with this aspect of sexuality and attraction after experiencing sexual violence, but you will have to deal with it.

A part of the healing process is knowing you are valuable, you are amazing and you deserve to find a partner that loves you.

You deserve to be loved.

That's the general information.

<u>My Experience With My Sexuality and Attraction After my Assault</u>

Please know I am going to share extremely non-graphic but personal details about my own journey in this regard. I am feeling very vulnerable and honest but I am doing this just in case you find this useful and relatable.

I know a lot of people will find this relatable but still, I am nervous to share my story.

<u>Immediate Aftermath And The First Week</u>

For the first few days after my assault, I flat out couldn't look at male private areas at all and I couldn't look at dicks. I seriously couldn't because looking at a dick was way too triggering for me and I hated my own dick to be fair.

As I've mentioned before for those first few days, I wanted to cut my own dick off.

Personally, this was really annoying and concerning, because I am gay. I normally find dicks and men and male private areas very attractive and I am a massive fan of them. Yet given how I couldn't get hard, looking at male private areas made me feel sick and experience a lot of physical sensations.

This was a major problem for me and it was distressing.

It made me feel hopeless for the future because it made me think I could never date, never love and never ever be in a relationship. A fear that was only compounded by my child abuse and homophobic family.

As you can guess, this took a massive, dangerous toll on my mental health.

That's the sexuality angle.

In terms of attraction, I seriously couldn't be attracted to anyone for a few weeks after my assault. I go to a trans group (because I'm non-binary) and I have friends there and there are some trans-girls I find attractive (okay, okay I'm technically androsexual- attracted to masculinity and there are a few transwomen that are a little masculine at my group) and I'm normally attracted to them, but I wasn't attracted to them.

I'm still not particularly, so at this point in my journey, attraction was basically dead.

I was still attracted to what I call my "Core Four" and this is such an autistic thing (at least I hope so otherwise, I'm really weird) and these are the four people I love, trust and want relationships with. In other words, I know without a shadow of a doubt that these four people in my life (two of them aren't in my life anymore) would never ever hurt me.

I was glad about this attraction because I found reassurance in the fact that I could still feel attraction to some extent.

Between The Second Week Of My Assault And Now

Then as I've mentioned before, for the next few weeks, my attraction to my best friend was causing me a lot of distress, panic attacks and utter fear because they were going to be staying with me over my birthday weekend. This was going to be hard for me and it was as I mentioned before.

Therefore, in this sense, being attracted to someone was extremely distressing and it was triggering all my assault stuff really badly. Thankfully, this has abated completely when it comes to my best friend but it has morphed into something else now.

Additionally, I went through my massive disempowerment part of my journey where I felt so disempowered to do anything in my life. I felt like I couldn't do anything, I couldn't make any decisions and my life was in complete and utter freefall. This was awful as I've spoken about in previous chapters and this did connect to sexuality and attraction.

Even now one of the massive areas I feel disempowered in is anything to do with dating, being attracted to someone and wanting some kind of relationship in the future. I seriously do not feel like I can do this.

Therefore, me and my best friend (because my best friend knows I'm attracted to them and want to be with them) we're always said I should try to be proactive and date. Granted that was a tiny reason why I got raped in the first place, but that's life.

Anyway, my best friend has a friend that I think is really attractive and I find them rather hot. So I've been trying to get an introduction with this person for ages and my best friend has been trying (but failing a lot).

So a few weeks after my assault, my best friend was hanging out with this person and my best friend tried to put a plan in motion by getting this person to come to our trans group (we're all non-binary). This person said no.

Now I was angry and annoyed even though I didn't really have a right to be.

I was really angry during this period of time because whilst this person did not know about my assault, they didn't even know my best friend was inviting them so we could meet. I was really angry because I was trying to make a choice to make me feel empowered after what my bastard attacker did to me, and this person was denying me that choice.

I always knew I had no right to be annoyed but I was just angry and upset that I was trying here to be empowered and make my own decisions, something I can barely do at times, and this person said no.

That's another way experiencing sexual violence can impact attraction.

Current Relationship With Sexuality And Attraction

As a result, if we fast forward to this current point in time, my relationship with my sexuality and attraction is very difficult in some areas and easier in other areas.

Personally, I'm okay again about being gay (that was mixed in with my child abuse) and I have no problem being attracted to, loving and wanting to be with men. That is no longer a problem thankfully and I do want a boyfriend and partner.

This want and acceptance of my sexuality again was encouraged by me not committing suicide a few weeks ago. That is a good thing and I know I have a future, I am just not 100% sure what that future is yet, but I want to find out.

In terms of attraction, the reason why I wanted to talk about this topic in the first place was because I realised recently my attraction has gone to the other end of the extreme. I am trying to find a lot of people attracted to try and feel more empowered.

For example, I am not trying to be offensive here, it is just personally I do not find feminine women (or 99% of women) attractive whatsoever. This is simply down to my personal taste and preference. I am flat out NOT hating on women.

Last Wednesday, I had to quickly pop up into my best friend's DnD session to give them a birthday card and present for a friend of ours before I left Canterbury for the evening. I was going on holiday to Wales the next day so I couldn't see our friend.

Yet I went in there, saw the DnD game because my friend was talking to me in the corner and there was a woman and she smiled at me. She was only one that acknowledged me entering the room (turns out everyone was way too into DnD to even notice me) and I only saw her for a second or two but I thought she was really attractive and pretty.

Granted, looking back I realise Wednesday I had been crying, had a lot of social anxiety and I was a delicate wreck (more on that next chapter).

I was talking about her the next day with my best friend, I learnt her name and later on I checked her out on Facebook to see what she looked like. And I wasn't attracted to her, but she was lovely so I do wish her the best of luck in that department.

It still made me realise that I was being attracted to people a lot more than I actually should have been, and it made me realise something was a little wrong with my attraction in general.

So I thought about it more and more over my holiday and realised, my attraction was moving towards the extreme because I feel like I want to be attracted to someone, anyone so I can pretend to have a choice about my attraction, relationships and everything.

This isn't healthy.

And it is all fake.

As I said to my best friend when we went out for dinner and had this conversation, I'm not really attracted to anyone at the moment in any real sense. And even if this was "real" attraction, I am seriously not in a mental position where I could even consider dating and getting into a relationship.

Ultimately, this is me unhealthily wanting to feel in control because I still feel so disempowered in this area of my life. And I have no idea whatsoever about how to date as a sexual assault survivor, and that is annoying but I need to stop trying to be attracted to someone just so I can feel empowered for a second or two.

That seriously isn't healthy.

And as my best friend said, it can lead to some pretty risky situations if it goes to the extreme and if I don't have self-control. This connects to the sex obsession I mentioned earlier.

A Potential Solution

As an aspiring clinical psychologist, you know I'm going to say the only real solution for this sexuality and attraction issue caused by sexual violence is professional help. There is no way around that and you will need professional help no matter what, so do it as soon as possible.

In the meantime, I am going to tell you what me and my best friend are currently doing and this helped me in the sense that, it gives me a little bit of practical hope to focus on. So I don't get hopeless about relationships, my mental health doesn't die and I won't get suicidal again.

My best friend is demisexual and pansexual. In other words, they can only be attracted to you if they're friends with you first of all (not that it helped me get with them anyway. Ha) and they're attracted to all genders, and they're on the asexual spectrum too.

I'm mentioning these facts because it helps put this into perspective and why I understand this solution but I am not entirely sold on it, because I am not demisexual at all.

Again, I am still writing about this in case it helps others.

Therefore, me and my best friend are going to go to the LGBT+ coffee morning and other events during Freshers Week next academic year, we're going to go to new societies (adult social clubs formed around a particular interest) at our university and we're going to keep meeting people.

Then the plan is overtime, hopefully I will become friends with someone I am attracted to, and because friends hug, I can get used to hugging someone new as a friend first, and then if they're attracted to me I can enter a relationship that way.

This would solve a few issues for me in terms of sexual violence stuff, because I cannot abide the thought of being touched or hugged by anyone else at the moment. I only let my best friend touch me regularly when we hug goodbye, and I let my Mum hug me from time to time after she shouted at me a week-and-a-half after my assault for not letting her hug me.

Supportive and understanding as always. Not.

Also, it would allow me to form a relationship with someone I trust and I think it would help a lot of stuff generally.

Of course, the only problem with this is going from friend to relationship, I think is somewhat uncommon and unlike my best friend, I am not demisexual. Meaning I would like to go out, maybe use dating apps and whatever to meet people in the future.

However, for now, I think this is a solution that will help me focus on the future and realise that a future is possible.

Mini-Conclusion

Overall, I wrote this chapter to show you that after experiencing sexual violence, it is perfectly normal for your relationship with your sexuality and attraction to change and keep changing for a while. As you heal, it will change and it will almost certainly go back to whatever it was before your trauma as you near the end of your healing journey.

Just be kind to yourself, be careful and if you realise you are heading towards or you are at one of the extreme ends of the spectrum. You need to talk about it, get professional help and keep yourself safe.

And most importantly, you deserve to be loved, in a relationship and have everything you ever wanted.

It will take time, but it is very, very possible.

ACCEPTING THE WEIRDNESS OF TRIGGERS

In previous chapters, I've spoken about various triggers I've had and how distressing, upsetting and awful they are. One such example was a few chapters ago when I discussed what happened on my birthday on the London Tube, that was a surprising trigger that distressed me a lot.

Another surprising trigger soon after my assault was how whenever I thought of my best friend, it would trigger all the rape stuff and how horrific it was.

Therefore, in this next chapter, I want to focus on triggers itself in terms of how surprising, annoying and disempowering they can be at this point in my healing journey. Again, please, it has "only" been 9.5 weeks since my sexual assault so everything said in this chapter is a reflection of this point in my healing process.

In addition, as my best friend said the other night, from what they know from other sexual violence survivors, the triggers do get less common and distressing over time. Yet for now, triggers are a major part of the aftermath of sexual assault.

This brings me to what happened last week.

What Happened In Week 8?

In week 8 after my sexual assault, I only had three days to do things before I was going on holiday to Wales for 4 days, and I couldn't do anything the weekend before because I was at Canterbury Pride then I stayed at my best friend's house.

I only had three days to do a lot of business and writing things. To say I was busy was an understatement but I was really happy because I was busy and I was so focused on getting things done that I didn't have time to think about The Event or something assault related.

Anyway, so the night before I went to Wales I needed to go down to Canterbury anyway to pick up a psychology book from the library that my supervisor wanted me to read. Afterwards, I was going to go to the trans group I always go to because it was at the university.

This is where the triggers started.

I was so happy that it was Wednesday evening and I hadn't been triggered whatsoever this week, and I was so excited about maybe this was the week where I would be okay. A stupid idea if there ever was one.

This is my first tip for you.

Tip

You need to accept or find a way to accept that maybe the first three months or longer, there will probably be distressing stuff that pops up every single week without fail. This is scary, distressing and it might seem hopeless, but I promise you I am living proof that you can survive this and life is seriously worth living.

It gets better over time.

Back To Week 8

I was driving down to Canterbury and in case my best friend was done with their DnD game at 6 pm (they weren't really sure when they were going to be free and I needed to see them anyway to give them our friend's birthday card and present), I didn't have time to connect my phone to my speaker so I could listen to podcasts. So I was stuck listening to the radio.

I listen to Heart by the way.

There was good music, good adverts and good other stuff. Then Heart does the 6 pm news and it's always local rubbish that I don't really care about until the news told a local story about how a rapist had been convicted after abusing a young boy for years, and the police were praising that young boy for having the courage to report it. I won't say anymore because it made me feel awful so it might trigger other people too.

Thankfully I was just finishing up parking my car when I had to turn off the radio so I had a panic attack, I cried and I just shattered in my car. It brought up all my feelings about feeling worthless, a failure to other survivors and my mind went mad at the idea that I was a bad person for not reporting my assault and prosecuting him.

I managed to calm myself down enough so I could get out of my car, then I started walking out the university car park and towards the library.

Now the problem is that there were a good amount of people so I was really anxious anyway. I wanted to cry again so badly and my mind turned against me again saying that because I wasn't like that young boy, I was setting up other people to be attacked and assaulted because I was a failure.

I went to the toilets in my main university building and I just cried my eyes out, and I used Bing Co-pilot (just think ChatGPT) to answer some questions about reporting rape.

I Need To Stress

Now, I need to stress here that it is totally up to you if you report your sexual assault or rape to the police. It does not matter what other people do, it does not matter what other people say to you and it certainly does not matter what other survivors have done.

It is your choice.

And if someone tells you, you HAVE to do something then tell them to fuck off.

It is your choice. No one else's.

Furthermore, all my thinking was wrong after I heard that radio report. It is perfectly okay that I did not report my assault and my attacker because to legally prove it was sexual assault would have been extremely difficult, I did not want the public shame and embarrassment of a trial and I did not want to be ripped apart on the stand by a solicitor.

Also, I have no proof that what happened that night actually happened at all, much less that it was non-consensual and there was no informed consent. Not that there was consent at all in the first place.

If you want to report it then please go ahead, but if you did not report then that is fine too. You did nothing wrong and if you want, you can always report it in the future.

Back To Week 8

After I finished crying and I spent easily 25 minutes in the toilet, I went to the library. That was a nightmare in itself because I could not find this book for love or money so that took another 30 minutes to find a single bloody book.

Anyway, I was about to call it quits when I found it because I realise I hate narrow and enclosed spaces these days. I hate narrow library rows of books because they make me anxious and my mind goes "hey you know if anyone wanted too, they could grab you, pin you up against the bookshelves and do whatever they want to you,"

This fear was also reinforced on my trip to Wales when I was walking under a short tunnel with a narrow walkway with a canal next to it. That was an enclosed space and my traumatised mind loved it.

Not.

That was difficult then I realised how anxious, scared and panicked I was about going to my trans social group. This is a great group of people, I have a lot of friends there and I like talking to people there.

However, as I was talking to where the social group was, I was getting more and more socially anxious so back to the toilets I went. I spent another 20 minutes in there and I was scared, panicked and all my triggers were popping up again. Because there are a lot of people there, there are some fat people there and in my mind, any one of them could hurt me.

That wasn't nice for me.

If we fast-forward to three days later, me and my parents had had a lovely day in Wales doing some hiking, exploring and we went to the local town. We came back early, my parents had a crime drama on and they feel asleep.

I kept on watching the crime drama and it turned out that the killer was getting revenge on her rapists. I got distressed, I couldn't change over the channel so I shouted and got even more distressed. My parents woke up, helped me change over the channel and then they shouted at me, because I was overreacting, I woke them up and I was being an idiot.

Yeah, my parents are amazing supporters of me after my sexual assault. (They are great in a lot of other areas though)

That was annoying that I got triggered by something as simple as a crime drama, and I didn't have the social support from my parents.

I know there were other triggers on my trip to Wales, I think there were daily triggers because all the distress, fear and depression mixed into one. I know I was distressed on the Sunday because in Wales they do horse-drawn canal boat trips and the guy leading the horse was a spitting image of my attacker.

I made sure just not to look at him and I was with my parents so I forced myself not to react. I was dying inside but I dared not show it.

I didn't want to get shouted at again.

One Trigger For This Week (So Far)

Lastly, a final trigger I want to mention from this week is, and this goes back to social anxiety, is me and my best friend are working what's known as Summer Core at our university. We're both student ambassadors for the Outreach and Widening Participation department. This means we help out and support events that ultimately help to promote the idea of coming to university to students from schools that have a below-average number of pupils that go on to university.

For example, yesterday I helped out with a finance talk at a local secondary school, on Tuesday I helped out at a Future Human day that gets students to do a small research project at a university for the day and gets them to experience a lecture and what a seminar is (helps develop a sense of belonging amongst other pedological outcomes), and next Thursday, I'm helping at a World Languages Day.

Anyway, there is Outreach every working day for the next four weeks.

Therefore, on Saturday, me and my best friend are working a KS3 (just think 13 and 14 year old students) Family day so students and parents come to the university to do fun activities. Thankfully, when Outreach emails us from time to time I can see who else at the university is included in the email and I recognised one of the names.

Let's call him Rory (not his real name) and I know Rory because we used to do scouts together, he's about 5 years younger than me and our parents get on great. We haven't really spoken for years but we did talk when I was Session Lead at another Future Human event back in May.

So I was going to offer him a lift down to Canterbury, because we live in the same town in Medway, and this would mean I could get an extra 5 pence petrol allowance, so it's a win-win for everyone.

Then I thought about it. That would mean I would be alone in a car for over 40 minutes with a man that is slightly overweight and I haven't seen and spoken properly with him for ages.

Just thinking that again made my anxiety shoot up.

Equally, I know if I made this offer, I would not sleep for the next three nights, in turn this would make my mental health worse and I would be even more triggered again and again.

So even offering an old friend a lift and car pooling like so many people do every day (hell I know a few people carpooling at the moment and I'm picking up my best friend anyway on Saturday), is something that triggers me.

Especially as my mind when I'm getting triggered imagines Rory doing stuff to me. Stuff that would never ever happen in real life, Rory is straight for starters.

That's annoying. It makes me angry and it is so fucking disempowering that I cannot even do those simple, nice things for people like I used to be able to.

What Was The Point Of This Chapter?

On the whole, the point of this chapter was to help normalise how random, annoying and common triggers are. I found the triggers were more intense for the first few weeks after my assault but now they are a lot more common and random.

This is disempowering because I just want to live my life and do whatever I want. Yet I know and mostly accept that this cannot happen until I get professional help in the future so I hope that comes sooner rather than later.

Furthermore, I want to help normalise how common and random these triggers can be. I want you to know you are normal, there is nothing wrong with you and triggers are an unfortunate part of Post-Traumatic Stress Disorder. This is just something that will happen to us for a while until we get professional help and we can work through it.

And you can work through this.

Life can get better. Life is worth living and you are an amazing, brave survivor who will recover and heal.

REMEMBER AND FOCUS ON THE GOOD TIMES

Before I talk about the brilliant topic of this chapter (I'm really excited to be back writing after having to deal with a lot of Real Life stuff for the past week), I want to take a moment to be honest about why I want to be truthful that I have no idea where this chapter is going in the book.

I don't want everything in this book to be perfectly organised, structured and flow without a single problem.

That isn't how sexual violence recovery works in the slightest.

Therefore, I strongly believe it would be a massive disservice to myself and you wonderful readers if I pretended that this subject material wasn't chaotic at times. It is and that's okay.

Your life might be chaotic on certain days, certain hours or certain minutes. But you will be fine, you can recover and you will survive this.

And most importantly, please remember that you are never going insane when experiencing the effects of trauma.

You are simply experiencing normal effects to an extremely abnormal situation.

Why Do You Need To Remember and Focus On The Good Times?

If you're a survivor or if you know a survivor then you are probably way more aware than you want to be that there will be tough times ahead. I'm currently writing this chapter at week 11 after my assault, and it is tough.

There hasn't been a single week since my sexual assault that there hasn't been something major pop up. And hell, for the past four days, it has been major.

However, I'm doing okay at the moment because I'm focusing on the good times because they make me smile, they make me feel like a teenager again (which is a weird saying for me because my teens weren't that great) and they remind me that life is brilliant.

I'm not going to pretend that you're going to be able to focus on the good times when/ if you experience panic attacks, nightmares and flashbacks.

Even though, please make sure you ground yourself by saying out loud what you can see, hear, touch, taste and smell. As well as make sure you do any other grounding techniques you want.

Nonetheless, in those moments where you feel safe, secure and you aren't experiencing a flashback or panic attack. Or do this straight after one, please remember and focus on the good times.

Personally, I would be extremely careful about focusing on memories and good times from the distant past and I would attempt to keep them as current or close to the present as possible. This is just my opinion and what works for me.

However, the reason why you might want to stay out of the distant past is because flashbacks, panic attacks and all the other trauma responses of sexual violence take you back to the past in a bad way. And sometimes focusing on the past can be triggering and it can take away from the external sense of safety of the present.

In addition, these moments don't actually have to be massive things. Like the examples I'm going to list below. They can be tiny positive things that make you feel good, grounded and positive about your life. For example, right now, I am finally back writing after dealing with moving house, dealing with the crisis of the Psychology Society at my university and working so much Outreach work as a student ambassador at my university. As well as trying to get two podcast episodes out.

I flat out love writing, I love my business and I love being back at my keyboard doing what I love. That is an amazing feeling and I am happy.

Moreover, I haven't had a Tassimo coffee for at least five days and I haven't had a Coke of some sort for a while. These were just part of my normal routines when I lived with my parents. So I'm introducing them tonight and I like them. I do recommend the Costa Cappuccino in case you're interested.

These might be tiny positive things but you know what, they make be smile, feel good and feel positive in between all the trauma responses.

That is worth remembering.

Penultimately, for this section, two things you might want to do is write down 5 positive things that happened to you today before you go to bed. I'm pretty sure I've already mentioned it in this book, but a woman I talked to a lot does this and I've started doing it (I need to remember it better) and it works. It makes you realise there are a lot more positive things that happen to you than you remember.

These can be really small things too.

For example, if I was thinking about today my five (you can try to do more too) would be:

1. I've started writing again.
2. I helped my best friend by driving them to and from work.
3. I had a Tassimo
4. I had some Pepsi Max
5. I listened to the Handsome Podcast with the wonderful Mae Martin.

On the whole, making yourself focus and remembering the good times, helps you to realise that life does have some great, fun, positive moments. Sure, sometimes they are tiny moments, but they can remind you that you are so much more than your trauma and there are moments in life that can make you smile.

It is those moments that are amazing.

What Was The Inspiration For This Chapter?

I want to write this chapter for a very specific reason but I want to use another example first. As I mentioned earlier I'm working a lot of student ambassador events at the moment at my university because it's the Summer Core period and the university is really busy.

Last week, I worked a lot of great events. Including a forensic science event where I got to support kids doing fingerprinting, indentation taking, a forensic search of a crime scene and more. Those were really interesting events because I never normally get to do them.

In addition, I got to work as a Lead Ambassador at a Care Leavers event at Mote Park. I was essentially getting paid stupid money to sit around for 8.5 hours. I didn't do much because the event was so quiet in the end (250 people were meant to turn up, only 50 people did) but it was fun. I got to have a lot of lovely conversations with my fellow students, care leavers and university staff.

It was a fun day.

There were other highlights of Week 10, but even now as I'm writing this section, I'm smiling because they were really positive times. And after the past few days and how bad my mental health has been, it is honestly lovely to think about good times.

Please make sure you focus and remember these good times too.

What's The Second Reason?

This is the real reason that I wanted to write this chapter because it reminded me that there will be positive moments in amongst all the chaos of recovering from sexual violence.

I sort of, kind of met someone yesterday.

There are a few points here I want to make in a moment after I tell you what happened.

I can't mention their real name (obviously) but let's call him Henry. Me and Henry were working as student ambassadors yesterday at a Business Challenge event (basically it was a day of just babysitting 17-year-old students because the school wanted to bring them to university for a day.

I arrived there early because I had dropped my best friend off too as their event started earlier than mine. I got to the meeting place and there was a cute guy sitting there, I didn't have a trauma reaction which was nice but I didn't give it anymore thought.

Until it turned out he was another ambassador.

Henry was cute so I was glad he was working the event but I did not think at all about him anymore in between sessions. I don't know why I just didn't, I was dealing with enough stuff that it seemed impossible to talk to them.

Anyway at lunch time, we were eating with the students outside, it was sunny and I put my hat on. It was a branded hat for Kent International Jamboree which is a major global scouting event. If you don't know what "scouting" is it's similar to Boy Scouts of America.

Henry started talking to me about it, we talked all throughout lunch and it was lovely. I felt good, positive and I actually felt like a teen again. And I admit I wasn't flirty but you could tell I was gay by how I was acting and yeah, I just wasn't acting straight at all.

We could to the end of the day, we spoke some more and Henry seemed really, really interested in what Outreach events I was working so he could see me again. We found out we were both working together for 3 days next week and he seemed really pleased.

I'm not doing the experience any justice but Henry is cute, he's really nice and I do want to explore something with him.

Now I do not know if Henry is gay, bisexual or even into males whatsoever. I also don't know if he actually likes me or anything like that, and on a serious note, I have no idea how dating works as a rape survivor.

Come on, who does?

However, it is still lovely to experience being seriously into someone and just feeling like anything actually is possible for a few hours. And I honestly thought this wouldn't be "real" attraction because as I've mentioned at other points in the book, I have been attracted to people before since my assault but it wasn't real. It was simply me wanting to be empowered in an unhealthy way.

This is different though.

My main piece of evidence for this "difference" is something that has happened over the past 24 hours. Whenever I talk about Henry, I feel really positive and I *might* act like a teenager with a first crush. Since I am not embarrassed (that much. Grin) to admit that below is a real extract from an email I sent earlier to the sexual violence specialist at my university. She emails every few weeks and I say I hate these emails, but they are lovely and they are really good. I just like talking to someone other than my best friend about life.

Honestly, I only say I hate them because it means I have to repeat everything that has gone on lately and it makes everything real. I know this is part of recovery and it is important and I want to do it, but it's annoying.

Here is the extract:

"Finally, I sort out of met someone yesterday. He's called Henry, and I know this is the rape survivor and trauma talking but I doubt he's gay or even into me at all. But he's cute, really nice and he really likes talking to me. He was really pleased to know we're working the same Outreach event for three days straight next week. It was lovely feeling normal for a few hours yesterday considering the hell of moving. But as I said, I doubt he's gay or even into me, and it isn't like I can date at the moment. My mind tried to imagine me and him doing stuff together and it turned into a full-on rape scene. Not very nice at all.

Overall, I am doing okay today and honestly, sure a lot of triggers are popping up. Yet I am focusing on the positives like my Outreach work, living and spending time with my best friend, meeting Henry even if it leads to nothing, and I'm slowly getting back into my routines."

So the fact that I mentioned Henry in an email to a mental health professional stresses how positive I feel, and I promise I am not the type of person to do this normally. I don't go round mentioning my crushes or people I find attractive. I seriously don't, but this time was different.

I just felt really good.

Chapter Conclusion

Therefore, whilst I have no idea if Henry is gay or into me or if a relationship is even possible. But I actually will ask for his phone number or social media just so maybe I can explore a friendship or possible relationship.

And honestly, I know in the dark times, I will just say what I said last night to my best friend (something I am not repeating in this chapter because this is a positive chapter), and most of the time I might believe I cannot date.

Yet yesterday proved me wrong.

I am capable of real attraction and want, and that is all you actually need for the seed of a relationship to form. Anything physical or psychologically intimate can change or develop and grow safety and securely over time in response to the boundaries YOU need.

That is the truth and as a survivor, I always need to focus and remember that because life isn't all doom and gloom.

It is amazing and there are certainly tiny, positive moments in amongst the darkness.

YOU HAVE THE RIGHT TO MAKE A CHOICE

One of the biggest themes of this stage of my sexual violence recovery is disempowerment, and one of the hallmarks of being disempowered is that you cannot make decisions. I originally wanted to write this chapter at the Week 9 mark but it's now Week 11. However, as I've switched the order of these chapters, you've already seen why it is important you remember "you have the right to make a choice".

Previously, you've seen how I wasn't going to make any sort of decision about where to put my kitchen items, and even deciding where to put my things in my bedroom at the new house was a major challenge. I needed to get my best friend to talk to me whilst I put stuff away so I could distract myself and continue to make progress and those sort of micro-decisions that this activity requires.

In addition, even though, technically, I could "only" manage 40 minutes of these micro-decisions before I needed a major break. That is actually brilliant progress compared to the day before, and sure it took longer than I would have liked, but I still did it.

And on a self-compassion note, I am proud of myself for doing it. I could have just thrown in the towel but I didn't. I made sure that I continued and *I* managed to put everything away for myself.

Therefore, this is a lesson for all of us, survivors. We need to be kind to ourselves when things go wrong, we need to reward ourselves when we accomplish things and most importantly, we just need to keep going.

That is the key to the aftermath of sexual violence.

Why Am I Talking About *You Have The Right To Make A Choice*?

As you might know already, after sexual assault or another type of sexual violence, you feel guilty, you don't trust your own judgement, have low self-worth and so on as I spoke about in the past chapter. However, you might find yourself having a moment when you can make a decision and you want to make it.

You can do that.

You can absolutely tell someone your decision and stick with it.

That is your right given as a human being and you have every single permission you need to make a decision.

If you want to decide something, just do it.

I'm talking about this because at the Week 9 mark after my assault, me and my friend had spoken earlier in the week about attraction and my best friend's relationship. My best friend was saying about they could keep it discreet, they could do it in secret so I didn't have to see it because it could be triggering. I'm missing out a lot of the conversation but you get the gist.

In other words, my best friend was willing to keep their relationship very secret so I wouldn't be triggered and rape stuff popping up.

I really wasn't sure and my best friend was brilliant because they let me make the decision entirely.

Of course, that is exactly what you should do when it comes to survivors. It is critical that survivors are allowed to make their own decisions.

Therefore, a few days later, originally me and my best friend had wanted to hang out on the Friday but they were tired so we didn't. Instead because I had made a decision, I sent the following text to them that night telling them about my decision:

"I want to tell you that rape-related thing now. I don't want to sit on it for another night and we might not have time tomorrow. That's just life though. I'm almost cried twice thinking of this message.

I don't want you being discreet with your partner because I want to make a choice for myself and there's 2 more reasons. So I am disempowered because of what he did to me. I can't start new social activities and I can't go to London because of my meltdowns and anxiety. I struggle going to something like Group because of the amount of people. I can't even drive a guy I've known for a decade down to campus tomorrow because I keep imagining me getting raped in my own car over and over.

There are a thousand more examples of me being disempowered and things I can't just do because they make me feel sick, have a meltdown or make me feel like I'm getting raped again.

But you are off-limits to him.

I am not letting him affect you and me. You're too kind, lovely and a great friend to let him do anything to us. I'm glad you'll never know how hard that first week was for me with whenever I thought of you it triggered all my rape stuff. My birthday was bad enough. I was terrified (Someone we both know) was right about us not being able to be friends anymore.

You are off-limits to my rapist affecting me. You can do whatever you want, live your life normally and let us just be us. Let us just be the great close friends we are without him making us change anything.

So I don't know want you being discreet because I will NOT let him affect us, your partners might not be that triggering for me anyway. And just let me make a choice for once. In a world where I can't do and make any choices please let me make one. I choose to make this one also because after all the shit you've been through, I want you to live normally with the freedom to do and have over whoever you want.

I'll be fine. If I haven't killed myself yet, there's a 99.9% chance I won't."

That was a very intense, raw message that fits who I am at times with people I am extremely close with, but it proves a point.

You can make a decision if you want.

If there is something you want to do, if there is something that you want to go a certain way then that is okay. You are allowed to say it, communicate it with others and you have the right for other people to listen and respect it.

Another great example was I'm writing this chapter in Week 11, and last night, me and my best friend spoke about anything and everything for about 6 hours straight. Something that popped up was my guilt about them being the only person I have, and me wanting to meet new friends.

I said to them (because they're half-French and I'm learning French on Duolingo) that I want to go to French Society at our university. This would mean I could meet French people and other people with an interest in French. It is something I've spoken about before but I want to do this, I have made the decision that I want to go to French Society.

I'm partly joking when I say this but I want to go to French Society because I might meet an attractive French guy, fall in love and marry him. So I can have an EU passport again. (Hell, French guys can be attractive).

Joking aside, it is okay for you to say what you want and other people have to respect your wishes even if they don't agree with it. If they love you, care about you and support you fully then they will respect your decision even if they don't agree with it.

You have the right to make a choice.

Sometimes you might not be able to make decisions like me when it came to moving things into my new place. Yet sometimes you will be able to make a decision like me going to French Society and me wanting my best friend not to be discreet about their relationship.

You can make any choice you want. It might seem impossible at times but you seriously can.

I believe in you.

GUILT AS A SEXUAL VIOLENCE SURVIVOR

It might be Week 11 for me at the time of writing but I wanted to put this chapter earlier in the book, because guilt is a major part of the healing process and the aftermath of sexual violence. I've experienced guilt in a massive number of ways, and I've experienced a wide range of ways how I've dealt and overcome with this difficulty.

Therefore, in this next chapter, we're going to be exploring guilt after sexual assault, how it's impacted me and how I've dealt with it. Then I'll talk more generally about some other ways how you can deal with guilt as a survivor.

In addition, I'll talk about my experiences in a moment, but research shows (references included in the back of the book) that survivors feel guilt because of three main factors. Firstly, they feel guilt because of self-blame. For example, if they hadn't done something then it wouldn't have happened so they feel guilt about that.

I used to struggle a lot with the idea that "if only I hadn't been in a hurry and wanted to be gay" then I wouldn't have made the mistake.

Even though in reality, not a single survivor reading this book has made any sort of mistake whatsoever.

None of us are to blame, It is the bastard that attacked us that is the only person we can blame.

Moreover, another reason why survivors experience guilt is because of the cognitive impacts of sexual assault. For instance, the disturbed sleep and the intrusive thoughts. These trauma responses can make us feel guilty and this feeds into the self-blame too.

Finally, survivors can feel guilt because of their interactions with medical, legal and other professionals or people. This links to retraumaisation and if other people give us negative reactions then this certainly does not decrease the guilt.

Personally, the stuff that has been said to my face by people who should have loved and respected me has only increased my guilt, my self-hate and at times my suicidal idealisation. Thankfully, that doesn't pop up now.

<u>How Has Guilt Impacted Me?</u>

I've already hinted at a few ways how guilt has impacted me, but there are two ways that have had a major negative impact on me. I want to share them because I doubt I am unique enough to be the only person experiencing them.

The first one is dark, and the second one is very true that I know a lot of survivors experience.

Firstly, I used to get angry my attacker didn't physically beat me or just kill me when he did what he did to me. If he had done that then I would have had physical evidence and it would have made a prosecution easier, and if he had killed me then I wouldn't have had to deal with everything for the past 11 Weeks and onwards.

I wouldn't have to be in so much pain when everything pops up and I wouldn't have to deal and struggle and cry so much.

This is extreme guilt and I call it guilt because I feel guilt at times that this didn't happen.

Life gets better though.

If someone had told me that at the beginning of this book and shortly after my assault, I really wouldn't have believed them because life seemed impossible back then. And honestly, yes, life can seem a little impossible now at times.

But there are a lot of fun, joyous and exciting moments after sexual assault that is so worth living for.

In future chapters, I talk about how much fun I'm having with my Outreach work as a student ambassador, I'm having a lot of fun doing what I love with my writing, business and podcasting. And it was so, so lovely to possibly meet someone romantically on Monday at an Outreach event.

Even if meeting this guy doesn't turn into a relationship, it was still such a lovely moment because it proved that my sexual assault hasn't killed that part of me. I can still be genuinely attracted to people and that is a lovely thing to realise.

So please if you're suicidal, get professional help, contact a helpline and most importantly, remember that life is so worth living for.

Secondly, I experienced a lot of guilt as a survivor towards my best friend, because they are the only social support system I have in place. I don't have that many close friends I can lean on for support, my family doesn't know how to handle (or have a willingness to search online) me being assaulted. And they've said more than enough damaging stuff that it isn't worth it.

So I lie and say I'm perfectly okay whenever I talk to them, even if I've had the most hellish few days of my life.

Therefore, my best friend is literally all I have as a support system until my therapy starts and that is going to take another few months before that begins. To say I've felt extremely guilty about that is an understatement.

Because I felt like that was a hell of a burden on my best friend, knowing that they are all I have and if they leave or go back home for a few weeks then I have no other close friends. Thankfully, they are still living their life independently of me, which is what I want, but I still feel so guilty because they have to listen to me when I want to talk about my experiences and how I'm feeling.

There is no one else I can talk to.

And the following WhatsApp message highlighted how much guilt I had a few days ago towards my best friend:

"I'm really sorry about the hot water. If I wasn't so scared and traumatised, I could have listened and I might have heard something. I don't think he mentioned much. I know you know I'm trying and dealing with a lot but I want to be useful and I just still useless and draining at the moment. I promise I'll have more fun conversations soon."

I wanted to share this message because it highlights how as a survivor, there are times when you might feel extremely guilty for no reason, or you might feel really guilty about the smallest things. It's normal to feel that way and I hope this message shows you that if you feel guilt over the smallest "mistakes" then it doesn't matter, it's normal so you aren't going insane and most importantly just be kind to yourself.

In a future chapter, I'm going to talk about the importance of positive self-talk because you can see how negative I'm being towards myself here, and that isn't good for your mental health at all.

A final message is one that I typed out but I never sent it because me and my best friend spoke about this stuff later on in the night. The context for this text is on Monday, I had had a really rough day for reasons you'll read in a moment, I couldn't do any projects or anything because my desk hadn't arrived so I was left to ruminate about my assault and its consequences. I asked my best friend after an hour of giving them alone time if I could come up and talk, they said they wanted some more alone time (which is fair, they need their own space) so after three hours of really bad mental health I wrote out this message to send later on.

I'm sharing this message because it shows how survivors can feel guilt over the smallest of things and how I show immense guilt over this friendship. As well as I'm sharing this because it highlights how triggers can surprise you and it's normal (even if its really distressing) for triggers to surprise you.

Yet I am also sharing it because it highlights hope for future relationships (something I talk about in more depth in the future and before you ask Henry isn't his real name) and it shows how survivors can have very negative self-talk towards themselves. Again, this isn't good for mental health so I'm sharing this here for you to set up a future chapter.

"I'm sorry I bothered you earlier. I know it was okay but I'm not. I promise when I get my desk sorted, I'll be better. I'll be playing in stories and doing business stuff. You don't know the guilt I feel about you being my only support thing. It is not fair on either of us. Come September I promise I'll work hard to make more friends, be out more away from you and more.

I almost ruined a lot today. Um, I was in Wolfe Lecture theatre. Easily fits 400, we had 150 students. That was enough anxiety. But we were doing outreach registers and Wolfe has like 20-seat long rows so a group of girls had packed the back row. The second to last one was empty except for a stupid boy who stayed on the edge. I asked to pass him but he wouldn't get out of the row and stand to one side. He just stood up so there was a small gap between his front and his desk. I went past the first time okay. He just sat down. I got the registers from the girls in the middle. Maybe 10 just fine.

Then I went back.

I asked him to stand up again but he didn't give me much room. I slid past him, my ass facing his front and I think I had to bend over slightly to move past. Then it triggered anything because I was in a vulnerable position, I shot out of the row, I was tensed, I might have started to shake. Henry quietly asked if I was okay as he passed me his registers. He said it so quietly I just thanked him for the registers. Handed them to Judith, went to the toilet to calm down.

I just never want to have a public meltdown at Outreach. If they bench me because I'm a risk to the image of the uni or I "need time away from work to recover". Then I'm screwed. I need Outreach to keep me okay sometimes.

P.S- when I was downstairs, I couldn't find Henry on Facebook, Insta, LinkedIn, followers of ChemSoc or LGBTSoc on insta or the ambassador FB group. My mind tried to imagine some stuff happening between us but my mind turned it into a full-on rape scene. So I'm interpreting this, yes, I can find Henry as interesting as I want and in a fantasy world, he can like me too. But I can't do anything unless he's extremely patient and prepared to deal with so much shit. It's too much for 18/19 year to deal with."

The Solution For This Friendship Guilt

Thankfully, last night me and a friend spoke for hours upon hours and this was something we spoke about. We spoke about my guilt towards them and they reassured me that is was okay, they were happy to do it and we do have a healthy relationship. I am not so dependent on them and I am in no way so suffocating that they cannot live in their own life.

Also, they mentioned how this is what friendship is. Friendship is about supporting and enjoying the time with your friend even when they're going through hell and back. Friendship is just as much about the bad times as they are about the good times.

As a result, my unofficial tip for this experience of guilt, is please make sure you communicate with your friend about why you feel guilty. Your friend can support you, tell you why that isn't true and why you have nothing to worry about.

That conversation made me feel a thousand times lighter.

General Ways To Decrease Guilt In Survivors

After talking about my personal experiences, I want to mention some more general ways about how to decrease guilt within survivors. These are very useful ideas that you might want to try out.

Firstly, be fair to yourself and use self-compassion. Since we all need to understand that guilt is a very normal response to trauma but it is often biased because the guilt we feel doesn't reflect our responsibility.

I've mentioned that what happened to all of us wasn't our fault, we shouldn't feel guilty for something we didn't choose or do willingly or want.

There is nothing for us to feel guilty about because it wasn't our fault. This feeling of guilt is a trauma response, nothing more.

Also, in my experience, a very effective and easy way to be self-compassionate is to be kind to yourself and imagine what you say to a friend in a similar situation. In other words, never talk to yourself in a way that you wouldn't talk to a friend.

Secondly, therapy is a great way to decrease feelings of guilt. I wanted to grab my old therapist for an appointment so she can help me with my feelings of guilt but she was on holiday, and my availability is too bad when she's back.

Still therapy is a brilliant way to get professional help with these negative feelings, and honestly, therapy is a great way to help you process what happened to you. As well as trauma-focused therapies like Eye Movement Desensitisation and Reprocessing (EMDR) and Cognitive Behavioural Therapy (CBT) can help us to process our feelings of guilt.

We all need therapy because of what people have done to us.

Thirdly, education is an effective way to deal with guilt and trauma as a whole, because we need to understand that guilt is a natural part of the healing process. As well as a lot of people find (myself included) that the more you learn about sexual violence and trauma, the more empowered you become and you can reduce self-blame.

Another added benefit is you find out what you're going through is normal and you aren't going insane.

Even as a psychology student who lives and breathes clinical psychology, this is still a very scary and annoying part of sexual violence. Since when everything pops up and everything gets intense and dark and you feel like your life will never be good again, you do feel like you're going insane.

Education helps to prevent the worst of that feeling.

Furthermore, support networks are a great way to reduce feelings of guilt. These include support groups, trusted friends and family members as well, because sharing with a support network can validate your experiences and decrease the feelings of guilt.

Mainly because you'll learn that there is nothing to feel guilty about because you did nothing wrong and people will support you.

Penultimately, using grounding as well as mindfulness techniques can be effective ways to reduce guilt. Since by practising mindfulness, you're helping yourself stay in the present and manage any overwhelming emotions you're experiencing. As well as I find grounding techniques some of the best ways to keep yourself in the present and remind yourself that you're safe whenever you go through a distressing moment.

Finally, journalling is a good way to write down your thoughts and feelings so you can process your guilt, trauma responses and it helps you to gain perspective. Honestly, that is one of the reasons why I'm writing this book because I want to help you and I want to record how I'm feeling and what I'm learning about clinical psychology, sexual violence and myself as I go along.

This is essentially a massive journalling exercise and I've found it helpful for me to process my trauma and what He did to me.

On the whole, as a sexual assault survivor, guilt is a normal and natural part of the healing process. All of us feel guilt for a wide range of different reasons, there are some general trends, but there are individual reasons too.

However, there are ways to overcome and deal with the guilt so you can heal, thrive and take back control of your life.

Healing is possible if we deal with one thing at a time.

Useful reference:

Ullman, S. E., & Peter-Hagene, L. C. (2014). Social reactions to sexual assault disclosure, coping, perceived control, and PTSD symptoms in sexual assault victims. Journal of Community Psychology, 42(4), 495–512. doi:10.1002/jcop.21618

TRYING TO LIVE YOUR LIFE AS MUCH AS POSSIBLE AFTER SEXUAL VIOLENCE

It might seem impossible, but there comes a point when you need to try to live your life as much as possible after what happened.

As sexual violence survivors, especially if you go on to develop Post-Traumatic Stress Disorder like I have, living a life seems flat out impossible or it is extremely stressful. For example, going out, seeing friends, going to crowded places can all be extremely triggering and distressing.

But it can be fun too.

Since something I've noticed at Week 14 is that you do need to live your life as much as possible after sexual violence to some extent. The reason why it's taken me so long to realise this is because of a few different reasons. For example, I find new things distressing, I find small spaces very scary and triggering and I find one-on-one situations almost impossible and they make me want to cry.

Yesterday I returned with my best friend and another friend of ours (who's a housemate too and let's call them Ruby, again not their real name) from Brighton, because Ruby lives down there and we went to see them. Also, we went to Brighton Trans Pride, we stayed at Ruby's mum's flat and we had a lot of fun.

However, it was extremely distressing for me, because we went Friday to Sunday. It's bad enough that Pride was extremely busy and packed and there were some very large people there who triggered me badly. Yet it was in a new environment, the flat was very small and choking so I couldn't really sleep, but on Thursday me and my best friend went to a BBQ with some work friends and rape stuff was mentioned.

Including a very innocent joke that played on my mind for ages. And I want to mention here that if you ever hear someone make a joke, feel free to correct them or tell them that isn't okay. I didn't do that because I didn't want these work friends to know I was raped and I know it was from ignorance, it wasn't them trying to be nasty.

That BBQ content meant I didn't sleep Thursday night, so I didn't really sleep for three nights straight. This only added to my distress.

However, there are great moments too, and this is what I want to focus on in this chapter.

Yes, triggers, distress and PTSD can be a major part of life before you go on to get specialist rape counselling or another form of psychological support. The sooner you start that process and get onto a waiting list, the better in my opinion because you will need the support.

However, if you allow yourself to be controlled by the fear, the anxiety and the panic attacks then in my opinion, it only increases your suffering, your hopelessness and decreases your mental health even more. For example, whilst I will always describe going to Brighton to see Ruby as hellish and the same goes for the first week when I moved into my student accommodation. I always focus on the positives too, because there are always lovely moments.

When we saw Ruby in Brighton, I took some lovely photos of the three of us on the beach, we saw some great, affirming content and there were tons of other great or funny moments too. Including getting gelato, racing to get the train before it left without us and my best friend being nauseous and vomiting because of a bad chilli.

Therefore, whilst I don't know what stage of the healing journey you are at, I don't know how you're feeling and I don't know how your mental health is (it might be better or worse than mine). I do know that it is so tempting to simply stay inside and stay in your safe space forever, and there are times when being in your safe space is your best option. For instance, it is best for me to limit my "new things" this week to basically nothing, because I need to recover after the past few days.

And if Ruby wasn't staying with us for the week because they wanted to see the house before they moved in in September, then I seriously would spend days in my safe space without going anywhere. That would be okay because I'm not isolating myself away from the world, I am just taking a few days to recover.

Therefore, my point is, over time as you start to heal a little bit more, it is okay to try new things and do more social stuff. You can do baby steps and you can adapt it to whatever you need. You can ask a friend to come with you, you can tell a friend point-blank what you need and don't need (I've mentioned that earlier in the book) and you can simply take it one step at a time.

But please don't trap yourself away from the world.

For me, going to Brighton was one of the biggest things I've done since I was raped and it was mostly hellish, but there were great moments too. And I know if I didn't go or if I stopped myself from going out of fear then my mental health would have been even worse, because it would make me feel trapped, isolated and hopeless about the future.

In addition, Brighton is even more proof for the future, because by going out, you're proving to yourself that you can go out, you can live and you can have fun after sexual violence. You can be a person again who enjoys their life.

That is something that seems impossible at times.

Finally, at this moment in time, there are reasons why I talk about living your life as much as possible. Since for all of us survivors, there are different limits to what we can do at our current stage of healing. For instance, I cannot go out and do major things by myself. Like, I flat out cannot do one-on-one or group social situations with new people, I cannot go to London by myself and I cannot go on any trips by myself.

I just can't because it's too much, too scary and it kills my mental health too much. Also, in these situations, it's okay not to do these things because doing these things by myself will do so much more damage to me, my mental health and my recovery than me not doing it or doing it with friends.

That's why at the moment, my best friend is the person I basically do everything with. Although, my best friend is going home to the Midlands for a month in a few weeks so I will be alone for a month. Granted, we need to have a conversation about a "safety plan" for when they go away, but we've agreed I need to see people, be social and have things to look forward to during that month so I don't become suicidal. Therefore, we have talked about me and Henry doing things as friends (it turns out he wasn't into me after all and he's straight), and that is something I am scared about, but in the interest of protecting my mental health and proving to myself I can do it, I want to try it.

And I do know Henry would never ever hurt me so going out with them and doing something will be fine and fun. Even though I will be taking me and Henry doing things together very slowly and one step at a time.

Overall, at the end of this chapter, I want to stress to you that it is okay to struggle, it is okay to take baby steps and adapt "going out" to whatever you need, and it's okay to go slow with reclaiming the going out part of your life.

In my experience, the going out part after sexual violence is scary, anxiety-provoking and it can be hellish. But I am reclaiming that small part of my life, so I can feel safe, secure and happy to be out in the world again living my life and showing my rapist hasn't taken that part of me.

I am my own person and I can do whatever I want given enough time. I am nowhere near "healed enough" (whatever that means) to do grand things on my own and that's okay. Yet slowly but surely, I am finding ways to go out, have fun and make great memories with great friends.

And that is a wonderfully powerful thing that brings me a lot of joy in dark times.

It could do the same for you.

IF YOU CAN'T MAKE DECISIONS, THAT'S A NORMAL TRAUMA RESPOSNE

For the majority of these experience-based chapters, I try to write them in chronological order because I want you to see the ups and downs of sexual violence recovery as the weeks and months go on.

However, this chapter I want to bring forward because it complements and improves a chapter and something that happened from Week 9.

What Happened?

On the 29th June 2024, I moved to Canterbury with my best friend and I was already struggling a little because it was a lot, my bedroom is basically an enclosed space and my self-talk was very negative. And I realise I should have stopped, focused on the self-talk going on in my head and changed it from "I don't want to get raped again now I'm living in Canterbury" to "You'll be fine by living in Canterbury. No one will hurt you".

Anyway, my best friend had their partner over so they were upstairs unpacking my best friend's room. I was downstairs I flat out could not handle going upstairs because it was too triggering for me.

I needed to unpack but I was struggling with triggers, flashbacks and I was really depressed. I cried a few times and I finally wanted to put my kitchen stuff away in a cupboard but I couldn't decide.

I seriously could not decide what I wanted to do with my stuff. Should I put my stuff in the left-hand or right-hand cupboard? What should I put wear? What should I do at all?

I had also struggled to make any sort of decisions for that entire late afternoon and evening of moving in.

Afterwards I simply broke down and cried my eyes out and I Whatsapped my best friend immediately asking them to come downstairs alone, we hugged and I explained everything to them. All I really remember about that conversation was how I talked about how much I hated my rapist, He stole my ability to make decisions and he was stealing everything from me.

And so on.

Thankfully, my best friend just talked to me as we both put away our kitchen stuff together, and it was a lovely hour before they went back upstairs to unpack their room.

After a while, I forced myself to go upstairs into my enclosed space of a bedroom because I was going to make decisions and unpack. That did not happen for a single second because I listened to music through my earphones to distract me from my fear. Then my bedroom popped open by itself, hit me and I realised how seriously jumpy I am so I got depressed and I laid on the floor of my room with all my boxes around me for a few hours.

I will admit Duolingo is a brilliant break from rumination, so maybe try that.

The next day my friend talked to me as I unpacked a little and we both kept our bedroom doors open so and that helped a lot. Granted I could only manage about 40 minutes of decision-making at a time and it took me a lot longer than I wanted to finish unpacking but I managed.

Granted that is the tip of the iceberg of my mental health over the past four days, but I wanted to focus on the decision-making aspect of disempowerment.

In addition, whilst the above paragraphs capture what happened, the Whatsapp message below helps to highlight the sheer distress and emotion I was feeling at the time. And again, I'm sharing this message with you so you understand that it's normal to be distressed, you shouldn't feel guilty for being distressed or triggered and I'm trying to normalise what we all go through.

Also, please note, this message connects to chapters on negative self-talk and guilt. This is something we shouldn't say to ourselves because we should be kind to ourselves, so please note that the negative self-talk and guilt I feel in this message is something I have thankfully worked on.

Yet it goes to show how distressing new situations can be and negative self-talk and guilt is something we all need to work on.

'Before I try to get some sleep, thank you for comforting me earlier and helping me. I hate the disempowerment part of rape and making choices. I can decide on anything business or writing related, but not normal stuff. It's shit.

I never did anymore unpacking. I tried to listen to music to get upstairs then my door opened by itself, it hit me, I jumped and I got depressed. I hate how jumpy I am so I got tired and depressed and couldn't really move. I just laid on my floor for a few hours thinking and being depressed. Duolingo was a short relief.

I try to live my life. This week proved that with Outreach, moving and the chaos of Psychology Society. But at this point in time, I can't make decisions, I doubt I'll ever have a relationship or anything like you and Nathan have. I'm going to die alone, unloved and useless. I just want to live but I've never been able. From my child abuse from intensely homophobic family leading to mental breakdown last August to my friendship abandonment to my rape. I only survive. I don't want this anymore. Honestly part of me would love to die, but I care about you too much and I'll never hurt you. There are lovely, positive moments too that I love. So I won't do it but it's annoying a small part of me wants to.

Tonight I wanted to do a fun thing with you. We write down 3 things we want in our lives by the end of the tenancy.

I've seen different people do this for other things. The only thing I genuinely wanted on my list was still be alive. It took me at least 10 mins just to undress tonight. Only managed because I listened to music.

I'm sorry you had to move in with a raped person. I'm sorry for everything that will come up. I'm sorry this always gets dumped on. I hate it. I hate I have no one else. I just want this to be better for you than your last house for you and I'm scared it won't be.

Now I try to sleep and hopefully I'll have energy in the morning. Sleep well.

Over To You

Whilst nothing in this book is any sort of official advice, I want to mention a few things I have read or found useful myself in case you are struggling to make "basic" decisions because these decisions do not feel basic or easy at all.

In addition, it is worth mentioning that the reason why sexual assault survivors have difficulty with decisions is because of a range of reasons. For instance, guilt and shame about their attack and the notion that it was somehow their fault when it wasn't, they have low self-worth, they become perfectionists, they no longer trust their sense of judgement and so on.

That is why us survivors feel disempowered.

It is also our job, our professional help, determination and our social support network to move beyond all this in time.

Even though it takes a hell of a lot longer than we would like.

Therefore, I believe there are two main important things to remember when it comes to making decisions. Firstly, be kind to yourself and I know how impossible this is in the moment but please try. Remember that isn't your fault, it is the fault of your rapist/ attacker and you ARE capable of making decisions. As well as you will only get better at making decisions in the future, and these powerless moments are simply that, mere moments in the grand scheme of things.

You will be empowered again because you are brilliant.

Secondly, get some support. This can either be professional help and/ or support from friends or family. Get a friend that makes you feel good to talk to you either in-person, over the phone or over a video call as you make decisions. Get them to support YOU making the decisions so you can make your own decisions with a little bit of support.

The worse and most disempowering thing for survivors of sexual violence is for other people to make decisions for you.

For example, it was lovely my best friend just talked to me and helped me make decisions about where to put my kitchen stuff. It helped *me* to make the decisions and it was lovely to feel empowered for a while.

And the more you make decisions, the more natural it will feel and the more empowered you will feel over time. This will make you feel good, improve your mental health and it will help your recovery.

On the whole, if you're struggling to make decisions, even the so-called "most basic" decisions ever. Then this is a normal reaction to an extremely abnormal situation and you are seriously not alone. A difficulty making decisions is something the vast majority of sexual assault survivors experience and it never makes you flawed, a problem or anything else negative.

It makes you human.

And the fact that you're reading a book and looking for ways to help yourself and improve your life, that truly makes you a strong, amazing person that will recover in time because it is possible.

I remember that no matter how dark, lonely or isolating a moment is where I cannot make decisions, there is always a way to make a decision and steal back a little grain of power from my rapist. Sometimes I need a friend or something else.

But I can reclaim my power.

And so can you.

THOUGHTS ON VIRGINITY LOSS AFTER SEXUAL VIOLENCE

As a writer, I process and think about topics by writing about them, considering the perspectives and writing about them in a way that is useful to other people. Originally, I was going to put this chapter earlier in the book, but I wanted to keep this chapter around the Week 14 mark because I believe some people might not be ready or even consider this option until a lot of the "initial" trauma responses have decreased.

I wrote that line smiling because I still have way more trauma responses than I would like, but that is the mind trying to help me process what happened.

Anyway, when I was in Brighton and dealing with everything I was going through, I don't know why this popped up but I got very scared that I wasn't a virgin anymore and I had effectively lost my virginity to my rapist. This was something I did not want, I was scared and a little distressed. I think I would be more distressed if I wasn't so exhausted, so this was a topic I wanted to explore in this chapter from different angles to help me understand if I am a virgin or not, and I want to help other people decide this for themselves too.

Also, I will end this chapter with a specific "Over To You" section so you can get something aimed at you, the reader, from this chapter.

Note: in the second section of this chapter on Definitions, *there are references to sexual acts. I have tried to keep it as light and non-graphic as possible, but please be careful if sexual references are triggering to you.*

Why Am I Writing About This Topic?

I've done a lot of online reading about virginity loss through sexual violence over the past few days, and this is something a lot of survivors struggle with to process and it is something that a lot of people have differing opinions on. All these differing opinions are important and good, because they work for different people. Therefore, I'm going to be writing about all the major different opinions I've read about because it is hard after experiencing sexual violence to process the concept of virginity, due to the way how society puts such importance on losing your virginity.

A lot of people see losing your virginity as a rite of passage into adulthood. I talk more about the social aspects of losing your virginity in the next section.

Furthermore, for a lot of sexual violence survivors, their rape or assault or whatever term you want to use for it, the Event was their first sexual encounter. This is what happened to me and after spending years of my life hearing from classmates, friends and family members about how great your first time can be and how it is such a big, wonderful thing, having *that* as your first sexual encounter, it is fucked up and wrong on so many levels.

It is that tragic realisation where you can realise or consider your attacker has stolen something from you. That is what's distressing and it makes survivors struggle with the idea of virginity loss, and this is why we need to talk about it in this chapter.

Personally, I struggle with the concept of losing my virginity because after suffering a lot of homophobic child trauma for a decade, I built up the idea of my virginity as something exciting, precious and it kept me alive. When I was really struggling, suicidal and I lost all hope that I could ever be gay, the idea of having a boyfriend that might love me and want to be with me (including having sex) kept me going.

Moreover, the idea of losing my virginity was the ultimate act of defiance against my family. The idea of gay sex where two men love each other, have passionate sex and want to be together is every single thing that my family hates and despises and finds an abomination. So the idea of utterly defining them and doing something they found so disgusting was exciting and it kept me going.

On the whole, the idea of losing my virginity to someone who was attracted to me and I was attracted to back gave me such hope in a childhood that was often hopeless.

As a result, the very notion or idea that I lost my virginity to an idiot rapist is disgusting, outrageous and I fucking hate my rapist. How dare he take that from me, how dare he lives and how dare he touch me.

I still want to be a virgin but after reading some opinions, I think there is a chance I might not be a virgin.

And if that is true, if I am no longer a virgin then that will only add to my pain, my suffering and my profound sense of loss because of what that bastard did to me.

Why Virginity Is A Social Construct And Its Social Purpose?

I know as a university psychology Masters student, I shouldn't read Wikipedia but I read up on virginity, and it meant the social purpose and constructive nature of virginity.

In essence, we all know that virginity doesn't actually exist, and it isn't real. There is nothing biological, there is nothing you can touch and there is nothing you can actually measure about virginity.

In truth, virginity is just a concept that people have made up to give importance to an event that happens in someone's life. Sometimes this "Importance" is given for religious reasons and other times virginity is "important" for social reasons. For example, the silly idea that virgins are more pure, better and more moral than non-virgins. Also, the silly idea that virgins are worth more, having sex with a virgin can cure aids and other Sexually Transmitted Diseases (a horrible myth that leads to a lot of women getting raped in Africa), and there are a lot of bunch of other reasons.

Furthermore, especially when it comes to young women, virginity is a concept used to control them and other people. Since there are certain people that want women to remain virgins because they believe virgin women are more valuable, more worthy and purer than non-virgin women. Therefore, by stressing the importance of being a virgin, it allows men and other people to socially control women and their behaviour so *they* can reap the rewards instead of the woman herself.

The final reason I'll look at in a little more depth is that in western societies, losing your virginity is seen as a massive deal amongst young people because it makes you an adult. It is a way for young men to brag and bond with their friends, they can talk about their sexual conquests and there is a lot of pressure on young men to lose their virginity sooner rather than later.

This is even more true for boys belonging to the popular social groups or more "laddie" groups in my experience.

On the whole, the concept of losing your virginity is important in society for no "real" reason. Instead people believe losing their virginity is important because of a wide range of social and religious reasons. This doesn't mean wanting to lose your virginity isn't important and it doesn't invalidate you wanting to lose it to someone you love or have a fun time with. Yet I want you to know that it is only important for these social reasons.

And for some people, it might be immensely useful to know that virginity lost is a social construct as it might allow them to move past these non-existent social expectations and decrease its importance as a result.

This might work for some people, it might not for others.

<u>The Different Ways To Lose Your Virginity According To Different People</u>

Before the first 14 weeks of after my rape, I was very content with the definition that you needed something to be inside you for you to lose your virginity. Yet I must have read something that caused me to start questioning that definition, then I started reading things online and I realised that a lot of people have differing definitions of virginity lost.

Now I'm going to explain the top three definitions.

Firstly, you have the "traditional" definition as I'm calling it. This is where you can only lose your virginity if a penis (a real or fake one) has entered your body. The most extreme traditional version is when a penis enters a vagina, but that definition isn't useful for LGBT+ people. Therefore, you can lose your virginity if someone puts something in you.

Secondly, you can lose your virginity if you have any sort of sexual contact. For example, if someone performs oral sex on you, you're naked and you touch each other, you give someone anal or penetrative sex without them doing the same to you and so on.

Personally, this is the definition that caused me a lot of distress because this definition means I am not a virgin, and my rapist has already taken so much from me, I don't want him to take away my virginity too.

Finally, you can define it as you see fit and some people believe something extremely interesting. Some people believe that losing your virginity is impossible during rape because losing your virginity is a consensual act that you enjoy, and considering that sexual violence is not consensual and it is far from fun, it means you absolutely cannot lose your virginity during rape.

I cannot help but smile when I write about this reason.

If you adopt this definition then it means you can never lose your virginity to sexual violence, your attacker can NEVER take that from you and your virginity will always be yours until you decide this is the time and person you want to lose it too.

This definition is a great way to reclaim a small amount of power from your attacker. Your attacker will never take your virginity because they never had your consent and you did not enjoy it.

Your virginity is yours to keep, control and only *you* can "lose" it because it is yours and your attacker can never take it away from you.

What Do I Think Virginity Loss Is?

This is why I love writing about topics I am struggling with, because I am a virgin and I can't help myself but smile at that realisation. I am choosing (the fact I am actually making a decision is amazing to be fair) that my virginity can only be lost to someone I choose, someone I consent with and someone I can have fun with.

To me, you are only not a virgin if you have actual sex. Rape, sexual assault and any form of sexual violence is not sex.

Sex is when you form sexual acts with consent, enjoyment and attraction. To be able to have sex, there has to be a want, an interest and an attraction, so rape is never sex.

Rape seriously is not sex and that is a great thing to realise.

Therefore, all those years where the idea of having sex with a guy I was attracted to is still alive and that is still achievable. I can lose my virginity to someone I consent too and everything that kept me going during my extremely homophobic adolescence is still there and strong, and my rapist has not taken that from me.

He has taken so much away from me but I have something. I have something he will never take from me and after everything I have been through and after everything he has stolen from me, I can keep something.

And I love that. It is a great feeling to have.

Over To You

On the whole, at the end of this chapter, if your experience of sexual violence was your first sexual encounter like me, then you might want to think about your own personal definition of virginity, and how someone loses it. You've read a lot of different ideas and definitions in this chapter, so you might want to mix-and-match them, pick certain definitions and you can decide for yourself.

And even if you decide that after what happened to you makes you no longer a virgin, then please remember, that being a virgin is a social construct. It doesn't mean anything, so it's okay.

I hope this chapter gives you the information you need to make a decision about your virginity if you need to. Also, if you don't need to make this decision, then I hope it gave you some food for thought about our fellow survivors and what they might need to know to heal a little bit.

What's your definition of virginity?

DEALING WITH EXISTING FRIENDSHIPS AFTER SEXUAL VIOLENCE

As I continue this introductory section of topics that I want to say upfront so regardless of the point of your healing journey, you understand these critical basics. I want to talk about friendships in this chapter and then in a future chapter, I'm going to talk about making new friendships. Originally, I was going to put both friendship chapters together, but it took me until Week 12 or Week 14 to be ready to make new friendships and I would have panicked if someone mentioned new friendships at any point before then.

Therefore, in case you're like me and the very notion of making new friends makes you want to have a panic attack at this point in your healing journey, then that's okay. That chapter comes later and you can skip it and come back to it later if you want.

Existing Friendships After Sexual Violence

I know from my psychology degree that friendships and your social support network is a critical protective factor when it comes to your mental health. Typically, the more friends you have, the better your mental health will be and the following is a short extract from an academic article I wrote yesterday for a different project:

"This is critical considering people have a fundamental need to belong where they can experience ongoing relational bonds and these bonds have a plethora of mental health benefits (Baumeister & Leary, 1995). For example, social groups are protective factor against depression (Hellzen et al., 2011), stress (American Psychological Association, 2022), and Post-Traumatic Stress Disorder symptoms (Flanagan et al., 2016) amongst other benefits."

As a result, you can see how friendships and other social relationships help to protect us against negative mental health, and I've read articles over the past few months about how friendships are critical for rape survivors.

Personally, because of my child abuse and my autism, friendships are a very difficult topic for me naturally. At the time of writing, I only have two or three friends and there's only one friend (my best friend is referred a lot in this book) who I can talk about my rape with in any great depth.

You'll see through the book this led to a lot of guilt, bad mental health and it really doesn't help that I am very, very attracted to my best friend. This is a trigger for my rape stuff too so shortly after my rape, the friendship was very challenging for me but thankfully, it isn't any more and it is a brilliant friendship.

The only real "benefit" (the wrong-est word if there ever was one) of my assault was that it brought me and my best friend even closer together.

What Is The Point Of This Chapter?

Anyway, in the aftermath of sexual violence, when you're panicking, you're distressed and you have no idea what the fuck just happened to you. Your existing friendships can be utterly terrifying because you feel like you need to tell them because you want the support, someone to talk to and you want to process what happened. Yet you're scared of being judged, blamed and you might be scared your friends might cut-off contact with you.

As a result, the point of this chapter is to explain how I dealt with existing friendships after my sexual violence experience, and give you some more general tips about existing friendships.

By the end of this chapter, you'll understand some ways to tell your friends, why friends are important and how a disclosure of sexual violence might impact friendships.

This isn't as scary as it seems but it is so important to your healing process that you have friends you can rely on.

Always Start With Your Closest Friends

Even though I reference a lot of friendship content in the rest of the book, I want to spell it out clearly here that after you realise you've experienced sexual violence, I would recommend you tell your closest friends.

I say this because your closest friends are the people that know you best, the people that care about you the most and these are the friends that should be happy to support you, because you're a close friend to them.

You'll see in more detail in other chapters how my best friend was the first person I told about my assault. Granted it was stressful because they didn't see my messages for two days so I was very lonely in that time, I had to deal with a lot myself and it was rather hellish because I was processing what the hell happened to me.

However, my best friend is amazing, brilliant and they are one of the most caring people I know. Over the past few months, they have always been there for me no matter how distressed, self-critical and bad my mental health was. They were there for me.

They were always just a text away before we lived together, and now I'm living with them, they're always happy to listen to when I need to talk.

They are the ideal friend to have after experiencing sexual violence.

I truly hope everyone has a friend like mine.

In addition, when it came to how I told them, because they're my best friend I was extremely honest with them. Surprisingly enough, I know I share a lot of copies of WhatsApp messages I've sent in the other chapters (and I include some more below), I am not sharing these ones in this chapter.

Mainly because you can see how raw, panicked and distressed I was. You can see how I was in denial too for the first two days, and I hated rereading them.

However, when telling your best or closest friends about what happened to you, depending on the type of friendship you have, you can just be brutally honest. You can tell them the details, how it happened and just talk to them. Tell them whatever you need to be able to cope.

In my original text to my best friend, I was honest enough so they got the gist about how bad it was for me. Then whilst they were in Switzerland for the next three weeks, I texted them whenever I needed it and they learnt just how much I was struggling with everything and they might have been 600 miles away but they supported me.

Overall, when it comes to telling your closest friends about your sexual violence experience, just tell them and go into as much depth as you need to for you. You have all the power here and your closest friends will support, love and help you because your dear friends to each other.

Your closest friends are the people you're meant to feel safe with.

Finally, in terms of reaction, my best friend was extremely "sorry" about what had happened to me, and my best friend is not normally the type of person to send an extremely angry message directed at anyone. Yet to say my best friend was pissed off at my rapist was an understatement and it was actually lovely to read.

It was validating and that is what good friends do. They support you, validate you and listen to you.

How To Tell Other Friends?

Even though I don't have *that* many friends, there were still three other friends that I felt like I needed to tell. Yet unlike my best friend, I told these three friends when the situation popped up and I didn't really have a choice anymore.

Telling A First Friend

For example, I talk about this in another chapter but I have another friend who experienced sexual abuse as a kid and we are good friends. And as much as I didn't want to talk about it with him, my best friend wasn't getting back to me so I had to contact him and tell him.

I'll add a copy of the two messages I sent below that were sent about 30 minutes apart because I want you to see the differences between the messages I sent different people.

"Hi, hope you're okay.

Is there a chance I can talk to you about something that happened Saturday night please?

Yet this is to do with really bad sex stuff so you can say No. That is perfectly okay and I do have others to talk too. Your mental health and you are far more important. Say no if that's best for you. It's okay."

The second message.

"I've emailed the uni support services now so they'll help so it's okay. Sorry to bother you. I know this is a sensitive area. I shouldn't have mentioned it.

Hope you're doing well in general."

You see in this message I did want to talk to him but I was unsure about it, I was gently bringing up the topic to see how he would react and if this was an okay topic. I partly did this because I wanted him to know I respect him, his past and his mental health yet I wanted to gauge his reaction too.

You can see I got increasingly distressed in between these two texts being sent, and that's okay too. Telling someone about sexual violence is very scary and I was utterly terrified because of a possible negative reaction.

Thankfully, none of my friends gave me a negative reaction. They were all supportive, kind and lovely to me.

On the whole, what I learnt about doing a disclosure after talking to this friend was it's okay to go slow, approach the subject gently and it's okay to be distressed. Sexual violence is very distressing so it's okay to tell someone in a distressed way because you're processing a lot, depending on the friendship, you seriously don't need to downplay it.

In fact, you should never ever downplay sexual violence.

<u>How I Told A Second Friend?</u>

In a chapter later in the book, I talk about one of my friends Ruby (not their real name) and how they're living with me and my best friend next academic year. I really like Ruby, they are a great friend and I have a lot of great conversations with Ruby. Yet because of their age and their looks, I see them as a very innocent child (Ruby is 19 by the way) and because I didn't know anything about Ruby's mental health experiences up until two days ago. I was very nervous and resistant to have conversations with Ruby about what happened to me.

However, a few days before my assault I had contacted Ruby to see they wanted to meet up where they lived. That's about a two-hour drive for me but I wanted to see Ruby as I hadn't seen them in over a month.

Two days after my rape (yes Ruby is that bad at responding to texts), Ruby said to me they were excited to see me and that would be great. Yet the idea of one-on-one, going out and doing a lot of different things just seemed impossible to me.

So I had to tell Ruby what had happened to me in this text:

"That's okay about not responding sooner. Sorry, I'm no longer free next week because all I'll say is I was sexually assaulted a week ago, so I've got my therapy booked, I'm working Outreach at the uni and getting to get my life back to some sort of normal. Also, I'm a little sensitive to one-on-one situations at the moment.

In May when you're back, we'll meet up and do something.

Have a lovely rest of your easter."

Therefore, when it came to telling Ruby about my sexual assault, I was much more careful and limited in the details because besides from Ruby's reply about how sorry they are that happened to me and they hope I'm okay. This is all we spoke about it until very late May when me and my best friend met up with Ruby for dinner.

I choose to keep details light with Ruby because up until recently I didn't feel like I could have serious or traumatic conversations with them. I didn't feel like me and Ruby had that sort of friendship and I didn't want to keep having to tell different people.

Overall, whilst Ruby has been very supportive and lovely towards me, if you don't feel like you have the sort of relationship where you can talk in-depth about something as traumatic as rape and other forms of sexual violence. You can keep it very light so the other person has a general idea of what happened to you and then if you need certain things from that friend then you can ask and talk about it. For instance, in my text, I am essentially asking Ruby to be patient and understanding about why I cannot see them one-on-one for a while.

Thankfully, Ruby is very understanding.

How Did I Tell A Friend I Work With?

A final friend that I told in the initial aftermath of my assault was a friend who was my former supervisor for my psychology dissertation in my undergraduate degree. We became friends because we worked together really well, he knew I had great project management skills and he was the first person I told about my mental health, my extremely homophobic family and he was a great listener. He was there for me.

Granted he is still more of a work friend because of our age gap, we're different people socially and other factors, we wouldn't spend time together outside of a university environment together. But we still class each other as good friends.

Anyway, because he knows about my mental health, my past and he is honestly lovely and supportive. I would have liked to see him in the aftermath, so telling him was a little complicated. Since he is more of work friend than a personal friend, telling someone that you experienced sexual violence is a lot and I really, really didn't want him to see me differently because we have some great projects lined up together.

Therefore, I decided to tell him in a subtle, light way where I was asking more to keep myself busy and see a friend rather than wanting to have an in-depth conversation with him. Even though he did offer to have an in-depth conversation with me and I told him I would think about it.

"Hey, hope you're okay.

What days are you at the centre next week please?

Just asking because I was sexually assaulted Saturday night.

I've spoken to the specialist uni service, C and another friend of ours Y. I'm better than I was and this week I'm focusing on myself, chipping away at projects and seeing Y on Thursday (X's away). But I was wondering if next week I needed something else to do like helping at the centre, would that be possible?

I probably won't need it as I'm doing a lot of Outreach work but still. Thought I'll ask."

One major difference between this message and the message I sent Ruby was I went into slightly more depth because me and this work friend do have the type of relationship where bad things can be spoken about. Also, this friend knows a lot about other aspects of my life so I was okay going into a little more, and I know without a shadow of a doubt that this work friend is so lovely that he would support me no matter what.

Overall, when it comes to telling different friends about your sexual violence experiences, here are some tips for you:

- Tell your closest friends everything you want and you're comfortable telling them so you can process what happened.
- Only tell people you trust.
- It's okay not to tell people everything until later on.

- You can leave details out if that makes you more comfortable.
- Do what is right for you
- Think about the level of friendship you have with that person.

Ultimately, trust your friends to give you the support, love and listening ear that you need.

How Did My Disclosure Impact My Different Friendships?

This is the scariest aspect of telling your existing friends about sexual violence because I was concerned that my friends would:

- Not believe me.
- Blame me for what happened.
- Not want to be friends with me anymore.
- Tell other people without my permission.

I'm sure there were other concerns but these are the main ones, and from what I've read and heard from the past few months, these are the standard concerns of survivors.

Honestly, in my experience, my friends have been flat out amazing. I haven't had a single negative comment, a single piece of judgment and all my friends still want to be friends with me. All my friends have done nothing but love, support and listen to me whenever I needed it. They've been amazing.

In terms of specific friendships, me and my best friend have always been close but because of past friendships, I was very skittish because I was just waiting for my best friend to abandon me because everyone does that to me in the end. I was relatively insecure in that friendship until this happened. Also, my best friend wasn't entirely all-in in this friendship because I could be very intense at times and my best friend used to say a lot of "I need to get to know you more" in certain situations.

We were both close friends beforehand but both of us had things holding us back before truly committing to the friendship.

Thankfully, the disclosure about my rape made me and my best friend grow very close together. And we were talking about it the other night and my best friend agreed with me when I said my rape brought us closer together because neither one of us are letting things hold us back anymore. We're just enjoying being really close friends.

All because we've bonded through this trauma.

Besides from that effect of closeness, there haven't been any other noticeable effects on my friendships. My other three friends are very supportive and I know I can turn to them whenever I need it to some extent. I'm still not really close enough with my other three friends to have in-depth conversations about my rape, but they are there for me. As well as Ruby is a great listener even if they don't say too much because they have no idea how to respond.

I do have great friends and I'm glad I didn't isolate myself after what happened, I leant on my friends and thankfully it worked out brilliantly.

Make Sure To Tell Your Friends What You Need

In this penultimate section, I wanted to quickly mention that as part of dealing with existing friendships after sexual violence, it is perfectly okay (and needed) for you to tell your friends what you need from them.

If you need them not to touch you (like a hug), mention certain names or places or talk about certain topics (like sex or dating) then that is okay, your friends should/ will respect your wishes and you need to do what is right for you.

Some of my boundaries with my friends are:

- Not mentioning the name of my rapist (even if someone else shares the same name)
- We can talk about sex, dating and love but I have the power to shut down these conversations quickly if needed.
- Don't hug or touch me unless I give you clear permission

That's all the boundaries I can think of but my friends respect them and it helps to make spending time with them easier.

Furthermore, if you're going somewhere that is very triggering for you then feel free to tell them. Below is the text I sent Ruby when me and my best friend where coming down to visit them for a weekend. And I don't do well with crowded places, sleeping in new rooms and I just don't do well with going out much. I explain in a later chapter how hard this weekend was for me, but I explained to Ruby what might happen so everyone was on the same page.

"Hi Ruby, I like being honest and I know you're brilliant so you'll be okay with me telling you this, but I just want to be honest. Mainly so I don't feel horrific guilt if stuff pops us.

I am excited and really looking forward to seeing you, but I am nervous. Because coming to Brighton and Seaford for a weekend is one of the biggest things I've done since I was raped. I went on holiday to Wales with my family but that was a disaster.

So I know if rape stuff pops up for me, it's okay, I can manage it and if I need to say no to doing stuff it's okay. And I do want you to stay for next week so you can see the house, do tourist things with me and more. But the first week after moving in was hell for me because it triggered so much rape stuff.

Point is, it will be a lovely weekend in Brighton because we're doing fun stuff and seeing you. And I'm looking forward to you living with us next week, but I'm reminding myself that if rape stuff pops up a lot, it's okay.

I have no clue if this text makes sense. And because you'll probably wonder, no thank you, there isn't anything extra I need from you. I can't predict my triggers so let's just have a fun weekend like normal and we'll deal with stuff if they pop up.

Looking forward to seeing you."

You can tell I was a little distressed by sending this text but it was okay to send and it was me doing what was best for me so I could have a nice time too.

You always need to give yourself permission to put yourself first so you can have a nice time too and live your life. Something else I talk about later on in the book.

<u>Conclusion</u>

Ultimately, I know following sexual violence, you're dealing with a hell of a lot of really, really scary shit from panic attacks to processing what the hell happened and your mental health changes too. This is why friendships are so critical but the idea of telling your friends is terrifying.

I hope after reading this chapter, you can see some different ways to tell different friends depending on your level of friendship with them.

In addition, I hope you can see how the vast, vast majority of friendships have positive reactions towards you after a disclosure. This means they'll want to support you, listen to you and help you with whatever you need.

That is what friends are for.

Sexual violence might seem like the end of everything and it can seem like it messes up your entire life and it seems like it can ruin friendships. Yet your friends love you, want to support you and your friends are the people you can hopefully feel safe with. So please, tell them, lean on them for support because you will need them so badly in the weeks and months to come.

But you can survive sexual violence with a little help from your friends.

Finally, just as a reminder, here are my tips again for when it comes to telling different friends about your sexual violence experiences:

- Tell your closest friends everything you want and you're comfortable telling them so you can process what happened.
- Only tell people you trust.
- It's okay not to tell people everything until later on.
- You can leave details out if that makes you more comfortable.
- Do what is right for you
- Think about the level of friendship you have with that person.

Ultimately, trust your friends to give you the support, love and listening ear that you need.

MAKING NEW FRIENDS AFTER SEXUAL VIOLENCE

Something I really struggle with these days is the idea of meeting new people, forming new friendships and spending time with new friends. A lot of this comes back to me developing Post-Traumatic Stress Disorder and me associating new people with danger because my attacker was a new person, so as you can imagine I have a lot of social anxiety too.

This means the idea of making new friends is extremely hard for me to understand and it is a very scary idea.

As a result, it is only at Week 14 I am willing to talk about it because I have made a new friend and I am slowly approaching this friendship and developing it. Since even though Henry wasn't into me (he's straight), he was just very intense about wanting to get to know me and make a friend. And like me, he is very autistic so that explains a lot.

Therefore, as Henry is a new friend and he wants to be friends with me, this raised a lot of interesting points, including some scary ones about how to navigate certain things and I want to talk about it openly in this chapter.

Due to I know the idea of making new friends seems terrifying to a lot of survivors and a lot of us have social anxiety, so this makes it even worse for us.

Ultimately, in this chapter, I'll talk about my experiences of social anxiety, The R Conversation and managing friendships after experiencing sexual violence. This will obviously be based on my own experiences so it might be different for other people, and I will make more general useful points along the way too so this chapter can be useful for as many people as possible.

Social Anxiety

At this point in time, I don't do well when it comes to meeting new people, being in new situations and being out of my safe place. I've already spoken before about making sure you continue to live your life as much as you can and making sure you don't isolate yourself. This is why I put up with the anxiety even if it wrecks my mental health for days.

I want to limit how much my rapist steals from me, and each time I go out, live my life and experience happiness is an act of defiance against him.

In addition, when my best friend asked me why I found going to Brighton so stressful and triggering the other week from a social anxiety point of view, I explained that a few stressors run through my head at a million miles an hour:

- If I'm in a large crowd, that's a lot of people who could hurt me or rape me.
- I don't want to get trapped again.
- I don't want to get hurt.
- I don't want to get touched and groped and raped again.
- A crowd limits your options to escape.
- If I'm with new people then they could rape me again.

Of course, I acknowledge every single one of these is a biased, illogical thought that has no evidence supporting it. As well as a lot of these fears and thoughts aren't based in reality or what happened to me, they're actually based in the emotions I felt during the assault.

For example, I wasn't physically limited on me being able to escape, but I was so scared that my rapist would beat me, hurt me and pin me down if I made a wrong move. Since he was a lot bigger and heavier than me, it wouldn't have been hard. That the fear paralysed me and stopped me from being able to escape.

I never want to experience that feeling again.

Therefore, I have a lot of social anxiety about accidentally finding myself in another situation where I could get hurt and abused again, even I know in the grand scheme of things that is very unlikely.

Furthermore, I have a lot of anxiety about meeting new people because I know my pre-existing friends are not going to hurt or abuse me, but I am scared that new people will. As well as it doesn't help when my intrusive thoughts and dreams twist what happened to me to show me new friends (and sometimes old close friends) are beating and raping me.

All these different factors make meeting new people difficult for me.

However, I know I have to allow myself to meet new people, live my life and I never want to isolate myself. I recently found that the woman who attacked me because of her persecutory delusions was sexually abused as a kid by a woman and she started to isolate herself recently. I saw how she attacked anyone who did even the slightest thing wrong in her eyes and unless you supported her 100% she dropped you. She dropped my best friend (someone who moved heaven and earth for her constantly) just because my best friend defended me once against her.

I never want to end up like her so I will always be subtly open and try to make new friends, new connections and I want to live my life regardless of how many barriers my sexual assault puts up.

<u>The R Conversation</u>

As much as I hate to say this (and believe I wish I didn't have to), at some point in the friendship you have to have the conversation about what happened to you. And this does not have to be a detailed conversation, you never have to reveal anything you don't want to and actually, you don't have to tell them if you don't want to.

However, there might be a situation, a comment or a joke that makes you realise you need to have that conversation with your new friend so you can enjoy the friendship without getting triggered, have bad mental health and you can live your life without suffering.

There is no timeline for this conversation. You might want to or need to have the conversation within a few weeks of the new friendship, you might be able to wait months or you might never want or need to tell them.

Nonetheless, if you do want or need to have the conversation about what happened to you, my advice is the following:

- Be sure you want to tell them.
- Only tell them what you are comfortable sharing.
- Remember you are in full control of the situation, so you can tell them however you want to. For instance, in-person, on the phone or by text.

In addition, I would mention based on my own experience, this is actually more terrifying than telling your pre-existing friends. Since the friends you had before what happened to you occurred, you were already friends with them, your relationships were solid and your friends love you so a disclosure shouldn't have changed anything in that regard.

On the other hand, when it comes to new friendships, they don't know you before your sexual violence experience, they don't know what you're like and there is a fear they will react badly because your friendship is new.

Personally, before I told Henry about what happened to me (I'll show you how I did that in a moment), I was very scared that he wouldn't want to be friends anymore, he wouldn't just leave or he would react negatively to my disclosure.

I always knew I was going to have to tell Henry about what happened to me, because my best friend is going back home for a month, and we both want me to hang out with Henry so I get some social contact. As well as I have something to look forward to so I won't get hopeless and severely suicidality again.

Therefore, I wanted to push this conversation as late as I possibly could, so Henry could get to know me, the fun, cool person (I am so not cool) and not me The Rape Survivor. That is what I would have preferred.

Nevertheless, life doesn't always stick to my plans.

As a result of with Ruby being at the house this week and them bringing their Nintendo Switch, I knew Henry wanted to hang out this week and Henry is a massive gamer. And as me, Ruby and my best friend were playing Mario Kart 8 Sunday night, I was considering asking Henry to come round so I could get used to them without my best friend being there.

Something that would be very useful for when they go back. Since I am concerned about spending time with Henry one-on-one when my best friend isn't down here in Canterbury.

Therefore, I asked Henry if he wanted to come round and I wanted to get ahead of this so I effectively ripped off the bandage. This is what I sent on Instagram:

"Hey, are you free anytime this week? Maybe Wednesday?

My housemate Reuben's down for the week and they brought their Nintendo Switch and I know you're a massive gamer. I was wondering if you wanted to come round, catch up and play games for a few hours.

And you're a friend so I want to be honest with you. So I have PTSD because I was raped back in April and it can cause me panic attacks, intense social anxiety and so on. So one-on-one stuff is really difficult for me especially with a guy, so that's why I invite you to group things. Yet I really like you as a friend so even when X goes back to Solihull for a month in a few weeks, I will try to do things with you. And if there's anything you want to do, please ask and feel free to invite me.

I don't need you to treat or see me differently but I'm just telling you this because if I say no to things or ever have a meltdown in front of you (granted I rarely have meltdowns in public), it's nothing against you, you've done nothing wrong and I think you're a great guy. I do want to be friends with you."

The point of this message was to be honest and explain why I might struggle when my best friend goes back home for a month, so he doesn't feel like I don't want to be friends with him.

Originally, I was slightly annoyed at Henry's response because he disregarded my PTSD comments completely. Yet my best friend pointed out, he is very autistic (like both of us) so he might not know how to respond at all and he doesn't come across as the most emotionally mature person, so it's fine he didn't react.

At the time I completely disagreed with my best friend, because I wanted at least an acknowledgement. Yet now it doesn't bother me because we've still been texting, he shared a funny reel with me yesterday and he still wants to hang out with me.

He still wants to be friends.

Honestly, him still wanting to be friends is actually all I care about because Henry is still a friend I can do things with, have fun and I can live a little. Another act of defiance against my rapist.

Tips For Managing New Friendships

On the whole, when I was telling Ruby about me disclosing my sexual violence experience to Henry, they mentioned the following "if (a new friend) doesn't take your disclosure well then they aren't a person you should be friends with".

That is seriously true to be fair because we can want all the new friends we want, but unless they're respectful, kind and caring then I don't want them to be my friends. I am not so desperate for new friends that I am going to allow myself to experience disrespect and negativity from idiots who pretend to be my friends.

Friends are people who support me, care about me and are interested in knowing more about me.

If people react badly and unsupportively about my rape then I don't want them in my life.

In addition, when you find people who do respect you, are interested in you and want to support you as you deepen your friendship over time. Then here are my tips based on my own experience at Week 14:

- Go at a pace that is comfortable for you.
- You don't have to do anything you don't want to do.
- You can bring another friend along for in-person hangouts or whatever.

- Only have the R conversation when you're ready and if you want to have it.
- When you hang out, pick places and options that make you feel comfortable.
- Enjoy it.

Personally, the idea of picking places and options that make you feel comfortable is really important to me. For example, I flat out will not hang out at Henry's house for months because my sexual violence happened at a new person's house in their living room. So the idea of going into Henry's living room is terrifying.

Furthermore, it will take me ages to do something with Henry one-on-one but being in public is also distressing. Therefore, I will need to decide what's going to make me more comfortable because at some point, I will have to carefully spend time with him one-on-one.

Overall, making new friends is very possible after experiencing sexual violence and it is something you absolutely should do when you are ready and when you meet someone you want to be friends with.

Finally, please put yourself first. Protect your mental health, do what you need to do and make sure you enjoy the process of making friends. New friends are a great way to live your life a little after what happened and it can be a very rewarding process, if not a little scary to us survivors.

But just like surviving sexual violence, making friends is certainly possible, and making friends can certainly be fun, funny and very enjoyable indeed.

WHY DIDN'T I REPORT MY SEXUAL ASSAULT?

There are a good amount of chapters in this book that I seriously avoid writing for as long as humanly possible, because as you can imagine, a lot of these chapters are really hard and draining for me to write. Yet I want to get this content written down, I want to process what happened and I want to help people.

Therefore, I mention a lot of my triggers throughout the book but whenever I heard about someone reporting their sexual violence, I get very triggered because I feel inadequate. I feel like a failure for not standing up for my fellow survivors, I feel like I'm the reason why my attacker *might* hurt other people and so on.

Of course, none of these thoughts are realistic at all because if my attacker hurts anyone else, it is because of His decision to hurt them, not me. And I am not a failure for not wanting to report it because I know because *how* everything happened, reporting it would be relatively pointless because I fly in the face of so many rape myths and I am far from the "perfect" rape victim.

Hell, I am not even a victim, I am a survivor.

As a result, I'm finally comfortable enough to write this chapter exactly 15 weeks after what happened to me, because last night I read a woman's article from Candan on this exact topic. And it gave me peace of mind that I had made the right decision for me.

Important Note:

Despite everything I am going to say in this chapter, you absolutely have to do what is right for you, your situation and your mental health. If you want to report your sexual violence to the police then DO IT, if reporting it to the university, your workplace, wherever will help you then please DO IT and if you want to report it to see what happens then DO IT.

Everything in this book is just my experience, and you will have a different experience to me, so if you want to report your sexual assault then please do it.

This chapter is just to explain why *I* didn't report it in case a fellow reader finds this reassuring and comforting in case they didn't want to report it. As well as if you do want to report it, then this might encourage you to do so, so you can challenge some of these ideas.

And most importantly, hopefully put the bastard who did this to you behind bars.

The Article From Last Night

I want to share the article that I read last night because it's another perspective on everything I've spoken about in this book and it helps to show that whoever you are, the vast majority of us sexual violence survivors experience the same thing over time. Therefore, the article is "I was raped at university. Here's why I never reported it" by Meghan Simard, and I've added in the website link at the end of this section before I talk about my own reasons.

Essentially, Meghan consistently tried to report her rape to her university, the police and a range of other places but no one took notes, no one took her seriously and no one wanted to press charges against her attacker.

Mainly because what happened to her didn't fit with the idea that a lot of people had about rape, so even if it went to court, it probably wouldn't have ended up with a guilty verdict because she wasn't the typical "victim" in laypeople's eyes.

Even though in reality, she actually was the typical rape survivor in terms of she did what happens in 99% of rapes and sexual assaults, and her reaction during her rape was the same as mine. I really do recommend reading the article if you're up for it.

Personally, it just annoys me that laypeople (and honestly I was probably no exception before I was raped too) are so convinced they know what rape is and they have such fixed ideas that you are only a rape survivor if you kicked, screamed and fought off your attacker. And when someone who was actually raped comes forward, the laypeople call them a liar because their experience goes against all the myths.

On a little side note, this is so common in clinical psychology when we have to deal with laypeople too. Some clients believe they know what therapy is, what mental health is and they know what they need to do to improve their mental health, but when clinical psychologists try to help them, some clients think we don't know what we're talking about. Just because how therapy actually works is different from the myths.

I flat out hate myths.

Anyway, there is one paragraph in the article I love because it sums up my life and how much I love my best friend because they support me so well. As well as I am really grateful Meghan has a much larger social support network than me and I hope she's doing better now.

"The rest of my school year was more or less a garbage fire. Attending university classes with newly developed, untreated, and severe PTSD is hard enough, but I also had to see my rapist regularly on and around campus. I am indebted to my friends who held my hands through panic attacks and to my family who picked up the phone in the middle of the night when all I wanted to do was die."

Source- https://www.cbc.ca/news/canada/first-person-campus-sex-assault-1.6189141

On the whole, you can experience massive challenges from the healthcare, university and Criminal Justice System when it comes to reporting your rape. This should never happen, it is outrageous and it is flat out disgusting that the very systems that are meant to protect us are failing us survivors so badly.

However, there are initiatives and policies and survivors fighting to change this, so hopefully over time this will change. For now, I will stick to doing occasional podcast episodes and books on sexual violence in an effort to change people's minds and reveal the truth about sexual violence, but it is a very uncomfortable topic for a lot of people. And I lose a lot of listeners each time I try to do these topics, but I need to do them sparingly unfortunately.

Why I Did Not Report My Sexual Assault?

When it comes to how sexual violence investigations work, like everyone else, my knowledge is limited but because I watch a lot of crime dramas, and a goodish amount of True Crime programmes and some of those episodes featured rape, I had an okay understanding of what to expect.

I knew I was the physical evidence and I understood that the "worst" thing I could do was shower, clean my teeth and the rest. Yet I was in denial about what had happened to me was classed as sexual assault and sexual violence until two days after it had happened.

Furthermore, I think I knew it was sexual violence because I refused to shower and clean my teeth when I got home. Maybe I was thinking I would realise what had happened in the morning and I would report it then. Yet these were not conscious thoughts of what I was intending to do because I was pretending I was perfectly okay and nothing had happened whatsoever.

However, when I got up the next morning as you read earlier I was so distressed that I would have been happy to cut off my own dick, so I did have a shower and I washed away the evidence on me.

That was one reason why I didn't report it because there was no physical evidence left. In all honesty, I still have my boxers from that night and there is a small chance His spit is still on them but I am not going down that road.

Another reason why I decided not to report it was because I was far from the stereotypical rape victim that jurors would expect. I'm male for starters and in society there is the stupid myth that males do not get raped.

Therefore, I would have to go through the embarrassment and stigma and social judgment from everyone that I (someone born male at birth) "allowed" themselves to get raped. Like fuck did I allow myself to get raped, but it is still what people believe.

In this situation, the myths and misconceptions that people have about male rape and male victims were massive factors that stopped me from being safe enough to report it to the police. This was only confirmed and reinforced by the negative reactions I've had from certain important people in my life who blame me completely for what happened and they think I'm making up how badly this is affecting me.

Also, I'm gay and transgender non-binary so there are times when my opinion is hardly positive about the police considering the heavy bias they have against gay and trans people.

Moreover, I know more than enough about the criminal justice system from my forensic psychology interest to know that in court, the defence would have to call me a liar. Now I have been called a liar before by important people in my life and I have no desire whatsoever to be called that disgusting term again.

Moreover, when I was being raped, I now realise all I wanted to do was survive as well as I was so scared to make a wrong move that I didn't fight back when he did stuff. Since I did not want to "offend" him and for him to turn violent. I was just focusing on surviving but that reason flies in the face of all the rape myths and misconceptions. Therefore, whilst that is what the vast, vast majority of rape survivors do during their attack, the defence would eat me alive through their stupid questions. Like:

- Why didn't you fight back?
- Why didn't you scream?
- Why didn't you leave after he grabbed you the first time?
- Why didn't you report it that night?
- He never actually hit you or threatened you so why are you making up that you felt in danger? Are you too sensitive?
- And on and on and on.

As much as I want to say in a court of law that the defence can fuck off because I just wanted to survive and the posh twat of a defence barrister could never even imagine what being raped is like, I know that would hardly make me look good and contemptible.

The criminal justice system itself was another reason why I didn't report it.

Finally, my main issue with reporting what happened to me was simply a lack of other evidence. The entire case would be "They said, he said," because I can't even prove I was actually there that night and we engaged in sex.

My rapist deleted the Grindr messages by the time I got home because I was going to take screenshots of them. Then without the messages there were no signs he wanted to have sex with me and I have no idea how you prove it wasn't consensual.

I've tried researching it online but consent is a very hard legal area to define and I don't know how you prove that the sexual activity I was forced to have against my will wasn't consent. I said it firmly wasn't but he would say it was (because he would have to unless he wanted to go to prison).

Therefore, without those Grindr messages, I have no idea how you prove I was there that night, let alone that he never asked for my consent, that he grabbed me against my Will a second time after I had said no and the rest.

There is no evidence that I could submit to a court of law so that's why I didn't report it because there would be no point.

<u>How Has This "Decision" Affected Me Over The Months?</u>

Firstly, I wouldn't call this a "decision" at all because a decision makes it sound like I had more than one option. I could have reported it but I have no evidence and there are other reasons above why I didn't report it, and I know there is a risk I could be charged with force reporting of a crime. And there would be a lot of dicks online that would twist my story and make it sound like I was "yet another" person making up rape stories.

In reality, so, so few people make up rape stories that it was outrageous that people think individuals would lie about this disgusting event.

Anyway, me not reporting what happened to me wasn't something I could control and because of the lack of evidence I couldn't take another option.

Over the past few months, me not being to report it didn't bother me until the end of Week 13 because it just started to annoy me and I felt a little grief towards that was yet something my rapist denied me and took away from me.

Also, before Week 13, it only played on my mind whenever I would hear news reports about how great, brave and courageous a sexual violence survivor was for reporting it to the police. I completely agree that survivor was amazing, especially because there was one time when it was a child) but I always felt like shit after hearing that. Then I would have a few panic attacks and so on.

At this current point in time at Week 15, I'm relatively okay about not being able to report it, because I'm still struggling. I am trying to move on, I know I couldn't handle the criminal justice system and I don't want to get called a liar by the defence.

And I'm at peace with the decision that my rapist might never see the inside of a courtroom and I will never get justice, but here's the thing. I'm alive.

I am alive.

Sure, as you'll see in future chapters, my rapist has taken so bloody much from me over the past few months and he will continue to interfere in my life so damn much. He has caused PTSD, severe social anxiety, suicidality and so on.

Yet I will recover, I will live a good life and I will date in the future. I have no idea how long that will be and who it will be with but I will not allow my rapist to ruin my life. He can make it as difficult as he wants because of that single outrageous event, and he will cause me many difficulties going forward.

Yet I am alive, I am sort of living and I am slowly accomplishing stuff over time. And I will continue to slowly get better at a snail's pace.

So yes, I am okay with not reporting my rape because I am alive and I am going to keep living in spite that what that bastard did. And each positive thing I do in my life is a middle-finger up to that bastard and everything he did to me.

Conclusion: Over To You

When it comes to deciding whether to report your experience or not, I know this is not an easy decision and you will have a million questions racing around inside your head.

You will be processing what the hell just happened to you, you will be wondering about how your friends and family will see you, and what the response will be from different areas of society including what your experience of the criminal justice system will be like.

Just stop and take a breath.

I strongly believe that the only aspect you need to be thinking about when you're thinking about whether to report it or not is you.

Just focus on yourself.

I would suggest you think about what do you need, what do you want and how are you going to feel if you report it versus not reporting it.

If you want to report it then you absolutely should and more power to you, because you are more courageous than I could ever be and I admire you for that.

However, if you decide not to report then that is absolutely okay too. It is what I've done, it is what 95% of survivors do and that's okay. It doesn't mean what happened to you matters or impacts you any less, and it still means you have a lot of healing to do.

Whatever decision you make, me and the rest of us survivors will support you because this is one of the hardest decisions you will ever have to make. And this is such a personal choice that is decided by a million different factors that only you can make this decision.

Let me repeat that, only you can decide whether to report what happened to you. No one else can or should ever decide it for you.

No one.

YOU HAVE THE RIGHT TO BE VULNERABLE AND CONFUSED

Originally I put this on my list of chapter ideas a few weeks ago so maybe around Week 12/ 13 because I felt so vulnerable all the time, as fragile as a child and I really didn't like this feeling.

However, once I accepted this feeling dealing with everything got a little nicer because sexual violence is so traumatic, so foul and so disgusting that it will rattle you to your very core. Hence, you will feel very vulnerable and fragile like a child because you might not know what your triggers are so you might be reacting to the so-called smallest of things and then you become anxious about becoming triggered and dealing with all the panic attacks and other trauma responses.

Nonetheless, I want to stress that this is okay. You need to remember that what you went through was traumatic, horrible and it will scar you but you can and will heal if you get professional help and you work through the trauma.

You will feel extremely vulnerable and fragile for a wide range of reasons. Including Post-Traumatic Stress Disorder so if you develop the condition, you'll be experiencing flashbacks, severe anxiety and nightmares so you'll be constantly on edge and hyperalert. This only makes you feel more vulnerable and fragile.

In addition, you might feel vulnerable and fragile because you might be scared that your attacker will hurt or harm you again or you might be scared other people won't believe you. Then it is this sense of fear that makes you feel vulnerable.

Personally, my main feelings of being vulnerable and fragile come from my anxiety and utter fear that someone else will hurt me again, and there is a minor concern that my rapist will find me again and do what he did to me again over and over.

The fear is where most of my psychological distress comes from.

Moreover, something I seriously struggle with is the sense of loss of control because rape is an awful act of violence that takes away our sense of control over our lives and our bodies. Thus, the lack of control that we feel leads us to feel helpless and very vulnerable.

Another reason why survivors feel vulnerable is because a lot of us struggle with guilt and shame even though what happened to us was never our fault. The fault only lays with the bastard that did this to us. And as I discovered a few weeks ago when me and my best friend moved in together, the feelings of guilt can be crippling and they are another major source of vulnerability in my experience.

By the way, I do expand upon these points in different ways in other chapters, but right now I want to give you the information.

Penultimately, the social stigma, myths and misconceptions surrounding rape is another reason why survivors feel a lot of vulnerability. Since the social stigma can lead to a lack of support and for us to feel isolated. This is definitely an issue I face because my best friend is literally all I have in terms of social support and as much as I love my best friend for always being there, I still want other people to support me.

Finally, physical injuries are another reason why survivors can feel fragile because if their assault included them getting injured physically then this only adds to the pain they experience. As a result, the physical healing process, something that sadly takes time, can be painful in itself but it can be a painful reminder of the trauma too.

On the whole, in this section of the chapter, we've looked at a wide range of reasons explaining why survivors feel vulnerable and fragile and I want you to know that feeling this way is okay.

It feels horrible, you might feel like a child, you might feel weak and you might feel like you will never be strong or normal again. Yet I promise you that when you process things over time, when you accept yourself and your trauma responses then things get easier. This might take you weeks or months like it did for me, but you can get there and you can start to feel a little stronger over time.

And just remember, each time you get stronger, each time you experience joy and each time you can feel a little less fragile is a major act of defiance against what your attacker did to you.

Feeling vulnerable and fragile is a part of the healing process, and it never defines you.

HOW DOES SEXUAL VIOLENCE IMPACT EMPLOYABILITY AND PERSONAL FINANCES?

Last night one of my dear friends sat down with me and my best friend and told us some very personal things about their mental health, their past trauma and what had happened to them about a decade ago. I knew something had happened to them because of our conversations throughout this week and I had been laying the groundwork so my friend felt safe enough to talk about what was bothering them.

And last night, they thankfully trusted us enough to talk about it.

It was a very personal, deep and emotional conversation that brought all of us closer as friends, and the future should be a lot easier for this friend now whenever they stay with us.

However, I realised something very troubling during that conversation. I don't have the same level of empathy and emotions as I once did before I was raped. I still love this friend, I still said a lot of useful things and I've shown all week how I would happily move heaven and earth for them.

Nonetheless, when they were revealing what had happened to them, how it had impacted them and how they were refusing to talk about it and get professional help the one time I gently pressed them for it. I couldn't help but feel a little less empathetic for them because they couldn't see how much this event was hurting them, damaging their mental health and reducing them to a shell of the great friend I had spent the week with.

I understand this makes me sound like a bad person and a very bad friend. Yet there were tons of similarities between the symptoms me and my friend were experiencing. My friend wasn't raped but it was still trauma and they were having a lot of trauma responses.

And I understand this is just my psychology degree, psychology books and podcast that have helped me to understand how important talking, processing and getting professional help is for people. Yet it bugged me that I could see how much my friend was struggling and they didn't want to get help. They wanted to pretend it never happened and they were denying everything.

It brought up a lot of other feelings, including a lot of distress for me because hearing about their trauma experience was difficult for me. It triggered a lot of my own trauma about my rape and it caused a lot of things to pile up so I didn't sleep last night.

Considering I want to be a clinical psychologist in the future and improve lives, decrease psychological distress and give clients more adaptive coping mechanisms where I will have to hear a lot about other people's mental health, this is a major problem.

Leading us onto the topic of this chapter.

How Does Sexual Violence Impact Employability And Personal Finances?

After I panicked about me not being able to be a clinical psychologist anymore as well as work in the mental health sector, I calmed down and I decided to look at the facts and any academic research on employment after sexual violence. There isn't a lot of research on the topic but I managed to find an excellent paper that I'll share below. It's very accessible, easy to understand, and I highly recommend reading it if you want to learn more.

Loya R. M. (2015). Rape as an Economic Crime: The Impact of Sexual Violence on Survivors' Employment and Economic Well-Being. *Journal of interpersonal violence*, *30*(16), 2793–2813. https://doi.org/10.1177/0886260514554291

Honestly, I almost cried reading this paper about four times because it revealed some hard truths about employment after experiencing sexual violence. Therefore, I'll take you through the results of the academic paper and then I'll explain my own situation.

The paper mentions how after experiencing sexual violence, employment can become very difficult for survivors for a range of reasons. For example, as mentioned previously, a lot of survivors go onto develop Post-Traumatic Stress Disorder including severe anxiety and flashbacks, and they experience other mental health difficulties or conditions. Such as depression, anxiety, substance abuse disorder amongst others.

As a result, the mental health impacts of sexual violence can cause survivors to feel the need to quit their jobs, especially if they were attacked on the way to or from work or if their attacker was someone they worked with. Also, a decrease in mental health can lead to decreased job performance so the survivor ends up getting fired in the end for no fault of their own.

In addition, the paper mentioned that survivors who told their bosses about being a survivor of sexual violence did better than the survivors who did not. Since the bosses and leadership team were able to attribute the signs of the survivor's mental health and decreasing performance to the sexual violence and not the survivor being bad at their job.

Moreover, the paper explains how dealing with the aftermath and mental health difficulties of sexual violence leads to a lot of costs over time. For example, needing days, weeks or years off work to recover, see doctors, liaising with the police and other members of the criminal justice system and so on. This cost or loss of money only increases if hospital and doctor's visits are needed, even more so in places that don't have free healthcare like the United Kingdom at the time of writing.

In addition, the aftermath of sexual violence can make some survivors need to quit work altogether because it is too much for their mental health, it is too triggering and they cannot hold down a job. For instance, the paper mentions how one woman who was raped 30 years ago has only been able to do minimum wage work ever since. As well as another woman had to do temporary work for 3 years after her rape because her mental health couldn't handle doing more than a week's work at a time.

This is why survivors who lived in states with progressive public benefits managed to do reasonably well, because they could get income support even if they were raped by an intimate partner.

On the other hand, the paper did explain how survivors who managed to access mental health support as well as counselling for their assault did manage to do better than those who couldn't access support after their sexual violence experience. For example, the woman who's sadly still doing minimum wage work after 30 years was never able to afford counselling for her rape, so she was never really able to recover. Whereas another woman who was able to afford counselling did *better* over time and she managed to return to full-time employment even though she's never managed to return to the same levels of earnings before her rape.

This is why counselling and mental health support is so critical, and more must be done to make it available to all survivors.

A final discovery in the paper that I want to talk about is the idea of Major and Modest Trajectory Shifts within a survivor's life. Due to it's very common for a survivor's life to change a lot after their sexual assault so their life effectively changes trajectory, so they don't end up doing what they wanted to do before they were raped.

One example in the paper is that one survivor needed to delay herself going to college by three years because she wasn't ready to do so before then. Another woman had to delay herself going to college by a year and the paper explained this took a year away from her future high earnings from her.

These two examples show you what a Modest Trajectory Shift looks like because these were temporary delays in what a survivor wants to do. As well as the definition the paper uses is as follows:

"modest trajectory shifts or delays, which are changes to survivors' employment or economic stability from which they eventually recovered and returned to their prior level of economic well-being."

This is a type of shift that makes me very happy and almost hopeful for the future because it shows that given the right amount of support (and a bunch of other factors), a survivor can go back to what they wanted to do before their rape in the end. Thankfully, modest shifts show that sexual violence doesn't have to change your employability forever, there is hope that you can reclaim your career choices given the right professional support and time.

In addition, there are lots of survivors who unfortunately experience major trajectory shifts, and this is something I am flat out terrified about. This is how the paper defines these types of shifts:

"major shifts, employment consequences that permanently changed survivors' occupational or earning pathways, 2806 Journal of Interpersonal Violence 30(16) including long-term unemployment, career change, and permanent disability. A lawyer explained major trajectory shifts this way: "It really spirals. Like I've talked to clients, literally, who 20 years later after the assault . . . the trajectory of their life is so totally different than it was the 10 seconds before the rape happened"

(Provider 100)."

As you can imagine, this quote made me cry my eyes out because I'll talk about this more in a moment, but it goes to show that sexual violence can seriously interfere with every single aspect of our lives. Also, considering I have a future career in mind, I am terrified that I am never going to be able to do that, help people and improve lives.

I want to do my future career but I am scared that my sexual violence experience will stop that from ever happening.

How Has My Rape Impacted My Employability?

The major caveat to this section is that I am a Masters student but I still need to earn money, I am still a business owner and I am still a student ambassador with the university.

Therefore, it was only last night hearing my friend talk about their trauma experience and reading that academic paper that I realised just how badly my experience of sexual violence has impacted my employment over the past few months. In terms of being a student ambassador, it hasn't really impacted me too much because I am still doing the work, I am still signing up for work opportunities and Outreach still loves me because I always do an amazing job.

That is what external observers see.

In reality, I still love Outreach work, I love interacting with students and I really enjoy the wide range of work I get to be involved in to promote higher education. As well as give young people from disadvantaged, poor backgrounds hope that anyone can go to university regardless of their postcode.

However, I still have extreme social anxiety, panic attacks and I get triggered a lot at Outreach events. For example, I've had to hide in toilets to calm down at times, I've had to avoid certain students and teachers from outside the university like the plague and Thursday was very rough and you can see how bad I was in the following WhatsApp message:

"Mythbuster session was really good and I enjoyed it. There were only two people which is a shame but still.

Except the guy was fat, had long brown hair, jeans and a brown checked overshirt. He looked like a younger version of my rapist. Panicked a little in the session but managed to keep it under wraps. I've been sitting on the toilet for 20 minutes trying to calm down and I'm about to head back.

I'm going co-op now for some stuff now."

Therefore, as you can see this was a work situation because I was getting paid to deliver a Mythbuster session to a bunch of students (only two signed-up to the session but money is money and it was fun) but I was really distressed by the end of it.

And sometimes Outreach work does knock me out for a few days afterwards and sometimes it can trigger me for days. Thursday did kickstart a whole bunch of smaller events that led to me not sleeping last night, so I am very glad that Outreach work isn't 40 hours a week and I can pick and choose when I work, but that doesn't make it any easier.

Furthermore, when it comes to my writing business, this has been heavily damaged by my sexual violence. I have had to take a lot of time off to recover, to mentally and emotionally process what the hell happened to me and this all has a knock-on effect with my writing. I have written a lot less than I would have liked to at this point in the year, and this has a massive impact on my future income.

That's why I am so thankful and grateful for my readers because you buying books helps to support me.

Then this lack of writing and lack of business work really negatively impacts my mental health, so I'm dealing with bad mental health on two fronts. The lack of writing and business because this is what I flat out love and it makes me so happy, and I'm dealing with the rape itself.

I have no idea how much money I've lost because of a lack of writing and business work as I try to process my sexual assault, but by the time I'm "okay" (whatever that means), it will be a lot unfortunately.

Finally, if we look towards the future and my possible career as a clinical psychologist where I get to help people improve their lives, give them control back and give them more adaptive coping mechanisms, then I am scared.

I used to be fine hearing about people's mental health, trauma and their maladaptive coping mechanisms. I used to be able to listen to these conversations in such a caring, compassionate and understanding way that I could offer really good tips, advice and other things to my friends and family. Yet I can only do this now with my best friend.

If I talk or listen to anyone else about their mental health and trauma then I find it distressing, triggering and all my rape stuff gets triggered over and over again. Hell, I tend to feel all the horrible physical sensations of me getting raped multiple times and my brain twists it horrifically so last night I had intrusive thoughts about my best friend beating and raping me.

I think listening to my friend talk about their trauma and bad mental health was the thing that broke my back and led to a terrible night of bad sleep.

I cannot do that every day and every night, but if I wanted to work as a clinical psychologist then I would have to. Especially when it came to building up my clinical experience when I would really need to work full-time to try and get as much experience as possible.

Last night, I went outside to process everything I had read in the academic paper and I really did cry.

I know not everyone reading this book will be psychology students or psychology professionals, but I flat out love clinical psychology. I love how it gives us the theories, the therapies and the interventions to transform people's lives. We can give them hope in their darkest hour, we can give them new ways to deal with stressful situations and we work with clients at every step of the way because our clients are proud, courageous and they deserve our full respect.

That is why clinical psychologists work so hard to improve the lives of our clients because they're great people that want to live their lives and we can support them doing that.

So the very idea that my rapist, that fat, ugly bastard could take that away from me is fucking outrageous. I flat out hate the idea that he could take away my ability to help so many amazing people who are suffering or are in need of psychological support.

I can deal with him impacting me, raping me and sabotaging my life. But how fucking dare he impact the lives of other innocent people who have nothing to do with him.

In the future, I should be helping them, supporting them and giving them hope, but if I cannot do that because of the hurt and trauma he has inflicted upon me then I hope he suffers somehow in the end.

I cannot stand leaving innocent people to suffer and live in pain, but unfortunately, if this is a major trajectory shift for me then I am concerned that I will not be the one to help clients in the future.

And that kills me inside.

You only have to read my books, listen to my podcast and talk to me in person to know how much I love clinical psychology and I want to be a clinical psychologist in the future.

However, unless I can find a way to work in mental health in a wide range of settings and be okay listening to trauma, psychological distress and maybe even the worst of humanity without it destroying my own mental health instantly then I am scared I cannot do the career I love.

And if that is the case then I know I will have to grieve that as well as everything else I am grieving as part of my rape.

Personally, if clinical psychology isn't available to me as a career path, I have considered going into academia and focusing on research. I do enjoy research these days and I do have ideas for a lot of different mental health studies for rape survivors and transgender individuals. I would enjoy researching my ideas, writing up papers and getting academically published.

This would require me to get a PhD so I would have the safety and security that being at the university gives me, as well as I could continue my Outreach work for another 3 or 4 years.

However, I know I don't actually want this, I have never thought about this before my rape and even for months after my rape I never considered or wanted this. I have always thought that a PhD was seriously not something I want and I do not want to work in academia because it is not my world.

This is just a rape reaction and it is not what I want for my life.

In a small way, it's funny because it was only the day before I met up with a friend I haven't seen since my rape and he asked me about future careers after my Masters. My words were basically "in an ideal world, it's still become an assistant psychologist, gain my years of experience and then apply for the doctorate of clinical psychology so I can become a fully qualified clinical psychologist. But in reality, it's what job I can hold down because I doubt I can do full-time work at the moment,"

It's weird that I already knew that deep down about how much I was struggling, hurting and not being able to function.

Thankfully, I should have my rape counselling starting next month but this is still hard. I want this to be a modest shift in my career trajectory but I'm concerned that it isn't, and maybe my rapist stole my chance of doing the career I flat out love and the one I've been working so hard for years to be able to do.

Yet I am not giving up on my future career without a fight.

Conclusion: Over To You

At the end of this chapter, I want you to know that if you're struggling with your employment after your experience of sexual violence that is normal, expected and if you get professional help, maybe talk to your employer and get other forms of support then things might be okay in the end.

This includes accommodations for you so you can get the support you need and stay employed. For example, you might need extra time off if you need to talk to the lawyers or police or you might need to work from home for two days a week so you can work and get paid but you can look after yourself too.

Personally, reading this section within the academic paper was a massive relief because at the time of writing, tomorrow I have training for the Year 10 Residential summer school where over 50 14- and 15-year-olds will be staying at the university in halls for three days and two nights to experience university life. I'll be with other ambassadors but I am extremely nervous.

This will be a very intense four days for me because I have the training on the Monday and the summer school starts at 8 am on Tuesday and runs straight through until 5 pm on Thursday. Sure, I get a 1-hour or 2 hour break per day but that is it.

That is not a lot of time for me to look after myself if (when) something triggers me.

Additionally, I am very nervous about there being a student at the summer school with the same name as my rapist. Especially if this student is in my corridor that I have to look after, because I refuse, I just can't say his name over and over again this week when I'm looking after students.

I don't think I can handle that, but thankfully Outreach does love me, all the staff working at the summer school think I am amazing (their words actually) and I know they will support me. Therefore, this academic paper was a great reminder that it is okay to talk and ask for accommodations.

That is exactly what I will do this week if I need to. Please do the same for yourself if you need it.

Never suffer in silence.

Trajectory Shifts

You might experience a modest or major trajectory shift in your career and that is normal too. I understand you might be angry, rageful and you will grieve for whatever you feel like you have loss. I know I will in the end too.

However, the same guidance applies when dealing with employment issues than when it comes to mental health. Please be kind to yourself, be compassionate towards yourself and get professional help so you can work towards your recovery. Once your recovery is well underway your employment and job might get easier and your economic wellbeing might improve too.

To wrap up the chapter, here's some unofficial tips and advice you might want to do:

- Think about talking to your employer about what happened so accommodations can be made.
- Get professional mental health support
- Think about what would happen if you experience a modest and major trajectory shift.

- Process your feelings about your employment situation.
- Read the academic paper below.

Loya R. M. (2015). Rape as an Economic Crime: The Impact of Sexual Violence on Survivors' Employment and Economic Well-Being. *Journal of interpersonal violence*, *30*(16), 2793–2813. https://doi.org/10.1177/0886260514554291

IF YOU DON'T DEAL WITH TRAUMA, IT WILL DEAL WITH YOU

It's been at least three days since I've had a good night's sleep. I am currently emotionally and physically exhausted, I am a little depressed and I am terrified about going to sleep tonight because whenever I stop doing something and I lay down, I get intrusive thoughts and half-dreams about rape.

It is very rare that I write a chapter from the outset intending it to be for two different audiences that will find this content very useful. Therefore, this next chapter will be written with aspiring and qualified clinical psychologists as well as other people interested in psychology, and my fellow sexual violence survivors in mind. Since this next chapter will be packed full of useful insights for both groups of individuals.

This chapter focuses on the importance of processing and dealing with your trauma and realising you cannot deny your traumatic event ever happened. As well as for the psychologists reading this chapter, this chapter focuses on the lived experience of people who have gone through traumatic events, and the chapter helps to shine a light on some of the avoidance techniques that people with trauma go through.

In addition, another reason why I am using this chapter for both audiences is because I want to show survivors of sexual violence that psychologists only want to help you, support and there is no magic going on. In other words, a lot of the myths and misconceptions you have about therapy are just that. Anything weird and negative you've heard about psychologists and therapy almost certainly isn't true.

Overall, in the rest of the chapter, you're going to learn the heartbreaking experience I had with a friend recently that led me to write about this topic. Then I'll talk about why I allow myself to deal with my rape no matter how hard and distressing it is (and why I sometimes don't, which is not a good thing but I am still human) as well as through the chapter, I'll be adding in details and paragraphs for survivors and psychologists alike.

This is a very eye-opening and flat out critical chapter to read and enjoy.

<u>What Recent Experience Made Me Want To Talk About This Topic?</u>

I know I mentioned I haven't slept in three nights and this was a tiny factor in that massive problem. Since me and my best friend sat one of our friends down the other house because they were distressed, struggling and I had been laying the groundwork down all week helping our friend to realise that our house (they'll be our housemate in September) is a safe space and they can talk about whatever is troubling them.

Three nights ago, their last night at our house for a while, they told us about their trauma, what had happened to them and a whole bunch of other things that I was surprised about. I wasn't surprised something was causing their bad mental health because the conditions and experiences and even odd phrases they mentioned in passing made me know something had happened. Yet my friend wasn't telling us what had happened and I never pushed it.

Thankfully, they felt safe around me and my best friend to open up and explain everything.

However, the reason why this experience made me want to talk about this topic is because the trauma my friend experienced happened roughly 8 years ago. Now aspiring and qualified clinical psychologists know that to deal with trauma, time does NOT heal all wounds as well as it takes processing, professional help and talking openly and honestly about your trauma for you to heal.

Nonetheless, this friend, my dear sweet friend who I often refer to as a child and a baby because they are so young (okay, they're 4 years younger than me but they're very baby-faced and innocent) has believed for the past 8 years that if they simply didn't talk about it. Everything would magically be healed and they would be fine.

That is not how trauma works.

And what makes the whole situation even more troubling and concerning is that my friend was scared to death about talking about their traumatic experience. They kept saying how talking about it was "bad", "wrong" and they shouldn't talk about it because it's only going to get them hurt.

My friend had internalised so much shame, guilt and pain about the traumatic experience that they were refusing to talk about it for 8 years. And even when I gently and very subtly asked about going to therapy (which is free at the university), they didn't want to do that because it would make it real, it would involve talking about it which is "bad" in their eyes and it would involve telling others about their shame and guilt.

Yet from my perspective, as a friend, I hated seeing how shattered my friend was. This is the type of friend that is pure innocence, so kind and the person who you can laugh with about everything. My friend is always there for others, always kind and they never have a bad word to say about anyone.

My friend is the type of person who you want to protect at all costs because they are so innocent, so kind and so good. They are the sort of person the world needs more of.

However, three nights ago, my friend was so shattered, so broken and they were crying so much that I basically didn't recognise them. I could see their distress as they cried, I could hear their terror in their broken voice and I could feel them shaking on their end of the sofa.

They were really anxious, scared and they were having a major breakdown.

And yet my friend still believes not talking about their trauma, not processing it and not dealing with their trauma in any way is a good idea.

Me and my best friend gently and subtly suggested ways like therapy, talking about it whenever with us, learning about trauma responses and trying to understand why they've been depressed, anxious and occasionally suicidal for 8 years. Yet my friend doesn't want to do that and my friend is suffering so much.

On the whole, I understand why this is scary for my friend, and I am extremely privileged to know the power of psychotherapy and processing trauma because of my degree. As well as to some extent I am just as guilty of this when it came to my child abuse and trauma, I didn't get therapy until I had a breakdown in August 2023.

Nonetheless, my point is that my friend understands how badly they are struggling. They have crippling depression, anxiety and that only makes their physical conditions worse. They understand this all links back to their trauma but they are refusing to process, talk and heal from their trauma in any way, shape or form.

They simply want to pretend their trauma never happened.

And I can see the result as clear as day now.

My friend is continuing to decide not to deal with their trauma, so their trauma is making them process the event in the worst possible way. And the saddest thing is that I know this isn't going to stop anytime soon unless my friend processes what happened to them in therapy and starts their healing journey.

Note: I highly recommend survivors read the section below as well.

Why Is This Important For Clinical Psychologists To Understand?

This is going to be a shorter section because I've already told in a range of places, including The Psychology World Podcast, my other books and my clinical psychology reflection books, about how clients can be resistant to processing their trauma and mental health.

Largely this connects to the topic of capacity to change where a client needs to be motivated and already to undergo the therapeutic process so they can talk, process and ultimately heal.

We can give clients all the tools and techniques that they need to improve their lives, decrease their psychological distress and develop new adaptive coping mechanisms. Yet unless they have the drive to bring about lasting therapeutic change and they put the effort in to use these tools and techniques, then the therapy will fail.

And that is heartbreaking.

Currently, therapy would be useless for my friend because they don't have the drive, motivation or capacity to change. They could go to therapy but they aren't at a point in their life where they would be engaged or motivated to let us work *with* them to improve their lives and start their healing journey.

My friend would be too resistant for therapy for any good to come from it.

Which is heartbreaking because all of us aspiring and qualified clinical psychologists are driven by our desire, need and I think it's a fundamental drive of our profession to help people. We know clinical psychology and different forms of psychotherapy can be immensely powerful and they can and do help millions of people each year.

Therapy has the power to transform lives for the better and our clinical work is some of the most rewarding work there is, in my opinion.

Because we make a difference using our expertise, working with clients and helping them to improve their own lives with the tools and techniques we give them.

Therefore, when someone is in distress like my friend and they are so clearly struggling and they would benefit immensely from therapy, and they don't want it, think it's valuable or a worthwhile use of their time. It is honestly soul-crushing.

I would love my friend to go to therapy because it means they could heal, they could feel better and they could feel safe around me and my best friend. Yet they don't want therapy and I cannot make them go to therapy as much as I would like to.

As a result, as their friend, this makes me sad because I want them to be okay but they aren't allowing themselves to process what's happening. So their trauma and brain is making them process it for them with devastating consequences.

Overall, whilst I lengthened this section so I could bust some myths about therapy and show to survivors therapy is a kind and collaborative process, my point is that when it comes to clinical work. We can give a client everything they need to improve their lives but unless they are willing to put in the work and have the motivation to change their lives then there is only so much we can do.

And it is heartbreaking but we are not miracle workers or gods or goddesses, we are just normal humans with human powers and a lot of psychology knowledge behind us.

We cannot make someone do anything they aren't ready for. Just be aware of that, that sometimes a person will not seek out therapy when they're struggling.

But when they are ready, we must always be ready to welcome them into our therapy room so we can help them improve their lives, decrease their psychological distress and help them develop more adaptive coping mechanisms so they can heal.

Maybe for the first time in their life.

Why Do I Allow Myself To Process My Rape?

If you're reading this in my book written for rape survivors (it doesn't even have a working title at the moment to be fair) then you'll be aware that in basically every chapter of the book, I explain how my rape negatively impacts my mental health, how it causes me extreme distress and I explore different aspects of my experience as a rape survivor.

I never really try to stop myself processing this stuff no matter how distressing it is. Although because I am human and I might be an aspiring clinical psychologist as well as a psychology author and podcaster, but I am still human. There are times when I do actively avoid processing stuff, like I sometimes only go to sleep when I'm so exhausted I can't process them in bed.

And you know what happened, if I delay processing an emotion, an experience or a trigger. It turns up at the next opportunity and it's ten times worse.

Therefore, I allow myself to process my rape and all the extremely distressing and wide ranging impacts it has on me because I want to heal. I can only heal if I allow myself to process what the hell happened to me, and I need to process this event by thinking about it, talking about it with my best friend and me writing about in this book. As well as hopefully starting next month at the time of writing, I will finally be having rape counselling so I can talk about it with a professional.

That will be brilliant.

As a result, as distressing as everything is, I know if I want to be okay, if I want to get to a point where I can live my life and have a boyfriend (the idea of that made me really smile) and live a relatively normal life then I have no choice but to process my rape.

For example, right now, I get horrific intrusive thoughts and times when I'm in bed and I'm in a light dream state and I imagine that people in my life that I'm even subtly attracted to are beating me, raping me and then killing me. I know this is me processing my fears and the emotions I was experiencing during my rape, and I fucking hate when this happens.

It's why I haven't slept much in three days,

However, I could be extremely unhealthy and go to bed at 2 am and get up at 7 am so I was purposefully so tired I cannot think about these thoughts. Yet I know this will have a worse impact on my physical and mental health over time.

I need to process this stuff as much as I can and I can process it more in therapy. And I am getting better and I am slowly healing over these 15 weeks (the time since my rape. In fact, it's 15 weeks and 2 days) so allowing yourself time to process stuff does help.

There are a lot of things I used to get extremely triggered by that I don't anymore. For example, whilst I have still have chronically bad social anxiety basically whenever I go outside and whenever I go somewhere I haven't been to before, I can get on the London metro system (the Tube) without having a full-on meltdown in public and crying my eyes out.

That is progress.

Overall, I will always hate every single little thing that bastard of a rapist has caused me to experience because it is so distressing and it wrecks my mental health so badly. Yet I am not going to avoid processing this trauma because I can see how badly it is affecting me and I don't want this to affect me for the rest of my life.

I know I cannot process my rape fully until I get my rape counselling next month (there was a 3-month waiting list) but I can take small steps to help me in the meantime. Like talking to my best friend, writing this book and researching and thinking about rape myself.

I can see how badly it's impacting and destroying my friend's mental and physical health. I don't want that for myself and as I keep supporting my friend and gently pushing them towards therapy over time. I hope that I can fully process my rape and I heal so I can live a full, relatively normal life that involves love, going outside and just living how people who haven't been raped do.

That is my dream, and I will only reach that dream by processing my rape myself and not allowing my rape to force me to process it in the only destructive way possible.

Conclusion: Why Is This Important For Survivors?

The purpose of this chapter flat out wasn't to say processing trauma was easy if you decide to do it yourself. That also isn't how trauma works because your brain will surprise you with intrusive thoughts, flashbacks and a whole range of other distressing mental health difficulties. Thus, the point of this chapter wasn't to say processing trauma was easy, that was the last thing this chapter would ever try to say.

Instead the point of this chapter was to highlight how rape is extremely distressing and it can damage your mental health in very scary ways. For example, earlier today, I was paralysed with fear for an hour because I had the intrusive thought that was my best friend's brother (who I have never actually met but I saw a topless photo of them yesterday and they have a great body) and a fellow university student who I'm working with this week were taking turns raping me.

For basically 65 minutes I had to live through the intrusive thoughts and physical sensations of two people who I find attractive raping me and occasionally beating me when my mind said no.

That is how distressing rape can be at times and processing this stuff is not easy.

No one will ever say processing is easy.

Nonetheless, in the long term, you have to process your sexual violence, and you need to take steps towards facilitating this processing. At first you might only want to talk to close friends then you might talk to a therapist and other people.

I would highly recommend that you talk to a therapist specialising in rape as soon as possible because that professional support is flat out critical in trauma recovery.

Just please make sure you take steps to deal with your trauma no matter how scary they seem. They never have to be big steps because they can range from you writing about your thoughts, feelings and your sexual violence to talking with close, trusted friends to seeing a therapist.

Just start your healing journey please somehow, and take steps towards processing what the hell happened to you.

Please don't be like my dear, sweet, innocent friend who breaks my heart by suffering, struggling and having extremely distressing thought spirals but not taking any steps towards healing.

You can heal if you seek out support.

Don't deny yourself healing. You deserve to heal because you are worthy, you are loved and there are people who care about you.

HOW TO CHANGE NEGATIVE SELF-TALK TO POSITIVE SELF-TALK AFTER SEXUAL VIOLENCE?

This is definitely a chapter that reveals that whilst I have a degree in psychology focusing on mental health, I am currently a Masters student in clinical psychology (mental health) and I live and breathe mental health through my podcast, I am still human at the end of the day. As well as just because I *know* all of this psychological knowledge about how our self-talk impacts our mental health, it doesn't mean I follow it.

Thankfully, I do now and my mental health is a lot better.

As a result, after rape and experiencing sexual violence, us survivors can have very negative self-talk. For example, we can call ourselves useless, pathetic, weak and a lot of other very negative words that are not healthy and it doesn't do anything good for our mental health.

<u>What Is Self-Talk And Why Is It Important?</u>

In fact, whilst I cannot go into too much depth about our self-talk impacts our mental health because this isn't a strict psychology book. Our self-talk impacts our feelings of self-esteem and self-worth so this leads to how we feel about ourselves. Therefore, if we talk negatively about ourselves then we feel down and we hate ourselves. Whereas if we talk positively we feel better about ourselves and it improves our mental health.

This is one of the reasons why you might notice a shift in language in the book towards the third month after my assault, because this is when my self-talk became more positive. I had to change the language I used to describe myself and who I am so I could improve my mental health and focus more on healing, instead of hating myself.

Moreover, this is why I prefer the term "survivor" instead of "victim". Since unfortunately, because of our society and the culture we live in, the term "victim" has a lot of negative connotations. For example, weakness, victim-blaming and it is a very disempowering term. Thus, "survivor" is a more helpful term as this has connotations of strength, courage and empowerment. Something that all rape survivors need to realise because we are strong, we are brave and we are empowered to deal with what happened to us.

So please use the term "survivor" instead to describe yourself, because you have survived.

Believe me, I know at times your mental health will make it seem like you haven't survived your sexual assault at all. Yet you are alive and you have survived so you are a strong survivor.

Finally, a lot of rape survivors develop negative self-talk because we have low self-worth so we doubt ourselves, we question ourselves and whether *we* could have done anything differently to stop our assaults, and we experience a lot of shame and guilt and even feelings of responsibility over what happened to us.

None of these negative self-talks have any accurate basis in reality but I know, God I know when our mental health decreases it is impossible to see that.

On the whole, so far in this chapter, I've explained why self-talk impacts our mental health and why rape survivors experience negative self-talk. Now in the rest of the chapter, we're going to be deep diving into some examples of negative self-talk, why the negative things I said to myself wasn't right or helpful as well as how I changed my negative self-talk into positive self-talk using some examples from actual distressed messages I sent my best friend over time.

This is a critical chapter to read for your own mental health.

Most Important Tip In The Chapter

I wanted to put this here at the start of the chapter before I repeat it at the end too because this is the most important tip in the chapter and it will not make sense first of all but by the end of this chapter, it hopefully will. As well as when the penny does drop around this tip then your life and your mental health will improve, even if it only feels like a little bit.

You need to treat yourself how you would treat a dear friend.

This is what my best friend said about self-talk. If you wouldn't say it to a dear, close friend then certainly don't say it to yourself.

Of course, originally I didn't listen to my best friend but over the next week, I really tried and I kept trying to improve how I treated myself. Honestly, it was hard but now I am a lot kinder towards myself and my mental health is a lot better from a self-critical perspective.

That is a sign of progress and a win and I will happily take any wins I can get.

In other words, if you wouldn't say it to a dear, close friend, do not say it to yourself.

What Shouldn't You Say To Yourself?

I know I reuse this WhatsApp in a much later chapter but I wanted to put the message here because this is the worst, most self-critical message I have ever sent. This message wasn't healthy in the slightest and looking back with hindsight, I cannot imagine I would ever send a message like this nowadays at Week 15.

I'll copy the message below and then I'll explain what parts of the message wasn't healthy, why they're not accurate and what I would say instead:

"I don't think I can go to the Warhammer painting event Friday night. 5 hours is too long with new people in a small seminar room and there might be the person that looks like my attacker there judging from the Facebook photos of the club. Friday's causing me a lot of social anxiety, I don't want to have a meltdown, I don't want to suffer and I don't want to feel like I'm getting raped over and over again.

I know I'm just being a weak, pathetic victim but I just don't think I can. I've already done tons since my rape like endless outreach work, hanging out with friends, going to Group, playing DnD despite Tallis possibly being there and I've done well. The woman from the rape charity was pleased I'm still doing stuff. I'm just scared of going to this Warhammer thing.

I'll go in September to the Warhammer club for a normal session when it's easier to pop in and out instead of having to paint for a few hours. My counseling would be started by then too. I'll honestly probably find it a little boring too. I just wanted to do something new and different because I'm different now.

I'll rather just go to my great-aunt's for the evening, see her, get a goodnight sleep for Saturday so me not being tired slightly reduces the chance of Saturday going badly for me because of my child abuse, rape and Someone From My Past.

I'm sorry I'm a weak, pathetic victim at times. I'm trying I promise. (I know you don't doubt me but this is a lot to deal with and you're the only person I can talk to).

I hate waiting for counselling because I don't want to feel like a victim anymore.

P.S- Saturday's 8 weeks since The Event, and I had a nice day at Outreach today. Stuttered more than normal but it was a lot of fun being session lead. Tomorrow will be brilliant with my Psychology Society meeting.

Thanks for reading. I don't know how you can respond but thank you for always being there. I look forward to when counseling starts so this fear can go."

There was one very unhelpful and unhealthy idea I kept having during this text. *"I know I'm just being a weak, pathetic victim"* I used to say that so much up until my best friend basically moaned at me strongly for constantly hating myself. And I used to feel like this because of the Post-Traumatic Stress Disorder, the intense social anxiety and the sheer debilitating nature of rape. Even now I flat out hate how my rape stops me from doing perfectly normal things.

However, calling myself "a weak, pathetic victim" isn't healthy and it isn't positive. It shifts the blame, the pain and the focus of my rape to me. Yet it wasn't my fault, I am NOT the problem and there is nothing "weak or pathetic" about my actions. I am having perfectly normal trauma responses to an extremely abnormal situation.

I am not the problem so there is no reason to call myself a victim. I am a survivor, not a victim.

Over To You

I recap this discovery about positive self-talk later in the book but I want you to think about how you talk and describe yourself, both in your head and out loud. If you're not being positive towards yourself and if you're being self-blaming then you need to change because self-blame and negative self-talk only harms your mental health and make you feel worse.

Of course, I am flat out not saying you need to speak positively about your sexual assault (no one would ever do that), you don't need to talk positively about your trauma responses and you don't need to say you're okay when you're struggling.

That isn't what I'm saying at all.

Instead what I am saying is that you should never attribute your sexual assault, your trauma responses or your struggles to yourself.

You should **never** say or think:

- I caused my rape so I hate myself.

- I'm pathetic for always being anxious.
- I'm useless because I can't go to work without having a panic attack.

Instead a more positive self-talk version would be:

- I hate the bastard that raped me.
- I'm anxious because of what the bastard did to me, but I'll get professional help and improve over time.
- I struggle with work and panic attacks because of my sexual assault.

Even though these are fairly "basic" examples and believe me, I know us survivors have a much larger and more nuanced range of negative self-talk than that, but you see how I wasn't blaming myself in any of that. I was talking positively about myself by not self-blaming or self-criticising and I was laying the blame where it should be.

You should always blame your attacker.

Finally for this section, this is a skill that you will need to practice and improve over time. You're going to need to practice being kind to yourself, talking positively about yourself and this takes a lot of acceptance about whatever happened to you is NOT your fault. As a result, something you might want to do is practice saying kind things to yourself. For example:

- I am lovable.
- I am not to blame for what happened.
- I deserve happiness.

These might seem really simple and easy to say but these are equally extremely hard to say after experiencing sexual violence. I seriously wouldn't have been able to say these things until 2 or 3 months after my assault.

My point is, it's okay to have moments where your self-talk is negative but you need to learn that you aren't to blame, you deserve to be happy and you need to be kind towards yourself.

It's hard, I seriously know that, but you need to practice.

Improving A Little

I wanted to show how improving your self-talk is a process and it isn't a magical overnight thing. I never want to pretend dealing with anything around sexual violence is easy so me revealing a personal mistake on improving my own self-talk is another way of doing this honesty.

"Hope DnD was fun. I look forward to hearing about it Tuesday.

I think I just want to vent or something. Mum innocently saying "suck it" really fucked me up. I've had a good night. I recorded the podcast and me and Dad talked for hours in the garden. Still had flashbacks for 10 mins in the uni toilets, then even more throughout the whole evening. All leading to a really bad panic attack an hour ago.

I already sort of believe I'll die alone. So few would want to date me, the rape survivor. But what if I can never give or receive oral? Will guys and non-binary peeps hate me? I don't think they will but this is just disempowerment again. The cunt stole oral stuff from me. I don't know if I was ever into it. I can't remember or decide.

I looked at a job description earlier for the future. It would have been brilliant for me... Then I just got scared and triggered about the future. If a simple word can trigger me this bad, how am I meant to work in the profession I love in clinical psychology? Can I hold down a real job? What if he's stolen that from me too?

I'll probably recover well enough in the future but it's scary to think what if I don't. Will my life be worth living? And stop that silly thought train there.

Sometimes I just feel like a weak child and I don't want to.

That's the ultra-brief version of the few hours. Thanks for reading. I really liked dinner today. It was nice. Sleep well."

Whilst this message wasn't as bad or self-blaming as the last one, because I didn't call myself "pathetic" and I wasn't too hateful towards myself. I imagine if I sent this type of message a few weeks earlier I think I would be ripping myself apart about the employability and future stuff.

In addition, there is still a fair amount of negative self-talk, so there's an improvement but this isn't perfect. And honestly, no one is going to be "perfect" all the time but we need to be kind to ourselves.

In this message, I still called myself "weak" and "like a child" and I did a little self-criticism around other aspects of my life.

This message was progress but I still needed to work on getting better.

Example Of Good Self-Talk

Please note whilst these examples are a little dark because I was updating my best friend on what had happened the night before, these are still good examples of self-talk because I never blame myself for what I'm experiencing. None of these trauma responses are my fault and it is simply my brain trying to deal with an extremely abnormal situation.

Also, I know for some people these might seem to be very, very honest and intense messages. Yet this is perfectly fine within the context of mine and my best friend's relationship, so me being this honest isn't a problem at all.

"I guess I should tell you, last night was another rough night. It was better in the sense I wasn't getting beaten and killed. It was worse in the sense that because I think Your Brother has a great body (he doesn't do much for me in the face department), I kept having dreams and intrusive thoughts about Your Brother raping me, saying stuff like because I like his body that's consent and he kept doing stuff to me. Including saying how he enjoyed me struggling against him.

I know he is lovely in real life but I got fairly suicidal.

I hate it how whenever I find someone attractive even in passing. I get intense rape thoughts about them. Killing myself would be so much easier. I don't want to live if I'm constantly scared about finding someone attractive. Being attracted makes me feel good and normal until I go to sleep where I imagine them raping me.

How the fuck am I meant to meet your parents, hang out with A Certain Friend and go to Manchester if all I'm going to get is no sleep and rape stuff. That isn't a life.

But I know I can't kill myself because I do have things to live for and I can't hurt you. I despise anyone that hurts you so I never want to become one of those people. And if I don't do things then that makes me more hopeless and suicidal, and I enjoy living even if I have to deal with the consequences later.

I just want everything to stop. I want to be normal allo-romantic and be able to admire attractive guys without imagining how they'll rape me, beat me and kill me.

I'm nervous about this week enough without my A Cute Guy I Work With concern. He is really attractive in a strange way. My mind tried to get him to rape me last night but Your Brother was scarier focus (because of his strength) so my mind went with that.

Enjoy your week. Text me if you need anything."

This is a good example of talking about distressing experiences without blaming yourself, because I never say these dreams or intrusive thoughts are my fault and I'm a failure for having them. Since I am not a failure for them at all.

Instead I say they're annoying, I don't like them and I find them deeply distressing, but I never imply they're my fault.

Additionally, whilst I "lash out" at my distress because me and my best friend are planning to go to meet their brother up in Manchester with another friend of ours. I know there's no reason to talk badly about myself because this is my brain trying to process what the hell happened to me.

Two Final Workplace-Based Examples

For context this week I'm working at my university at a summer school residential so 14 and 15-year-old students are staying overnight for two nights, but I stayed over the Monday night too. I was fairly concerned about the event and I had to do a lot of work around this event for my mental health, something I talk about in future chapters.

Yet even though I had a really distressing Monday night, I didn't blame myself as seen in the text below:

"Last night before bed was enjoyable. Got a lot of publishing work and writing done. Did about 3 hours total done then I wrote an email to My Three Supervisors about the accommodation I might need. I cc'd you in the email because I was so tired. Then because the other ambassadors made a group chat and An Ambassador put an implied rape image as the profile pic earlier in the evening that distressed me. I had to put a little message on the group chat. Everyone reacted well and 3 Ambassadors hoped I was okay.

I was extremely tired last night so that made my intrusive thoughts and dreams a little less intense. Yet it was still the normal A Cute Guy raping me (I'm definitely attracted to him in real life, and he's not completely my type but he's a little cool. He's autistic, plays DnD and yeah. I think I had internalised homophobia around him before) and your brother still rapes me in the dreams. I think because he has the strength and power that makes him a scary option in my mind. And there's still violence in my dreams. Like A Cute Guy killing me when I say no and dream Your Brother made threats against you if I said no. I still said no and... I dreamt about him doing his threat.

That was distressing as fuck.

Anyway I need to go for breakfast, catch up with the others and talk to A Cute Guy a little more if I can. Believe me, I know nothing can happen but he's nice. And I want to catch up with Another Ambassador and the others too.

Enjoy your day."

A final message example is:

"I've just finished 65 mins of lying on the floor paralysed by intrusive thoughts and half-dreams of Your Brother and A Cute Guy taking turns raping me.

I'm so emotionally and physically exhausted but I can't sleep or nap at the moment. I can't even ask Outreach for accommodations because there's nothing they can actually do, but if I think of something then I'll talk to them. I will break at one point because of the lack of sleep but I have energy now and the rape stuff has gone. So I need to do something to stop the rape stuff coming back for a while.

Thankfully I brought my laptop so I can write and do business things."

Brief Conclusion

On the whole, when it comes to self-talk, you need to remember:

- Never blame yourself
- If you wouldn't say it to a friend, NEVER say it to yourself
- Never criticise yourself for your reactions.

Moreover, having positive self-talk is never ever about undermining how distressing and traumatic your experience was and how you're dealing with it. That's why I picked these particular messages because they're filled with distressing content that different survivors might connect with, whilst showing you can still be kind to yourself.

This isn't easy and it has taken me months to learn it and even now I still slip up. Yet my mental health is better now because I am not hating myself because I am worthy, I deserve happiness and nothing that has happened to me was my fault.

You can have positive self-talk, it's hard but it is so doable with practice.

Most Important Tip In The Chapter

I wanted to repeat it here again because this is the most important tip in the chapter and it will not make sense first of all but by the end of this chapter, it hopefully will. As well as when the penny does drop around this tip then your life and your mental health will improve, even if it only feels like a little bit.

You need to treat yourself how you would treat a dear friend.

This is what my best friend said about self-talk. If you wouldn't say it to a dear, close friend then certainly don't say it to yourself.

Of course, originally I didn't listen to my best friend but over the next week, I really tried and I kept trying to improve how I treated myself. Honestly, it was hard but now I am a lot kinder towards myself and my mental health is a lot better from a self-critical perspective.

That is a sign of progress and a win and I will happily take any wins I can get.

In other words, if you wouldn't say it to a dear, close friend, do not say it to yourself.

WHAT IS DISEMPOWERMENT IN MENTAL HEALTH?

Disempowerment is a concept I've sort of heard a lot about in clinical psychology lectures, textbooks and in my own reading for The Psychology World Podcast, but no one has actually highlighted just how important it is to understand.

Since disempowerment refers to the lack of control and, well, power that a person feels like they have over their own life, decisions and what they do.

Furthermore, disempowerment targets a person's self-worth, self-perception and it can lead to feelings of shame and guilt. Granted I'm remembering what I read about disempowerment from sexual assault, but the same applies to other events and conditions too.

In turn, these feelings of guilt and shame that disempowerment can create and/ or reinforce can lead to a multitude of maladaptive coping mechanisms. Like alcohol and substance abuse, self-harm, suicidal ideation and more.

As a result, this idea of disempowerment is flat out critical to understand in mental health, because a wide range of mental health conditions are very disempowering. To some extent, this is probably why we don't really focus on disempowerment in mental health and clinical psychology, because we just know our clients are disempowered in their own lives so us, as aspiring or qualified mental health professionals, we don't really need to know or focus on it.

I agree to some extent.

However, I do believe we should think about mental health in terms of disempowerment from time to time, because once you start thinking about mental health conditions or difficulties as something that disempowers our clients. Then this opens up new ideas about how to conceptualise, understand and even empathise with our clients.

In addition, I should note that clinical psychology sometimes focuses on disempowerment in terms of minority groups and mental health services. I think I've actually spoken or reflected on this topic in a previous volume. Therefore, whilst it is flat out critical that therapists and services never disempower our clients, this isn't what we're focusing on in this reflection.

Instead, to give you some examples of mental health conditions as disempowerment, let's talk about social anxiety. This is the easiest example to understand but if a client has social anxiety then they likely feel like they can't go outside, they can't go out with friends and they can't do something that they want to because they're scared of feeling anxious, having a panic attack or being judged negatively.

Normally, we think about this in terms of normal social anxiety because these are symptoms, biased cognitive processes and some of the safety behaviours seen in social anxiety.

Nonetheless, if we think about this in terms of disempowerment, we can see that social anxiety as a condition and the biased cognitive processes has actually decreased the control and ability of the client to live their own life. The client wants to go out, be social and do things that bring them pleasure but it is the social anxiety that makes them feel like they don't have the power to do that.

Another example is depression, because a client feeling unable to get out of bed, they catastrophizing about everything and the client has a low mood. Through a disempowerment lens, you could argue that that isn't the client feeling that part, it is the depression taking away the client's power and ability to control what they do in their own life.

A final example which serves as a minor segway into our next section is Post-Traumatic Stress Disorder. Since the intense thoughts, flashbacks and panic attacks seen in PTSD robs a client of the control they have over their lives to the point where they get extremely distressed when triggered and they avoid potentially triggering stimuli all together.

Overall, my point is that a wide range of mental health conditions robs clients the control they have over their lives. Due to our clients want to improve their lives, they want to be able to do whatever they want and they want to regain their independence so their mental health difficulty or condition is no longer ruling their lives.

Of course, in an attempt to be balanced here, you could argue that there is no point thinking about mental health in this way because disempowerment is obvious. Of course, if you're anxious, depressed, whatever you're going to lack control over your life.

Therefore, you might argue that disempowerment is a waste of time and it's better to think of mental health in terms of the symptoms, interventions and what you're going to do to improve the client's life.

All of those points are valid.

Although, I would counter-argue by saying that thinking about disempowerment is important too for a very simple and important reason. Thinking about mental health as disempowerment is extremely humanising.

Instead of thinking about a client in terms of their symptoms, what can be done to help them so we can move onto our next client to reduce waiting lists (which is a very real, valid and understandable pressure we all face in mental health). If we think about a client in terms of what *they* have lost and how *they* are disempowered. Then we're taking a moment to think about the client and that's it.

And actually, I'm not going to explore it here but you might be able to get some useful information from disempowerment-thinking for your clinical formulation.

On the whole, I would argue disempowerment-thinking helps us to take a moment to think about the client, what they've lost and what they want to gain from the therapeutic work. This might help you understand the client so you can phase things in a certain way, help them and benefit the therapeutic alliance somehow.

Ultimately, disempowerment work is the main point of therapy.

Therapy is about subtly empowering our clients so using the tools and techniques we give them, the client can go back out into the world and conquer it. By empowering our clients we can obviously improve their lives, but we can decrease their psychological distress and give them control over their lives again.

And it is that sense of control that I'm focusing on in this reflection.

Since I'm actually going to come back in the next one and talk about why I'm discussing this and give you some examples about my own disempowerment in terms of my assault (which was a short extremely intense event) and my child abuse and trauma (a long-term, low intensity trauma that happened every single day for a decade).

Definitely turn over the page to see this disempowerment thinking in action.

WHAT DOES DISEMPOWERMENT LOOK LIKE AFTER SEXUAL TRAUMA?

The reason why I'm writing this chapter looking at disempowerment is because in the past two days, I've realised, truly realised how disempowering sexual assault can be. I've felt this way for a while but it took me some time and a good few internet searches to find the terminology.

Of course, once you know the terminology you feel like an idiot because you knew it all along.

Anyway, I'll get to the disempowerment I feel because of my assault later in the chapter, and please relax, I don't even talk about the assault itself so it isn't graphic at all.

Therefore, in this chapter, I'm going to be sharing my own experience of disempowerment in hope that this helps your own understanding, it might help you with your clinical work in the future and it might reinforce what we spoke about in the last chapter.

Disempowerment From Long-Term Trauma

I have to admit here that my long-term abuse and trauma that started in my childhood and went on for a decade thankfully stopped nine months ago, so my memory might be blocking some of the nuances of disempowerment but I remember the it for the most part.

And in fact a lot of my current difficulty actually stem from that disempowerment.

As a result of because my social world (a slightly vague term for who abused me) taught me, drummed it into my skull from 12 years old onwards and made threats and perform actions that made me believe those threats, I was terrified for my life for that decade if these people found out I was gay.

Therefore, because I couldn't afford to be gay because I didn't want to die, I didn't want to be beaten and I didn't want to be homeless. This was actually extremely disempowering and it's really interesting to look at my childhood in terms of disempowerment.

Since I basically had no control over large aspects of my life.

I couldn't really afford to have any gay friends because I wanted to protect gay people, and I didn't want these people to think I was gay. That would have been a direct threat to my life and safety.

Also, I couldn't date, have a first kiss or have anything that heterosexual teenagers enjoy as a matter of course. Again, experiencing any type of normal adolescent behaviour would have been a risk to myself, the person I was kissing or whatever and I didn't want to die.

It was as simple as that.

Also, these people in my social world were very critical of my friendships as it was so friendships were difficult enough as a young, gay autistic kid who struggled anyway.

Moreover, my entire family were deeply homophobic so combined a lack of familial support with a tiny and basically non-existent friendship network. My emotional dependency (you can hear more about that on the Psychology World Podcast) is seriously no surprise.

Since if we think about emotional dependency and how I was (to some extent) "addicted" to a close friend I made who accepted me for me. You might argue that my emotional dependency was me trying in an extremely unhealthy way to take control of my life again. In terms of me having a gay friend that liked me for me and wasn't berating or abusing me.

Overall, my current relationship and friendship difficulties certainly come from that disempowerment and lack of control I had over my own life. Since with disempowerment impacting someone's self-perception and self-worth judgment. I am awful for saying that I don't deserve love, no one will ever love me and I don't deserve happiness.

If not believing you deserve the same happiness everyone else has the right to feel isn't disempowerment, then I seriously don't know what is.

<u>What Might Disempowerment Look Like After A Sexual Assault?</u>

Ever since my assault, even though I didn't realise it until yesterday, I've been feeling really disempowered because there are times my life feels like it's in freefall. I don't feel like I have control over my life and I am fearful what might happen in certain situations.

As I mentioned a few chapters ago, this mainly manifested itself after my assault as a crippling, intense fear of seeing my best friend again because I'm into them romantically. I was fearful of being alone with them, I was scared of sleeping in the same room as them and I was scared they would do something to me.

Of course that would never ever happen because they are the nicest person you would ever meet. Yet as much as it annoys me, sometimes when I think about my best friend it triggers thoughts of my assaulter. According to one of my other friends, that's a normal assault/ rape response because both are to do with physiological arousal.

As a result, when everything happened over my birthday weekend like my panic attack on the Tube, like my inability to sleep comfortably in the same room as my best friend and me having panic attacks at the social group I go to. That is such a disempowering feeling.

I don't know what I can do, where I can go and who I can be with so I don't have a panic attack or something else.

Below is a Whatsapp message I quickly sent my best friend and then I'll explain the context in terms of disempowerment:

"I acknowledge this isn't a logical concern but X isn't the type of person to touch and hug people she's only just met right?

I know she's lovely from our conversations. She's Y's girlfriend, right? I want to meet her.

I'm generally okay. Past few days have been nice.

Last night was tough. I'm just a little nervous about Friday. I'm coming no matter what but that's a lot of people in a (maybe locked) room. And I don't want to spoil it for people if I have a panic attack or something. If needed, I'll ask Z not to lock the door but I hate drawing attention to my discomfort. It just makes what happened even more real and reminds me I'm disempowered and it will take time to heal and get empowered again."

Firstly, I want to focus on getting back to a sense of empowerment does take time because it takes time to heal and for therapy to happen and for you to process stuff.

Also, the context for Friday is I'm going to a one-shot game of Dungeons and Dragons because a friend is doing it, he invited me and some others and I am refusing to let my social anxiety and assault control my life too much.

I don't want to accidentally lock myself away in my room because I'm too scared of being assaulted and hurt again.

Yet I am nervous about Friday for illogical reasons but to me they are very real. I mentioned some of the reasons in that text to my best friend, but there's another reason I will probably keep exclusively for these pages. I am scared about someone who's going to be playing this one-shot with us will be triggering to me.

There's a player and he's kind, very nice and we've spoke a few times. Yet he has long hair and he's slightly on the larger side of life and he has an oval-type of face. All those 3 things are similar to my attacker.

I think he might trigger me so there are very real but illogical reasons why I might have problems on Friday. Then I'm scared that a lot of negative thoughts will pop up about me not being able to enjoy my life anymore and stuff like that.

Personally, I know if something happens, no one will actually care in the sense that they won't judge me for it. Everyone but two of the seven people at the game knows to differing extents what happened to me. And that's something else I'm not thrilled about, I think I'm scared people are going to see me as a weak victim.

Of course, I know as an aspiring clinical psychologist that victims are flat out far from weak. But as a person, I feel a little weak, violated and I'm still reeling from what happened. I don't wish it on anyone and I don't want this to ever happen again.

That is why I feel disempowered because I feel like I don't have control over my reactions, my decisions to do things and I have this constant fear to be honest. Fear that something bad's going to happen, fear that people will judge me for having a panic attack and a fear that people will stop inviting me to stuff because they don't know how I'll react.

I know none of that is logical because my friends are amazing and even though I don't really care much about Dungeons and Dragons (sorry friends and readers), I want to be social and make sure I don't retreat into my room for the rest of my life.

Disempowerment isn't always pretty but if you give a client (or myself) time to process, heal and go to therapy then they can be empowered once more so they can retake control of their lives, decisions and more once again.

And that is an amazing feeling to have after being disempowered for so long.

ACCEPTING YOUR MENTAL HEALTH TRAUMA RESPONSES FOR WHAT THEY ARE

Now my best friend would probably be extremely proud of this next chapter because they would be seriously happy that I've finished accepting a lot about my mental health, my trauma and what I am able and not really able to do at the moment.

Of course, I'm referring to the outcome of my assault and my own frustration that my mental health simply cannot handle certain things, and I have certain trauma responses.

I've written about a lot of them in previous chapters, but when I wrote those chapters, I hadn't accepted that and I had been really annoyed that they were popping up.

In addition, what kicked off my acceptance of my trauma responses was a lot of small things that happened last week at the time of writing. Yet the following WhatsApp I sent my best friend was what really kicked it into high gear:

I don't think I can go to the Warhammer painting event Friday night. 5 hours is too long with new people in a small seminar room and there might be the person that looks like my attacker there judging from the Facebook photos of the club. Friday's causing me a lot of social anxiety, I don't want to have a meltdown, I don't want to suffer and I don't want to feel like I'm getting raped over and over again.

I know I'm just being a weak, pathetic victim but I just don't think I can. I've already done tons since my rape like endless outreach work, hanging out with friends, going to Group, playing DnD despite (Someone's Name) *possibly being there and I've done well. The woman from the rape charity was pleased I'm still doing stuff. I'm just scared of going to this Warhammer thing.*

I'll go in September to the Warhammer club for a normal session when it's easier to pop in and out instead of having to paint for a few hours. My counselling would start by then too. I'll honestly probably find it a little boring too. I just wanted to do something new and different because I'm different now.

I'll rather just go to my great-aunt's for the evening, see her, get a good night's sleep for Saturday so me not being tired slightly reduces the chance of Saturday going badly for me because of my child abuse, rape and Someone's Name.

I'm sorry I'm a weak, pathetic victim at times. I'm trying I promise. (I know you don't doubt me but this is a lot to deal with and you're the only person I can talk to).

I hate waiting for counselling because I don't want to feel like a victim anymore.

P.S- Saturday's 8 weeks since The Event, and I had a nice day at Outreach today. Stuttered more than normal but it was a lot of fun being session lead. Tomorrow will be brilliant with my Psychology Society meeting.

Thanks for reading. I don't know how you can respond but thank you for always being there. I look forward to when counselling starts so this fear can go.

So as you could tell from that message I was distress to say the least, I was blaming myself for a lot and I was a little angry I was having these sort of reactions. I just wanted to be normal, able to do things and I wanted to start doing things.

That isn't possible at the moment.

Of course, my best friend was a little annoyed at me for blaming myself for so much. I cannot put their reply in these pages for copyright reasons but they wanted me to stop blaming myself and they mentioned I have PTSD.

Me being me was very dismissive (not to my best friend) about the idea of me having PTSD. Yet I looked into it and it turns out that about 81% of sexual violence survivors have PTSD in the first month and then that doesn't really drop too much even after the first month which is when you can actually get the PTSD diagnosis.

Again, I looked into PTSD itself a little more and let me include a list of PTSD symptoms from the NHS website:

- Flashbacks
- Nightmares
- Distressing and repetitive sensations and images
- Physical sensations
- Constant negative thoughts about the experience
- Including pondering the event
- Avoidance of being reminded about the traumatic event
- Hyperarousal
- Sleeping problems
- Difficulty focusing
- Mental health difficulties (like depression and anxiety)
- Self-harm or destructive behaviours
- Other physical symptoms

Well, even that list was rather fun (not) because over the past two months, I have certainly had the vast, vast majority of these symptoms. As you could tell from my WhatsApp message I'm no stranger to the physical sensations, especially when I feel like my sexual assault is happening over and over.

Therefore, me realising that I have PTSD followed by me having a lovely time at my Great-Aunt's and some other things that happened over Pride weekend just made me realise I am sort of stuck for a bit.

And even as an aspiring clinical psychologist, I am willing to say this. I think this is okay for now because yes, I firmly do not believe I can do any *NEW* social situations at the moment. For example, I just cannot go to any new societies, meet-ups or group things, for the time being.

Even a social group I've been going to for months and months now I am finding harder and harder to be at, because there are a lot of people there, some of them are fat and it triggers a lot of assault stuff for me.

So yes, I have social anxiety when it comes to new things and that is okay. I have accepted that until my therapy, it is okay if I don't do any new things.

Yet I will not allow this to continue after my therapy because I need to start living fully again and I want to banish this social anxiety because of my assault. Even now to be honest, I am still doing a lot of things like being President of the Psychology Society at my university and I'm getting into a new situation in August. I'm working a year 10 residential at the university as part of my Outreach work.

That I am a little nervous about but I applied to work that before my assault and I'm committed to that now. I wouldn't really change it anyway.

In addition, I've accepted that I really don't bloody like enclosed spaces filled with people. I've already mentioned how I had a meltdown and cried on the Tube on my birthday because of the sexual violence notices on the Tube.

Well, I went on the Tube again yesterday and I thankfully didn't have a meltdown or cried and shook in public. Yet I was uncomfortable and I seriously hated the Tube coming back to the O2 arena (where my car was parked) because it was packed, I couldn't sit down and I couldn't have my personal space.

The problem I have with standing up is that my assault took place standing up, so sometimes it's like I can still feel him touching me and doing things if I stand up for a while.

Thankfully, my best friend was there so I sort of had to touch their coat and stare at them a little to ground myself in the present moment instead of the memories and physical sensations.

And once we got back to the O2, I basically sped-walked out of the underground station and didn't stop until I was past the pay barriers where I waited for my friend to catch up.

Therefore, I've accepted enclosed spaces with lots of people will be an issue for me. I am not avoiding going on the Tube, I am avoiding going to London by myself if I have to travel on the Tube, but if I'm going with my best friend then that's okay.

Granted, I am going to Kew gardens with my family at some point soon that will involve the Tube. But it's my family so I'll have to act like things are perfectly fine and just feel like I'm dying and getting raped inside.

The one silver lining about the Tube ride was I did not have a meltdown, cry or shake. That means the effect was less than it was before on me, so the more I travel on the Tube, the better I might be.

There is hope in that realisation.

Hope I am very happy about to be fair.

Another negative that made me realise I needed to accept I have PTSD is that my best friend, their friend and a mutual friend of ours were in the Pride Parade. The original plan was to have me and my best friend's friend stand together, watch the Parade and chat.

The mutual friend didn't know this but it was to make sure I was okay given my child abuse and my last reaction to Pride.

That didn't happen because the mutual friend wanted to join the Parade, there were spare wrist bands and I pushed him towards going in the Parade. I always like putting other people's joy ahead of mine.

So I was alone in Canterbury High Street watching the Parade.

It was a great Parade with great groups, great people and great music. Yet there were two sexual violence charities and I now know (and accepted) that I find anything referring to sexual violence to be extremely triggering.

So I had to self-harm to keep myself grounded and I had to bleed a little. It didn't stop all of the assault stuff coming back and the physical sensations taking over, but it sort of kept me grounded and there wasn't anything else I could have done.

I couldn't think of another way to distract myself.

Again, being alone in public without a way to distract myself, maybe this isn't something I can do at the moment either. Especially when my mind does just turn to those sort of things.

I need to keep myself busy, and I've accepted this difficulty.

My Point For Aspiring And Qualified Clinical Psychologists

My point is there comes a time in trauma, mental health and waiting for therapy that you just have to realise and accept what is happening to you. Now, I've truly accepted that I just cannot do certain things at this moment in time, I do feel more positive, happy and kinder to myself.

I no longer think of myself as a weak, pathetic victim. I am just a victim and I suppose a survivor, and I know in time when I start counselling with the charity that things will get better for me.

I will be able to do new things and I will be able to go out and do perfectly normal things without my best friend or anyone I lean on for support.

And in the meantime, what will I be doing?

Like always I will be writing, podcasting and running a business. I will also be having in-person meetings, emailing people and continuing to set up the Psychology Society for a September 2024 launch.

AND I will be seeing, meeting up and doing things with friends and I will be conducting and writing up my psychology research. As well as in September I'll be conducting research, supervising volunteers and helping Parkinson's clients at my university's Parkinson's centre.

Therefore, whilst I have extremely dark days and there are moments that I just hate because I feel like I am getting assaulted over and over again and I can't do anything to stop it. I am still living my life as best as I can and I am doing what makes me happy.

I will be even happier in the future when I can do whatever I want without a threat of a meltdown, self-harming or anything else.

That time will come. It will.

However, until that time comes, I need to accept that things will be challenging, difficult and there will be some things that will cause me too much distress to be worth it.

Yet there are a thousand other things that I can do, and it is the positives that I am focusing on and accepting.

Acceptance really is a powerful tool and it certainly has the power to make you feel more positive, happier and content with your situation until you start therapy. Just make sure you get the professional help you need because *that* is the thing that will truly change your life for the better.

APPRECIATING THE TRUE POWER OF SOCIAL NETWORKS

Whilst this isn't one of my clinical psychology reflection books where I normally reflect and tell aspiring and qualified clinical psychologists things that I've learnt through my own mental health experiences, this next chapter is partly based on a reflection. Therefore, I wanted to use this next chapter as a chance to partly reflect and write about something I have learnt after my sexual assault.

Due to you really learn who your friends are and how powerful social networks are after something as traumatic as a sexual assault.

I encourage you to keep reading because this isn't graphic and this helps you to deepen your understanding about how useful social networks actually are in mental health recovery and supporting victims. Since again, we can read as much as we want about mental health research and how important social groups are, but it isn't until something happens that we realise just how critical they are.

Especially when it comes to the darker side of sexual assault.

Also, I will add here that I wrote the previous reflection on lived experience 19 days ago and I haven't felt like finishing this reflection until now. A lot has happened in those 19 days and I am even more grateful for my friends and how I am building my social network over time.

Why Are Social Networks Important?

I won't spend too long on this section because we're all aspiring or qualified psychologists here, so we all know the benefits of having friends. For example, people with friends tend to be happier, have better mental health outcomes and have higher life satisfaction compared to people with few or no friends.

In addition, friends are great sources of support when something bad happens in your life. For instance, the death of a loved one, a major negative life event or you're struggling with something. Friends are people you can turn to for advice, they can listen to you and they are the people you can do fun stuff with to make you feel better.

We all know those basics and when it comes to mental health, sometimes I feel like a lot of our work is about human connection, and helping clients build better, more successful relationships in the future.

Such as, when it comes to social anxiety work, we are basically working with a client to give them the skills and coping mechanisms so they can go out into the world, make friends and get all the benefits of having a social network.

The same goes for depression, because we're working with a client so they have the techniques and coping mechanisms to stop isolating themselves, criticising them and stop their biased cognitive processes from limiting their social interaction. This allows them to go out into the world, rejoin their friends doing fun activities and they can deepen their friendships.

Finally, in Post-Traumatic Stress Disorder or any trauma-based work, we're giving client tools and techniques so they can move past their trauma, reclaim their life and they can start living again. This includes the part of life that involves going out with friends, doing silly things and just laughing until your stomach and jaw hurt.

That's my point of view on a lot of mental health work.

How Did My Social Network Help Me?

For the sake of context, I need to be upfront here and say I naturally have a very small social network. I have one close friend who I see often, we talk a lot and we're living together next academic year. I have another friend that we get on great when we're together and I am their closest friend, but they don't text me back. It isn't anything against me, they just don't respond and they always forget to reply to messages.

Then I have another friend which we aren't that close but we talk a fair bit, and I have more of a university friend who's a PhD student. We've helped each other a lot over the years and we are friends.

Anyway, I only really have two close friends. A lot of that is because of child abuse, trauma and undiagnosed autism to be honest.

And even though, I don't have endless amounts of friends, I am still so grateful to have each and every one of them in my life. They actually are some of the best people I know and they are all there for me in their own special way.

I love them for that.

Firstly, the morning after my assault when I realised how distressed I was I contacted my close friend despite them not being available. So the next day when they were available, we spoke and because they weren't back in the UK for another three weeks, we spoke a lot. They were very understanding, very calm and they were really supportive.

I seriously needed that because I was so scared of my best friend. Since I'm attracted to them and that was triggering a lot of assault stuff for me as I've mentioned before.

And ever since my best friend has been back in the country, they have constantly been there for me. We've had a lot of conversations, we've been out a lot and they've been interested in every step of my "recovery". Like tomorrow after I have my counselling assessment with a sexual violence charity, I'll be texting them about it because they want to know.

It's been lovely having a friend who is *that* there for me, and I know for a lot of people this is normal. Yet because of everything that's happened to me in the past, including a fair amount of friendship trauma and betrayal, this is surprising for me.

My other close friend, let's call them, Luke for the sake of ease. Even though Luke never replies to any messages because they forget, they were really nice about messaging me back quickly. We were planning to meet up a few times but I've had to cancel, because one-on-one situations with them was too hard for me. And Luke isn't the type of person I would want to have a meltdown in front of.

It's not because Luke wouldn't be nice about it, it's more because I would feel bad.

Yet I know Luke is a really good friend because they don't mind, they understand why I cancelled and why it took me so long to meet up with them. Then we went to a social thing and we were talking for hours and it was great.

That's what I appreciate about a social network and having different levels of closeness with people. Since my best friend is the person I tell everything to and who I panic and stress with in the moment and I have meltdowns in front of, but Luke is the type of person I talk to after the fact and we just have fun.

Thirdly, my PhD friend was lovely to because he works as a researcher in the Parkinson centre at my university, so I was going to spend some time helping him at work. It never happened because he was ill and then my mental health just died so I wasn't able to help, and I had exams anyway.

However, he was still there for me, he was still willing to listen and talk and I could talk to him about slightly different things compared to the others.

Finally, my last friend was able to offer me a very good perspective because he's a victim of sexual violence. He was raped constantly as a kid so it was actually something we bonded over. When I was feeling so distressed and whatnot and I wanted to give my best friend a little break, I could talk to him. We related a lot with each other, what we were going through and he told me different ways about how to cope with it.

That was nice and it was good hearing from someone with lived experience.

Of course, the "problem" with this friend is there are massive limits about what we can talk about because he's still reeling from his child sexual abuse and there are things he just couldn't process. Which I understand even if I was a little disappointed about because I wanted answers to certain questions and he couldn't give them to me.

Yet considering this was the first time me and this friend have hung out just the two of us and we talk a lot. It has been lovely having another friend who I can talk so openly with about some really dark stuff.

Conclusion

Overall, even though this has been a bit of a different reflection, I still hope you found it useful because you've been able to see the importance and the positive impact that my social network has had on me over the past six weeks. This is a useful reminder that our friends are great, we should always treasure our friendships and we should always be able to turn to our friends in our darkest hour.

Personally, I would hate to imagine what the past six weeks would have been like if I didn't have friends or the friends I have right now. The past six weeks would have been awful, lonely and I am willing to say, I doubt I would still be here.

I don't think that's inaccurate at all, because sexual violence is awful.

Moreover, this experience and this reflection on my own social connections will be useful in future clinical work. Since I'll be able to draw on examples when appropriate with clients about the power and the benefits of friends in difficult times. And this will make me focus and have a lot of enthusiasm for the social skills and the relationship part of our work.

Since I now truly appreciate the power, the hope and decrease in suffering that a good social network can provide, and I wish that everyone has the same opportunities that I do.

Friends really can be the light in the darkness of our lives.

ENJOY THE GOOD TIMES

You have to recognise, enjoy and celebrate the good times.

A lot of the content in this book deals with a lot of distressing topics like rape, negative mental health and occasionally suicidality. And whilst this reflects what the vast, vast majority of sexual assault survivors go through, I don't want this book to seem all doom and gloom because this isn't the message of the book.

This entire book is about showing you that your recovery and your healing will be tough and you will experience a lot of distressing mental health outcomes, but you can heal, you can thrive and you can have good times in between.

That's what I want to remind myself and you in this next chapter.

Today I've had an absolutely lovely day that marks a lot of progress to in my own recovery. Since Henry came around today to my student accommodation and I spent probably 3.5 hours with him, one-on-one and we had a lovely time. We spoke about video games and film lore. More specifically we spoke about Halo lore, his hangover, our student ambassador work a little more and so on.

He found it really nice as well, because he had to have a little nap because of his hangover. Yet before he went to sleep on my sofa, he mentioned he was really happy that he came round today because it was really nice talking to me. Something he repeated when I dropped him off home.

Personally, it was just such a lovely experience just being with a new friend in the comfort of my own home in a one-on-one situation without any rape stuff popping up. I didn't have a panic attack, I didn't have intrusive thoughts about him raping me and I didn't have any of my normal reactions to the idea of spending time with someone.

And as I write this shorter chapter, I couldn't stop smiling because this means a hell of a lot for me. It means I am healing, it might be slow and I might have seriously distressing hours, but I can actually do something that I flat out couldn't do even last week.

I *can* and I will spend time with new friends, just talking, being normal and just enjoying my life.

In addition, it proves that I don't *need* my best friend with me all the time in social situations. Our original plan was to have Henry around with me and my best friend talking to him, playing games and having fun.

However, my best friend has some resit assignments to do for their degree so they were going to be upstairs in their room working on that. They asked me if I wanted them to do downstairs sitting at the kitchen table so they were in the room to make me feel comfortable. I said no to that so I was comforted by the idea of them being in the house.

So my panicked mind could calm down about the fact that if Henry tried to hurt me (he never ever would) then my best friend would stop it and protect me.

The world had other plans.

Since my best friend took out of the university's rentable laptops and no one told them, the laptop does not work until you're on campus. Meaning my best friend had a serious conversation with me about whether I was comfortable being alone and if I wanted them to be here.

Honestly, if I really wanted them to be here, I could have said just work on my laptop.

I didn't really want them here just for me and my mental health, because I was feeling okay about Henry coming round. I told my best friend to go to campus so they could work on their assignments (which are a lot more important to be fair) and that's how a one-on-one situation happened.

And those three hours with Henry were some of the best, most positive moments I've had in weeks.

It isn't even because I had a nice time, because I've had a lovely week at the Year 10 summer school with my fellow ambassadors. And I've had lots of wonderful conversations with other people this week.

I think what made this time with Henry so lovely was it surprised me and gave me hope. It gave me hope that I seriously don't need my best friend to give me my social opportunities, I don't need them to accompany me whenever I want to do something social and when they go back home this week, I don't need to cut myself off from the world until they return.

I can be social and hang out with Henry in the meantime.

Of course, me and my best friend will still spend tons of time together and still do almost everything together because we are really close. Yet I am no longer restricted to only doing things with them.

I still know I will struggle socially in other respects. At the Year 10 summer school on Wednesday, we had a disco and that was extremely distressing for me, so I know I am not healed in certain ways.

However, I can trust people, I can enjoy spending time with them and I can enjoy my life after sexual violence. That is a win and I am grateful that I have these moments in my life.

Moreover, it probably helps that Henry is the complete opposite of my rapist because he's average and fit (not overweight), he's younger than me (unlike my rapist) and he's intensely kind (so not like my rapist). That was a massive help in making today successful, and I still know because of my best friend's Role-Playing Game group that I'll be joining in September for their Halo campaign that I still find very overweight men very triggering and distressing.

Therefore, this definitely isn't the end of my social anxiety and Post-Traumatic Stress Disorder. Yet it is still a win, a sign of progress and a sign of hope for my future.

Finally, as a quick note, a very small aspect of today that I'm excited about is I didn't realise that I could be genuinely attracted to Henry. Since he is lovely, he is fit and he is an attractive guy. Also, whilst he isn't gay so nothing can ever happen between us, the interesting thing for me was it didn't trigger anything for me. Me feeling attraction did not trigger any rape stuff for me.

That has never happened before.

Again, I know from the Year 10 summer school that this flat out isn't a fixed rule because attraction can make me severely distressed most of the time. Yet spending time with Henry goes to show that if I feel safe with someone, if I enjoy spending time with them and if my mental health is good then there is hope I can experience attraction without anything bad happening.

That is another massive sign of progress.

Two perfect discoveries to mark exactly 16 weeks since my rape.

On the whole, when it comes to your recovery, please focus, enjoy and celebrate the good times. You'll need to remember these moments in the dark times and sometimes these good moments will be uncommon, but that makes them even more special when they do happen.

You deserve to be happy, you deserve to be loved and you deserve to experience lovely times.

I know they can happen to you because if they can happen to me then they can happen to anyone, and most importantly, I believe in you.

MY EXPERIENCE OF REVEALING MY RAPE TO THE WORKPLACE

Week 15 was major for me in my recovery, my healing and me telling other people what had happened to me, because I told my bosses and the people I work with that I was raped.

Whilst I know I don't work in any "typical" job because I work as a student ambassador at a university on a very flexible contract where I work with students across Kent who come from schools with typically a low number of students who go on to higher education by supporting and/or delivering a wide range of fun activities with them. There is a lot all of us can learn from this chapter, my experience and what response I got.

As a result of being a student ambassador is still a working environment where there are rather high expectations of me where I have to complete certain duties, responsibilities, behave in a certain way, report to a boss and so on.

Just because this isn't a typical office job, physical labour or anything that non-students would ever be doing, please do not dismiss this as me not having a job. Since this is a part-time job and revealing I was raped to my bosses was just as terrifying as it would be in any other job or profession.

If not more so because I was concerned if I revealed my rape and my bad mental health to my bosses then I would be put "on leave" because they might not have wanted me interacting with young students (under 18s) where I could possibly damage the reputation and image of the university.

That was a very honest concern I had.

Therefore, in the rest of the chapter, I'll give you the context for why I revealed my rape because I technically could have done it 15 weeks ago, but I didn't want to. Then I'll reveal how I did it and what the response was. As well as I'll explain why I told the other student ambassadors too and what their response was as well.

Why Did I Reveal My Rape?

This week I worked what's known as the Year 10 Residential summer school at my university. This was where 55 year 10 students (15-year-olds) came to the university from across Kent to stay for three days and two nights to complete a wide range of fun activities, so they could experience university life and they could take part in fun projects.

The overall theme of the summer school was Breaking Barriers, so showing students through some games, some group work and a group presentation that whatever barriers a person faces to their goals and future dreams. There is support for them at university or in other ways so they can overcome them and achieve whatever they want to.

In addition, there were other academic taster sessions, like law, forensic science, biology and film studies. They were all really good and the students loved them. As well as there were society tasters (for our international audience just think university social clubs formed around a particular interest) like singing, fantasy fiction, photography and mindfulness art (also known as painting).

Then we did quiz nights, meals and sports with them too. I would have loved to have been on the Nerf gun sport option but I was on the non-sport option. There was volleyball and ultimate Frisbee too.

As you can see we did a lot of things with the year 10 students over the three days. As well as there was a disco on the second night too.

Anyway, this was going to be an intense week and as I've mentioned before, I don't tend to do well meeting new people, doing completely new things and sleeping in new places. Hell, sleep is a fight that I lose most of the time.

I was very concerned about the summer school before I went and my concerns were only getting more founded.

Due to on the Monday (the day before the summer school), we had "training" so all 10 ambassadors who were working the event had spent 6 hours on the training. We went through the plan for the next three days, health and safety, safeguarding and a whole bunch of other things.

However, something I've read a lot about when it comes to rape survivors but I haven't really experienced it until the training was rape survivors struggle with concentration.

I kept zoning out of the training and that was a problem throughout the week. And I laugh about it now because whenever someone would give me or a group of people an instruction I would zone out and very quickly have to remember or figure out what the instruction was from the reaction of other people.

Thankfully no one noticed my zoning out but that was only because of some miracle.

That was a warning sign.

Then on the Monday night we could stay over at the university so we didn't need to travel back to the university the next day for the start of the summer school. Also, for context, there was an ambassador that I'll call Oaks (not his real name obviously) that I'm attracted to, and I've always been attracted to him before my rape. So my attraction to Oaks is genuine and not rape-related.

I checked into my room at 4:45 pm and I started having problems immediately. It's a student accommodation room so a sort of cheap hotel room. That means it's an enclosed space with only one way out and it had a double bed. I have massive problems with double beds because my mind twists them to say "oh, that bed's big enough for someone to climb in and rape you again".

Very helpful, not.

I tried to ignore my fears so I sat on the wooden chair and I started to take my shoes off like any normal person would. Yet I started getting intrusive thoughts about Oaks giving me a lap dance and sexually touching me.

This was distressing enough so I knew I couldn't sit on the wooden chair and flick through my phone after taking off my shoes. Also, I knew laying or sitting on the bed was a no-go so I laid on the floor and I quickly became paralysed for the next 65 minutes as the intrusive thoughts of Oaks and my best friend's brother took turns raping me.

I was so emotionally exhausted that it was just hell and you've seen the message I sent to my best friend about this distressing time in a previous chapter.

I knew my mental health was only going to get worse unless I did something. As well as I knew the disco was going to be extremely distressing for me and there was a genuine risk of being me finally having a very public and messy meltdown.

In reality, it was distressing but I managed. I did almost have a public meltdown and I was visually distressed at least twice and I did have to hide in the toilet twice. I did have full permission to go into the quiet room the university had setup but my normal reaction is hide in the toilets.

I knew I had to do something.

I knew I was finally going to have to tell Outreach about my rape so if anything happened then I had an explanation they were already aware of in place, so this would never be interpreted as something I was making up to explain away "bad" behaviour. Outreach would never be like that but I was distressed and so tired when I made this decision. As well as in case I needed anything from Outreach this week, I wanted them to know over an email what had happened because I am not brave enough to tell them to their faces.

So at 11 pm Monday night I sent the following email, and for context, please know I have a very good relationship with the three people in charge of the summer school. We're all very friendly (except for one woman in charge of the summer school who she just isn't approachable but I included her in the email anyway) and I am very well-liked within Outreach. Everyone is always happy to have me on an event because I'm very good at my job.

"Hi all, hope you're well.

I know we're all extremely busy getting ready for the summer school so I'll keep this as short as possible.

I would appreciate the possibility of a small "accommodation" please this week in the rare case I need it, and please appreciate this is a very hard email for me to write as this contains extremely sensitive information.

So I was raped 15 weeks, 2 days ago and all I'll say is as you can imagine it kills your mental health and affects you in basically every single part of your life. Some of the mental health consequences alone include panic attacks, severe social anxiety and Post-Traumatic Stress Disorder. So when these mental health difficulties get added to my mild autism, this is a very fun for me (not).

Therefore, whilst I would greatly appreciate you treating me like normal because Outreach work and the staff have been a lifesaver in the past 15 weeks for giving me normality in an extreme abnormal time and whilst I go through the waiting list for specialist rape counselling. I would appreciate the following:

- *If I ask to supervise or if an ambassador is needed for the quiet room when we're doing a major event (like the quiz or disco), then unless it is seriously inconvenience and it risks making the summer school not run smoothly. Then please let me do to the quiet room for a while and supervise whatever students are in there (or let me have a little bit of time in there please).*
- *If you need an ambassador for the quiet space, maybe ask me as a first pick or something please. I know this sounds nit-pricky but don't assign me the quiet space (if that's something you were going to do for ambassadors. I know it wasn't but I'm panicking as I write this email) because rape is extremely disempowering and I have enough trouble making basic decisions in my everyday life. So having someone innocently make a decision for me about my own mental health makes me feel even more disempowered.*

Besides from that, I don't think there is anything else I need or would like.

However, as an employee of the university, you've all worked with me over the past 15 weeks so you know I can do Outreach work really well and none of you have ever had been issue with me and my work on behalf of the university. Yet because this is a residential with a lot of intense parts, and it is effectively a new environment (especially looking after students in a corridor), this summer school might be challenging for me. As well as I haven't had a good night's sleep in three days because of trauma stuff and that might continue throughout the summer school.

In other words, chances are I will cope, the event will run fine and you won't be able to tell I'm a rape survivor with a lot of difficulties. But if there is a chance of me seriously struggling, I am telling you now so I feel able to ask for help.

I understand this is probably a tough email to read but thank you for reading. I was really hard for me to tell you all as my bosses. Yet all of you are lovely people and I enjoy working with each of you so I feel safe enough to tell you.

Thank you for reading.

I look forward to the summer school starting soon,

Connor."

With this email, I wanted to strike a balance between being seen as fully competent so there was no chance they would request I didn't work the next few days, and whilst emphasising I am not okay and I might need support.

In addition, I wanted to stress the need for them to treat me normally because if they followed the myths and misconceptions about rape survivors or so-called "victims" being weak, broken or any other negative myth about us. Then there was a very real chance of them making me feel worse and negatively impacting my mental health even more.

Of course, I am sure some of you reading this could never imagine being a mixture of formal and informal with your boss, and you will need to adapt your email or you revealing your assault to your bosses to suit your situation. Yet I've included this email in this chapter to give you a starting point or an idea.

<u>What Was The Response From My Three Bosses?</u>

At 7:30 am the next morning, I got an email from Nat, let's call her, and she is already a lovely lady that I have so much time for because she's been in constant contact with me for different Outreach events over the past few months and she cares about us ambassadors a lot.

Now I didn't see her email until an hour later after I had had breakfast with the other ambassadors and I had already seen her. I honestly hadn't realised she had read or seen my email because she treated me normally. She asked me *how was I* and *how did I sleep* but for her, that isn't an odd thing to ask at all.

Her response was basically something along the lines of *I can only imagine how difficult that email was to write so thank you for trusting us. That information will be handled sensitively and if there is anything you need just ask and we'll do it. You're really important to us and we're really lucky to have you on the summer school.*

I have a lot of time for Nat and later on in the day she did mention the quiet room to me and she said if we set it up, we'll ask you and only if you want you can do it. The conversation was half-serious because she wasn't sure it was even needed for the students and half-me-focused because she wanted me to be okay.

Then the other woman I sent my email too. She didn't treat me any different over the next three days and she didn't even talk to me about my email nor did she reply. Honestly, I wasn't expecting her to because the idea of her having an emotional or heartfelt conversation with anyone is funny. She has her nice moments but no one really likes her anyway because she is a very militant boss.

Anyway, the man I sent my email too was another great example of people treating me normally because I didn't think he read my email at all. Yet on the Wednesday night he spoke to me and it turned out he had read it Tuesday afternoon and simply hadn't had a chance to speak to me before the disco. Then he said he was really sorry for what happened to me and if there was anything I needed he wanted me to ask for it.

I asked where the quiet room was because I knew I was going to need it that night. It was even worse that after all the distress of the disco, I needed to start packing up my room because we were checking out straight after breakfast the next day. Yet I couldn't make any decisions so I had to text my best friend my thinking process so I could then make a decision. Thankfully, my best friend was asleep so I didn't have to have a reply.

Yet sending that text did help me a lot and I was able to pack.

On the whole, when it came to disclosing my rape to my bosses, it was hard but I am so glad I did it. This took a lot of the stress away and the summer school was a lot of fun. I do love Outreach work, interacting with students and doing a lot of fun activities.

It was nice to know that Outreach supports me no matter what and if you ask people not to treat you differently then they'll do it, and support you.

It was a brilliant thing to realise.

<u>How Did I Tell My Peers About My Rape?</u>

In an effort to be completely open and transparent with you, there has been a rough 5-week gap between me writing this section and the last section, because of my mental health. Yet that will be explored in a future chapter as well as the tips and tricks I used to manage my mental health as best I could.

Anyway, on the Monday night of the year 10 Residential, we created a WhatsApp group chat so we could all talk, relay information and sort out any problems during the Summer School if needed.

As I mentioned earlier by the time Monday night came along, I was already really struggling with everything and I knew there was a good chance I was going to get a lot worse, so I needed to protect my mental health.

This was made even worse when one of the less mature members of the Summer School, another student ambassador, made the group chat profile picture to be one of implied rape. Why the hell people working a school event would pick that is beyond me.

Well, this ambassador was a bit of an idiot too.

Therefore, when I saw that profile picture I got distressed, it triggered me and I was paralysed with rape sensations for another 30 minutes. I knew I had to get them to change the profile picture so I was going to have to tell them the reason why.

I posted the following on the group chat.

"Hey everyone, can we change the group chat image please?

Because all I'll say is (as hard as this is for me), I was raped in April so that sort of image is rather distressing to me and because this summer school is intense enough, there's a chance this event will be difficult for me. And I need to look after myself.

Apologies for this tough message, and please don't treat me any differently now you know I'm a rape survivor. I really like talking and working with all of you and I don't want that to change. Working with all of you over the past 15 weeks has helped me tons, so thank you all. Especially the summer core lot.

Sleep well everyone."

I went for this tone and sort of message in retrospect because I've worked with these people for a good few years, I really like them all and I was concerned they were going to treat me differently. Also, I had just spent the past month working with most of them every single working day on a wide range of Summer Core activities, and we had all become good friends.

As a result, the point of the message was to make sure they changed the image, that they knew what had happened to me and my biggest point was so they didn't treat me differently.

The worst thing for my mental health would have been for them to infantilise me, blame me or have a negative reaction.

How Did My Peers React To My Revelation?

I sent the message above at about 12:15 am because I was struggling too much to sleep beforehand and I had to get up at 6:30 am. I sent the message, put my phone on extreme power-saving mode so I couldn't receive notifications and I went straight to sleep.

Even when I got up the next morning, I showered, got changed and did French Duolingo before I even remotely thought about checking the messages.

Thankfully, there were lots of supportive messages considering the size of the group chat. There were 11 of us in the group chat so minus myself that's 10. When I checked the messages, there were 3 people who messaged saying how sorry they were that had happened, they're there for me if I needed any support and one of them changed the profile picture.

The idiot ambassador who made the silly profile picture in the first place never commented on this message. In all fairness, he probably felt too bad and I suspect he felt guilty because on the Thursday night (the end of the Summer School) we were all at a bar on campus and he made a comment and then he apologised to me. So he read it, remembered it and tried to change his behaviour.

That's good on him.

Then the next morning when me and another ambassador who I get along with brilliantly went into Canterbury city centre to pick up a student in a taxi, whilst we were waiting we were talking about random things then she suddenly said how brave I was, it was good I spoke up about it and she's sorry I had to go through that.

It was lovely.

That was all I got in terms of messages but 40% of people acknowledged it and made sure I was okay. That is still really good. As well as 0% of people treated me differently, negatively or judged me for my message.

That's all I care about.

In addition, one ambassador who I've known for years and we get on well he kept looking after me the next day. He would sit next to me and talk to me, he would subtly ask if I was okay and once we were in a talk and it was boiling hot so he kept giving me his tiny handheld fan.

It was really nice and I was surprised, but it was lovely.

Over To You

Ultimately, I know being a student ambassador who works part-time whilst being a university student isn't similar to your job. Yet there are still strong parallels because if you get on with your peers, if they actually care about you (a brilliant, resilient survivor) and if they're good people. Then they will listen, acknowledge and act on what you need to feel safe and get your work done.

I hope this chapter has shown you that it is possible to get support at work from your bosses, your peers and accommodations can be made.

It will still be difficult at times but if you need it, if your rape is impacting your ability to work then please consider telling your employer and asking for accommodations to be made.

If I didn't reveal my rape to my peers and bosses, I would have found the Summer School next to impossible and I think I would have had a very public and very bad meltdown that would have put my job at risk.

Please do what you need to do to keep yourself happy, able to work and safe.

You are more important than you'll ever realise.

THE GREAT COLLAPSE OF MY MENTAL HEALTH AND ALWAYS READ TRIGGER WARNINGS

Note: there are tricks and techniques layered throughout this chapter about how to cope with negative mental health, safety plans and how to heal from PTSD. Especially after the first two sections.

It pains me to admit this, but there's been a massive, very dark, very painful and extremely difficult 4-week gap in the writing of this book.

All because my mental health collapsed.

Of course, you've seen for the past 22 weeks how my mental health has ebbed and flowed, weakened and strengthened and how I've focused on the odd light in the darkness of this part of my life.

My mental health completely and utterly collapsed for the past four weeks, so much so my best friend has been really worried for me. They didn't sleep last night because they were so worried about me and so much has happened.

It's been impossibly dark most of the time between suicidal ideation, depression and even more depression. This is the worst my mental health has ever been and I have struggled so much just to function. It's one of the reasons why I haven't written this book for ages because I've been trying to focus on writing my academic paper, which I'm calling: *We Are Our Names: Transgender Individuals on Chosen Name Strategies and Mental Health Implications.*

I've managed to do everything for the paper except finish the discussion section, conclusion, abstract and formatting it to be sent off to my supervisor. Since the past month has literally been a case of I have enough energy and mental capacity to do one major thing a day.

That is it and that is not how I normally am at all.

Anyway, in this chapter, I want to give you a brief overview of the past 4 weeks for me including my triggers, my experiences and how me and my best friend moved heaven and Earth to keep me alive.

What Happened?

My best friend went back up to the Midlands (for our international audience, this is the name of the region in the middle of England. Yes, the English are extremely creative with their names) to see family for 3 weeks starting on the 10th August. I met their parents for the first time on the 9th and it was lovely.

Yet me and my best friend, I finally need to give them a fake name so let's call them Purple (in all fairness that is trans and colour-blindness inside joke), were both concerned how I would cope being home alone for 3 weeks. I was going to see my parents, see my friend Henry and do some Outreach work but still.

We were concerned.

Anyway, that first week was really good. I flat out loved being home alone because I was being extremely productive, I was doing a ton of really fun writing and business projects and I was enjoying myself. I was doing 7-hour days, something I hadn't done since my rape.

However, my mental health kept dipping badly in the evening. It didn't help that I watched the first episode of *Young Royals*, two days after Purple left. It's a great gay royal romance TV series on Netflix set in Sweden. I'd been meaning to watch it for years but I hadn't and Purple had never really wanted to watch it.

They were gone and I needed a series to watch whilst I ate dinner.

Of course, in my 23 years of life, I have never ever had to read trigger warnings before so I watched it. At the 20-minute mark of the first episode there was straight sexual content, I screamed, jumped, had a panic attack and got depressed for 20 minutes until I texted Purple.

That is basically how my mental health started dipping and it kept dipping throughout the entire week. I really took a turn for the worse when Purple mentioned they were heading up to Liverpool to meet someone they met online for four days.

Now that actually did kill my mental health. 5% of it was probably jealousy that Purple wants to date someone who isn't me but 95% of it was just pure and utter grief that I cannot do that myself. I want to meet people, have a normal romantic life and enjoy that part of my life.

I will one day but when I'm depressed and struggling that just seems flat out impossible.

It was the Friday night of the first week that I learnt that Purple was going to Liverpool on Sunday to Wednesday. I knew my mental health was bad but I seriously didn't know how bad it was going to get.

<u>When The Depression Started</u>

On the Saturday morning, I woke up and really felt that something was wrong because I was so depressed, I couldn't get out of bed and I didn't see the point in anything. Luckily, I had Henry coming round at 2 pm so I had to be ready before then so I forced myself to shower and do a little bit of hoovering.

And honestly, seeing Henry was lovely and it as exactly what I needed, but I didn't realise how the following message I sent Purple later on was just the tip of the iceberg in terms of me spiralling:

'It was lovely seeing Henry. He stayed for 4.5 hours just talking. We talked about Halo, Elden Ring, his parents and friends and social history. I spoke about my abusive upbringing and mentioned my parents' reaction to my rape. He was speechless about my parents both times.

A guy asked him out once. Edward kept talking to the guy but they drifted apart after that. I didn't have the heart to tell him, we thought he was bi.

He has a transwoman friend. Even though he only remembers her dead name which he knows how bad that is and he needs to talk to her more. She's great on a night out. Anyway, we had a trans conversation. He couldn't care less about my gender and his Mum thought I was a transman.

He has tons of friends, at least 20. He considers you a friend and there was my normal social awkwardness when he left. I think he wanted a handshake, I tried a hug then we settled on a hug. I think that was a bad idea because I think that's triggered me badly and I'm spiralling again.

I'm irritated you're the only one I can hug without having bad reactions.

It was nice seeing Henry. We're going to do something practical next time. He wants tennis. I firmly want something else but that involves me making a decision. Something... I will have to do it when I'm better.

I'm glad I have a friend I can see down here whilst you're away. It's a tiny light in the darkness."

Then as soon as Henry left I got slightly depressed because I was alone again and that set me up perfectly for the Great Collapse the next day. Below is a little extract from a podcast episode that summarises that particular Sunday for me:

"On the Sunday, it was even worse. And because it was so dark and so bad, I can't actually go into all of the details, but it was absolutely horrific.

All I'll say is it took me 3 hours and 20 minutes just to have a shower because the interesting thing about depression is that because it's a low mood, it really impacts your energy levels. So then what happened was that around 2:00 pm, I finally decided, right, I am gonna have a shower. I'm gonna move heaven and earth to have a shower.

Well, the issue with that is that you need to get up from the sofa, then you need to go upstairs, then you need to get your clothes, get your towel, go into the bathroom, have a shower, get changed, etc. So, when you think about it, there are actually quite a few steps to anything that we do. And normally, I can normally do that all in, like, 20 minutes.

On Sunday, it took me 3 hours, 20 minutes to have a shower. I mean, that was just like... It took me 15 minutes just to get up the stairs. But then I actually had to come back down, so I was depressed about that, and it was ridiculous. It wasn't until I actually got in the shower at 5:00 pm, and I was just like, there's no point in me actually having a shower because it's 5:00, and to me, that's pointless. But I was like, I've been trying to do this for three hours. I've got to try."

Afterwards, as the night went on my mental health got worse and worse. I self-harmed, I smashed my favourite mug in the entire world. It was a brilliant mug that I've had for 5 years now ever since I started my undergraduate degree and it was a 500 ml mug so it was great. I smashed it because I was so angry with my life, my rapist and my failing social support network. I still hate it that Purple is everything I have but it really got to me that night.

I was really bad and I wanted to kill myself and it just got to the point where I couldn't do anything.

Before Purple left, we had a discussion about how I could always text and call, and we had been texting every day that week. It was how they knew I was dipping throughout the week.

I called them on the Sunday night and we spent the next 75 minutes talking about me, we came up with safety plans and what we were going to do.

Moreover, it was so bad that I had to wrap up Purple's sharp knives in kitchen roll (I didn't want them to get dirty) and I had to throw them behind our tumble dryer because I kept trying to self-harm and kill myself with them.

We agreed to call every night basically regardless of what Purple was doing because they were going to make the time for me. And it worked out fine anyway because they could do whatever they wanted in the daytime, afternoon and evening and we would call between 10 pm and 11:30 pm depending on what they were doing.

In addition, we agreed that I would come up to the Midlands on the 30th August, because Purple would be back from a family holiday, seeing all their friends and Liverpool by that point. Then I would come up for the day and I would take them back to Canterbury the day after because one of our housemates (and really good friends) were moving in that day.

Furthermore, Purple made me go back to my parents for a few days so I wasn't alone, as well as I had a counselling appointment booked with my old therapist just so I could talk to someone in the meantime. And it was lovely talking to Purple because we spoke about how important we are to each other, how much better our lives are for having the other in it and we are just really good friends and Purple really, REALLY wants me around.

Therefore, I went back to my parents for three nights and three days and it was good. I wasn't alone when they were back from work, me and Purple called every night but I was still really depressed when I was alone. I couldn't do anything, I struggled to watch stuff and that was bad.

So that's basically how the next two weeks went, I was extremely depressed. I was still dealing with tons of PTSD, intrusive thoughts and "extreme" reactions to media and small triggers. I was a complete and utter mess most days and it was just impossible to function.

I had two really good therapy sessions but the "problem" was that my old counsellor isn't a rape specialist, so she couldn't help me too much. Yet it was lovely to talk to someone who wasn't Purple and to someone who had psychological training. Therefore, the first session was more me talking to her and educating her about the effects of sexual violence. Then in the second session, she gave me the following resources that are VERY useful and I **highly** recommend that you check them out for yourself:

- YouTube- Justin Haven All Trauma Is Treatable
- Dream Completion Technique- a technique to help PTSD nightmares
- Flash Technique- a great technique from EMDR.

As well as whilst I couldn't really do too much, I could manage one major thing a day which I dedicated to focusing on my academic paper and my psychology podcast.

Those two things were very important to me and I realised if I didn't try to focus on my academic paper then it would never be done and it's too "important" for that to happen.

<u>A Potential Productivity Trick Whilst Depressed</u>

One trick I did discover thankfully was I could manage doing one session/ sitting on my laptop before my depression and executive dysfunction kicked in. Then I would be depressed, disassociated or just spiralling for hours at a time.

However, I did learn after a while that if I wanted to force myself to do another session on my laptop or try to be productive. I could make myself a really nice Toffee Nut Latte with my Tassimo machine and promise myself that if I allow myself to have their luxury drink. Then in exchange, I need to do some stuff on my laptop.

It worked.

It was a good productivity hack on my "bad but not horrific" days and it allowed me to get some extra things done for my paper.

A Lovely Respite: Seeing Purple Again Wasn't The End of My Struggles, It Was The Midpoint

I thought Friday 30th August 2024 would be the end of my mental health struggles, and I would go back to what I was like before Purple went back to see their family and friends in the Midlands. In other words, still struggling, still having PTSD and everything I've spoken about in previous chapters. Yet not be depressed, unable to function and struggle as much as I had been.

I was wrong.

However, first of all, I went up to Midlands leaving at 7:20 am and arriving at Purple's house about 3 and a bit hours later but Purple was having an Osteopathic massage so I met their brother for the first time and spoke to him for ages. I'd been wanting to meet him for months because him and Purple got on well, he really supported Purple being non-binary and queer and that was such a violently alien concept for me that I wanted to meet him. And I thought I might be attracted to him (he's straight) but I'm still interested. I wasn't attracted to him in the end.

Anyway, Purple came back and we had a lovely lunch with their brother and Mum. We spoke for ages then me and Purple went Ice Skating, which was interesting.

Now I stressed to Purple in quite a few of our calls that I wanted to live, have fun and I wanted to be anywhere but indoors. Because I'd been stuck depressed and suicidal indoors for the past three weeks. Purple had suggested ice skating because there wasn't a great amount to do in the town they lived in that was filled with Rich Old White people.

Also, I am many things but I am not a sporty person. I've always wanted to go ice skating so I went and me and Purple had a brilliant 1.5 hours of skating. I laughed a lot, had a lot of fun and Purple really enjoyed it too.

However, the current joke (more like reality) is that I do not do sports because I am good at them. I do sports because I am so bad at them that I make everyone laugh.

I fell off so many times that I have 3 massive swallowed lumps on my right elbow, my right hip and under my right rib. Also, I had a minor swallowed lump at the base of my spine when I fell, hit my tailbone and let out an extremely loud scream that made everyone in the arena stop, look at me and go deadly silent until I got back up.

Anyway, it was great fun and I wouldn't change it for the world.

Afterwards, Purple showed me round their town and it was very nice. Then we went to Café Nero and had a coffee and something to eat, and I asked Purple about how worried they've been and how they're feeling.

They stressed that they're better now I was with them because they could keep an eye on me, but they were… they are worried about me. That change of tense was what they actually did in the conversation.

Only neither one of knew I was going to get worse still.

Following our coffee break we went to the park because Purple wanted to teach me some skateboarding, and because I wasn't in the ice ring anymore I took my hoody off.

The park itself was really nice with lots of young families laughing, smiling and running about as did young couples and dogwalkers. There was a nice warm breeze and the air was really refreshing, clean and calming.

So Purple talked to me about skateboarding, I tried, fell off immediately and scraped my already-swollen elbow on the path. So much so that there was a lot of dark red rich blood and we went straight back to their parents and their Mum fussed over me.

I bleed for a fair while.

We returned to Canterbury the next day.

The Next Week: It Gets Worse

At this point in the chapter, you need to realise that my mental health can be absolutely horrific, but one of my many superpowers is the ability to mask and act extremely well in front of other people. That is the survivor in me, it is what I have always had to be just to survive. It started in childhood and it is something I have just had to continue.

Then I crumble and collapse when I'm alone with someone I trust.

Therefore, me and Purple returned to Canterbury the next day and it was lovely seeing our other housemate and friend again. We caught up, we laughed, we talked and it was great.

Even though I realised I was still dipping very badly.

Over the course of the next week, I actually had some Outreach work. The first proper work I had in the past three weeks so it was nice seeing people again, but I was struggling. It was whenever I wasn't at Outreach work and I was home with my two friends. I was depressed and barely able to function.

I felt guilty that I was so bad, I was annoyed that I was openly being depressed in front of Purple and our other friend. It was awful.

However, Purple and our friend didn't mind, they understood and they were there for me. They're both really good friends even though Purple is the only one I can really talk to about stuff.

Honestly, most of that week is a blur because I was so depressed, it was two weeks ago and most of it was Outreach work and just crippling depression.

Nonetheless, we did go out and play Tennis with Henry and one of Purple's friends on the Thursday evening. It was "interesting" weather for it because the sky was grey, the air was moist and had a slight chill to it and the tarmac outdoor court had a slight slippiness to it.

Now, I am not good at Tennis but thankfully Purple's friend is horrific and even worse than me. It was a great, really fun and enjoyable time. It was a good escape from my depression and executive dysfunction for two hours.

Even though, my mental health was never going to leave me alone for two full hours especially when I was playing a game like tennis. A game that requires more mental capacity than I realised.

Around the 90-minute mark, I knew I was in trouble because I couldn't focus, I couldn't make decisions, I was terrified. Purple had already picked up something was wrong so we had a break and I went to the toilet.

Normally escaping to the toilet, getting depressed or calming myself down works when my executive dysfunction kicks in when I'm not at home. Yet that wasn't really an option at the tennis centre so I tried what I could in the toilet but I knew I was in trouble.

I went back we played light tennis for another 20 minutes including Henry and Purple (the two best tennis players) played against each other. Purple won.

Afterwards, we headed back to mine and Purple's place to hang out, but my executive dysfunction was so bad I couldn't talk. I needed to tell Purple that Henry wanted to do something about dinner but I didn't have the mental capacity to cook so I needed Purple to help me.

In the end, I wrote it on an email draft so they could read it.

Later on, I found out that Purple was really worried that I would go non-verbal for the evening. That's happened to them before.

Thankfully, I didn't go non-verbal and it was a lovely evening filled with talking, laughter and I just really, really like hanging out with Henry. He's cool and it's just brilliant to have another friend.

Highlighting A Tip

Just to make this tip very, very clear to all you wonderful readers, if we're experiencing executive dysfunction and you cannot talk to other people. You can **text** them or you can **write it down** so you can still communicate if you cannot form words.

Our Housemate Leaves, Purple Leaves, The Final-ish Week

It's honestly weird saying that it was the last week because the rest of this chapter covers the past 9 days but honestly it feels like a decade ago. I actually had to look at my calendar to remind myself what had happened because it was so bad and I've tried to block it out for the most part.

Saturday I can summarise shortly as our housemate left, me and Purple had a nice day together just talking, watching stuff and having some time just the two of us as close friends and we spoke about some stuff we couldn't talk about in front of our other friend. It was nothing bad or about my mental health, it was just other stuff.

Anyway, because my mental health was only getting worse, I said to Purple, the idea of me being alone for a week makes me want to kill myself. I was deadly serious about that.

Granted we had our final housemate moving in on the Wednesday (someone we kind of know but not really), and I was concerned I would feel even more lonely and depressed with our other housemate because they might be out a lot, they might be in their room a lot and so on.

Also, it really isn't the other housemate's job to provide me with social contact.

Purple suggested I come up on to the Midlands on Thursday because I had to be here on Wednesday to let our final housemate in, I had Outreach work Wednesday evening and all day on Thursday and Purple was seeing friends up until Thursday night anyway.

We both agreed that four days with Purple should be perfectly fine.

We were seriously wrong.

I went out with my "social environment" (I am trying to be anomalous here) on Sunday and that was a disaster. I realised just how negative, homophobic and disrespectful they were. It was a nice day with them in the sense that we caught up, we had a coffee, lunch and we did some sightseeing in Canterbury.

However, my "social environment" never asked me how I was because they don't want to know about my rape trauma because it hurts them too much, they were still homophobic and they don't respect my boundaries.

For example, I simply ask do NOT touch me without answering and do not touch me in certain ways.

They took me clothes shopping (I didn't want to go anyway) and I was already depressed and suicidal at this point anyway. And they kept touching me in certain ways that I will not tell you in case it triggers you, so I had a PTSD reaction and they shouted at me.

They believed they should be allowed to touch me because they are my "social environment" and I'm simply overreacting.

They dropped me off at my student house and I just disassociated for two hours, I was depressed, suicidal and Purple left 9 am that morning and they weren't available to call that night.

Sunday night was really bad.

When it came to Monday and Tuesday, they were only 8 and 9 days ago but I don't really remember them. I know me and Purple called Monday night and Purple was so angry with my "social environment" and we spoke for a good hour on the phone, and I was constantly dealing with PTSD reactions and intrusive thoughts about my "social environment" touching and doing things to me.

Then Tuesday, I spiralled so badly because I was so terrified of going to sleep. This sums up how horrific Tuesday night was for me and this is what I sent Purple at 2:30 am:

Please note: Purple later said to me, it's okay that you spiralled. You need to be kind to yourself when this happens. Please listen to Purple yourself.

"I'm sorry okay. I'm an idiot. I spiralled badly for the past 4 hours all because the images of Mum raping me because of those stupid touches and her shouting at me. I just wanted the thoughts and physical sensations to stop.

I kept disassociating but I was scared. I just wanted something else to focus on when the thoughts flooded me.

Nothing happened but I went on Grindr and talked to guys with the intention to have sex. I got close to setting stuff up. I didn't.

Maybe a fucked up part of me wants to get raped properly like Mum keeps saying. Maybe I want to prove I was raped whatever that means. Maybe I just want to get raped and killed.

I JUST WANT THE THOUGHTS TO STOP.

I'm sorry. I just can't do this anymore. I don't want to have images of every single person I meet raping me. No one cares about my rules, no one cares about talking to me. It feels I have to shout at the world to be heard even slightly.

That's why I need to die.

No I'm sorry. I'm so sorry.

I didn't mean it. I'm just spiralling. I need sleep but if I sleep the thoughts return.

I'm sorry. I'm probably hurting you and that's why I won't kill myself because I never want to hurt you.

I'm going to sleep and I'll wake up and have a better day. I won't but I want to wake up and be alive.

I'm sorry it's always you. I'm more sorry than you'll ever know. You never deserve this.

Good night. Hope you'll sleeping okay."

As you can see I was in a right state and I had terrified myself.

Wednesday was just more of the same sort of bad and depressed mental health, but Outreach work was fun. As well as I had a good two-hour conversation with our new housemate getting to know them and it was good.

In addition, I got my first rape counselling session scheduled because they phoned me. Yet the problem was I was too depressed to feel anything about the session that I've been wanting and hoping for for months. Purple was a lot more excited about the appointment than I was.

Then on Thursday, I had a fun day at the particular Outreach event I was working then it took me 4.5 hours to get to Purple's parents. Purple had another friend round when I arrived so I met this friend for about an hour (her and Purple don't see each other often) then I literally collapsed and let everything out when it was just me and Purple.

Purple held me for an hour whilst we watched stuff and I was really "out of it". I was shaking, disassociating and nothing felt real at times.

It was bad.

Fortunately, the next few days in the Midlands was fine in the daytime. Friday, me and Purple relaxed and watched stuff whilst their Dad was away on one of his projects. We watched the Dungeons and Dragons: Honour Amongst Thieves movie and it was good. Then I introduced Purple to a livestream of the game Space Marines 2.

It is brilliant.

Then Purple's Mum came home from being in France and it's always lovely seeing her.

My mental health always dies in the evening and at nighttime, which wasn't fun but I managed.

And the Saturday was surprisingly lovely because Purple was meeting up with a very old friend from secondary school who they hadn't seen for two years. This was arranged before my mental health died and me coming up to the Midlands this week wasn't planned until 4 days before I arrived.

So originally I was just going to do some academic work (and more than likely spend tons of hours depressed until Purple came home). Thankfully, Purple's Mum really likes me and I really like her so for the next seven hours (not including the two hours I spent doing laptop things) until Purple came home. We went for coffee and cake in town, we picked up medication where the pharmacist thought I was Purple, we went for a toastie, went in some shops, went for an hour long dog walk and then we spent a few hours in the garden with Purple's Dad. And because Purple's Mum is French we had an aperitif for an hour (just think a starter. Sorry, French people for the extremely cruel and slightly wrong definition)

Now the funny thing is that Sunday and Monday were literally two and three days ago. Sunday was just cooking a nice brunch for me and Purple before we drove back to Canterbury and Monday was working on my academic paper (for the first time in two weeks). I do not remember anything else about those days.

Then everything went to hell yesterday.

The Climax Of Horrific Mental Health

At the time of writing, it's Fresher's Week here in the UK so all the new university students are coming along to fun welcome events and trying to make new friends. Even though me and Purple are not first years, everyone still goes to these events to have fun and try to make new friends.

I was looking forward to yesterday because it was the LGBT+ coffee morning and then there were Board Games and other events going on. I wanted to make friends and I was going to try so hard.

However, I forgot how bad my mental health was so me and Purple went there, then me and Purple managed to attract a group of different people and they're very nice. Purple got on like a house on fire with them, I felt extremely lonely sitting at that table surrounded by my best friend and 8 others.

I didn't feel like I could connect with any of them because I don't share their interests. Purple later said they think I could but I need to try, keep contributing to conversations and effectively "use" going out with this social group to get introduced to other people I could connect with.

Anyway, during board games I went to the toilet, then I got depressed on the toilet for a surprising 45 minutes. I should have known I was in trouble but I kept going. I had a psychology neurodivergent event I was supporting too.

However, afterwards, I met back up with Purple and the group of friends we had made earlier in the day and we talked and did arty things for the next 2 hours. Then one of the friends mentioned they've been raped (they did ask for trigger warnings but I was silly and didn't mention it. I didn't want anyone to know I've experienced sexual violence. I had only just met them) so that distressed me.

Also, I got so depressed and suicidal sitting doing arty things and they had already made plans for the evening to continue late into the night. I couldn't do that and then sex conversations popped up.

I had to left then and I basically cried all the way back to my car, Purple had stayed thankfully and the rest of the night went to hell until Purple came back four hours later.

Now I cannot accurately describe how bad last night was myself so I'm going to show you what I sent Purple when I was extremely out of it. Thankfully, texting Purple helps me but sending these texts were next to impossible and then I want to caveat all this too afterwards:

"I do NOT want you home. I want you to enjoy your evening.

Make a decision for me please. I absolutely can't and I don't want to eat because if I don't eat I die sooner.

Should I cook or finish livestream?

Actually tell me to cook please. I'll do both. I'm likely to actually attempt the intensely difficult task if you ask me to do it.

Also, your small sharp knife is behind the microwave. I kept trying to slice my left upper arm but your knife isn't sharp enough to do that with small blade movements. So I splashed boiling hot water on my hand instead.

I'm sorry. I'm texting you. Everything's starting to feel real again, so I'm slightly better. I'll probably just be depressed. It's fine.

Please just do NOT come home until the evening's naturally ended. I WANT you to live your life with friends and do anything that makes me want to kill myself.

If you want a lift text me. I probably won't sleep tonight so yeah....

I better start cooking before the depression returns fully."

And I should note that I do send Purple very intense messages but we do have a healthy close friendship and I do leave them alone for the most part. For example, last night I was going through hell, depression and really wanting to kill myself, I didn't call them. I wanted to leave them alone and just allow them to have a nice evening with their new friends.

And even now, Purple's been out with another friend for 4 hours and I haven't texted them once. I haven't needed to. Granted they have just texted me saying they're on their way home.

My point is, these are extremely intense messages that make Purple seriously worry about me but we do have boundaries, we are healthy and Purple knows and will tell me if they need to step back.

Ultimately, when they came back, they were extremely fatigued because of socialising, health stuff and it was a long day. We spoke about their day, my mental health and we made enough safety plan because their sharp knives keep becoming an issue.

I'm banned from opening the draw and they're in and if I want anything in there for cooking I need to text permission.

It's a good safety plan. Annoying, but it will be effective.

And I know Purple was terrified for me because we always hug before we go to bed, it's what Purple does with their friends. Normally, their one to break the hug first and then I do. Last night, I went to break the hug and Purple just hugged me tighter and they spoke to me for a minute whilst tightly hugging me.

Then I learnt I was a big reason why they couldn't sleep last night. In addition to social anxiety and something they were doing this morning.

Overall, my dear readers, that is the past four weeks of my life. Just over 6,000 words on how my mental health has just died and the safety plans and other tips and tricks I have done just to still be alive when all I have wanted to do is kill myself at times.

However, life does get better and there are small positive moments that make everything worthwhile and worth living for. Because if I had killed myself, I never would have gone up to the Midlands and gone ice skating, I never would have had such a lovely time with Purple's Mum and I wouldn't have had the lovely conversations with Purple over the past month.

I am happy to be alive, and I want you to keep living too regardless of how bad your mental health is.

There is light, happiness and hope at the end of the tunnel no matter how pitch black the tunnel is in the meantime.

Never give up.

WHAT IS IT LIKE TO EXPERIENCE A MAJOR DEPRESSIVE EPISODE?

In the last chapter, I spoke about horrific my mental health has been for the past month and even though my rape counselling started today thankfully, I only gave you a brief overview. In our next chapter, I want to give you a more focused look at how mental health collapsed in the first week of this on-going depressive episode.

I wanted to include this aspect of my mental health in the book. Again, because I want you to know whatever you're experiencing it is normal, okay and you CAN survive it.

In addition, I normally say this to my psychology audience but whilst we learn a lot of content about different mental health conditions. It is only lived experience that can possibly help us to truly understand what a condition is like for a client or service user. Since we can all read as many academic papers or resources on depression but until you talk or listen to people who have or are currently experiencing depression then you will never be able to fully understand how depression impacts a person. Especially in their everyday life.

As a result, I am including this very personal chapter in this even-more personal book to help you understand what you might be experiencing. I hope it helps you, your loved one or the survivor in your life.

Why Am I Talking About Experiencing Depression?

Note: this is a cleaned-up audio transcription from the recording I made when I was experiencing a wave of depression. I did not realise I was as depressed as I was when I was making the record, so there will be grammatical errors. Since this is spoken word and not written word.

I've hinted at my depression and declining mental health in the past two episodes. Therefore, the reason why I'm talking about this is because since Saturday, so seven days now, I've been having quite a major depressive episode, and I've never actually had this before. Sure, I've had one or two days of being depressed, and I mean going through quite crippling depression, but I've never had it for seven days.

And yes, it's sort of gotten a little better, but I'm still quite depressed now, though. For example, the only reason why I can actually record this and sound relatively normal in terms of this is what I normally sound like, at least I hope so, is because I've just been texting my best friend because they wanted to know about what plant pot they had in their bedroom. And I was like, "Oh God, I'm gonna have to go and look."

So, I did that, and we were talking, and we were texting to and fro for a bit, and I was making fun of them for their mason jars here. Thankfully, this helped me to have quite a bit of energy. But I know that will seriously dip, though. I thought, right now I feel good, I've got to do this.

Overall, the reason why I'm talking about this is, one, because of the practical issue that I just spoke about. Two, as a future clinical psychologist, or maybe even qualified psychologists and people interested in lived mental health experiences, it is really important that we do understand not only what academia says about a mental health condition, but we also hear about it from those people with a life experience. Of course, I do not have a depression diagnosis. To be honest, I do have a scary feeling that I'm not actually gonna get any better by saying "over the next week." And because I have been feeling depressed for two weeks, this is just off the top of my head, so don't quote me on this, that's actually all you need for a depression diagnosis, of course, as long as you meet the other criteria too, though.

So, at the moment, I don't have a depression diagnosis, and I'm hoping that I won't ever have to get one. So, I'm talking about this just so we can all understand lived-like experiences here.

An Overview Of My Week

I already mentioned earlier that this all started on Saturday, but there's something larger that's going on here. So, as you guys know, I experienced sexual violence back in April, and that has really messed with my mental health. That has been quite debilitating, and I've been doing tons of different bits to try and get better in that sense. But I'm still on a waiting list for specialist rape counselling, which is taking a toll on my mental health because I need this support, but I can't get it because it turns out there's a lot of people that get raped. So, it takes a while for a place to open up for you, which is tragic. And I'm basically coping as best I can with my mental health getting worse as the months go by, especially my PTSD. And I mean, like, I think I've had two days of depression since my, so to like 19 weeks ago tomorrow at the time of recording.

I've not had it for seven days before.

In addition, what happened was that on Saturday, I started to feel quite depressed. I started to feel really down, and it was a struggle to get out of bed. Thankfully, I had a friend coming round at 2:00 just because we had already planned it, and I wanted to spend time with him because we get on really well. But the problem was, was that I couldn't get out of bed. It took me a long time to have a shower, not as much as the next day though. And it took me a while to do everything. So, thankfully, I was ready for when he came around at 2:00, but I wanted to do stuff before then. I wanted to do some writing, I wanted to do some podcast work and other stuff, but that really didn't happen.

Me and my friend had a really nice four and a half hours. It was really nice talking. We spoke about Halo Lore. We basically talked about a bunch of nerd stuff, then we talked about relationships and other bits and pieces, basically stuff you normally talk with your friends about. Then he left, and then I was just like, oh, right, I'm actually quite sad now. I'm actually feeling ridiculously lonely and everything. And then it was a full-on night of just PTSD. I mean, if there was a sound, I would have a massive reaction. There were tons of intrusive thoughts about sexual violence.

That was not fun.

On the Sunday, it was even worse. And because it was so dark and so bad, I can't actually go into all of the details, but it was absolutely horrific.

All I'll say is it took me 3 hours and 20 minutes just to have a shower because the interesting thing about depression is that because it's a low mood, it really impacts your energy levels. So then what happened was that around 2:00 pm, I finally decided, right, I am gonna have a shower. I'm gonna move heaven and earth to have a shower.

Well, the issue with that is that you need to get up from the sofa, then you need to go upstairs, then you need to get your clothes, get your towel, go into the bathroom, have a shower, get changed, etc. So, when you think about it, there are actually quite a few steps to anything that we do. And normally, I can normally do that all in, like, 20 minutes.

On Sunday, it took me 3 hours, 20 minutes to have a shower. I mean, that was just like... It took me 15 minutes just to get up the stairs. But then I actually had to come back down, so I was depressed about that, and it was ridiculous. It wasn't until I actually got in the shower at 5:00 pm, and I was just like, there's no point in me actually having a shower because it's 5:00, and to me, that's pointless. But I was like, I've been trying to do this for three hours. I've got to try.

And then, as the night went on, my mental health deteriorated. I broke my favorite mug. I smashed my favorite mug ever. Oh, God. I mean, I was actually quite devastated because it's this half-liter mug, which is just amazing. I've had it since 2019, since I first came to university, so I broke it, and then I just called my best friend, and we spoke for, like, an hour and a quarter, and then they were just like, "Right. You need to go home. You need to be around people," and, etc. So, I went...

I got back to my parents at half past midnight that night because me and my friend had a really heartfelt conversation. We'd had a really detailed one. Over the next two days, it was just constant depression. I was in and out of it because my parents work during the days, I was alone. Again, quite depressed. I couldn't really do anything. I had no energy. And then when they were back, it was fine because I was around people, so we could talk and stuff. Some stuff happened, but, I mean, that's just family.

And then I came back Wednesday because I saw my great aunt, who lives, like, nearby. Then I came back. Now, bear in mind, when my mug had shattered that night, I actually hadn't cleaned it up because I was just like... My mental health was so bad, I didn't have the capacity to actually clean it up. So, then I walked in at Wednesday, and I was just like, "Oh, my God, I'm back here. I've got to clean the mug. I've got to do tons of stuff." It took me an hour and 40 minutes just to clean that mug up. And that did not make me feel great. So that all happened.

Following on from this, yesterday, thankfully, I was able to do a few bits, but it was the energy levels that were really concerning me, because it was more of a thing about being in and out of depression and it basically not stopping and me not being able to reliably do stuff. I managed to do,

I don't know, let's say four hours of stuff. It really wasn't that, it was more, like, two and a half because I tried to do some stuff. It was so unproductive. And considering I'm normally used to doing seven hours with ease of different bits and pieces, that was quite shocking, and that was actually quite bad. Quite bad.

Unfortunately, today it's just been more of the same. There has been a lot of other very traumatic things going on in the background. But again, just to keep this podcast easy to listen to, or at least nice to listen to, I'm not gonna go into it.

I just had to pause the podcast because I thought I heard a noise outside. I thought I was going to have a bad reaction. And then I felt a massive hit of depression almost hit, though. So, I've got to keep going with this, otherwise, it's not gonna get done.

<u>What Triggered This Depressive Episode?</u>

As with all mental health conditions and difficulties, there are always goning be triggers and different aspects of this which make your mental health worse. Thankfully the only highlight of being depressed for seven days is that there are moments when you can actually think clearly. Oh, believe me, it happens extremely rarely, but they still happen.

As a result, the thing that really triggered my depression and the thing that keeps making me feel worse is one, of course, the sexual violence. Two, just being really lonely because I really don't have many friends. And my best friend, they went back to the midlands to see their family and spend time with their friends. As well as basically, everyone I know is out there doing really cool stuff. They're going away, they're having fun, they're seeing their other friends. And because of my PTSD, because of everything else, my issue is that I actually can't do the same.

Then there's also been some relationship stuff that were present. My best friends have been doing some relationship stuff. The LGBT+ society at my university, some of those conversations have been about past and current romantic relationships. And as someone who's been through sexual violence and also child abuse that was very homophobic, it's sort of like... I don't know if I can have that.

I know logically, I can, but I mean, like, there's gonna be so much work to actually do that for. So that really didn't help me. And also, PTSD is bad enough, but when it comes to going outside, that doesn't help. But also, something I've been finding a lot lately when I've been going outside, like, going shopping is a nightmare. For instance, I tend to forget a lot. I find it really hard to focus. So as you can expect, it's really tough going out. As well as in my mind, if you're going go out properly, like, you're going to go somewhere, you do tend to need a friend just to make it more, enjoyable. And you can do it as a shared experience.

But because my only real friend is actually not here at the moment, that's really tough.

<u>What Are The Challenges Of Experiencing Depression?</u>

Moreover, there are four main challenges which I'm really struggling with at the moment. The first one is an inability to watch stuff because it's bad enough when I'm in and out of being depressed, which is another major problem because I can just be going along, then a wave of depression can just hit me. It can also be linked to triggers. For example, I can be doing stuff, then an intrusive thought comes out that's really bad, quite traumatic. Then it knocks me for six, and then I get depressed, and I just lay on the stairs, on the sofa, or wherever I am for half an hour to an hour.

That's bad enough.

But when I'm depressed, I also have a massive problem. I can't watch stuff because I can't watch things on the TV or any streaming service because of sexual references and sex scenes, which never used to bother me whatsoever. But because that's how bad my mental health is at the moment, I can't watch any of that because it's too distressing, it's too triggering, which is annoying.

As a result, that was another reason why me and my best friend, we were on the phone for two and a quarter hours last night, as they were going through and compiling me a list of different series and films which I might be able to watch. But as I said to them, the main problem with that is, and just know I am extremely grateful that they did that. And I'm definitely gonna start watching some of it at some point. But some of it is that, yeah, you can have this list, you can have stuff to do, but you don't have the energy to actually do it, or you don't have the executive function to do it, which is an issue.

My third major challenging of experiencing depression is loss of pleasure. I've always known this is a depression symptom, but I've never had to experience it before. So, you can be doing stuff which you normally flat-out love. Like earlier today, I was flat-out loving doing some business stuff, but I wasn't enjoying it. It was just like, "Wow, this is actually quite boring." And sure, I sort of picked the more mundane aspects, but I still enjoy it. I still don't mind doing it. It's so important to me. I did not enjoy it.

Normally, I can do some reading, I can do a hobby, or I can do anything that I find really fun. No, not this week. I've just lost pleasure in most things, which is why I'm a bit concerned about this list that my friends put was they really love all of these programs. I don't wanna be the type of person who turns around and says, "Oh, thank you for doing this, but I really don't like this. I couldn't really care less about this." I'm pretty sure that's just the depression, but still, I don't want to do that even though I think that might be the case. But I will honestly try and enjoy this stuff.

But the main issue that I've been having is energy.

I know this is linked to a low mood, but the energy is that I really only have so much energy to be able to do stuff in the day. And I like to think of this in terms of spoons theory.

I've done an autism podcast episode maybe two years ago on spoons. So, the idea of this, and this is done by Christina someone, is that there's the idea that you only have so many spoons in terms of energy throughout the day, and every time you do something, you take away a spoon.

Let's say you have 10 spoons. Then what happens is that if you get up, then you could lose a spoon. If you go to work, if you have a shower, then you lose another spoon. Then if you get the kids ready, take them to school and get to work, that's another spoon. Then you have a really hard day at work, you have lots of meetings, you're working a very high-pressure job.

Let's say that actually takes five spoons away from you. That means you've only got two spoons left by the time you get home from work. But then let's say you've got to pick up the kids, and then you've got to do dinner. Both of those activities takes away your two spoons. Therefore, after you've cooked dinner, you might not have even served it up yet. You're completely exhausted, and you have no energy whatsoever. That's how you can think about energy levels in terms of spoons. That's something I found quite annoying yesterday, was that I was trying to do stuff, I wanted to do stuff, I had no energy after a while to do it whatsoever.

What am I trying to do to feel better?

I'm between a rock and a hard place.

The reason why I'm sort of in a rock and a hard place is quite simply because what I need is my rape counseling to start.

Nonetheless, that can't happen because I'm still on the waiting list. And my contact at this charity that I'm gonna be seen by, she's on annual leave until the 27th of August. That's five days away, at the very least. And in the meantime, I sort of keep suffering. Of course, it's not the charity's fault. This is just how life works. But she can't chase it, and she can't say, "Right, this person needs help ASAP. Can we please try and fit them in?"

So that's what I really, really need, and that's the sort of the solution. As soon as I start processing my rape and everything, then everything will get better. But until then, I am trying to do one or two things. I'm calling my best friend every night. We're having quite long conversations about each other's day, how I'm doing. And it's nice because it's social connection when I normally wouldn't get any social connection, which is quite a depressing fact, but that's just my life at the moment.

And then the only other thing which I'm really doing because this week's been quite difficult because, I mean, I can't go back to my parents again because they're away, and the whole point is that I'm lonely. So I can't just go somewhere else to be lonely. That defeats the whole point.

The only other thing I'm doing is I'm seeing my private therapist this week and next week. Both of us have agreed she's not a rape specialist. So, it's a case of me just talking to her. To be honest, like, I'm educating her about sexual violence because I've done so much research in the past 19 weeks. And I mean, it's nice just having someone to talk to, but I know it's sort of just sticking plaster on a very crumbling wall at the moment.

Oh, no. Actually, the only other last thing that I'm doing, though, is that next week, I'm going up to see my best friend in the midlands. So, we can see each other, we can go to this city that I've always wanted to go to, more for a laugh than anything else. But this got quite a reputation. And originally, I wanted to go by myself, but my best friend was like, "You can't. You just can't. Like, I don't think you'll be able to cope."

Of course, they said in much more polite terms than this, but I was just like, "You're right," and I'm really annoyed that I just can't go out without having a meltdown, without having an inability to make decisions and just getting overwhelmed, anxiety, PTSD, etc.

So, all fun, not.

As a result, I'm going up to see them, and their parents are going be there. And, I mean, I get on great with their parents. Their parents are lovely. And I might be able to meet their brother, which would be nice because I've been wanting to meet him for ages.

Ultimately, there's a lot's going on. I'm just trying to hang in there. And I don't know if this was a useful podcast episode, but I hope you got something out of it.

WHAT IS RAPE GRIEF?

Previously in the book, I've spoken a lot about how after my rape I researched sexual violence and Post-Traumatic Stress Disorder, because I wanted to understand what was happening to me, why I was having such extreme trauma responses and how I could heal. A lot of people who experience various types of trauma and mental health conditions do this and we all find various psychology facts, techniques and revelations that stick with us. For me, understanding rape grief was profoundly helpful, stabilizing and for the first time, it gave me words to describe a unique aspect of my rape and its consequences that no one had spoken about.

Therefore, in this chapter, you'll learn what is rape grief, why is this a powerful concept for rape survivors and more. If you enjoy learning about trauma recovery, healing from sexual violence and mental health, then this will be a great chapter for you.

What Is Rape Grief?

I think I found the concept of "rape grief" extremely powerful and important to me because it captured so much of what I was experiencing in the early days after my rape.

Therefore, grief is an intense emotional response to significant personal loss, and this painful emotional experience can include us wanting what we had lost back, concerns and fears about the future, as well as remorse for what we did and didn't do in a given moment.

Now everyone experiences grief at some point in their life and it isn't always around death despite popular opinion. For instance, yes, when someone dies we want our loved one back, we get fearful and concerned about how we will deal with them no longer being there in the future and we question whether they knew we loved them or not.

Equally, when it comes to jobs, we can yearn for that job promotion we never got, we can question if we said the right thing or not in an interview and we might question how we will work at the company now someone else is your boss or got the promotion.

We can experience grief around anything as long as there is that personal loss.

In addition, grief isn't a bad thing. Whilst it is a painful emotional experience, grief is a natural part of our lives and everyone will go through grief at some point in their life. It only becomes a clinical difficulty or "condition" if the grief causes clinically significant levels of psychological distress and impaired functioning in multiple domains of life. Like home life, work and school. As well as if it generates thoughts of self-harm, self-neglect and sometimes grief can be powerful enough to harm our own immune system.

As a result, when it comes to rape and other examples of sexual trauma, this "rape grief" follows the initial shock of the attack. This shock eventually leads to feelings of loss and fear amongst the sexual assault survivors because the survivors can lose a lot because of the attacker. For instance, survivors can feel a loss of their sense of safety and the following too:

- Loss of their lifestyle
- Loss of their physical and mental health.
- Loss of trust in other people
- Loss of their ability to work
- Loss of their hopes and dreams about the future
- Loss of virginity if their rape was their first sexual encounter
- Loss of important relationships. This is mainly if the attacker belongs to their family or group of friends.
- Loss of interest in physical intimacy
- Loss of ability to resume their normal roles like going to school.
- Loss of self-esteem

Personally, I don't believe there is a single one of those bullet points that I haven't experienced myself. Although, I will add in my book *I Am Survivor, Not A Victim* I do comment in there I firmly reject the idea that rape counts as losing your virginity. That was a very healing moment for me.

However, during the first 7 months of my rape, I felt a massive sense of loss because I had lost my sense of safety, my sense of hope about the future and the idea that I could ever work again or live a normal life. As well as I completely lost my ability to live my lifestyle and do my normal roles.

Moreover, when we consider how significant and how many of these sense of losses combine, it is no surprise that sexual assault survivors experience rape grief to extreme levels. The process of healing from rape grief isn't linear or easy or straightforward in the slightest. When I consider my own mental health journey, there have been major breakthrough moments where I thought my life was changed and healed forever, then new triggers, new fears and new experiences cause that all to change so this requires more healing. Trauma recovery ebbs and flows and it depends on the triggers that the client experiences as these act as reminders of what the client has lost.

In addition, one of the most annoying things but equally, it was this fact that I found healing. It is the fact that survivors experiencing rape grief will have conflicting emotions. For example, I remember this clearly because I had just found out about rape grief, I was sitting on the ugly red sofas in our shared house and me and my best friend had moved in together whilst the other two didn't until two months later. After a month, we were sitting on the sofa in the afternoon, I was depressed and I wanted to be alone. Yet I wanted to be with my best friend. I wanted to share everything with my best friend including the nightmares about them raping me (my best friend would never ever do that to me) but I didn't want to tell them because it would hurt them. And so many more conflicting emotions and thoughts.

I felt insane half the time.

And it is that simple realisation that it is okay for rape survivors to feel so many conflicting emotions.

It is normal. As difficult, insane and awful as you feel when you're experiencing all these different emotions, you are reacting normally to an extremely abnormal situation.

Why You Should NOT Tell A Rape Survivor "Time Heals All Wounds"?

There are a lot of different phrases and other rubbish that has been said to me as a rape survivor that have been the opposite of helpful. I cover a whole bunch of them in my book *I Am A Survivor, Not A Victim* but I flat out hate the phrase "Time Heals All Wounds" and "Give It Time".

Interestingly when it comes to this "well-intentioned" advice, this isn't helpful but it isn't done with malice. These pieces of advice simply reflect myths and misconceptions that people have about trauma and rape. Since this bad advice can create self-doubts within survivors as survivors can get concerned and fearful and their mental health can be further harmed if they believe they should be healing more because it's been months or more since their attack.

This was one of my major struggles after my rape.

In addition, "time heals all wounds" is a bad phrase because whilst it takes time to heal from grief and trauma, what actually impacts healing the most is the degree of support and acceptance that the survivor receives in the long term. I completely agree with this because it seriously wasn't the time since I was raped that healed me. It was living in a supportive and loving environment as well as my rape counselling. It was the support I got that made the difference, not the time.

Furthermore, if you tell a rape survivor to "just give it time" then this can seriously trivialise the gravity of the situation for the survivor and everything they are going through. As well as "just giving it time" doesn't help the emotional turmoil and hell that the survivor is going through and it makes the survivor feel powerless. Due to it explains to survivors that it doesn't matter what they do or how they try to cope, time (a factor that they do not control) will determine how long it takes for them to heal.

This suggests to the survivor that waiting is the only way to cope instead of any deliberate action.

Why You Should NOT Say "Don't Think About It" To A Rape Survivor?

When my mental health really got bad during August 2024 and I had to go back to my parents to stay with them for a few days, I remember one of them saying "Just don't think about it" and it annoyed me so much. I flat out hate this silly saying or piece of advice. Since the issue with "don't think about it" is that you are telling someone to ignore or bury these powerful feelings and it doesn't allow a survivor to create an emotional space where they can process what happened to them and heal. Instead "just don't think about it" encourages the survivor to not feel a certain way so this denies the survivor the right to truly feel how they feel and it can even imply that the survivor isn't good enough because they can't control their emotions.

This is similar to why "keep busy" isn't a good piece of advice either. Due to why I strongly encourage survivors to do self-care things that make them happy, give them structure and purpose. It is important not to "keep busy" because keeping a survivor busy doesn't make them "snap out" of the trauma, it simply allows them to escape processing and healing from what happened to them. I always like to mention that you can only go without processing trauma for so long. If you don't deal with your trauma, your trauma will deal with you. This can be depression, a mental breakdown, severe Post-Traumatic Stress Disorder (as if any form of PTSD isn't severe) amongst others.

Of course, like I mentioned in the last paragraph, there are mental health benefits to having structure and engaging in normal activities and routines. Like I found it extremely helpful during the worst of my PTSD to have my Outreach work at the university, my writing and my business. Then again, this is only useful if the survivor has a good support system around themselves, because keeping busy does not and will never eliminate the intrusive thoughts, feelings and other trauma responses.

"Keeping busy" is only ever a temporary distraction and trauma will be dealt with. It can be by the survivor with a social support network and therapy, but the trauma can make you deal with it.

What Are The Outcomes of This Misguided Advice?

When dealing with rape grief, this so-called advice that people give rape survivors just isn't helpful and it can be very harmful to their healing and recovery. For example, it can lead to the survivor becoming guarded in expressing how they feel to others out of concern for being judged or being hurt further. This is what happened to me because I only really open up to my best friend because I know they would never ever hurt me. It's only recently I've started to become less guarded around my family and a new friend that I'm making.

In addition, this unhelpful advice can make a survivor feel guilty about feeling or acting or not in a certain way. As well as this silly advice suggests that rape survivors should ignore or bury their powerfully distressing and negative emotions. This leads to the survivor becoming confused about what they're feeling or how they're expected to feel.

Ultimately, the reason why this is so harmful to survivors is because trauma healing is all about living in an environment that is supportive and allows the survivor to be honest with themselves and get in touch with their true emotions. If a survivor lives in an environment that isn't supportive and encourages denial, guilt as well as an inability to share their feelings with other people then they will not heal and their mental health will die.

Their sense of rape grief will only be prolonged and as a survivor myself, that is something we cannot allow.

That is why supportive friends, family and therapists are the most important thing in trauma healing. Especially after sexual violence which for me is the ultimate act of betrayal and violation. A violation so severe it creates an immense sense of loss and grief that must be overcome in order to heal.

It might feel impossible to heal from sexual violence but it is possible. It might be cheesy but this always makes me smile. I don't know who said it but I like the saying "Nothing is impossible because impossible actually reads I'm Possible,"

And that is even truer when it comes to sexual trauma recovery.

CONCLUSION: YOU WILL HAVE YOUR HEALING MOMENT

Right now I am 100% sure I am meant to be doing my Seminar Report for my Neuropsychology Ageing module that is due in in less than 3 days, but I wanted to write this conclusion first. Due to it has been at least 6 weeks since I last wrote in this book, or I did any sort of sexual violence writing because my mental health has simply been too bad.

Yet I had my Healing Moment today.

What is a Healing Moment I hear you ask, well originally this conclusion was meant to be about how Therapy Is Hope, and therapy is an absolute must for any survivor, and this moment only came about because I'm in therapy and I got back to reading *Healing Sexual Trauma Workbook by Erika Shershun* today.

However, that original idea for the conclusion never felt concrete enough and at the time, I never really believed it myself and it didn't feel right me writing something I didn't believe in. Therefore, I wanted to try something else because I have had a Healing Moment.

A Healing Moment is when something just snapped inside you and your entire world changes for the better. It does not mean you are "cured" (whatever that means and that isn't how mental health works anyway), it does not mean everything will be plain sailing anymore and it does not mean you will never be in pain again.

I am actually tearing up as I write this section.

A Healing Moment simply means you realise that there is hope that everything can get better, you are definitely not a victim and if everyone is telling you that life gets better (hopefully they are or they shouldn't be in your life) that you realise it and internalise it as the truth that it is.

In addition, Healing Moments look different for everyone and what mine looks like will probably be completely different to yours. Your Healing Moment might be tiny, yours might be massive, yours might make you cry or it might not.

It is *your* Healing Moment for a reason.

As a result, my Healing Moment happened today because I tried to kill myself twice last night in two different ways. I also found out I hurt my best friend by accident and I had done something wrong with a housemate that really hurt them. It was truly awful and I tried to kill myself.

Moreover, my mental health has been so bad for so long that I just couldn't see another way out. I've self-harmed, been suicidal for months and I have an eating disorder and on and on and on.

So I tried to kill myself.

Thankfully, my housemates subtly rallied around me and when I woke up this morning, I still felt suicidal but the idea of me hurting my best friend. Who I love romantically, who has always been there for me and the one person I have lived for for so long, I realised I had two choices.

Either I could keep trying to kill myself and ruin my best friend's life forever or I could find a new way of healing.

My best friend went to the gym with a new friend that I've made and getting close with, so I went into the library and started reading *Healing Sexual Trauma Workbook* again. I have not read this book in months because I used the possible "excuse" that my mental health was too bad that I didn't want to try it.

I had forgotten how great this book is for me personally. This book truly makes me feel understood and validated.

There was a simple exercise that changed everything.

The first chapter of the book focuses on feeling safe in your own skin and after the first few pages, the exercises focus on helping you to focus on the *feelings* of safety. For example, what does your body feel like when you feel unsafe then there's another question on what does your body feel like when you feel safe.

Those are not the actual wording of the questions and there are questions on thoughts during these times too, but you get the gist.

As a result, this is what I wrote for my answers:

When I feel unsafe, my body panics. My breathing increases but goes shallow, I shake and my thoughts go a million miles an hour.

When I feel safe, my body just feels 100% relaxed and untensed.

Now my counsellor has been wanting me to focus on my body for ages but maybe I was resistant to it, maybe I needed it to be worded differently, but that did not work for me.

However, me thinking and writing down how my body actually felt when I was safe was brilliant. It got me to label this feeling so I could savour it when I felt safe and I could focus on getting my body to that state.

In hindsight I did some weird stuff to savour that feeling. I went and sat in two different toilets at the university and I went into a very busy Co-Op (just think corner shop on campus) and each time I focused on feeling completely relaxed and untensed. I savoured that wonderful feeling of being relaxed and my body just not caring or being in survival mode.

I am relaxed because I am safe. I am always safe.

Then of course, I felt depressed and bad for the next few hours because I felt awful about hurting my best friend. Granted, they had already forgotten about it at that point, but I read a bit more of the workbook.

I did some more exercises but I did something interesting. I focused on feeling 100% relaxed in my own home in Canterbury with my three housemates in the house.

I realised ever since mid-August when I had my mental health collapse and everything happened. I had not felt safe in this house, this has never been my home and I know I haven't enjoyed living with two extra housemates as much as I love them. In a way, I suppose I have never felt safe in this house either.

I 100% relaxed today in my own home and I could do it so easily.

And this is my home now. I belong in this house with my three housemates, I belong in Canterbury and I am not a problem and all the million other things my mind tries to tell me.

I am not a problem.

It is a lovely feeling to know that I am home.

Something else I've been struggling with lately was my best friend has been focusing a lot more on another housemate who is going through hell-and-back at the moment. Also, my best friend deals with us in extremely different ways and I think I have been a lot more jealous than I want to admit.

My mind has tried to twist it repeatedly as my best friend not liking me, hating me and my best friend wanting not to be friends anymore.

But the following message highlights a large part of my Healing Moment:

I'm really sorry I'm chronically insecure a lot of the time because you're all I have in terms of real support.

And that it's taken me so long to realise that you focusing more on, spending more time with and doing more tasks for R isn't a reflection of you not liking, you hating me or our friendship breaking down so much so you're a carer, not a friend.

Mine and R's mental health manifests in very different ways and you are more comfortable with them anyway. R needs the constant help and support right now and for the next few months, and that's okay. Because you've offered the same to me since June without me realising it and now you can't be in two places at once.

I need to focus on my healing for me and I know you are always there for me when I need it most, but now I need to take back control because otherwise something might genuinely happen to this friendship without even one of us seeing it until it's too late.

So what I'm saying is... Thank you for being the most amazing and patient friend I can ever ask for. And I understand what I need to do to heal now a little better.

You're still there for me and I am ALWAYS there for you and it will still hurt like hell at times for me because of my trauma, but I now realise I don't need you to make me feel safe in my own home.

And here with R, L and especially you, you're all my home.

(Yes I teared up writing this. I hope this makes sense and I don't come off as a dick)

Thankfully, my best friend found that message really cute and sweet, and I need to send one to R and L later (don't you just love how creative I am with pseudonyms).

Ultimately, my Healing Moment boiled down to finally, finally realising that I am worthy of people liking me for me. I don't need to think I'm a burden, I don't need to think unless I am a certain way I'll be safe and I don't need to rely on other people to make me feel safe, because I am safe. And as long as I focus on that 100% relaxed and untensed feeling in my body then I know, I will truly know that I am safe.

Since when I'm distressed, it doesn't matter what I tell my body or tell myself, unless I *feel* safe in my own skin then I won't be safe and I will continue to be distressed.

That's why in the next book that focuses on therapy and rape counselling, I have a lot of new and exciting unofficial tips and tricks to share with you, because my life is worth living.

It will never be perfect, I will always carry this rape trauma with me and I will always be distressed at times. But I no longer have to feel unsafe in my own body and house and around other people, I am safe. I am loved. I am me.

And that's a great thing to me.

So I hope after reading this book as distressing as some parts would have been to both of us, you can see three things. Firstly, in whenever you are experiencing you are never alone, that as horrific as the past 6 months have been for me, there is light in the darkness and actually, there is healing.

It might take months or years and a lot more therapy than you ever imagined but it is possible to heal.

And never forget you are loved and worthy and you are so amazing.

You're not a victim, you are a survivor.

REFERENCES AND FURTHER READING

Linehan, M. M. (1993). Skills training manual for treating borderline personality disorder. Guilford press.

American Journal of Psychiatry

Annual Review of Psychology

Au, T. M., Dickstein, B. D., Comer, J. S., Salters-Pedneault, K., & Litz, B. T. (2013). Co-occurring posttraumatic stress and depression symptoms after sexual assault: A latent profile analysis. *Journal of affective disorders*, *149*(1-3), 209-216.

Biological Psychiatry

Brown, A. L., Testa, M., & Messman-Moore, T. L. (2009). Psychological consequences of sexual victimization resulting from force, incapacitation, or verbal coercion. *Violence against women*, *15*(8), 898-919.

Bullock, C. M., & Beckson, M. (2011). Male victims of sexual assault: Phenomenology, psychology, physiology. *Journal of the American Academy of Psychiatry and the Law Online*, *39*(2), 197-205.

Campbell, R. (2009). Trauma, Violence, & Abuse, Vol. 10, No. 3.

Campus Sexual Assault Study, 2007; Matthew Kimble, Andrada Neacsiu, et. Al, *Risk of Unwanted Sex for College Women: Evidence for a Red Zone*, Journal of American College Health (2008).

Canadian Journal of Psychiatry

Centers for Disease Control and Prevention. Intimate Partner Violence, Sexual Violence, and Stalking Among Men.

Cunningham, S., Hudson, C. C., & Harkness, K. (2021). Social media and depression symptoms: a meta-analysis. *Research on child and adolescent psychopathology*, *49*(2), 241-253.

David Cantor, Bonnie Fisher, Susan Chibnall, Reanna Townsend, et. al. Association of American Universities (AAU), *Report on the AAU Campus Climate Survey on Sexual Assault and Sexual Misconduct* (January 17, 2020). ("Victim services agency" is defined in this study as a "public or privately funded organization that provides victims with support and services to aid their recovery, offer protection, guide them through the criminal justice process, and assist with obtaining restitution." RAINN presents this data for educational purposes only, and strongly recommends using the citations to review any and all sources for more information and detail.)

Davies, M. (2002). Male sexual assault victims: A selective review of the literature and implications for support services. *Aggression and violent behavior*, *7*(3), 203-214.

Department of Justice, Office of Justice Programs, Bureau of Justice Statistics, Rape and Sexual Victimization Among College-Aged Females, 1995-2013 (2014).

Department of Justice, Office of Justice Programs, Bureau of Justice Statistics, Campus Law Enforcement, 2011-2012 (2015).

Diagnostic and Statistical Manual of Mental Disorders, Fifth Edition

DiMarco, D., Mizzoni, J., & Savitz, R. (2022). On the sexual assault of men. *Sexuality & Culture*, 1-9.

Dworkin, E. R., Menon, S. V., Bystrynski, J., & Allen, N. E. (2017). Sexual assault victimization and psychopathology: A review and meta-analysis. *Clinical psychology review*, *56*, 65-81.

Fuchs, S. F. (2004). Male sexual assault: Issues of arousal and consent. *Clev. St. L. Rev.*, *51*, 93.

Hippocampal Volume in Women Victimized by Childhood Sexual Abuse.

https://www.eurekalert.org/news-releases/630084

https://www.psychologytoday.com/us/conditions/post-traumatic-stress-disorder

https://www.verywellmind.com/symptoms-of-ptsd-after-a-rape-2797203#toc-symptoms-of-ptsd-after-sexual-assault

i. National Crime Victimization Survey, 1995-2013 (2015); ii. Department of Justice, Office of Justice Programs, Bureau of Justice Statistics, Rape and Sexual Victimization Among College-Aged Females, 1995-2013 (2014).

Jarero, I., & Artigas, L. (2016). Instruction for the Butterfly Hug Method.

Journal of Psychopharmacology

Journal of Traumatic Stress

Jubb, H. (2017). The effectiveness of self-soothing techniques for people with PTSD in secure units. Mental Health Practice, 20(5).

Khalfa, S., BELLA, S. D., Roy, M., Peretz, I., & Lupien, S. J. (2003). Effects of relaxing music on salivary cortisol level after psychological stress. Annals of the New York Academy of Sciences, 999(1), 374-376.

Malgaroli, M., Calderon, A., & Bonanno, G. A. (2021). Networks of major depressive disorder: A systematic review. *Clinical Psychology Review*, *85*, 102000.

Mohammed, G. F., & Hashish, R. K. (2015). Sexual violence against females and its impact on their sexual function. *Egyptian Journal of Forensic Sciences*, *5*(3), 96-102.

Mok, M. C., Schwannauer, M., & Chan, S. W. (2020). Soothe ourselves in times of need: A qualitative exploration of how the feeling of 'soothe'is understood and experienced in everyday life. Psychology and Psychotherapy: Theory, Research and Practice, 93(3), 587-620.

National Center for PTSD, U.S. Department of Veterans Affairs

National Comorbidity Survey Replication

National Institute of Mental Health

National Institutes of Health - National Library of Medicine

O'Callaghan, E., Shepp, V., Ullman, S. E., & Kirkner, A. (2019). Navigating sex and sexuality after sexual assault: A qualitative study of survivors and informal support providers. *The Journal of Sex Research*, *56*(8), 1045-1057.

Panisch, L. S., & Tam, L. M. (2020). The role of trauma and mental health in the treatment of chronic pelvic pain: a systematic review of the intervention literature. *Trauma, Violence, & Abuse*, *21*(5), 1029-1043.

Petreca, V. G., & Burgess, A. W. (2024). Long-Term Psychological and Physiological Effects of Male Sexual Trauma. *The Journal of the American Academy of Psychiatry and the Law*, *52*(1), 23-32.

Psychiatric Clinics of North America

Rice, S. M., Easton, S. D., Seidler, Z. E., & Oliffe, J. L. (2022). Sexual abuse and mental ill health in boys and men: what we do and don't know. *BJPsych open*, *8*(4), e110.

Shorey, S., Ng, E. D., & Wong, C. H. (2022). Global prevalence of depression and elevated depressive symptoms among adolescents: A systematic review and meta-analysis. *British Journal of Clinical Psychology*, *61*(2), 287-305.

Smith, M. M., Sherry, S. B., Ray, C., Hewitt, P. L., & Flett, G. L. (2021). Is perfectionism a vulnerability factor for depressive symptoms, a complication of depressive symptoms, or both? A meta-analytic test of 67 longitudinal studies. *Clinical Psychology Review*, *84*, 101982.

Steffen, P. R., Bartlett, D., Channell, R. M., Jackman, K., Cressman, M., & Bills, J. (2021). Integrating breathing techniques into psychotherapy to improve HRV: which approach is best?. Frontiers in Psychology, 12, 624254.

Thomas, J. C., & Kopel, J. (2023). Male victims of sexual assault: a review of the literature. *Behavioral Sciences*, *13*(4), 304.

University of Kent Student Service Instagram Post on 16th February 2024

US Department of Health and Human Services

Vidal, J., & Soldevilla, J. M. (2023). Effect of compassion-focused therapy on self-criticism and self-soothing: A meta-analysis. British Journal of Clinical Psychology, 62(1), 70-81.

Whiteley, C. (2022) Psychology of Relationships: The Social Psychology of Friendships, Romantic Relationships and More. CGD Publishing. England.

Whiteley, C. (2024) CBT For Anxiety: A Clinical Psychology Introduction To Cognitive Behavioural Therapy For Anxiety Disorders. CGD Publishing. England.

Whiteley, C. (2024) CBT For Depression: A Clinical Psychology Introduction To Cognitive Behavioural Therapy For Depression. CGD Publishing. England.

Whiteley, C. (2024) Social Media Psychology: A Guide To Clinical Psychology, Cyberpsychology and Mental Health. CGD Publishing. England.

Whiteley, C. (2024) Working With Children and Young People: A Guide To Clinical Psychology, Mental Health and Psychotherapy. CGD Publishing. England.

Widanaralalage, B. K., Hine, B. A., Murphy, A. D., & Murji, K. (2022). "I didn't feel i was a victim": a phenomenological analysis of the experiences of male-on-male survivors of rape and sexual abuse. *Victims & Offenders*, *17*(8), 1147-1172.

Wright, J. (2009). Self-Soothing—A recursive intrapsychic and relational process: The contribution of the Bowen theory to the process of self-soothing. Australian and New Zealand Journal of Family Therapy, 30(1), 29-41.

HEALING AS A SURVIVOR

CONNOR WHITELEY

DEDICATION

Thank you to all my readers without you I couldn't do what I love.

INTRODUCTION

This is a book about healing, recovery and thriving after being raped and experiencing sexual violence.

You don't need to have read my past two books on sexual violence to read and enjoy this one. *I Am Not A Victim, I Am A Survivor* is a very personal book that details my mental health, my trauma responses and how I navigated life for the first five months after my rape before my specialist counselling started. This book might provide a lot of context for why I needed this specialist counselling so badly but it is not needed to appreciate this book.

Whereas *Breaking The Silence* is a psychology-focused book on the research, facts and figures of sexual violence so why does it happen, what makes men and women commit sexual violence against others, how can we support survivors and more.

Both books are brilliant additions to this one.

What Does This Book Cover?

Healing As A Survivor is a deeply personal, moving and potentially heartwarming book about my recovery and healing from sexual trauma. It covers each of my specialist counselling sessions, the insights I learnt about myself that allowed me to heal and a lot of useful techniques and concepts that I learnt along the way.

Nothing in this book is any sort of official mental health advice, but I still talk about everything that I found helpful and all the extra things that I was going through as I healed from sexual trauma.

If you want to understand what it's like to recover from PTSD, anxiety, hypervigilance, depression and more trauma responses that sexual violence can cause, then this is a brilliant book for you.

Who Is This Book For?

Mainly, I wrote this book for survivors and for anyone who wants to understand what survivors go through and what it takes to heal. For instance, friends, family and therapists working with survivors of sexual violence.

Survivors might find this insightful, engaging and very relatable book useful because it clearly shows that recovery is possible. It isn't easy, it isn't linear and it can be painful at times, but healing is possible. Also, this book will show that what you're experiencing isn't abnormal, strange or messed-up.

You are trying to deal with an extremely abnormal situation so what is happening to you is normal given the situation.

This book helps to show you how recovery can happen, how counselling works and it demystifies the process for you.

Loved ones and friends could find this book useful too because this book helps to show you what your friends and loved one might be thinking, feeling and experiencing. As well as you can show this engaging and conversational book to the survivor in your life so they know that healing is possible.

In addition, therapists might find this book a useful guide to some of the concepts you might want to explore with clients, and this book will help you gain a deeper understanding of what it takes to recover from sexual violence. This includes the psychoeducational and physical aspects related to the trauma.

Everyone has the potential to find this book interesting, heartbreaking and useful.

Who Am I?

In my other psychology books, I include this section because I like to know who the author is so I know the information is coming from a reliable and good source, but I'm including this section for a different reason.

I'm Connor Whiteley, the internationally bestselling author of over 40 psychology books, I am the host of *The Psychology World Podcast,* a weekly show exploring a new psychology topic each week and delivering the latest psychology news. Available on all major podcast apps and YouTube. As well as I am a psychology graduate who studied a Clinical Psychology undergraduate and Masters at the University of Kent, England.

I am a survivor, not a victim.

I love psychology, spending time with my friends, going out and living. Also, I like fiction books of all types especially books by Dean Wesley Smith, and I like watching films with my friends.

I am a normal person with a normal, fun, exciting life but when I was raped, he took everything from me.

Originally, I thought I was a weak victim but I am not. I have healed from what he did to me.

I am a survivor, not a victim, but it wasn't always that way.

This is my story of recovery and this is my truth.

MEETING THE THERAPIST, CONTRACTS AND MORE: LESSONS FROM A GREAT FIRST SESSION

This book is going to be an honest account of my therapy sessions starting with my first to my twelfth specialist counselling session designed to support sexual violence survivors to heal and thrive.

Of course I'm not going to pretend that I wasn't nervous, scared and a little numb before my first session. Since if you've read my previous book *I Am Not A Victim, I Am A Survivor,* then you know the month before my rape counselling started, my mental health just died.

I had already been experiencing severe Post-Traumatic Stress Disorder, severe panic attacks, nightmares and on and on and on. My mental health was a mess so I was very nervous about starting counselling because I needed the support more than ever, and a part of me was scared that it wasn't going to work.

I was scared that if my counselling didn't work then I was going to be "messed up" for life and there was no hope that I would be able to survive, heal and thrive from my trauma. Also, I was scared that if that happened then He had won, my rapist had won over me and I would never be able to move on from the messed-up rubbish he did to me that night.

That was why I was scared and nervous about my first counselling session.

In addition, the weirdest thing about it was that even though my mental health was dead in the month of August 2024 and that continued for a while afterwards. I still placed so much hope on getting my rape counselling and I was always waiting for that phone call telling me when my first appointment was.

However, I remember when the call came, it was 10:30 in the morning on the Wednesday before my first session. I was grateful for it and I thanked the lady on the phone, but I felt numb and I couldn't feel anything.

I couldn't *feel* happiness, relief or any sort of emotion whatsoever, and that was odd. It was weird to me that for the past three months, I had been waiting and fighting to be okay enough to have these sessions that I was expecting to feel more when I received them.

I did not. I felt absolutely dead inside.

Therefore, I'm telling you this because I want you to know that it's okay if you react to finding getting professional help in a counterintuitive way. Some people will cry in happiness, some people will feel so hopeful and other people will feel the best they have in months because they've finally got an appointment.

However, it's okay if you don't. After experiencing sexual violence, it's okay if you experience emotions differently to how your brain tells you you should logically feel. If you feel nervous, scared or even concerned about your therapy or counselling. That is okay.

It is just your body and your brain reacting in a normal way to an extremely abnormal situation.

Sexual violence is never ever your fault and there is nothing you could have done to stop or change what happened to you. The fault always lies with whoever did it to you.

You never should have had to go to therapy because your sexual violence experience never should have happened, and that's on your attacker.

It is never on you.

What Happened During My First Session?

Meeting The Counsellor

I already mentioned that I was nervous about my first counselling session and thankfully it turned out I had absolutely nothing to be nervous about. Since my counsellor was a really lovely lady, let's call her Kay (a fake name) for the purpose of this book. She was really kind, happy and positive person who happened to be a humanistic counsellor.

In other words, she focuses on you doing a lot of your own healing outside of sessions, and she believes that you already know the answers to your own healing and thriving, sometimes you just need a little support getting to those answers for yourself.

In the next chapter, you'll learn about what Person-Centred Therapy is, because that therapy contains a lot of ideas that humanistic counsellors draw on and use in their work.

Personally, as a clinical psychology Masters student at the time of writing and a survivor, I really like this model. Since it's very client-focused so I know I'm in control, she is working *with* me and never ever against me and it's an empowering model. I have all the answers, I do know myself and I am strong enough to heal. I just need some guidance and help from a counsellor.

That's why I am an empowered survivor, not a victim.

Moreover, I want to mention here that even if you feel like you cannot be an empowered survivor, and only a victim that has connotations of being weak, helpless and broken. I want you to know that I used to think the same, and I talk a lot more about my own experiences of powerlessness and all the mental health consequences of my rape in my book.

Yet I want you to know that as you continue to heal, get professional help and you continue your trauma recovery. You can become empowered and you can stop seeing yourself as a victim.

The Contract, Confidentiality And Explaining Specialist Counselling

Now I have to admit that as a clinical psychology student, I always rather enjoy these first sessions because I know how important they are in developing what's known as the therapeutic alliance. This is essentially the relationship you have with your therapist or counsellor and how good this relationship is can be a powerful predictor in the success of the therapy.

Nonetheless, it's impressive how you need to create a good enough relationship in the space of 50 minutes that the client trusts you enough that they want to come back, and trust you enough that they're willing to open up to you.

Due to it is perfectly acceptable for you not to open up with someone who you don't like or aren't comfortable with. If that is the case then you might need a new counsellor or therapist.

Therefore, when it came to my counsellor, we spoke a little about ourselves so we could get to know each other a little more. As well as this is the ultimate aim of the first session, it is all about establishing that therapeutic relationship and for you both to get to know each other, and how the therapy will work.

In terms of the contract, you will have to sign a counselling contract because this lays out how the therapy sessions work, how your allocation works, what happens if you miss a session, what happens if you need to make a complaint and so on.

This might sound scary but this is a simple document that is designed to protect you as the client and the mental health service.

My counsellor explained the contract in a very easy-to-understand way and it was really nice.

She did something very clever too.

This might sound simple but in my future clinical work, I am definitely doing this with my own clients. She left the contract on the table next to the chair I was sitting on, so I could simply reach over to the contract, get it and read it. The counsellor did not need to move from her chair and she did not need to get close to me in any fashion.

As a survivor, I flat out love that little technique. It made me feel really safe, protected and I was much happier to engage with her. It showed me that she did respect me, she wasn't going to presume anything about my boundaries and she was going to give me the space I needed to heal and process what He had done to me.

I respect that a lot.

Especially, in my traumatised state, I would have had a panic attack, my nervous system would have activated and I would be way too focused on survival instead of the therapy if she had come anywhere near me. That didn't happen so I was happier and calmer.

After explaining the contract, she moved on to the confidentiality section of the first session, which is always good. It basically reaffirms that everything you say within session is completely confidential and will not leave the therapy room unless in a few situations. She will need to tell a safeguarding professional if I am experiencing ongoing sexual violence. As well as in mental health practice, there is something called "Supervision". In supervision, a mental health professional might talk about their caseload with a supervisor to get ideas about how to help the client or if a case is negatively impacting their mental health then they can talk about it in supervision.

In essence, supervision is all about the mental health professional making sure they are okay in the long term so they can keep helping clients.

Information On The Sexual Violence Itself

You don't cover the rape or sexual violence itself in your therapy, at least not directly.

I know for the vast majority of sexual assault survivors, they are very concerned, nervous and anxious about specialist counselling or therapy because they're concerned that they will have to relive the memories of their sexual trauma. Thankfully, in rape counselling, you never have to tell the counsellor exactly what happened to you in any detail.

Since the main focus of rape counselling is that you focus on stabilising yourself, your nervous system and process the trauma in indirect ways that means you never have to reveal exactly what happened to you.

Personally, I was very surprised about this aspect of the counselling, because I was "happy" to talk about what happened to me. Especially because I thought that was critical to the therapy, but as the sessions have gone on I realised how that wasn't correct. I have done so much healing and therapy working without having to explain my rape in any detail.

The closest I've come to explaining to my counsellor what exactly happened to me was when I was telling her about the situations that led to me meeting my attacker. Then again, she never asked for that information and I only told her because it was useful for context in something I wanted help with.

In addition, at the time of writing, which is a little while after this first session, I helped a good friend of mine access the same rape crisis centre as me. Their main concern was having to tell the counsellor, effectively a stranger, everything that happened to them.

Therefore, when I told my friend that they wouldn't need to reveal any detail of what happened to them. They were a lot more relaxed and happy to progress with the self-referral.

I want *you* to know that you never have to tell your counsellor anything you don't want to. You are in full control of the counselling.

<u>Other Things Of Note</u>

To start wrapping up this chapter, I wanted to mention some of the other things we spoke about in case they're useful to you for context.

My favourite thing that we spoke about was "call it what *you* want. Only you can decide". If you've read my other sexual violence focused books then you'll probably be aware that I've experienced a lot of invalidation surrounding my rape. A lot of people refused to allow me to call it rape and they only wanted me to go by legal definitions because legal definitions made it less severe and less scary for *them*.

Because I was *only* sexually assaulted, I wasn't raped.

In reality, I call it rape because if the guy's dick worked it would have been considering what he tried to do.

Anyway, experiencing constant invalidation and having people deny that I was raped really took a toll on my mental health. It made me feel very isolated, slightly insane and I was gaslighted because I was going through all these PTSD, depression and anxiety symptoms but people were saying the root cause never happened.

That really hurt me.

Therefore, I brought this up in the counselling session and she mentioned that it doesn't matter what other people call it, because it happened to me, it's impacting me and I am the one that is hurting. Only I get to decide what I call it and that thankfully reinforced the conclusion I had already drawn on my own, because as I've researched sexual violence survivors more and more. I've realised how interchangeably the definitions are and can be used depending on how comfortable a survivor is with a particular word.

Moreover, there was a lot of talk about my trauma responses (both sexual and childhood trauma) and she mentioned the 5-Steps to mindfulness. Which is a very good technique focusing on setting you to name 5 things you see, 4 things you can touch, 3 things you can hear, 2 or 1 things you can smell and taste. That helps you to ground yourself in the present moment instead of any trauma memories or flashbacks or trauma responses you're experiencing.

I really do recommend that technique.

Finally, something very small that I appreciated was she reinforced something I was doubting. Ever since I was raped and since my own mental health died as my psychological distress grew to such intensity I was experiencing hourly trauma reactions. Even going outside was problematic. I doubted that I could ever be a clinical psychologist in the future because whenever I heard someone's mental health experience it would cause me extreme levels of distress and it would trigger a very wide range of responses in me.

As a result, I had considered going into academic research because I enjoy it, I'm good at it and I know how to run studies very well. By the end of April 2025, I'm hoping to have run 5 studies in total independent of my Masters, because me and my supervisor at the university get on great so she lets me research a bunch of topics related to transgender mental health.

Nonetheless, at the time, I was scared that this wasn't a valid career path because I didn't know if it was important and I was scared or if this was just a trauma reaction. Thankfully, she reminded me how important research is in psychotherapy and counselling work. Our treatments and interventions have to be evidence-based because it is the evidence-based approaches that save lives.

She made me feel a lot better about that decision.

Ultimately, the first session was brilliant because she made me feel listened to, respected and I could see she was someone I could work with. Sure, I knew it wouldn't be easy in the future and I would struggle because of my trauma but I was interested and driven to heal.

And that was only possible because of a great first session.

WHAT ARE SOME SELF-SOOTHING STRATEGIES?

In the last therapy reflection, I mentioned how my counsellor wanted me to start focusing on self-soothing techniques so I could do something to help myself relax when I get distressed. Now the issue I had with this therapy conversation was that I had no idea what self-soothing actually involved and I had no clue how to self-soothe.

I have never ever been good at it before so I needed to learn. Hence, the research and chapter that you're about to read, and these techniques and a few more that my counsellor gave me have been rather life changing.

As a result, the ability to self-soothe is beyond critical to mental health because it allows us to calm ourselves down, we can relax and return to our window of tolerance. Yet some people aren't able to self-soothe so to relax, calm down and maintain their mental health they need others to soothe them. This is a strategy that works for a time but it is far from perfect and it doesn't solve anything.

I struggle a lot with my inability to self-soothe because this was the focus of the topic this week in my specialist counselling session. Therefore, in this chapter, you'll learn what is self-soothing, how can you self-soothe and why it's so important to your mental health.

What Is Self-Soothing?

A person's ability to self-soothe is their efforts to calm themselves down when they're in an emotional state as proposed by Wright (2009). As well as this is beyond critical for our psychological well-being because it helps people to stay calm and emotionally regulated.

I know this is a massive issue for me because my ability to self-soothe has always been bad, but after my rape, over time it got worse and worse. Currently, at the time of writing, I essentially cannot self-soothe at all, which is a massive problem. This is why I'm focusing on this in therapy.

Moreover, a lot of people learn how to self-soothe when we're babies because when our caregivers soothe us, we internalise this soothing and learn how to do it ourselves (Wright, 2009). Yet there are a wide range of reasons why people (like me) are unable to learn these self-soothing skills and use them as adults.

Thankfully, it is perfectly possible to learn how to self-soothe as an adult and that's the focus of this chapter. Granted, self-soothing requires self-insight, we need to develop our skills and we need to be able to effectively use these skills in an effort to calm ourselves down.

This is an important bit I believe because we can read and learn everything we want to about self-soothing. Yet unless we practice and get better *over time* then we will never actually improve our self-soothing skills.

What Are Some Self-Soothing Strategies?

Take Some Deep Breaths

I wanted to start us off with an extremely simple one because I know from personal experience, it is this extremely simple and extremely useful technique that we tend to forget the most. As well as I want to take advantage of the primacy and recency effect. Therefore, whenever we want to self-soothe we need to deactivate our sympathetic nervous system. This means we need to activate our parasympathetic nervous system because this nervous system helps to stop the fight-or-flight response and helps us to calm down.

Thankfully, the parasympathetic nervous system can be very easily activated by taking a few long, deep breaths, including box breathing. Box breathing involves you breathing in for a count of 4 then you hold for a count of 4 and breathe out for a count of 4. Finally, you hold for a count of 4.

You do this a few times until you start to feel calmer.

Again, you need to practice this, so let's try it right now together.

- Breathe in for a count of 4.
- Hold your breath for a count of 4
- Breathe out
- Hold

You would do this a few times but I hope you already start to feel calmer. I know I do.

You Need To Listen To Relaxing Music

Something I've only just realised is that when my mental health is bad and I cannot focus on doing something on my laptop, I play relaxing music as a matter of habit. I never do it when my mental health is good, but I still do it to self-soothe. I never realised that until now. In fact, on YouTube, I'm currently listening to "*Cozy Autumn Vibes, Beautiful Relaxing Music, Peaceful Soothing Instrumental Music, By Tim Janis*".

It's very good by the way.

Anyway, listening to relaxing music is a good idea for self-soothing because this type of music helps to reduce the stress hormone called Cortisol (Khalfa et al., 2003). As a result, if you're feeling distressed and you're spiralling, try listening to relaxing music because this calming music might help you change your mood, help you to breathe deeper and decrease the negative emotions that you're experiencing.

If you have a Go-To music service that you love (my friends still don't understand why I prefer YouTube for my music over Spotify), then maybe create a playlist of relaxing music so you can listen to it when you're distressed.

Then remember to actually play it and listen to it.

You Should Do Pleasant Activities To Self-Soothe

Personally, I know how difficult, impossible and awful it can be when you're depressed, spiralling or in a mental health crisis, because we all know we need to do pleasant activities to maintain our mental health. Yet when we're spiralling and urgently need to self-soothe, it can be so impossible to do these things that we enjoy.

However, Dialectical Behavioural Therapy suggests that we can self-soothe by doing activities that bring us joy and make us happy (Linehan, 1993). Especially as us doing a pleasurable activity when we're distressed can make us feel better.

As a result, when you're distressed, try to do activities you enjoy. Be it reading, gardening, exercise, whatever. Just try to do something that makes you happy.

When I'm distressed, I try to watch something I'll enjoy, listen to podcasts, cook, read or hang out with friends. Since these are the activities that make me happy and they help to make me feel better. Of course that doesn't mean they're easy to do in the slightest when I'm distressed but over time as you practise to self-soothe more and more then these strategies become a lot easier.

Conclusion

In my opinion, none of these strategies are useful alone and in isolation. In reality, whilst all these are highly effective self-soothing strategies, they feed into each other. For example, when you're distressed you cannot simply start doing pleasurable activities because in my experience, you cannot focus and you cannot enjoy them. Therefore, you can start to self-soothe by doing box-breathing to activate our parasympathetic nervous system so you can calm down or listen to relaxing music. Then you can start to do pleasurable activities to help you self-soothe for longer.

So much of psychology and mental health advice can never be done effectively in isolation.

Therefore, to end this chapter, I want to finish by saying that having an inability to self-soothe can be very damaging to your mental health, and it is so annoying. Yet it is more than possible over time to practise and improve your self-soothing skills. I never thought I would be able to self-soothe but last night I got triggered by a stupid sex ad on YouTube and I got distressed yet I practised box-breathing and managed to self-soothe for the first time in my life.

And I am very proud of myself for managing that.

Now I just need to keep practising, keep trying and keep strengthening my ability to self-soothe. It is possible regardless of how impossible and scary it seems. Just keep trying and using the strategies included in this chapter and one day you will get there.

And it will be a wonderful feeling when you do.

WHAT IS PERSON-CENTRED THERAPY?

In the last chapter, I mentioned that my counsellor was a humanistic counsellor and in my experience, a lot of humanistic counsellors draw on concepts from person-centred therapy. Therefore, in this chapter, adapted from a psychology article from The Psychology World Podcast, you'll learn what is person-centred therapy, some of my own experiences and what you might experience as you engage with a humanistic counsellor or therapist.

Enjoy.

***

Interestingly enough in August 2023, I started four weeks of psychotherapy to help me deal with trauma and abuse from my past and I have only recently learnt that the counsellor (or as I call her 'therapist') uses a person-centred approach to therapy. I have only just heard about this approach to mental health to be honest, so I want to explore it further. Since I found it rather useful. Therefore, in this clinical psychology podcast episode, we'll explore what is person-centred therapy, how does it work, what to expect and so much more.

What Is Person-Centred Psychotherapy?

Person-centred therapy is a client-based psychotherapy that uses a non-authoritative approach to mental health difficulties that allows clients to take the lead in therapy sessions so they can discover their own solutions to their difficulties.

This particular approach to mental health was started by Carl Rodgers because he believed that every person is unique (which we are) and everyone's view of their world should be trusted. In other words, he believed we should never ever doubt our clients and how they describe the world, because to them that actually is how the world works.

Personally, I do understand this because everyone interprets different situations and events differently depending on their past experiences. This is basically what the cognitive approach is saying just with different words. Due to the cognitive approach believes it isn't the events themselves that cause mental health difficulties it is our beliefs and interpretations of them that lead to difficulties.

Furthermore, Carl Rodgers firmly believed in self-actualisation. This is the idea that all of us have the solutions, knowledge and power to make the changes we need in our lives. As well as this therapy is non-directive so the therapist doesn't take the lead and instead follows the client and doesn't engage in any direct discussions.

However, something I am seriously starting to notice is that all these different approaches to mental health are basically just rehashing what another has already said. For example, every single psychotherapy I can think of is about self-actualisation and making sure the client realises *they* can make the changes needed in their lives using the tools and guidance the therapist gives them. Yet only they can make the changes for themselves.

This actually isn't unique to any approach.

Moreover, I will admit that the non-directive part of person-centred therapy does require a bit of getting used to. Since I love cognitive-behavioural therapy, which is very structured, I had to let go of the idea that she was going to lead, and I had to lead instead. Thankfully I have so much mental health difficulties tied up in different parts of abuse and trauma that I have more than enough things to talk about, but it still did require a bit of relearning.

Anyway, during person-centred therapy, a therapist isn't the lead as we know. Instead the therapist is known as a "compassionate facilitator" because they listen to the client without judgement, they acknowledge the client's experiences without changing or moving the conversation and they are there to support the client without interrupting them. Or impacting on their own process of self-discovery.

In my experience that acknowledgement and "validation" in a fashion is extremely important and it does feel great to have someone else call your abuse and trauma, well, abuse and trauma. And I will happily admit that the process of self-discovery it is scary how much you can actually discover about yourself when we free yourself up. Like I literally cannot share everything I've discovered about myself on the podcast because that's like another twenty episodes in itself, but it's a lot of fun. And honestly, as much as really don't want to discover anything more about myself, I know I will and that's okay.

Overall, the reason why the therapist doesn't interrupt this process of self-discovery and lead is because it is down to the client to uncover what hurts them and what they need to do to repair it. That is a very powerful realisation when it hits you.

<u>How Does Person-Centred Therapy Work?</u>

The entire point of person-centred therapy is to step away from the more traditional psychotherapeutic models where the therapist is the leader and expert and instead the client is the expert in themselves. Again that is something I have mentioned a thousand times before on the podcast and in books.

Therefore, person-centred therapy has three central tenets that allow the therapy to be successful. Firstly, the therapist has an unconditional positive regard so they are empathetic and non-judgemental. Due to the therapist accepts what the client is saying as true and they want to convey to the client that they are understood, confident, trusted and they are valued. As well as the client is free to make their own better choices and decisions in their life.

This tenet I think is very powerful and helpful because I have tried to talk about my past before and there are only ever three outcomes really. None of which I blame on people. Firstly, they call me a liar because they don't want to hear it because what I have to say is too painful. Secondly, they are sorry for what's happening but they can ultimately never ever understand it at a deep level. Thirdly, they understand it but the problem with that is it is common trauma and abuse so they aren't comfortable listening to it and because of emotional dependency and other difficulties, I burn them out too much.

That's why having a therapist that can just listen to me talk is extremely helpful.

Secondly, there is congruence or genuineness so the therapists have no air of authority to them. Instead they present themselves as an accessible and their true self that clients can see is honest and transparent. And this is definitely true, I might be autistic so reading and understanding people is always going to be hard but I know my therapist is very honest and transparent.

Finally, there is empathetic understanding where the therapist wholeheartedly accepts and understands the client's views as well as feelings in a way that can be helpful in reshaping the client's sense of their experiences.

Normally, I think this final part is done by "accident" in a fashion because just by talking and listening and offering up good psychological insights. My therapist has helped me to realise a lot about myself and how I view my Self and my past and my relationships.

On the whole, in this therapy, whenever the therapy is working well the clients feel they are better understood in these sessions and this leads them to feel better understood in other areas of their lives as well. This does have research support, especially whenever a client identifies the unconditional positive regard in their therapist there is an increased chance in positive outcomes. Since the therapeutic relationship between the therapist and the client is a type of therapy in itself.

When Is Person-Centred Therapy Used?

A person-centred therapeutic approach might be used with groups and individuals, be it adults or adolescents in a short- or long-term fashion. The people that tend to take this approach and benefit from it are people that want more self-confidence, a stronger sense of identity and authenticity, increased trust in their own relationships and more success in establishing (and maintaining I will add) their interpersonal relationships.

In addition, like other approaches to mental health, the person-centred approach doesn't have to be used only because it can be combined with other therapies to treat depression, grief and anxiety. Although, it can also be treated to treat trauma, family stressors, abuse and so much more.

And because this is a client-led psychotherapy, it is the more motivated and determined clients that tend to do better and be more successful at the therapy.

Personally, even though I didn't choose person-centred therapy, I am more than glad I ended up with it. Since I've only had two sessions so far and I have found it so useful in understanding my own relationships, my identity, self-confidence and it has basically taught me to let go of what other people want from me and their expectations. I talk about this a little more next week in the Emotional Dependency and Locus of Evaluation podcast episode but person-centred therapy has been immensely useful to me.

What To Expect In Person-Centred Therapy?

Even though I've mentioned my own experience through the podcast episode, the only other thing I want to say is that the therapist might repeat your words. This isn't them trying to be annoying or anything, it is simply them trying to understand what happened, what you mean and how you feel. It is them trying to draw out a little more information from you too.

Of course, they might have misunderstood you and I think that's happened once or twice with myself. One time was when, because I laugh as a coping mechanism when I have seriously screwed up, she didn't understand why I was laughing about something extremely serious (well at least it was to me). This allowed me to rephrase my response in a way both of us could understand.

Moreover, there might be moments of silence in the therapy and this can be good because it allows us to process our thoughts and realisations. Since person-centred therapy is all about self-acceptance and self-discovery. Or if you're like me and you have so many things to unpack, you basically don't stop talking for the entire session.

Then you end up at the end of the therapy feeling a little overwhelmed because of everything you've learnt, discussed and it can take a little while for you to realise what the takeaways are for you.

Conclusion

Overall, person-centred therapy is all about allowing a client to talk, explore their difficulties and find the solutions for themselves. This is extremely helpful in my experience but then again I've learnt recently I have very high emotional intelligence, which is funny because I used to be extremely bad at it.

A Person-centred Therapist should always have the ability to be calm in sessions and they need to let a client verbalise their frustrations and disappointments too. Since this can all help a client to gain insights into what's hurting them and most importantly how they can move forwards.

Personally, I am willing to say that person-centred therapy has already changed my life for the better and I still have two more sessions, so I am actually really excited to see what will happen, what will I learn and most importantly how else can *I* change my life for the better.

Therapy can be seriously fun, interesting and life changing if you want it to be.

WINDOW OF TOLERANCE, SOCIAL SCRIPTS AND CHILD TRAUMA HEALING: LESSONS LEARNT FROM A SECOND SESSION

There were a lot of technology issues between the first and second session of my specialist counselling. My counsellor was meant to send me a bunch of things but when I didn't get them, I was feeling let down and I was nervous about how good my counsellor actually was. Yet thankfully, she had sent them, there was just an issue with the email so I never got them.

Therefore, in the next chapter of the book, I will explain Window Of Tolerance a lot more and in a lot more detail, but we focused on this topic by me watching a video that she had sent me. I didn't mind spending the first 6 minutes (I watch videos on 2-times speed) of the session watching the video because I wanted to try and I knew this was a useful concept.

In essence, Window Of Tolerance is about the area of stress we can handle and function in without trauma reactions kicking in and making us anxious and fear or depressed and us freezing.

That is a very cruel explanation of the topic but in the next chapter, you get to explore this topic in a lot more depth.

In addition, we spent a lot of time on Window of Tolerance, because it's a useful psychoeducation tool. It teaches you about the body's reactions, the nervous system and *why* we have trauma responses after sexual trauma. Once this was explained to me, I was much "happier" because I know my body's reactions weren't my fault. It was simply my body reacting in normal ways for an extremely abnormal situation.

After you read the next chapter, you'll find it really useful too.

Moreover, in the second session, I mentioned how when I start shaking, getting anxious and terrified because of a trigger. I tried to stop the shaking in its tracks, which my counsellor said might not be a useful thing to do. Due to the body shakes because it's released adrenaline into the bloodstream and that extra energy that the hormone gives you needs to go somewhere. Hence, the shaking so when I try to stop this I'm storing up that energy.

Instead it's a good idea to simply allow my body to shake, release that energy and adrenaline and everything will be fine.

At the time, I was rather surprised by her saying that it was useful to know, and I did tend to find that after I started doing this technique (if you can call it that) that my shaking was shorter and the aftermath wasn't so intense. It was useful.

Furthermore, during the first half of my counselling sessions I was severely anxious, depressed and I was not having a good time at all. Every single night without fail I would get depressed, my anxiety would skyrocket and I would be constantly plagued with intrusive thoughts, physical sensations and nightmares that I would be getting raped over and over again.

It was awful.

That was my life every single night for 7 months. At the time of my second session, it had been 5 months since my rape so I was going to suffer and my mental health was going to get a lot worse in the next two months. Honestly, I didn't even think that was possible at the time.

As a result, I mentioned this to my counsellor and she mentioned it might be a good idea if I have a "Good Things" box. This is a box, be it physical or digital like a folder on a phone, that is filled with things that make you smile and help you when you're having a bad day. For example, you might want to fill it with pictures of loved ones, friends and good memories. Equally, you could fill it with loving and positive messages, basically anything that makes you happy.

It is all about having and being able to access good things that make you feel better when you're having a bad day.

Therefore, I included things like pictures of my best friend, good days out, messages from friends and loved ones over the years and positive messages from my readers that make me happy.

I highly recommend that you do this too because as a survivor, you will have bad days (probably a lot of them) and you will need the positivity. I know that so please create a box or something you can access when you need it most.

Before I talk about the third counselling session, we'll learn about *How To Survive A Major Depressive Episode* to give you some extra techniques too in case you experience an episode. Something I did for about two- to three months because of my rape.

<u>Childhood Trauma and Social Scripts</u>

Something you need to know about me is that I suffered a decade of unintentional abuse and intense homophobia. My family flat out hated gay people and thought gay people were the scum of the earth. One side of my family was deeply religious and the other side just didn't care enough about gay people to defend them or say anything nice about them.

It wasn't exactly abnormal for me to hear "we need to beat the gay out of them" at least once a week and then there were all the other homophobic comments in between. As well as there are the very public outrage that my parents had whenever they used to see a gay couple, let alone a transgender couple, in public.

It was rough and that utter fear and terror that I felt every single day of my life for a decade took a massive toll on my mental health. This went on for about a decade before I had a massive breakdown, got immensely suicidal and my life fell apart. My family had to get better at supporting me and being less homophobic.

It took my rape to stop it completely.

I mention this about my life and childhood that I've written a lot about in other places, because this directly impacted my trauma recovery for my rape. All the trauma, pain and lessons I had learnt during my childhood just to survive was impeding my trauma healing even more.

Especially, as I believed that if my family found out I was gay then I would be beaten, kicked out of my house or worse.

This was made even worse by my family constantly invalidating my trauma, and telling me that my rape wasn't impacting me as much as it was and I simply needed to move on.

Who the hell can just "move on" after being raped?

In addition, the typical advice recommended for the families and friends of rape survivors is to research sexual violence, sexual trauma and investigate how to help the survivor as much as possible whilst looking after yourself too. My family are not the type of people to actually do that no matter how much I'm struggling, jumping at any sound and my trauma responses getting worse and worse.

They wouldn't help me.

This continued to have a greater and greater impact on my mental health, so I mentioned it in counselling.

We had a long conversation about my family, my childhood trauma and what I needed to do now about it. The conclusion was that because I was scared of standing up to them, because if I did that in my childhood then I would be shouted at, berated and accused of a bunch of stuff. The issue was that I didn't have boundaries with them, because I would set them, they would step over them and I would get too scared of them to stand up to my family.

That is a major difficulty after sexual violence that lots of survivors have, it is even worse if you never developed setting boundaries anyway.

Also, it's worth noting that my family blames me for everything that happens in regards to my mental health. It was my fault I was raped, my rape was a "lesson learnt" about not being gay, me being suicidal and scared of my family because they were actively telling me they wanted to beat up gay people, that was all my fault.

They will never take responsibility for their actions.

As a result, towards the end of the session, we spoke about setting boundaries with them, the importance of reinforcing boundaries they crossed and developing social scripts so I knew what to say when things didn't go to plan.

This is what I explore in two later chapters about family boundaries and healing from childhood trauma.

As a result, whilst over the next week, this caused me a lot of concern and fear because for the first time ever I was going to tell my family some boundaries so I could heal, I learnt a lot.

I did a lot of online research which is where the next few family-based chapters come from, as well as I found the following online:

- What boundaries do I want to set?
- What could their responses be?
- Write down everything parents have done that's crossed a boundary

- How will I keep myself safe?
- Train yourself to counter these responses

Personally, I highly recommend that you think about these questions and you write down your answers. This will allow you to always check-in with yourself about what your boundaries are, and they will help remind you why boundaries are important, and why and how your family crosses them.

This is a great, but tough, exercise to do. I really benefited from it though so I hope it can help you as well.

To wrap up this therapy session that seriously benefited my mental health in the long-term, I wanted to share with you a text message that I sent a family member after they accidentally crossed a boundary two days before. This was the first time I stuck up for myself and it is this text that changed our relationship for the better as it led to a longer conversation.

"Hi, how's work? Is *Co-Worker* still there?

I've had some good times this week. I finished making my Outreach lecture, seminar and library research task on How To reduce Reoffending? As part of a Degree for A Day programme. A Whitstable school has already booked the event for Jan/ Feb. I'm excited.

And I hung out with *New Friend* and *Best Friend* for over 3 hours on Tuesday. Which was really fun and good considering.

Also, it was lovely you calling me Friday to check if I was the stabbing victim *(Context, there are a stabbing in my local area).* Yet please remember what I said to you about checking up on me. Please do check up on me because I love you and I enjoy talking to you, but if you're going to check on me please actually hear how I am. Because you don't know about my eating disorder and that's the main way I'm struggling this week.

And me and *Best Friend* are going into Canterbury today to enjoy some French cafe food. It'll be really good."

It might not be the most naturally worded text I've ever sent but it was important, because it led to a texting conversation about how I was really struggling, what I needed from my family and so on.

It is immensely scary setting boundaries but it is so, so worth it in the long-term as you will see in the following chapters.

WHAT IS WINDOW OF TOLERANCE?

Normally as an aspiring clinical psychologist, I don't really focus too much on how our biological processes and the nervous system impacts our mental health. I should focus on this area a lot more than I do because our physical reactions to trauma, anxiety and depression are very important. Instead I tend to focus on the psychological processes that interact with our physical processes to produce behaviours. Yet as I deal with my sexual trauma more and more, I've realised I can no longer ignore the impact our nervous system and the role it plays in our mental health.

Therefore, in this chapter, we'll be focusing on window of tolerance, hyperarousal and hypoarousal during psychological distress. And how importantly we can get back within our window of tolerance to improve our mental health. If you enjoy learning about clinical psychology, biological psychology and the nervous system then you'll love this chapter.

What Is The Window of Tolerance?

This is a topic that has been critical in my rape counselling and once I understood this psychological concept, things started to get a little easier. You or your clients understanding the window of tolerance isn't a magic bullet that will suddenly make everything better but it can be immensely useful in healing from trauma, including sexual violence.

Therefore, Window of Tolerance was a term coined by Daniel J. Siegel who was a clinical professor at the UCLA School of Medicine. He created Window of Tolerance to describe the optimal emotional "zone" that people can best exist in so they can thrive and function in their everyday lives. When someone is within their Window of Tolerance then they have a sense of groundedness, openness, curiosity, presence, flexibility, an ability to emotionally self-regulate and a capacity to tolerate any stressors that pop up in their everyday life.

However, either side of the Window of Tolerance are two different states where we do not function and thrive in our daily lives. These states are called the hypoarousal and hyperarousal states.

When someone is in hyperarousal then they are in an emotional state that we can characterise as panic, anger, high energy, anxiety, irritability, overwhelm, chaos, hypervigilance, startle responses and fight-or-flight instincts. For example, I know I'm in a hyperarousal state running my panic attacks, anxiety and my thoughts running a million miles an hour about how unsafe I am and how I need to escape or I am going to die or get raped again.

On the other end of the spectrum is the hypoarousal state where someone effectively shuts down and experiences numbness, withdrawal, depressiveness, flat affect, disconnection, shame amongst others. For instance, when I'm in a hypoarousal state (like an hour before I started writing this post), I was severely depressed, shut down and I didn't want to move. I effectively wanted to play dead so I couldn't be hurt again like he did to me that night.

Why Is The Window of Tolerance Important?

If we are outside of our Window of Tolerance then we cannot function and thrive in our everyday lives. For example, when my mental health died in August and September (and probably October) 2024 because of my rape, most of the time I was too hypervigilance, anxious and terrified to function on most days. I was always in a state of hyperarousal, or I was too depressed and shut down to function (hypoarousal).

Therefore, when we're in our Window of Tolerance, we can access all the prefrontal cortex as well as executive functioning skills we need to be able to thrive. Like, our ability to organise, plan and prioritise complex tasks that we need to complete. Also, being within our Window of Tolerance means we can emotionally self-regulate, start projects and actions and focus on them and practice good time management.

These executive functions are critical to our functioning because they allow us to work, problem-solve whatever issues and challenges we face and they allow us to be present and work in our relationships.

This is a major problem I had during my mental health crisis. I was too anxious, terrified or depressed to do much work, problem-solve and I wasn't able to have or maintain many social relationships. I wasn't able to do much Outreach work at my university because a lot of it was brand-new students and staff that I had never worked with before, and the specific type of Outreach activities, because it was the school holidays, were so different to what I was used to. I couldn't deal with it.

Then it was even worse for my own business. I couldn't write as much, I couldn't do a fraction of the business tasks that I needed to do and I can see the impact it has on my bottom line and the podcast audience.

This is why being within our Window of Tolerance is so important.

Moreover, we lose access to these skills when we're outside of our Window of Tolerance because we lose access to the prefrontal cortex and our executive skills. Since instead of relying on these brain areas, we default to panic, action or a freeze response. Sometimes this can even manifest as self-sabotaging behaviours so we might gravitate towards choices and patterns that undermine or erode our relationship with ourselves, others and the world.

Ultimately, it's important that we try to stay within our Window of Tolerance so we can support ourselves, function and live in a healthy way. Yet there will always be times in our lives when we fall outside our Window of Tolerance and we end up in some non-deal emotionally regulated way.

Thankfully, this is just a part of human behaviour and it's natural and normal.

Therefore, the ultimate goal of this chapter isn't to make sure we never ever fall outside of our Window of Tolerance. That is never going to happen, but instead I want to show you why it's important to expand our Window of Tolerance. This allows a person to effectively bounce back quicker and be more resilient over time, so we can better deal with being outside our Window of Tolerance.

In my opinion, this is a critical area of mental health and trauma work because as my Window of Tolerance has expanded I have been able to deal with more and more. For example, I used to have thousands of triggers (probably not a joke) but everything has been toned down recently in terms of my PTSD. Like a few months ago, if I even saw a reference of sex in a film or book, my mental health completely died and I would have major intrusive thoughts and flashbacks. Now I can tolerate sex references and even the odd light sex scene in a film or book and I only experience mild intrusive thoughts and flashbacks.

It's still a little distressing but it is nowhere near as bad as in the past few months.

How Do You Increase Your Window of Tolerance?

Whilst there are several effective therapeutic techniques and activities that can over time increase your Window of Tolerance, everyone's Window of Tolerance is rather different because of a range of biopsychosocial factors. For example, whether or not you have childhood trauma and social support can impact the size of your Window of Tolerance as well as your physiology, personal history and your temperament.

All these factors and more interact with each other to make your Window of Tolerance, and no two Windows of Tolerance will ever be the same.

As a result, it's important to mention that people, like me, who come from trauma backgrounds will have a smaller Window of Tolerance than people who have not experienced trauma. This shrinking of the Window of Tolerance isn't unique to any type of trauma, like physical, childhood or sexual trauma, your Window of Tolerance doesn't discriminate. Trauma is trauma and it is the unfortunate gift that keeps on giving.

The reason why trauma shrinks your Window of Tolerance is because trauma gives you triggers that are more likely to rapidly and more frequently push you outside your Window of Tolerance and into hypoarousal or hyperarousal.

Consequently, it's important that as part of trauma work (even though anyone can benefit from this knowledge) is that we work to expand a client's Window of Tolerance. This allows the client to practice resilience and bring themselves back into their Window of Tolerance when you're in a hypoarousal or hyperarousal state. The only reason difference in this regard between people with and without trauma is that a person with relational trauma might need to work worker, longer and dedicate more time and effort into expanding their Window of Tolerance.

Personally, I can relate to this because it is normal for a person's Window of Tolerance to expand as they get older, experience more things and stressors, and they learn more techniques without realising it about to bring themselves back into their Window of Tolerance. However, ever since I was raped up until 7 months later when I learnt how to feel safe in my own body. I just couldn't bring myself back into my Window of Tolerance and it required a lot of therapeutic work, a lot of effort and a lot longer than I wanted to to be able to bring myself reliably back into my Window of Tolerance.

There are still times I cannot achieve this but 90% of the time I thankfully can.

In addition, there are two main ways how someone can recognise that their Windows of Tolerance are unique and how to expand it. Ultimately, we need to understand the foundational biopsychosocial elements that contribute to a healthy nervous system and that's why I flat out love *Healing Sexual Trauma Workbook* by Erika Shershun because it handles this topic very well. Also, we can give ourselves this knowledge by providing our minds with supportive experiences. This can include providing ourselves with good amounts of stimulation, focus and engagement whilst we balance this with good amounts of play, rest and spaciousness. This was a mistake I made this week at the time of writing because I overbooked myself with Outreach work at my university so I had plenty of stimulation, focus and I was really engaged with helping students change their lives, but I didn't give myself enough rest time.

Hence, I found myself very outside my Window of Tolerance on two occasions this week.

Moreover, we need to provide our bodies with supportive self-care. For example, we need to get enough sleep, exercise, eat nutritious foods, attend to our medical needs and avoid substances that damage our health. Since if our bodies aren't looked after then our nervous system won't be healthy and it will be easier to go outside our Window of Tolerance. As well as we need to provide ourselves with supportive experiences like being in a connected relationship and being connected to something bigger than ourselves.

I know this sounds like religion and I suppose some people find this helpful, but you can be connected to other things greater than yourself. For example, I connect to my Outreach work at my university because I'm helping to inspire and show young people that it doesn't matter what background or area they come from, if they want to they can go to university and thrive. As well as I connect to my books and my podcast because I am providing people with a psychology education, entertainment and hopefully I'll inspire some people to enjoy mental health and clinical psychology as much as I do.

You can connect to anything that you are passionate about.

Finally for this first part, you can tend to your physical environment to set yourself up for success. You can do this by working and living in places and ways that reduce your stressors instead of increasing them. As well as you can design an external environment that nourishes you instead of depletes you. I did this when I moved into my shared house with my best friend back in June because as one of our housemates wasn't moving in for another 3 months, I made their room my office (with their permission) and that was great for me. It gave me a stress-free, non-triggering environment for me to do what I loved.

Secondly, we need to work with ourselves to cultivate and use a wide range of tools to bring ourselves back inside our Window of Tolerance when we inevitably find ourselves outside. You can do this by developing tools, habits, practices and internalised and externalised resources that help you to self-soothe, self-regulate and ground yourself. I'm smiling as I write as I write this because these are aspects of Window of Tolerance that I've been reading about lately in Erika Shershun's book, and it's very helpful to learn about.

Maybe I'll dive into these aspects of Window of Tolerance in a future chapter.

Conclusion

I cannot stress enough the importance of Window of Tolerance in trauma work, because it actually did change my life. There are a lot of concepts in clinical psychology that are useful to some clients but not all, and there are certain concepts that are useful to the vast, vast majority of clients. Window of Tolerance is certainly one of the latter, because it is a very useful tool for psychoeducation and explaining to trauma explains why their body is reacting in the ways that it is.

It was a relief to understand why my body was doing all these extreme trauma responses and it was nice to put a name to the psychological framework. Therefore, it meant now I understood what I was dealing with it, I could research, read and practice how to expand my Window of Tolerance and how to reduce the volatility of my nervous system.

If I didn't know about Window of Tolerance, I certainly wouldn't be as far along in my recovery as I am now.

Ultimately, the Window of Tolerance might "only" be a psychoeducational concept but it is an extremely powerful tool to use in clinical trauma work. Therefore, I unofficially suggest to my fellow aspiring and qualified psychologists that you embody this Window of Tolerance in your own life and especially in your clinical trauma work. Your clients and yourself will openly find it more useful and life-changing than you ever thought possible.

I know I did, and that's one of the entire points of our profession.

Clinical psychology is all about changing one life for the better at a time.

HOW TO HEAL FROM FAMILY TRAUMA BY SETTING BOUNDARIES?

In the last chapter I mentioned how I needed to start learning how to deal with family trauma a lot more and the next two chapters are the result of my research and my efforts to thankfully try and build better relationships with my family.

Since when it comes to healing from family trauma, it's flat out critical to learn how to set effective boundaries. These boundaries allow you to heal, protect yourself and build healthier relationships with family members that might have treated you badly before. Their bad or inappropriate treatment doesn't always have to be intentional or malicious, but it can be. My abuse wasn't intentionally malicious but it had done a lot of psychological damage to me over the past decade. As well as it was massively amplified by my rape, and even if you haven't been through additional trauma as you try and heal from the damaging impact of dysfunctional families, setting boundaries is beyond critical. Therefore, in this clinical psychology podcast episode, you'll learn why setting boundaries is important with family members, how to do it and more. If you enjoy learning about trauma healing, distributional families and now then this is a great episode for you.

How Does Setting Boundaries Help Heal Family Trauma?

The reason why setting boundaries helps clients to heal from family trauma is because by setting boundaries, you're helping yourself and other people to understand what is and what is not okay in your relationship. As well as with you being an adult child, it means you have a lot of freedom to set boundaries and limits with your family that will help you to improve your relationships over time. For example, you could set a limit on how much time and energy you invest with them. Also, you setting boundaries might involve invoking your right to self-care and personal autonomy and this is perfectly okay even if it does mean creating a certain distance from particular family members.

Additionally, by setting boundaries, you aren't saying that you don't love your family. Instead setting boundaries means that you are trying to stay connected as well as have a healthy, mature relationship with your family.

Of course, it is worth noting that unfortunately some people just aren't able to have healthy relationships so you may need to distance yourself from them.

Moreover, it's important to know that your boundaries act as a protective shield around you so you are less likely to be hurt by the dysfunctional, immature relationship that your family trauma has caused. Ultimately, setting boundaries with family members helps to protect yourself against further harm and they allow you to reclaim a sense of agency over your life.

And because this is a topic that I struggle a lot with, I want to stress here that asserting your own needs might be incredibly scary but it is so important. Asserting your needs helps you to break free from the patterns of dysfunction as well as co-dependency that effectively made up your upbringing.

I talk about this struggle more in my Work-In-Progress book that focuses on my rape counselling. When I first had the conversation with my Mum about what I needed, the struggles I was facing and everything I was dealing with. I was shaking, terrified and I felt sick, but it worked out okay and everything has improved in the past week. Of course, there will always be challenges ahead but it is progress and it is the small victories you need to celebrate.

How Else Can Boundaries Help Trauma Healing?

Some other ways how setting boundaries can help clients heal from family trauma includes reduced stress. Setting boundaries helps to reduce stress because let's face it, toxic family interactions are extremely draining so boundaries help you to manage the level of stress that these interactions create and you can limit your exposure to these interactions. Therefore, you can focus on your health and wellbeing instead of focusing on the fallout and draining nature of these toxic interactions.

Secondly, setting boundaries can help your sense of safety because boundaries give you a safe space to heal. Since by limiting contact with toxic family members as well as friends and any other toxic people in your life, you can minimise any further emotional harm. I definitely agree with this point because as bad as my mental health is at the time of writing, setting boundaries and expectations with my family has given me one less concern or stressor in my life. This means I can focus, heal and think about other things instead of negative interactions, and I'm already seeing how my interactions with my family are becoming a lot more positive and better for my mental health.

Thirdly, setting boundaries can help to reduce your triggers because toxic family members tend to engage in behaviours that trigger your negative memories or negative emotions. As a result, boundaries help to minimise your exposure to these triggers so you can process your past trauma in a safe and controlled environment. And this is a great point because there have been times when my family have seriously triggered me because of my sexual trauma with some comments, a non-consensual touch or hug and some invalidation. Yet because I set boundaries, I have to deal with these triggers less and that has had a good impact on my mental health.

In addition, self-care is a great benefit of setting boundaries, because boundaries help you to focus on your own mental health and wellbeing. As well as boundaries allow you to treat yourself with the respect and kindness you deserve and this is a critical part of healing from trauma. Something I am needing to get better at. Also, boundaries can free up your time, energy and even money so you can partake in healing activities.

Building upon the last point, setting boundaries helps you to improve your self-esteem because boundaries help you to communicate and truly *feel* your self-worth. Because I know firsthand how people not respecting your boundaries, your consent and your self-worth makes you feel useless, awful and like dirt. Yet you are worth so much, you are clever, brilliant and a great person who deserves so much more. Therefore, by communicating your healthy boundaries, you are showing that you deserve to be treated respectfully by others and you will never tolerate being mistreated ever again.

This reminds me to mention that you need to reinforce your boundaries too, but that's something we mention again later.

Finally, setting boundaries helps you to break the cycle of dysfunction in your life. Since dysfunctional family dynamics and patterns of behaviour are often passed down the generations so setting boundaries helps to disrupt this cycle. Thus, you can build healthier relationships that focus on respect and genuine connection instead of these maladaptive dysfunctional patterns of behaviour.

As well as it's useful to note that every time you stand up for yourself by focusing on your own health and wellbeing, you are becoming a powerful example for future generations. Due to you are truly showing it is possible to overcome these dysfunctional family patterns of behaviour.

How To Deal With Resistant Family Members?

As much as I wish I could tell you that all your family members will be perfectly happy with you setting boundaries, I cannot. There will be a few or maybe the majority of toxic family members and loved ones that think you are being outrageous, unfair and evil for wanting to set boundaries. For example, my family was annoyed at me and very defensive at first when it came to me setting boundaries because everything was my fault.

Furthermore, the strategies that your toxic family members use on you, like guilt, will make you enforcing your boundaries even more difficult. Since you'll be dealing with your own fears of abandonment, guilt and familial duty and loyalty. As well as you might have to deal with internalised core beliefs about that family harmony is more important than your own wellbeing. It is not, but you may still have to deal with those beliefs.

Again, I was utterly terrified when I started to put boundaries in place with my own family because I was scared of being shouted at, hated and being guilt-tripped into submission.

However, there are strategies to help you overcome and deal with resistant family members.

What Are Some Strategies To Deal With Resistant Family Members?

Firstly, you need to start small. This is something my best friend kept banging on about because they could see how distressed and scared I was about setting boundaries, so they encouraged me to start very small. You should start small because this helps make the task of setting boundaries more manageable and then you can gradually build from there. For instance, the only real boundaries I have currently set with my family is something along the lines of *Don't ask me how I am if you aren't going to listen.* That is a very small and manageable boundary that I can and will build on over time.

Think about a small boundary you could set and go from there. Rome wasn't built in a day so neither will boundary setting.

Secondly, you need to be clear and direct. To do this, you should use "I" statements so no one can accuse you of being influenced by other people and you are definitely saying this is what *you* want during this conversation. This is very important in setting your boundaries. For example, you could say the following to your family, "I don't feel comfortable having this conversation right now. I want to take a break and we can talk about this again in the future,"

Thirdly, you need to focus on yourself. As much as I would love to tell you that you can control how others will react that isn't possible and you can only control your own responses as well as actions. It reminds me of something that happened in my friendship group back in May 2024 when a person with persecutory delusions attacked me very publicly and repeatedly over text. I knew right in this moment she was in the wrong for attacking me and I could have ripped into her just as hard but that wouldn't have helped the situation. If I had attacked her back then everything would have gotten a lot worse and there was a very good risk I would become just as guilty as her. My point is what you do when family members are being resistant and possibly attacking you when you go to set boundaries matters. Don't engage, don't make things worse.

If your family members are being resistant and horrible then please, just walk away. You can always return to conversations later on when they are calmer.

Always focus on meeting your own needs and not the needs of others. Sometimes people will change, sometimes they will not so don't waste your energy getting people to change when they will not.

Fourthly, expect pushback. I hope by this point in the podcast episode that you're starting to realise that you will get pushback because toxic family members will not like you setting boundaries and reclaiming your life. Therefore, expect that they're going to manipulate, guilt-trip and use other strategies to try to get you to back down. Yet you need to stay firm, set and enforce those boundaries and take all the time and space you need so you can heal.

This is about you, not them.

Finally, you need to seek support. Not only from a dear friend or non-toxic family member that knows what you're going through, but healing from trauma is hard. It is very possible to heal from trauma but you never have to do it alone. Therefore, please seek support from a therapist, a dear friend and a support group.

Setting boundaries is just one part of the journey towards healing from trauma, but it is a very rewarding part indeed.

<u>Conclusion</u>

Ultimately, when it comes to setting boundaries, it is extremely important to your trauma healing and your life that you never give up. Sure, there will be struggles, setbacks and there will be family members that never want you to set boundaries, but you need to do it for you. You are so much more important than you realise.

Also, it's important to realise, truly realise that healing isn't linear. There will be setbacks, you will dip and you will rise so high that you think the worst is behind you, and that's okay. That is how healing works. I know that better than most.

As a result, I would suggest that you learn from your setbacks and you celebrate your successes.

Every single step you take towards healthier boundaries is a step closer towards you creating a space within yourself and within your social world where you can develop self-compassion, post-traumatic growth and you can heal.

Healing is more than possible as much as it seems impossible most of the time, but if you set boundaries then you might be a lot closer to starting to truly heal than you ever thought possible.

WHAT ARE SOCIAL SCRIPTS TO HELP SET FAMILY BOUNDARIES AFTER TRAUMA?

Building upon the last chapter, in this next chapter, you're going to learn the sort of things to say to family members to help set and reinforce your boundaries.

What Are Social Scripts Important?

Social scripts are lines or sentences you practise so you know what to say to family members or other people you are trying to set boundaries with. As well as social scripts are sentences you remember so you can counter and practise defending your boundaries against family resistance.

For example, a boundary I want to set is something along the lines of *if you're going to ask me how I am, actually let me talk about how I actually am.* Yet my "social environment" would have a lot of different excuses about why they shouldn't or wouldn't do that. Mostly it boils down to my trauma is too painful for them, so me being depressed, having PTSD and being suicidal at times is too much for them.

Therefore, developing useful and effective social scripts would allow me to come up with a good counterargument or statement.

Ultimately, survivors of developmental trauma typically experience some form of unsafe, unsupportive and unhealthy family dynamics. This is why as a survivor of trauma, you need to establish boundaries with your family to protect yourself and chances are, they will improve your family relationships too. Yet this can feel like one of the hardest things you will ever do.

To be honest, the night my counsellor recommended this to me I had such a bad mental health spiral because I was so terrified of this idea, and I've been uncomfortable about this setting boundaries idea for days now. Thankfully, I see my "social environment" tomorrow so I can set one or two small boundaries then, I seriously hope I can.

As a result in the rest of this chapter, we'll going to be looking at some scripts you can use in different situations to help set and reinforce your boundaries.

General Social Scripts

In a moment, we're going to look at some social scripts to protect you and set boundaries during specific topics. Yet I want to start us off with some general social scripts that will help you in everyday conversations if your family members try to disrespect your boundaries.

Some general social scripts are:

- *I don't have to explain myself to you.*
- *I prefer not to say.*
- *No, that's why I'm not going to share.*
- *No.*
- *Silence (just don't say anything)*
- *I can't do this, I'm sorry.*

Scripts For Emotionally Charged Conversations

There are certain conversations that will be very emotionally charged, causing yourself and/ or your family members to be very emotional and reactive. These conversations can include death, politics and trauma. For example, my "social environment" firmly denies they have ever done anything wrong whatsoever, so trauma is a very, very emotionally charged topic. Mainly, it involves a lot of gaslighting.

Although, when it comes to these emotionally charged conversations YOU get to decide how you contribute and interact with these topics. You don't actually have to and then you need to communicate your choices to your family members.

Some possible scripts include:

- *My thoughts and opinions are just as important as yours so if you want me to listen then you need to listen to me as well. Can you do that?*
- *That hasn't been my experience.*
- *Let's agree to disagree*
- *I'm embarrassed that you brought that up in front of everyone. Please talk about this topic in private with me next time.*
- *I'm overwhelmed right now so it's difficult for me to focus on feedback. I need a break.*

Equally, I think a bunch of the General Social Scripts are useful here too because if you're talking about trauma or why you don't want to go out and do something. Then you can simply say *I don't have to explain myself to you.* Even though I have to admit because of my trauma that is a really scary idea.

Social Scripts For Safety

For a lot of trauma survivors, safety is a very weird concept because I do feel a lot safer than I used to and I truly understand in my head what safety is, but I don't always feel it. There are only certain situations I feel truly safe in and that no one will hurt me at all, even though I have never actually been physically hurt. There was always the threat because I'm gay but emotional safety is important too. Something I have never really had.

Therefore, you might not feel physically or emotionally safe when you're with your family so you might need to establish boundaries to secure your safety and the safety of other people.

Some Safety Social Scripts can include:

- *I'm not attending that family event if This Person is going.*
- *I'm happy to come but I will not be left alone with This Person.*
- *Whenever I visit you always invalidate me so I feel hurt and unsupported. If you want me to continue visiting hen you need to stop invalidating me.*
- *I'm happy to spend time with you but it has to be outdoors, not indoors.*
- *I know you can take me but I want to drive there myself. That way I can leave when I need to.*
- *No thank you, I don't want to be touched.*

Personally, this is a category I'm going to be focusing on for my own conversations because social stuff is all about safety and I want to feel more comfortable doing social things with my "social environment". Instead of them always invalidating me, my rape and my trauma. As well as I need to get so much better at reinforcing my no-touch-without-permission rule because last time my "social environment" did that, it was bad. And it's an awful example of how my childhood trauma comes up so I'm too scared to reinforce my boundaries.

<u>Social Scripts To Use About Children</u>

Whilst I really want to have children in the future, I don't have any children at the moment. However, a caregiver's main job is to ensure their child is safe and they have good welfare so your family members might or might not be biologically related to your child, they may or may not be close or expect to be in charge of your child. Yet ultimately, these family members are not responsible for your child.

You are.

As a result, it's up to you to set any boundaries you deem necessary to take care of your child.

Some Social Scripts About Children Include:

- *Do not use those words in front of my child.*
- *That (Specific Thing) is not up for debate when it comes to my child.*
- *As their caregiver, I made the final decision because I am responsible for their welfare and wellbeing.*
- *Thanks for the feedback. I'll deal with it with (other parent or child) and I'll reach out if I need extra feedback.*
- *You can ask my child if they want to hug you but please don't force them. Respect their physical boundaries.*

<u>Conclusion</u>

As a survivor myself of two types of trauma, I understand how scary this is. The idea of setting boundaries with my family that I need to reinforce after 22 years, absolutely terrifies me because it is so new, unknown and I know I am going to be met with so much resistance. Yet I know this is critical to my mental health going forward and I cannot heal from my trauma and my rape without these boundaries being reinforced so it's hard.

Just please give yourself a chance to make these boundaries, enforce them and start to heal. You deserve to have a healthy relationship with your family, regardless of how impossible, scary and intimidating it may seem.

START OF AN EATING DISORDER, FEEL THE FEAR BUT EMBRACE, DISCOVER WHO YOU ARE: LESSONS FROM A FOURTH SESSION

I need to start off this chapter by apologising and being even more honest than I am in the rest of the book. Since normally at the end of each therapy session or in the next few days afterwards, I write an email draft with what we covered, some lessons learnt and other useful things that will help me write out these chapters.

That did not happen whatsoever for the third session of my rape counselling.

Whilst I cannot be sure of the reason why because that was around 9 weeks ago, it was probably because for the first four or five specialist counselling sessions, they were really hard on me. I would come home from counselling and later that evening I would have a complete and utter mental health crisis because it was so hard for me to process, calm down and my counsellor did say at least one wrong thing a session.

This chapter really proves that.

Looking back I think these crises were because I was struggling so much with my mental health anyway that it wasn't massively difficult to say the wrong thing. Therefore, I think it was the stress of dealing with my PTSD, other trauma responses and something she said that made me just not have the mental capacity or even remember to write down anything useful that week.

That's why there are no reflections or lessons from my third session.

The "Start" of An Eating Disorder

Personally, I cannot really say that my eating disorder (anorexia) started around the time of my third counselling session, because I have always struggled with eating in recent years. I was clinically obese as a young teenager so of course, I got bullied for that a lot at school, scouts and everywhere I went I was bullied for it. Thankfully, I managed to drop down to an average weight during the middle and late parts of my adolescence, but I later developed problematic eating.

During my first year of undergrad in 2019/2020, I lived on campus accommodation because without realising it, I was eating barely 1,000 calories a day without thinking about it. I simply didn't want to put on any weight and I was fine. Sure, I was very fatigued around 5 pm every night but I didn't see that as a problem.

Then in March 2020, COVID-19 hit and I went home to my parents, started eating normally again and I put on all the weight I had dramatically loss.

That's the historical context but the issue I had in 2024 was that my rapist was a very fat man. He was massive and that was a God's sent in a way because it meant his dick didn't work properly which is something I will always, always be grateful for. Yet it quickly became apparent that I was terrified of fat men because it reminded me too much of my rapist and I was obsessed with the idea of making sure I reached 10,000 steps a day for a whole month directly after my rape.

I did not want to gain any weight under any circumstances.

Leading us to the present situation and my fourth counselling session.

Around the time of my fourth session, me and my housemates had noticed that I was eating less and less. I was barely hitting a 1,000 calories a day and I had been losing a kilogram a week. Therefore, my best friend highly suggested that I mention my eating to my counsellor so we could work on it as it is a trauma response.

That did not go down well.

Note: as with everything in this book, these are only my experiences with my rape and with my counsellor. You should always talk to your counsellor about anything you want because the majority of the time they will know exactly what to do or they will least listen to you and signpost you to the correct service or support.

I mentioned to my counsellor that I have my eating disorder, I eat a lot less than I should and I think this is linked to my rape because he was a massive fat guy and I never want to end up like him.

She denied I had an eating disorder and she said that I was okay. She stressed that if I wanted to lose weight then I need to own it and do it for me, not because of my rape. As well as we explore my past eating and found that it was based in my childhood trauma of bullying over my weight then my rape had simply magnified that trauma and pain.

In all fair, my rape trauma had magnified a lot of my past trauma. Especially considering how I had to survive, cope and I want to say constantly fight in my childhood as I dealt with a family that hated gay people, and a social world that didn't understand me because of my undiagnosed autism.

In addition, I mentioned to my counsellor that another driving force behind my lack of eating was my ideas about wanting to be attractive. I wanted to lose weight so I could be more attractive so I could possibly find a partner and for someone to love me for the first time. Then maybe if I lose weight I could find someone who would actually like me for me and not rape me.

A slightly unhealthy view of attraction.

Therefore, my counsellor helped me to understand that "attraction does what attraction does". In other words, she helped me to understand that weight doesn't determine attraction because two people can be attracted to each other through more than weight.

If two people are attracted to each other then that attraction will be there regardless of weight. So I don't need to worry about my weight being linked to my attractiveness because that isn't how it works in the real world.

I will note that at the time of writing, my eating disorder has gotten a lot worse and I am showing more signs of anorexia than ever before, and eating is becoming a lot more difficult. I even went to the GP (doctor's) about my eating disorder but the GP and the counsellor both said I was fine because I haven't lost *enough* weight to be treated. The doctor put me in for a blood test but I passed the blood test so medically I am fine and I need to get a lot, lot worse before I can be helped.

Personally, I am completely fine with that but my best friend and my other housemates are getting really worried about my weight loss and my eating. They want me to find a therapist this week and I will but I just don't want to get told yet again that I am fine when I am really not.

Anyway that might be a future topic of a future book perhaps.

Camouflaging, Finding Out Who You Are And Feel The Fear But Do it Anyway

Building upon the eating disorder section of the session, we spoke about camouflaging and how I need to try to cut down on it. Now camouflaging is the term she used to describe how I pretend that I am perfectly okay, I ignore my emotions and I act like nothing is wrong when the opposite is the case.

She helped me to understand how I've been camouflaging my entire life and she is right, too right actually. I camouflaged my entire adolescence, I had to hide and mask the fact that I was gay with such fierce devotion and commitment that I didn't know who I was anymore. The same goes for my autism, I had to mask and fight and study others with such intensity just to survive and function in a world that did not want me to be autistic. That was largely a mixture of friends and family but it was a constant fight just to survive.

And of course, I wasn't always successful so I was bullied, mocked and people thought I was a creep at times. All because they didn't know I was autistic and didn't understand how I struggled with the basic social graces that they took for granted so easily.

Back when I had my mental breakdown in August 2023 and I had my counselling back then, I mentioned how I didn't know who I was anymore because all I know is how to survive and fight. I don't know how to live, I don't know how to relax and I don't know how to live.

Or even be at peace.

All I knew how to do was camouflage my emotions so I could survive. Hell, it was exactly what I did the night I was raped. I just wanted, needed to survive.

And that's what I did. I survived.

Therefore, my counsellor explained to me how learning to uncamouflage involves me listening to my body, paying attention to my anxiety and everything that my body and mind is trying to tell me. Then if I need to leave or change something or ask for something to help me cope then that's what I need to do.

It was a hard conversation to have because all I know is camouflaging so identifying it was going to be impossible. Yet she mentioned how I need to start finding out who *I* am and that I need to make sure I am not scared to find out, because once I know who I am then it will help me to camouflage less.

Instead of camouflaging to survive by making my decisions based on what will help me to survive. I can make more decisions based on who I am, what my values are and how I am feeling in a given moment.

Decision making is about surviving, it is about doing what's best for me and up until that counselling session I had never really thought about it like that before.

And I'm grateful for that lesson. Actually am, I haven't really thought about that lesson much in the past 9 weeks but given how much better I've been doing and the sorts of decisions I've been making, I've been doing it.

And whilst my counsellor really messed up with the eating disorder conversation so badly that it's negatively impacting me now, she did teach me a great lesson that session.

That's a win and in counselling and in the early stages of trauma recovery, you really have to take all the wins you can.

Thankfully, this was a great win to have.

HOW TO SURVIVE A MAJOR DEPRESSIVE EPISODE?

From our clinical psychology lectures, watching the media and talking to friends and peers at university or in the workplace, we know that depression is serious and can even be life-threatening. Depression can lead to increases in self-harm, suicidal ideation and it can be crippling. Therefore, it's important to know how to survive a major depressive episode. Even if you don't have depression yourself, this is still a useful chapter that will give you a lot of useful ideas and unofficial tips and techniques to help someone in the future. And if you are depressed then this chapter will give you a lot of ideas to think about for the future.

Why Is Depression Serious And Potentially Life-Threatening?

Before we talk about the five main ways how you or a client can survive a major depressive episode, I want to remind people how serious Depression is and how dangerous it can be. Granted, I was reminded of this yesterday because even though I'm not clinically depressed, there have been two times in the past 6-months where I've been so depressed I simply couldn't move. There were other consequences too but I want to keep this chapter light as always.

Therefore, depression is the leading cause of disability in the world according to Friedrich (2017) as well as about 34% of people with bipolar disorder and about 31% of people with major depression disorder will attempt suicide in their lifetime (Dong et al., 2019; Dong et al., 2020). On the whole, when we add those percentages to the fact that depression is most associated with suicide, it makes us realise that depression can be life-threatening.

Hence, why we need to think about and make it common knowledge about how to survive a major depressive episode.

In addition, major or severe depression can be linked at times to changes in a person's information and sensory integration. This is called Psychosis, and this type of psychosis tends to take on a dark, depressive-congruent quality. For instance, a person experiencing this type of psychosis might experience persecutory delusions so they truly believe that the people around them are trying to harm them and they hate them or they can hear unkind voices too. Interestingly, about 10% of people with major depressive disorder (Dold et al., 2019) as well as 63% of people with bipolar disorder experience psychotic features (Aminioff et al., 2022).

Overall, I know you're all psychology students, professionals and people interested in psychology here, but we absolutely cannot underestimate depression. That is half the problem I think is the world at times, because we hear ignorant people saying they're "depressed" about the weather or that their football team is losing and they actually don't understand what their talking about. Instead they are just using a word with a critical, vital meaning outside of a clinical context and this doesn't help our clients. This only waters down the meaning of an important term so people don't think depression is as important as it is and this stops people from seeking help when they need it and it creates extra barriers for our clients too.

Thankfully, it's important to note that people can recover from depression regardless of its severity, and there are more treatments than ever before to help people. I've spoken about them in podcast episodes before and in my books, with different forms of psychotherapy and anti-depressants being first-line treatments.

How To Survive A Major Depressive Episode?

It Will Not Always Be This Way

I have to admit that when you are going through a major depressive episode, you seriously don't remember this and I always forget it. I don't remember that this is a temporary thing and I think this is how my life will be from now on because in the moment or the hours or day that it lasts, this is how my life seems.

And it doesn't help that when you are healthy again, the experiences of depression just feel so disconnected from you because it feels completely foreign.

Therefore, it's good to remind ourselves and our clients that the vast majority of major depressive episodes are temporary, as well as even with the longer-lasting depression episodes, there are usually moments of happiness.

If your client is in a major depressive episode, remember that this is temporary and there will be moments of happiness again.

Sometimes it can help to look over pictures and other memories from times when you were happy. Also when your client is healthy again, get them to write a note of encouragement to remind themselves of these times when they don't feel happy.

Depression never lasts.

Seek Meaning

This is an interesting one because even when a person is in a depressive episode, they can normally find meaning in small things or they can take steps towards their values. Since depression is an oppressive force so clients might want to find out what they can do and look for opportunities to live how you see as meaningful.

Yesterday, I was sort of reminded of this because at my university, I want to reform the Psychology Society and I had emailed a final-year student on the 1st of May and she replied the same night. It was the 24th of May yesterday and I still hadn't replied and I noticed her and a group of people had tried to message me on Teams. So I forced myself to go onto my laptop and look at what had happened in the email and on Teams. It was a nice reminder that people wanted to talk to me, be with me and work with me for the long term. And I seriously do want to start up the psychology society again and be President.

Equally, I had a specialist appointment at the university again on Monday and this is basically what the woman said. She stressed that I should do a lot of self-care, throw myself into my interests and stick to my values and what would bring me joy.

Ask For Help

Last night me and a friend went to go and play Tennis because my friend was probably a little worried about me, and when we got back to their place, we were talking. I still hate their kitchen. I know it's a student house but I hate their kitchen with a passion and I'm also glad the house we're moving into together has a nice kitchen.

Anyway, we were talking about mental health and my friend said that based on their experience, they realised that when it comes to mental health you never really notice how bad of a place you were in until you look back later on. I largely agree with the comment and depression is very good at hiding that from you. This touches on a different topic altogether.

However, my point is that when you realise you need help, it's okay to ask for it.

If you haven't received mental health support before then contact different services, find a therapist by searching for it online or ask for help in other ways. Just make sure you get the professional help you.

If you're already in therapy or getting another form of mental health support then asking for help means asking for more or different help than what you're currently getting. This is something I'm struggling with at the moment because my normal therapist was brilliant for helping me with my child abuse and trauma. She isn't so good at helping me now, which isn't her fault because sexual violence work is so specialised at times so I reached out to charity and I have a counselling assessment next Friday.

Additionally, if there's a risk you or your client is at risk of self-harming or suicide then reach out to crisis services like the 988 suicide prevention lifeline. Also, a therapist and even a primary care doctor can help you.

When it comes to asking for help, you can also reach out to your natural support systems like your family and friends too.

In addition, one of the most annoying feelings in the world is when you don't feel like you're able to get help straight away or you're told "no" in different ways. For example, I hate it when my therapist doesn't have an appointment for me for a week and a bit, that is just annoying because I want support now and I'm not able to get it. Another form of this is when clients are looking for inpatient programmes and the programmes they want to get into don't have any "beds" available.

When this happens, you need to keep trying and realise that you reaching out for support is an act of defiance against your depression, so keep doing it. Keep looking for therapists, support and other options.

Just please make sure you get the help and support you need.

Remember Your Reasons For Living

I know from personal experience how extremely difficult this can be during a depressive episode.

When it comes to reasons for living, a lot of people want to live so they can see their friends and family, they have hope for the future so they want to see what happens and they believe that they'll find something worth living for in the future. Yet during a depressive episode, it can seem like a client doesn't have any of these options and they can't even start to think of these things.

For example, being brutally honest about yesterday, I do have a good number to live for coming up. I have Summer Core at my university from mid-June to mid-July as a student ambassador so that's a lot of fun, really easy work with a great pay check attached. Me and my family are going to Kew Gardens somewhere I've always wanted to go, I'm going to Canterbury Pride with some friends and I'm moving in with my friends at the end of next month.

In addition, me having a lot of normal reasons to live for because my life is good.

I couldn't remember a single one of those reasons yesterday and even when I did remember, my depression or my mental health twisted it so these things didn't look like a reason to live.

As a result, when it comes to surviving a depressive episode, you need to remind yourself of reasons to live. You need to write down your reasons so you can read it and remember you have plenty of reasons to live for, as well as you can hang up pictures of the people that are close to you and love you too.

Just give yourself as many reminders that life is worth living as possible.

Conclusion

I never really intended to do a chapter on depression but I wasn't really inspired or bothered about any of the other topics I have on my list after what happened yesterday. And I have to admit that I like chapters like this because even though nothing in this book is official advice, I still like that I can do slightly more practical and applied chapters that will hopefully help a student, professional or another person entirely.

Going through a depressive episode is awful and I don't wish it on anyone, but there is always hope and you are never alone.

There is always support available and whilst it might seem difficult to find, it is there and there are lots of people happy and ready to help you, because you deserve it.

You never deserve to suffer in silence and you can survive a major depressive episode.

You seriously can.

WHAT TO DO WHEN DEPRESSION MAKES IT IMPOSSIBLE TO GET OUT OF BED?

I wanted to include this next chapter because during the worse of my mental health because of my rape, it was very typical for me to take hours upon hours to get out of bed in the morning. For me, getting out of bed felt like it would take way too much energy and it feels impossible.

This was awful, scary and it made me feel even worse about myself. I felt useless, pathetic and I meant I was laying in bed with nothing to do except ruminate about my sexual trauma even more, leading to me trauma responses. Over time, this only created an evil cycle of me not being able to get out of bed so I thought rape and I experienced more trauma responses, so it felt even more impossible to get out of bed and so on.

As a result, I wanted to include this next chapter to help you understand this consequence of sexual trauma and how might be able to support yourself if you encounter this difficulty.

Of course, whilst nothing in this book is any form of official advice, this will hopefully still be very interest, useful and insightful.

Enjoy.

***

With depression being one of the most common mental health conditions in the world, a lot of a clinical psychologist's workload will be supporting people with depression. A common depression symptom is what's known as "Leaden Paralysis" and one of the effects of the symptoms is that everyday tasks take a million times more energy to complete. This can make the "simple" task of getting out of bed feel impossible for people with depression. Therefore, in this chapter, you'll learn what is leaden paralysis, why leaden paralysis impacts people's mental health and what to do when depression makes it impossible to get out of bed.

<u>What is The Weight of Depression?</u>

If you've ever experienced depression then you might be aware that there are some days where your depression will weigh you down so much that it feels like your body is made of lead and concrete. This makes the very notion of doing anything, much less leave your bed feel flat out impossible. As well as the sheer weight of depression might make you cancel plans, spend more time at home and/ or you might miss or be late for work.

This weight of depression and a struggle to get out of bed can take a massive toll on your work, relationships and your quality of life.

Personally, during August until October 2024 when I had quite severe depression, it always took me about two hours to get out of bed in the morning. Getting out of bed just felt hard because I had fun things to do, I could see my friends and everything but it wasn't good enough motivation to actually want to get out of bed. I just wanted the day to be over so I could sleep and I didn't have to deal with all the trauma responses that I was having every single hour of every single day.

What Is Leaden Paralysis?

As a result, there is a symptom of depression called "leaden paralysis" that causes people with depression to experience a severe drop in energy and as Qi et al. (2020) highlights this makes everyday tasks a million times harder for the individual. This is important to bear in mind because a lot of people who have never experienced depression or severe depression before might argue that people should just get up. Yet it isn't that easy. And this is one of the reasons why depression is a leading cause of disability round the world (Friedrich, 2017).

One of the clearest examples for me of leaden paralysis was on the very first day of my severe depression when it took me 5 hours just to have a shower. After struggling to get up for two or three hours, I managed to eventually make breakfast and at midday I decided to try to have a shower. Yet everything felt so heavy, I was so drained, I had no energy and my body might as well have had 20kg kettlebells tied to it.

It took so long to go through the living room, up the stairs, grab my towel and clothes, go across the landing, go into the bathroom, undressed, etc, etc.

Every one of those steps felt so impossible and each one took so long.

That is what leaden paralysis is like and that's why supporting people with depression is so important. You can probably imagine but having leaden paralysis doesn't make you feel great and it can make you feel even worse about yourself as your quality of life starts to crumble, so this is why mental health support is critical.

What To Do When Depression Makes It Impossible To Get Out Of Bed?

Here are three strategies to help people with depression overcome leaden paralysis and get out of bed in the mornings.

Firstly, you can break the day down into "hoops". This strategy involves breaking down your day into sections then you visualise these tasks as hoops. For example, getting up or brushing your teeth can be seen as two hoops that need to be conquered. After completing each task, you could imagine yourself jumping through each hoop and this can be an encouraging visual so you get a sense of achievement, and it helps to make the day less overwhelming. As well as on the really difficult days, seeing tasks as hoops can help you determine what tasks or hoops can be done on other days.

Secondly, you need to try to be kind to yourself because one of the ways how depression impacts us is makes us criticise ourselves more often. Therefore, to define your depression and how it criticizes you every chance it gets, you might want to practise self-kindness by using compassionate words when you realise your self-dialogue is getting more negative and harsher.

For example, today is actually a good example for me because my mental health definitely dipped today, and I was tired, overwhelmed and I was anxious about seeing my partner tomorrow because of trauma responses. My partner has done nothing wrong by the way. This meant I didn't get up for over an hour this morning and when I had a nap in the late afternoon in an effort to make myself feel better, I napped for 40 minutes but I didn't get out of bed for another two hours.

At first I was judging myself harshly because that was such a waste of time, I had so much to do and on and on and on. But I realised that it's okay I couldn't get out of bed earlier because this is what happens when my mental health dips. I need to listen to myself, figure out what's causing my mental health to dip and just keep going. Things will get better later on or tomorrow and as long as I focus on just going forward then that's okay. As well as I am hardly alone because this happens to everyone at different times in their life, even more so when you have depression and other mental health difficulties.

This is what works for me, you might need other self-compassionate and self-kindness thoughts.

The key is to not feed into your depression by criticising and hating yourself because you can't get out of bed. This will only make it feel even harder to do everyday tasks.

Finally, reach out for mental health support, because if you're experiencing depression that is so severe you find it really difficult to get out of bed. It is important that you seek mental health support as soon as possible because if you don't get support then your symptoms might get worse and your risk of suicide and self-harm increase. I really don't want that for you. As well as your depression might make you want to be alone and isolate yourself, but when you're struggling, it is a really good idea to be surrounded by other people. These people can include friends and family, but make sure you reach out to mental health professionals like a therapist or a mental health helpline too. Since if you isolate yourself then you might quickly find yourself in an echo chamber surrounded by your negative thoughts and inactivity and this will only maintain your depression.

And make you feel worse and worse until you don't see another way out.

Whenever I go through depression and mental health difficulties, reaching out to mental health support is always the best thing I could have done. It is always nerve-racking, I try to put it off as long as possible and I try to deal with things on my own at first. Yet ultimately seeing a counsellor, therapist or another form of mental health support is always best and I grow and develop so much and I flat out love the process too.

Conclusion

Whether you're an aspiring or qualified psychologist or person with depression, we've learnt a lot in this chapter. For psychologists, a lot of our future work will be with people with depression and we will encounter leaden paralysis the majority of the time because it is a common symptom. I know as someone who has experienced the inability to get out of bed frequently in the past, this is very distressing, it makes you feel awful about yourself and it can play into suicidal thoughts.

Especially, when every single other everyday task seems to require so much effort that your quality of life just crumbles and is reduced to nothing.

This is why learning about strategies to support clients with leaden paralysis is so important.

For people with depression, I hope you now have some strategies to help you get out of bed in the morning and I hope you realise that you aren't alone. What you're experiencing is normal for depression and it is a normal response for whatever is causing your difficulties and that's why talking to a mental health professional is critical.

Here are some questions at the end of this chapter:

- Have you ever encountered leaden paralysis before? Either through personal or clinical experience.
- How have you dealt with these experiences of leaden paralysis?
- Do you know how to practise self-kindness?
- How could you learn more about self-kindness?
- What would you say to a loved one and/ or client who struggles to get out of bed in the morning because of their depression?

SOMETIMES IT GETS WORSE BEFORE IT GETS BETTER: LESSONS FROM FIFTH SESSION OF RAPE COUNSELLING

Around the time of my 5th counselling session, my mental health was really taking a turn for the worse because at this point, the rape counselling wasn't helping as much as I needed. I didn't feel like it was working, I felt my counsellor was always saying the wrong thing and my PTSD was getting worse and worse.

So, this is really hard to write but I want you to know dear reader that a lot of the so-called "dark" or "negative" trauma responses that happen to a rape survivor are normal reactions to an extremely abnormal situation. As well as I want you to see over the course of this book that my mental health has dramatically improved and my PTSD, anxiety and all my other trauma responses have basically gone at the time of writing (week 11).

Yet I tried to kill myself that week.

It's 8 weeks ago so I don't really remember it clearly but I just remember that my best friend was helping one of our housemates Ruby (a fake name) because their mental health wasn't the best that night. Then me and my other housemate were simply sitting on the two sofas just talking and I felt so bad I just started scratching my wrist.

I kept going until it was painful and then I realised my best friend (yes, not me) was going to get really stressed about this and it was going to impact them badly. So I went upstairs and grabbed a plaster and stuff and the night got worse and worse for me, I was getting more and more suicidal but I didn't try again too much.

Then my best friend had a long conversation with me because they were scared that I hadn't called them, they explained how me dying would ruin their life and they care about a lot. I already knew all this but it was nice to hear it again I suppose.

My mental health was still horrific for another week.

In addition, as part of our conversation, me and my best friend spoke about how we need to continue to plan fun things together so I have something to look forward to. This is why even now we schedule time together every Tuesday and Sunday. For example, last Sunday we went to see Wicked: Part One and we went to a Vietnamese restaurant in Canterbury. It was a lovely six hours together.

Moreover, they made me write down the following on a Note on my phone:

'No I'm not a burden. They're my friend

No we don't only talk about my mental health. Then List other stuff we talk about

IT WILL RUIN THEIR LIFE IF I KILL MYSELF"

You can see one of the reasons why I was suicidal in that note. I just felt like all we were talking about was my mental health and it wasn't a good friendship anymore, because I felt like my best friend was a carer and not a friend. As well as because I felt like all we were doing was talking about my mental health was I felt like a massive burden.

That's why I tried to kill myself that night and thankfully I didn't, because life is really good now and you'll see that in the future chapters.

NEVER KILL YOURSELF.

Furthermore, me and my best friend spoke about me looking into my savings or asking my parents for money for a therapist, because at that point in time, my rape counselling just wasn't having much of an effect on me. At least not a positive effect.

PowerPoint Night

Then two days later on the Tuesday, I had another mental health crisis as did Ruby, because we went to Neurodivergent Society PowerPoint presentation night at my university. Basically, a bunch of autistic and ADHD people give a 20-minute max presentation about their special interest (something they are REALLY passionate about).

Someone was interested in witchcraft and spells and the Society committee hadn't thought to check exactly what content was covered in the PowerPoint. The witchcraft one covered a lot of non-consensual love spells and erotic-binding spells.

My mind went mad at that so when I got back with my housemates I had a full-on mental health crisis because non-consensual stuff was so triggering for me.

It was so bad that I sent the following message to the President of the Society:

"Hey thanks for doing the presentation night earlier and letting me present. It was great to see the other presenters, but could the society please screen the PowerPoints first for trigger warnings?

Because the first presentation mentioned a lot of non-consent and erotic-binding spells. It was a great topic but considering I was raped a few months ago, I find non-consent sex and romance extremely triggering. And I had full on mental health crisis when I got back.

Please know I'm not blaming the presenter, the society or anyone else. It's just a trigger warning would have been nice. I'm probably just as guilty even referencing trans mental health."

I got a very supportive message back and I was surprised that the very next day, the society started advertising for two welfare officers. One of them became my best friend so it all worked out in the end but it was an extremely rough night.

My Fifth Counselling Session

Now that you know the context behind my fifth counselling session, we can move onto the session itself and it did not go well. I should mention here that it takes a lot of courage to actually go to counselling or therapy in the first place because you aren't sure if it's going to work, you have to reveal personal details to someone who is effectively a stranger and it is a tense time. Especially after sexual violence, but I always recommend therapy and counselling because mental health professionals do have the skills to help decrease your distress, improve your lives and give you new adaptive coping mechanisms.

It takes even more courage to tell a counsellor that you tried to kill yourself.

That's what I did and it didn't go well.

She seemed concerned (clearly) but there was a judgmental undertone and her voice sounded angry. I'm not sure if it actually was but she wasn't happy and her words only confirmed it. "Well Connor, that's a big statement to make,"

I've been a psychology student, podcaster and I've read more than enough about therapy to know what her response should have been. So I felt scared and nervous so whilst I should have challenged her, I didn't.

I explain a lot more in the next chapter about how a mental health professional should respond to a suicide revelation. She helped me to explore what led to the suicide attempt and why I felt like that was the only way out.

I didn't really want to talk to her too much after her reaction but I was there for counselling and I was there for psychological support, so I was going to talk for the sake of it.

She helped me learn 3 things that I could take away by the end of the session (but when I made more dramatic attempts on my life 5 days later, I didn't tell her. something I seriously do not recommend for you to do).

You'll see in the next therapy chapter how I had a major breakthrough but that's not the focus of this chapter.

Anyway, she helped me to understand that I need to allow myself to feel what I need and want to feel. Since the event that started the chain of events that led to my suicide attempt was 2 days before the attempt on the Friday, I had a meeting with a friend of mine who's doing his PhD and he works at my university's Parkinson's clinic. He had spoken to the clinical psychologist at the clinic who I had been talking about my PhD idea with, and he had some news to give me.

He said that the clinical psychologist (who is the national leading expert on Brief Psychological Interventions) said that my idea for a Brief psychological Intervention for rape survivors wasn't practical. Since it wouldn't get through ethics because it could be unethical to give rape survivors some mental health support that has an end date and ethics wouldn't allow me to do clinical work with such a vulnerable group. As well as she wasn't sure that Brief Psychological Interventions would be useful for rape survivors because they need a lot more support than BPIs are designed to give. Finally, she didn't think the project was practical because it would require someone at the university to be clinically trained and able to clinically supervise me.

She would have liked to but her contract didn't allow it.

The issue with this rejection of my PhD proposal was that I didn't allow myself to grieve. This was an idea I was extremely excited by because I knew this had the potential to stop so, so many rape survivors from going through what I went through over the summer.

I knew I felt grief, I was upset and I was really devastated that I wasn't able to do this amazing project. My error was that I didn't allow myself to feel these emotions because I knew they were going to hurt so I simply let them build and build and build along with everything else going on in my life.

In addition, she encouraged me to use the Three Good Things technique from positive psychology and even now I still do this because it is a great technique that helps you to understand and appreciate that even on the darkest days, there are good things to celebrate.

Below is an extract from a psychology article I wrote that explains what this technique is:

"What Is The Three Good Things Techniques?

Interestingly enough I learnt our next technique when I was talking to a Final Year undergraduate student one afternoon when we were both sitting in a psychology area that only researchers have access to. She had my older placement and Final Year Project supervisor as her own so we were talking about her project.

She mentioned one of her experiments that her group was working on was using this next technique in a two-week intervention to improve depressed mood.

That was my first encounter with technique and it's interested me ever since, and it's appeared back in my life again recently as I still reel from my trauma and mental health.

As a result, the Three Good Things technique was introduced in 2005 by Martin Seligman for clients with low self-esteem and/ or depressed mood so they could do this in 5 or 10 minutes a day. The technique involves a client writing down three positive things that happened that day. Also, what's really good about this technique is that even on the roughest of days, there will be some positives as well as these positives don't have to be great.

For example, my mental health was truly, truly horrific last Tuesday at the time of writing, but my positive things would still be:

- I allowed myself to hug my dear friend so they touched me.
- I gave a presentation at neurodivergent society.
- I brought myself some Biscoff chocolate.

You can see in this example, there are two "big" positives and a small one and that's okay.

If we look at the next day, which was another bad day. There are no "big" positives but there were still positives in the day.

- I got up to go to counselling as much as I didn't want.
- I saw my parents.
- I brought back supplies Dad had brought me from Costco.

Therefore, whilst there were no "big" positives in that list. It was still really nice seeing my parents, seeing that Dad brought me a lot of Tassimo pods for my machine and I went to counselling.

We all need to take the wins and this technique helps you to realise that there are always positives in your life. No matter how dark the world seems.

Moreover, the advantage of this technique is that it encourages clients to be positive and it improves their mood. Yet these three good things can feel forced or artificial at times.

Lastly for this technique, my counsellor just calls this technique "adding some positive psychology" into your life. Now, I am have major issues with her calling the technique that because positive psychology is an entire massive discipline, you cannot put an entire discipline into your life. But she recommends I start using the technique so I can focus on the positives and this is something I seriously need to start doing.

Maybe we all do."

Ultimately, whilst I didn't like how she responded to my revelation that I tried to kill myself because it was judgmental and there wasn't the level of support in terms of empathy and compassion that I needed in that moment. I still learnt some important things like the Three Good Things technique that still benefits my mental health even now.

Yes. Sometimes your mental health will get worse before it gets better but counselling and social support are always useful for helping you get through it.

HOW SHOULD THERAPISTS REACT AFTER A SUICIDE REVELATION?

In the last chapter, I mentioned how I don't feel like my counsellor handled my suicide revelation very well so I wanted to investigate how therapists and other mental health professionals *should* handle this revelation. Since I understand that this might be the worst case scenario for any aspiring or even qualified psychologist, because when their client reveals they want to or they have attempted suicide. This naturally feels any psychologist with dread and fear because this is a very serious situation.

That's why I've added in this chapter adapted from a podcast episode because it is ultimately, a therapist's words, actions and body language to a suicide revelation that determines what happens next. Since if they react negatively then this can make the client feel invalidated, silly and stupid so this makes them more distant and disengaged in therapy. Also, it harms the therapeutic alliance as well as if a client feels alienated from their therapist (the one person in the world who is meant to support them, help them and be there for them) then the darker option can be a lot, lot more tempting. On the other hand, if a client feels supported by their therapist's "positive" reaction to their revelation then this can deepen trust and ultimately allow the therapist to get through to the client to help them heal in a very dark time in their life. Therefore, in this chapter, you'll learn how therapists should react to a suicide revelation and some tips and techniques to help therapists in this situation. If you enjoy learning about mental health, suicide and clinical psychology then this will be a great chapter for you.

Why Am I Talking About This Topic?

For context and as much as I don't want to admit it, I did do a suicide attempt in mid-October 2024 and it was a hellish night for me. As well as my best friend when they eventually found out about it. Granted a lot happened that night for other people and it gave me the shock that I needed to know I had to start looking after myself better because what I was currently doing wasn't enough, even though I thought it was.

Therefore, after a rough Tuesday night and Wednesday morning, I had specialist counselling on Wednesday at 12 pm. I told my therapist that I attempted suicide but I really didn't like her reaction. I wanted or imagined a therapist to clearly be shocked, concerned and maybe even scared internally.

Yet externally, I wanted her to take a deep breath and simply say something along the lines of this, *Okay, firstly, thank you for telling me. I know that couldn't have been easy but I'm glad you told me. Secondly, you know this is serious so, can you please tell me what happened?*

A therapist is meant to be non-judgmental and 100% supportive in this situation. Yet my counsellor wasn't and she messed up with me because her first thing was "Well Connor, that's a massive statement you made. You tried to commit suicide," and I didn't like her tone or her facial expressions because they were not non-judgemental.

And because her tone was slightly angry, I did disengage. I went into flight-freeze-fight in her therapy room for a little bit. And I calmed down as we spoke about what happened, what led up to the event but even now I am not okay because of some of the things she said during this conversation.

For example, she accused me of playing games with myself because I keep trying to do small distressing things when I can't. Instead I would have preferred her to say something kinder. Maybe something like "Do you think it's a pattern that your PTSD gets triggered by, in your own words, *small* things?" then I would like to imagine this would start a conversation getting *me* to realise that I need to just leave as soon as I get distressed so I can handle the little things.

Anyway, that's a topic for another day.

Ultimately, my counsellor made me feel bad, unsupported and very judged at a time when I seriously did not need to be judged. Therefore, I wanted to learn about how therapists should react to suicide revelations and whilst the rest of the chapter isn't an exhaustive and ultimate guide. It will surely help you be a million times better than my counsellor.

Let's begin.

How Should Therapists React To A Suicide Revelation?

In the rest of the chapter, we're going to look at 7 points explaining how therapists should respond to clients with suicidal thoughts. Yet when it comes to each of these points, it is critical to remember that clients must be treated with empathy, compassion and professionalism. These three things are the most important aspects of this situation.

You Need To Actively and Empathetically Listen To Suicidal Clients

Whenever you're faced with a suicidal client, you absolutely need to listen actively and empathetically because the client has decided to be extremely brave and tell you about this fact. The client will most probably be scared and utterly terrified that something bad will happen to them now. Sometimes they might be scared that you'll cart them off to a psychiatric ward, you'll prescribe them drugs or you will make them do something.

Whilst none of these fears are logical or based in reality in a general sense, the media, books and films have implanted these rare possibilities into our collective minds. Making these fears very real to our clients.

This is why our clients are extremely brave for telling us what's happening to them.

Therefore, it is important that you allow the client to express their feelings without any interruption as well as that you show empathy and you validate their emotions.

My counsellor tried to do this because she seemed angry at first, I interpreted them in my vulnerable state as judgment and invalidation. As well as I didn't feel like she was very empathetic to my reasons and my situation so I felt like she had put a wedge between us. This isn't what you want with clients.

<u>You Need To Assess The Risk</u>

There are a lot of different tools and ways how you can do this and please stick to whatever your organisation uses, so I will talk more generally about this topic. Whenever you have a suicidal client, you seriously need to assess the risks because research shows that once a client tries to kill themselves, they are a lot more likely to have a suicide attempt and the last thing we want is for clients to keep trying and one day actually be successful.

This is a major area that my counsellor messed up in because she didn't do a risk assessment, she didn't do anything that I'm about to tell you and I honestly think even if she did I would have lied to her. Simply because she had put that wedge between us by making me feel judged and not understood. Since I first tried to kill myself three days before the appointment I told her in then there was her judgement and I tried to kill myself again 5 days later using two different methods.

Thankfully, I had a very healing day the following day so it will not happen again.

Anyway, a therapist or clinical psychologist should always carry out a thorough risk assessment to help you fully understand the severity of the suicidal idealisation within the client. It's useful to know about the duration, frequency and the intensity of the suicidal idealisation, and if there are any plans or means to carry out the suicide attempt.

My counsellor didn't ask me a single one of these basic questions.

<u>You Need To Create A Safety Plan With Suicidal Clients</u>

Professional training and different organisations have more detailed tips and guides about how to do this, but as a general overview, when a client reveals their suicidal idealisation, you need to create a safety plan with them. This is so the client has a guide or ideas about what to do instead of trying to commit suicide.

Therefore, in the development of this safety plan, you should include emergency contacts (like helplines), coping strategies so the client knows how to deal with suicidal thoughts and what steps they need to take if the suicidal thoughts get more intense and they want to make an attempt.

Again, my counsellor didn't do any of this kind of work with me and that was very dangerous. If she had calmly created a safety plan with me then things might have been different and I might not have tried again, so please make safety plans with your clients.

<u>If The Client Agrees, Involve Support Systems</u>

On the podcast and in my different rape-focused books, I've often spoken about how my best friend has been a major, major support system in my life since I was raped. My best friend has done a lot for me to ensure that I was safe, I was as okay as I could be and that I had hope for the future. We've spent a lot of time together, we've laughed a lot and we've created some really good memories together since I was raped.

Support systems are critical to everyone going through a mental health crisis.

As a result, if the client agrees, you can involve family members and the client's friends in the process so they can support the client. If this does happen, then the family members and friends need to understand the importance of their role in the client's safety. For example, they might be needed to sit with the client when you're suicidal, they might need to take away objects or do other things to prevent the client from killing themselves or they could do something else entirely.

The details change for every client and what their support system is like, but you get the general idea.

Therapists Should Provide Resources and Follow-Up To The Suicidal Client

Something else that my counsellor should have done as standard but she didn't was provide me with a list of resources. These resources are designed to help clients when they're suicidal and they need help the most. For example, these resources can and should include details of crisis hotlines, support groups and essentially anything that can help clients get immediate help.

This is something that will help the client when you're suffering the most and this could be the difference between an attempt and no attempt, let alone a successful or unsuccessful attempt.

The issue I had with my counsellor was that she didn't give me anything. I didn't know any hotlines, any ways to get additional help and I was just left still feeling a little suicidal after the appointment. My suicidality only got worse after that appointment.

Thankfully, I am okay now and I wouldn't do it again but at that time I was in so much pain.

Yet life gets better. I know that now.

In addition, therapists should follow up with suicidal clients by scheduling regular follow-up sessions to monitor their progress and adjust the intervention plan as needed.

Conclusion: Continue Your Professional Development

Once I was talking to a clinical psychologist who lectures at my university and he said something that I hope is going to stay with me. It doesn't matter what mental health service you work in, be it children and adolescents, eating disorders, depression or Obsessive-Compulsive Disorder. Suicidality and suicide risk will always be on your workload at some point in your career, because this is the unfortunate reality of mental health and its negative consequences.

Therefore, I firmly believe that as part of your Continued Professional Development, you keep learning, investigating and researching about suicide prevention, and even postvention. It is critical for you as a therapist, and your clients, that you have the most updated knowledge and best practices about suicide prevention.

At some point in your career, you will meet and have to work with a suicidal client, and your training will matter more than ever. It's beyond critical for you to remain composed, calm and you are sure that clients feel heard and supported during this extremely difficult process. Hearing that a client is suicidal will be difficult for you and you will have an emotional reaction to such a revelation, but for the sake of the client, you need to remain calm and you need to focus on the client.

Make sure look yourself later on, use your clinical supervision to your benefit and make sure you don't get burnt out.

Yet ultimately, as a therapist, your response can and will make a significant difference to the client's journey towards recovery.

Your actions, your words, your response matters, so please keep learning, stay calm and remember to act with empathy and compassion. Two elements that are more important than ever.

GREAT HEALING MOMENT, A BRILLIANT SESSION. THINGS ARE LOOKING UP: LESSONS LEARNT FROM SESSION SIX

Everything in my life went to sh*t after my last therapy session and that is a large part of the first half of this chapter. I tried to kill myself in two very different ways but equally I had an extremely healing moment that I'll explain in a moment.

Now I will admit that I did not tell my counsellor about my two other suicide attempts after she reacted with such judgment without empathy or compassion, the last time that I made a revelation to her.

Therefore, in a moment, I'll explain what happened in the therapy session itself because there were a lot of major breakthroughs and I am extremely grateful that this therapy session happened.

Below is a long but fascinating extract from the conclusion of *I Am Not A Victim, I Am A Survivor* and I'm including it in the chapter, because you can see how happy I was the night it happened. Also, this was written the night before session 6 of my rape counselling.

It shows a lot of useful insights and lessons for sure.

<u>Extract</u>

"A Healing Moment is when something just snaps inside you and your entire world changes for the better. It does not mean you are "cured" (whatever that means and that isn't how mental health works anyway), it does not mean everything will be plain sailing anymore and it does not mean you will never be in pain again.

I am actually tearing up as I write this section.

A Healing Moment simply means you realise that there is hope that everything can get better, you are definitely not a victim and if everyone is telling you that life gets better (hopefully they are or they shouldn't be in your life) that you realise it and internalise it as the truth that it is.

In addition, Healing Moments look different for everyone and what mine looks like will probably be completely different to yours. Your Healing Moment might be tiny, yours might be massive, yours might make you cry or it might not.

It is *your* Healing Moment for a reason.

As a result, my Healing Moment happened today because I tried to kill myself twice last night in two different ways. I also found out I hurt my best friend by accident and I had done something wrong with a housemate that really hurt them. It was truly awful and I tried to kill myself.

Moreover, my mental health has been so bad for so long that I just couldn't see another way out. I've self-harmed, been suicidal for months and I have an eating disorder and on and on and on.

So I tried to kill myself.

Thankfully, my housemates subtly rallied around me and when I woke up this morning, I still felt suicidal but the idea of me hurting my best friend. Who I love romantically, who has always been there for me and the one person I have lived for for so long, I realised I had two choices.

Either I could keep trying to kill myself and ruin my best friend's life forever so I could find a new way of healing.

My best friend went to the gym with a new friend that I've made and getting close with, so I went into the library and started reading the *Healing Sexual Trauma Workbook* again. I have not read this book in months because I used to the possible "excuse" that my mental health was too bad that I didn't want to try it.

I had forgotten how great this book is for me personally. This book truly makes me feel understood and validated.

There was a simple exercise that changed everything.

The first chapter of the book focuses on feeling safe in your own skin and after the first few pages, the exercises focus on helping you to focus on the *feelings* of safety. For example, what does your body feel like when you feel unsafe then there's another question on what does your body feel like when you feel safe.

Those are not the actual wording of the questions and there are questions on thoughts during these times too, but you get the gist.

As a result, this is what I wrote for my answers:

When I feel unsafe, my body panics. My breathing increases but goes shallow, I shake and my thoughts go a million miles an hour.

When I feel safe, my body just feels 100% relaxed and untensed.

Now my counsellor has been wanting me to focus on my body for ages but maybe I was resistant to it, maybe I needed it to be worded differently, but that did not work for me.

However, me thinking and writing down how my body actually felt when I was safe was brilliant. It got me to label this feeling so I could savour it when I felt safe and I could focus on getting my body to that state.

In hindsight I did some weird stuff to savour that feeling. I went and sat in two different toilets at the university and I went into a very busy Co-Op (just think corner shop on campus) and each time I focused on feeling completely relaxed and untensed. I savoured that wonderful feeling of being relaxed and my body just not caring or being in survival mode.

I am relaxed because I am safe. I am always safe.

Then of course, I felt depressed and bad for the next few hours because I felt awful about hurting my best friend. Granted, they had already forgotten about it at that point, but I read a bit more of the workbook.

I did some more exercises but I did something interesting. I focused on feeling 100% relaxed in my own home in Canterbury with my three housemates in the house.

I realised ever since mid-August when I had my mental health collapse and everything happened. I had not felt safe in this house, this has never been my home and I know I haven't enjoyed living with two extra housemates as much as I love them. In a way, I suppose I have never felt safe in this house either.

I 100% relaxed today in my own home and I could do it so easily.

And this is my home now. I belong in this house with my three housemates, I belong in Canterbury and I am not a problem and all the million other things my mind tries to tell me.

I am not a problem.

It is a lovely feeling to know that I am home.

Something else I've been struggling with lately was my best friend has been focusing a lot more on another housemate who is going through hell-and-back at the moment. Also, my best friend deals with us in extremely different ways and I think I have been a lot more jealous than I want to admit.

My mind has tried to twist it repeatedly as my best friend not liking me, hating me and my best friend not wanting to be friends anymore.

But the following message highlights a large part of my Healing Moment:

I'm really sorry I'm chronically insecure a lot of the time because you're all I have in terms of real support.

And that it's taken me so long to realise that you focusing more on, spending more time with and doing more tasks for R isn't a reflection of you not liking, you hating me or our friendship breaking down so much so you're a carer, not a friend.

Mine and R's mental health manifests in very different ways and you are more comfortable with them anyway. R needs the constant help and support right now and for the next few months, and that's okay. Because you've offered the same to me since June without me realising it and now you can't be in two places at once.

I need to focus on my healing for me and I know you are always there for me when I need it most, but now I need to take back control because otherwise something might genuinely happen to this friendship without even one of us seeing it until it's too late.

So what I'm saying is... Thank you for being the most amazing and patient friend I could ever ask for. And I understand what I need to do to heal now a little better.

You're still there for me and I am ALWAYS there for you and it will still hurt like hell at times for me because of my trauma, but I now realise I don't need you to make me feel safe in my own home.

And here with R, L and especially you, you're all my home.

(Yes I teared up writing this. I hope this makes sense and I don't come off as a dick)

Thankfully, my best friend found that message really cute and sweet, and I need to send one to R and L later (don't you just love how creative I am with pseudonyms).

Ultimately, my Healing Moment boiled down to finally, finally realising that I am worthy of people liking me for me. I don't need to think I'm a burden, I don't need to think unless I am a certain way I'll be safe and I don't need to rely on other people to make me feel safe, because I am safe. And as long as I focus on that 100% relaxed and untensed feeling in my body then I know, I will truly know that I am safe."

My Sixth Counselling Session

Overall, it was a brilliant session because it was the most positive session I had had up to that point, and it felt great that it was a session that focused on myself, what I needed and it celebrated the major success I had made that week.

It wasn't a session that made me feel bad, traumatised and it didn't make me feel hopeless. Granted, none of the sessions themselves ever made me feel like this, it was more the aftermath of the sessions and me still having to deal with PTSD, anxiety and other trauma responses.

That was not easy to still have to deal with after each of the other counselling sessions, but I actually didn't need to experience those things as much after this breakthrough and session.

In addition, during this session, I asked her about wanting to process more of the trauma instead of doing stabilisation work. In the next chapter, I explain more about the Trauma Recovery Model that my rape counselling is based on, at least, so you can understand how it works.

My counsellor mentioned how even when we're doing stabilisation work, I'm still processing the trauma and slowly integrating it into my everyday life. All three of those components are important parts of the Model that you'll look at next.

Personally, I really liked that explanation. Not only because she named the model so I could later research it on my own (granted it took me 9 weeks to research that model), but I liked knowing I was still making good progress. I liked processing what He had done to me that night and it was comforting to know that I wasn't "stuck" in the stabilisation stage, I was actually processing and progressing towards healing.

Ultimately, she explained how the aim of the specialist counselling as well as Recovery Model is to help me integrate the sense of safety into my life amongst a few other things so I can heal, thrive and live the life that I want to choose. In other words, I control my life, not my trauma.

3 Main Areas To Work On

The next part of the session really focused on the final stage of the trauma Recovery Model, focusing on integrating that sense of safety into your everyday life. I was really happy that we were focusing on this aspect because this is where I wanted to put my focus on now.

I wanted to focus on living, thriving and actually doing more than just surviving for the first time in my life. Therefore, we worked together to identify three major areas of my life that I wanted to focus on for now.

Dungeons And Dragons

Firstly, my best friend is in charge of a Dungeons and Dragons Campaign (DM) and they run this with our other housemates and some of our other friends. Amongst these other players with an overweight guy with longish brown hair (both of which are similar to my rapist) so being in the same room as him makes me very tense and over time it chips away at my mental health.

It was only a Friday or two before this sixth session that I just couldn't deal with DnD because my mental health just got too bad. Mainly because this player at no fault of their own was triggering my PTSD and other trauma responses too badly.

As a result, me and my counsellor discussed how I would in future use grounding techniques and focus on that physical feeling of safety to make DnD more manageable. Then over time as I get better at this skill and I'm able to desensitise myself further, I'll be able to stay in the room longer and longer.

Interestingly, I'm writing this chapter six weeks after this session and whilst I could argue that I have made no progress in this area because the triggering player hasn't joined us again (I doubt he will). I am actually going to celebrate how I have made a lot of progress in this area because the trigger I've been working on here is to do with fat men. In reality, my trauma responses are a lot better towards seeing, being in the same room and even being close to fat men.

Fat men no longer cause me to have trauma responses, experience intense anxiety or intrusive thoughts.

That is a major progress because I can go outside and live my life without being scared of my trauma responses around fat men.

<u>Going To The Gym</u>

Secondly, I really wanted to be able to go to the gym because it's something I can do with my friends, it's a way of seeing people and it means I can keep healthy and in shape.

In case you haven't read my book *I Am Not A Victim, I Am A Survivor,* the reason why the gym triggers a lot of trauma responses within me is because of the sportswear. I was raped in sportswear so seeing it all and having to see hot guys in sportswear is very hard for me.

It reminds me too much of my rape.

Therefore, a lot of me and my counsellor discussed is the same as the DnD content in terms of remembering and holding onto that physical feeling of safety. As well as take small steps so over time I can spend more and more time in the gym.

In addition, she did mention how I could desensitise myself to the sensory experiences of a gym too. For example, the smell, the sounds and more that's associated with the gym. Even if it's someone taking their belt off because that was an extremely distressing noise for me that me and my best friend found out the hard way. I had no idea that was such a triggering sound until it was far too late one night.

As a result, my idea was that I would sit in the gym café when there are all the gym people in their sportswear walking around, and I would do some work on my laptop. This would allow me to become desensitised to sportswear as it shows I can be around sportswear without anything bad happening to me.

Then I could build up going into the gym and working out.

Fast-forward six weeks later, I have only sat in the gym café once but that was at least a month after this session and by that time, my PTSD and other trauma reactions were dramatically reduced so it was fine. As well as I think I could easily go to the gym now and work out with my friends but given my eating disorder, I don't want to risk it.

As much as I have anorexic thinking, I am trying not to dramatically lose too many calories.

<u>Social Groups</u>

Finally, the Thursday before this counselling session, I went out with a new friend that I had made, let's call them Joe and their boyfriend. Originally, me and my housemates were meant to be going out with them for dinner but they all had to go back. Ruby was struggling so my best friend went to support them and my other housemate had a society event on then they went home afterwards as me, Joe and their boyfriend were talking.

Joe's boyfriend was an overweight man with long brown hair, exactly like my rapist. It was difficult for me for sure so I focused on Joe and the three of us chatted for two or three hours.

However, around nine o'clock in the evening, I started seriously dipping and I knew I needed to go. I forgot to mention that in my previous counselling session she had spoken to me about how I need to just go whenever I'm feeling down.

The issue on this particular night was that I had already offered them lifts home and I had never asked someone to just leave before. So I hung it out for another 15 minutes until I texted Joe (yes, the person sitting straight across from me) about me dipping and can we go.

If I had just left them that night then I might have been okay, but I didn't. We all walked back to my car and I drove them home. The walk to my car (on the other side of campus) was the longest part but I kept dipping more and more.

When I eventually got home, I had a mental health crisis, I couldn't stop shaking, my PTSD was kicked into high gear and it was a rough night. It was something about being stuck with two people in the enclosed space of my car that really bothered me. In my mind, Joe and their boyfriend could have done whatever they wanted to me and I wouldn't have been able to stop it.

That is what caused my crisis.

Anyway, I explained this to my counsellor and she was very empathetic and compassionate, because that was the first time I had ever practised the skill. As well as it's great that I did want to leave at some point, I didn't make it last any longer than needed.

Overall, in the future, I needed to do the same remembering and focusing on the physical feeling of safety as previously mentioned. Also, I needed to remember that if I am dipping then I NEED to go immediately. Then over time as my trauma responses get better and better, I can work myself towards being able to take people home.

Thankfully, 6 weeks on I have done that very well. I have driven new ambassadors at my university to and from work opportunities without a breakdown and everything is really good.

In a few chapters' time, you get to see how I met up with someone one-on-one for the first time since my rape.

Finally, I made my counsellor cry because I have had such a powerfully healing moment this week that I was able to change something in my perspective towards December. You see my best friend is going to Thailand to see some new family members for the first time so they won't be here for 10 days then they'll be staying with their family in the Midlands afterwards.

Therefore, we both found that us calling every day worked really well in August 2024. I was so depressed, suicidal and I was not able to do much of anything. At the start of the collapse of my mental health, it took me 5 hours just to have a shower.

We were going to call every day again when they were in Thailand and back in the Midlands for mental health support. Yet this particular week, I was able to say to my best friend "I don't want to call because you're my mental health support or you're my carer, I want to call every day because you're my best friend,"

I was only able to say that and make my counsellor cry because I had had a healing moment. You can have your healing moment too with the right support, counselling and friends.

WHAT IS THE THREE STAGE TRAUMA RECOVERY MODEL?

As a psychology Masters student at the time of writing with a massive interest in clinical psychology, I really like looking into therapies. This is even more true when I'm undergoing therapy and counselling for trauma, so when I found out my rape counselling was based on the Three-Stage Recovery Model by Judith Herman, I wanted to learn more. Granted, it took me 9 weeks to finally get round to researching the model in-depth but better late than never. Therefore, in this chapter, you'll learn what are the three stages included in this recovery model, why are they useful and how does the model work to treat trauma. If you enjoy learning about mental health, clinical trauma work and psychotherapy then this is a brilliant chapter for you.

What Is The Three-Stage Recovery Model By Judith Herman?

The more I read about trauma work and the psychological models designed to explain how to treat trauma, the more I realise how important American psychiatrist Judith Herman's recovery model actually is. This model forms the foundation of a lot of psychotherapies as well as it is the basis of the specialist rape counselling that I underwent between September and December 2024. I technically have one session left at the time of writing but we've done all the therapeutic work.

Personally, whilst I'll explain this model in a moment, as a psychology student, podcaster and writer, I find this model immensely useful. Since it explains how to deal with the trauma responses and gradually helps a client to return to a clinically normal life where they can control their actions, do the activities they want to do and they can enjoy life again.

As a client with sexual trauma, I found this model even more useful. It isn't a linear model which bugged me and my autistic brain, but it is very helpful. It allowed me to basically get rid of my Post-Traumatic Stress Disorder, decrease my triggers dramatically and I can actually do things again with my life. For example, last week, I went out with a new friend one-on-one for the first time since my rape. That was amazing and so major for me because before the very notion of spending one-on-one time with anyone but my best friend would cause me to have a mental health crisis.

Ultimately, the three stages of the recovery model are:

- Safety and Stabilisation
- Remembrance and Mourning

- Reconnection and Integration

During each of these stages, the therapist works with the client to create an environment where the client can safely process what happened to them without any sense of urgency. This helps to ensure the recovery is sustainable as well as empowering.

<u>What Is the Safety and Stabilisation Stage?</u>

The first stage of the recovery model is the "Safety and Stabilisation" stage and when I've looked into trauma work in a psychotherapy context I've always heard rumours about stabilisation work, but it is only through my counselling that I was able to see what that looks like. Therefore, stabilisation work is the very bedrock and foundation of all the therapy work that happens afterwards. The client absolutely needs to feel physically and emotionally safe before they can ever hope to engage with their trauma.

There is a real-world caveat here but I'll address it later.

In addition, a large focus for the therapist during stabilisation work is to build a rapport and ensure that clients feel comfortable with them. I always say how as therapists we are asking clients to reveal their own personal, dark moments to us, people who are effectively strangers. That takes a lot of courage and a lot of trust, so we need to earn that trust quickly and effectively.

One technique of helping clients feel comfortable is that trauma-informed counsellors must be prepared to disclose small amounts of personal information about themselves if the client asks a question. This is useful in building trust. Especially, as there is a relationship between the client and therapist called the therapeutic alliance, and if I adopt a marketing term "we buy from people we know, like and trust". We can adapt this idea to psychology because "we like working with therapists, we know, like and trust". Therefore, having a therapist open up to us about themselves helps us to know them so we can hopefully like them and trust them after a while too.

Judith Herman herself uses the comparison that clients like to know who's "holding the rope" during their therapy sessions so they can develop their sense of safety. Just like how a climber likes to know who's holding their rope (safety line) during a climbing challenge.

Moreover, stabilisation work involves reducing chaos and crisis in a client's life so this might involve helping them to create a sense or environment of normalcy within the therapeutic environment. This helps the client to feel secure enough to explore their trauma. Especially, because trauma survivors typically feel unsafe internally (within themselves) as well as externally (in the physical world). This is why trauma-informed therapists work with clients to understand the difference between their internal and external realities and help them to learn techniques to manage hyperarousal and other trauma responses.

In another chapter, you'll learn about Window of Tolerance for this reason.

On the whole, stabilisation work focuses on stabilisation techniques like psychoeducation, self-regulation and boundary-setting strategies. As well as therapists don't force disclosures or force progress too quickly because clients need to be able to progress their trauma at their own speed. Also, therapists help clients during stabilisation work to reduce chaos and crisis in their life, create a safe space and give the clients tools to help them separate their internal and external realities.

Something that is highly useful for dealing with flashbacks and other trauma responses.

What Is The Remembrance and Mourning Stage?

The second stage of Herman's recovery model is the Remembrance and Mourning stage that focuses on reconstructing the trauma through remembrance and then mourning. Unfortunately, clients can experience this stage as a timeless descent with no clear endpoint.

Interestingly enough, I actually experienced this sense and it was painful because it felt like I was processing things, remembering a lot of awful details about my rape but I didn't know what I was working towards. I didn't even know where the counselling was heading towards and I felt confused that I wasn't expressively telling her what happened during my rape.

Additionally, during this second stage, it isn't unusual for clients to experience grief over various losses in their lives. For example, their loss of innocence, some failed relationships and even loss of family support or friends. This is important to remember when we consider that a lot of survivors, even more so for survivors abused within families, are often rejected or are faced with disbelief when they disclose their trauma. This leads clients to feel isolated as trauma can sever family ties.

This connects to the topic of Rape Grief that I talk about in *I Am A Survivor, Not A Victim.*

Moving onto the mourning aspect of this stage, I was no exception to this issue, a lot of clients mourn over the loss of years (or months) that their trauma has controlled their life. Clients feel like the trauma has robbed them of time that could have been spent in healthy relationships, personal growth and fulfilling careers. This is why it's important that therapists support clients with empathy and without judgment so the client isn't rushed.

Personally, when it came to my childhood trauma, I was angry for so long that I wasn't able to form healthy friendships, relationships, get a boyfriend, kiss and enjoy so many normal things that normal teenagers are allowed to do. I mourned that loss for so, so long. Equally, when it came to my sexual trauma, I mourned for months that I was going through my PTSD, intense social anxiety, depression and all my other trauma responses. I mourned for the lost friendships, the lost ability to do fun things and I mourned for the impact it had/ has (still present tenses to be fair) on my writing, podcasting and everything else that I flat out love.

During this second stage, the therapist's main job is to help a client process these losses and provide a safe space for a client to recount their trauma without the pressure of time or any expectations. Clarity, courage and trust are all needed for therapists and clients throughout this stage.

What is The Reconnection and Integration Stage of The Recovery Model?

In the final stage of the model, therapists work with clients to help them work towards reconnecting with their world as well as integrating their trauma into a new sense of self. For example, during this stage, clients regain trust in their relationships because they've learnt how to extend their trust and when it's best not to extend trust to someone. As well as this stage involves something called "reparenting". I first came across this term in my counselling during August 2023 and this is a term that describes the therapist's role in modelling healthy boundaries as well as relationships. When it comes to trauma survivors, this can include relearning what are, how to have and how to recognise healthy sexual relationships. Something that myself and a lot of different survivors find immensely difficult, because this "reparenting" is often the first time that someone has spoken to us about what on Earth healthy relationships look like.

In addition, a major part of reconnection during this stage is the survivor developing and maintaining their ability to form and sustain healthy relationships. This doesn't only mean sexual relationships, but it can include friendships and familial relationships too. I talk a lot about these aspects of my trauma recovery in my book *Healing As A Survivor.* Also, for survivors of sexual abuse and sexual violence, a lot of survivors have to rediscover their sexual identity and sexual preferences, which is immensely challenging, because this only adds to the struggle that survivors have around their sense of self.

Furthermore, you tend to be able to see progress in this stage of trauma recovery in a few different ways. For instance, as clients progress, they can enjoy intimacy or new experiences without associating it with their abuser or feeling like they need to be protected from their abuser. And the reason why these are amazing, wonderful moments for survivors is because they show the client is growing in their autonomy and ability to live without the fear and trauma responses that have ruled their life for so long.

I know for me, being able to go out with a newish friend one-on-one was an amazing experience, because for the past 7 months that would have been flat out impossible. It would have caused me to have a panic attack, a breakdown and I would have had constant trauma responses. That had happened a good few times.

However, this is a difficult and scary stage of trauma recovery because it's an immensely weird and disorienting feeling to know that you don't need to be protected from your attacker. Also, it is so disorienting to feel safe, secure and able to experience life and pleasure without trauma responses. I talk more about this in my healing book, but I found it weird because I had been having severe PTSD for 7 months and then I wasn't.

It was weird to experience such an extreme change.

<u>Conclusion</u>

As much as I love the trauma recovery model because I have experienced it in the real world and I know how it can transform lives for the better, it isn't the best applied psychological model. Since the model itself proposes that these stages are very linear, but in reality, you tend to work through all these stages at the same time to different extents. When I was talking to my counsellor about this model, she explained how we work a lot on Stage 1 at the beginning but during stabilization work, you are processing the trauma too, and doing a little integration work too. Whereas towards the end of the therapy, you're working more on integration work and less on processing trauma and stabilisation work, but those stages are still present too.

Ultimately, the Three-Stage Recovery Model is a humane and thorough model that provides a helpful framework for trauma therapy. It focuses on client safety and respecting client autonomy during the healing process because the model stresses it is the client that controls their pace, not the therapist. Then the therapist facilitates the client's recovery by respecting the complex nature of trauma and provides the client with a safe space. As well as therapists and clients need to understand what can be achieved in the limited number of sessions that a mental health service provides so it's easier to maintain realistic therapeutic goals.

Yet we need to remember as aspiring and qualified psychologists that trauma work is not easy on *us*.

I know I always talk about how important focusing on our clients are but honestly, we are so important too. We cannot help people if we don't look after ourselves and if our mental health isn't as good as it could be. Therefore, clinical supervision and self-care are critical for therapists because trauma work takes an emotional toll on us so we need to practice good self-care and we need to balance what our clients need with our capacity. As well as trauma-informed therapists should receive ongoing professional support so regular discussions in supervision and peer consultations can be useful in maintaining their effectiveness and well-being. Finally, a supportive work environment is important too so therapists and clients can work in a safe environment and have the time needed for meaningful, sustained healing.

That will ultimately change our client's life for the better.

INTENSE TWO WEEKS, HEARTBREAK AT HOME AND PTSD IS NOT FUN: LESSONS FROM A SEVENTH SESSION

Note: you absolutely have to read the "Self-Compassion Steps" section in this chapter. It was a major healing technique for me, so it should help you too.

As a fellow survivor, person who works with survivors or you have a survivor in your life then you might be extremely well aware at this point that everything in healing depends on context. Therefore, for context, there was a two-week gap between my last session and this one because my counsellor needed to go away for a week to deal with a family matter.

Originally, I thought these two weeks were going to be great, really easy and great for my mental health because I felt safe, I felt secure and my PTSD was really starting to decrease. Whilst that was completely true in the second week, the first week did not want to follow my hopes and dreams.

My mental health died yet again for another few reasons that I will mention in this chapter, because they're insightful, they're helpful for understanding sexual trauma and its impact and there is a certain comedy in one of these events looking back.

Learning About A Massive Change In My Personal Life

I fully admit that looking back this was almost funny that I reacted this way to this specific event, but at the time, this was one of the most intense, awful and shocking 48 hours of my life. A lot happened and it was awful.

On the Sunday night of the first week, me and my housemates were hanging out in my best friend's bedroom talking, catching up and just spending time together. I was already feeling really low and my mental health wasn't great because sexual trauma is horrible. As well as me and my best friend had scheduled to spend some time together just the two of us and it was nine o'clock at night and it hadn't happened yet. I later found out we needed to plan something specific so it would happen and thankfully we've done a lot of great things since.

Yet at the time one of my very old friends from school had contacted me so I was writing out a message to her (after talking to her for the first time in years, no one can accuse me of writing too long messages again).

However, as I was writing this message, I started hearing kissing sounds that two people were making out. Bearing in mind I have never been kissed, no one has even made out with me and my rapist was the first person to ever kiss me.

My PTSD kicked in and I ran out the room after shouting out "No!".

Afterwards my best friend came to check on me and we went out into their room to spend some time together just the two of us and talk about it and then my best friend just dropped a bombshell.

Now bear in mind, that I love my best friend romantically. They are the kindest person you will ever meet, and they are sweet, thoughtful and they are attractive too, but it's *them* and their personality that I love.

I asked them back in October 2023, they said no but they wanted to become good friends with me anyway.

My best friend told me that they were dating Ruby, our other housemate, and I felt so bad, so awful and it felt like my world was collapsing down around me.

I think I felt this way because I am so used to my best friend's partners being online, living hundreds of miles away or them dating dickheads. And most importantly, I never had to see their partners and see another person kiss, hug and sleep with the person I wanted to.

Yes, I am only human after all.

Yet we kept talking, spending time together and I was relatively okay when they went to bed with Ruby, but the problem was that my mind spiralled with distress. It brought up all my child abuse, all my sexual trauma and all my crippling grief about never being able to find love, be in a relationship and find someone who would love me without raping me.

My mind kept running a million times an hour so I wanted to self-soothe. The breathing wasn't working, I was too distressed to listen to music or read so I went for a walk.

I know going for a walk is a good way to calm down.

Everything got even worse.

As summarised in this message I wrote out in an effort to talk to a helpline:

"What happened tonight was I was already feeling depressed and distressed because I found out my best friend and another friend of ours are dating. And it's naturally hard because I romantically love my best friend and we're both open and accepting about that fact and that Blue will never love me romantically but they love me as a friend.

And I realised a PTSD trigger for me is hearing constant kissing. One or two kisses is fine so that's why no one knew, including me, thought it was a trigger before.

Then I went to bed, I couldn't self-sooth so I went for a walk. I got triggered and went into full survival mode with panic attacks and everything because I remembered like tonight, I was raped on a cold night, all the houses in the dark looks like my rapist's house and I went for a walk around the time I was raped. Then there were other people about who I perceived as dangerous and so on.

I came back to the house my best friend comforted me for 25 mins. They didn't want to go but they were really tired and they encouraged me to use a helpline if needed.

I'm too exhausted and scared and nervous about a helpline to use it.

That was all 2 hours ago and I'm still distressed."

Interestingly, my best friend kept saying to me to try a helpline but I didn't know how to use one so I contacted one via the online chat, it went through but I instantly logged back off it because I didn't know how it worked.

I simply kept panicking, getting more and more distressed and I felt like I was going to die because the little bombshell of my two friends dating had brought up so much trauma for me.

The Next Day: Even Worse Bad News

After three hours sleep, I woke up still very distressed, constantly shaking and I went downstairs to make myself some breakfast. I panicked so much when I was downstairs I collapsed to the ground then I went upstairs to get ready for a shower but my thoughts were still going so fast and my heart felt like it was going to explode so I collapsed again and I couldn't get back up.

I was meant to take my best friend to therapy that morning but I was collapsed on the floor in my doorway so they helped me back into bed and took the bus to therapy.

I felt awful. I felt like such a failure as a friend, an idiot and I hated that I was reacting so badly to the fact that they were in a relationship with such a lovely person.

I fell off my bed whilst they were out and when they texted me saying they were almost back I tried to go down the stairs but I collapsed going down them. Thankfully, I managed to grab the stair rail so I wasn't injured too badly.

Then me and my best friend spoke and they broke my heart yet again.

They told me they couldn't support me as much anymore.

The one singular constant in my life, the one person who was the only person I could turn to and the one person I trusted to let touch me was stepping away from me.

My heart shattered.

Why did they say this I hear you ask.

As a result of their mental health was starting to decline now and they flat out hated seeing me so distressed, me trying to kill myself and they kept having panic attacks over the thought of me dying. They said how they were terrified that I was going to die because of their inaction.

And they were only just realising that they weren't entirely comfortable with us cuddling so that was starting to impact them too. That was something that has always bugged me about my best friend, because one of the ways their autism manifests is that they don't realise something is bothering them until it's become part of our friendship.

They've done this before and it always hurts me, but I know they genuinely don't mean to do this on purpose. As well as, as soon as they find out something is hurting them, they do find a solution so our friendship is okay.

I still get hurt in the end anyway.

Nonetheless, it would be easy for me to protest and say that anyone who hurts me isn't worth being in my life. Then in the next chapter, we're going to be talking about the Traffic Light system and I explain there how people can do Yellow Lights without meaning and as long as they learn from their mistakes and try then it is okay in the end.

And friends hurting you by accident isn't ideal, but that is part of friendship and interacting with other humans.

If we lose ourselves off and cut off everyone who makes a mistake and hurts us, then all our lives would be extremely lonely and boring indeed.

Nonetheless, in this moment, I was extremely hurt and I was in so much emotional pain because honestly… I was annoyed at my best friend. I was the one that kept asking for permission and consent, I was the one holding back for asking what I needed because I wanted my best friend to be okay.

They went to Yellow boundaries with me to make sure I was okay. I was grateful for it in the moment but looking back this was one of the massive mistakes they made with our friendship.

Online Rape Crisis Chats

As a result of my best friend taking a major step back, they wanted me to start using helplines so I found one and they sat with me whilst I used it. I still had no idea how to use a helpline so I wrote out the following message and it helps to capture a lot of my raw emotion on the day:

"I got extremely triggered last night that my best friend (who I have unrequited love for) and my housemate were making out (I didn't know they were a couple before that). None of us knew kissing was trigger for me before because it's happened before but not making out. So I had severe PTSD reactions to the kissing.

Then after this PTSD episode my best friend told me they're dating.

I feel silly but that made me worse because I want both of them to be happy but it's dating in the house when I already struggle with feelings that I'll never be loved, able to date or anything and this changes everything in the house and my relationship with them.

They're both confirmed to be everything is fine, nothing is going to change (and honestly it actually won't) but it's hard.

Then I went for a walk. Before remembering something I had repressed. I was raped on a cold night and I walked some of the way there in the cold. And a lot of the houses where I recently moved look like my rapist's house in the dark.

I have been having panic attacks for 18 hours with only 3 hours not because I was sleeping. I'm exhausted, and struggling."

As you can see, I was really distressed and I was not hopeful about the effectiveness of online chats. I really wasn't hopeful because I had no idea how using an online chat and texting a random stranger would be useful.

Turns out it was useful.

I used the Rape Crisis England and Wales online chat and you're allowed to use it twice a week for 45 minutes. By the end of the 45 minutes, I was much more relaxed and I wasn't panicking quite as much and I felt relatively okay.

Since that night, I have probably used the online chat four times. I've had one bad experience because there was a worker who clearly didn't understand that men could be raped too, I've had two good experiences and I a flat out amazing experience.

Therefore, if you are struggling, definitely contact a helpline because these people are trained to listen to and believe you and signpost you to mental health and other services.

I cannot recommend them enough.

Finally, for this section, the next day I was actually bed-bound because I was so malnourished I felt like I was going to die. I think it was a mixture of malnourishment from my eating disorder, the extreme stress of Sunday night and Monday and me not sleeping enough.

PTSD Is Not Fun: A Birthday Celebration and a London Bus

The rest of these sections should be shorter as I highlight specific situations. For example, a week before my seventh therapy session, it was my best friend's birthday celebration so they had their nine friends around to watch the first Lord of the Rings film extended edition.

There were a lot of people, I was still adjusting to my new reality of needing to make decisions myself and me supporting myself more. I used the online chat again to calm myself down and I used some self-care techniques and other self-soothing ideas to get myself ready for the birthday party.

I was calm but it did not last long.

When you get a group of young people together, there were bound to be sexual comments made and my PTSD at this point in time does not respond well to sexual references.

I was already severely distressed so it only took one comment and I ran out the room as fast as I could.

My best friend came to check on me and I just couldn't deal with their birthday anymore, and I certainly couldn't make a decision about what to order for dinner. That alone caused me to have a panic attack, so me, Ruby and my best friend shared a massive pizza together.

The advantages of me and Ruby both having eating disorders. We can support each other in tiny ways.

What was meant to be a birthday celebration turned into a nightmare for me, my trauma and my PTSD.

Then the day before my seventh counselling session, we went up to London together and whilst my best friend spoke on a London bus, I heard a woman reporting sexual harassment and sure, my PTSD kicked in. Yet it wasn't as intense as before as much as my mind tried to tell me I was in danger, I was going to die and I was going to get raped again.

My PTSD had decreased and that was a weird feeling in its own right.

Self-Compassionate Steps

This was a critical part of my own healing journey because I have never been very self-compassionate but once you realise it is okay to show compassion with yourself. Your life will change forever in a very, very good way and it takes a little bit of time to practise but it is a great technique to use.

Therefore, Doctor Kristin Neff developed the following five steps to help you become self-compassionate:

1. Understand shame is normal and it doesn't need to be eliminated. It is okay to feel shame.
2. Acknowledge you are hurting and you are distressed.
3. Understand other people go through the same thing.
4. Pretend you're talking to a dear friend that is going through the same thing as you. What would you say to them?
5. Say that to yourself and take it in. Internalise what you would say to a dear friend.

Be your friend for a change. Treat yourself as you would a friend, never treat yourself as an enemy.

So to use these self-compassionate steps with the PTSD example at the birthday celebration, I would:

1. Acknowledge that I was distressed about being in a large group, having to support myself as much as I could and I was hurting that my best friend was in a relationship with someone who wasn't me.
2. It's okay to feel like this because other people hurt when people who they are interested in are no longer available, and lots of other survivors experience anxiety.
3. I would ensure my dear friend that it's okay to feel like this. It doesn't make them a bad person, a bad friend and it doesn't make them weak. It just means they are a survivor of something awful and they are healing. They can come down whenever they want, they can choose to say upstairs and they do whatever they need to do. Because they are important too.
4. And I would say that to myself and accept it, because it is all true.

Self-compassion often requires practice but it is so important.

<u>Quick Note On Session Itself and A Transactional Analysis Technique</u>

After all the chaos of the past two weeks, it was a really good session that was positive, we were both really pleased with my progress and how much I was healing and everything I had discovered about myself.

We did some extra paperwork using the centre's CORE outcome measurements which was a questionnaire about the severity of my symptoms, ability to function and more.

Moreover, I learnt about something called "Okay Corral". It's an idea that comes from an approach to therapy called Transactional Analysis (TA). I don't like a lot of what TA does because it's psychodynamic but there are some good concepts.

"Okay Corral" is about there are four types of interpersonal situations:

- Me and the other person are okay.
- I am okay but the other person is not.
- I am not okay but the other person is.
- We are both not okay.

My counsellor mentioned this to me because she thought this technique might be useful to remember if I'm feeling tense, awful or nervous in a social situation. I can think about which category this situation falls into and what I need to do to be okay.

Using the order listed above, I might do the following:

- Not change anything because we are both okay.
- I would try to help the other person but I would prepare to leave.
- I would use my self-soothing and other therapy techniques. If they didn't work then I would leave the situation. I might consider asking for social support but that depends on the other person.
- We should both leave because no one is okay.

Overall, I think this is a useful tool if you're struggling in a social situation and your trauma starts making you feel unsafe or like the other person hates you. That is a train of thought my brain loves to tell me, but that's not entirely related to sexual trauma.

Remember it for the future.

Finally, we agreed that in the next session, we're going to look at interpersonal red flags so I can recognise abuse and manipulation in the future.

A very important and critical life skill for everyone. Especially, survivors and I hope you learn as much as I did in the next chapter.

Turn over the page and let's find out.

SELF-COMPASSION, ADJUSTING TO A NEW REALITY AND LEARNING TO RECOGNISE ABUSE: LESSONS LEARNT FROM SESSION EIGHT

This next week proved that I was partly struggling to adapt to the new reality of me and my best friend wanting a healthier relationship where they supported me less, but I was still able to talk to, text and call them if needed.

The theme of the week was certainly me taking their boundary too far (I may have accidentally cut myself off completely from them in terms of support) with sprinkles of self-compassion and recognising abuse in the process too.

Therefore, I wanted to share this chapter with you because I want you to realise that it is okay if you take actions a little too far after someone imposes a boundary. It is okay if you misinterpret things and it is okay if you get distressed and "overreact" to what a dear friend has said.

Whilst you are healing, you are going through hell and back and you are trying to survive as best you can. The world already seems like a dangerous place, the world is confusing and every single thing you thought you knew about the world gets turned on its head after sexual violence.

It is normal to react in ways that other people think are overreacting.

You are surviving and that is why you are so amazing, because you are able to survive. Now the next stage of healing is to calm your body down and retrain your brain so it doesn't need to go on survival mode so often when it doesn't need to.

Proved I Can Do Self-Compassion and Triggers Majorly Decreasing

After my best friend told me they need to take a step back last week, we spoke about how I need more friends that over time I could deepen those relationships and I could have additional people to turn to for support.

I had no idea how to do this because friendships were always messy, complicated and everyone always seemed to leave me in the end anyway. Between childhood trauma and autism, making friendships always feels like an impossible task, but thankfully my best friend understood to.

Everyone in my shared university house is autistic.

However, one option we did come up with was that my university has a Warhammer 40,000 society (just think a social group formed around a particular interest for our international audience).

As a teenager, I had loved Warhammer 40,000 because it's a great science fiction fantasy game and even now I listen to a Warhammer podcast, watch lore videos and I still keep a pulse on the hobby.

As a result, my best friend managed to begrudgingly convince me to go on Saturday, so my parents thankfully paid for me to get some models (they are stupidly expensive. Another great reason why I stopped playing Warhammer. My bank account didn't like it), so I tried to go.

Now I hadn't realised until I tried to go to Warhammer society that Saturday that this was the first time I had tried to go to a brand-new event alone since my rape.

I had always gone to events or work opportunities that I was familiar with pre-rape. I could easily manage those events or situations because they weren't new and I was familiar with them before my rape, but this was a brand-new situation. I didn't have any friends with me, I didn't have any support and so my PTSD kicked in.

I hid in a university toilet for a few hours constantly cycling between pure fear, anxiety and panic attacks. Then I tried more and more to get up the courage to get going again and I couldn't.

I was trapped in a cycle of fear, panic and rape memories so I never ended up going.

I spent around three hours at the university before my best friend was done with their Dungeons and Dragons game, so we went back to our place together.

We spoke about how terrified I was that I was going to get raped again by going to the Warhammer society alone. And they reminded me that's it's okay that it takes time to build up the courage and confidence to do new things, and after it became clear I wasn't able to go *today*, I should have left and gone home to self-soothe.

That was a great note for future reference.

Over to you dear reader, I want you to know that it's okay if you can't do things straight away. I mention all the distressing times when I tried to do basic or social things I simply couldn't in my book *I Am Not A Victim, I Am A Survivor*. Yet I want you to be aware that you will fall into the trap at some point of "oh I've healed a little that means I am cured and I can do everything,". Whilst it is definitely true you will be able to do so much more as you heal, there will be limits as you edge towards the tail end of your healing journey.

For example, at this point of my healing journey, I could be in the same room and talk to a fat man, I could hear sexual references and see implied sexual scenes in films amongst other things. Yet at this point, I couldn't do something brand-new by myself.

Like a lot of these chapters, I'm writing them a good few weeks after the session happened based on my notes, but now I am able to go out to brand-new things. Such as, I just came back from a brand-new "Winter Showcase" at my university where PhD students were presenting their research. I saw two presentations on "carbonwashing" and "how Working From Home impacts Fertility rates". Both of them were very good presentations and I was talking to a guy I found attractive in the break before I went home.

It was a good few hours out, I got to talk to a few really nice people and it was something I wouldn't have been able to do a few weeks ago. I am only able to do it now because I am healed enough to do new things.

Around the time of my seventh session, I wasn't healed enough but now I am. Therefore, please know that things do get better if you keep slowly working towards healing, be kind to yourself and keep trying in the future.

Finally, for this section, a major sign that my triggers are decreasing was when Chloe (a fake name) came round the Thursday before this session for some video games and a catch-up. I walked them back. It was a cold, dark night through where I live, exactly the same as the night I had been extremely triggered and had panic attacks for 18 hours.

I was fine, because I was just that little bit more healed and I had spent a lovely evening with my housemates and Chloe.

Adjusting To A New Reality

Since my best friend took a massive step back in terms of supporting me, my brain was struggling to cope with this new reality so it made me take their boundary too far and I cut myself off from their support. This wasn't great for my mental health as you can imagine because it left me feeling very isolated, lonely and like I had no one I could turn to when I needed it.

I was still using the rape crisis online chat, self-soothing techniques and other tools I had at my disposal, but it was hard for me. It was hard for me to adapt to a massive change in our relationship.

As a result, on the Sunday before this session happened, we both spoke about it during our scheduled time together (no autistic signs there, ha.) and my best friend was worried that I had cut them off and I was distressed that I was completely alone. Especially, as since they had started dating Ruby, they weren't talking to me about emotional stuff so I felt less close to them and like our friendship was nothing compared to what it had been.

The conclusion of our conversation was that my best friend needed to talk to me more so I could get what I needed from the relationship, and my best friend wanted me to lean on them more. It was all about trying to find a middle ground as we explored what a healthy relationship looked like.

Now this connects to the counselling session because she helped me to realise (and one of the women on the rape online chat had helped me with the same thing) that it's okay that my best friend hurt me, that we both made mistakes and it was bad that they didn't tell me when they weren't comfortable with something we were doing or consider the consequences of what we were doing, like cuddling for support.

Then towards the end of this segment of the session, my counsellor mentioned if we've spoken about what a healthy relationship looks like for both of us. Thankfully, we had the Sunday before this session.

For us, a healthy relationship evolves over time and it is where we support each other. We can always text, talk to and call the other for support, but there are boundaries. We still hug because that's what my best friend likes doing with their friends, but we don't cuddle, I don't stay in their room anymore and then I added that we focus on our actual friendship.

We focus less on support for mental health, and more on why we're actually friends and that takes centre stage of "us" instead of my best friend effectively being a carer. We focus on all our shared interests, our shared points of view and we do things together because we like hanging out. Not because I need the support.

I won't lie, this was and still is a tough reality to get used to, but over time I have gotten better and our relationship is lovely. It can still be distressing when I want support but I know I need to do a lot more for myself these days and that's okay.

They are still my best friend, they are still there for me and we are still great together. Which is brilliant news considering we recently extended the tenancy agreement for another year.

How To Recognise Manipulation

We spent about the final twenty minutes of the session discussing how to recognise manipulation and abuse. In the next two chapters, I'll include content on coercive control and gaslighting because it goes into more depth than I can in this chapter.

Understanding gaslighting and control is very important for survivors.

In the session itself, there was a lot of to-and-fro because I didn't understand signs of abuse. No one ever taught it to me in school because you never get taught about what healthy relationships look like and you never get taught about abuse. That is a massive failure of the education system, similar to what I talk about in *Breaking The Silence* with teenage dating violence.

As a result, abuse and manipulation is a pattern that can be very sophisticated. It isn't often mean things that typically align with the "traditional" view of abuse and manipulation. In reality, abuse are often nice things that the abuser uses to isolate you from your social support system.

For example, in my case, it would be my abuser would be trying to separate me and prevent me from spending time with my best friend and other housemates. He might "treat" me to a nice dinner, maybe surprise cinema tickets and so on.

Anything that he can disguise as a so-called nice treat to continue to isolate me away from my support system until I become dependent on him. That is how abuse and manipulation typically works in the real world.

My counsellor went to say that when I notice this pattern, I need to have a conversation to correct it and remember to balance my time between myself, my partner and my social support network.

This connects to skills you learn about in specialist counselling about saying no and setting boundaries. I would need to say no to my abuser because if I had plans to spend time with my housemates that night and my abuser would surprise me by taking me away from them. I should say no to him and continue my plans with my housemates.

And resist any emotional manipulation he tries.

Please note, I'm using *he* because I'm attracted to mainly men and transmasculine individuals but women and transfeminine people could do this just as easily.

Therefore, it's important to have a conversation to correct this behaviour and set up boundaries. In the current example, I could set a boundary saying my partner needs to stop surprising me, needs to respect the time I spend with other people and I need more room for myself.

In reality, I might only set one of those boundaries for starters, because it's okay to be nervous about setting new boundaries. Especially after what you, the reader, and me have been through.

Yet boundaries are so important to set and reinforce like I mentioned in previous chapters.

If the partner doesn't respect your boundaries and this person continues to manipulate you and isolate you from your social support system. Then you need to leave and end the relationship as hard as it seems, and thankfully there are a lot of great resources available online for you if needed.

The final activity my counsellor wanted us to discuss was considering what makes actions and partners go from "Green Light" (meaning everything is okay) to "Yellow Light" (meaning you're uncomfortable and you might withdraw consent but it isn't an automatic No) to a "Red Light". This means the other person has crossed a line and you want to withdraw consent immediately.

This was a hard activity because I had never thought what actions or what could make someone go through these different boundaries.

I highly recommend that you think about this yourself. Both in terms of sexual consent and what partners are allowed to do in everyday life.

Personally, an action is Green Light if I am okay with it and it doesn't make me uncomfortable at all. My Healing Sexual Trauma Workbook made me write about what this feels like in terms of my body and I wrote "when it's a *yes* boundary, I feel happy, relaxed and excited." These activities depend on the person but these can include kissing, hugging and cuddling.

In addition, for me a Yellow Light is something I am not entirely comfortable with and I need to think about it. It is perfectly okay to stop during sex, think about it in another room and then continue.

Your safety is the most important thing.

If a partner makes me uncomfortable then I will talk to them and set a boundary on it so we might not do it at all or we can do it in a way that makes me feel safe and respected.

This can apply to the relationship itself too, because if my partner accidentally tells a secret to someone I know, that doesn't make them a bad person. People are not perfect in relationships and both of you will make mistakes, and it doesn't make you a bad person if you learn from them.

Therefore, if my partner made a mistake that made me feel uncomfortable then I would talk to them so they wouldn't do it again.

Finally, in terms of Red lights, for sexual relationships, this would be anything I am not comfortable with and any sexual acts that make me feel scared, nervous and make me start or want to start shaking. In terms of romantic relationships, this is whenever someone crosses a boundary that they are aware of and they don't listen or respect me when I reinforce it.

People who go into Red Lights and don't learn from their mistakes do not deserve to be in your life.

It is as simple as that because you are the most important person in your life and your safety is beyond vital.

Never forget that dear reader.

WHAT IS COERCIVE CONTROL?

After learning about recognising buse and manipulation in relationships, and coming across a woman's domestic violence survival story and her wish to raise awareness about domestic violence and Coercive Control. I really wanted to help honour her survival in a way so I wanted us to look on the podcast at this critical topic. So we can understand the psychology behind this outrageous behaviour, and in future episodes hopefully focus on helping ourselves avoid Coercive control.

Why Psychology Needs To Look At Coercive Control And Abusive Relationships?

I always think it's important to highlight why these are important topics to discuss on the podcast because that way I know I tend to focus on them, and you might enjoy them more because of their importance. I don't know why I like to lay down a psychological foundation too before we dive into the meat of the topic.

In terms of Coercive Control and abusive relationships, many people simply ask questions: *why don't victims simply leave the relationship?*

And of course that is a reasonable question, I think when I was younger I wondered that too. Yet from social psychology and the Need To Belong Theory, humans are resistant to breaking any relationship even ones that are bad for us.

In addition, as we are all hopefully outside the abusive relationship the answer seems so simple to the abuse. Just report it and leave the relationship. But this is where the reality is different from the ideal and it was a lot, lot more complicated than this.

As well as whilst there are many different reasons why victims don't leave the relationship. One of the most common reasons is fear, and whilst the exact definition of fear is hard to pin down. A good definition is something along the lines of a very unpleasant strong emotion caused by a person's anticipation and/ or awareness of danger.

Due to like most emotions, fear can range from minor to severe, and the fear could be real or perceived to be real. And what's critical to understand here is that the victim's perception and whether the danger is real or not doesn't matter. What does matter is that fear can be psychological or physical and it can be rather incapacitating and debilitating. Making leaving the relationship quite impossible.

And I want to mention that the reason why I'm not mentioning gender here is because whilst women are the victims in the vast majority of cases. They are not in every single case and men can be and are still abused in some cases, so I don't want to put a gender here instead of the word *victim* and help to reinforce a damaging stereotype.

Additionally, to help show the importance of this topic some more, here are some numbers from the United States' National Coalition Against Domestic Violence. For example, 1 in 9 men and 1 in 4 women experience severe intimate partner physical violence, intimate partner contact, sexual violence, intimate partner stalking with impacts. These impacts include fearfulness, post-traumatic stress disorder, use of victim services, injury and more.

Furthermore, 1 in 3 women and 1 in 4 men have experienced some kind of physical violence in the past by an intimate partner. This includes a range of behaviour, like slapping, pushing and shoving, and in some cases might not be considered "domestic violence" when it actually is.

1 in 4 women and 1 in 7 men have been victims of severe physical violence. For example, beating, strangling and burning by an intimate partner in their lifetime. As well as 1 in 7 women and 1 in 25 men have been injured by an intimate partner.

Therefore, as you can clearly see (or hear) regardless of the situation (except maybe the last one) regardless of gender a sadly high number of both have experienced domestic violence. And this only highlights why it's critical to increase awareness of the topic.

What Is Coercive Control?

Moving onto the next section of the episode, one of the leading authorities on this area is a person called Dr Evan Stark and he defines Coercive Control as the following:

"a strategic course of oppressive behavior designed to secure and expand gender-based privilege by depriving women of their rights and liberties and establishing a regime of domination in personal life."

As well as one of the problems with the literature on Coercive Control is that there is no, or no easy to find studies that have men as the victims. Now it would be great to imagine that meant no men fall under this area, but given how the myth of men being domestically abused is false. I personally doubt this and think this is a massive gap in the literature. You cannot seriously imagine that out of every single man on the planet, not a single one of them is being Coercively Controlled.

Moreover, Stark adds in his work that 60% to 80% of all abused women experience Coercive Control beyond the use of physical abuse. Meaning the physical abuse might have stopped but the Coercive Control continues.

And Coercive Control can have deadly consequences as Stark argues Coercive Control is strongly correlated with murder. For example, for the sake of illustration only, between the years 2000 and 2006 3200 American soldiers were killed in combat, but during the same time three times as many women were murdered by their husbands or boyfriends. As well as 1 woman is murdered every 16 hours in the United State either by a current or former male partner.

With the victims most at risk of being murdered are the people in which domestic violence, stalking and Coercive Control happen at the same time. And domestic violence and stalking is common.

The Role of Narcissistic Personality Disorder:

Interesting, there is some evidence that Narcissistic Personality Disorder is involved in Coercive Control alongside antisocial personality disorder, as all three of them are common among perpetrators of domestic violence. With people having Narcissistic Personality Disorder being described as manipulative, demanding, arrogant and self-centred. And they exhibit at least 5 of the following traits:

- Exploitation of others
- A lack of empathy
- Envy of others
- Have a need for excessive admiration
- A grandiose sense of self-importance
- Busy with fantasies of unlimited power, beauty, ideal love, success and brilliance.
- A belief about themselves being special and can only be understood by or associated with special people and institutions.
- Arrogant, condescending attitudes or behaviours
- Sense of entitlement

How Is Coercive Control Criminalised?

Moving onto the last section of the episode, we need to address the very harsh topic of Coercive Control and the legal system. Due to very few elements of Coercive Control are technically a crime and criminal and psychological abuse is always harder to get evidence for and prosecute compared to physical abuse. And yes, I know physical abuse getting prosecuted is hard enough.

This sadly results in the identification, criminally charging and prosecution of the Coercive Control cases is very much beyond challenging.

To make matters worse, successfully prosecuting Coercive Control cases are incredibly rare.

Yet there is a bit of hope because if a case does move forward to trial then the case will most likely be plea-bargained.

In addition, if you live in Ireland, England, Wales, Scotland and France. Then you're in luck because those countries have criminalised Coercive Control but the United States does not. New York State has become the first state in the entire country to start introducing criminalising legalisation for Coercive Control as a class E felony. Which for myself and our non-US audience, it means that Coercive Control is punishable by a maximum fine of $250,000 dollars and/ or a maximum of 5 years imprisonment but more than 1 year.

And I just checked the New York State Senate Website for the bill and it says it is currently in committee. So it has another 4 stages to pass until it is signed or vetoed by the New York governor.

Conclusion:

At the end of this episode, I want to say that Coercive Control isn't just another facet of abuse to look at it. It is very serious that we need to address and I truly hope that none of you listening or reading this will ever experience it. And whilst we didn't look at how to avoid it and recognise the signs in this episode, I do want to do that in the future just to help protect all of us a little more.

But until then, Coercive Control and abuse might be a dark topic to look at. But it is fascinating and very much worth investigating, because you never know when it might be useful.

WHEN IS IT GASLIGHTING?

Concluding our look at recognising abuse and manipulation in relationships, we need to look at the scary, horrific and subtle form of abuse known as gaslighting.

Now, gaslighting is a very popular term in recent times and it is reasonably common to some extent, and it allowed victims and sufferers to name what was happening to them. But as the term started to gain popularity and currency, it started to lose its meaning. In this chapter, we look at what is gaslighting and most importantly, when is it gaslighting and when isn't it. This is a great chapter, you need to be aware of.

What is Gaslighting?

Gaslighting is a form of emotional abuse where someone uses psychological manipulations to cause another person to question their reality. It can happen between two people in any relationship. Like friendships, working relationships and romantic relationships. The gaslighter preserves their own sense of self and power over the other person who ends up adopting the gaslighter's version of reality over their own.

The reason why we need to look at this is because it's important to distinguish gaslighting from normal and healthy behaviours. Like disagreeing and we need to understand when a conflict turns into gaslighting.

When Is it Gaslighting?

Therefore, to understand this harmful behaviour, the easiest scenario to see when something is not gaslighting is something similar to this fictional one below.

Harry and his sister Claire used to spend a lot of time together and every Saturday you would go together, and bring your families along. Then when the pandemic struck they were forced to move their Saturdays together to a few hours on Teams together and they would catch up, play games and have dinner together.

However, when the pandemic eased and the restrictions were relaxed. Harry started going back out, going out on day trips and living life again to the fullest. Yet Claire wasn't comfortable with that and she doesn't feel like going out too much. So, the siblings spoke and they don't agree on where to go for their Saturdays together, because Harry wants to go out-out somewhere nice and Claire wants to stay in.

Resulting in the siblings being judgemental about each other, and each one is calling the other selfish, inconsiderable and horrible. As well as Claire might accuse Harry of not wanting to spend time with her and her family.

Now this isn't gaslighting because even though both siblings are interpreting the same facts very differently, and they want the other sibling to adopt their perspective. They aren't causing each other to question their own reality and they aren't trying to manipulate each other.

However, this could turn into gaslighting if one of the siblings were so insistent on their interpretation that it caused the other one to start doubting themselves. This would create a power imbalance in their relationship that would allow the gaslighter to undermine the victim's sense of self. As well as the gaslighter's need for control, the very act of manipulating and leveraging of power of this relationship are essential components in gaslighting.

And hurt feelings and challenging each other's viewpoints is not gaslighting.

On a personal note, I think it would be rather tragic if those things were gaslighting because it means you could never question other people or challenge their views on anything. I suppose that would also put clinical psychology in a difficult spot considering it's our job to challenge the client's maladaptive coping mechanisms, and cognitive processes.

As a result, if we apply this knowledge to our fictional example, if Claire was the sibling who was more powerful and pushed Harry around. Then Harry would be vulnerable to Claire gaslighting him in adulthood. Especially if Harry really does start to believe he is selfish, awful and horrible person by not submitting to Claire's wishes. Then he might start withdrawing from their relationship.

Again this would result in a gaslight dance if you will, because if Harry ends up being unable to sleep at night at night because he's wondering if Claire is right and he is selfish. Because he fears she's right about him not wanting to spend time with her then he's starting to question his own character and the very integrity of her relationships.

Then gaslighting is very much present.

<u>You Need Two People To Gaslight</u>

Moving onto the last section of the episode, I want to mention that gaslighting happens when there is a power dynamic within a relationship that ends up causing the person being gaslighted to question themselves, along with their sense of reality.

Typically, the gaslighter is constantly manipulating and attack the gaslightee as well as being verbally aggressive towards them.

In addition, the gaslighter is very likely to turn a discussion between the two into a blaming game against the other person. And they will most probably outright lie about what took place just to further their own manipulations because if the gaslighter is so certain about something then it's easy to make you question if you're memory or perception is right.

Then it all ends up leaving the victim of the gaslighting to feel worn out, unsure of themselves and wondering if they are crazy like the gaslighter said, and they might even end up avoiding future discussions out of fear of disagreements escalating this already disorienting discussion.

Additionally, the most concerning thing is that over time the victim may even accept the gaslighter's views of reality as their own. And these are critical defining elements of gaslighting.

However, the most critical to remember when it comes to gaslighting is that it can only work if there are two people taking part in it. The gaslighter and the victim. In other words, gaslighting can only happen if the victim allows it to.

You can keep yourself from ending up in a gaslighting relationship by being aware of the topic and the sort of language used in arguments. As well as how it makes you feel, and noticing how you react to it.

Some helpful phrases that might be helpful to stop you engaging in a verbal loop or power struggle include:

- "What you said hurt my feelings and I'm too upset at the moment to talk about it,"
- "Let's agree to disagree,"
- You're twisting what I said. Let's take a break and talk about it later,"

Conclusion

To wrap up this social psychology episode, I must admit that as more and more people use the word "gaslighting" in our world, we risk its meaning becoming blurred or forgotten. Therefore, it is critical that we clearly understand what it actually means and when something is and isn't gaslighting. Sometimes you will be involved in disagreements, it's natural, but sometimes you might meet person who wants to gaslight you.

And that's when you need to be aware of what's going on for your own sake, but just remember sometimes a disagreement is simply that. Two people disagreeing and not gaslighting in the slightest.

EXCITED FOR NEW THINGS, GOING TO LET BOUNDARIES DOWN (YOU'RE HUMAN) AND THINKING ABOUT ENDINGS: LESSONS LEARNT FROM SESSION NINE

This next session was definitely a mixture of positives and negatives, as is most of the therapeutic and healing journey. Thankfully, a lot of really positive things had happened in this past week and there were a lot of exciting things happening in the next few days.

For example, the day after this therapy appointment, I was going out and spending one-on-one time with a friend I made back in September. And that went really well actually, we spent four hours together, we spoke constantly and it was lovely that I was able to spend one-on-one time with them without me having a mental breakdown or mental health crisis afterwards.

We spoke about everything and nothing whilst we had lunch together, then they went off to a seminar at 5 til 6 in the evening. Personally, I still think that is a brutal time for a seminar but it meant we could spend a lot of time together, which was nice.

When it came to the counselling session, the day before I spent one-on-one time with this new friend, we focused on celebrating and acknowledging the fact that this was major progress. It was great that I was able to do this and I was looking forward to it.

Of course, I was nervous and anxious about spending time with this friend. My mental health had proven time and time again that this could end very badly, I could get seriously hurt and this could really decrease my mental health.

However, I wanted to do this for me, for my recovery and I wanted to try and prove to myself that I was ready. In reality, you probably shouldn't try to "prove" things to yourself because I have done that before it has been awful and my mental health has died because of it.

Thankfully, because I feel safe, because I have my therapy techniques and because I *know* I am safe with this friend, I was willing to try it. And thankfully, everything was fine and me realising that I am okay to try new things has really helped me, my mental health and my life because I have tried a lot of new things since this day and it has been great.

Another positive that I was excited about was I was no longer distressed and I didn't have PTSD reaction to the sound of kissing anymore. Since my best friend and Ruby could be kissing and being a couple in the same room as me and I didn't have to run out the room being distressed as hell.

I will admit that there has been one or two times when I have had to leave a room by casually walking away just to make sure that I was okay. I wasn't overly distressed but I needed in that moment to leave so my mental health didn't tip over.

This is a good reminder that us survivors are the most important people to ourselves and we need to do what we need for us. For example, I could have stayed in the room and there was a chance that my distress would build and build over time and I would have a mental health crisis. Yet I decided it was best for me to take a few minutes out, do some self-soothing techniques and then go back downstairs into where my best friend and Ruby were.

As a survivor, you are the most important person to you and you have to do what is best for you and your mental health in the moment. It is always best if you take a few minutes or an hour compared to staying in a situation that will trigger and distress you.

Please focus on yourself.

You are more important than you will ever know.

Personally, it felt really weird that I could sit in the same room as two people lightly kissing and not get triggered or reminded of my rape. And my counsellor mentioned it might be a good idea to decrease my use of the word "trigger" because I am not getting triggered as much anymore. Instead I am being reminded.

Being triggered means you have PTSD or trauma responses. For me, this means feeling like I was going to get raped again, I would feel terrified, I would feel physical sensations of him touching me again and so on.

However, at this moment in my recovery, I am actually not experiencing those responses. Instead, sure, the sound of kissing will remind me more often than not of what He did to me that night. That will never be okay but it is just a memory, just an event and just something that happened to me a few months ago.

I survived, I am healing and He can never touch me again.

In a moment, I'll mention a topic my counsellor was concerned about and we had a long conversation about it, because she didn't want me to get hurt again. Yet a final area that we celebrated was a day this week, I managed to sit in the gym café without being triggered or even reminded of my rape.

You might remember from a few chapters ago that I mentioned that the gym, sportswear and athletics in general was very triggering for me because I was raped in sportswear. Which being completely honest was a massive inconvenience because guys in sportswear are a major turn-on for me.

Therefore, my best friend was in the gym and I was up at the university anyway because I took them and I wanted to get some work done anyway, so I went to the library then sat in the gym café afterwards. I saw lots of guys and women in sportswear and I remember some of the guys looked hot and stunning.

Yet I wasn't triggered, I didn't feel scared and I didn't feel like my life was in danger. That was a massive sign of healing, progress and it was a little weird because this major, major trigger for me wasn't a trigger anymore.

That opened up a lot of great opportunities for me, because it means I can go to the gym, I can happily go to places where sportswear is a probable option and more.

I love healing and it just goes to show that healing is possible if you put in the work, have a good counsellor and in my experience, a very good workbook.

Spoke About Talking To A Guy

For context, the Saturday before my 8th counselling session I was feeling very lonely, I was struggling with my mental health and I was readjusting to the new reality that my best friend needed to take a step back as I spoke about in previous chapters. I felt like I didn't have any friends (even though I do) and I really wanted to make some extra friends.

So I did something that was a little dramatic when you take the context of my rape into account.

I've mentioned before that the context for my rape was I was sick and tired of never being allowed to be gay because I had been in fear for my life for so long during my adolescence and young adulthood. I simply wanted a hookup so I could have sex but it was a hookup that went wrong so he grabbed me, didn't ask my consent and so on. I've written about it in my other sexual violence psychology books.

Yet this hookup happened on the gay app, Grindr.

Therefore, this Saturday, I was feeling very lonely, my mental health was relatively good but not amazing so I downloaded the app with the sole aim of meeting people on it and finding friends. Of course, 99% of the people on this particular app only want sex, as a survivor that is not something I was after at that point. Even now maybe 4 or 5 weeks after this counselling session, I want to talk to people for a while before I even start thinking about having sex with someone.

I am still a virgin at the time of writing and I am okay with that. Virginity doesn't actually mean anything. You can read more about my thoughts on sexual violence and virginity in *I Am Not A Victim, I Am A Survivor.*

Anyway, between that Saturday and this ninth counselling session, I was talking to a particular guy and we spoke every day about a range of things. None of these things actually touched on sex. We mainly spoke about our degrees, where we were from, our thoughts on different topics like religions, philosophy (he studied them for his degree), games, movies and so on.

Given the context of my rape, my counsellor was concerned then I assured her that I was not looking for a relationship. In hindsight, maybe I was lying because I wouldn't mind a relationship with this guy but I was always going to pursue a friendship first and foremost.

Over the course of the session, me and counsellor spoke and I mentioned that my best friend recommended that me and this guy call first to see if we wanted a friendship and it removed the scariness (and possible dangers) of meeting a stranger one-on-one. This was before I went out with my friend the next day so we didn't know if I could handle a one-on-one situation.

My counsellor agreed this was a good idea and then I mentioned that my best friend had stressed that they were going to tell me when I was allowed to meet this guy one-on-one. At first (as

I mentioned to my counsellor) that I wasn't happy with this, because surely my best friend was taking my autonomy away from me. Then I realised my best friend has experienced in this area so I probably should listen to them.

My counsellor agreed with me that I should request a call when I was ready.

That was interesting and a feature in next week's counselling session for sure.

You're Human So You Are Going To Let Your Boundaries Down

This event focuses on the Wednesday before this session, so this happened on the same day as my eighth counselling session.

I've mentioned before that I'm transgender because I'm non-binary, so I go to a trans social group where I talk to my friends, hang out with people and just meet others like me. It's where I met my best friend amongst some of my other closest friends.

In addition, the 20th November every year is known as Transgender Remembrance Day to remember all the trans people that have been murdered all over the world in the past year. Sadly, the number of trans people being murdered is only increasing year-on-year and given the state of the world, this number will only increase in the coming years.

A lot more innocent people are going to be murdered for no reason. It's disgusting. This is why supporting trans people, survivors and other minority groups is so important.

Anyway, the trans group I go hold to a Trans Day of Remembrance service on the 20th November and they need people to read the names of the dead out for each month of the year. Therefore, the organiser of the group was struggling to find a final person to read out the month of December, so she asked me.

Now I am dyslexic (even though I wouldn't be officially diagnosed for another two weeks), I struggle with saying names and I did not want to do this. Yet she kept asking me, I kept saying no but then I gave in.

I wasn't happy but I was okay until I made the connection between consent, boundaries and fear. I was so scared that there were parallels between the organiser wearing me down, me not standing up for my own boundaries and reinforcing them and there were a lot of other rape parallels that I was struggling with.

I was scared for the future because if a lovely woman who I have known for maybe 16 months wore down my boundaries and I didn't reinforce them with someone I trusted. How the hell could I reinforce them with a stranger?

Was I a failure for not reinforcing boundaries? Was I failing in my counselling? Was I making a mistake that could play out in a different situation and get me raped again?

I was distressed as hell.

However, as my counsellor mentioned in the ninth session, we are all only human and we are going to lower our boundaries at times. It doesn't make us flawed, failures and it doesn't mean that we aren't recovering.

It just means that we are human.

Of course, we should always try to make, reinforce and challenge others when they cross our boundaries. Yet ultimately, if we let a boundary slip from time to time, then that is normal. Especially when it comes to our friends and loved ones.

Not reinforcing boundaries only becomes a problem if you consistently let people walk over your boundaries.

Personally, this did help me feel better because since then I have reinforced other boundaries so I know this was just a slip. And that's okay because that is natural.

We need to be kind to ourselves and remember the self-compassionate steps I've mentioned before.

Thinking Of Endings

The charity that I get my specialist counselling from allows you to have up to 12 sessions of counselling with the possibility of more, but that isn't generally needed. Yet because I have been doing so well, my counsellor was wondering if I could finish early so I agreed to finish at week 11 instead of Week 12, because I wanted it, I didn't think I needed it anymore and I was happy to end it.

I had to make sure that I wanted to end it early for me instead of someone else's need. For example, I did have to think about whether I should end early so someone else could have my slot, but then my counsellor reminded me that I am just as important as the next person who fills my slot. I needed to make this decision for me.

After I realised I did want this to end early for me, my counsellor started to talk about what are endings like for me. Personally, endings are very abrupt for me. A lot of people just tend to abandon me, a lot of people and relationships just end without me knowing and there is never a sense of closure. For example, my childhood best friend was ripped away from me because of the lies and concerns of other people who didn't understand I was autistic and not a danger.

My nephews and nieces were ripped away because of my brother's girlfriend's toxic family stopping us from seeing them. that's actually happened twice now with two different girlfriends, so I have nieces and nephews that I was really close with but I no longer see. That's hard for me.

And there are countless other examples too.

Of course, I suspect a lot of this friendship and relationship stuff is because of my perception as outlined in the cognitive approach to mental health, but still. These endings were never nice.

As a result, my counsellor wanted to know what my idea of a good ending of the counselling would look like. This made me very excited as a clinical psychology student because I've heard a lot about how endings are critical in therapeutic work otherwise it can completely undo all the gains and success in a therapy.

I wasn't sure how I wanted this ending to look.

My counsellor explained that one client watched the last ever episode of Friends with her and they were both crying their eyes out. Another client wrote a poem and another one a story about how the counselling had impacted her, and another client had wanted coffee and cake. As well as one client had wanted a certificate so my counsellor had made that for her.

I still had no idea what I wanted for the ending of the therapy, but I have always liked coffee and cake. So I mentioned that was what I wanted for my final session in two weeks' time, then we could talk about anything and do paperwork in the final session.

She would bring the cake, and I asked for a coffee and walnut cake because I hadn't had one of them for years, and I was tasked with bringing the coffee.

It was going to be a wonderful way to end my counselling and that just gave me something else to look forward to in the future.

Something I never ever could have imagined nine weeks before.

FRIENDSHIPS, DISTRESS, TRAUMA: LESSONS LEARNT FROM SESSION 10

This had to be one of the most impactful and important counselling sessions and thankfully, it was the penultimate one. Since if you've been a long time reader of mine then you might be aware that friendships cause me a lot of distress. A lot of this comes from autism and my family refusing to get me diagnosed as a child as I could never access any support, people would think I was a creep and an idiot instead of an autistic person who didn't understand how the social world worked, and I have a lot of friendship trauma too.

I have been abandoned by a lot of friends over the years for different reasons, the majority of them not my fault and they happened because of the misunderstandings of other people (not actually my friends) so that led to people leaving and trying to ruin friendships etc.

That's a topic I've written about in other places.

Therefore, even now, I struggle with social relationships and I generally struggle with friendships. Both in terms of maintaining them by developing deeper, more meaningful friendships as well as developing them in the first place.

Now I am very grateful that in specialist counselling for sexual violence, you can talk about anything that brings you a lot of distress besides the sexual violence trauma. Making friends and being one-on-one was a major trigger and difficulty I had because of my sexual trauma, so this was connected.

The reason why I brought it up in this tenth session was because I asked for a phone call from the guy I had been talking too online, and that didn't go to plan so my autistic and traumatised mind went into overdrive. And my best friend made a cutting revelation about me that caused me a lot of distress for no reason.

Firstly, the Wednesday after my ninth counselling session, I texted the guy I had been talking to and I asked him something along the lines of, in the future would he be up for calling so we can see about being friends, meeting up in person and perhaps developing a relationship. Neither one of us had mentioned a relationship but I was curious.

He messaged back saying he wasn't sure what he wanted at the moment because he wasn't going on dates as much as he used to, he was focusing on his university presentations and assignments and he wasn't looking for anymore friends at the moment because he had enough and he didn't want to devalue anyone.

My traumatised mind went slightly panicked at this, because this wasn't how I intended this conversation to go. I did not understand how someone could talk to a person every day for at least nine or ten days and not be interested in a friendship, and I was seriously confused that people could have too many friends.

My trauma and my autism said that was impossible.

To make matters worse, we were talking on Snapchat which I have never used before. I screenshotted his message to send to my best friend because I had no idea how to respond. But the interesting thing about Snapchat is that it alerts the other person if you screenshot a message.

That created some tension and made me even more distressed because the other guy apologised he had hurt me, so I needed to explain what I'm bad at this friendship stuff, I didn't know what to say so I asked my best friend for advice and then later on I mentioned that I had a lot of trauma around relationships and that I was raped, so I was so new to this.

In other words, I was a wonderful chaotic mess.

He was very nice, kind and we spoke a little more that night over text but then I didn't talk to him for another week until after this counselling session. The only reason I started talking to him again was I do like him, I think he's cute and we both admitted that we like talking to the other because we had good conversations. And even though I doubt an in-person or an actual friendship would form, I would like to be friends in the future.

And he's just someone else to talk to and in the past few weeks, my mindset has changed. I do have a lot of good in-person friendships so having an online one isn't going to harm me.

In fact, I messaged him a few days ago and he replied to me earlier (normally he replies on the same day but it's near Christmas so everyone is busy) that I need to reply to.

That was the first part of my friendship distress in the week before this session.

The second part was I was very stressed, anxious and worried about meeting with my friend one-on-one the day after session eight. Since I did not want it to go wrong under any circumstances, but I did put a lot of pressure on myself which maybe I shouldn't have.

Instead it might have been a good idea if I had used my compassion steps and other self-soothing techniques. However, given what had happened with this guy the day before, how I was so distressed I couldn't calm down because I was working a Postgraduate Open Evening outside in the freezing cold so I couldn't use any self-soothing techniques. As well as an interview for a good additional role at my student ambassador work went wrong because there was an admin and communication error, I was severely distressed.

If those things had not happened the day before then I don't think I would have been so distressed about meeting up with a friend one-on-one (that wasn't with my best friend) for the first time since I was raped.

The final friendship-related distress was because my best friend made a very cutting revelation about me, and I do not believe that they meant this as a bad thing, or that it was something I needed to move heaven and earth to change. Yet I was so distressed, so anxious and my mental health around friendships was not the best that I took it as a major character flaw in myself.

My best friend mentioned how I only get to form friendships and want to get close to people that I am attracted to and want to get into a relationship with. Then they listed the five relationships that I have formed (and tried to form before the other people drifted away) since I was raped where that had been the case.

And this shouldn't be the case because this isn't healthy.

My traumatised mind went even more panicked about that because it was so true, and my best friend had been right about a lot of other things about my mental health and trauma so surely they were right about this too.

In reality, they weren't a hundred percent right and it is best if I don't take everything they say as truth even if it is right to some extent.

These three major stressors about friendships and social relationships really damaged my mental health for the next four days. My mental health was better for the counselling session but it seriously hadn't been for about half of the week.

My counsellor said that people who go through typical development without childhood trauma tend to go through certain stages of making friends. Around the ages of 13 to 16, teenagers make a lot of friends based on romantic and sexual attraction and they go through a lot of friends as they try to figure out what they like and don't like in people and potential partners. My counsellor explained this as remember how most teenagers have partners that last a week or a day at most and then they change it again with someone new.

Then around the age of 16, teenagers start to think beyond looks and physical attraction as well as they want something more permanent. As well as, this continues into adulthood moving away from physical attraction being the most important thing and they continue to develop their thoughts, feelings and emotions towards personality and psychological characteristics that they're attracted to.

However, when someone experiences childhood trauma, like I was in fear for my life because my social world was so homophobic so I thought if I made friends, got into a relationship amongst other things that I would be killed. This leads to stunted development so I was never able to do these stages that a typically developing child or teenager gets to do.

Therefore, my best friend was right in the sense that I do have a tendency to form friendships and want to become close with people I want to form relationships with. Yet they were wrong to say this wasn't entirely healthy or good, because developmentally I am still moving through the stages that other people go through.

And I am passing through the stages.

Because I am basically 10 years behind on this social development because it's only been recently that I am even remotely safe enough to start exploring who I am, who I like and what sort of people I am looking for. I'm still exploring the 13- and 16-year-old side of friendships.

Although, nowadays, I am starting to form relationships and friendships with people who might not be physically attractive but I think they're great people that I would really enjoy being in a relationship with because *they* are great people on the inside. For example, the friend I made back in September and I spent one-on-one time with them for the first time in this particular week. They are not my normal type but I like them because they're interesting, we both study psychology, we're both passionate about trans mental health research and we have other things in common too.

Another example is that I briefly had a friendship with a guy over the summer who I met during student ambassador work, and sure, he was physically attractive with his slim body, longish brown hair and boyish looks. Yet I was actually attracted to him because we could talk for hours upon hours about certain topics without getting bored and I liked *him* for him.

Therefore, it was so helpful for me to understand that I wasn't deeply flawed, I wasn't weird and I wasn't as toxic as people in my past had made me out to be. I am a traumatised person simply trying to recover and I am healing and recovering my life. This friendship forming is just part of the process.

In addition, as my counsellor said, David and Victoria Beckham, the main bond between them is physical attraction. For some people, physical attraction is important and the main driving force behind their relationships and friendships. It doesn't make them bad people, weird people or messed up.

Physical attraction just works for them.

So if physical attraction is my main driver in friendships and attraction then it doesn't matter, because it works for me and I do have deep and meaningful relationships in my life.

The main takeaway that my counsellor mentioned after the above was that I shouldn't accept everything my best friend says as truth. Yes, they've been a lot of trauma counselling themselves and they're had a lot of traumatised friends too. Yet they don't have a degree, they don't have any qualifications and they don't know the psychological theory and research behind everything.

Whereas the mental health professionals do.

Personally, even now about three weeks after this counselling therapy, I am not sure if I am angry or upset with my best friend about this. I suppose I am a little because they caused me so much distress because they thought they knew better about me and how I made friends (even though they were the exact same as me up until recently). So I am annoyed that they added to my distress for no reason.

Equally, I am sort of glad that they did mention it because it allowed me to learn about this development, that I am okay and I am making progress through these developmental stages. So maybe, all the distress was sort of worth it to some extent.

Quick Notes On Self-Soothing Techniques

As a result of me getting very distressed last Wednesday, my counsellor recommended that it would be a good idea if I made a list of self-soothing techniques that I could do in different situations so I could self-soothe even if I was very busy. Since I believed that I simply couldn't self-soothe because I was working Outreach then I was at a remembrance service so there was no time for me to focus on myself.

However, there are different self-soothing techniques I could do in different situations that help me better cope with being very distressed.

Therefore, if I was distressed when I was with other people, like my friends, besides from leaving the room and calming down that way. I could talk to my friends about what was troubling or distressing me, or I could talk to them about anything else, so this would get my mind to stop thinking about whatever's distressing me.

If I'm distressed and I'm home alone, then I can self-soothe by listening to music or one of the many podcast episodes that are always on my downloads. As well as I could do work on my laptop to help me relax, feel better and to get me to stop thinking about whatever's distressing me.

Me going on my laptop was a useful technique that I realised after talking to a woman on a rape support online chat before the servers crashed and the chat was ended. Just before the chat was terminated because of the technical issue, I realised that I was distressed because I kept ruminating about it so I needed to go on my laptop, do some things and that would help me not to focus on it as much.

Finally, when I'm busy and there isn't time for me to go on my laptop, talk to friends or do any of the other techniques that I mentioned in earlier chapters. Then I can do my breathing exercises to help me to calm down a little, I could play short songs through earphones (like I flat out love the Nezuko theme song from the anime Demonslayer), I could listen to short podcast episodes and I could imagine something relaxing and then make sure that I actually do it later on.

That could be a very powerful and useful technique that I need to try out when I get distressed again.

Overall, whenever it comes to distress and dealing with the negative emotions that trauma brings up, it is very useful to know at least a few self-soothing techniques that you can use in different situations.

An unofficial tip for you is after you read this chapter come up with your own list of self-soothing techniques that you can use in the following areas of your life:

- When you're with other people
- When you're with strangers
- When you're at work
- When you're home alone
- When you're outside alone

You might not believe you need this list of self-soothing techniques now but it is always better to have them and never need them, then need them because you're distressed and not have them.

<u>Useful Quotes:</u>

I wanted to end this chapter by mentioning two useful things that my counsellor said through the session. It was helpful because it helped me realise that I just need to let my emotions out, I need to allow myself to experience whatever my mind and body want me to experience, as well as experiencing these emotions are better than not. Keeping emotions bottled up is never a good idea.

"Let emotions flow and let it all come out,"
"There's nothing wrong in going to uncomfortable places,"

HOPE, HEALING AND EXCITEMENT: CONCLUSIONS FROM A FINAL COUNSELLING SESSION

There isn't a better way to wrap up this book that has been difficult, heartbreaking and distressing as hell to write at times than to finish off with a conclusion based on the final counselling session. I was partly surprised how great I felt, how excited I was for the future and how lovely the ending was.

It really was the perfect end to a great course of counselling that had allowed me to heal, thrive and get excited about the future. Not only because my PTSD, anxiety and other trauma responses were greatly reduced to the point where it doesn't cause me much distress.

Yet because it was a course of therapy that had changed my life forever and it had given me a lot of valuable skills that I can use with my own future clients too.

Therefore, as I start to wrap up this final chapter and conclude this great healing journey that I have been on for eight months now, I want to tell you what you can expect from a final session as well as all the great things that happened in that session.

The start of the session really highlighted how much progress that I've made over the past 11 weeks because there was nothing to actually report on or talk about. Sure, I had gotten distressed a few times by different things but I had my self-soothing techniques. I listened to my music so I didn't continue getting distressed, I went on my laptop to do some fun projects so I could disengage my brain and I talked to friends outside of my mental health.

I enjoyed talking to them and spending time with them, not because I needed mental health support but because they're my friends and I like them for them, and they like me for me. That was a very useful mindset shift that I had, because I can still lean on my friends from time to time but as my best friend said, I needed to support myself more.

And thankfully because of my rape counselling, that Healing Sexual Trauma workbook and my own research on the podcast that you have full access to over the course of these three sexual trauma books, I have all the skills I need to be able to cope on my own.

I can go back to having friendships because I love my friends, I enjoy hanging out with them and we have fun together.

That is a brilliant result to have after the past 11 weeks when my best friend was my lifeline, and we both made mistakes that led to us having an unhealthy relationship, and now I can feel closer to my other friends. I understand that I can be closer to people without us going through some mental health stuff together, and that people can care about me without being able to support me.

I know a lot of this might sound obvious to some people but as someone who's autistic and been raped, this was a very hard concept to understand.

Overall, I am really proud of myself that there was nothing to report, talk about or things that I needed advice for at the end of this session. That is major progress considering every single session for the past 10 weeks there has been something important or distressing I wanted to talk to her about.

Now I am back in control of my life, instead of my mental health controlling me.

Final Bits of Paperwork

Whenever you go for specialist counselling, you will need to complete a final set of paperwork so the mental health service can use it in their research, fundraising and reporting. For example, whilst we had our coffee and cake (more on that in a moment), we completed another set of CORE measurements so she could see how my distress had decreased and ability to function increased. Thankfully, I scored a 12 and anything below a 21 is deemed as clinically normal, so I was more than happy with that.

And interestingly, that is a massive decrease since the 7th session (the last time) I did the CORE measurements because I had scored around a 35 at that point and now I'm a 12. That's a great improvement.

Of course, you might not have such dramatic reductions in your symptoms, levels of distress and increases in your ability to function. That's okay.

We are all different people and it's okay if you're healing "better" or not as well as someone else. Healing is a journey and most of the time, progress will be immensely small, so small at times that you won't be able to notice it but you are in counselling, you are trying and you are using the skills and techniques that counselling teaches you in your own life.

You are making progress, and over time that progress will add up to something amazing.

In addition, I completed a form that I've completely forgotten about, and the final form was designed to be a part of the centre's fundraising statistics. You were given three answers out of "Improved", "Stayed The Same" and "deteriorated". Then the questions were along the lines of:

- Over the course of this counselling, my mental health has…
- Over the course of this counselling, my symptoms have….
- Over the course of this counselling, my ability to function has…

Those types of questions so the centre say in fundraising efforts something along the lines of "Give us money because 90% of survivors found our counselling improved their ability to function".

As you can see I do not work in a marketing department and I probably should never work in a fundraising department, but you get my point.

Personally, I'm more than happy to take part in this research and answer these questions, because I know it's important. As a researcher myself, I know how important data is so these sort of questionnaires can give mental health services invaluable insights into the effectiveness of their work.

In addition, I know how tight budgets are and how much pressure mental health services are under, so if there is any way that I can help them. Then I want to take it, not really for myself because filling in these forms has no real impact on me.

Yet I do it for you and all the other survivors.

I want to give the service data so they can campaign, receive money and so many other clients can receive the same, great support as I did.

And so other people's lives can change for the better too.

Overall, in the final session of your specialist counselling, you will have to do some paperwork. Not only so you can see how much progress you've made but to help the centre (which is probably a charity) so they can see their work is important and they can receive money to keep helping fellow survivors.

Coffee and Cake

There are two things I really love in this world besides writing, business and psychology. Okay maybe I love a lot of great things in this life, but I really love my coffee and exploring different types of food. Unfortunately, in the UK, it is very hard to find coffee cake anymore so when my specialist counsellor asked me what I wanted to do for my final session, I said coffee and cake.

A few of my friends have laughed at the idea because they were so surprised and it was so different from their mental health sessions, but they didn't experience sexual violence thankfully.

Therefore, I chose coffee and cake because to me that was the best way to end a series of counselling sessions about something as awful and evil as sexual violence. It's almost like the end of a good story, I had been fighting like hell for 8 months with my mental health, my PTSD and just struggling to stay alive.

However, after all the pain, all the agony and all the trauma that my idiot rapist unleashed on me, there I was. I was alive, happy and my mental health was so good I could happily sit down and eat cake without any fear, any worries and I could just talk to my counsellor like a close work colleague.

The ability to have something as normal as coffee and cake was a major achievement for me, because that was honestly the most normal thing I had done since I was raped.

And it felt amazing.

So after the paperwork as we sat there drinking our Nescafe coffee (yes I had brought seriously good coffee for the final session) and we ate the great cake that she had found, we talked, chatted and laughed about the state of mental health services.

She picked my brain about mental health services, what needed to improve, how bad the state of the UK's National Health Service was and how it needed to change in the future to be fit for the 21st century.

I was in my element as we debated and talked about my degree and this area of psychology that I am seriously passionate about, because this is why I want to work in clinical psychology. I want to help people, I want to transform lives and I want to help make the world a better place.

It might be a grand idea and hope, but even small actions can have a massive impact, so I am excited for the future.

I never would have said that 11 weeks ago.

Moreover, we discussed how she's learnt a lot from me over the past 11 weeks. She's started reading research papers again because she wants to learn, she wants to see what new methods are about and she is excited to learn again. That was only because of me, and that is a great thing to know.

Therefore, dear reader, when it comes to the end of your counselling or therapy for sexual violence, even if your therapist doesn't do this sort of thing, think about how you want to celebrate your journey.

You have done amazing because you are healing, you are alive and you have had to deal with more than most people have to deal with in their entire life, but you have survived.

It probably felt impossible, draining and like life could never ever get better but you survived and you went through therapy to start your healing journey. That is amazing progress so celebrate it.

Think about what *you* want to do to celebrate and mark this great event. The end of your therapy and end of the most intense part of your healing journey is a sensational achievement.

Celebrate it.

Some of the ideas that my counsellor gave me when I was talking to her included one client had watched the final ever episode of Friends with her. It was emotional and she was watching the end of an era on her final counselling session. It was poetically beautiful.

Another client had my counsellor make her a certificate, another client wanted to do drawings and yet another wrote a story about how therapy had impacted her and her emotions and she read it to my counsellor.

You can celebrate and mark the end of counselling however you want to. Whatever helps you mark this as an ending for you and will help you move on.

The Actual End

Ultimately, as we reach the end of this book, as I said to my counsellor, thank you for everything you have helped me to do and I wish you all the best for the future.

Without you, you wonderful reader, I couldn't have written this book, there wouldn't have been any motivation and there would have been no motivation for me to think of lessons to reflect on each week. You are the sole reason this book came into being and you have helped my healing more than you could ever know.

So thank you from the bottom of my heart.

And now that you've seen all my ups and downs, struggles and triumphs, you know that the healing journey isn't linear and there will be hardships ahead. Yet it is worth it, it is wonderful and it is one of the best things you can ever do for yourself.

So please, as we end this book, embark on your healing journey, find a professional who works with sexual violence survivors and start your journey towards healing and recovering from your trauma.

It is time to take back control of your life instead of your trauma controlling you.

You've already picked up this book so you must be interested in healing, and with that drive and determination and sheer willingness to start healing, I don't doubt you can heal fully.

Thank you for everything dear reader, and I wish you all the best with your future.

And I am proud of you for finishing this book and starting your healing journey.

REFERENCES

Linehan, M. M. (1993). Skills training manual for treating borderline personality disorder. Guilford press.

Linehan, M. M. (1993). Skills training manual for treating borderline personality disorder. Guilford press.

Almaliah-Rauscher, S., Ettinger, N., Levi-Belz, Y., & Gvion, Y. (2020). "Will you treat me? I'm suicidal!" The effect of patient gender, suicidal severity, and therapist characteristics on the therapist's likelihood to treat a hypothetical suicidal patient. Clinical Psychology & Psychotherapy, 27(3), 278-287.

Alshehri, T., Mook-Kanamori, D. O., de Mutsert, R., Penninx, B. W., Rosendaal, F. R., le Cessie, S., & Milaneschi, Y. (2023). The association between adiposity and atypical energy-related symptoms of depression: a role for metabolic dysregulations. *Brain, Behavior, and Immunity*, *108*, 197-203.

Aminoff, S. R., Onyeka, I. N., Ødegaard, M., Simonsen, C., Lagerberg, T. V., Andreassen, O. A., ... & Melle, I. (2022). Lifetime and point prevalence of psychotic symptoms in adults with bipolar disorders: a systematic review and meta-analysis. Psychological medicine, 1-13.

Blanchard, M., & Farber, B. A. (2020). "It is never okay to talk about suicide": patients' reasons for concealing suicidal idealisation in psychotherapy. Psychotherapy Research, 30(1), 124-136.

Bower P., Byford S., Sibbald B. et al., Randomised controlled trial of non-directive counselling, cognitive-behavior therapy, and usual general practitioner care for patients with depression. II Cost Effectiveness. British Medical Journal. Dec 2000;321:1389.

Brockways, Laura Hale. 12/30/21. 59 Phrases to Help You Set Boundaries. PR Daily. https://www.prdaily.com/59-phrases-to-help-you-set-boundaries

Brown, S., Rodwin, A. H., & Munson, M. R. (2023). Multi-systemic trauma and regulation: Re-centering how to BE with clients. *Journal of Human Behavior in the Social Environment*, 1-18.

Chae, W. R., Baumert, J., Nübel, J., Brasanac, J., Gold, S. M., Hapke, U., & Otte, C. (2023). Associations between individual depressive symptoms and immunometabolic characteristics in major depression. *European Neuropsychopharmacology*, *71*, 25-40.

Choi, K. J., & Kangas, M. (2020). Impact of maternal betrayal trauma on parent and child well-being: Attachment style and emotion regulation as moderators. Psychological Trauma: Theory, Research, Practice, and Policy, 12(2), 121.

Coleman, J. (2024). Rules of Estrangement: Why Adult Children Cut Ties & How to Heal the Conflict. Random House.

Collins, K. A., Eng, G. K., Tural, Ü., Irvin, M. K., Iosifescu, D. V., & Stern, E. R. (2022). Affective and somatic symptom clusters in depression and their relationship to treatment outcomes in the STAR* D sample. *Journal of Affective Disorders*, *300*, 469-473.

Corrigan, F. M., Fisher, J. J., & Nutt, D. J. (2011). Autonomic dysregulation and the window of tolerance model of the effects of complex emotional trauma. *Journal of psychopharmacology*, *25*(1), 17-25.

Craparo, G. (2014). The role of dissociation, affect dysregulation, and developmental trauma in sexual addiction. *Clinical Neuropsychiatry*, *11*(2).

De Luna, J. E., & Wang, D. C. (2021). Child traumatic stress and the sacred: Neurobiologically informed interventions for therapists and parents. Religions, 12(3), 163.

Deaton, J. D., Wymer, B., & Carlson, R. G. (2021). Supervision strategies to facilitate vicarious post traumatic growth among trauma counselors. Journal of Counselor Preparation and Supervision, 14(4), 12.

Deutsch, R., Drozd, L., & Ajoku, C. (2020). Trauma-informed interventions in parent–child contact cases. Family Court Review, 58(2), 470-487.

Deutsch, R., Drozd, L., & Ajoku, C. (2020). Trauma-informed interventions in parent–child contact cases. *Family Court Review*, *58*(2), 470-487.

Dold, M., Bartova, L., Kautzky, A., Porcelli, S., Montgomery, S., Zohar, J., & Kasper, S. (2019). Psychotic features in patients with major depressive disorder: a report from the European group for the study of resistant depression. The Journal of clinical psychiatry, 80(1), 16309.

Dong, M., Lu, L., Zhang, L., Zhang, Q., Ungvari, G. S., Ng, C. H., ... & Xiang, Y. T. (2020). Prevalence of suicide attempts in bipolar disorder: a systematic review and meta-analysis of observational studies. Epidemiology and psychiatric sciences, 29, e63.

Dong, M., Zeng, L. N., Lu, L., Li, X. H., Ungvari, G. S., Ng, C. H., ... & Xiang, Y. T. (2019). Prevalence of suicide attempt in individuals with major depressive disorder: a meta-analysis of observational surveys. Psychological medicine, 49(10), 1691-1704.

Dubue, J. D., & Hanson, W. E. (2020). Psychologists' experiences conducting suicide risk assessments: A phenomenological study. Canadian Journal of Counselling and Psychotherapy, 54(4), 819-845.

Frankl, V. E. (1992). Man's search for meaning: An introduction to logotherapy (4th ed.) (I. Lasch, Trans.). Beacon Press

Friedrich, M. J. (2017). Depression is the leading cause of disability around the world. Jama, 317(15), 1517-1517.

Friedrich, M. J. (2017). Depression is the leading cause of disability around the world. Jama, 317(15),

1517-1517.

Gunter, E., Sevier-Guy, L. J., & Heffernan, A. (2023). Top tips for supporting patients with a history of psychological trauma. *British Dental Journal*, *234*(7), 490.

Guo, Z. P., Chen, L., Tang, L. R., Gao, Y., Qu, M., Wang, L., & Liu, C. H. (2025). The differential orbitofrontal activity and connectivity between atypical and typical major depressive disorder. *NeuroImage: Clinical*, *45*, 103717.

Harrison, L., & Wright, J. (2020). The experiences of person-centred counsellors working with suicidal clients online through the medium of text. British Journal of Guidance & Counselling, 48(4), 576-591.

Hazler, Richard J., Counseling and Psychotherapy Theories and Interventions. Chapter 7: Person-Centered Theory. 6th Ed. 2016. American Counseling Association.

Herman, J. L. (1998). Recovery from psychological trauma. *Psychiatry and Clinical Neurosciences*, *52*(S1), S98-S103.

Herman, J. L. (2015). *Trauma and recovery: The aftermath of violence--from domestic abuse to political terror*. Hachette uK.

Herman, J. L., & van der Kolk, B. A. (2020). *Treating complex traumatic stress disorders in adults: Scientific foundations and therapeutic models*. Guilford Publications.

Hershler, A. (2021). Window of tolerance. *Looking at trauma: A tool kit for clinicians*, *23*, 25-28.

https://www.health.nsw.gov.au/mentalhealth/psychosocial/strategies/Pages/communicating-response.aspx

https://www.livewellwithsharonmartin.com/boundaries-healing-childhood-trauma

https://www.psychologytoday.com/gb/blog/making-the-whole-beautiful/202205/what-is-the-window-of-tolerance-and-why-is-it-so-important

https://www.psychologytoday.com/gb/blog/the-crime-and-justice-doctor/202107/coercive-control-entrapped-fear

https://www.psychologytoday.com/us/blog/beyond-mental-health/202407/when-it-feels-impossible-to-get-out-of-bed

Jarero, I., & Artigas, L. (2016). Instruction for the Butterfly Hug Method.

Jarero, I., & Artigas, L. (2016). Instruction for the Butterfly Hug Method.

Jenkins, S. (2018). Increasing tolerance for calm in clients with complex trauma and dissociation. In *Equine-assisted mental health for healing trauma* (pp. 44-53). Routledge.

Jubb, H. (2017). The effectiveness of self-soothing techniques for people with PTSD in secure units. Mental Health Practice, 20(5).

Jubb, H. (2017). The effectiveness of self-soothing techniques for people with PTSD in secure units. Mental Health Practice, 20(5).

Khalfa, S., BELLA, S. D., Roy, M., Peretz, I., & Lupien, S. J. (2003). Effects of relaxing music on salivary cortisol level after psychological stress. Annals of the New York Academy of Sciences, 999(1), 374-376.

Khalfa, S., BELLA, S. D., Roy, M., Peretz, I., & Lupien, S. J. (2003). Effects of relaxing music on salivary cortisol level after psychological stress. Annals of the New York Academy of Sciences, 999(1), 374-376.

Luby, R. R. (2024). Sexual violence: a trauma-informed approach for mental health nurses supporting survivors. *Mental Health Practice*, *27*(4).

McCormack, B., McCance, T., Bulley, C., Brown, D., McMillan, A., & Martin, S. (Eds.). (2021). *Fundamentals of person-centred healthcare practice*. John Wiley & Sons.

McCormack, B., McCance, T., Bulley, C., Brown, D., McMillan, A., & Martin, S. (Eds.). (2021). *Fundamentals of person-centred healthcare practice*. John Wiley & Sons.

Mearns, D., Thorne, B., Lambers, E., & Warner, M. (2000). *Person-centred therapy today: New frontiers in theory and practice*. Sage.

Mendelsohn, M., Herman, J. L., Schatzow, E., Coco, M., Kallivayalil, D., & Levitan, J. (2011). *The trauma recovery group: A guide for practitioners*. Guilford Press.

Mok, M. C., Schwannauer, M., & Chan, S. W. (2020). Soothe ourselves in times of need: A qualitative exploration of how the feeling of 'soothe'is understood and experienced in everyday life. Psychology and Psychotherapy: Theory, Research and Practice, 93(3), 587-620.

Mok, M. C., Schwannauer, M., & Chan, S. W. (2020). Soothe ourselves in times of need: A qualitative exploration of how the feeling of 'soothe'is understood and experienced in everyday life. Psychology and Psychotherapy: Theory, Research and Practice, 93(3), 587-620.

Monahan, M. F., Crowley, K. J., Arnkoff, D. B., Glass, C. R., & Jobes, D. A. (2020). Understanding therapists' work with suicidal patients: An examination of qualitative data. OMEGA-Journal of death and dying, 81(2), 330-346.

Podlogar, T., Poštuvan, V., De Leo, D., & Žvelc, G. (2020). The model of dynamic balance in therapists' experiences and views on working with suicidal clients: A qualitative study. Clinical Psychology & Psychotherapy, 27(6), 977-987.

Qi, B., MacDonald, K., Berlim, M. T., Fielding, A., Lis, E., Low, N., ... & Trakadis, Y. (2020). Balance problems, paralysis, and angina as clinical markers for severity in major depression. Frontiers in psychiatry, 11, 567394.

Renger, S. (2023). Therapists' views on the use of questions in person-centred therapy. *British Journal of Guidance & Counselling, 51*(2), 238-250.

Rogers, C. (2000). Person-centred therapy. *Six key approaches to counselling and therapy*, *1*, 98-105.

Scupham, S., & Goss, S. P. (2020). Working with suicidal clients: Psychotherapists and allied professionals speak about their experiences. Counselling and Psychotherapy Research, 20(3), 525-534.

Siegel, D. J. (2010). *The Mindful Therapist: A Clinician's Guide to Mindsight and Neural Integration (Norton Series on Interpersonal Neurobiology)*. WW Norton & Company.

Steffen, P. R., Bartlett, D., Channell, R. M., Jackman, K., Cressman, M., & Bills, J. (2021). Integrating breathing techniques into psychotherapy to improve HRV: which approach is best?. Frontiers in Psychology, 12, 624254.

Steffen, P. R., Bartlett, D., Channell, R. M., Jackman, K., Cressman, M., & Bills, J. (2021).

Integrating breathing techniques into psychotherapy to improve HRV: which approach is best?. Frontiers in Psychology, 12, 624254.

Stern, R. (2018). *The gaslight effect: How to spot and survive the hidden manipulation others use to control your life*. Harmony.

Tudor, K., & Worrall, M. (2006). *Person-centred therapy: A clinical philosophy*. Routledge.

Vidal, J., & Soldevilla, J. M. (2023). Effect of compassion-focused therapy on self-criticism and self-soothing: A meta-analysis. British Journal of Clinical Psychology, 62(1), 70-81.

Vidal, J., & Soldevilla, J. M. (2023). Effect of compassion-focused therapy on self-criticism and self-soothing: A meta-analysis. British Journal of Clinical Psychology, 62(1), 70-81.

Vreijling, S. R., Fatt, C. R. C., Williams, L. M., Schatzberg, A. F., Usherwood, T., Nemeroff, C. B., ... & Lamers, F. (2024). Features of immunometabolic depression as predictors of antidepressant treatment outcomes: pooled analysis of four clinical trials. *The British Journal of Psychiatry*, *224*(3), 89-97.

Whiteley, C. (2024) CBT For Anxiety: A Clinical Psychology Introduction To Cognitive Behavioural Therapy For Anxiety Disorders. CGD Publishing. England.

Whiteley, C. (2024) CBT For Depression: A Clinical Psychology Introduction To Cognitive Behavioural Therapy For Depression. CGD Publishing. England.

Wood, K. M. (2023). Setting Boundaries: 100 Ways to Protect Yourself, Strengthen Your Relationships, and Build the Life You Want... Starting Now!. Simon and Schuster.

World Health Organization. (2021). Guidance on community mental health services: promoting person-centred and rights-based approaches.

Wright, J. (2009). Self-Soothing—A recursive intrapsychic and relational process: The contribution of the Bowen theory to the process of self-soothing. Australian and New Zealand Journal of Family Therapy, 30(1), 29-41.

Wright, J. (2009). Self-Soothing—A recursive intrapsychic and relational process: The contribution of the Bowen theory to the process of self-soothing. Australian and New Zealand Journal of Family Therapy, 30(1), 29-41.

Zaleski, K. L., Johnson, D. K., & Klein, J. T. (2016). Grounding Judith Herman's trauma theory within interpersonal neuroscience and evidence-based practice modalities for trauma treatment. *Smith College Studies in Social Work*, *86*(4), 377-393.

https://www.subscribepage.io/psychologyboxset

CHECK OUT THE PSYCHOLOGY WORLD PODCAST FOR MORE PSYCHOLOGY INFORMATION!
AVAILABLE ON ALL MAJOR PODCAST APPS.

About the author:

Connor Whiteley is the author of over 60 books in the sci-fi fantasy, nonfiction psychology and books for writer's genre and he is a Human Branding Speaker and Consultant.

He is a passionate warhammer 40,000 reader, psychology student and author.

Who narrates his own audiobooks and he hosts The Psychology World Podcast.

All whilst studying Psychology at the University of Kent, England.

Also, he was a former Explorer Scout where he gave a speech to the Maltese President in August 2018 and he attended Prince Charles' 70th Birthday Party at Buckingham Palace in May 2018.

Plus, he is a self-confessed coffee lover!

All books in 'An Introductory Series':

How To Improve Your Relationships
How Does Ageing Affect Us?
Introduction To Psychotherapies
I Am Not A Victim, I Am A Survivor
Breaking The Silence
Healing As A Survivor
Clinical Psychology and Transgender Clients
Clinical Psychology
Moral Psychology
Myths About Clinical Psychology
401 Statistics Questions For Psychology Students
Careers In Psychology
Psychology of Suicide
Dementia Psychology
Clinical Psychology Reflections Volume 4
Forensic Psychology of Terrorism And Hostage-Taking
Forensic Psychology of False Allegations
Year In Psychology
CBT For Anxiety
CBT For Depression
Applied Psychology
BIOLOGICAL PSYCHOLOGY 3RD EDITION
COGNITIVE PSYCHOLOGY THIRD EDITION
SOCIAL PSYCHOLOGY- 3RD EDITION

ABNORMAL PSYCHOLOGY 3RD EDITION
PSYCHOLOGY OF RELATIONSHIPS- 3RD EDITION
DEVELOPMENTAL PSYCHOLOGY 3RD EDITION
HEALTH PSYCHOLOGY
RESEARCH IN PSYCHOLOGY
A GUIDE TO MENTAL HEALTH AND TREATMENT AROUND THE WORLD- A GLOBAL LOOK AT DEPRESSION
FORENSIC PSYCHOLOGY
THE FORENSIC PSYCHOLOGY OF THEFT, BURGLARY AND OTHER CRIMES AGAINST PROPERTY
CRIMINAL PROFILING: A FORENSIC PSYCHOLOGY GUIDE TO FBI PROFILING AND GEOGRAPHICAL AND STATISTICAL PROFILING.
CLINICAL PSYCHOLOGY
FORMULATION IN PSYCHOTHERAPY
PERSONALITY PSYCHOLOGY AND INDIVIDUAL DIFFERENCES
CLINICAL PSYCHOLOGY REFLECTIONS VOLUME 1
CLINICAL PSYCHOLOGY REFLECTIONS VOLUME 2
Clinical Psychology Reflections Volume 3
CULT PSYCHOLOGY
Police Psychology

A Psychology Student's Guide To University
How Does University Work?
A Student's Guide To University And Learning
University Mental Health and Mindset

Other books by Connor Whiteley:

Bettie English Private Eye Series
The Landlord Problem
Death of Blackmail
The Good Friday Murder
Three's A Pattern
A Very Private Woman
The Russian Case
A Very Urgent Matter
A Case Most Personal
Trains, Scots and Private Eyes
The Federation Protects
Cops, Robbers and Private Eyes

Just Ask Bettie English
An Inheritance To Die For
The Death of Graham Adams
Bearing Witness
The Twelve
The Wrong Body
The Assassination Of Bettie English
Wining And Dying
Eight Hours
Uniformed Cabal
A Case Most Christmas

<u>Gay Romance Novellas</u>
Breaking, Nursing, Repairing A Broken Heart
Jacob And Daniel
Fallen For A Lie
Spying And Weddings
Clean Break
Awakening Love
Meeting A Country Man
Loving Prime Minister
Snowed In Love
Never Been Kissed
Love Betrays You
Love And Hurt

<u>Lord of War Origin Trilogy:</u>
Not Scared Of The Dark
Madness
Burn Them All

<u>Way Of The Odyssey</u>
Odyssey of Rebirth
Convergence of Odysseys
Odyssey Of Hope
Odyssey of Enlightenment

Lady Tano Fantasy Adventure Stories

Betrayal
Murder
Annihilation
Rising Shadow
Coming of Demons

Agents of The Emperor

Deceitful Terra
Blood And Wrath
Infiltration
Fuel To The Fire
Return of The Ancient Ones
Vigilance
Angels of Fire
Kingmaker
The Eight
The Lost Generation
Hunt
Emperor's Council
Speaker of Treachery
Birth Of The Empire
Terraforma
Spaceguard

The Rising Augusta Fantasy Adventure Series

Rise To Power
Rising Walls
Rising Force
Rising Realm

The Fireheart Fantasy Series

Heart of Fire
Heart of Lies
Heart of Prophecy
Heart of Bones
Heart of Fate

City of Assassins (Urban Fantasy)

City of Death

City of Martyrs

City of Pleasure

City of Power

Lord Of War Trilogy (Agents of The Emperor)

Not Scared Of The Dark

Madness

Burn It All Down

OTHER SHORT STORIES BY CONNOR WHITELEY

Mystery Short Story Collections

Criminally Good Stories Volume 1: 20 Detective Mystery Short Stories

Criminally Good Stories Volume 2: 20 Private Investigator Short Stories

Criminally Good Stories Volume 3: 20 Crime Fiction Short Stories

Criminally Good Stories Volume 4: 20 Science Fiction and Fantasy Mystery Short Stories

Criminally Good Stories Volume 5: 20 Romantic Suspense Short Stories

Connor Whiteley Starter Collections:

Agents of The Emperor Starter Collection

Bettie English Starter Collection

Matilda Plum Starter Collection

Gay Romance Starter Collection

Way Of The Odyssey Starter Collection

Kendra Detective Fiction Starter Collection

Science Fiction Short Story Collections

Rivetingly Great Stories Volume 1

Rivetingly Great Stories Volume 2

Rivetingly Great Stories Volume 3

Rivetingly Great Stories Volume 4

Rivetingly Great Stories Volume 5

www.ingramcontent.com/pod-product-compliance
Lightning Source LLC
LaVergne TN
LVHW082017200926
848481LV00010B/2874